My Galitzianer Ancestors:

Geiger and Turnheim Families from Subcarpathia Province, Poland

Judith C. Goldsmith, Ed.D., M.S.W.

My Galitzianer Ancestors:
Geiger and Turnheim Families from Subcarpathia Province, Poland

Requests for permission to make copies of any part of this publication should be addressed to:

Judith C. Goldsmith
101 Crescent Moon Drive
Groveland, Florida 34736

Printed in the United States of America

First Printing

Includes bibliographical references and index

ISBN: 979-8-9861182-0-8

Dedication

To My Beloved Family and Future Generations

Acknowledgments

There were so many wonderful relatives who were kind enough to offer information about their family stories. Without their contributions our Geiger and Turnheim ancestors would only be names and dates. I especially want to thank my relatives for their past and recent contributions of family history, documents, stories, and photographs. I apologize to anyone who was inadvertently omitted from this list.

Gabby Bate	Gary Geiger z"l	Carol Lebeaux z"l
Helen Bialik z"l	Lotke Geiger z"l	Elizabeth Lifschitz
Martin Bialik	Bertha aka Bess Gerber z"l	Lisa Margolis
Eddy Bikales	Frank Gerber z"l	Evelyn Mast
David Brainin z"l	Sylvia Gerber z"l	Steven Messner
Pearl Bronz z"l	Arthur Goshin	Debra Polsky
Martha Cantor z"l	Marion Goshin z"l	Dora Ritzer
Mark Cantor	Herbert Goshin z"l	Mikki Rolland
Lois Chertoff	Harry Holly z"l	Olivia Schwartz
Clara Chopp	Mina Keenan z"l	Jeanne Shenkman
Cathy Cohen	Helen Keenan	Daniel Stern
Julie Ann Estabrook	Suzi Kleiman z"l	Jane Stern
Elisha Geiger	Karen Lashman	Georg Turnheim
		Minnie Geiger Weiss z"l

My special appreciation extends to my cousin Elizabeth Lifschitz for her prescient safe-keeping of important correspondence between her father George Bronz with Abraham Geiger, Charles Geiger and others during WWII. Elizabeth kindly shared those documents with me giving her permission to include them in this book. They are testimony to their efforts to save those relatives in Europe who were at immediate risk of murder during the Shoah. Please refer to Appendix A World War II Letters. The correspondence is also discussed in the chapters for Abraham Geiger, Charles Geiger, Mariem Geiger and the Turnheim Family.

Some cousins participated in my autosomal DNA study by donating their atDNA to www.familytreedna.com. Their generosity provided important data for finding additional cousins for building a more complete family tree as discussed in chapters eleven and twelve. Gary Geiger z"l also donated his Y-DNA to www.familytreedna.com for my research, to find ancient genetic roots of the male Geiger lineage as discussed in chapter six. I also contributed my Mt-DNA to www.familytreedna.com to research my ancient genetic maternal lineage as discussed in chapter ten.

There were so many people who generously provided me with guidance and valuable information essential for my research progress. My deepest gratitude is extended to the following individuals. Rabbi Joshua Segal gave his time and expertise with Hebrew to English translations from family matsevahs in Poland and the United States. Researchers Israel Pickholtz and Krzysztof Malczewski were instrumental in helping me to obtain vital records from Polish archives. The Israelische Kultus Gemeinde Wien (IKG) in Vienna was most helpful with photographs of graves and my research questions, especially Debora Kravtschenko, Irma Wulz, and Chaim Tetruashvili. The Weiner Stadt-und Landesarchiv of Vienna was a wonderful research source. The organizations JewishGen.org., JRI-Poland.org, Gesher Galicia.org, Yad Vashem.org, Ancestry.com, Family Search.org provided me with invaluable information and documents that made my research possible. I also accessed many other helpful genealogy organizations and archives in the United States and in Poland that are listed as sources at the conclusion of each chapter.

Researcher David Priever generously investigated probate records from the New York Municipal archives. Domicella Grossman Klima from Przemyśl, Poland photographed Turnheim family matsevahs at the Przemyśl cemetery; she also helped me with Polish translations and research. Genealogist Marla Raucher Osborn provided additional sources for my Przemyśl research. Genealogist David Semmel assisted me with Przemyśl research and answered my many questions. Translator volunteers from Viewmate on www.jewishgen.org were generous with their time. They provided me with translations of German, Hebrew and Polish languages written on documents and on matsevahs. My sincere appreciation extends to the following translators: Scheindle Cohen, Odeda Zlotnick, Fredel Fruhman, Jonathan Michael Wein, David Rosen, Laurence H. Kleerekoper, David Ziants, Zipora Neustadt, Tomasz Jerzy Nowak, Witold Wrzosinski, Yitschok Tzvi Margareten, Abraham Marmorstein, and Dror Haim Bereznitsky.

A special thank you goes to the Re'ut School in Jerusalem for their excellent Gidonim Project that provided me with photographs of family matsevahs, translations as well as their restoration of the cemetery at Błażowa. Researcher Alter Raubvogel sent me photographs of difficult to find family records and matsevahs from the United Jewish Cemetery at Cincinnati, Ohio. Genealogists Estelle Guzik and Suzan Wynne shared their family information and their research experiences in Błażowa. Suzan Wynne kindly sent me her photographs taken at Błażowa for this book. Suzan Wynne's invaluable book *The Galitzianers: the Jews of Galicia, 1772-1918* was my bedrock. Researcher Brenda Habshush, an Israeli genealogist, generously gave her time to research my genealogical questions and connect me to lost relatives in Israel.

My appreciation extends to our beloved daughter Abby Goldsmith who helped me with her considerable technical skills and artistic expertise. Thank you Abby for your launch of the website: sites.google.com/site/galitzianerancestors/; your cover design for this book and for your continuous support. I appreciate the interest and encouragement offered by our beloved daughter Jennifer and by our dear son-in-law Jonathan Friedman.

This book is my special legacy to our darling grandchildren Ora and Aaron. My deepest gratitude extends to my beloved scientist husband Michael Goldsmith, my soulmate, who was generous with his time reading my chapters, contributing astute editorial suggestions, and guiding me through the science of DNA research and analysis as applied to my research within certain chapters. I am truly grateful for Mike's constant support as a true partner in our study of genealogy and mutual quest for finding our respective family roots.

Contents

Introduction

My ancestors were ordinary yet extraordinary people. For many centuries they adhered to Judaism in the face of intolerance, ignorance, persecution, violence and genocide. They loved their families, nurturing and raising children, some even adopting orphaned children, despite poverty and scarcity. They gave of themselves to help others in need even when it was inconvenient and often dangerous. They courageously served in the armies and navies of the countries where they lived. My ancestors faced many challenges of illnesses such as typhoid and cholera without benefit of modern medicine, enduring risky childbirths and primitive surgeries. They continued to survive and to pass down their basic values of piety and prayer, love for Judaism, charity, and repentance. In addition, I sought to honor those ancestors who were so cruelly murdered during the Holocaust; they will not be forgotten. Certain chapters include their names, and they are also included in a memorial list. It is my purpose to honor ancestors who came before me, to remember their lives, their values, and contributions, and how they shaped future generations.

My research took me to the 18th–20th centuries mainly in Poland, then to Austria, other parts of Europe and to Israel. Many ancestors immigrated to the United States during the 1880s to post-WWII, settling mainly in New York. Those immigrants left the Old World for the New World to rebuild their lives in freedom and prosperity. They soon realized that they would never again see their families. They occasionally kept in touch by letters, postcards, photographs however so many were lost to the ravages of time. I treasured surviving letters, photographs and stories that added to my deeper understanding and appreciation of my courageous and resourceful immigrant ancestors.

The challenge was to consolidate twenty-five years of research and exploration of my family history together in a book. The amount of material collected quickly became encyclopedic and even overwhelming. I did not want this material to be lost. I realized that it was valuable enough to disseminate in a comprehensible format within a family history book. The value of genealogy research certainly helped me to understand how my ancestors passed down their core values to help form who I am. It has been my hope that other descendants might also gain this perspective. In addition, there was a thrill of discovering the pieces of a research puzzle and then putting together facts to see how they fit together for an ancestor and their families. My engrossing hobby swiftly grew into an obsessive pursuit with never-ending searches. Clues led to more answers that raised more questions.

It soon became apparent that such an accumulation of family history was valuable for my own family as well as for other researchers. I view this as my legacy for my children, grandchildren, my cousins, near and distant relatives as well as for genealogy students and researchers to serve as inspiration and even to provide links and clues for others who may want to research their families.

While growing up as a child in Brooklyn and Queens Counties in New York City, my only living grandparent that I knew was my maternal grandmother Minnie Weiss née Geiger. I have little memory of my paternal grandparents or my maternal grandfather Oscar Weiss. I adored Minnie and always looked forward to the special times we were together when she took me to visit her umbrella factory in Manhattan. I sometimes helped with some simple tasks in the factory such as putting handles on the umbrellas. She sometimes took me to lunch in a distinctly Jewish style cafeteria that sold borscht, potato latkes, gefilte fish and other such Jewish delicacies. The customers spoke Yiddish and read Hebrew and Yiddish language newspapers and books. Sometimes Grandma liked to spoil me by taking me to Radio City Music Hall, to Rumplemeyers and to Schraffts restaurants.

I enjoyed watching her make gefilte fish during Passover. I sometimes sat with her in my aunt Martha's spacious backyard and listened to her softly accented speech as she spoke of her fond memories when she hiked in the hills where she grew up in Europe. Such stories reminded me of Heidi in the Swiss Alps. She often read and prayed from a Hebrew siddur (prayerbook). She would fast for the required 25 hours and pray all day at the synagogue during the most sacred day of Yom Kippur, even when she grew older. Although I felt close to her, I also felt that there were so many unknowns pertaining to her life. She told me that she immigrated to New York from Austria and being a child, I never thought to ask her more questions. I was 16 years of age when she died and by then my chances of asking her more questions about her family history were gone. Other family members were only able to give sketchy information about Grandma or about her Geiger family. None really knew very much except for snippets of stories handed down.

My genealogical research grew from my exploration of my maternal grandparents, great-grandparents, and great-great-grandparents. The maternal lineage of my family includes the families Geiger, Unger, Turnheim, Weiss, Zuckerberg, Frankel, Borgman as well as other family surnames associated through marriage. I learned that my maternal ancestors came from Galicia, an area that no longer exists today by name. I later learned that when Grandma told me she came from Austria, she meant that she was from Galicia, a territory that was annexed by the Austro-Hungarian Empire from 1772 until 1918. It was known as the Kingdom of Galicia and Lodomeria. Since WWII, the western part of Galicia can be found in Poland; the eastern part of Galicia lies within the Ukraine. For the purposes of this first book, I decided to focus on my Geiger, Unger and Turnheim families from Poland. The Jews from Galicia referred to themselves as *Galitzianers*.

I began to realize that my Geiger and Turnheim ancestors and their descendants came from various towns in Poland within a certain geographical area in a province known today in Polish as *Województwo Podkarpackie* or the Subcarpathia Province, located in southeastern Poland. This region includes large cities as Rzeszów and Przemyśl and smaller towns such as Błażowa, Jarosław, Leżajsk, Lańcut, Kolbuszowa, Kańczuga, Pruchnik and Sokołów Małopolski. The name of the province is based on the location near the Carpathian Mountains; the geography is described as mountainous to hilly. I titled my genealogy book *Geiger and Turnheim Families from the Subcarpathia Province, Poland* to include various ancestral locations within this specific area in Poland.

Steps taken to do this family research were many interviews with family members asking them what they remembered and what they were willing to share, specifically family stories, photographs, and documents. Next steps were taken to obtain primary sources, such as ship manifests, naturalizations, Federal and state censuses, birth, marriage and death records, cemetery information, SS5 applications, military records, draft registrations, land records, probate records. Such records were obtained from the LDS, AGAD, other Polish archives, NARA, state and city archives in the USA, city directories, yizkor books, newspapers, research organizations such as www.jewishgen.org, www.ancestry.com, www.jri-poland. org, fhc.familysearch.org, www.geshergalicia.org, www.yadvashem.org. The various Jewish Gen SIG groups (special interest groups) for Poland were also accessed for information.

Understanding foreign language records was a challenge and this book will illustrate how I made use of books to read the Polish and German text. A helpful book was *In Their Words-a Genealogist's Translation Guide to Polish, German, Latin, and Russian Documents Volume I: Polish* by Jonathan D. Shea and William F. Hoffman as well as Polish and German dictionaries. My many requests for translations from Hebrew, Polish, and German on the website www.jewishgen.org/viewmate.org often yielded good results.

Since the many shtetls and towns were unfamiliar to me, I frequently consulted the excellent *Genealogical Gazetteer of Galicia* by Brian J. Lenius for spelling and locating towns also to visualize distances and proximity of certain towns on maps within the 82 administrative districts in Galicia during 1906–1914.

Among my many sources, I referred to the comprehensive books by Alexander Beider: *A Dictionary of Jewish Surnames from Galicia* and *A Dictionary of Ashkenazi Given Names* for discussion of the origins and meanings of names. Suzan Wynne's seminal book *The Galitzianers: The Jews of Galicia, 1772–1918* discussed how Jews often had surnames such as an occupation either chosen by Jews when they were required to choose a surname by law in 1787 or possibly assigned to them by a government official e.g. the name Geiger is German for violinist or fiddler.

My genealogy book begins with the earliest known ancestors i.e. "first generation." This was as far back as I could research. For the purposes of this book, my family trees continued through several generations omitting information about living descendants. Relevant family trees and charts are included to help guide readers through the many names and descendants.

Finding "lost cousins" was especially rewarding and was a joy to see how cousins appreciated learning about their roots, and how quickly they connected with others on the family tree. The additional information and photographs they provided was indeed priceless and helped me to break through "brick walls." In many cases, my cousins did not realize that they had other living family members. I extend my deepest appreciation to so many relatives who graciously allowed me to copy their family documents and photographs, as well as share their knowledge of our family history. Many relatives extended a warm welcome when they learned of my mission. There were several instances when I decided to honor requests by certain descendants to keep sensitive facts confidential and therefore such facts were not included in this book.

Many cousins obliged with my requests to donate their autosomal DNA (atDNA) to the testing company www.familytreedna.com for extending knowledge of our family history through atDNA matches, especially important when paper trails ran dry. I discussed how I confirmed "lost cousins" by using various research methods including analysis of atDNA.

Whatever good results from this book, I share it with all those who have helped me. I also take full responsibility for any errors, inconsistencies or misunderstandings that may come from my work.

If this genealogy pertains to your direct ancestors, it is my hope that you dear readers will learn much. I also hope that this book proves useful and will provide inspiration for others who may want to research their Jewish ancestors from Poland.

Detail Subcarpathia Province, 2009 Michelin Map Poland

Chapter One

Background

My genealogical research and DNA testing combined with what I knew of my heritage confirmed that I am descended from Ashkenazi Jews from both sides of my family. I am proud of the remarkable history of Jews as the first people to establish a monotheistic religion as written in their sacred books of Judaism. Jewish achievements over the centuries have been remarkable in such fields as literature, philosophy, music, science, law, and medicine despite being a small population marked by much suffering throughout their long history from slavery, expulsions, discrimination, persecution, and genocide.

After the destruction of the Second Temple in Jerusalem 70 CE by the Romans, sporadic warfare continued by Jews against the Roman legions. During the last Jewish Roman War 132–136, Jews were led by the Jewish commander Shimon Bar Kokhba against the Romans that ended with Roman victory. During this period many Jews were sold off as slaves to Rome. With the reign of Roman Emperor Caracalla 198–217, freed Jews became full citizens of the Roman Empire. Eventually Jewish communities rose in many regions belonging to the Roman Empire including Spain, France, South Germany, Italy, Greece, and Asia Minor. During this Jewish diaspora documents indicated by the 10th century Jewish communities were already established in the Germanic cities of Cologne, Mainz, Worms and Speyer.

The Crusades in Europe (1095–1192) became increasingly anti-Semitic with allegations of crimes committed by Jews, such as blood libel, poisoning of wells and treason. Jews became impoverished under oppressive laws and hundreds were burned at the stake or were expelled from Britain, France, and Germany. For example, this researcher and her husband Mike had the opportunity to visit a site at York, U.K. where the entire Jewish population of York consisting of 150 individuals committed suicide in 1190 while they sought refuge in the royal castle (known as Clifford's Tower) rather than be put to death by the angry mob or surrender to forced baptism.[1] The incident was driven by anti-Semitism and the greed of those who owed money to the leading Jewish moneylenders. It was sadly only one of countless incidents of mob-violence against Jewish communities across England and Western Europe during the Middle Ages. There developed a steady flow of Jews during the Crusades from the Rhine and Danube provinces eastward into Poland and Lithuania to escape from persecution and worse.

The plague known as the Black Death became a widespread event throughout Europe and Asia in 1348–49 and returned repeatedly between 1346–1671 with no cure or treatment. People did not understand the plague was caused by the bacterium Yersinia pestis, carried by fleas living on rodents. The rodents travelled on merchant ships that disembarked at European ports. The fleas spread the plague by infecting huge populations in crowded and filthy cities. Millions of people died horrible deaths. European Christians observed that fewer Jews were affected by the plague as they failed to understand how Jewish isolation being forced to live in ghettos prevented some Jewish deaths and blamed the Jews for causing the plague by poisoning wells. Jews were also accused of blood libels, that is the murder of Christian children to use their blood for Jewish religious rituals during Passover such as making wine and matzot. Those accusations incited pogroms that resulted in the annihilation of whole populations of Jews in many communities. Discrimination, pogroms, and continuing persecution against Jews resulted in their increased migration eastward into the Kingdom of Poland and the Grand Duchy of Lithuania.[2]

Jewish Migration to Poland

Jews were welcomed by the Polish nobility for their literacy and adept financial abilities. Polish territory came to be viewed by Jews as the land of protection with guaranties of freedom of worship, initially granted by Boleslaw the Pious, Duke of Kalisz in 1264. He declared a statute defining the rights of Jews, forbidding harassment of Jewish merchants and attacks on Jewish cemeteries, synagogues, and schools. He refused to allow blood libels that accused Jews of murdering Christians for use of their blood for baking matzos or for any other purpose.

In Poland additional opportunities for Jews besides moneylending included leasing arrangements with nobles called *arenda* as well as increased employment in commerce and the trades. Arenda leasing arrangements included use of land owned by the nobility to obtain lumber, grain to make liquor, and hides of cattle for leather.[3] Nobles also granted Jews the rights to collect taxes and customs duties. Jews were prominent in occupations as peddlers, artisans, traders, innkeepers, brewers, and merchants.

A new language emerged among Jews known as Yiddish. It began to emerge when Jews living in Poland invited rabbis and Talmudic scholars from Germany to educate their youth and to conduct religious services. Through this interchange with Germany, a German dialect evolved during the 10th–13th centuries in the language that we know as Yiddish, as an amalgam of German, Hebrew, Aramaic, and Slavic influences. Yiddish eventually became the lingua franca among Jews throughout Europe. Yiddish as a language remained dominant amongst Jews in Eastern Europe until the Holocaust.[4] It is still spoken by thousands of Ashkenazi orthodox Jews. My Jewish grandparents who immigrated to the United States all conversed primarily in Yiddish and read Yiddish newspapers.

During the 14th century more Jews emigrated from Western Europe to Poland fleeing pogroms in Germanic territories. A progressive Polish ruler Casimir the Great (1333–1370) founded and fortified new cities and welcomed Jews into Poland for their expertise with capital. He placed Jewish legal cases under his own jurisdiction out of the hands of municipal and ecclesiastic authorities. Casimir the Great applied the progressive Magdeburg Law to Jews in Lemberg. He granted Jews the right to be judged by their own laws and to have autonomy in their communal matters.

The Kingdom of Poland and the Grand Duchy of Lithuania was formed following the 1396 marriage of the Polish queen Hedwig with Lithuania's Grand Duke Jogaila. This became known as the Polish-Lithuanian Commonwealth, an enormous land area with much ethnic diversity known for religious tolerance for all faiths later reinforced by the Warsaw Confederation Act 1573. After decades of prosperity, there began a period of political, economic, and military decline that led to the Commonwealth being partitioned and annexed by the empires of Austria, Prussia, and Russia during the late 18th century.[5]

The Austro-Hungarian Empire ruled by the Hapsburg monarchy annexed the territory known as Galicia from the Polish-Lithuanian Commonwealth during the first partition of Poland in 1772. Galicia was the largest province of the Austro-Hungarian Empire, bordering on Moravia to the west, the Russian Empire to the north and east, Hungary and the Ottoman Empire to the south. During the second partition of Poland in 1793, Russia and Prussia seized land leaving only one-third of the 1772 population in Poland. With the third partition of Poland in 1795, the Austro-Hungarian Empire annexed additional land including Lublin and Kraków. Russia gained Vilnius and Prussia gained Warsaw.[6]

Detail Map of Eastern Hungary and Galicia 1908

When Galicia was part of the Austro-Hungarian Empire, it was ruled by various monarchs including Charles VI, Empress Maria Theresa and her son Josef, Josef II and Franz Joseph. Although the largest, Galicia was also the poorest province in the Austro-Hungarian Empire. Taxes imposed on Jews were much higher than for non-Jews; there were taxes on candles, on synagogues, on kosher meat, on trading, and on marriage. The Jewish marriage tax was onerous and discouraged civil registered marriages of Jewish couples who were usually religiously married.[7] The 1880s and 1890s were marked by endemic poverty with mounting anti-Semitism and violent outbreaks against Jews in western Galicia.[8]

During WWI, Galicia became a fierce battleground with many Jewish Galitzianers moving to Vienna for safety. When WWI ended, the Treaty of Versailles 1919 set Poland as an independent country and western Galicia became incorporated into Poland. The territory of eastern Galicia was contested 1918–1919 between Polish and Ukrainian armies and was marked by fierce fighting. Polish forces won the war, and the Treaty of Riga 1921 gave Poland the territory, however in 1939 the Soviet Union annexed the territory that was eastern Galicia until 1991 until it became incorporated into the independent state of the Ukraine.

Galicia as a territory no longer exists in name except for the purposes of historical and genealogical research. My maternal Galitzianer ancestors married and raised families in western Galicia mainly in the region within southeastern Poland now called the Subcarpathia Province. This area encompasses cities and counties as Rzeszów, Przemyśl, Mielec, Jarosław, Sanok, Błażowa, Przeworsk, Ropczyce, Leżjask, Nisko, Łańcut, Kolbuszowa, Jaslo, Dynów, Kańczuga, Sokołow.[9]

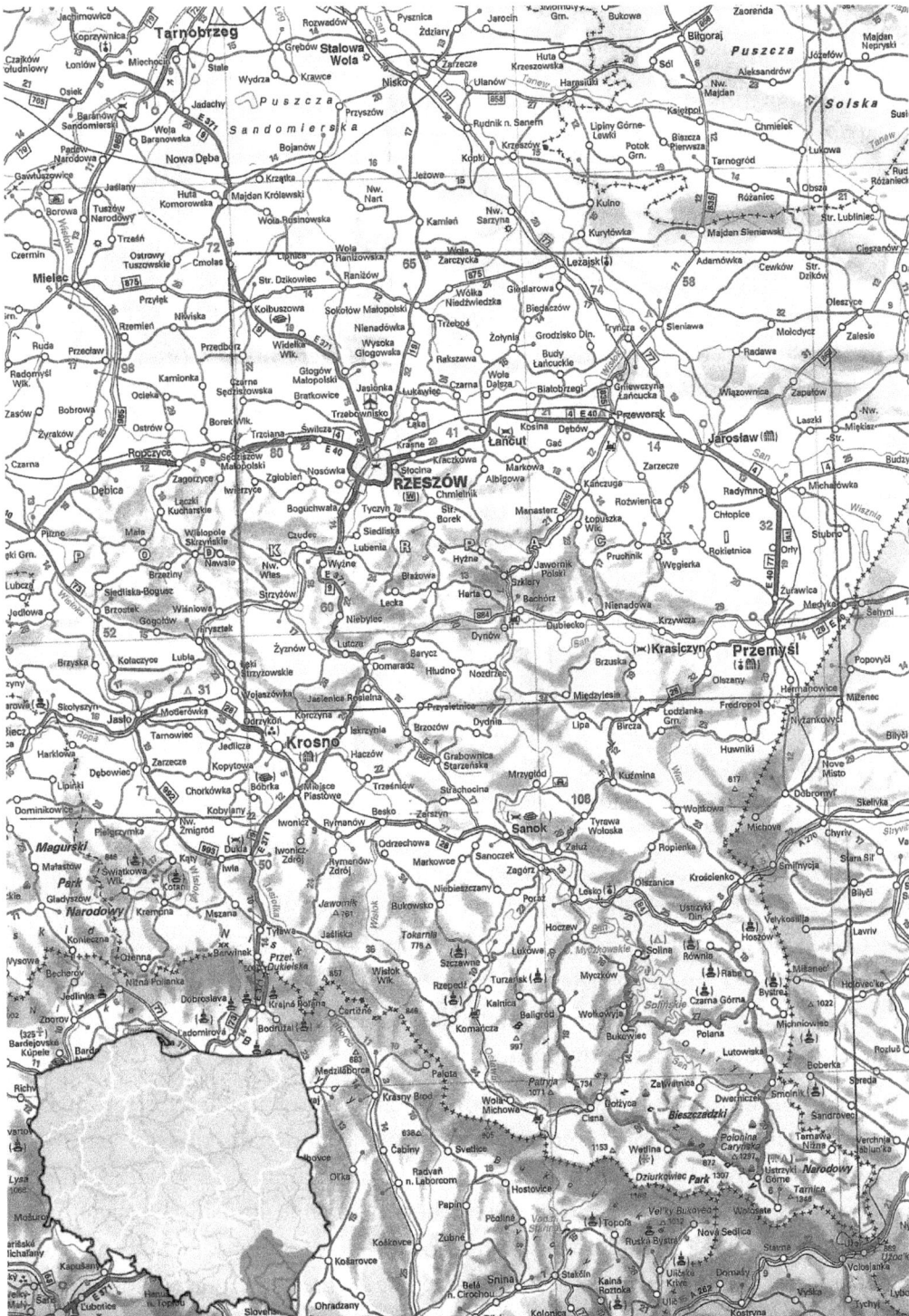

Subcarpathia, Poland

Jewish Life in Galicia

The Austro-Hungarian Empire conducted the following censuses to compare Jewish populations with the total populations in Galicia: in 1789 there were 178,072 Jews (6 percent of the total population); in the census of 1827 there were 246,146 Jews (6 percent); the census of 1850 counted 317,227 Jews (7 percent); and the census of 1900 indicated there were 811,371 Jews living in Galicia (11 percent of the total population).[10] There was probably an under estimation of the Jewish population since Jews did not want to be counted in the census for many reasons including targeted conscription and harsh tax policy. Jews tended to live in the larger towns and cities in Galicia and were often more than 50 percent in urban populations due to economic opportunities and reasons of safety by numbers as there was scattered violence from false accusations of blood libels and anti-Semitism incited by clergy.

Prior to WWI the Jewish population in Galicia was subject to Austro-Hungarian law. There was a *familiant* law that was imposed in 1726 on the Jews granting only one male in each family the right to establish a legitimate household, under a quota system. Those who only had a religious marriage found it very difficult to obtain permits for business licenses or to move elsewhere. A law in 1734 set the minimum age for Jewish brides and grooms at 15 and 18 years respectively. This *familiant* law for Jews was established by Charles VI in 1726 to keep Jewish population at low levels. It gave only one male of a Jewish family the right to establish a legitimate household, to register and pay a substantial tax. No other male in the family was permitted to have a legitimate household. This may explain why brothers changed their surnames. Each community had a quota for the number of legitimate households.[11] Harsh marriage laws such as the *familiant* were abolished in Galicia by 1869. A law was passed in 1875 to reinstate the civil marriage requirement; marriages had to be performed by official rabbis from the *Gemeinde* (local government of Jewish leaders) in each community working cooperatively with the Austrian government.[12]

Children born to couples who were not married under civil registration were considered illegitimate. Such births were registered under the mother's surname without the father being identified unless he appeared in person with two witnesses, thus attesting that he was the father. Any child considered illegitimate could not automatically inherit property from the father. Some parents obtained a civil marriage many years later even when they were middle-aged so that their children could obtain travel documents, inherit, or acquire business licenses.

Jewish traditions held if a Jewish woman did not bear a child within a few years of marriage, Jewish law allowed a husband to divorce and seek a new wife who could give him children. It was assumed that it was the woman's fault when there were no children. Women could obtain a *get* (a Jewish divorce) if the husband was impotent or uninterested in fulfilling sexual obligations. If the husband was missing or disagreed with the divorce, then the wife's marital status was *agudah* (left in limbo), making it impossible for her to be able to remarry in a religious ceremony.[13]

There were frequent Jewish marriages between relatives in Galicia, often between first cousins, also between uncles and nieces. Such marriages ensured that the religious backgrounds of the parties were well known, and that money and property would be retained within the family. Engagements were often arranged by families when the parties were infants. Typically, the groom moved to the bride's town, unless the groom was financially established elsewhere. Marriages commonly occurred between parties from within the same or adjacent districts.[14] There were also arranged marriages among rabbinical lineages.

When Poland was first partitioned by the Austro-Hungarian Empire in 1772, there were very few Jewish surnames in use, and most Jews used patronymics; based on the given name of one's father or male ancestor such as Aron ben Sholom David. The Hapsburg Emperor Joseph II signed a law on 5 July 1787 requiring all Jews living within the border of the Hapsburg Empire to adopt fixed family surnames. The deadline to choose a surname was 1 January 1788. The selection of names was administered by a government commission, to make certain that each family living within a local area was to receive a different surname. Unmarried children living in their parent's house received the same surnames as their parents. Married sons were directed to choose a surname different from the father. In some cases, people in the same family living in the same house had to choose different surnames.[15]

If a Jew did not choose a surname, one was assigned to him by officials in Galicia. Such surnames could be based on occupation, personal characteristics, rabbinical lineages, artificial (compound surnames based on dissimilar nouns), place names, or drawn from masculine or feminine given names. I considered that my maternal Geiger lineage indicated they were originally musicians or violinists, since Geiger means violinist or fiddler in German (occupational). My maternal Turnheim lineage means gate + home in German. Many Jews delayed choosing a surname because they suspected this process was to make a census of the Jewish population to enforce conscription, to impose new taxes, etc. In addition, officials used their power to extort bribes from Jews for favorable and pleasant surnames.[16]

Jewish husbands often spent much of their married life travelling for religious or economic purposes. Women managed their home and often the marketplace. Men were not expected to participate in housework or in child rearing, apart from religious and moral instruction and guidance. A high value was accorded to men who pursued a life devoted to religious study and scholarship. Men who were drawn to this life were often supported by their father-in-law or by their wives as the primary breadwinners.[17]

Jews in Galicia were not peasants, and they were not from the *szlachta* or land-owning nobility. They were in the category of "other;" prohibited from owning land and from many occupations and were dependent upon the nobility. They were often excluded from joining artisan and craft guilds that controlled much non-agricultural commerce. More than two-thirds of Jews were involved in trade, handicraft, and small industry. Certain productions were entirely in Jewish hands, such as flourmills, alcohol distilleries, taverns, small oil refineries in eastern Galicia, sawmills, tanneries, brickyards, soda water factories, and production of religious items such as talliths. Jews were well represented in the liquor trade before 1911, and they also dominated in trade of cattle, horses, poultry, feathers, and bristles.[18] An economic boycott against Galitzianer Jews was proclaimed in 1893 during a Catholic convention in Kraków. Special licenses were imposed on Jews for trade in items such as spices, paint, and old clothes. By 1910 Jews were forbidden from selling alcoholic beverages. The economic situation of Galitzianer Jews worsened and poverty became endemic. In addition, sanitary conditions deteriorated during cholera outbreaks in 1831, 1873 and 1894. Homelessness and unemployment among Galitzianer Jews became widespread.

It is no wonder that Jewish emigration from Galicia reached a peak during the 1880s through 1910 when 236,500 Jews from Galicia emigrated to the United States including my Geiger ancestors: Charles Geiger, Israel Geiger, Miriam Geiger, and my grandmother Minnie Geiger. Other Galitzianer Jews such as my Geiger ancestors Aron Geiger and Abraham Geiger moved to Vienna during WWI. They were initially welcomed in Vienna and were aided by Viennese Jews with soup kitchens and subsidies. During WWI Galitzianer Jews in Vienna numbered 77,000. Before WWII Vienna had 175,000 Jews and was the third largest Jewish community in Europe. After WWII, only a few thousand Jews remained.[19]

Within Poland, during the 1920s, Jews were permitted to engage in professions, acquire land, and enter the civil service. This short period of opportunity and hope ended abruptly during the Holocaust with tragic and catastrophic consequences for Jews and other targeted groups, not only in Poland but also throughout Europe. Many *yizkor* (memorial) books and memoirs have been written about those lost communities and cruel fates of the Jews. The yizkor books are sentimental, nostalgic as well as sad and bitter.

Błażowa

My Geiger ancestors lived in Błażowa, within the Subcarpathian Voivodeship or Subcarpathia Province in Poland. Błażowa is located at coordinates 49° 53´ N and 22° 06´ E within the southeastern corner of Poland, in the green and hilly foothills of the Carpathian Mountains along the Ryjak River. Błażowa lies 12 miles SSE of Rzeszów, the main administrative and industrial center for this province. Today, the total population of Błażowa is 2,100 mainly Roman Catholic with no Jewish presence. In 1890 the Jewish population of Błażowa numbered 942 (20 per cent) out of a general population of 4,760.[20] During the interwar period (1918–1939) the province was part of the Lwów Voivodeship. During 1999 Poland created the territory Subcarpathian Voivodeship or Subcarpathia Province; in Polish it is *województwo podkarpackie*.

Błażowa was an example of a typical *shtetl*, a town or village where Jews settled in Galicia and throughout Eastern Europe. The *shtetl* consisted of wood houses clustered around a marketplace called a *rynek*. The marketplace had shops, booths, and tables where peasant women would sell their live-stock, fish, vegetables, and where they would buy items produced by the Jews such as hats, shoes, textiles, tools.[21] Jews living within the *shtetl* were traditional and orthodox, praying to G-d in

Beit Ha Midrash Błażowa

Hebrew with Yiddish as their spoken language. Pious Jews in the *shtetl* adhered to following the 613 *mitzvot* or commandments molding an inner discipline for rituals of daily life. The world of Jews living in the *shtetl* revolved around G-d as a living force and a familiar divine presence.[22] Orthodox Jewish religious education was reserved for males in *cheders* (elementary grades) and in *yeshivas* (high school and beyond) where students were immersed in the study of traditional religious texts such as the Torah and the Talmud in the *beit hamidrash*, a building set aside for this education.

A Jewish community existed in Błażowa by the 18th and 19th centuries. The early occupations of Jews in Błażowa were mainly agriculture, crafts, and home-based manufacture of cloth and textiles. Jews worked in small-scale commerce, labor, and peddling.[23] If a peasant could not barter or pay for goods, the Jewish merchant could offer credit to those who lacked enough cash.[24] Jews in Błażowa also raised chickens and grew their own vegetables for their sustenance.

Jewish vital records, tax records, etc. were unfortunately destroyed in Błażowa during a huge fire 27 May 1907. Much of the town was destroyed, and four hundred Jewish families were financially ruined.[25] A fund was established to assist the poor Jews living in Błażowa, by affluent Jews and by charity donations, as well as help from abroad.[26] During 1918, two hundred Jewish homes were pillaged by local peasants who then initiated a boycott on sales of food to Jews.

Such anti-Semitism afflicted the Jews of Błażowa from 1918 through the horrors of WWII. Pogroms against Jews began in nearby villages and roads that led to Błażowa during November 1918. Jews were beaten and robbed. When this news first broke out, Jews in Błażowa wanted to set up a militia, but the suggestion was rejected. Masses of armed farmers and local non-Jews, including women from surrounding villages, began to stream toward Błażowa with loaded weapons. At least two hundred Jewish families were plundered and left with nothing. The police stood aside while incidents of rape and murder occurred.[27]

Once again, in 1919 bands of farmers organized another pogrom against the Jews, but this time they were dispersed by the police. The mob then destroyed much of the Jewish cemetery and continued plundering other Jews. Attacks on Jews were daily occurrences on the road from Rzeszów to Błażowa.[28] The farmers imposed a boycott against the Jews by not selling them food. The wave of anti-Semitism did not abate and worsened in 1924 under the leadership of the Endek (Polish Democratic Party) located in Rzeszów. Leaflets and pamphlets with strong anti-Semitic content were distributed. To make matters worse, the government imposed substantial taxes upon the local Jews, destroying their sources of livelihood and confiscated the property of small-scale Jewish merchants.[29]

Life for Jews in Błażowa came to an abrupt and tragic end during WWII. Early in the war, The Nazis tortured and murdered twenty-two local Jews. Jewish refugees from other towns arrived in Błażowa during the last months of 1939, as the Nazi regime occupied Poland. The Jewish community of Błażowa set up a soup kitchen, and by 1942 the numbers grew to three hundred destitute Jews. A *Judenrat* (Nazi-administered Jewish council) was formed in Błażowa. Jews were drafted for road construction and forced labor. Police were empowered to search Jewish homes and stores; they missed no opportunity to seize goods from affluent Jews. A Jewish bakery was put out of business and the flour was auctioned off. Stocks of tobacco and cigars were confiscated. The Germans imposed monetary "contributions" from Jews. The Mayor and Judenrat listed assets owned by Jews, such as cash, gold, jewelry, and real estate.[30]

In June or July 1941 more than twenty Jews from Błażowa were arrested, and transferred to a prison in Rzeszów, where Jews from nearby Kolbuszowa were also imprisoned. Concerned family members and others from the Judenrat travelled to Rzeszów, bribing guards to give food packages to the prisoners. The prisoners from Błażowa were finally released for a large ransom.

The liquidation of the Jewish community from Błażowa began in June of 1942, with their deportation to the Rzeszów ghetto. Many elderly and sick people were murdered during this action. Grand Rabbi Meir Spira was among the victims. In July of 1942, most of the Jews from Błażowa were deported to the Bełżec Extermination Camp, along with Jewish deportees from other towns in the district. [31]

Why My Geiger Ancestors Settled in Błażowa

My research indicated that my Geiger ancestors settled in Błażowa, Poland for religious reasons. Błażowa became a magnet for Hasidim because the charismatic and respected Hasidic Grand Rabbi Tzvi Elimelech Spira (1841–1924), the author of *Tzvi Latzadik*, moved to Błażowa in 1874 from Rybotycze, Poland.[32] Grand Rabbi Tzvi Elimelech Spira of Bluzhov was born into a distinguished lineage that began with his grandfather Rabbi Tzvi Elimelech of Dynów (1783–1841) who wrote an important Hasidic text *Bnei Yissaschar*, both a scholarly and mystical work.

R'Tzvi Elimelech Spira One Room House Błażowa

Middle figure R'Tzvi Elimelech Spira Błażowa

Grand Rabbi Tzvi Elimelech Spira of Bluzhov was known as an extremely intelligent man who had a large following of Hasidim from Dynów and even from Hungary and Congress Poland. He drew hundreds of worshippers to his house which became the center for Hasidim in Błażowa. My great-grandfather Rabbi Aron Geiger was among his Hasidic congregants in both Błażowa and Rzeszów; his son Rabbi Abraham Geiger, worked closely with Grand Rabbi Tzvi Elimelech Spira as a rabbi, *gabbai* and community *mohel* in Błażowa. My great-grandparents Aron and Hinde Geiger travelled from Vienna to Rzeszów in 1924 to pay their respects to the ailing Grand Rabbi Tzvi Elimelech Spira.

Grand Rabbi Israel Spira (1889–1989) was another grandson of Grand Rabbi Tzvi Elimelech Spira. Rabbi Israel Spira survived imprisonment and torture in concentration camps through a series of miracles during the Holocaust, including his escape from the extermination camp at Bergen-Belsen. After WWII he immigrated to the United States in 1946 as a remnant of the Błażowa rabbinical dynasty and continued as the Bluzhover spiritual leader in Brooklyn, New York until his death.[33]

Błażowa Jewish Cemetery

I initially learned about Błażowa and the Błażowa Jewish cemetery through genealogists Suzan Wynne and Estelle Guzik, who shared their detailed experiences and photographs with me since 2008. In addition, Estelle and I share a genealogical link with the Geigers from Błażowa. Please see my chapter *Yehezkeil Geiger and Fradal Landesman.*

The Błażowa Jewish cemetery exists in the eastern part of the town, up a hill at the end of Mickiewicz Street. The cemetery occupies a land area of 5455 sq. meters.[34] About half of the headstones are toppled and the cemetery has no sign or marker. It is reached through private property, through a broken masonry wall and a broken fence with no gate. It was vandalized during WWII and occasionally thereafter. Security and vandalism remain serious threats, with vegetation overgrowth as continuous problems.[35]

Gidonim Project

A contributor to the Gesher Galicia SIG digest relayed important information about a new website with tombstone photos from Błażowa, www.gidonim.com/English/.[36] Please view the website for a complete listing of all the matsevahs and graves in the Błażowa cemetery. The Gidonim Project originated 2004 at the Re'ut School, Jerusalem, Israel under the auspices of the founder Dr. Aryeh Geiger. This was a valuable program that sent young adult volunteers to various cemeteries in Poland including Błażowa. Funding for the program was raised by the school and participants. The youth helped restore cemeteries and headstones, documented, and photographed the matsevahs. In this way they honored the mitzvah of showing respect for the dead.[37] Thus far, I have no knowledge of a family relationship between Dr. Aryeh Geiger with my Geiger family. Thanks to the work of those able volunteers and teachers, I was able to view on-line the matsevah of my ancestor Chaim Yehuda son of Szlomo Dawida Geiger who died 1 Adar 5692 or 1932 at Błażowa. The Hebrew inscription for Chaim Yehuda was translated, confirming my research that Szlomo Dawida Geiger was my great-great-grandfather as it corresponded with the name from the matsevah in Vienna of my great-grandfather, Aron Geiger who was the son of Shlomo Dawid. Chaim Yehuda was therefore a brother of my great-grandfather Aron Geiger. I was also able to view another Błażowa matsevah for Yehezkeil son of Eliezer Geiger who died 5697 or 1937. I discovered after years of research that this person also known as Chaskel Geiger, was a cousin of my Geiger ancestors. Both Geiger families were living in Błażowa during the same time, and this was not a coincidence.

Endnotes

1   jewishencyclopedia.com/articles/15122-york.

2   Wikipedia.org (en.wikipedia.org/wiki/Black_Death).

3   Suzan Wynne. *The Galitzianers: The Jews of Galicia, 1772–1918*. (Kensington,MD: Suzan Wynne, 2006). 29–30.

4   Jewish Virtual Library.org (www.jewishvirtuallibrary.org/history-and-development-of-yiddish).

5   Wikipedia.org (en.wikipedia.org/wiki/Polish-Lithuanian Commonwealth.

6   Wikipedia.org (wikipedia.org/wiki/Partitions _of_ Poland.

7   Suzan Wynne. *The Galitzianers:The Jews of Galicia, 1772–1918*. (Kensington, MD: Suzan Wynne, 2006).48.

8   YIVO Institute for Jewish Research. Galicia.

9   Jewishgen.org. Gesher Galicia-the Special Interest Group for Galicia. Province of the Former Austrian Empire.

10   Galician Jews. jewishencyclopedia.com/articles/3453-bochnia-austria.

11   Ibid., 56.

12   Wynne, Suzan. *The Galitzianers:The Jews of Galicia, 1772–1918*. (Kensington, MD: Suzan Wynne, 2006). 55–63.

13   Ibid. 62.

14   Ibid.,63.

15   Ibid., 34–39.

16   Alexander Beider. *A Dictionary of Jewish Surnames from Galicia.*(New York: Avotaynu, 2004).10–21.

17   Suzan Wynne. *The Galitzianers: the Jews of Galicia, 1772–1918*. (Kensington,MD: Suzan Wynne, 2006). 61-62.

18   Piotr Wrobel. *The Jews of Galicia under Austrian-Polish Rule 1869–1918* (Boston: Cambridge University Press, 1994).8.

19   Henry Wellisch, Email. (Vienna: The Archives of the Jewish Community of Vienna). groups.google.com/group/soc.genealogy.jewish/browse. 20 October 2008.

20   sztetl.org.pl. Virtual Shtetl is a bi-lingual Polish-English portal of the Museum of the History of Polish Jews, located in Warsaw.

21   Irving Howe. *World of Our Fathers*. (New York: New York University Press, 2005).10.

22   Ibid.,11–13.

23   Shmuel Spector, editor. *Pinkas Hakehillot—Polin. Encyclopedia of Jewish Communities in Poland, Volume III, Blazowa*. Jerrold Landau, translator. JewishGen Coordinator: Judith Goldsmith (Jerusalem, Israel: Yad Vashem). 90–92.

24   Suzan Wynne. *The Galitzianers: The Jews of Galicia, 1772–1918*. (Kensington, MD: Suzan Wynne, 2006). 30–34.

25   Henrietta Szold, editor. *American Jewish Yearbook*. Vol. *9* (1907-1908). 516. Blazowa destroyed by fire. (www.ajcarchives.org/AJC_DATA/Files/1907_1908.

26   www.sztetl.org.pl/en/article/blazowa.

27   Shmuel Spector, editor. *Pinkas Hakehillot—Polin. Encyclopedia of Jewish Communities in Poland, Volume III, Blazowa*. Jerrold Landau, translator. (Jerusalem, Israel: Yad Vashem).91.

28   Ibid.92.

29   Ibid.

30   www.sztetl.org.pl/en/article/blazowa.History Section.2.

31   Shmuel Spector, editor. *Pinkas Hakehillot—Polin. Encyclopedia of Jewish Communities in Poland, Volume III, Blazowa*. Jerrold Landau, translator. (Jerusalem, Israel: Yad Vashem). 90–92.

32   Suzan Wynne. *The Langsam-Spira Family*. (New York: Center for Jewish History, 1986). AR 10234.

33   New York Times Archives. Obituary published 1 Nov 1989. *Israel Spira, 99, Leader of Bluzhov Hasidim died 31 Oct 1989 at Maimonides Hospital, Brooklyn, New York.*

34 www.kirkuty.xip.pl/blazowa.htm. Discussion of the cemetery in Blazowa with a list of names and photographs.

35 International Jewish Cemetery Project. International Association of Jewish Genealogical Societies. Blazowa: Rzeszowskie.

36 Tomer Brunner. Email 4 May 2007. Gesher Galicia SIG Digest. (www.jewishgen.org).

37 Re'ut School: Jerusalem, Israel. (www.gidonim.com).

Chapter Two

Solomon David Geiger and Chaje Mindel Unger

First Steps

My mother Sylvia Gerber née Weiss dutifully recorded in my Life Journal book "after consulting with Uncle Abraham Geiger we named our darling Hensha Hinde in Jewish and Judith Carol. The first child is always named after the mother's family." She recorded that Hensha and Hinde were my great-grandmothers. I began my genealogical journey knowing my maternal grandparents were Minnie Geiger and Oscar Weiss but wondered about the names Hensha and Hinde. My first step was to obtain my grandparent's marriage certificate from the New York City Municipal Archives.

This important document yielded the names of my four maternal great-grandparents and opened new avenues for my genealogical research. On their marriage certificate, my grandmother, Minnie Geiger, listed her parents as Hinde Turnheim and Aron Geiger. My grandfather Oscar Weiss listed his parents as Hannie Zuckerberg and Fischel Weiss. (See the chapter *Minnie Geiger and Oscar Weiss.*) I now learned that I was named for my two maternal great-grandmothers; Hensha aka Hannie Zuckerberg and Hinde Turnheim.[1] Now that I had the names of my great-grandparents, I decided to pursue the trail further back in time and focus on researching my maternal lineage who lived in the Austrian ruled province of Galicia. (See the chapter *Aron Geiger and Hinde Turnheim.*)

I first found mention of my great-great-grandfather Solomon David aka Sholom Dovid while searching for the burial place of my great-grandfather Aron Geiger. I found a reference for him on the JewishGen.org JOWBR (Jewish On-line Worldwide Burial Registry) and discovered that Aron Geiger's matsevah and final resting place was in the Weiner Zentralfriedhof Cemetery, Vienna, Austria. In June 2009, I exchanged emails with a genealogist, Celia Male z"l who made frequent visits to Vienna from her home in London, and she offered to take photos of the matsevah that I requested for Aron Geiger. Another researcher, Australian Daniela Torsch, also generously provided me with photographs of his matsevah.

I discovered that my great-grandfather Aron Geiger was the son of Sholom Dovid Geiger from Błażowa! The Hebrew inscription on the matsevah was difficult to read from the photographs but what was visible indicated that Aron was the son of Sholom Dovid Geiger of Błażowa. I now had the name of one of my great-great-grandparents. This evidence was confirmed by death records sent to me from the archives of the Israelitische Kultus Gemeinde Wien (known as the IKG-Wien) and the Wiener Stadt und Landesarchiv in Vienna for my great-grandparents Aron Geiger and Hinde Turnheim. Aron Geiger was born 1850 at Błażowa, Poland and died 1924; Hinde was born 1850 at Przemyśl, Poland and died 1931. They are buried side by side in the Jewish Cemetery Weiner Zentralfriedhof at Vienna, Austria.

Discovering Rabbis in the Family

I contacted the Israelitische Kultus Gemeinde Wien (IKG), the Jewish Community cultural center of Vienna, and asked if they could send clear photographs of my great-grandparents' matsevahs. Ms. Debora Kravtschenko of the IKG agreed to take photographs of my ancestors' matsevahs in that cemetery: Aron and Hinde Geiger, Fischl Weiss, Sigmund and Salomon Turnheim. True to her word, Ms. Kravtschenko sent me photos of their matsevahs with improved clarity of the Hebrew inscriptions on the matsevahs.

My next step was to post photos of my Geiger matsevahs to ViewMate on JewishGen.org for translations from the Hebrew. I was surprised to learn that both Aron Geiger and his father Solomon David Geiger were rabbis and religious teachers. I had no idea of this, as none of my relatives knew this fact, only that Aron's son Abraham Geiger was a rabbi. I saw there was a rabbinical line extending from father to son, from generation to generation. I do not know how far back the profession of rabbi could extend with the Geiger family but here it was for me to discover and to tell you. Any crumbs of information are clues to the character and lives of our ancestors who we never met, therefore quite valuable. I was moved when I learned that some of my Geiger ancestors followed an unbroken chain of Judaic spiritual practice and tradition.

The Rabbi

I researched the vocation of Rabbi as it pertained to my Geiger family. It is interesting that the title Rabbi does not appear in the Hebrew Bible, such men were referred to as priests and scribes. The earliest reference to "rabbi" was during the first century CE. The word "rabbi" derives from the Hebrew word *rav* meaning "great one or master"; and *ha-rav* for "the master." A *Rav*/rabbi consciously takes on the role of "raising" sons by teaching them the Torah and Jewish law. The *Rav* or rabbi becomes like a second father in the religious and spiritual sense. Jewish tradition also encourages Jewish fathers to teach their sons a practical trade to support their families.[2]

Studying the Torah is a rabbi's lifelong undertaking that does not end with receiving ordination. A Rabbi is expected to set aside time daily for study; acquired Torah knowledge must be passed on to students and disciples. Teaching by rabbis occurs in the elementary *heder*, intermediate *yeshivah*, and advanced *kollel*. Prior to modern times, progressive Polish rulers designated legal matters pertaining to Jews should be settled within the Jewish community or *kahal* by the town rabbi. Those rabbis with extensive knowledge of Torah law (*halakhah*) presided as Head of the Jewish Court (*av beth din*) and judgments were enforced with fines and even with degrees of communal excommunication when necessary.

Rabbis legislated with other rabbis in a *beth din* to debate solutions and enact regulations in matters as diverse as matchmaking, matrimonial law, relations with gentiles, utilizing civil courts, education of orphans, hiring of schoolteachers. Rabbis often supervised Jewish slaughter of animals (*shekhita*) to ensure this practice was in accordance with Jewish law. They supervised Jewish kosher regulations in shops that sold food for their compliance with *kashrut*. They supervised rules for the ritual bath (*mikveh*), the elementary school (*heder*), the Sabbath community boundaries (*eruvin*) and the burial society (*hevra kadisha*). Rabbis provided counseling including visiting the sick and officiated at life-cycle occasions. Among Hasidic Jews it is still common to turn to the *rebbe* for advice on personal matters.

Unlike modern times, traditionally the rabbi did not lead prayer services since the Jewish liturgy is fixed and printed in prayer books (*siddurim*). The vocal portions were often chanted by a cantor (*hazan*) and the Torah portion was read by a trained reader (*ba'al koreh*). If the rabbi was present, he would be seated in front near the Ark. If halakhic questions rose about the prayer service, the rabbi would address them.

Being a rabbi was uncompensated in early days; often rabbis needed other occupations to support themselves and their families such as merchant, woodchopper, sandal-maker, carpenter, farmer, tanner, etc. The birth record for Chaje Mindel Finder, a granddaughter of Solomon David Geiger and Chaje Mindel Unger, indicated that Sholom David Geiger was a merchant in addition to being a rabbi and a teacher.

Within a Hasidic dynasty, positions of spiritual leadership were transmitted from fathers to sons. If there were no sons, then leadership could pass to sons-in-laws, to nephews or to another male family member. The curriculum for study to become a rabbi included study of the Torah, the Talmud, Responsa and Musar. The profession of rabbi was vital to the transmission of Jewish knowledge of sacred texts, spirituality, Jewish moral, and ethical values. It was a highly valued role in the community. I am impressed that my great-great-grandfather Rabbi Solomon David Geiger and great-grandfather Rabbi Aron Geiger were so committed and respected by their community. Aron Geiger passed on this tradition to his son Rabbi Abraham Geiger.

My grandmother Minnie was raised in a Hasidic orthodox home with her father as a rabbi. Her advice to me was "do all the good you can, for all the people you can, in every way you can". I interpret this to mean even if one does not become a rabbi, one can certainly fulfill tzedakah and mitzvahs and in general, practice Jewish values for honesty, piety, charity, justice, compassion, spirituality, family cohesion, with moral and ethical living.

Paths of Research

Researching JRI-Poland and JewishGen provided me with valuable information concerning birth records from the Przemyśl Archives, not only for my grandmother Minnie but also for her siblings as they were all born at Przemyśl, Subcarpathia Province, Poland. My great uncle Israel Geiger's birth record was significant for containing additional evidence about my great great-grandfather. Israel Geiger was born 16 January 1874 to parents Aron Geiger and Hinde Turnheim. Solomon David Geiger was recorded as the *sandek*. This was an honor often reserved for the grandfather. The responsibility of the sandek was to hold the male baby for the circumcision ceremony or *brit milah* performed on the eighth day of life. (*See the chapter Israel Geiger and Esther Perlberg.*)

My grandmother Minnie's ship manifest in 1904 listed her home as Błażowa, under the Rzeszów administrative district, Poland that was in Galicia. I later learned that other Geiger relatives also lived in Błażowa. I was fortunate to obtain photographs of matsevahs in the Jewish cemetery of Błażowa from the Gidonim project.[3] There were two headstones at the Jewish Cemetery in Błażowa both with the surname Geiger; one was Chaim Yehuda who was a son of Shlomo Dovid and the other was Yechezkiel who was a son of Eliezer. (See chapter *Yechezkiel Geiger and Fradal Landesman.*) I subsequently learned there was a family relationship between both Geiger families from Błażowa.

There emerged additional evidence for the identification of my great-great-grandparents with records located through JewishGen and JRI-Poland of births for parents Lazar Finder and Cipra (Zipora) Geiger. The records indicated that Cipra (Zipora) was a daughter of my great great-grandparents Sholom David Geiger and Chaja Mindel Unger from Błażowa. One of their children was named Chaje Mindel Finder, born 4 November 1891 at Bagienica, Dabrowa District, Malopolskie, Poland to parents Lazar Finder and Cipra Geiger; Cipra was recorded on the birth record as the daughter of Salomon Dawid Geiger and Chaje Mindel Geiger of Błażowa. Their baby Chaja Mindel was named for Cipra's mother Chaja Mindel Unger, who was probably deceased by that date.[4]

Could I go further back to find my great-great-great-grandparents? Not without records or other direct evidence. I have not yet encountered vital records for Sholom Dovid Geiger or for Chaje Mindel Unger which may have yielded more clues. I learned that Solomon David Geiger (ca. 1823–ca. 1891) and Chaje Min-

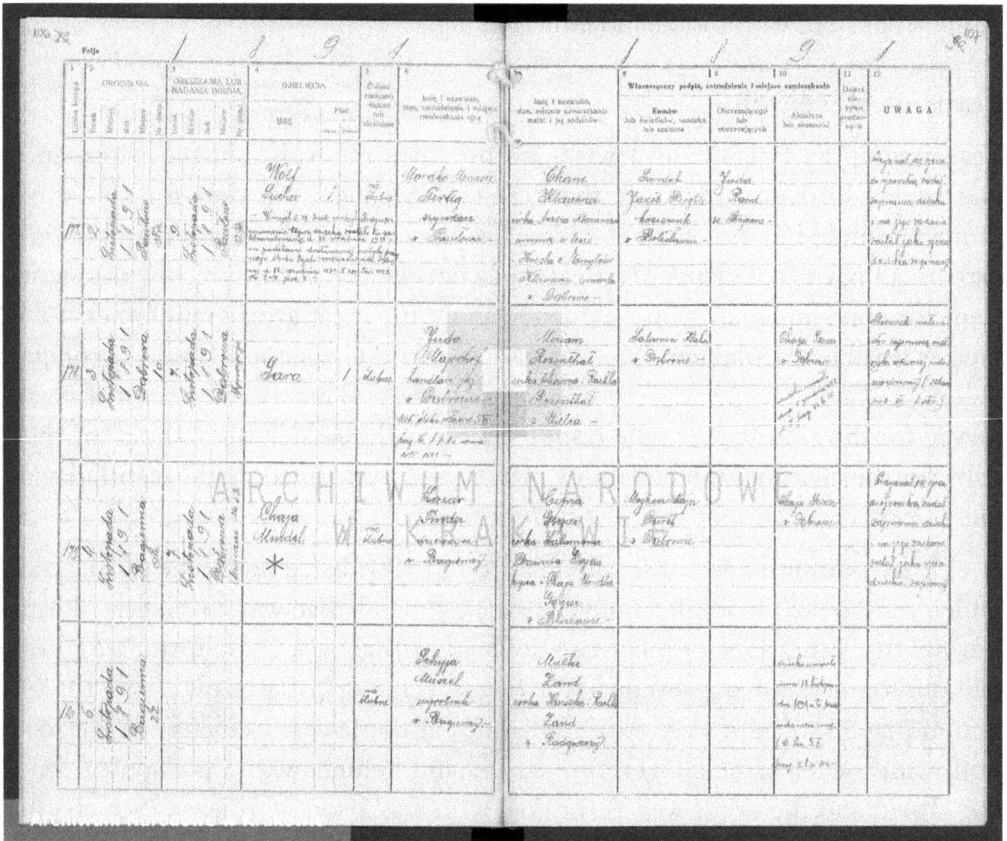

Birth record for Chaje Mindel Finder

del Unger (ca. 1825–ca.1886) were my great-great-grandparents. They had the following children: Moses Geiger (1841–1912); my great-grandfather Aron Geiger (1850–1924); Zipora Geiger (ca. 1860–unknown date of death); and Chaim Yehuda Geiger (ca.1866–1932). Two of the children of Solomon David Geiger and Chaje Mindel Unger, Chaim Yehuda Geiger and Cipre Geiger are discussed in this chapter. Aron Geiger and Moses Geiger are discussed in chapters *Aron Geiger and Hinde Turnheim; Moses Geiger and Laje.*

I speculated that my great-great-grandfather Rabbi Sholom David Geiger was either born at Błażowa or moved to Błażowa as a youth due to religious and/or marital reasons. It is possible that he was drawn to Błażowa by the presence of the Bluzhover Rabbi Tzvi Elimelech Spira (1841–1924). Sholom Dovid Geiger was born ca. 1823, locale unknown.[5] He was a merchant, a rabbi, and a religious teacher. He died ca. 1891 or 1892 at Błażowa in the Rzeszów District. This estimate is based on available records and matzevahs as evidence discovered over the years. Some records were obtained directly from the Rzeszów Archive with the assistance of a Polish researcher, Krzysztof Malczewski. Sources pointed to Błażowa as the place where my grandmother lived, as well as my great-grandparents and my great-great-grandparents. There are no surviving Jewish records from Błażowa.

Chaje Mindel Unger and Her Family

Chaje Mindel Unger was born ca. 1825 and she married Sholom David Geiger ca.1841. She died ca. 1886 at 61 years.[6] The couple lived in Błażowa and their children were Moshe, Aron, Zipora and Chaim Yehuda. Jewish grooms in Galicia would usually live in the same town where the bride and her family lived, unless the groom was financially established in another town and then the bride would move there.[7] An arranged marriage could involve betrothals promised at birth. There is not enough evidence yet to determine whether Chaje Mindel Unger moved to Błażowa from another locale because Sholom David Geiger was established there, whether she was originally from Błażowa or whether Sholom David came from another town and moved to his bride's shtetl of Błażowa. I was puzzled why my great-great-grandparents chose Lazar Finder as husband for their daughter Cipre since he was born at Dąbrowa Tarnowska within the Malopolskie Province. The distance to Błażowa is 76 miles. I found additional birth records for the children of Cipre and Lazar Finder indicating that Lazar was born in Grądy, a small town within the region of Dąbrowa. He established his young family there after he married Cipre Geiger from Błażowa.

The Hasidic Jewish population in Dąbrowa were mainly followers of the respected Unger rabbinical dynasty. Dąbrowa Tarnowska is approximately 48 miles east of Kraków and 10 miles north of Tarnów. In 1830 the Jewish population was 978, by 1880 the Jewish population in Dąbrowa was 1,882. [8] Was the connection of the Finders living in an area known for Unger Hasidim a coincidence or an explanation why there probably was an arranged marriage of Chaje Mindel Unger's daughter Cipre Geiger with Lazar Finder?

The *tzadiks* from the Unger family established their rabbinical dynasty at Dąbrowa by the beginning of the 19th century. Ungers were often listed as sandeks and rabbis in vital records, not only for the Finder family but also for other families in Dąbrowa.[9] A synagogue was built by the Hasids at Dąbrowa Tarnowska in 1865 that later deteriorated and fell into derelict condition. It was once known as the Pearl of Hasidic Architecture.

Old Postcard Dabrowa Synagogue

The Dąbrowa Tarnowska synagogue was fully restored in 2012 with EU, national and local funding and contains beautiful Italian-painted frescos. It was dedicated as a new Jewish cultural center.[10] I took note of Unger names on Dąbrowa records to see if I could find Chaje Mindel Unger and her family. Although there were Unger records, I could not find a familial relationship between my great-great-grandmother Chaje Mindel Unger of Błażowa with the Ungers of Dabrowa as the few surviving records were of much later dates.

Chaim Yehuda Geiger was a Son of Sholom David Geiger and Chaje Mindel Unger

The Gidonim.org project provided me with information for my Geiger family from Błażowa based on their research and photographs of matsevahs taken at the Jewish Błażowa cemetery. One of the matsevahs was for Chaim Yehuda Geiger. Since his matsevah was in Hebrew, I requested a translation from Rabbi Joshua Segal.[11] His translation from Hebrew to English for Chaim Yehuda Geiger's matsevah is the following:

> He is covered by the Crown of Torah. Here lies a man who walked the straight
> path, Mr. Chayim Judah Geiger, son of Shlomo David of blessed memory. G-d will

surely avenge the spilling of Jewish blood on the first day of the new moon of Adar 5692. May his soul be bound up in the bonds of the living.

I learned that Chaim Yehuda Geiger was a son of my great-great-grandfather Sholom David Geiger, and he was murdered on 8 February 1932. The murder of Chaim Yehuda Geiger likely occurred by some anti-Semitic person or persons, perhaps by a vicious mob, as violent actions were being stirred up by propaganda emanating from Adolf Hitler and the Nazi party. At that time there was a world-wide recession, the Polish economy was in shambles and unemployment was at record highs. There were two million unemployed Poles and anti-Semitic feelings were being roused blaming the Jews for all their problems. I noted that Shlomo Dovid must have been deceased prior to his son's Chayim Judah's death since the phrase on his matsevah stated Shlomo Dovid was *of blessed memory.*

After an extensive search of records, I came across additional information from the Rzeszów Archives. Judah Geiger and Golda Lea Gruenstein were a couple with a family of four children listed in the 1910 census of Rzeszów.[12] Juda (Yehuda) was born 1866 at Ruska Wieś, Rzeszów, married and head of the household. His wife, Golda, was born 1870 at Kolbuszowa. Their children were: Berel, born 1899,[13] Joachim, born 1904,[14] Sara, born 1906,[15] and Chaskel, born 1908.[16] A notation in the Comments section indicated that Juda and Golda had their marriage registered by civil authority on 31 August 1902.

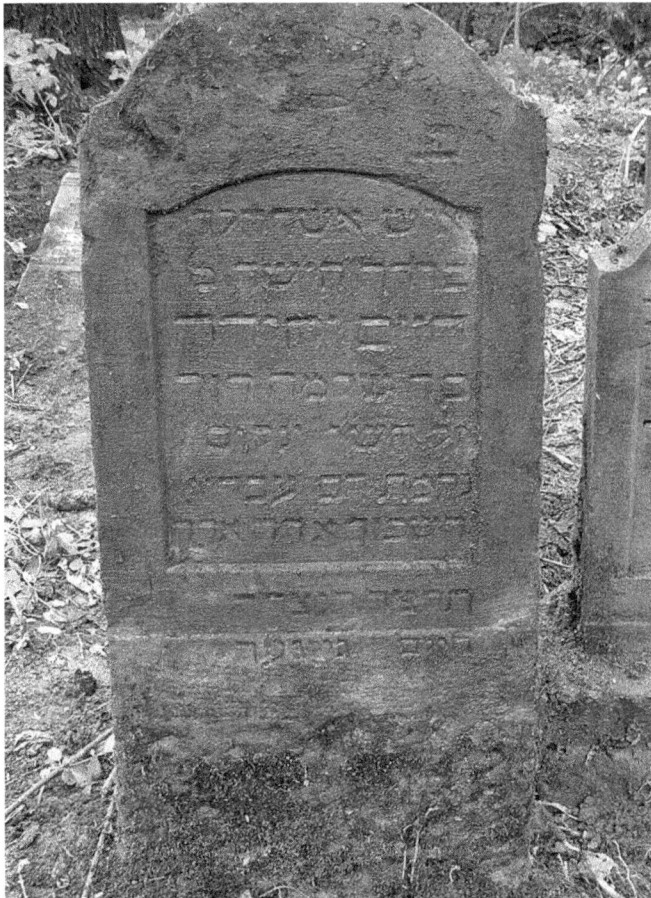

Chaim Yehuda Geiger matsevah Błażowa

Juda Geiger and Golda Lea Grunstein had another child named Salomon Dawid (1892–1898). This record was listed under the mother's surname Gruenstein probably due to their marriage not being registered, the given name of the mother was Golda. I sent away for that record from the Rzeszów Archive because the name Salomon Dawid could be evidence that the baby was named after Juda's father Sholom Dovid, following the Ashkenazi Jewish custom of naming after a recently deceased close relative. This record fit with my estimate for the death of Solomon David Geiger in 1891 or 1892. Juda Geiger signed the record under the Comments section establishing that he was the baby's father.[17]

Birth record for Salomon Dawid Grunstein

I discovered another birth record for a child named Mendel, born 1911 to parents Juda Geiger and Golda Gruenstein.[18] A death record came to my attention, the death of Golda Lea Geiger in 1930, at age 60 thus correlating with her birth year of 1870.[19] Some of the Rzeszów records in Fond 533 for children born to Yehuda Geiger and Golda Gruenstein listed Juda Geiger with an additional name, Juda Mendel Geiger. This additional name left me confused. Could I conclude that Chaim Yehuda Geiger was indeed Juda Mendel Geiger? Could this mean that he had three given names-Chaim Yehuda Mendel? Alexander Beider noted that Ashkenazi Jews in Europe often had double and even triple given names because names from deceased close relatives were often handed down through generations.

Children of Chaim Yehuda Geiger and Golda Lea Gruenstein

Three marriage records were found for children of Chaim Yehuda Geiger and Golda Lea Gruenstein. Bernard aka Berl Geiger born 1899 at Rzeszów, married Fania Ernestyna Goldmann 1923 at Rzeszów, Podkarpackie, Poland. Her mother was Rosa Goldmann.[20] Joachim Geiger born 1904 at Rzeszów, married Rachela Krebs 1928 at Rzeszów, Podkarpackie, Poland.[21] Her parents were Jakub Marcus Krebs and Chana Gruenthal. Joachim Geiger worked as a policeman in Radom, a city near Warsaw, Poland during the Shoah.[22] Mendel Geiger born 1911 at Rzeszów, married Sprinca Brueckner 1936 at Rzeszów. Her parents were Jakub Hersh Brueckner and Ruchla Sufrin.[23]

Zipora Geiger was a daughter of Shlomo Dovid Geiger and Chaje Mindel Unger

Zipora, also known as Cipre, was a daughter of my great-great-grandparents Shlomo Dovid Geiger and Chaje Mindel Unger from Błażowa, Podkarpackie, Poland. This fact was confirmed when I found 8 birth records for Cipre and Lazar Finder's children, indicating that Zipora aka Cipre was the daughter of Shlomo Dovid Geiger and Chaya Mindel Unger of Błażowa, Podkarpackie, Poland.

I estimated that Cipre was born ca.1860, based on dates of births for her siblings: Moses Geiger born 1841; Aron Geiger born 1850; Chaim Yehuda born ca. 1866. Cipre Geiger and Lazar Finder were married ca.1885 most likely in Błażowa, Podkarpackie, Poland. Cipre was approximately 27 years of age when she had her first child Nechuma in 1887 and 41 years of age when she had her last child Zecharje Leib in 1901.

Children of Cipre Geiger and Lazar Finder were: Nechuma born 27 October 1887 at Grądy, Dąbrowa, Małopolskie, Poland[24]; Nuchim born 28 July 1889 at Bagienica, Dąbrowa, Małopolskie, Poland.[25] Chaja Mindel born 4 November 1891 at Bagienica, Dąbrowa, Małopolskie, Poland,[26] died 1897 at Wola Postolowa, Lisko, Podkarpackie, Poland,[27] Israel Ber born 20 June 1895 in Bagienica;[28] died 1897 at Wola Postolowa, Lisko, Podkarpackie, Poland,[29] Taube born 1897 and died 1897 at Wola Postolowa, Lisko, Podkarpackie, Poland,[30] Alte Marjem born 25 April 1900 at Zurawiczki, Jarosław, Podkarpackie, Poland,[31] Zecharje Leib born 24 April 1901 at Zurawiczki, Jarosław, Podkarpackie, Poland.[32] I noted that Cipre's mother Chaja Mindel was probably deceased prior to November 1891. Cipre and Lazar suffered the deaths of their children at Wola Postolowa in the Lisko District during 1897; Taube died at 4 weeks; Israel Ber aka Srul died at 2 years and Chaje Mindel aka Mindzia died at 6 years. There may have been an outbreak of a disease or a calamity at Wola Postolowa that claimed the lives of their three children in 1897.

The Finder Family

There was likely an arranged marriage between Cipre Geiger and Lazar Finder as that was the tradition for Ashkenazi Jews and continues to this day among the Hasidim. Lazar Finder was born ca. 1860 at Grądy, within the Dąbrowa District, Małopolskie, Poland. This was a shtetl about 83 miles from Błażowa and was near a larger town Dąbrowa Tarnowska, Małopolskie, Poland. I needed to learn more about Lazar Finder's family background.

By reviewing Finder birth and marriage records, I noted that Lazar had several Finder family relatives within the Dąbrowa District. I found four other Finder individuals in the same generation as Lazar, living within the Dąbrowa District and observed they all shared the same parents: Nuchim and Nisli Finder who were from Grądy therefore they were also Lazar Finder's parents. Nuchim Finder was born ca. 1835 and he died ca. 1889. As further circumstantial evidence, Lazar Finder and Cipre Geiger had a son named Nuchim who was born 28 July 1889 at Bagienica, named after Lazar's deceased father Nuchim.[33] I located a possible Finder descendant who put this Finder family on their *Rubin Web Site* at www.myheritage.com. This web site agreed with my own research that parents of Lazar and his siblings were Nelly aka Nisli Nissel and Nuchim Finder.

I searched the JewishGen Online Worldwide Burial Registry Database to find a descendant of Cipre Geiger and Lazar Finder. I found a Nuchim Finder who died at Vienna on 2 July 1925 and was buried at the Wiener Zentralfriedhof cemetery. I became excited about this information thinking this could be Nuchim, the son of Lazar and Cipre. I contacted the Jewish Community of Vienna (IKG) to obtain his death record.[34] After I filled out the requisite paperwork and wired money to the organization, they sent me Nuchim Finder's marriage and death records. Nuchim Finder was born at Bagienica 6 August 1889; however, his parents were listed as Simche Diller and Blima Finder, not Lazar Finder and Cipre Geiger. This Nuchim Finder married his first cousin Frimet Finder whose parents were Isak Finder and Betti Schapira in Vienna, 1921. He died 2 July 1925 at 35 years. He was buried in the Wiener Zentralfriedhof cemetery, Tor IV, Group 6, Row 17, grave 91. He was a first cousin to Lazar and Cipre's son Nuchim who was also born 1889 at Bagienica.

Yad Vashem Records

I researched the names from the Finder family to see if they appeared in the Central Database for Shoah Victims at Yad Vashem. I found a record for Lazar Finder's nephew Abraham Wolf Finder born at Radwan, Poland 27 March 1884 and who lived at Kraków when the Shoah began.[35] He was married to Beila Gemeiner and she was born at Kraków 08 May 1884. They were merchants. This married couple, Abraham Wolf and Beila Finder, also appeared on a list compiled 1940 of Jews from the Kraków Ghetto.[36] They were deported with 200,000 Jews during 1942–1943 for extermination at Auschwitz, Kraków-Płaszów, and Bełżec.

Finder Occupations

I was curious about occupations for the Finders. There was a record held in the Central Archives of Historical Records in Warsaw (AGAD) from the Austrian Ministry of the Interior Tax on Alcohol Production and Sale database for 1900–1914. Several records were found for a David Finder paying taxes to the Austro-Hungarian government for the sale or production of alcohol with a business address Plac Kleparz 25, Craców for the years 1903–1905.[37] I could not be certain if this David Finder was Lazar Finder's brother. David Finder was either a producer or retailer of alcoholic beverages and was approximately 45 years of age. Furthermore, Kraków is only 47 miles from David Finder's home region Dąbrowa Tarnowska. Another occupational clue was found on Lazar and Cipre's son Izrael Ber's birth record from 1895 in Bagienica listing the godfather as Chanina Blazenstein, a tavern-keeper. It is probable that some Finder family members had occupations to do with alcohol sales and production.

The Museum of the History of Polish Jews in Polin published a virtual shtetl about the history of Dąbrowa Tarnowska.[38] There were 147 Jewish families living at Dąbrowa by the middle of the 18th century. Jews worked as traders and craftsmen. They also produced and sold vodka and beer; they opened inns and taverns in Dąbrowa Tarnowska and surrounding villages.

Another occupation listed on the vital records for Lazar Finder's family in the Dąbrowa District was that of *mohel*, a person who was skilled at performing circumcisions for the *brit milah*. Lazar's father Nuchim Finder from Grądy was listed as the mohel on many Finder family birth records.

Conclusion

Marriages at Dąbrowa between Finders and Ungers happened from time to time. The records for the Finders in Dąbrowa led me to consider that my great-great-grandmother Chaje Mindel Unger was possibly a relative of the Ungers, who were living at Dąbrowa. That may be how an arranged marriage occurred between Cipre Geiger and Lazar Finder. I conclude that it is possible that Cipre's mother Chaje Mindel Unger had family connections with the Unger Rabbinical Dynasty at Dąbrowa and that is how Lazar Finder may have been selected for marriage with Cipre Geiger from Błażowa. Vital records for Solomon David Geiger or for Chaje Mindel Unger were either destroyed or lost. The children of Chaje Mindel Unger and Solomon David Geiger, Chaim Yehuda Geiger and Zipora Geiger were reviewed in this chapter. Please see additional chapters for their other children: *Aron Geiger and Hinde Turnheim, Moses Geiger and Laje.*

Josef Israels, A Jewish Wedding, 1903, Rijksmuseum

Descendants of Nuchim Finder

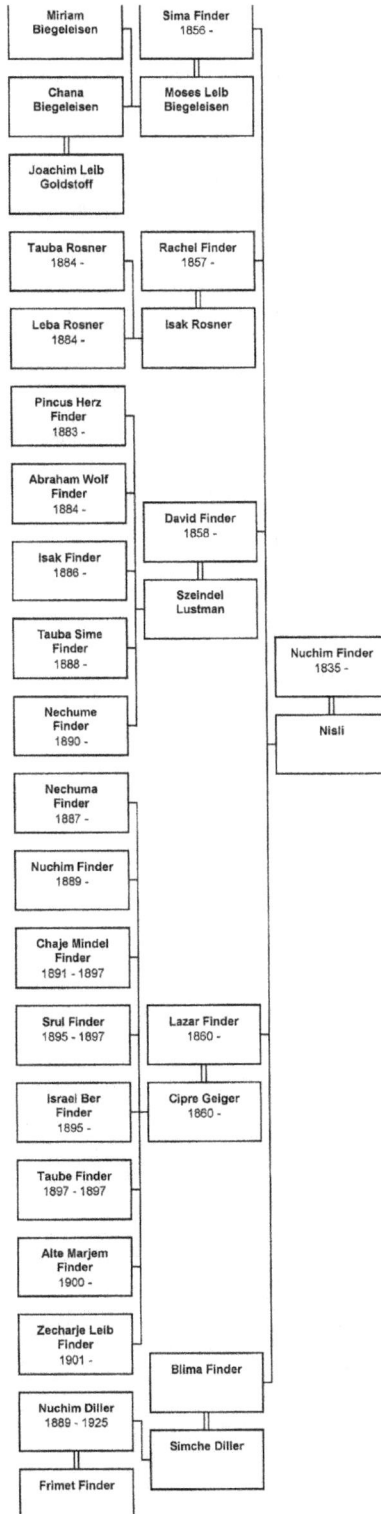

Miriam Biegeleisen	Sima Finder 1856 -
Chana Biegeleisen	Moses Leib Biegeleisen
Joachim Leib Goldstoff	
Tauba Rosner 1884 -	Rachel Finder 1857 -
Leba Rosner 1884 -	Isak Rosner
Pincus Herz Finder 1883 -	
Abraham Wolf Finder 1884 -	David Finder 1858 -
Isak Finder 1886 -	Szeindel Lustman
Tauba Sime Finder 1888 -	
Nechume Finder 1890 -	
Nechuma Finder 1887 -	
Nuchim Finder 1889 -	
Chaje Mindel Finder 1891 - 1897	
Srul Finder 1895 - 1897	Lazar Finder 1860 -
Israel Ber Finder 1895 -	Cipre Geiger 1860 -
Taube Finder 1897 - 1897	
Alte Marjem Finder 1900 -	
Zecharje Leib Finder 1901 -	Blima Finder
Nuchim Diller 1889 - 1925	Simche Diller
Frimet Finder	

Nuchim Finder 1835 -

Nisli

Descendants of Solomon David Geiger

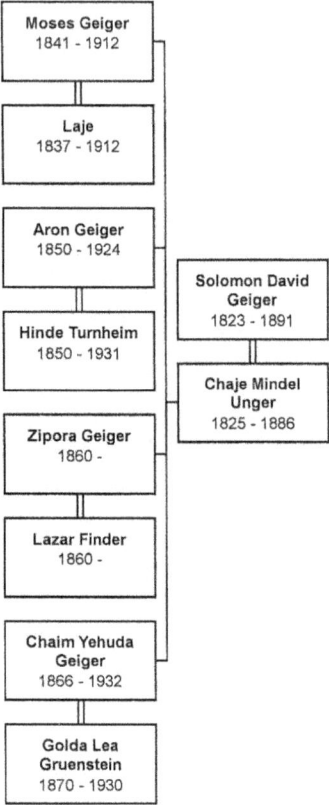

```
Moses Geiger
1841 - 1912

Laje
1837 - 1912

Aron Geiger
1850 - 1924
                          Solomon David
                          Geiger
                          1823 - 1891
Hinde Turnheim
1850 - 1931
                          Chaje Mindel
                          Unger
                          1825 - 1886
Zipora Geiger
1860 -

Lazar Finder
1860 -

Chaim Yehuda
Geiger
1866 - 1932

Golda Lea
Gruenstein
1870 - 1930
```

Endnotes

1   Alexander Beider, *A Dictionary of Ashkenazic Given Names*. (Bergenfield, New Jersey: Avotaynu, 2001). 520–521; 516–517. Hannie, Hensha, Hencsze were all variations for Hannah. This name was based on the biblical Hannah, the mother of Samuel; Hannah means gracious in Hebrew. The name Hinde is from the German language and means doe.

2   Rabbi. (www.wikipedia.org).

3   www.gidonim.org This is a project from the Reul School at Jerusalem, Israel where students photograph Jewish cemeteries in Poland. Blazowa was one of the places.

4   Kraków Archive-Tarnów branch. *Dabrowa Tarnowska Births 1882–92*. Birth Chaja Mindel, Akta 179, 1891.*Jewish Records Indexing-Poland* (jri-poland.org/jriplweb.htm).

5   Alexander Beider. *A Dictionary of Ashkenazic Given Names*. (Bergenfield, New Jersey: Avotaynu, 2001). 423; 296–298. Sholem derives from the Hebrew word for "peace" and from the biblical King Solomon. Dovid or Dawid derives from the Hebrew Dovid, referring to King David. In Jewish history Solomon was the son of King David and Bathsheba. Solomon became ruler ca. 967 BCE and was known for his wisdom, wealth, and writings. He wrote the Song of Songs, the Book of Proverbs and Ecclesiastes.

6   Alexander Beider, *A Dictionary of Ashkenazic Given Names*. (Bergenfield, New Jersey: Avotaynu, 2001).525–526; 543–544. Chaje derives from the Hebrew word Khaye for life and Mindel derives from Middle High German word Mine for the word love.

7   Suzan Wynne. *The Galitzianers: The Jews of Galicia 1772–1918*. (Kensington,MD: Suzan Wynne, 2006). 63.

8   Abraham Wein and Aharon Weiss, editors. Yissocher Marmorstein, translator. *Pinkas Hakehillot Polin. Encyclopedia of Jewish Communities in Poland, V.III. Dombrowa Tarnowska.* (Jerusalem, Israel: Yad Vashem, 1984) 107–111.

9   The first Unger rabbi in Dabrowa was Grand Rabbi Zevi Hersh Unger in 1800. His son was Grand Rabbi Mordecai Dov Unger in Dąbrowa and he was a disciple of Rabbi Yaacov Yitzchak Horowitz, the Seer of Lublin (1745–1815). After Rabbi Mordecai Dov Unger's death in 1843, he was succeeded by his son Grand Rabbi Yosef Unger who died 1876. His son, Grand Rabbi Yisrael Elimelech Unger, moved to Żabno and was known as the Żabno Rabbi.

10   kehilalinks.jewishgen.org/dabrowa_tarnowska/.

11   Joshua L. Segal. *A Field Guide to Visiting a Jewish Cemetery*. (Nashua, New Hampshire: Jewish Cemetery Publishing, 2006).

12   Rzeszów Archive. Fond 1. Rzeszów PSA 1910 Census. Jewish Records Indexing-Poland (jri-poland. org).

13   Rzeszów Archive. Fond 533. *Rzeszów Births 1866–1919*. Birth 1899 Bernard Berl. Parents Juda Geiger and Golda Lea Gruenstein. Akta 64. (jri-poland.org).

14   Rzeszów Archive. Fond 533. *Rzeszów Marriages 1896–1914, 17–1939*. Marriage 1928 Joachim Geiger. His date of birth recorded as 1904. His parents were Juda Geiger and Golda Lea Gruenstain. Akta 36. (jri-poland.org).

15   Rzeszów Archive. Fond 533. *Rzeszów Births 1866–1919*. Birth 1906 Sara Geiger. Akta 119. (jri-poland. org).

16   Rzeszów Archive. Fond 533. *Rzeszów Births 1866–1919*. Birth 1908 Chaskel Geiger. Akta 154. (jri-poland.org).

17   Rzeszów Archive. Fond 533. *Rzeszów Deaths 1877–1939*. Death 1898 Salomon Dawid Gruenstein, age 6 years. Akta 25. Jewish Records Indexing-Poland (jri-poland.org).

18   Rzeszów Archive. Fond 533. *Rzeszów Births 1866–1919*. Fond 533. Birth 1911 Mendel Geiger, akta 66. (jri-poland.org).

19   Ibid., Fond 533. *Rzeszów Deaths, 1842–75, 77–1935*. Death: 1930. Golda Lea Geiger. Akta 61. (jri-poland.org).

20   Rzeszów Archive. Fond 533. *Rzeszów Marriages 1917–1939*. Marriage: 1923 Bernard Geiger and Fania Ernestyna Goldmann. Akta 64. (*jri-poland.org*).

21   Rzeszów Archive. Fond 533. *Rzeszów Marriages 1917–1939*. Marriage: 1928 Joachim Geiger and Rachela Krebs. Akta 36. (jri-poland.org).

22   Yad Vashem.org. The Central Database of Shoah Victims' Names. Joachim Geiger and his family were deported 1942 to Treblinka. (yvng.yadvashem.org).

23   Rzeszów Archive. Fond 533. *Rzeszów Marriages 1917–1939*. Marriage :1936 Mendel Geiger and Sprinca Brueckner. Akta 34. (jri-poland.org).

24   Kraków Archive Tarnów Branch. *Dabrowa Tarnowska Births 1882–98*. Fond 374. Birth Nechuma Finder 1887, akta 171. (jri-poland.org).

25   Ibid., Birth Nuchim Finder 1889, akta 131. (jri-poland.org).

26   Ibid., Birth Chaja Mindel Finder 1891, akta 179. (jri-poland.org).

27   Sanok Archive. Fond 448. Lesko Deaths 1877–1900. Death Mindzia (Chaje Mindel) Finder 1897, akta 58. (jri-poland.org)

28   Kraków Archive Tarnów Branch. *Dabrowa Tarnowska Births 1882–98*. Fond 374. Birth Israel Ber Finder 1895, akta 74. (jri-poland.org).

29   Sanok Archive. Fond 448. *Lesko Deaths 1877–1900*. Death Srul (Israel Ber) Finder 1897, akta 62. (jri-poland.org).

30   Ibid., Death Taube Finder, 1897, akta 58. (jri-poland.org).

31   Przemyśl Archive. Jaroslaw Births 1877–1913. Fond 154. Birth 1900 Alte Marjem Finder, akta 79. (jri-poland.org)

32   Ibid., Birth 1901 Zecharje Leib Finder, akta 67. (jri-poland.org)

33   Kraków Archive Tarnów Branch. Fond 374. *Dabrowa Tarnowska Births 1882–92*. Birth 1889 Nuchim Finder, akta 131. (jri-poland.org).

34   Israelitische Kultusgemeinde Wien (IKG), Vienna, Austria. Marriage and Death records, Nuchim Finder.

35   Yad Vashem.org. Central Database of Shoah Victims' Names. Card File of Jews in Kraków with German identity cards kennkarte 1941. Abraham Wolf Finder. Item 10249017. Beila Finder née Gemeiner. Item 10249005.

36   Museum of Jewish Heritage, a Living Memorial to the Holocaust. Krakow Ghetto. Abraham Wolf and Beila Finder. (www.jewishgen.org.).

37   Archiwum Główne Akt Dawnych (AGAD*). Austrian Ministry of the Interior: Tax on Alcohol Production and Sale Database 1900-1914*. Fond 307, file number 253, pp. 523-527. 1903. (www.geshergalicia.org).

38   sztetl.org/pl/en/towns/d/317-dabrowa-tarnowska/99-history.

Chapter Three

Aron Geiger and Hinde Turnheim

Background

I searched the JewishGen Online Worldwide Burial Registry to locate where my great-grandfather Aron Geiger was buried and that was how I discovered that my great-grandfather Aron Geiger was buried at the Weiner Zentralfriedhof Cemetery in Vienna, Austria. This is a huge interdenominational cemetery with two Jewish cemeteries for Jewish interments.[1] Aron Geiger died 17 August 1924 at age 74. I subsequently wrote to the Weiner Stadt-und Landesarchiv in Vienna and was able to obtain his death record with his birth, marriage, and death information.[2] The death date for Aron Geiger was 17 August 1924, his marriage was 1868 and his birth was 1850 at Błażowa, Galicia. Finding the grave and matsevah of my great-grandfather Aron Geiger proved to be the key to opening the door for further research on my Geiger and Turnheim ancestors. I later learned Rabbi Aron Geiger followed the same rabbinical tradition set before him by his father Rabbi Solomon David Geiger of Błażowa.

Hasidism reached its peak during 1815–1848 and by the middle 19th century Hasidism dominated all religious life in Galicia, where 6 out of 7 Jews were adherents, including my ancestors Solomon David Geiger and Aron Geiger. Observant Jews in

Aron Geiger in Vienna

the shtetl of Błażowa were Hasidic. Everyday life was regulated by religious doc-
trine including prayer, observance of the Sabbath and holidays. Work stopped every Friday night through Saturday night and only partially resumed Sunday. The
synagogue or prayer hall was central in the lives of Jewish people. There were
traditional ways of dressing, eating, bathing, with rituals for male circumcision,
bar mitzvah, matrimony, death, mourning and burial. The rabbi supervised all
religious customs and observances. Every Jewish community maintained several
chederim, religious schools, that usually consisted of one room with a teacher.
Children began the cheder at age three, learning Torah, Hebrew and some history
and geography.[3] Many rabbis were also religious teachers. There were charitable
organizations in every shtetl, including a *Chevra Kadisha* or burial society, another
society to collect clothing and financial assistance for the poor and a society to
aid orphans. Most Jewish communities had their own cemetery.

Aron Geiger age 18

Aron and Hinde Geiger, 1910, Rzeszów

Marriage

In addition to achieving *semicha* (ordination as a rabbi), Aron Geiger also followed the traditional path for marriage. A *shadchen* (matchmaker) was probably consulted and a bride was chosen for Aron as was the custom in those days. Aron married my great-grandmother Hinde Turnheim in 1868 at Przemyśl, Poland.[4] She was born 1 January 1850 at Przemyśl, Poland to a prominent Jewish merchant family. I discovered her death record after Viennese officials were unable to locate any information for Hinde Geiger. I reasoned there may have been a name mix-up and was proven correct when they found a record for Hinde Heiger who was my great-grandmother Hinde Geiger (1850–1931).[5] This record listed her maiden name as Turnheim, her birth and death dates and where she was buried, at the Weiner Zentralfriedhof Cemetery in Vienna.

My aunt Martha sent me a photo of Aron Geiger as a young man about age 18, possibly an engagement photo, wearing a kippa, a long coat, sitting on an elaborate chair, holding a cigarette, somehow looking both worldly and yet also religious. In another photo taken ca. 1904 at Rzeszów both Aron and Hinde appeared to be traditionally dressed as pious Hasids and Aron had a full beard. Aron was a rabbi and a religious teacher as well as a businessman. Hinde was a traditional Jewish housewife, accomplished in raising children, managing the household, and teaching her daughters the arts of needlecraft, sewing and cooking.

Przemyśl and Children

Aron and Hinde had seven children, all born at Przemyśl, Podkarpackie, Poland and were most likely raised in Przemyśl. I obtained their birth records from the Przemyśl Archive, Poland. According to the birth record of their last child, my grandmother Minnie born 1887, they lived at Przemyśl, Dobromilska Street 461 that was later changed to Slowackiego Street, known as a street with a high percentage of Jewish families. That is the street where the "new" Jewish Cemetery of Przemyśl is located. Aron and Hinde had two children who died relatively early, Naftale and Freude. Naftale was born 29 March 1871 at Przemyśl, Poland to Hinde Turnheim.[6] Naftale died 2 April 1877 at age 6, although the death record listed his age as 8 years. The cause of his death was typhoid fever.[7]

Aron and Hinde's daughter Freude was born 23 January 1882 at Przemyśl, Poland.[8] She was their sixth child and the second female in their family. In a family photograph taken 1904, Freude appeared to be afflicted with scoliosis.

My cousin Olivia inherited lovely needlework that was made by Freude, possibly indicating that Freude was skilled at needlecrafts. The family was listed in the 1910 Rzeszów Census. Freude lived as a single woman with her parents Aron and Hinde. They lived at 3 Krola Kazimierza Street in Rzeszów.[9] When Aron Geiger died in 1924, he left a will listing his beneficiaries including his wife Hinde and their five adult children: Charles, Abraham, Israel, Mariem, and Minnie. There was no mention of Freude. Although it is possible that Freude married and had a different surname, Aron's other children were listed with their married surnames.

Seated Hinde and Aron. Standing (L to R) Mariem, Getzel, Minnie, Freude and Salomea Neumark, 1904

I have not been able to find Freude's death record or any other records of Freude after the 1910 Rzeszów Census, therefore I estimate Freude died sometime between 1910 and 1924. I pose a hypothesis about the death of Freude Geiger. There was a devastating flu pandemic of 1918 (January 1918–December 1920) known as the Spanish Flu affecting 500 million people worldwide. It killed predominantly healthy young adults with very rapid and progressive respiratory failure. The Spanish flu morbidity and mortality was higher in Germany and Austria than in Britain and France. Freude Geiger may have been a casualty as she fit the demographic profile of deaths attributed to the 1918 Spanish Flu.

Aron and Hinde had five children who lived to full maturity: Chaskel, Abraham, Israel, Mariem, and Minnie. See the *Solomon David Geiger Family Tree.*

Move from Błażowa to Rzeszów

Aron and Hinde lived in Przemyśl with their children, however sometime after the birth of their last child in 1887, my grandmother Minnie, they moved back to Błażowa possibly to help care for Aron's aging father Solomon David Geiger. Aron's mother Chaje Mindel Unger was probably deceased. Aron may have want-

Rzeszów Synagoga Staromiejska

ed to be back in Błażowa for religious reasons, to join the congregation of the Grand Rabbi Tzvi Elimelech Spira of Bluzhev who had an enormous following of Hasids.

Aron Geiger, his wife Hinde, and his daughter Freude were listed on the 1910 Census for Rzeszów. A possible trigger for their move to Rzeszów was a devastating fire in Błażowa during 27 May 1907 that demolished the town including 400 Jewish families who owned homes and businesses.[10] The economy of the town was ruined by this fire thus Aron relocated to Rzeszów with his wife Hinde and daughter Freude. Although most of their children immigrated to the United States, their son Abraham Geiger continued to live close to his parents in Galicia and Austria until WWII.

Aron and his family were observant Jews and lived near the Old Synagogue in Rzeszów where they could walk to services on Shabbat and holidays. This is the Old (Stara) Synagogue at Boznica 4 is now used as the Rzeszów branch of the Polish State Archives. The Jewish population in Rzeszów numbered 5,820

Geiger residence, Króla Kazimierza 3, Rzeszów

in 1880 and 8,785 in 1910. By 1921 the Jewish population increased to 11,361.[11] Jews formed at least 35 percent of the total population.

Aron and Hinde Geiger's daughter Mariem married Getzel Holoszycer; their children were first cousins with Dr. Moshe Yaari Wald. (See the *Isak Holoszycer Family Tree* and the chapter *Mariem Geiger and Getzel Holoszycer*). Dr. Wald was a writer and educator who described his recollections of Rzeszów in the yizkor book for Rzeszów.[12] Rzeszów was the central administrative city for neighboring towns populated with thousands of Jewish families from Tyczn, Sokolów, Kolbuszowa, Łańcut, Kańczuga, Dynów, Leżajsk, Błażowa, Sienawa and hundreds of neighboring villages. Jews were always on the move on account of poverty as they struggled to earn a livelihood. A dwelling for an entire family consisted of one room, that served as kitchen, bedroom, living room, workroom. No house had a bath, running water or a lavatory. Water had to be drawn from the well that was next to the old synagogue. Gentile water drawers used pails and poles to bring water to the homes and poured water into barrels. The middle class lived in larger dwellings with tolerable sanitary conditions. Only the upper class lived in splendid homes, furnished, with closets and bathrooms.

Aron Geiger and his family lived at 3 Kazimierza the Great Street, also known as "Jew Street," in Rzeszów because of the high percentage of Jews living there. Dr. Moshe Yaari Wald described his memories living on that same street in Rzeszów. There were two houses with an adjoining courtyard that had one lavatory with two cubicles for the 14 families living in the houses. He wrote "There were three rooms in the cellar of the first building, each one housing a family. A shoemaker with his ten children lived in a damp room next to the lavatories…in the second room of the cellar lived a bagel distributor with his two daughters. His wife would prepare potatoes as the daily meal…In the third room of the cellar lived a lame writer of requests. For a few coins, he taught the children of the poor to read and write. My family lived in two rooms on the second floor…a hallway separated us from the two tenants. In one room lived an elderly man by the name of Reb Moshe Nota, a merchant of caustic lime for building, with his son and two spinster daughters who sewed linens. In the second room lived Reb Hershel Vitus, a tailor, with his son and wife Vita. The diligent old women assisted in the family livelihood by selling frozen goose fat *(grieben* in Yiddish). In the upper floor lived an extremely poor porter. I often saw his wife bring home intestines of fowl for dinner, to make kishke. On the left side lived a Hassid who was a distributor of bread, who was an epileptic, who instilled fear upon the children of the house when his mysterious illness struck."[13]

Dr. Wald went on to discuss Kazimierza the Great Street with old multi-story houses dating from the 18th or 19th centuries. "The roofs were covered with tin sheets or tiles. On one side of the road there were houses whose backs faced fields and gardens some distance away, toward the Wislok River; and on the other side of the streets were houses whose backs faced the main square of the city (Rynek). There was a system of cellars and tunnels under the houses, like cat-acombs, that were built for the purposes of defense in previous centuries and served as hiding places for Jews once the Gestapo murderers arrived. Our house had a common wall with the house of the *Admor* Reb Elazarel Weissblum, a descendent of Reb Elimelech of Lizhensk. On the first floor were a prayer hall and the living quarters of his son-in-law the rabbinical judge Reb Chaim Yonah Halpern, and on the second floor was his dwelling and guestrooms....The sound of prayer and song constantly rose from these prayer halls, along with the melody of those studying Talmud and the sound of children at cheder." [14]

Move from Rzeszów to Vienna

I do not know exactly when my Geiger ancestors left Rzeszów to escape from unfavorable conditions or if they were still residing in Rzeszów during the po-grom of 3 May 1919. I speculate that during or soon after the start of WWI, Aron took his family and left Rzeszów. They joined many Galitzianers moving to Vienna, Austria, for greater safety and improved economic conditions. Aron's son Rabbi Abraham Geiger and his family moved to Vienna with Aron and Hin-de. Aron's daughter Freude may have also moved with them unless she was al-ready deceased.

When the Austro-Hungarian Monarchy fell apart in October 1918, Rzeszów found itself in chaos, like other towns in Galicia. Rzeszów suffered impoverish-ment as food was confiscated and diverted to the army. Peasants did not sell their food for almost worthless paper money but instead dealt on a barter basis, such as trading vegetables for kerosene and salt. There was no security especially for Jews. Anti-Semitism surged again with open hostility. Streets remained dark at night due to lack of fuel. Violence was frequent at all hours. Jewish males were subject to abuse and violence by Polish soldiers from General Haller's Brigade. Here was another pogrom with the familiar formula of robbery, murder, bodily harm, and destruction of property.[15] While Jews were praying in the synagogue on the sabbath, explosions and heavy rocks came flying through the windows of the synagogue. The attackers surrounded them and fell upon the Jews with hate and fury.[16] Eventually the police and army took control restoring peace.

By 1915 there were already 340,000 Galician Jewish refugees fleeing from the war in Galicia and rising anti-Semitism. Most of these refugees were Hasidic. Of this population, a large group numbering 77,000 went to Vienna. The refugees hoped that in Vienna it would be easier to find jobs, better assistance and increased security. Vienna Jews initially provided relief for the Galician refugees in Vienna in the form of soup kitchens, financial assistance, and schools, however as the months went by severe food shortages appeared and the previously friendly atmosphere vanished. Anti-Semites increased their demands on the city to remove the refugees from Vienna. By the end of 1918, about 35,000 Jewish refugees remained in Vienna.[17]

There was no record of the existence of Hasidim in Vienna before WWI. The Viennese Jews numbered 300,000 and were largely assimilated into the German culture of Vienna. Some Viennese Jews gradually became influenced by the Galician Jewish refugees who dressed and lived differently, who spoke in the unfamiliar language of Yiddish and who acted in a strange manner. The values of Hasidim included humility, introspection, meditation, and absolute faith in their

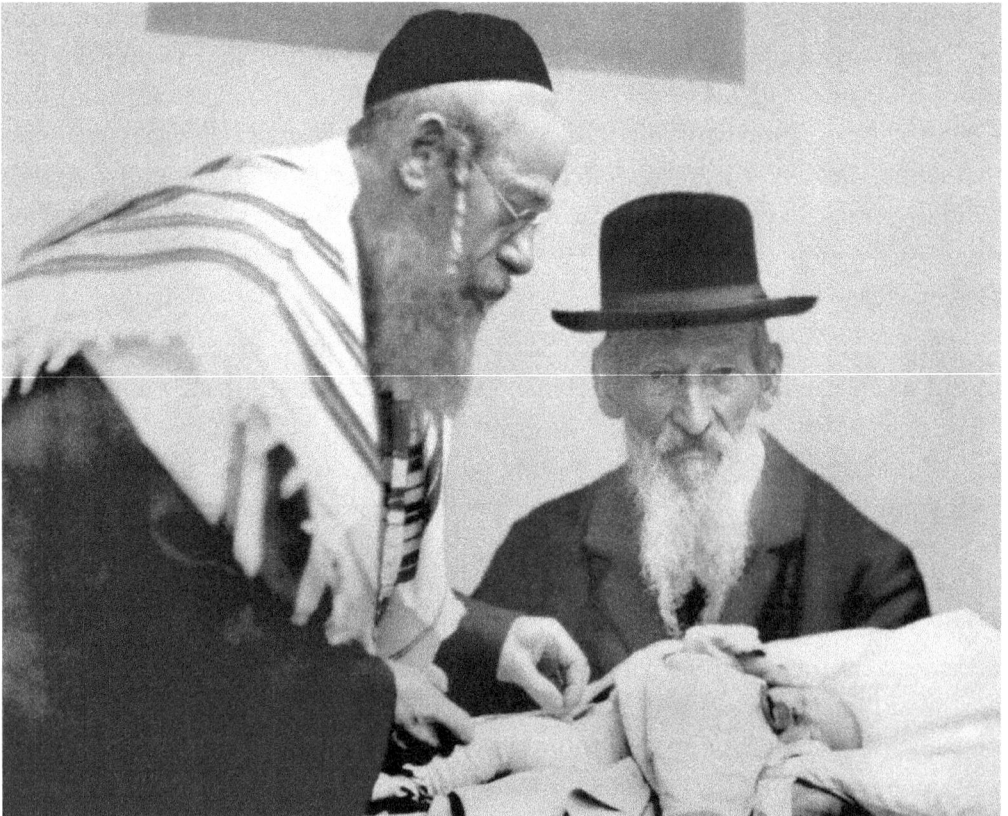

(L) Abraham Geiger (R) Aron Geiger, *brit milah*, Vienna, 1923

spiritual leader, their Rebbe. Hasidism took mystical concepts from the Zohar and brought them to ordinary Jews who began to see the Divine in ordinary life. Hasidism became a reservoir of strength for many Jewish people of Vienna.[18] Galician Jews in Vienna established their own Yiddish newspapers; Yiddish language writers and poets also flourished in Vienna.

Galician refugees did not receive adequate financial aid from the state or from private institutions. They needed to engage in business with most of their deals carried out in cafes in the center of Vienna. Numbers of Galician refugees succeeded in business, and they became an important factor in Viennese economic life.[19] Jews in Vienna, especially the Galician refugees resided mainly in the Leopoldstadt district II in Vienna, the district where Aron Geiger and my other Geiger relatives resided.

My great-grandfather Rabbi Aron Geiger and his son Rabbi Abraham Geiger continued to practice their Hasidism in Vienna and they established their own *shul* or synagogue. This was later destroyed by the Nazis. Geiger family members inherited a photo of Rabbi Aron Geiger with his son Rabbi Abraham Geiger. Rabbi Abraham Geiger was also a *mohel* (a professional who circumcises male babies on the eighth day after birth). In this photo Aron wears a hat in the Hasidic manner while Abraham wears a tallit and is performing a circumcision at a male baby's bris. Aron was given the honor of being the *sandek* (an adult male honored at a Jewish *brit milah* or circumcision ceremony by holding the baby boy while the mohel performs the brit milah. This photo was taken in the early 1920s in Vienna prior to Aron's death in 1924. It is in the photo collection at the Jewish Museum in Vienna.

Based on Aron Geiger's death certificate and will proceedings, both Aron and Abraham Geiger were residing at Leopoldstadt, a district in Vienna that had a high percentage of Jews before the Holocaust, about 38.5 per cent, and was nicknamed *Mazzesinsel* (Matzo Island). There is the Volksprater, a major amusement park in the center of the district with a large Ferris wheel that opened in 1897 and which featured prominently in the Orson Welles 1949 film *The Third Man*. Many synagogues and yeshivas could be found in Leopoldstadt, however none escaped destruction during the *Kristallnacht* pogrom by the Nazis during 9–10 November 1938. All synagogues and prayer houses were razed to the ground. By May 1939 approximately 130,000 persons considered Jews under the Nuremberg Racial Laws left Austria. Over 65,000 Viennese Jews were deported 1941 and subsequently murdered at extermination camps. They are counted among the six million victims of the genocide committed by the Nazis during the Holocaust.[20]

Aron Geiger's Business

Aron Geiger's death certificate from Vienna included information that Aron's occupation was a businessman and that he was married, however I did not know in what kind of business he was engaged besides being a rabbi in Vienna. My Aunt Martha recounted that she heard from her mother, my grandmother Minnie, that Aron Geiger owned a tavern with an inn where travelers would stay overnight. If Aron operated an inn it was probably prior to WWI.

The *YIVO Encyclopedia of Jews in Eastern Europe* had an interesting description of Jews as tavern and inn keepers.[21] Jews leased taverns and inns on royal and noble estates and this occupation was almost exclusively Jewish as Gentiles were

(L) Aron Geiger matsevah (R) Hinde Geiger matsevah Vienna

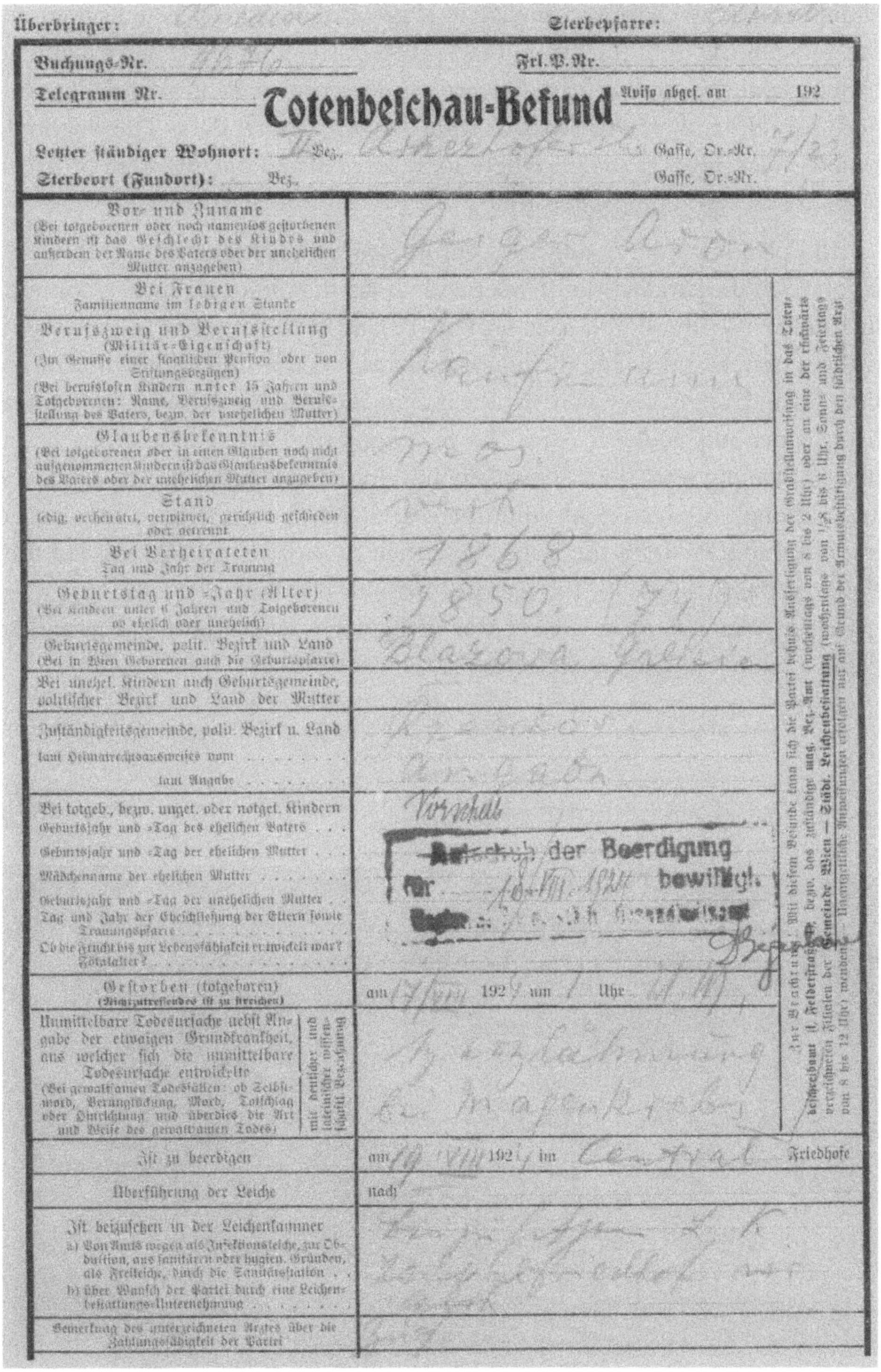
Überbringer: Sterbepfarre:

Buchungs-Nr. Frl.P.Nr.

Telegramm Nr.

Totenbeschau-Befund

Aviso abgef. am 192

Letzter ständiger Wohnort: II Bez. Gasse, Or.-Nr.

Sterbeort (Fundort): Bez. Gasse, Or.-Nr.

Vor- und Zuname (Bei totgeborenen oder noch namenlos gestorbenen Kindern ist das Geschlecht des Kindes und außerdem der Name des Vaters oder der unehelichen Mutter anzugeben)	Geiger Aron
Bei Frauen Familienname im ledigen Stande	
Berufszweig und Berufsstellung (Militär-Eigenschaft) (Im Genusse einer staatlichen Pension oder von Stiftungsbezügen) (Bei berufslosen Kindern unter 15 Jahren und Totgeborenen: Name, Berufszweig und Berufsstellung des Vaters, bezw. der unehelichen Mutter)	Kaufmann
Glaubensbekenntnis (Bei totgeborenen oder in einen Glauben noch nicht aufgenommenen Kindern ist das Glaubensbekenntnis des Vaters oder der unehelichen Mutter anzugeben)	mos.
Stand ledig, verheiratet, verwitwet, gerichtlich geschieden oder getrennt	verh.
Bei Verheirateten Tag und Jahr der Trauung	1868
Geburtstag und -Jahr (Alter) (Bei Kindern unter 6 Jahren und Totgeborenen ob ehelich oder unehelich)	1850. (74 J.)
Geburtsgemeinde, polit. Bezirk und Land (Bei in Wien Geborenen auch die Geburtspfarre)	Blazowa, Galizien
Bei unehel. Kindern auch Geburtsgemeinde, politischer Bezirk und Land der Mutter	
Zuständigkeitsgemeinde, polit. Bezirk u. Land laut Heimatrechtsausweises vom ... laut Angabe ...	
Bei totgeb., bezw. unget. oder notget. Kindern Geburtsjahr und -Tag des ehelichen Vaters ... Geburtsjahr und -Tag der ehelichen Mutter ... Mädchenname der ehelichen Mutter ... Geburtsjahr und -Tag der unehelichen Mutter ... Tag und Jahr der Eheschließung der Eltern sowie Trauungspfarre ... Ob die Frucht bis zur Lebensfähigkeit entwickelt war? Fötalalter?	Vorschuß; Aufschub der Beerdigung bewilligt
Gestorben (totgeboren) (Nichtzutreffendes ist zu streichen)	am 17/VIII 1924 um 1 Uhr
Unmittelbare Todesursache nebst Angabe der etwaigen Grundkrankheit, aus welcher sich die unmittelbare Todesursache entwickelte (Bei gewaltsamen Todesfällen: ob Selbstmord, Verunglückung, Mord, Totschlag oder Hinrichtung und überdies die Art und Weise des gewaltsamen Todes) — mit deutscher und lateinischer wissenschaftl. Bezeichnung	Herzlähmung, Magenkrebs
Ist zu beerdigen	am 19 VIII 1924 im Central Friedhofe
Überführung der Leiche	nach
Ist beizusetzen in der Leichenkammer a) Von Amts wegen als Infektionsleiche, zur Obduktion, aus sanitären oder hygien. Gründen, als Freileiche, durch die Sanitätsstation ... b) über Wunsch der Partei durch eine Leichenbestattungs-Unternehmung	
Bemerkung des unterzeichneten Arztes über die Zahlungsfähigkeit der Partei	

Zur Beachtung. Mit diesem Befunde kann sich die Partei behufs Ausfertigung der Grabstellenanweisung in das Totenbeschauamt (I. Felderstraße), bezw. das zuständige mag. Bez.-Amt (wochentags von 8 bis 2 Uhr) oder an eine der rückwärts verzeichneten Filialen der Gemeinde Wien — Städt. Leichenbestattung (wochentags von 1/2 8 bis 6 Uhr, Sonn- und Feiertags von 8 bis 12 Uhr) wenden. Unentgeltliche Anweisungen erfolgen nur auf Grund der Armutsbestätigung durch den städtischen Arzt.

Death Record Aron Geiger, Vienna

forbidden by the church to engage in alcohol trade. This was the situation from the 16th century until the mid-nineteenth century. Jews were also excluded from owning land and so they leased taverns and inns from nobles' lands. There was a need for inns and taverns as roads were dangerous after dark. The wagon drivers would direct travelers to inns where food, alcohol and lodging were provided and where horses would be cared for.

In Poland by the 17th and 18th centuries there was a larger proportion of Jews involved in the production of beer and vodka than in other Jewish communities in Europe. Wynne noted that Jews in Poland were engaged in distilling grain, making barrels and selling the liquor to consumers. By the mid-eighteenth century in Poland, many Jews were involved in manufacturing, wholesaling, or retailing beer, wine, and vodka.[22] After the partitions of Poland, numerous laws were passed banning Jews from selling alcohol. In Galicia, Jews tried to evade the ban and although the leaseholder numbers declined, Jews remained involved in the alcohol trade. By 1889 the nobles lost their monopoly on alcohol and the Jews also lost their exclusivity for that occupation. For however long, it is therefore quite possible that Aron Geiger was managing a tavern business in addition to being a rabbi and religious teacher.

Geiger residence Vienna Austria

Vienna Archives

Aron Geiger's death certificate was sent to me by the Weiner Stadt-und Landessarchiv, Vienna as Totenbeichau-Befund number 9676 with the following information. Aron Geiger was born 1850 in Błażowa, Galicia, within the Rzeszów District. He married in 1868, was a businessman and was of the Mosaic (Jewish) faith. He died 17 August 1924 and was buried 19 August 1924 at the Weiner Zentralfriedhof Cemetery. The immediate cause of death was listed as heart failure and he also had stomach cancer. He was living in Leopoldstadt, District II, Arnezhoferstraße 7, apartment 23. The Jewishgen Online Worldwide Burial Database provided the location of his grave at the Zentralfriedhof Cemetery gate 4, group 10, row 11, grave 66.[23]

I initially could not locate my great-grandmother Hinde Geiger's death record in the Vienna databases. I contacted Wolf-Erich Eckstein from the Israelitische Kultusgemeinde Wein (Vienna Jewish Records Office) to see if she could be listed under a different spelling. He replied through e-mail correspondence dated 14 June 2011 and confirmed that Hinde Geiger was misspelled Heiger and this error will be corrected in the database. Hinde died of senility and old age at the home for the Elderly of the Jewish Community at address Seegasse 9 in District 9, Vienna. Hinde was born 1 January 1850 at Przemyśl, married 1868, died 11 October 1931 and was buried 12 October 1931 in the Zentralfriedhof Cemetery gate 4 at location group 10, row 11, grave 65 next to her husband Aron Geiger.[24]

I obtained a clear photograph of Hinde's matsevah from the IKG-Wien and put the photograph on-line at JewishGen.org Viewmate, for a full translation. The following translation for Hinde Geiger's matsevah was provided by Mr. David Rosen.[25]

> *Here lies a dear woman honest, modest, and kosher, Mrs. Hinda Geiger daughter of reb Tzvi may he rest in peace; passed away 1 Cheshvan 5692. May her soul be bound up in the bond of everlasting life.*

I later confirmed that Hinde's father was named Tzvi (Hersch) Turnheim and that he was born in Jarosław, Poland, married Mariem Gems and resided in Przemyśl, Podkarpackie, Poland. (*See The Turnheim Family chapter and the Solomon Turnheim Family Tree.*)

The Vienna Archives provided additional information about Aron Geiger. On 30 April 2010 Frau Mag. Duizend-Jensen at the Archives sent me a record of the will proceedings for Aron Geiger, a businessman, having lived and died 1924 in the orthodox Jewish Leopoldstadt district in Vienna.[26] His widow, Hinde Geiger née Turnheim was listed as his lawful spouse. The will listed their five adult children: Heskel Geiger age 56, a businessman in New York; Abraham Geiger age 54, a businessman in Vienna residing at 7 Arnezhoferstraβe at Leopoldstadt District, Vienna; Israel Geiger age 50, businessman address unknown; Maria Holoschitz (Holly) née Geiger age 40, businesswoman in New York; Mindel Weihs (Weiss) née Geiger age 30, businesswoman in New York. The will proceedings stated that there were no minor children or other posthumous relatives declared. It should be mentioned that the ages listed were in error for Maria (Mariem), who was age 44 and Mindel who was age 37 at the time of Aron Geiger's death.

Aron Geiger Matsevah

A photo of Aron's matsevah was kindly sent to me by Celia Male z"l, a genealogist from the United Kingdom, who did not want to get in the foliage with ticks in the Weiner Zentralfriedhof cemetery so it is not a clear photo however from what can be read of the Hebrew stated that Aron, son of Solomon aka Shlomo David Geiger from the town of Błażowa lived to a good old age and he died at age 74. Another photograph of those gravestones was taken by Daniela Torsch, a genealogist from Australia and that photograph appeared to be clearer and the matsevahs in better shape. Finally, I obtained an improved photograph from the IKG-Wien for Aron and Hinde's matsevahs and subsequently obtained a full translation after submitting the photograph to JewishGen.org Viewmate. The translation for Aron Geiger's matsevah was provided by Mr. William Moskowitz:

> *Here lies a Respected/Honored man that walked the straight path; From a proper (or noteworthy) family. G-d fearing, He read (studied), reviewed and taught. He was immersed in the Commandments and Good Deeds. Our Teacher and Rabbi Aron son of our Teacher and Rabbi Shlomo Dovid Geiger, From the city of Bluzhev Galicia. He died at a ripe old age, On a Holiday (a play on words for 17th) of the month of Av 5684. May his soul be bound up in the bond of everlasting life.*

Aron Geiger was a rabbi and teacher who followed the same honorable profession of his father Shlomo David Geiger. Aron's son Abraham Geiger also had a predilection for the same profession as his father and grandfather. Rabbi Aron Geiger remained close with his son Rabbi Abraham Geiger. Aron and Hinde Geiger lived with Abraham and his family in Vienna. Following the deaths of Aron and Hinde, Abraham and his family left Vienna soon after Hitler came into power in Vienna.[27] Please see the chapter *Abraham Geiger and Sprynca Stark.*

Descendants of Aron Geiger

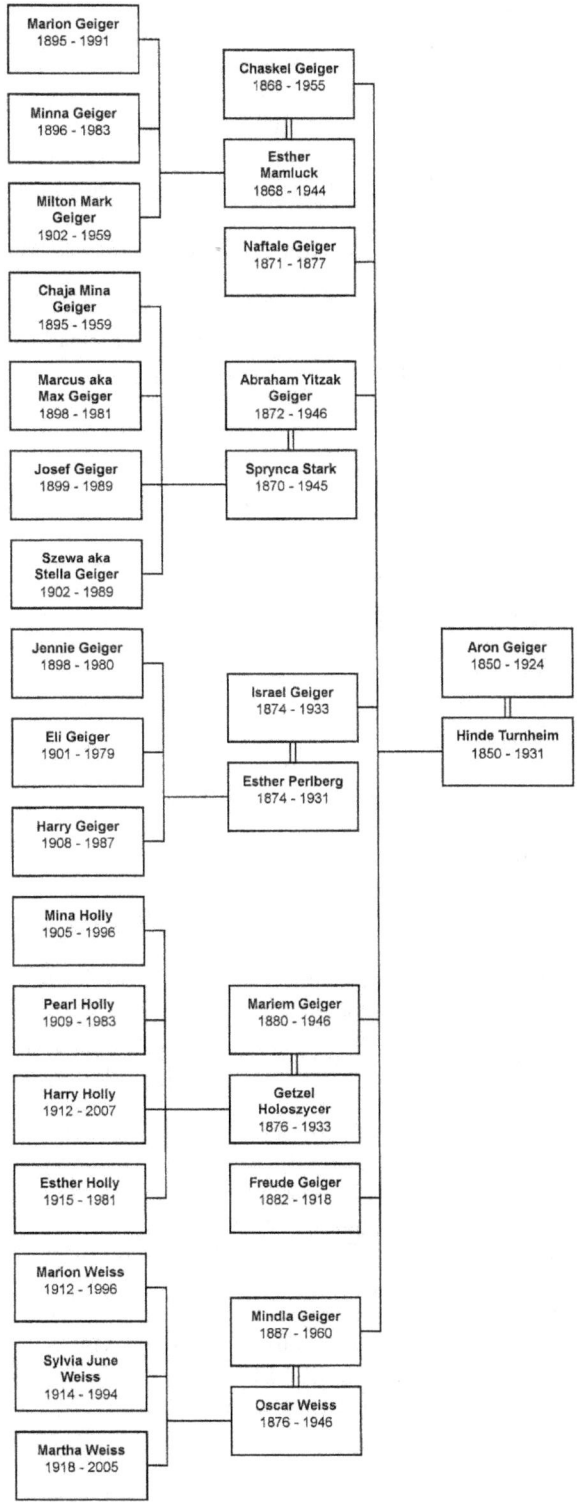

```
Marion Geiger
1895 - 1991
                    Chaskel Geiger
                    1868 - 1955
Minna Geiger
1896 - 1983
                    Esther
                    Mamluck
                    1868 - 1944
Milton Mark
Geiger
1902 - 1959
                    Naftale Geiger
                    1871 - 1877
Chaja Mina
Geiger
1895 - 1959
                    Abraham Yitzak
Marcus aka          Geiger
Max Geiger          1872 - 1946
1898 - 1981
Josef Geiger        Sprynca Stark
1899 - 1989         1870 - 1945
Szewa aka
Stella Geiger
1902 - 1989
Jennie Geiger
1898 - 1980                              Aron Geiger
                    Israel Geiger        1850 - 1924
                    1874 - 1933
Eli Geiger
1901 - 1979                              Hinde Turnheim
                    Esther Perlberg      1850 - 1931
Harry Geiger        1874 - 1931
1908 - 1987
Mina Holly
1905 - 1996
Pearl Holly         Mariem Geiger
1909 - 1983         1880 - 1946
Harry Holly         Getzel
1912 - 2007         Holoszycer
                    1876 - 1933
Esther Holly        Freude Geiger
1915 - 1981         1882 - 1918
Marion Weiss
1912 - 1996         Mindla Geiger
                    1887 - 1960
Sylvia June
Weiss
1914 - 1994         Oscar Weiss
                    1876 - 1946
Martha Weiss
1918 - 2005
```

Endnotes

1   Weiner Zentralfriedhof Cemetery, Vienna, Austria. This cemetery opened 1874 and covers 620 acres. It is one of the largest cemeteries in the world containing smaller cemeteries of all faiths. There are 79,833 Jewish burials as of 2011 in two Jewish cemeteries. (www.wikipedia.org.)

2   Weiner Stadt-und Landesarchiv, Vienna, Austria. Totenbeschaubefund 9676_1924 Aron Geiger. The death certificate indicated that Aron Geiger was born 1850 in Blazowa, Galicia in the district of Rzeszow and he married in 1868. He died 17 August 1924 and was buried 19 August 1924 in the Weiner Zentral-friedhof, Tor IV, Jewish Section.

3   Piotr Wrobel. The Jews of Galicia under Austrian-Polish Rule, 1867-1918. (haygenealogy.com/nagy/sources/Galicia-Jews.pdf), pp. 8-9.

4   Ibid.

5   Weiner Stadt-und Landesarchiv, Vienna, Austria. Dr. Michaela Laichmann, Oberarchivratin. Death records. Hinde Geiger listed as Hinde Heiger. Email dated 25 March 2011.

6   Przemysl Archive, Poland. Fond 1924. *Przemysl Births 1853–1900*. Birth Naftale (Tornheim) 29 March 1871, akta 69. Mother Hinde. Grandparents Hersch and Marjem Turnheim.

7   Przemysl Archive, Poland. Fond 1924. *Przemysl Deaths 1790–1899*. Death Naftali Geiger 1877. www.jri-poland.org.

8   Przemysl Archive, Poland. Fond 154. *Przemysl Births 1789–1827, 1853–1900*. Birth Freude Geiger, 1882, akta 39, mother Hinde Geiger.

9   Rzeszow Archive. Fond 1. Rzeszow 1910 Census. Aron, Hinde, and Fryda Geiger residing at 3 Krola Kazimierza Street, Rzeszow. (www.jri-poland.org)

10   Henrietta Szold, editor. *American Jewish Yearbook, volume 9, 1907–1908*, Review of the Year, p.516 (www.ajcarchives.org.)

11   Shmuel Spector, editor. *The Encyclopedia of Jewish Life before and during the Holocaust*. (New York: New York University Press, 2001). p.1111.

12   Dr. Moshe Yaari Wald. *Memories and Happenings: A Portrait of Rzeszow at the beginning of the 20th Century*. www.jewishgen.org/yizkor/rzeszow/rze132.html.pp 201.

13   Ibid., p. 204.

14   Dr. Moshe Yaari Wald. *Memories and Happenings: A Portrait of Rzeszow at the Beginning of the 20th Century*. www.jewishgen.org/yizkor/rzeszow/rze132.html.p.204.

15   Dr. Moshe Yaari Wald. During the Interregnum.www.jewishgen.org/yizkor/rzeszow/rze132.html.pp 134.

16   Naftali Hakhel. The Pogrom of Rzeszow. www.jewishgen.org/yizkor/rzeszow/rze132.html.pp. 137.

17   Piotr Wrobel. *The Jews of Galicia under Austrian-Polish Rule, 1867–1918*. haygenealogy.com/nagy/sources/Galicia-Jews.pdf.

18   Josef Fraenkel, Editor. *The Jews of Austria*. Rabbi J. Heshel. "The History of Hassidism in Austria." (London: Valentine, Mitchell and Co., 1967). Pp. 347–360.

19   Josef Fraenkel, Editor. *The Jews of Austria*. M. Henisch. "Galician Jews in Vienna". (London: Valentine, Mitchell and Co., 1967). Pp. 361–373.

20   City of Vienna. Expulsion, Deportation and Murder-History of the Jews in Vienna. (www.wien.gv.at.)

21   www.yivoencyclopedia.org/article.aspx/Tavernkeeping.

22   Suzan Wynne. *The Galitzianers: the Jews of Galicia 1772–1918*. Suzan Wynne: 2006. Pp. 33–34.

23   Jewish Online Worldwide Burial Database. (www.jewishgen.org.)

24   Eckstein, Wolf-Erich. Vienna Jewish Records Office. IKG-Vienna (Israelitische Kultusgemeinde Wien). Email dated 14 June 2011. Mr. Eckstein confirmed that Hinde Geiger died in the home for the Elderly of the Jewish Community and she was buried 12 October 1931 in the Zentralfriedhof Cemetery in Vienna gate 4, 10-11-65 next to her husband Aron Geiger.

25   Posted on ViewMate. (www. jewishgen.org)

26 Wiener Stadt-und Landesarchiv, Vienna, Austria. Email 25 Mar 2011. Leopoldstadt District (1) A 4/2
2 A 664/1924. Will Proceedings for GEIGER ARON, Businessman.
27 Google Maps, aerial view of Arnezhoferstraße 7, Vienna.

Chapter Four

Jews in Przemyśl

Introduction

Przemyśl is an ancient city in Poland existing from the 10th century to the present. It is located at Latitude 49.784° N and Longitude 22.781° E. It is approximately 24 miles from Jarosław, 36 miles from Błażowa and 54 miles from Rzeszów. Przemyśl is in the southeast region of Poland within the Subcarpathia Province, adjoining the border of the Ukraine. The city lies on the navigable San River in the foothills of the Carpathian Mountains. The population of Przemyśl today is approximately 66,600 with virtually no Jews. During 1939 the total population was 80,000 with 33% Jewish.[1] Jews lived in Przemyśl for hundreds of years until their genocide by the Nazis during WWII.

Przemyśl, Podkarpackie, Poland is the city where my grandmother Minnie Geiger and her siblings were born and raised. During my years of research, I also discovered that my great-grandmother Hinde Turnheim was born in Przemyśl where she married my great-grandfather Aron Geiger 1868 and raised their children in Przemyśl. My great-great-grandmother Mariem Gems was born in Przemyśl, married my great-great-grandfather Hersch Turnheim 1836 in Przemyśl and raised their children there. My great-great-great-grandparents Hinde Marberg and Gronem Gems were both from Przemyśl, married 1801 and raised their children in Przemyśl. Based on vital records my Jewish ancestors lived in Przemyśl for at least 240 years. I speculate that my earlier Jewish ancestors probably lived in Germanic lands before they arrived in Poland.

An important source of information about Jews in Przemyśl was found in the *Yizkor Book on Przemyśl,*[2] a collection of memories from people who were residents and who wrote their memories post WWII. Their memories are written in Hebrew and Yiddish and were translated to English at www.jewishgen.org/Yizkor/przemysl/Przemysl.html. Other sources of information were found in *The Genealogical Gazetteer of Galicia* by Brian Lenius[3]; *I Remember Every Day...the Fates of the Jews of Przemyśl During World War II* edited by John Hartman and Jacek Krochmal[4]; *The 11th AV* by David Semmel[5], *Jewish Roots in Poland* by Miriam

Weiner[6], *The Pinkas Hakehillot Polin published by* Yad Vashem,[7] *History of the Jews in Russia and Poland, from the Earliest Times Until the Present Day*[8] by Simon Dubnow; *The Encyclopedia of Jewish Life Before and During the Holocaust*[9]; and many on-line resources such as JewishGen.org.; YadVashem.org.; GesherGalicia.org.; JRI-Poland.org.; Virtual Shtetl of Poland.org; www.holocaustresearchproject.org/ghettos/przemysl.html. and the on-line State Archives of Przemyśl at www.nac.gov.pl/en/digital-archive/szukajwarchiwach-pl-search-the-archives/.

History

One of the oldest books of Przemyśl (1402–1445) includes the names of Jewish bankers and merchants in court documents and by 1419 there was mention of a street, Zydowska Street or Jew Street. A community of Przemyśl Jews occupied the Northeast section of town along the fortified embankment near the San River. The area was called Zasanie.[10] There was a record of a wooden synagogue in 1550 and a *mikvah* in 1538.[11] The legal status of Przemyśl Jews was defined by King Zygmunt Augustus in the Charter of 29 March 1559.[12] This charter granted Jews the permanent right to settle and to buy houses from the Christians. Another right was to conduct businesses and to trade freely in the city. It was also a fixed right that only the king or his representatives could judge Jews.

A Renaissance synagogue made of stone was completed in 1594 containing prayer rooms, a Hebrew school, a Talmud Academy, a Jewish court and kahal. A Jewish cemetery was also built ca. 1570 in Przemyśl. By 1563 there were 169 Jewish families living in Przemyśl and by 1578 there were 206 families.[13] A Jewish hospital was also built. Houses were mainly wood and arranged along eleven streets. The center of the Jewish district was a square called Targowica (Trade Center). Jews were involved in trade and credit matters and worked as artisans. There were Jewish trade guilds for barbers, tailors, furriers, and butchers.[14] Townspeople tried to deprive them of the right to settle and make a living through trade and business. Increased tense relationships grew between both sides, sometimes erupting in acute crises including pogroms.

In 1595 Jews signed an agreement with town authorities to pay a one-time sum of 500 zlotys to fortify the city, and in return they received permission to lease areas near the walls and build a hospital for the poor. This contract and others that followed were not always carried out by both sides. Lawsuits continued 40 years, with the verdicts of the courts often contradicting one another each time. There was a pogrom in 1628 at Zydowska Street that demolished Jewish homes and plundered the Jewish Hospital and stores.[15]

During 1630 a Christian woman was caught taking the consecrated bread and wine for the Eucharist from the Przemyśl Cathedral and she was tortured. During interrogation she claimed that she was persuaded to steal those items by a local Jew named Moszko Szmuklerz. She was then sentenced to death by burning at the stake. The Jew, Moszko Szmuklerz, was also tortured horribly and sentenced to death by burning. Although he denied the accusation and never confessed, the local court found him guilty. The court later reinvestigated the matter and learned that the woman stole the host for magic purposes to cure infertility on the advice of a local Christian midwife. Moszko never pled guilty and thus saved the entire Jewish community in Przemyśl from another pogrom. The day of Shmuklerz's burning, 30 Adar, was fixed for generations as a day of remembrance in the Przemyśl Jewish community until the mid-twentieth century.[16]

During the 17th century a city ordinance mandated that Jewish peddlers were only permitted to sell goods on streets inhabited by Jews. Jewish tailors could only work for Jewish clients. Jewish owned pharmacies were forbidden to sell medicines to Christians and Jewish barber surgeons could not bleed Christians who were ill. As the economy declined during the late 17th century, many Jews were forced to borrow money from the Polish nobility. The due dates for debt repayment were extended several times to slow Jewish emigration from Przemyśl however during the 18th century many Jews left the city due to indebtedness and severe taxation.[17] The Jewish community continued to grow in Przemyśl despite anti-Semitic barriers and crises.

Rabbinical Influences

Hasidism gained popularity in Przemyśl with residence of Hasidic dynasties: Błażowa, Dynów, Belz, Sadagora and Satmar. Rabbi Moshe Teitelbaum (1759–1841) was born in Przemyśl; he was one of the students of the renowned Hasidic rabbi Yaakov Yitzchak Halevi Horowitz (1745–1815) who was known as the Seer or Chozeh of Lublin. Rabbi Moshe Teitelbaum later became a rabbinical judge in Przemyśl and was also the progenitor of the Hungarian Satmar Hasidic dynasty. Rabbi Tzvi Elimelech Spira (1783–1841) from Dynów was the author of many important Hasidic books including the *Bnei Yissachar*. His eldest son Rabbi Dovid (1804–1874) was the author of *Tzemach Dovid* and he participated in the dedication of the *kloiz* at Przemyśl where his Hasidism had much influence.

Both traditional Jewish religious orthodoxy and Hasidism were opposed to a new Jewish intellectual movement known as the Haskalah (1770s–1880s) that began in Germany and originated with the Jewish philosopher Moses Mendelsson

(1726–1789). This became known as the Jewish Enlightenment movement that emphasized rational thought in religion. During this period, Przemyśl was under Austrian rule and the German language was widely used in government and in education. District rabbis were required to understand German and to use it. The Haskalah was mainly an intellectual movement that stressed the importance of secular education with Jewish history and cultural identity, study of European languages and use of Hebrew rather than Yiddish. The followers of Haskalah were called *maskilim*. Haskalah influenced the later movements of Reform Judaism and Zionism.

Rabbi Yitzhak Yehuda Schmelkes (1828–1904) was among the leading traditional orthodox Przemyśl rabbis and was a Talmudic scholar. He headed the Przemyśl rabbinical court in 1869–94 and wrote the well-known *Beit Yitzhak* on the *Shulhan Arukh*.[18] His nephew Rabbi Gedalya ben Mordecai Schmelkes (1857–1928) served as chief rabbi in Przemyśl from 1904 and worked to unify the community until his death in 1928.[19] Both Rabbi Yitzhak Schmelkes and Rabbi Gedalya Schmelkes were the rabbis during my Turnheim ancestors' life events in Przemyśl. Rabbi Gedalya Schmelkes became a Zionist and although Zionism was gradually accepted among the Jewish intelligensia it was not popular with the Hasidim or with many traditional orthodox Jews. He was selected for the rabbinical seat in Przemyśl in 1904 and began his long career there as spiritual and moral leader.

Rabbi Gedalya Schmelkes

He was a brilliant scholar with integrity. He did not hesitate to join the Zionist organization of Galicia despite the majority opinion against Zionism. He participated in the 9th Zionist Congress 1909 in Hamburg and the 10th Zionist Congress 1911 in Basel. Rabbi Schmelkes desired to make aliya to Israel despite his age and poor health however he died before he was able to make the journey. He was active as a Talmudic scholar, as a rabbi, a community leader and worked to improve social services for his community. His funeral was attended by hundreds at the Scheinbach synagogue.[20]

Przemyśl Synagogues

A synagogue called the Alte Shul (the ancient synagogue) on Jagiellonska Street was where my Jewish ancestors probably worshipped during the 18th and 19th centuries. The building was erected 1594, constructed in stone in the Renaissance style and was an architectural gem. Dr. Naftali Schneid described the beauty of the synagogue both inside and outside. He wrote how the synagogue was "unforgettable in the eyes of the beholder. The contrast between the simple modest exterior and the splendid, detailed interior emphasizes the strong impression of this monumental creation."[21] The interior was renovated after WWI however the Nazis burned and destroyed the synagogue in 1941.[22]

Two new synagogues were built during the late 1890s in Zasanie and on Slowackiego Street. Zasanie was a suburb of Przemyśl and due to difficult roads getting to the center of Przemyśl, the Jews of Zasanie decided to build their own synagogue. This synagogue was built near the San River and was opened 1909. The Nazis confiscated the synagogue to use as a temporary power station. After the war, the building was used as a garage. The building remains closed and abandoned.

The synagogue on Slowackiego Street in Przemyśl is often called the New Shul and the "Scheinbach Shul" because Moshe Scheinbach was instrumental in obtaining the financing to build it. He rose from being a wagon driver to having great wealth and he became a leader in the Przemyśl Jewish community. He had significant influence in the financial department at City Hall and in Jewish owned banks; he organized

Alte Shul, Jagiellonska St., before 1912

Interior Alte Shul

New Shul

plans and raised funds for the construction of the beautiful new synagogue. The synagogue opened for worship 1918.

Scheinbach chose a professional architect with a good record for building fine houses. The architectural style is described as Mauretano-eclectic. The synagogue's frame was completed prior to WWI and after the war stained-glas windows and beautiful interior paintings were added to walls and ceilings. The paintings depicted biblical scenes and landscapes evoking Israel at a time when Zionism gained increased popularity. The art was by Adolf Bienenstock, a Jewish artist from Przemyśl. This synagogue was not destroyed during WWII because the Nazis used it as a stable for army horses. It became a fabrics warehouse after the war. The building is now a public library.[23]

Hasidim of Belz, Błażowa, Buyowsko, Sanz and Sieniawa all worshipped in a building known as the large *kloiz* built during the 19th century. The *kloiz* was an informal Hasidic house of worship, often overflowing with huge crowds on special occasions.[24] Hasidim also worshipped in small *kloizes* and in private homes. Another synagogue named the Tempel, was built 1890 by the Reform Jewish community in Przemyśl on Jagiellonska Street. It was an elegant brick building in the Romanesque revival style. The Tempel had a choir, an organ and most of the service was in Polish. Songs and melodies were similiar to other progressive synagogues of Western Europe however the Tempel was destroyed by the Nazi army in 1939.[25]

My Turnheim Ancestors in Przemyśl

Economic prosperity came to Przemyśl during the second half of the 19th century, with the advent of the railroad. Jews supplied iron, grain, and foodstuffs. They set up flour mills, sawmills, brickyards, factories and served as building contractors. There was a well-to-do Jewish minority, however most Jews remained as petty traders who operated stalls in the markets. They peddled their wares in the villages or worked as factory employees. At this time, many Galician Jews immigrated to the United States during the 1880s in search of economic opportunities and freedom from oppression. By 1890 the Jewish population in Przemyśl was 10,998 and by 1910 approximately 16,000 Jews lived in Przemyśl.

The Yizkor Book of Przemyśl had several references to my Turnheim relatives. A section in the yizkor book *Economic Life in Przemysl during the Beginning of the 20th Century* mentioned the Gans brothers and their branches: Baumwald, Turnheim, Mieses, Majersdorf, Scharf and Astel, all working in foodstuffs.[26] The wholesale food business was mentioned as being on a national level and was on a par with other large businesses and factories. The Galicia 1891 Business Directory listed Benjamin Turnheim, my great-grand uncle, as the owner of a grocery/delicatessen in Przemyśl.[27]

The yizkor book also described a Jewish hospital founded 1842 at Przemyśl. The Jewish community decided that a larger, new hospital was needed. In 1900 Eliyahu Hirt purchased several houses intended to be the new hospital and registered them in the name of the Jewish community of Przemyśl. Money was raised by the philanthropist Moshe Scheinbach. The new hospital opened 1904 with 30 beds, new equipment, patient rooms and an operating theatre on the second floor. There were areas for a clinic, laundry room, chemical and bacteriological laboratories, and a kitchen.

During WWI, the Jewish Hospital was confiscated by the Austrian army for wounded soldiers. At the end of the war, the Red Cross used it for contagious diseases. When WWI ended the Jewish community eventually regained use of the damaged building with assistance of the American Joint Distribution Committee and prominent local leaders, to address the worsening health situation of the Jewish population. Increased poverty was triggered by raging inflation and a high cost of living. Such illnesses as typhoid, trachoma and skin diseases were rampant.[28]

Dr. Landau, as community leader, restored the hospital to ownership by the Jewish community. New equipment and modern medical devices were purchased

Jewish Hospital after WWI

and on 13 January 1924, the Jewish hospital re-opened. The hospital was located on a large park on a hill at Szaszkiewicza Street and had a building with 100 patient beds, a building for surgical operations and a building for administration.

The Labor and Delivery Department was the first one in Galicia. The medical skill and improved hygiene greatly decreased mortality during labor. The Dermatological clinic was directed by Dr. Samuel Turnheim, a son of Benjamin Turnheim. The hospital also served as a residency for young Jewish doctors who were not accepted into government hospitals for their residencies due to anti-Semitic discrimination. The hospital was funded by the Jewish community from income derived from *chuppa* registration, burial, and headstone fees; patient sick fees; donations; with assistance from the Przemyśl municipality. Despite running at a deficit, the hospital was going to expand in 1938. Plans for expansion were cut short due to WWII. Today the Jewish hospital building serves as a school for Polish nurses.

In the Yizkor book for Przemyśl, there was a description of early Zionist activities in the chapter *Political Movements in the Jewish Street.* A circle of young graduates from the Polish gymnasium in 1904 wanted to organize a new Zionist group. Together with university students, they founded an organization named

Agudat Herzl and among the 12 founders listed was Solomon Turnheim, a son of Benjamin Turnheim. It was noted that he later immigrated to the United States and worked there as an engineer.[29]

The old Jewish cemetery dating from ca.1570 on Zydowska Street was closed to new burials in 1865. A new Jewish cemetery was founded 1822 (Zydowski Cemetery) and is located on Slowackiego Street. This cemetery has approximately 1,000 graves and is where my Turnheim relatives were buried. They are: Sara Rifka Gans 1838–1917 (married to Meilich Gans and who was Benjamin Turnheim's mother-in-law); Elza Thurnheim 1889–30 August 1930 (Samuel Turnheim's wife); Benjamin Thurnheim died 18 April 1930 (my great-grand uncle); Roza Thurnheim died 15 July 1942 (granddaughter of Benjamin Turnheim); Edka Thurnheim died 15 July 1 1942(wife of Jozef Turnheim); Chaja Reizla Thurnheim died 13 March 1923 (Benjamin Turnheim's wife); Jozef Thurnheim died 15 July 1942 (son of Benjamin Turnheim); Samuel Thurnheim 4 October 1879–20 August 1957 physician (son of Benjamin Turnheim); my great-great-grandmother Mariem Turnheim died 4 August 1875 (the daughter of Rabbi Gro-

Przemyśl Jewish Cemetery

nem HaRav); Matitjahu Thurnheim 20 February 1886–1916 (son of Benjamin Turnheim) "died during horrible war".[30] The spelling of Turnheim was Thurnheim on the Przemyśl cemetery list. See the chapter *The Turnheim Family* and the *Solomon Turnheim Family Tree*.

World War I in Przemyśl

During WWI Przemyśl was the site of the heaviest fighting in the region; it had the largest and most important citadel in Galicia. Fortresses were built around the 28-mile circumference of Przemyśl to accommodate 85,000 soldiers and hundreds of cannons. The Russian Army advanced into Galicia and began a siege of the fortress of Przemyśl in October 1914. Due to lack of food and exhaustion of the defenders, the fortress surrendered 22 March 1915. During May 1915, the Russians ordered any remaining Jews to leave Przemyśl or be subject to violence by a Cossack battalion. Among the last Jews left in the city on 10 May 1915 was Rabbi Gedalia Schmelkes who refused to abandon the Jews of Przemyśl, and he survived the war. The Austrians and German armies recaptured Przemyśl on 3 June 1915. Many of the expelled Jews did not return to their city, and continued to live in Vienna, Budapest, and Czechoslovakia.

After WWI, in 1919 Przemyśl became part of independent Poland. By 1921 the total Przemyśl population was 47,958 including 18,360 Jews. The total population of Przemyśl increased to 51,038 with 17,326 Jews (34% of the total population) in 1931. Half the Jews were engaged in trade and about 100 Jewish doctors and 100 Jewish lawyers remained in the city. Jews were still discriminated against for state jobs such as occupations of police, post office, railroads, army officers and judges.

World War II and Przemyśl

Many Jews from Przemyśl were recruited into the Polish army during World War II. Others took part in the urban Civil Defense. The Nazis bombed Przemyśl 5 September 1939, and a mass flight of citizens took place in the direction of Hungarian and Romanian borders.[31] The city was captured by the Nazis on 14 September 1939, and they lost no time in executing 600 prominent Jews. The Nazis murdered 500 more Jews on 15 September 1939. The bodies were thrown into a mass grave, then after the war the bodies were exhumed and moved into a mass grave at the Jewish cemetery on Slowackiego Street where a memorial plaque was later placed.

According to German-Soviet agreement, the part of Przemyśl east of the San River was under Soviet control and west of the San River was under German rule. The Nazis set fire and destroyed the Tempel Synagogue and the Old Synagogue on 21 September 1939. They expropriated the New (Scheinbach) Synagogue and the Zasanie Synagogue and confiscated all commercial and residential real estate belonging to Jews. German soldiers also burst into Jewish shops and robbed their goods. Expelled Jews were permitted to take only a few possessions; few of them succeeded in getting carts or boats to move their families and possessions to the east side of the San River.[32] There were 20,000 Jews expelled by the Nazis to the Soviet occupation zone. The Soviets deported approximately 7,000 Jews to Siberia during April–May 1940.[33]

Jewish communal institutions immediately ceased to function, and the property of the community was nationalized. Jewish political parties stopped functioning; their clubs were closed and became the property of the authorities. The Jewish orphanages, old age homes, and hospital became the property of the municipality, converted into general institutions, and lost any specific Jewish affiliations.

The Nazis established a *Judenrat* in July 1941, and this consisted of Jewish men selected to be policemen to enforce Nazi dictates. The *Judenrat* was also responsible for supplying workers for forced labor. Jewish physicians issued exception forms to Jews for whom harsh labor would endanger their lives however the Germans did not honor those documents. Imprisonment and executions of Jews accused of cooperating with the Soviets continued during the winter of 1941–42. In addition, hunger, cold, disease and plagues caused many deaths.

The Nazi declaration for the establishment of the Przemyśl ghetto came at the beginning of July 1942. The population of 24,000 Jews were ordered to move there by 15 July 1942 and the population density in the ghetto was unbearable; people lived in every possible place, including attics, storerooms, and cellars. They died from inhuman treatment and extreme privation. I read the inscriptions on the matsevahs in the New Jewish Cemetery indicating many of my Turnheim ancestors died on that day 15 July 1942. The authorities forbade non-Jews to help members of the community under threat of capital punishment.

The Nazis ordered inmates in the ghetto to organize an orchestra and for a short time, the orchestra played public concerts three times a week. This emphasized the tragedy of the Jews of Przemyśl that in a condition of extreme hard labor, illnesses, hunger, and unceasing murder, they were humiliated and forced to perform concerts in the presence of their Nazi tormentors and murderers

The First *Aktion* began 27 July 1942 beginning with the murders of the disabled, sick, elderly, and children. Corpses of men, women, and children were found in piles on the streets of the ghetto at the end of the *Aktion*. About 7,000 people were delivered to Bełżec on the first day of the *Aktion* and 6,000 Jews were deported to Bełżec extermination camp 31 July and 3 August 1942. Thousands more were later sent to their deaths at Auschwitz or were summarily shot in Przemyśl in later *aktions*.

The Nazis entered the Jewish hospital and murdered all the patients; hospital personnel were expelled. There were many suicides, mainly among families of doctors. I cannot imagine how Dr. Samuel Turnheim survived the horrors of WWII and continued to live in Przemyśl during the post-war years until his death in 1957.

Post-War

The Soviet army captured Przemyśl on 27 July 1944.[34] The official end of WWII came when Nazi Germany surrendered to the Allied Forces on 7 May 1945. A border agreement between the Soviet Union and the Polish Provisional Government was signed in Moscow on 16 August 1945 that established the Curzon Line, a post war eastern border of Poland several kilometers to the east of Przemyśl. Przemyśl remained within the Polish People's Republic. During the war Jewish orphaned children were hidden by nuns and clergy in orphanages, monasteries, convents and were often provided with forged documents. After the war concluded in 1946 Jewish orphans were moved to Jewish institutions in Kraków, Lublin, and Łódź, where they continued their journey out of Poland. Surviving Przemyśl Jews who fled during the war to the Soviet Union returned to the city hoping to find someone from their family, but when it was clear that there were no survivors, they left and turned to the west. Gradually most of the remaining Jews of Przemyśl left the city, the majority left Poland for destinations overseas, especially to Israel.

Jarosław

During my investigations into my Turnheim family I found primary evidence through vital records that the first and second generations of the Turnheim family were born in Jarosław, Podkarpackie, Poland and lived there until my great-great-grandfather Hersch Turnheim from Jarosław married my great-great-grandmother Mariem Gems from Przemyśl. After their marriage Hersch and Mariem Turnheim settled in Przemyśl where they raised their family.

Jews first began to settle in Jarosław in 1464 but they were not permitted to work within the town. In 1608 fewer than 10 Jews lived there due to residence restrictions based on anti-Semitism. When Jews were permitted to reside within Jarosław; they initially worked as financiers and money lenders. Those trades were condemned by the church for Christians. By 1630 a small population of Jews lived in Jarosław and they built their first synagogue in 1640. One hundred and twenty Jews lived in Jarosław in 1648. Jews opened their own cemetery in 1699 even though they were still legally obligated to bury their dead at Przemyśl. During this time, Jews leased distilleries, flour mills, traded hides, and continued to trade food products with Danzig. Jarosław also became an important center for cattle trade, dominated by Jews. The famed August fairs in Jarosław attracted many Jewish merchants from the Polish-Lithuanian Commonwealth.[35]

King Augustus II of Poland (1670–1733) confirmed the right of Jews to settle in Jarosław in 1720. An independent kehilla was formed in Jarosław in 1774 after Jarosław was declared free of subordination to the Przemyśl Jewish community. Under Rabbi Jacob Ornstein (1775–1839) Jarosław became an important center of Jewish religious study. Hasidism soon took root, followed by the Jewish Enlightenment, and then Zionism.

During the 19th century Jews were dominant in the economy of Jarosław and owned most of the factories. By 1890 Jews in Jarosław numbered 4,820 out of a total population of 18,065. The Jewish community owned a hospital and a healthcare fund. The Jewish community of Jarosław also built a *beit ha midrash*, a school, a home for the elderly and a ritual slaughterhouse. They built a synagogue 1807–11 and another synagogue in 1900.[36] Up until 1931 the Jewish population of Jarosław remained at about 6,300.

There were 6,154 Jews living in Jarosław in 1910. After WWI ended, in June 1918 riots broke out against Jews. Another anti-Semitic riot occurred in 1920 by soldiers under General Haller with violence and looting. Anti-Semitism was always an under-lying current in Jarosław and this rose up again during the 1930s as Jews continued to lead in the commercial life of Jarosław, while the general economy of Poland was worsening.[37]

The Germans bombed Jarosław at the beginning of WWII. Jews were captured for forced labor and severely beaten by the German soldiers. Prominent

Jews were taken as hostages and were later murdered. Nazis seized Jarosław on 8 September 1939 and on 28 September deported hundreds of Jews across the San River to the Soviet occupation zone. That same day Jaroslaw Jewry ceased to exist. Jews were deported to Siberia, or they became prisoners in Nazi extermination camps. Some Jarosław Jews fought in the ranks of the Polish army or in the Red Army or with the partisans. Many chopped down trees in Siberia, mined coal in the Urals, and rotted in concentration camps or ghettos. By June 1942, the Jews who managed to survive in Jarosław were taken to Sienawa where the Gestapo established a prison on the grounds of a Benedictine monastery. Jews were methodically executed at this prison and the Germans removed the bodies so there would be no trace of the crime. Even when the war ended in 1945, gangs of anti-Semitic Poles in Jarosław murdered the few Holocaust survivors who returned to Jarosław.[38]

This excerpt was written by a survivor and was included the yizkor book for Jarosław:

"And now we are the survivors of the Jarosław's Jewry. We have no idea where the bones of our mothers and fathers are strewn, where the children are buried or where our relatives were murdered, whether in Bełżec or Treblinka or Auschwitz, Mauthausen or Bergen-Belsen. And now we are the remaining Jewish survivors of Jarosław, living in our homeland understanding the enormous obligation we have to perpetuate the memory of the magnificent Jewish community and how important it is to honor and respect those who are no longer with us; to hand down to our children and future generations a diligent description of Jarosław's Jewish community before its total destruction."[39]

Endnotes

1   Miriam Weiner. *Jewish Roots in Poland*. (New York: YIVO Institute for Jewish Research, 1997), 96–97.

2   www.jewishgen.org/Yizkor/Przemysl/Przemysl.html

3   Brian J. Lenius. *Genealogical Gazetteer of Galicia. 2ⁿᵈ. Ed. Updated. (*Anola, Manitoba, Canada: B.J. Lenius 1994).

4   John J. Hartman and Jacek Krochmal, editors. Translated by Agnieszka Andrzejewska. *I Remember Every Day—The Fates of the Jews of Przemysl during World War II*. (Przemysl, Poland, 2002).

5   David R. Semmel. *The 11ᵗʰ of Av.* (David R. Semmel, 2010).

6   Miriam Weiner. *Jewish Roots in Poland*. (New York: YIVO Institute for Jewish research, 1997).

7   Francine Shapiro, editor. *Pinkas Hakehillot Polin Przemysl-Encyclopedia of Jewish Communities in Poland, Volume II*. Translated by Shlomo Sneh. (Jerusalem, Israel: Yad Vashem). 424–440.

8   S.M. Dubnow. *History of the Jews in Russia and Poland from the Earliest Times until the Present Day*. Translated: I. Friedlaender. Vol. I.(Philadelphia, Pennsylvania: The Jewish Publication Society of America, 1916).

9   Shmuel Spector and Geoffrey Wigoder, editors. *The Encyclopedia of Jewish Life Before and During the Holocaust*. (New York : New York University Press, August 2001).

10   There is a legend from Zasanie that the Bishop of Przemyśl, Mikolay Blazejowski (1452–1474), was strolling in Zasanie when he was asked by a local Jew to help his wife in childbirth. The Bishop was willing to help and placed his ring on the Jewish woman's finger. The ring was believed to have facilitated the labor and a rumor spread about its miraculous power. The ring was called the "ring of women in childbirth" and was kept in the treasury of the Cathedral in Przemyśl. The local community believed in the miraculous power of the ring through the 19ᵗʰ century.

11   www.sztetl.org.pl/en/article/przemysl/5,history/

12   www.yivoencyclopedia.org.

13   www.sztetl.org.pl/en/article/przemysl/5,history/

14   John J. Hartman and Jacek Krochmal. 251–252.

15   Barbara U. Yeager and Blossom Glasser,editors. *Przemysl: Outline of Jewish History*. Kehila Links. (www.jewishgen.org).

16   John J.Hartman and Janek Krochmal., 253.

17   Barbara U. Yeager and Blossom Glasser, editors. *Przemysl: Outline of Jewish History*. Kehila Links. (www.jewishgen.org).

18   www.yeshiva.co.

19   www.encyclopedia.com

20   Arie Menczer, editor. *Przemysl Memorial Book. Chapter: Religious Life*. Dov Nitzani. (Israel: Irgun Yotzei Przemysl, 1964). Pp. 135–140.

21   Arie Menczer, editor. *Przemysl Memorial Book. Part I. Chapter 4: The Ancient Synagogue of Przemysl and its Place in Architectural History*. Professor Dr. Naftali Schneid. (Israel: Irgun Yotzei Przemysl, 1964). 50.

22   Arie Menczer, editor. *Przemysl Memorial Book. Part II. Chapter 4: Religious Life*. Dov Nitzani. (Israel: Irgun Yotzei Przemysl, 1964). Pp.122–124.

23   Arie Menczer, editor. *Przemysl Memorial Book. Part II. Chapter 4: Religious Life*. Dov Nitzani. (Israel: Irgun Yotzei Przemysl, 1964). Pp. 128–129.

24   Arie Menczer, editor. *Przemysl Memorial Book. Chapter: Religious Life*. Dov Nitzani. (Israel: Irgun Yotzei Przemysl, 1964). Pp.126–127.

25   Ibid. 130.

26   Arie Menczer, editor. *Przemysl Memorial Book. Part II. Section: Economic Life in Przemysl during the Beginning of the 20ᵗʰ Century. Chapter 2 In the City and Community*. Dov Nitzani. (Israel: Irgun Yotzei Przemysl, 1964). 85.

27   Galicia 1891 Business Directory. B. Turnheim. *Gemischtwaarenhandler*. Grocery/delicatessen. (www.jewishgen.org).

28   Arie Menczer, editor. *Przemysl Memorial Book. Part III. Chapter 7: The Jewish Health Institutions in Przemysl. Section: The Jewish Hospital*. Yosef Altbauer. (Israel: Irgun Yotzei Przemysl, 1964). Pp. 233–237.

29   Arie Menczer, editor. *Przemysl Memorial Book. Part II. Chapter 3: Political Movements in the Jewish Street*. Dov Nitzani. (Israel: Irgun Yotzei Przemysl, 1964). Pp. 95–96.

30   Cemetery List. Jewish Przemysl Cemetery. Slowackiego Street, Przemysl Poland.

31   John J. Hartman and Janek Krochmal. 260–261.

32   Shmuel Spector, Editor in Chief. *The Encyclopedia of Jewish Life Before and During the Holocaust*. 1034–1035.

33   Barbara U. Yeager and Blossom Glasser, editors. *Przemysl: Outline of Jewish History*. Kehila Links. (www.jewishgen.org).

34   Shmuel Spector. 1035.

35   sztetl.org.pl/en/towns/j/108-jaroslaw.

36   Ibid.

37   Ohad Levi-Zaloscer, translator and editor. *Jaroslaw. Pinkas Hakehillot Polin: Encyclopedia of Jewish Communities, Poland, Volume III*, pages 213–220. (Jerusalem: Yad Vashem).

38   Ibid.

39   Yitzhak Alperowitz, Editor. J*aroslaw Yizkor Book. Chapter: Holocaust and Heroism. Section: In Memoriam* by Alexander Silberman. Translated by Selwyn Rose. Published Tel Aviv, Israel, 1978). 280.

Chapter Five

The Turnheim Family

Introduction

My maternal great-grandmother was Hinde Turnheim, and this chapter will focus on her Turnheim family.

There are various spellings of the surname Turnheim; it is a German name for home gate and is most often found in Przemyśl.[1] The earliest records that I found for my Turnheim family indicated they lived in Jarosław, Poland. During the 16th and 17th centuries Jarosław gained importance as the marketplace where great fairs were held three times yearly. Jews were the main dealers, and many Jewish merchants visited the fairs from other communities. Jewish visitors set aside a place at the fair for daily prayers and for reading the Torah on Shabbat. By 1738 there were 100 Jewish families living in Jarosław; by 1813 the Jewish population numbered 2,355 of a total population of 9,007). Jews settled in Jarosław during the 17th century. At first the Jewish community of Jarosław relied on the larger city of Przemyśl for their religious requirements, for burial of their dead in the Jewish cemetery of Przemyśl and to borrow their Torah scroll for services in Jarosław. As the Jewish population grew, Jarosław became independent of Przemyśl with their own *kahal*.[2]

Matrimonial matches were sometimes made between Jewish families from Jarosław and Przemyśl, only 23 miles separated the cities. When Hersch Turnheim of Jarosław married Mariem Gems 1836 at Przemyśl, this event began a change of residence for future generations of Turnheims from Jarosław to residence at Przemyśl. There were frequent cousin/cousin and uncle/niece marriages within the Turnheim family during the 19th century. This was typical in Ashkenazi Jewish populations as they favorably viewed marriages between relatives for reasons based on affinity through kinship, continuity of religion and insurance that family wealth would be retained within the family. By the mid-19th century, the Turnheims were well established at Przemyśl, Poland as one of the preeminent Jewish families, successful in businesses and in professions while also adhering to traditional Jewish orthodoxy.

In the process of writing this chapter, I began with my earliest known Turnheim ancestor and proceeded forward in time, ending with the fifth generation of descendants. The databases www.jewishgen.org, www.geshergalicia.org, www.jri-poland.org, www.ancestry.com, www.yadvashem.org, and the State Archives in Przemyśl, Poland were invaluable sources for the Turnheim records. I found documents and vital records from other archives in Poland, the Ukraine, Austria, and the United States. I interviewed my cousins who are Turnheim descendants: Gabby Bate, Dora Ritzer, David Brainin and Georg Turnheim who shared their family histories. David R. Semmel provided me with valuable Przemyśl Jewish cemetery research and Domicella Klima née Grossman, a resident of Przemyśl, shared her family history and generously sent me cemetery photographs of the graves of my Turnheim relatives. Please refer to the *Solomon Turnheim Family Tree* and to the chapter *Jews in Przemyśl* including the section on *Jews in Jarosław*. Note that both Jarosław and Przemyśl in Poland are within the Podkarpackie Voivodeship also known as the Subcarpathia Province (in Polish it is *województwo podkarpackie*).

Generation One

1.Solomon[1] Turnheim, born ca. 1797 at Jarosław, Poland; died ca. 1857. He married ca. 1814 at Jarosław, Poland, Sara Feige.

Children of Solomon[1] Turnheim and Sara Feige:
i. Malie[2] Turnheim, born 1815 at Jarosław, Poland; died 1892, Jarosław, Poland. She married ca. 1833 at Jarosław, Poland, David Atlas, son of Sender Atlas and Feige.

ii. Hersch Turnheim, born 1818 at Jarosław, Poland; died ca. 1896. He married 1836 at Przemyśl, Poland, Mariem Gems, daughter of Gronem Gems and Hinde Marberg.

iii. David Turnheim, born 1820 at Jarosław, Poland; died 1883, Jarosław, Poland. He married ca. 1842 Chane Ruchel Lebenbraun, daughter of Moses Herz Lebenbraun and Basche Reisel.

Discussion

Solomon[1] Turnheim was born ca. 1797 at Jarosław, Poland. Both Solomon and his wife Sara Feige were my great-great-great-grandparents. I first noted the name Solomon Turnheim when I discovered a marriage record for my great-great-grandfather Hersch Turnheim, who married Mariem Gems 1836 at Przemyśl, Podkarpackie, Poland.[3]

The names Solomon Turnheim and his wife Sara Feige were noted on death records from Jarosław; as the parents of their son David Turnheim who died in 1883;[4] and as the parents of their daughter Malie Atlas who died 1892.[5] In the absence of vital records, Solomon's date of birth was estimated from the death record of his first child, Malie Atlas. Malie was 77 years at her death in 1892 thus born 1815. If Jewish grooms were typically age 18 at the time of their marriage, then Solomon was born ca. 1797. Circumstantial evidence indicated that Solomon Turnheim's death probably occurred prior to the birth of his grandson Schulem in December 1857 since the name Schulem is a variation for Solomon and followed the Ashkenazi Jewish tradition of naming a child after a deceased close relative. Solomon Turnheim was ca. age 60 if he died 1857 the year that Schulem was born.[6]

Generation Two

2. Malie[2] Turnheim (Solomon[1]), born 1815 at Jarosław, Poland to Solomon Turnheim and Sara Feige; died 1892 at Jarosław, Poland;[7] married ca. 1833 at Jarosław, Poland, David Atlas, the son of Sender Atlas and Feige. David Atlas was born 1812 at Jarosław, Poland; died 1889 at Jarosław, Poland.[8]

Children of Malie Turnheim and David Atlas:
i. Jacob[3] Atlas (Malie[2], Solomon[1]) born ca.1834 at Jarosław, Poland; died 1889. He married 23 February 1882 at Przemyśl, Poland, Zlate Turnheim, daughter of Hersch Turnheim and Mariem Gems.[9]

ii. Wolf Atlas, born 1838 at Jarosław, Poland; died 1894, Jarosław, Poland.[10]

iii. Joseph Atlas, born 1840 at Jarosław, Poland; died 1894, Jarosław, Poland.[11]

iv. Sender Atlas, born 1851 at Jarosław, Poland; died 1889, Jarosław, Poland.[12]

3. Hersch[2] Turnheim (Solomon[1]), born 1818 at Jarosław, Poland to Solomon Turnheim and Sara Feige; died ca.1896 at Przemyśl, Poland; married 1836 at Przemyśl, Poland, Mariem Gems, the daughter of Gronem Gems and Hinde Marberg.[13]

Children of Hersch Turnheim and Mariem Gems:
i. Zlate[3] Turnheim, born November 1839 at Przemyśl, Poland; married 23

February 1882 at Przemyśl, Poland, Jacob Atlas, the son of David Atlas and Malie Turnheim.

ii. Baruch Turnheim, born 1844 at Przemyśl, Poland; died 1914 at Drohobycz, Ukraine; married 5 December 1887 at Drohobycz, Ukraine, Chane Kreppel, the daughter of Chaim Kreppel and Chaje Wegner.

iii. Hinde Turnheim, born 1 January 1850 at Przemyśl, Poland; died 11 October 1931 at Vienna, Austria; married Aron Geiger 1868 at Przemyśl, Poland, the son of Solomon David Geiger and Chaje Mindel Unger.

iv. Moses Turnheim, born 1852 at Przemyśl, Poland; died 6 January 1890; married 17 January 1874 at Bolechów, Ukraine, Sara Hendel, daughter of Josef Hendel and Rechel.

v. Benjamin Turnheim, born 8 August 1854 at Przemyśl, Poland; died 15 April 1930 at Przemyśl, Poland; married 3 December 1882 at Przemyśl, Poland, Chaje Reisel Gans, the daughter of Meilech Gans and Sara Rifka Feldstein.

vi. Simon Turnheim (twin), born 7 December 1857 at Przemyśl, Poland; died 8 April 1858 at Przemyśl, Poland.

vii. Schulem Turnheim (twin), born 7 December 1857 at Przemyśl, Poland; died 30 August 1925 at Vienna, Austria; married (1) Sabina aka Sobel Pilpel 1879 at Lwów, Ukraine, daughter of Herz Jona Pilpel and Chaje Gittel Hand; married (2) Lea Turnheim 6 December 1887 at Drohobycz, Ukraine, daughter of Baruch Turnheim and Chane Kreppel.

Discussion

A birth record was found from Przemyśl where Hersch Turnheim was listed as the sandek for the *brit milah* (circumcision ceremony) of his grandson Solomon Turnheim during November 1881, therefore Hersch was still alive at that time.[14] Hersch was still living in 1896, when he was listed as the sandek for the *brit milah* of another grandson Ernest aka Chuna David Turnheim.[15] My hypothesis is that Hersch Turnheim died ca.1896 at Przemyśl, Podkarpackie, Poland or soon thereafter.

Marriage records contained the names of the parents for both groom and bride. The 1836 marriage record from Przemyśl for Hersch Turnheim (misspelled or misread as Furnheim) and Mariem Gems, included important information about my great great-grandparents. Hersch was age 18 and Mariem was age 17, indicating 1819 as her birth year. Hersch Turnheim was age 18 at the time of his marriage therefore born 1818. Based on this marriage record for Hersch Turnheim and Mariem Gems, I learned the names of my great-great-great-grandparents Salomon Turnheim and Sara Feige from Jarosław also my great-great-great-grandparents Gronem Gems and Hinde Marberg from Przemyśl. I found a marriage record for the groom Gronem Gems and the bride Hinde Marberg from Przemyśl dated 1802.[16] The surname Gems derives from the German meaning chamois and is a name found within the Subcarpathia Province.[17] The surname Gems was also recorded as Gans meaning goose in German. The surname Marberg was probably adapted from Marburg, the medieval town that was established in 1140 and in the German federal state of Hesse. It was a common surname in Rohatyn, formerly in Galicia now in the Ukraine.[18]

Death records from Przemyśl listed my great-great-great-grandmother Hinde Gems née Marberg who died at age 70 in 1847, therefore I estimated her birth year as 1777. [19]Another death record listed my great-great-great-grandfather Gronem Gans or Gems who died in 1846 at age 71; his birth year was 1775.[20] The name Gronem is a *kinnui* for the Hebrew name Samuel. The name Hinde was passed down from my great-great-great-grandmother Hinde Marberg to my great-grandmother Hinde Turnheim and then given to me as one of my Yiddish names.

A death record for my great-great-grandmother Mariem Turnheim contained information her death occurred in 1875 at age 61; her birth year would be 1814.[21] I prefer to use the date of her birth based on birth and marriage records since death records about age can be unreliable. I conclude that Marjem was probably born 1819 and she was age 56 when she died 4 August 1875 of cancer. I obtained a cemetery list from Przemyśl's New Jewish Cemetery with Miriam's date of death listing her father as Rabbi Gronem Gems.[22]

A photograph of Mariem's matsevah was obtained from the Jewishgen.org database Jewish Online Worldwide Burial Registry. I asked Rabbi Joshua Segal, an expert in reading matsevahs, to translate the Hebrew inscription seen on the photograph although some sections were not clearly legible. The translated inscription provided me with greater understanding of my ancestor Mariem Turnheim née Gems:

Here lies a woman, modest in her deeds, Mrs.
   Miriam, daughter of the learned scholar,
   our rabbi and teacher, Gronem
Died 3 Menachem Av, 5635 (corresponding
   to 4 August 1875)
What ails you O beautiful one, mistress of the
   house,
Who from among your children like olive trees
   (Psalms 128:3), one became head of our
   community.
They will ask of our mourning with mourning
   and moaning.
From the heights, she lay down in oblivion.
Daughter of Gronem, tears are legitimate in
   mourning for Miriam.
Much lamenting will penetrate the heart of heaven
Gronem ... burning tears
Her blessed memory and the ha-leil will say
She was G-d fearing and wise.
Miriam daughter of Reb Gronem of Blessed Memory.
May her soul be bound in the bond of everlasting life.[23]

Mariem Turnheim matsevah

4. David[2] **Turnheim** (Solomon[1]), born ca. 1820 at Jarosław, Poland to Solomon Turnheim and Sara Feige; died 1883 at Miłków, Dolnoślaskie, Poland[24]; married ca. 1842 at Jarosław, Poland, Chane Ruchel Löwenbrun, born 1821 at Jarosław, daughter of Moses Herz Löwenbrun and Basche Reisel; she died 1889 at Jarosław.[25] Note that Löwenbrun was also written as Lebenbraun.

Children of David Turnheim and Chane Ruchel Löwenbrun aka Lebenbraun:
i. Joseph[3] Turnheim, born 1843 at Jarosław; married 2 January 1866 at Przemyśl, Poland, Ruchel Glanz, daughter of Israel Glanz.[26]

ii. Jacob Turnheim, born ca.1850; married ca. 1888, Tillie Turnheim, the daughter of Joseph Turnheim and Ruchel Glanz. Tillie died 1909 at Jarosław, Poland.[27]

iii. Debora Turnheim, born 1852; married 1884 Leiba Tirk (also spelled Turk) son of Hersch Tirk and Diene at Jarosław, Poland.[28] She died 1892 at Przemyśl, Poland.[29]

iv. Leib Turnheim, born 1858, Jarosław, Poland. Married 25 November 1885 at Tarnów, Malopolskie, Poland, Ester Handgriff daughter of Chiel Dawid Handgriff and Feige Eisenberg.

Generation 3

5. Leib[3] Turnheim (David[2], Solomon[1]), born 1858 at Jarosław, Poland to David Turnheim and Chane Löwenbrun aka Lebenbraun. He married 25 November 1885 at Tarnów, Poland, Ester Handgriff, daughter of Chiel Dawid Handgriff and Feige Eisenberg.[30]

Children of Leib Turnheim and Ester Handgriff:

i. Sali Francziszka aka Salomea Turnheim was born 27 December 1886 at Tarnów, Poland, married Chaim Klein 21 October 1906 at Tarnów, Poland. Chaim Klein aka Schlachet was born at Nowy Sacz, Kraków, Poland, son of Maier Nathan Schlachet and Ester Klein.[31]

ii. Marya Turnheim was born 11 February 1888 at Tarnów, Poland, married Chajem Hochhauser 4 December 1910 at Tarnów, Małopolski, Poland, son of Abraham David Hochhauser and Czarna Luftglas.

iii. Abraham Chune Turnheim born 27 July 1889 at Tarnów, Poland.[32] He was murdered during the Shoah.[33]

iv. Anna Turnheim born 1892 at Tarnów; died 1893 at Tarnów, Poland.

v. Edward Turnheim born 1894 at Tarnów, Poland. He was a merchant in Tarnów and was murdered during the Shoah.[34]

vi. Gizela Turnheim born 1897 at Tarnów, Poland; died 1900 at Tarnów, Poland.

vii. Jozef Turnheim born 8 January 1899 at Tarnów, Poland; died 8 April 1915.[35]

viii. Maurycy Turnheim born 1901 at Tarnów, Poland.

ix. Menashe Juda aka Maks Juliusz Turnheim born 1903 at Tarnów, Poland.

x. Salomon Turnheim born 1907 at Tarnów, Poland. He lived in Tarnów and was murdered during the Shoah.[36]

Discussion

The 1885 marriage record from Tarnów for Leib Turnheim and Ester Hand-griff was translated by volunteers for the www.jewishgen.org ViewMate.[37] Leib Turnheim's father David Turnheim was a merchant of glassware in Jarosław. The groom Leib Turnheim was born at Jaroslaw and was a *prywatny* living in Jarosław. The Polish translation for *prywatny* means private. The bride Ester Handgriff was born in Tarnów and her father Chiel Dawid Handgriff was a grain merchant in Tarnów.

A page of testimony from Yad Vashem was found for Leib Turnheim and was translated from Hebrew. His last known address was in Tarnów, Poland, and he was the proprietor of a lamp store. The JRI-Poland archive coordinator for Tarnów, Howard Fink, generously shared Turnheim family records, although many were not yet available on-line. A death record for Leib aka Leon Turnheim indicated he died 1929 at Tarnów,[38] his wife Ester died 1932.[39] Leib and Ester Turnheim's children Abraham Chune, Jozef, Salomon, Marya and Salomea at-tended Tarnów public schools.[40]

A genealogical researcher, Linda S., contacted me with information that her relative Salamon Schlachet was born 22 July 1911 at Nowy Sacz, Kraków, Poland. His parents were Sali Francziska Turnheim and Chaim Klein. His maternal grand-parents were Leon (Leib) and Estera Turnheim née Handgriff; Linda connected this with my Turnheim family. Salamon Schlachet was a physician and married Ms. Spiro. Dr. Salamon Schlachet was included in the JewishGen database Polish Medical Questionnaire as a physician.[41] He was fluent in 4 languages. He was also included in the Yad Vashem Central Database of Shoah Victims' Names. Dr. Salomon Schlachet was murdered 1942 during the Shoah. Dr. Schlachet and his wife were living in Zborow, Tarnopol, Ukraine at Bazarna-boczna 17 during the war.[42]

Before WWII, Tarnów, Poland had a Jewish population of 25,000. The Jew-ish community was diverse with religious Hasidim, secular Zionists and many more. The persecution of Jews began soon after the German occupation on 8 September 1939. Synagogues were burned and Jews were drafted for forced la-bor. By 1941 Jews in Tarnów were ordered to hand in their valuables; there were increased labor roundups and arbitrary murders.

Deportations from Tarnów began June 1942 with 13,500 Jews sent to Bełżec extermination camp. An additional 10,000 Jews were tortured and murdered on the streets, in the Jewish cemetery and in the woods. A Tarnów ghetto was formed by the Germans to contain surviving Jews of Tarnów with thousands of Jews from neighboring towns. Conditions in the ghetto were perilous with severe food shortages and a lack of sanitation. The Germans used forced labor to produce goods for the German war industry. By September 1942, The Germans selected 8,000 Jews as "non-essential labor" and deported them to Bełzec. Another 2,500 were deported during November 1942. During the 1942 deportations, several young Zionists in Tarnów organized a Jewish resistance movement. They joined partisans fighting in the forests then subsequently died during battle with SS units. The Germans decided to destroy the Tarnów ghetto September 1943 first deporting 10,000 Jews to Auschwitz and to Plaszow concentration camps in Kraków. By the end of 1943 Tarnów was declared by the Nazis as *Judenrein* (free of Jews).[43]

Records were found for Marya and Chaim Hochhauser on www.geni.com. and JOWBR in www.jewishgen.org. The records indicated Marya and Chaim journeyed to Bolivia, South America and upon their deaths were buried in a Jewish cemetery at Cochabamba, Bolivia. Chaim Hochhauser was born 25 February 1884 in Poland and died 13 August 1943 at Cochabamba. His wife Marya Hochhauser née Turnheim was born 7 February 1888 and died 21 April 1984 also at Cochabamba. At the start of the Nazi era in 1933 Jewish families began to emigrate to Bolivia. By the end of 1942 there were 7,000 Jews in Bolivia primarily in La Paz and Cochabamba. Their benefactor was a German Jewish businessman, Maurice Hochschild, a businessman who had many investments in Bolivia. He arranged visas and employment for Jewish refugees to work in his Bolivian agricultural projects thus saving those Jews from genocide during the Shoah.

5. Zlate[3] **Turnheim** (Hersch[2], Solomon[1]), born November 1839 at Przemyśl to Hersch Turnheim and Mariem Gems; married Jacob Atlas 23 February 1882 at Przemyśl, the son of Malie Turnheim and David Atlas.[44]

Children of Zlate Turnheim and Jacob Atlas:
i. Schie[4] Atlas; born 9 June 1856 at Przemyśl, Poland.[45]

ii. Feige Atlas; born 1859 at Przemyśl, Poland;[46] married 7 March 1882 at Przemyśl, Poland, Israel Angerman, son of Hirsch Angerman and Ester.[47] Their children were Ester Angerman born 1883[48] and Freude Angerman born 1885.[49]

iii. Josef Atlas; born 8 December 1865 at Przemyśl, Poland,[50] married Malcia Gleicher 1896 at Rzeszów, Poland, daughter of Hersch Gleicher and Mindel Meister.[51] Their child Rebeka Atlas was born 29 November 1899 at Przemyśl.[52]

iv. Marim Atlas; born 16 October 1875 at Przemyśl, Poland[53]; married 19 June 1899 at Przemyśl, Poland, Szymon Mandel, the son of Jozef Mandel and Serka Katzner.[54] Szymon Mandel resided at Skałat, Ukraine and his occupation was bookkeeper.

Discussion

Zlate Turnheim was born 1839 at Przemyśl, Poland to Hersch Turnheim and Mariem Gems. Zlate was religiously married to Jacob Atlas ca.1855 in Przemyśl prior to their civil marriage of 1882. The purpose of their civil marriage was to legitimatize their children in the eyes of the law for the right to inherit, for business licenses, to own property or land and for travel documents.[55] Jacob Atlas was born ca.1834 in Jarosław and he resided at Przemyśl as a businessman.

6. Baruch[3] Turnheim (Hersch[2], Solomon[1]), born 1844 at Przemyśl; died 1914 at Drohobycz, Ukraine; married 5 December 1887 at Drohobycz, Ukraine, Chane Kreppel, the daughter of Chaim Kreppel and Chaje Wegner.

Children of Baruch Turnheim and Chane Kreppel:[56]
i. Lea[4] Turnheim; born 1866 at Przemyśl; married her uncle Schulem Turnheim 6 December 1887 at Drohobycz, Ukraine.

ii. Etel Turnheim; born 1870 at Drohobycz; married Moses David Schindler 8 July 1900 at Drohobycz, Ukraine.[57] He was a businessman from Bolechów, Ukraine and his parents were Abraham Schindler and Ryfke Gottlieb.

iii. Rysche Turnheim; born 1874 at Drohobycz, Ukraine; died 14 February 1896 at Drohobycz, Ukraine.[58]

iv. Maryem Turnheim; born 19 June 1879 at Drohobycz, Ukraine.[59]

Discussion

Baruch[3] Turnheim (Hersch[2], Solomon[1]) was born 1844 at Przemyśl to Hersch Turnheim and Mariem Gems; died 1914 age 70 at Drohobycz, Ukraine.[60] He married Chane Kreppel, 5 December 1887 at Drohobycz, Ukraine, the daughter

Marriages Baruch Turnheim and Schulem Turnheim 1887

Marriage Hersch Turnheim with Mariem Gems 1836

Marriage Gronem Gems with Hinde Marberg 1802

of Chaim Kreppel and Chaje Wegner. Baruch's marriage record noted that his father Hersch Turnheim was from Przemyśl and was a townsman/bourgeois trader. His mother Mariem Turnheim was deceased. Baruch's wife Chane Kreppel died 1 November 1895; she was buried 3 November 1895 at Drohobycz, Ukraine.[61] Their address in Drohobycz was listed as 43 Miasto. The occupation of Baruch Turnheim was grain merchant based on his wife Chane's death record. On his marriage record, Baruch was age 43 and Chane was age 46 and 9 months. This was obviously a civil marriage since the Jewish religious wedding would have occurred years before, probably before 1866.

There were many families listed at Drohobycz, Ukraine with the surname Kreppel. I found death records that listed Chaim Kreppel and Chaje Wegner as the parents of Chane Kreppel, and the names of Chane's siblings: Leizor Kreppel, born 1824,[62] died 1904; Israel Ber Kreppel, born 1838, died 1908,[63] Munisch Kreppel, born 1839, died 1905,[64] Chane Kreppel, born 1840, died 1895.

7. Hinde[3] **Turnheim** (Hersch[2], Solomon[1]), born 1 January 1850 at Przemyśl, Poland. She died 11 October 1931 at Vienna, Austria; married 1868 at Przemyśl, Poland, Aron Geiger, the son of Solomon David Geiger and Chaje Mindel Unger from Błażowa, Poland. Please see the chapter *Aron Geiger and Hinde Turnheim* for additional family information and the *Solomon David Geiger Family Tree*.

Children of Hinde Turnheim and Aron Geiger:
i. Chaskel[4] Geiger, born 18 May 1868 at Przemyśl, Poland; died 24 April 1955 at Manhattan, New York; married 6 March 1894 at Manhattan, New York; Esther Mamlock, the daughter of Meyer Mamlock and Caroline Sobel. See the chapter *Chaskel Geiger and Esther Mamlock* for additional family information.

ii. Naftale Geiger, born 29 March 1871 at Przemyśl, Poland,[65] died 2 April 1877 at Przemyśl, Poland due to typhoid fever.[66] See the chapter *Aron Geiger and Hinde Turnheim* for additional family information.

iii. Abraham Yitzak Geiger, born 19 November 1872 at Przemyśl, Poland; died 28 September 1946 at Manhattan, New York; married July 1894 at Kańczuga, Poland, Sprynca Stark, the daughter of Moses Stark and Sara. See the chapter *Abraham Yitzak Geiger and Sprynca Stark* for additional family information.

iv. Israel Geiger, born 16 January 1874 at Przemyśl, Poland; died 29 April 1933 at Chicago, Cook County, Illinois; married 27 November 1898 at Manhattan, New

York, Esther Perlberg, the daughter of Elias Perlberg and Sarah Malter. See the chapter *Israel Geiger and Esther Perlberg* for additional family information.

v. Mariem Geiger, born 22 February 1880 at Przemyśl, Poland; died 29 November 1946 at Manhattan, New York; married 31 March 1902 at Błażowa, Poland, Getzel Holoszycer, son of Jacob Holoszycer and Ester Jakubes. See the chapter *Mariem Geiger and Getzel Holoszycer* for additional family information.

vi. Freude Geiger, born 23 January 1882 at Przemyśl, Poland; died between 1910 and 1924. See the chapter *Aron Geiger and Hinde Turnheim* for additional family information.

vii. Mindla Geiger, born 3 April 1887 at Przemyśl, Poland; died 18 May 1960 at Woodmere, Nassau County, New York; married 17 October 1911 at Manhattan, New York, Oscar Weiss, son of Fischel Weiss and Hannie Zuckerberg. See the chapter *Minnie Geiger and Oscar Weiss* for additional family information.

Discussion

Hinde[3] Turnheim (Hersch[2], Solomon[1]) was born 1 January 1850 at Przemyśl, Poland to Hersch Turnheim and Mariem Gems.[67] My great-grandparents Hinde Turnheim and Aron Geiger were married 1868 at Przemyśl, Poland. Their marriage date was found on Aron Geiger's death record from Vienna. Aron Geiger died 17 August 1924.[68] He was a businessman and a rabbi. They moved from Rzeszów, Poland to Vienna, Austria, District II sometime at the beginning or during WWI. Prior to Rzeszów they lived at Przemyśl and Błażowa. While in Vienna, Hinde and Aron lived with their son Rabbi Abraham Geiger and his family. Their other adult children immigrated to the United States.

After Hinde became a widow, she continued living in Vienna with her son Abraham Geiger and his family until she became debilitated and needed additional care at the nursing home. Hinde died 11 October 1931 at Vienna, Austria where she was a resident at the Home for the Elderly of the Jewish Community of Vienna. She was buried 12 October 1931 in the Weiner Zentralfriedhof Cemetery at Vienna, Gate 4, group 10, row 11, grave 65 adjoining the grave of her husband Aron Geiger.[69]

8. Moses[3] Turnheim (Hersch[2], Solomon[1]), born 1852 at Przemyśl, Poland. His birth year was estimated from his death record 6 January 1890 at Przemyśl, Poland.

He married 17 January 1874 at Bolechów, Ukraine, Sara Hendel from Bolechów, Ukraine, the daughter of Jozef Hendel and Rechel. He died 6 January 1890 at Przemyśl, Poland from tuberculosis. His occupation was dealer/tradesman.

Children of Moses Turnheim and Sara Hendel:
i. Mariem[4] Turnheim; born 5 May 1877 at Bolechow, Ukraine.

ii. Chana[4] Turnheim; born 14 September 1880 at Bolechow, Ukraine; died 1887, Przemysl, Poland.[70]

iii. Josef Turnheim; born 1882 at Przemyśl, Poland. A notation for the civil marriage date for Moses and Sara Turnheim was written on the 1882 birth record of their son Josef Turnheim. Hersch Turnheim was listed as the sandek for the *brit milah* of Josef Turnheim. Jozef Thurnheim (alternate spelling) died 15 July 1942 during the Nazi occupation of Przemyśl. He was buried in the New Jewish Cemetery at Przemyśl, with his wife Edka and daughter Roza who also perished 15 July 1942. Edka née Schmidt was born 1910 at Sieniawa, Poland. She was a grocer and was married.[71] Their names were inscribed on the same matsevah as Benjamin Turnheim and his wife Chaja Reizla Turnheim.[72] Joseph Turnheim was Benjamin Turnheim's nephew.

iv. Ester Turnheim; born 1885 at Przemyśl, Poland; died 1895.[73]

9. Benjamin[3] Turnheim (Hersch[2], Solomon[1]), born 8 August 1854 at Przemyśl, Poland.[74] He died 15 April 1930 at Przemyśl, Poland. He married Chaje Reisel Gans on 3 December 1882 at Przemyśl, Podkarpackie, Poland, the daughter of Meilech Gans and Sara Rifka Feldstein.

Children of Benjamin Turnheim and Chaje Reisel Gans:
i. Freude[4] aka Francesca Turnheim; born 22 July 1875 at Przemyśl, Poland; married 3 June 1895 at Przemyśl, Poland, Herzil Schonbach, the son of Samuel Moses Schonbach and Blima. Herzil changed his name to Henryk Schonbach and died 1926 at Przemyśl, Poland.

ii. Mariem Turnheim; born 9 February 1877 at Przemyśl, Poland; died 12 October 1880 at Przemyśl, Poland.

iii. Debora Turnheim; born 22 April 1878 at Przemyśl, Poland; died 14 July 1959 at Manhattan, New York; married 7 June 1898 at Przemyśl; David Neumark, the son of Solomon Neumark and Shifra Schutz.

iv. Samuel Turnheim; born 4 October 1879 at Przemyśl, Poland; died 20 August 1957 at Przemyśl, Poland; married 1908 at Ivano-Frankivsk, Ukraine, Salcia Elza Halpern, the daughter of Nuchim Halpern and Ruchel.

v. Solomon Turnheim; born 21 November 1881 at Przemyśl, Poland; died 28 January 1960 at Louisville, Jefferson County, Kentucky; married ca. 1915 at Louisville, Jefferson County, Kentucky, Fannie Goodman.

Benjamin Turnheim matsevah Przemyśl

vi. Mathias Turnheim; born 20 February 1886 at Przemyśl, Poland; died 1916 during WWI and was buried in the New Jewish Cemetery at Przemyśl, Poland.

Discussion

Benjamin Turnheim was born 8 August 1854 at Przemyśl, Poland. He married Chaje Reizel Gans 3 December 1882 at Przemyśl, Poland. Benjamin was 28 years and Chaje Reizel was 26 years. They were probably married religiously ca. 1874. At the time of Benjamin Turnheim's marriage, the official rabbi was Isak Schmelkes. This record can be found in the Przemyśl Archives, Poland.

Chaje Reizel was born 1856 to Meilech Gans and Sara Rifka Feldstein.[75] The Gans family was one of the most prosperous Jewish families in Przemyśl. Chaje Reizel died 13 March 1923 at Przemyśl, Poland. Benjamin Turnheim died 15 April 1930 at Przemyśl, Poland.[76] An occupation for Benjamin Turnheim was listed in the 1891 Galicia Business Directory, as B. Turnheim in Przemyśl, owning a grocery/delicatessen, (*gemischtwaarenhandler*).[77] Benjamin Turnheim was also listed in the 1896 Galicia Business Directory as a spice dealer.[78]

The Yizkor Book of Przemyśl had several references to my Turnheim family. In the chapter *Economic Life in Przemysl during the Beginning of the 20th Century* there was a reference to types of wholesale, retail, and manufacturing businesses.[79] There was mention of the four Gans brothers with their branches: Baumwald, Turnheim, Mieses, Majerdorf, Scharf and Astel, all working in foodstuffs. They operated their wholesale and retail food businesses on a national level.

10. Schulem[3] Turnheim (Hersch[2], Solomon[1]), born 7 December 1857 at Przemyśl, Poland; died 29 August 1925 at Vienna, Austria. Schulem and Simon Turnheim were twins born 7 December 1857 at Przemyśl, Podkarpackie, Poland.[80] Simon Turnheim died as an infant, at four months in 1858.[81] The surviving twin, Schulem Turnheim, married (1) Sabina aka Sobel Pilpel 29 June 1879 at Lwów, Ukraine, daughter of Herz Jonah Pilpel and Chaje Gittel Hand,[82] she died sometime between 1885 and 1887. Schulem married (2) Lea Turnheim 6 December 1887 at Drohobycz, Ukraine, daughter of Baruch Turnheim and Chane Kreppel.[83]

Children of Schulem Turnheim and Sabina Sobel Pilpel:
i. Marya[4] Turnheim born 18 May 1880, Lwów, Ukraine.[84] Marya also known as Maria died 1941 during WWII.

ii. Kelman Jozef Turnheim born 8 November 1881,[85] in Lwów, Ukraine; died 1964, Vienna, Austria. He married Emilia Heine. They had two sons, Leopold, and Hans.

iii. Sigmund Salomon Turnheim born 1883 as determined by his death information; died 7 November 1909 at Vienna, Austria.[86] His occupation was forge assistant to a blacksmith.

iv. Lea Lorka Turnheim, born 10 October 1884, Lwów, Ukraine; died 19 February 1975, Vienna, Austria. She was a professor of vocational education in Vienna.

Schulem, became a widower sometime between 1885 to 1887. He subsequently married his niece Lea[4] Turnheim (Baruch[3], Hersch[2], Solomon[1]) 6 Decem-

Schulem and Sigmund Turnheim matsevah Vienna

ber 1887 at Drohobycz, Ukraine.[87] Schulem was 29 years 11 months and Lea was 21 years 5 months. Schulem was a leather manufacturer in Vienna.

Children of Schulem Turnheim and Lea Turnheim:

i. Freude[4] aka Freida Turnheim born 11 August 1889 at Przemyśl, Poland.[88] She died October 1942, Poland. Freida was a pharmacist and educated at the University of Vienna. She married 1925, Vienna, Austria, Betzalel Prisand, son of Abraham Prisand and Esther.

ii. Hugo Turnheim, born 2 May 1890, Vienna, Austria; died 1966, Israel. He was a businessman and married Anda, no issue.

iii. Valerie Turnheim, born 9 June 1891, Vienna, Austria.

iv. Max Turnheim, born 24 June 1892, Vienna, Austria. He was a leather manufacturer in Vienna.

v. Malka Elizbieta Turnheim[89] born 6 October 1894 at Przemyśl, Poland; Malka Elizbieta Turnheim died 1896 at 2 years.[90]

vi. Ernst Chuna Dawid Turnheim[91] born 14 April 1896 at Przemyśl, Poland; died 1973 in Israel. He was a chemist, married Tova Alexandrovitz, no issue.

vii. Hedwig Turnheim, born 30 March 1898, Vienna, Austria; died 4 January 1963 in England.

viii. Walter Turnheim, born 22 June 1899, Vienna, Austria; died 1985 in Tel Aviv, Israel. He was an engineer, married Hanna aka Hansi Neubauer, (1905–1989). They had two sons, Amiel and Joel Turnheim.

ix. Friedrich Turnheim, born 7 April 1902, Vienna, Austria; died 5 December 1980, Vienna, Austria. He was a chemist, married Irene Weiss. She was born 15 October 1907 and died 3 January 2007. They had two sons, Georg, and Fred Turnheim. Both are still living.

Discussion

Marya aka Maria Turnheim was born in Lwów and resided in Vienna during the war. A record for Marya aka Maria Turnheim was found in the Yad Vashem Central Database for Holocaust Victims. She lived at the same address as her father in Vienna and she was single.[92] The Page of Testimony contained her correct birth year 1880 and indicated that her parents were Shlomo and Lea (stepmother). Maria Turnheim was deported on Transport 10 from Vienna to the Lodz Ghetto during 1941.[93]

Schulem died 29 August 1925 at Vienna due to colon cancer. He was married, listed as a businessman and his last address in Vienna was 19, Pyrkergasse 38/5.[94] He was buried 31 August 1925 at the Weiner Zentralfriedhof Cemetery in Vienna, at Tor I, group 19 row 33 grave 084a in the same grave location as his previously deceased son Sigmund Salomon Turnheim.

During the rise of the Nazis, Friedrich Turnheim joined the Communist party and was arrested in 1933. He escaped prison in 1934 and fled to Kharkiv, Soviet Union where he lived until 1945 after WWII ended. He subsequently returned to Vienna with his wife and son Georg. One of my matches on www.myheritage.com was with Georg Turnheim. I discovered that I am second cousin once removed to Georg and that he and my mother are second cousins. Schulem and my great-grandmother Hinde were siblings; their parents were Hersch and Mariem Turnheim. Georg donated his atDNA to www.familytreedna.com however at the time of this writing his results have not yet been posted.

Walter, Ernest, Hugo, and Max emigrated to Israel during 1932–34. Walter Turnheim's children and their families reside in Israel.

11. Joseph[3] Turnheim (David[2], Solomon[1]), born 1843 at Jarosław, Poland to David and Chane Turnheim; died 1890; married Rachel Glanz in 1866.[95] She was born 1846 at Przemyśl, Poland and the daughter of Israel Glanz.

Children of Joseph Turnheim and Rachel Glanz:
i. Freude[4] Turnheim born 1864 at Przemyśl, Poland.[96]

ii. Leon Turnheim born 1866 at Przemyśl, Poland; married 26 July 1899 at Lwów, Ukraine, Antonina Kalmus, daughter of Nusyn Kalmus and Risie Thorn.

iii. Tillie Turnheim born 1867.[97] Tillie died 1909.[98] She married Jacob Turnheim son of David Turnheim and Chane Löwenbrun.

12. Jacob[3] Turnheim (David[2], Solomon[1]), born 1850 to David Turnheim and Chane Löwenbrun. Jacob married his niece Tillie Turnheim, the daughter of Joseph Turnheim and Rachel Glanz.

Children of Jacob Turnheim and Tillie Turnheim:
i. Josef[4] Turnheim born 1890 at Jarosław, Poland died 1890 as an infant.[99]

ii. David Turnheim born 28 August 1891 at Jarosław, Poland.[100] See section *Generation Four*.

iii. Moritz Turnheim born 1900.[101]

iv. Isidor Turnheim born 1893; died 1894.[102]

v. Anna Turnheim born 1895 in Bircza, Poland.[103]

13. Debora[3] Turnheim (David[2], Solomon[1]), born 1851 at Żołynia, Poland to David Turnheim and Chane Löwenbrun. Her birth year was estimated from her 1884 civil marriage record to Leiba Tirk at Jarosław, Poland, the son of Hersh Tirk and Diene.[104] They were probably married ca. 1877 in a religious ceremony, since the births of their children happened prior to their civil marriage. Debora died 3 December 1892 at Przemyśl, Poland due to cirrhosis of the liver.[105]

Children of Debora Turnheim and Leib Tirk:
i. Betty[4] Tirk born 1878 at Jarosław, Poland.[106]

ii. Sigmund Tirk born 1879 at Jarosław, Poland.[107]

iii. Alexander Tirk born 1880 at Jarosław, Poland; died 1880 at Jarosław, Poland.[108]

Generation 4

14. Kelman Josef[4] Turnheim (Schulem[3], Hersch[2], Solomon[1]), born 8 November 1881, Lwów, Ukraine and died 1964, Vienna, Austria. He married Emilia Heine. Kelman Jozef Turnheim was a coal merchant. They had two children, Hans, and Leopold Turnheim.

15. David[4] Turnheim (Jacob[3], David[2], Solomon[1]), born 28 August 1891 at Jarosław, Poland to Jacob Turnheim and Tillie Turnheim.[109] On David's birth record there was a notation that he died 25 May 1942. His date of death was also confirmed on the Polish Medical Questionnaire. He was married to Lotta Trattner.

Discussion

I located David Turnheim's record in the JewishGen.org database Polish Medical Questionnaires that listed his occupation as physician, he was married and his last address was 29 Kosciuzki Street, Lubaczow, Lwów, Ukraine.[110] His wife was listed with her maiden surname name of Trattner and date of birth 8 November 1905. Her paternal grandparents were Julius and Anna Trattner and her maternal grandparents were Osias and Ettel Malawer. David Turnheim's paternal grandparents were David Turnheim and Anna (Chane) Löwenbrun/Lebenbraun; his maternal grandparents were Josef Turnheim and Rachela Glanz.[111]

David Turnheim was in the Yad Vashem Central Database of Shoah Victims as a Jewish refugee from Poland living at Samarkand, Uzbekistan (USSR) during WWII. His wife Lotta was with him in Uzbekistan. Thousands of refugees arrived at Samarkand from all over Europe, especially Poland. They swarmed the streets starving and penniless. The lack of food was so severe people died in the streets of malnourishment. The religiously traditional orthodox refugees inhabited the old sections of Samarkand and Tashkent mingling with the Bucharian Jews who were also traditional and observant. Jews that were less observant lived in the new sections of Samarkand. All refugees looked for work since bread was rationed and only distributed through government issued coupons. Every morning there would be long lines of people waiting for bread.[112] Many refugees died of starvation and diseases. Dr. David Turnheim and his wife were residing at Ittifat 83 at Samarkand according to a list of Jewish refugees from Poland living in the Soviet Union.[113]

David Turnheim was included in the 1923 and the 1924 Polish Officers Handbooks at the rank of Captain.[114] He was listed in the 1932 Poland Telephone Directory as a physician and in the 1938 and 1939 Polish Medical Directories in Lubaczów, Lwów, Ukraine.[115]

16. Leib[4] Turnheim (Joseph[3] David[2], Solomon[1]), born 1866 at Przemyśl, Poland to Joseph Turnheim and Rachel Glanz.[116] He was an attorney and was referred to as Dr. Leon Turnheim, practicing law at Turka, Lwów, Ukraine. Leon Turnheim was listed in the 1907 Galicia Schematism under the heading for lawyers. He married 26 July 1899, at Lwów, Ukraine, Antonina Kalmus daughter of Nusym Kalmus and Risie Thorn, from Mariampol, Stanislawów, Ukraine.[117]

17. Etel[4] Turnheim (Baruch[3], Hersch[2], Solomon[1]), born 1870 to parents Baruch Turnheim and Chane Kreppel, married Moses David Schindler 8 July 1900 at Drohobych, Ukraine.[118] Prior to her marriage Etel lived at the same address, 43

Miasto at Drohobycz with her father, Baruch Turnheim. His occupation was trader/dealer. Moses David Schindler was born at Woloska Wies in Dolina Province, Ukraine and was living in Bolechów, Ukraine at 6 Koflarska Street, he was a trader/dealer and the son of Bolechów residents Abraham Schindler, dealer and the deceased Ryfki Gottlieb.

Children of Etel Turnheim and Moses Dawid Schindler:
i. Josef[5] Schindler born 10 December 1901 at Lviv, Ukraine.[119]

ii. Joachim Schindler born 27 December 1902 at Lviv, Ukraine.[120]

18. Freude[4] Turnheim (Benjamin[3], Hersch[2], Solomon[1]), born 22 July 1875 at Przemyśl, Poland to parents Benjamin and Chaje Reisel Turnheim.[121] She married Herzil Schonbach 3 June 1895 at Przemyśl, Poland.[122] Freude was 20 years and Herzil Schonbach was 33 years and 8 months. He was a merchant residing in Zurawnie (Zurawno), Poland. His parents were Samuel Schonbach and Blima Schonbach. Herzil later changed his given name to Henryk Schonbach and died 1926 at Przemyśl, Poland.[123]

Children of Freida Turnheim and Herzil Schonbach:
i. Klemens[5] Schonbach, born 1896.[124] He married 1925 at Kraków, Poland, Irma Liebeskind born 1899, daughter of Berish Liebeskind and Roza Apfelbaum.[125] Klemens Schonbach and Irma Liebeskind survived the Holocaust as they were listed in the Pinkas HaNitzolim I-Register of Jewish Survivors in Kraków.[126]

19. Debora[4] Turnheim (Benjamin[3], Hersch[2], Solomon[1]), born 22 April 1878 at Przemyśl, Poland to parents Benjamin Turnheim and Chaje Reisel Gans.[127]

Dr. David Neumark

She married David Neumark 7 June 1898 at Przemyśl, Poland. She died July 1959 at New York City.

Children of Debora Turnheim and David Neumark:
i. Salomea Neumark,[5] born 11 September 1899 at Przemyśl, Podkarpackie, Poland.[128]

ii. Marta aka Martha Neumark, born 5 May 1904 at Berlin, Germany.[129]

iii. Immanuel Kant Neumark, born 23 April 1914 at Cincinnati, Ohio.[130]

Debora and David Neumark ship manifest 1907

Discussion

I was privileged to obtain family history for Debora Turnheim through her descendants, Dora R. and Gabby B. Debora Turnheim married David Neumark, 7 June 1898 at Przemyśl, Poland.[131] David Neumark was born 3 August 1866 at Szcerzac, Ukraine to Solomon Neumark and Schifra Schuetz.[132] David Neumark died 15 December 1924 at Cincinnati, Ohio. Debora Turnheim died July 1959 at New York City.

Dr. David Neumark earned his Doctor of Philosophy degree in 1896 from the University of Berlin, Germany and was ordained as a Rabbi in Berlin in 1897. He served as a rabbi at Rakonitz, Bohemia from 1897–1904. Dr. Neumark was then slated to become president of the Collegio Rabbinico in Rome, Italy. The

Seated Dora Neumark. Standing (L to R) Salomea, Immanuel, Martha

leader of that Italian conservative Jewish community in Rome insisted that Dr. Neumark declare himself to be in favor of traditional orthodox Judaism. Dr. Neumark reasoned there was no firm basis either in Halacha or in logic for this theological stand.[133] The issue could not be resolved and Dr. Neumark moved back to Berlin.[134]

He became a professor of Jewish philosophy at Berlin in 1907. Two months later that same year he was appointed as a professor to the faculty of Hebrew

David Neumark Petition

Union College, Cincinnati, Ohio. The new position at Hebrew Union College prompted Dr. Neumark and his family to move from Germany to the United States. He became chair of philosophy at that college until his death 15 December 1924 at Cincinnati.[135] When Dr. David Neumark and his family immigrated to the United States, they travelled on the ship *President Lincoln* from Cauxhaven 16 November 1907 and arrived at New York 29 November 1907.[136] They were en route to Cincinnati, Ohio.

Dr. Neumark was a leading Hebrew scholar and a prolific writer contributing numerous articles to many important Hebrew journals. His magnum opus were his volumes written on the history of Jewish philosophy *Tolodoth Ha'ikrim B'Israel*

Passport Application Dora Neumark p.1   Dora Neumark Photo on Passport

(Toldoth Ha-Pilusufia B'yisrael) and a work in German *Geschichte der Juedischen Philos-ophie im Mittelalter.* Many distinguished rabbis were among his pupils.[137] He also fully supported his daughter Martha Neumark to attend Hebrew Union College to pursue her goal to become an ordained rabbi. This will be addressed in the section on Martha Neumark.

Dr. Neumark supported the Zionist cause and became a lifelong friend with another Hebrew scholar and writer, Reuben Brainin. Reuben Brainin (1862–1939) wrote biographies on important Jewish intellectuals as Theodore Herzl and Israel Zangwill. Dr. Neumark contributed articles to *Hatorem* published by Reuben Brainin. This close connection with the Brainin family extended to Dr. Neumark's marriage of his daughter Salomea with Reuben Brainin's son Joseph Brainin in 1921.[138] Dr. Neumark became a proponent of progressive Judaic theology and one of the first American reform rabbis.

David Neumark's German-Jewish ancestor, Rabbi Solomon Neumark, refused to join the 17th century Jewish intoxication with the false Messianism of Shabbatai Zevi. Rabbi Solomon Neumark as Oberrabineer was deposed from his position and exiled from the German-Jewish community. He migrated to Poland where some of his sons settled and remained. David Neumark was descended from that Polish Neumark branch; his parents were Rabbi Solomon Neumark of Bolechów and Schifra Schuetz. Schifra managed a small business in the village of Szcerzec so that her husband Solomon could devote himself to the study of Talmud and Kabbalah. Solomon taught his son David Neumark traditional prayers when David was two years old; by the time David was six he was studying the Gemara with his father.[139]

The Federal Census for 1910 indicated that David, Dora, Salomea and Martha lived at Cincinnati, Ohio, on Winslow Avenue, Number 2854-2856. David was a professor at Hebrew Union College.[140] David Neumark journeyed to Europe, and he was listed on the ship manifest for the *S.S. Rheim* sailing from Bremen to New York 11 August 1911.[141] David Neumark's physical description was listed as 5 ft., 2 inches, with red hair and blue eyes.

By the 1920 Federal Census the Neumark family moved to Rockdale Avenue East, in Cincinnati, in Ward 13, enumeration district 225. They declared on the census that they were naturalized in 1913. By this time, Dora and David had their third child, Immanuel Kant Neumark.[142] David Neumark suddenly died at Cincinnati, Ohio on 15 December 1924 at the age of 58.[143] He was buried at Walnut

Hills Cemetery, Evanston, Hamilton County, Ohio. By the 1930 Federal Census Dora Neumark and her 15-year-old son Immanuel Kant Neumark lived at 66 West Gun Hill Road, Bronx, New York.[144]

Dora Neumark was listed in the 1940 Federal Census as widowed, approximate age 61 years, a naturalized citizen, and lived alone in an apartment at Central Park West in Manhattan.[145] Dora died 14 July 1959 at the age of 81 and she was buried 17 July 1959 next to her husband Dr. David Neumark in the Walnut Hills Cemetery.[146] A passport for Dora Neumark was issued 9 May 1923 with a travel date scheduled for 28 June 1923 on the ship *Manchuria*.[147] Dora probably travelled to Przemyśl to see her widowed father Benjamin Turnheim and pay her respects for her recently deceased mother Chaje Reisel. A photo of Dora Neumark was found on her passport application. Her physical description was given as 5 ft. 4 inches, brown and gray hair, brown eyes, with a full face. Dora returned to America from Hamburg on 21 August 1923 to the port of New York on the ship *Resolute*.[148] Her destination was Cincinnati, Ohio.

Samuel and Elza Turnheim matsevahs

20. Samuel[4] Turnheim (Benjamin[3], Hersch[2], Solomon[1]), born 4 October 1879 at Przemyśl, Poland to parents Benjamin and Chaje Turnheim.[149] Samuel Turnheim died 20 August 1957 at Przemyśl, Poland.[150] He married Salcia Elza Halpern 1 November 1908 at Stanisławów, Ukraine, daughter of Nuchim Halpern and Ruchel Halber.[151]

Discussion

Samuel Turnheim was a physician and on the staff of the Jewish Hospital at Przemyśl, Poland. The Jewish Hospital was confiscated by the Austrian Army during WWI. After WWI, the Przemyśl Jewish community eventually regained use of the building with the assistance of the American Joint Distribution Committee to address the health situation of the Jewish population. Infectious diseases such as typhoid, trachoma and skin diseases were rampant. There was raging inflation and a high cost of living.[152] Eventually new equipment and modern medical devices were purchased by the local Jewish community and the hospital was restored.

The new Jewish Hospital officially opened on 13 January 1924. The Hospital was located in a large park on a hill on Szaszkiewicza Street and had three buildings: the main building, the surgical building and the administrative building. The main building had 100 beds. The Labor and Delivery Department was the first one in Galicia and greatly reduced mortality during childbirth.

Dr. Samuel Turnheim was the Director of the dermatological clinic for the Jewish Hospital in Przemyśl.[153] Among the physicians listed was Dr. M. Gans who directed the Ear, Nose and Throat Clinic perhaps related to the family of Meilech Gans. The Jewish Hospital also served as a residency for young Jewish doctors who could not do their residencies in government hospitals due to anti-Semitic discrimination. During the period between 1924 and 1938, the hospital admitted thousands of patients most of whom could not pay any fees. The Jewish community of Przemyśl provided funding with some assistance from the Przemyśl municipality. Despite running at a deficit, the hospital was going to expand in 1938. Plans were made for an additional building but due to WWII and the Shoah, the building was never completed. After the Shoah, the hospital became a school for Polish nurses.

Dr. Samuel Turnheim was listed in the 1914 Przemyśl Calendar under the listings for physicians. His business address was 43 Jagiellońska.[154] He was also listed in the 1932 and 1933 Poland Telephone Directories as a physician, and in the 1937, 1938, and 1948 Medical Yearbooks. His new business address was 1 Kazimierzowska Street, Przemyśl with a business telephone.[155] Dr. Turnheim was included in the 1937 Poland B'nai B'rith Membership Directory.[156]

Samuel Turnheim married Salcia Elza Halpern 1 November 1908, at Stanisławów, Ukraine. She was the daughter of Nuchim Halpern and Ruchel Halber.[157] Salcia Elza was born 10 June 1889, Ukraine;[158] died 30 August 1930 at Przemyśl, Podkarpackie, Poland.[159] According to the JewishGen Online World-wide Jewish Burial Registry, Samuel Thurnheim (Turnheim) died 20 August 1957, at Przemyśl and he was buried in the New Jewish cemetery on Slowackiego Street. Samuel Turnheim survived WWII and he resided in Przemyśl until his death. My Przemyśl contact, Domicella told me that her family loved, and respected Dr. "Tur" and she wrote in an email to me sent 4 August 2012: "Dr. Tur was a friend of my dad, came to us (when) I was sick to heal me… my mom and dad always said that he was the best! He was never wrong."

21. Solomon[4] Turnheim (Benjamin[3], Hersch[2], Solomon[1]), born 21 November 1881 at Przemyśl, Podkarpackie, Poland to parents Benjamin Turnheim and Chaje Reisel Gans.[160] He was an engineer, married Fanny Goodman ca.1915 at Louisville, Kentucky.

Children of Solomon Turnheim and Fanny Goodman:
i. Joseph Henry[5] Turnheim, born 13 February 1916 at Louisville, Kentucky.[161] He died 25 June 1974 at Louisville, Kentucky.

Discussion

In the Yizkor book for Przemyśl, there was mention of the founding of the Zionist party in Przemyśl in the years following the death of Theodore Herzl in 1904. Among the 12 founders of the Przemyśl Zionist organization Agudat Herzl was Shlomo aka Solomon Turnheim, who, according to the Yizkor book, later became an engineer in the United States.[162] Solomon Turnheim immigrated to the United States, and arrived in New York 28 August 1907, on the ship *Kaiser Wilhelm II*, from Bremen, Germany.[163] He worked as an engineer and manager of building materials at Louisville, Kentucky. Solomon Turnheim's wife Fanny Goodman was born 6 December 1891 and she lived in Kentucky.[164] She died 30

March 1976 at Louisville, Kentucky. Solomon Turnheim died 28 January 1960 in Jefferson County, Kentucky at age 79.[165]

Mathias Turnheim matsevah

22. Mathias⁴ Turnheim (Benjamin³, Hersch², Solomon¹), born 20 February 1886 at Przemyśl, Poland to parents Benjamin and Chaje Reisel Turnheim.[166] He died 1916 during WWI as a victim of disease while fighting as a soldier during the "terrible war."[167] He was buried in the New Jewish Cemetery at Przemyśl, Podkarpackie, Poland.[168]

Discussion

I posted a photo of the matsevah of Mathias Turnheim to Viewmate on www.jewishgen.org. for translation from the Hebrew. Both Fredel Fruhman and Yitschok Margareten kindly sent me their translations of the Hebrew inscription. The translations indicated that when Mathias died, he left his parents, his pregnant wife, and his son. Mathias Turnheim died a soldier and victim to a disease or illness contracted during the "terrible war."[169] The inscription was translated:

A stone shall scream from the wall
For the death of a man young in years
Matisyahu son of Binyamin, may his light continue to shine (referring to the father who was still alive)
He was born on the 15ᵗʰ of Adar I 5646
He died on … (crack in matsevah obliterated the date of his death) in the 30ᵗʰ year of his life
The deceased, in the prime of his life, left his parents, his wife the mother
Of his son, his child (seed) before development, too soon.
He weakened and fell victim to the turmoil and dreadful diseases that accompany the terrible war.
May his soul be bound in the bond of everlasting life.

23. Freida[4] Turnheim (Schulem[3], Hersch[2], Solomon[1]), born 11 August 1889,[170] died ca. 1942 at Chełmno extermination camp, Poland. Married 1925 at Alsergrund Synagogue, Vienna, Austria, Zallel aka Betzalel Prisand, son of Abraham Prisand and Ester.

Discussion

I found no birth or death records for Freida however based on other documents her parents were Schulem and Lea Turnheim who married in 1887. Schulem Turnheim died 1925 in Vienna.[171] He died at age 68 and was buried 31 August 1925, therefore his birth year was 1857. He resided in Vienna and that is where Freida also lived. Freida married Zallel aka Betzalel Prisand 1925 at the Alsergrund Synagogue, Vienna, Austria.[172] Betzalel Prisand was listed in the Vad Vashem Central Database of Shoah Victims, his parents were Abraham and Ester Prisand. He lived in Vienna, was a clerk and was deported from Vienna to Auschwitz where he died 1942.[173]

When I saw Freida's marriage record, there was an MAG. after Frieda Turnheim's name. This abbreviation indicated a graduate degree in German, equivalent to our Master of Science degree. Her marriage record included the name of the synagogue as Alsergrund. I learned Alsergrund was the 9th district in Vienna noted for the University of Vienna and departments such as economics, mathematics, pharmacology, biology, the medical college, and the largest hospital in Vienna *Allgemeines Krankenhaus* or General Hospital. This district was an intellectual center; with residents such as Sigmund Freud, Viktor Frankl, Theodor Herzl, Beethoven, and Mozart.

My cousin Harry Holly z"l and I spoke together by telephone shortly before his death in 2007. He told me that he had a cousin Freida Turnheim who lived in Vienna, who was very intellectual and attended lectures given by Sigmund Freud at the University in Vienna. This Freida is likely the same Freida Prisand née Turnheim, especially as she was university educated with a graduate degree.

I became curious about Freida Prisand when I saw the request for her Affidavit of Support written by my cousin Pearl's husband George Bronz in 1938 attempting to rescue Freida from Vienna to immigrate to the United States. George Bronz maintained that he would provide for her support so that she would not be a financial burden on the government. This affidavit was required for Jewish refugees fleeing from the Holocaust before they could enter the United States.[174] George Bronz was employed as Principal Attorney in the U.S. Department of Agriculture, Washington, D.C. However, in this instance George's political pull and efforts did not result in success since the Nazis were already in control in Austria. Please see the chapters *Chaskel Geiger and Esther Mamlock; Mariem Geiger and Getzel Holoszycer and Appendix A* for additional details about their rescue of relatives during the Shoah.

Freida Prisand was found in the Yad Vashem Central Database of Shoah Victims' Names. She was born 11 August 1889 and she lived at Wien 2, Tandelmarktgasse 12/19.[175] On 23 October 1941 she was deported from Vienna on transport train 8 to the Łódź Ghetto, Poland. She was among the names listed for Łódź Ghetto Inhabitants 1940–1944.[176] Most of the Jews in the ghetto population either died from starvation, disease, physical hardship, or were transported elsewhere for extermination. She worked as a pharmacist in the Łódź ghetto and was on the Łódź Ghetto List at address Pfeffergasse 4. Freida was moved from Pfeffergasse 4 to Fischstrasse 2 flat 1 on 31 May 1942.[177]

Freida Prisand was also listed in the JewishGen.org database *Last Letters from the Łódź Ghetto*. She wrote a letter addressed to the Ghetto administration's Office of Resettlement to be exempt from resettlement after being served with an eviction notice. The Nazi process was eviction first then deportation from the Łódź Ghetto to various extermination camps such as Chełmno, Buchenwald or Auschwitz. This letter from Freida was the last trace of her.[178]

Fritz Neubauer z"l was a genealogist who researched and collected information about the Łódź Ghetto. I wrote to Fritz Neubauer on 24 March 2016 and asked him if I could obtain a copy of Freida's last letter. He immediately sent me the actual letter written by Freida Prisand 11 May 1942, prior to her move to Fischstrasse. He translated her letter as:

> *I hereby ask to be exempted from the eviction order for the following reasons: Since 11 December 1941 I have been employed as a Master of Pharmacy in the drugstore No.4 of the Health Department. I enclose my nomination and the confirmation of the Health Department. I earn 150 marks per month, and I do not have to support anybody."*

The handwriting on top of the letter says "Papiere ausgefolgt", meaning the papers were returned. Mr. Neubauer said that there would have been a stamp on the application that the applicant was exempted, but the stamp is missing. Mr.

Neubauer thought that Frieda would have been exempted because the reason she gave would normally have been sufficient. However, another date Ausg. 23 October 1942 was written in a heading marked "Other Information". The notation "Ausg." and the date signified when Freida was deported from the Łódź Ghetto to Chełmno, an extermination camps where she was murdered. The list of Łódź ghetto names 1940–1944 was gathered by the Organization of former residents of Łódź in Israel and is on a database at Yad Vashem, Israel.

The Łódź Ghetto

The Nazis captured Łódź in 1939 and by 1940 a ghetto was created and sealed off with wooden fences and barbed wire. Transports kept arriving with Jews from many cities including Vienna. Approximately 60,000 inhabitants were packed into each square kilometer of the ghetto. There were 240,000 inhabitants in the Łódź ghetto. The ghetto became the main Jewish slave labor camp for the Nazis. Tailors made uniforms and civilian clothing. Jews labored in workshops for shoemaking, tannery, metal, electrical and furniture. The health department ran hospitals, pharmacies, and clinics. As the war progressed provisions became scarce, and famine and disease were widespread. Starvation and disease killed many of the Jews in the ghetto. The deportation and direct extermination of the Jews began in 1942. Many Jewish victims were sent to the death camp at Chełmno on the Ner River. When the Soviet Army approached in 1944, the Nazis had deported the last inhabitants of the Łódź Ghetto to Auschwitz and other concentration camps.[179]

Generation 5

24. Joseph Henry[5] Turnheim (Solomon[4], Benjamin[3], Hersch[2], Solomon[1]), born 13 February 1916 at Louisville, Kentucky to Solomon Turnheim and Fanny Goodman.[180] He died 25 June 1974 at Louisville, Kentucky age 58.[181] Joseph married Betty Zellner at Louisville, Kentucky. She was born 20 May 1920 at Louisville, Kentucky to Carl and Freda Zellner.; died 8 July 2005 at Atlanta, Georgia.[182] In the 1940 Federal Census for Louisville, Kentucky, Joseph was listed as a civil engineer, following the same career path as his father. They had two children who are still living.

25. Miriam[5] Turnheim (Mathias,[4] Benjamin[3], Hersch[2], Solomon[1]), born ca. 1917 at Przemyśl, Poland. I found additional information for Miriam Turnheim through www.geni.com. Her father was Mathias Turnheim, and her mother was Loti Silberbusch. Miriam immigrated to Israel and married Mendel Rosenbaum. Their surname changed to Rotem in Israel and although I estimate Miriam was born ca.1917, her birth year was given as 1920 by her son Ilan Rotem.[183] Miriam Rosenbaum Rotem née Turnheim died 23 March 2003 at Haifa, Israel. Miriam and Mendel Rotem had a son, Ilan, who resides in Israel.

26. Hans[5] **Turnheim** (Kelman Josef[4], Schulem[3], Hersch[2], Solomon[1]), born 11 April 1913, Vienna, Austria. Hans Turnheim was an engineer, married Meli and

Miriam Rotem née Turnheim

Standing Joseph Brainin with unknown soldier 1918

Detail Salomea Neumark with Aron Geiger family

they had two sons, Heinz and Klaus Turnheim. Hans Turnheim died in Salzburg, Austria.

27. Leopold⁵ Turnheim (Kelman Josef⁴, Schulem³, Hersch², Solomon¹), born 29 August 1911, Vienna, Austria; died 23 July 2012 in Vienna. He was a professor of medicine, married Henriette Drucker. They had two children, Maria Turnheim and Michael Turnheim. Michael Turnheim was a neurologist and psychiatrist in Paris. He was born 22 October 1946 in Vienna, Austria; died 27 November 2009 in Paris, France.

28. Salomea⁵ Neumark (Debora⁴, Benjamin³, Hersch², Solomon¹), born 11 September 1899 at Przemyśl, Poland to David Neumark and Debora Turnheim.[184] She married 3 October 1921 at Manhattan, New York, Joseph Brainin, son of Reuben Brainin and Masha Amsterdam. She died March 1985 at New York.

Discussion

I have a family photograph taken ca. 1904 of Salomea with her aunt Hinde Turnheim and her uncle Aron Geiger. The photograph also includes the Geiger's three daughters: Minnie Geiger, at age 17, Freude Geiger, Manya Geiger and her husband Getzel Holoszycer. Salomea appeared to be five years old in that photograph, a pretty child with blonde hair and delicate facial features. I think that she was temporarily staying with Hinde and Aron while her parents David and Debora were busy with the birth of Salomea's sister Marta in Germany. Her father, David Neumark, was studying at the university in Berlin where he completed requirements for his doctoral degree of philosophy. Salomea was named after her paternal grandfather Solomon Neumark.

Salomea and her family immigrated to the United States from Hamburg, Germany 16 November 1907. The ship *President Lincoln* arrived at New York on 28 November 1907.[185] The ship manifest listed David Neumark age 41, his wife Debora age 29, their two children Salomea age 8 and Marta age 3. Their destination was Cincinnati, to the Hebrew Union College where David Neumark had a job waiting for him as a college professor.[186]

Salomea graduated from the University of Cincinnati, Ohio. Salomea Neumark was listed as one of the contributors for a literary section "Blue Hydra" in the 1919 college yearbook *The*

Reuben Brainin
First Zionist
Congress 1897

Cincinnatian.[187] She apparently moved to New York after college. She married Joseph Brainin, on 3 October 1921 in Manhattan.[188] Joseph Brainin was born 19 June 1895 at Lyady, Russia. He died in February 1970 at New York City.[189] Information about the Brainin family was also obtained from the Dionne-Krosnick Family Tree on www.ancestry.com.

There must have been a close friendship between the Neumark and the Brainin families since they shared the same political ideology of Zionism and both families were living in Berlin at the same time. Joseph's father was Reuben Brainin. Both Reuben Brainin and David Neumark were delegates to the First Zionist Congress held in Basel, Switzerland in 1897. Both men were acquainted with Theodore Herzl who was synonymous with the Zionist movement. According to the Historical Jewish Press, Reuben Brainin was a celebrated Hebrew journalist and writer, born 16 April 1862 at Lyady, Vitebsk, Belarus.

Joseph, his brother Moses, and his father Reuben Brainin were volunteers in the Jewish Legion 1917–1918 to recruit other Jews to fight for Palestine. The Jewish Legion was an unofficial name referring to five battalions of Jewish volunteers serving in the Royal Fusiliers within the British Army to fight against the Ottoman Empire and Germany during WWI for regaining control of Palestine and to stop Axis forces. It should be noted Joseph Brainin was in the Royal Fusiliers in the City of London Regiment during the years 1914–1920. He received the British War Medal and the Victory Medal for his service.[190]

Jewish volunteers came mainly from Palestine, Russia, the United States and Canada. Fighting in 1918 took place north of Jerusalem, in the Jordan Valley and in the Battle of Megiddo against the Ottomans. After the end of WWI, the Jewish battalions were discharged back to their countries however many settled in Palestine including the future first Prime Minister of Israel David Ben-Gurion.[191] During the war the Brainins fought in a Palestinian battalion at Haifa, where their platoon collected German telegraphic and telephonic equipment along Turkish-German communication lines. They also guarded British engineering units along the Suez Canal during the outbreak of the Egyptian revolution.[192]

Salomea and Joseph Brainin were living in the Bronx, New York at the time of the 1930 Federal Census. Their address was 3405 Putnam Place, in the Bronx. The household consisted of Joseph, age 35, occupation journalist; Salomea age 30; son David age 5; daughter Miriam age 2 years 11 months and Mary McCann age 25, servant.[193]

Salomea filed a petition for citizenship that was completed 17 December 1931. This was in the Southern District Court in New York. Her current address was listed as 3871 Sedgwick Avenue, Bronx, New York. She stated that her husband Joseph Brainin was born at Lady, Russia on 19 June 1895. Note the correct spelling and location of the city was Lyady, Vitebsk, Belarus, and that was also where Joseph's father Reuben Brainin was born. Her children were listed as David and Miriam aka Mitzi.[194] As an interesting note, Salomea's physical description was hand-written on the petition, as being 5 ft. 5 inches, weighing 120 lbs., having grey hair and light blue eyes.

By the 1940 Federal census, Joseph and Salomea with their son David and daughter Miriam lived at 562 West End Avenue in Manhattan.[195] Joseph's occupation was public council with his own office and Salomea was his secretary. Their building was next to the building where their cousin Charles Geiger lived. See the chapter *Charles Geiger and Esther Mamlock*.

Other sources for the birthplace of Joseph Brainin were the U.S. World War II Registration Cards 1942 where Joseph wrote on the card that he was born in Lady, Russia.[196] He also listed his birth 19 June 1895 at Lady, Russia on the Manifest for Alien Passengers, Border Crossings from Canada to the U.S. His arrival date was September 1917 to Montreal, Quebec, Canada.[197] His occupation was journalist. Joseph travelled from Cherbourg, France to Montreal in 1929 on the ship *Andania*.[198]

After her husband Joseph Brainin died in 1970,[199] Salomea travelled to Israel to visit her daughter Mitzi. Salomea died at the age of 85 years, March 1985 at New York City.[200]

Children of Salomea Neumark and Joseph Brainin:
i. Miriam Brainin[6], born 14 June 1923, died 1924.

ii. David Brainin born 19 April 1925 at New York City; died 2015 at New York[201]

iii. Mitzi (Miriam) Brainin born 6 May 1927 at Manhattan, NY; married Zalman Y. Alper 6 June 1949 at Cook County, Illinois.[202] Zalman Y. Alper was born 18 Mar 1928; died 1 Nov 2008 at Chicago, Illinois.[203] Mitzi Alper is still living.

29. Martha[5] Neumark (Debora[4], Benjamin[3], Hersch[2], Solomon[1]), born 5 May 1904 at Berlin, Germany; died 21 September 1981 at Flushing, Queens, New York.[204] She was buried 9 July 1982 at Walnut Hills Cemetery, Ohio.[205] Martha

THE DES MOINES REGISTER: FRIDAY

She's to Be Only Woman Rabbi

MISS MARTHA NEUMARK.

Miss Martha Neumark of Cincinnati has the distinction of being the only woman in the United States who is studying to be a rabbi. When she completes her course at the Hebrew Union college in Cincinnati she will be the only woman rabbi in the country. She resides in Cincinnati and is also a student at the University of Cincinnati.

Martha Neumark in the newspaper

married 16 September 1924 at Marion County, Indiana, Harrison Goldberg aka Henry Montor.[206]

Discussion

Martha immigrated to the United States with her parents in 1907 from Berlin, Germany. Please refer to specific immigration information in the section for Salomea Neumark. Martha went to Hughes High School in Cincinnati and was listed as secretary for the Greek Club at Hughes High School in 1918.[207] In the 1920 Federal Census in Cincinnati she lived with her family on Rockdale Avenue East, with her father David Neumark, age 53, professor at the Hebrew seminary; her mother Dora age 41, sister Salomea age 20 and brother Immanuel Kant age 5. They were naturalized in 1913; Immanuel was born in the United States.[208] Martha graduated from the University of Cincinnati in 1924. She was listed with her photograph in the school yearbook The Cincinnatian.[209] She was also listed in the Cosmopolitan Club in the University of Cincinnati as Vice-President of the club, with her photograph.[210]

I found the marriage record of Martha Neumark to Harrison Goldberg on 16 September 1924 at Marion County, Indiana.[211] Harrison Goldberg later changed

Martha and Henry Montor

his name to Henry Montor. Henry Montor was born 27 December 1905 at St. Johns, New Brunswick, Canada.[212] He attended the University of Cincinnati and Hebrew Union College. He died 14 April 1982 at Jerusalem, Israel.[213]

By the 1930 Federal Census, Henry Montor age 24, was listed as a journalist for a Zionist organization. Henry and his wife Martha age 25 and their son Joris Karl age 4 years and 7 months were living at 3400 Tryon Avenue in the Bronx, New York.[214] By the 1940 Federal Census, the family moved to Queens County, New York. Henry was age 34 and listed as an executive for a charitable trust, Martha was age 35 and their son was age 14. [215]

Henry Montor made frequent trips to Europe as a fundraiser for Israel. In 1935 he sailed from Southampton, England on the *S.S. Majestic*.[216] In 1949 he sailed on the *S.S. Queen Mary* bound for Cherbourgh, France. He was naturalized in Pittsburgh, Pennsylvania. July 1914.[217] In 1950, Henry was listed on the ship

Martha Montor

Appeal Speaker

HENRY MONTOR, executive vice-
Henry Montor Fundraiser United Jewish Appeal

manifest for the *Queen Elizabeth* arriving in New York 19 September 1950. [218] In 1951 he travelled by Klm-Royal Dutch Airlines from New York to Hamburg, Germany.[219] Henry also travelled on airlines during 1952, from Israel to New York and in 1955 from Rome and then from Paris.[220]

The obituary for Henry Montor noted that he played a leading role in obtaining financing for arms and supplies for Israel specifically the Haganah, the Jewish underground army fighting to rid Palestine of British rule. He continued to raise money to buy arms during the 1948 war for independence when Israel faced seven Arab armies. He was a leader in the United Jewish Appeal and founder of the Israel Bonds Organization. Israel's first prime minister David Ben-Gurion stated he would put Henry Montor high on the list of 10 people most responsible for the creation of Israel.[221]

My Turnheim cousin Gabby B. informed me about Pamela Nadell's remarkable book *Women Who Would be Rabbis* covering the history of ordination for women to become rabbis. Gabby recommended this book because it included much information about my cousin Martha Neumark. I had no prior knowledge that Martha Neumark wanted to become a rabbi. While attending Hebrew Union College in Cincinnati she made headline news across the country as the only woman enrolled in a rabbinical program studying Hebrew, Aramaic, biblical texts, liturgy, Jewish history and Judaism in order to achieve ordination as a rabbi and become the first American woman rabbi in the U.S.A., if she completed her course of study.[222] She was a pioneer and paved the way for other women to enter this profession that was previously open only for men.

Martha first studied privately with her father Professor David Neumark, a professor of philosophy at Hebrew Union College. At the age of fourteen, she matriculated as a special student at Hebrew Union College Preparatory Division. Under the tutelage of her father, she was conducting Friday night services at age 16 years. She petitioned to be given a High Holiday pulpit after she completed three years at the college. This request raised much controversy about whether women should be ordained as rabbis. A two-year debate ensued by the faculty of Hebrew Union College about rabbinical ordination for women. Arguments against this issue were that it was an "absurd" innovation and was contrary to all Jewish tradition, since ordaining women would increase anger in congregations about becoming too feminist, also the college would need to install separate restrooms for men and women.

Additional arguments against allowing women to be ordained were that traditional Judaism expected women to marry therefore a woman could not follow her chosen profession as a rabbi and be a homemaker and mother. The college would have trained her for nothing and made a poor investment. The faculty agreed that women could be Jewish education teachers and leaders however rabbinical ordination was too radical.

Proponents of ordination for women included her father Dr. Neumark and other progressive faculty with arguments about previous departures of Reform Judaism from traditional orthodoxy such as abolition of the *get*, dismissal of the *agunah*, and suspension of dietary laws of Kashruth. The progressives felt that in the modern age, Jewish women could be professionals such as rabbis and have a family life. After a prolonged debate lasting two years, a decision was finally made by the Central Conference of American Rabbis that women cannot be denied the privilege of ordination.[223] They reasoned women were already counted in the number for a Jewish service, sisterhoods were adjuncts to congregations and women served on the temple Boards of Trustees.

Martha Neumark advanced to Hebrew Union College collegiate department in 1922 while also in her third year at the University of Cincinnati. However, the Hebrew Union College Board of Governors voted 1923 that no change should be made in permitting males only to matriculate for the purpose of entering the rabbinate.[224] Despite this set back, Martha courageously continued her religious studies as the only female in a class of 99 males and continued to argue for women to be allowed rabbinical ordination.

Ordination was within Martha's reach, however her world changed in 1924 after she married a classmate from the University of Cincinnati, Henry Montor, on 16 September 1924 at Marion County, Indiana. By that time, she completed 7 ½ years of the 9-year rabbinical course. Hebrew Union College awarded her the first certificate for Sunday school superintendent. After her beloved father David Neumark suddenly died 15 December 1924, she abruptly withdrew from Hebrew Union College in 1925.

Martha and Henry moved to New York City. While they were in New York City, Rabbi Stephen Wise, a liberal rabbi, and Zionist supporter, offered Martha private ordination if she completed the curriculum, however she turned down his offer. Many years later, she would "ruefully recollect her failure to follow through."[225] While living in New York City, Martha and Henry Montor worked together for Zionist and Jewish causes. Henry had his career with the United

Palestine Appeal as the executive vice-president (1939–50) and he worked with Henry Morgenthau, Jr. who became national chairperson in 1947. Israeli Prime Minister David Ben Gurion hailed the efforts of the Montor-Morgenthau team for providing the financial backing for the creation of the State of Israel.[226] Martha also worked with Henry to run a publishing house and two news agencies for the Zionist cause. Martha next earned a master's degree in musicology from Columbia Teachers College. She taught, composed, and wrote about music.[227] Martha and Henry divorced in 1956. After their divorce, Henry divided his time in Rome, Italy and Jerusalem, Israel.

Martha described her many careers as research specialist, publicist, psychologist, teacher, clinical social worker, and administrator. She was a prolific writer and wrote thousands of articles including sermons. When Martha retired in 1975, she was a counselor for the New York City Department of Corrections.

In 1964 Martha approached the Dean of the Hebrew Union College about reopening the question of women in the rabbinate. She wrote "I have a feeling that the time is ripe for active recruitment of women students…now I'd like to complete the circle by helping some more mature young woman to set the precedent." [228] Martha Montor née Neumark lived to see Sally Preisand ordained as the first American Jewish woman rabbi on 3 June 1972. Martha died 21 September 1981 and she was buried at Walnut Hills Cemetery, Hamilton County, Ohio.[229]

My Turnheim cousin Gabby B. also shared an important memoir written by Martha Montor née Neumark in December 1966 titled *Papa was a Philosopher.*[230] Martha donated this essay to the American Jewish Archives in Cincinnati. She wrote an engaging biography of her father David Neumark including his memories about Galicia.

Children of Martha Neumark and Henry Montor:
i. Rae Montor[6], born 24 July 1942; died 13 Sept 1999 at Oak Bluffs, Massachusetts.[231]

ii. Joris Karel Montor, born 24 Nov 1925; died 13 Mar 1998 at Severna Park, Maryland.[232] He was a professor at the U.S. Naval Academy, Annapolis, Maryland.

30. Immanuel Kant[5] Neumark (Debora[4], Benjamin[3], Hersch[2], Solomon[1]), born 23 April 1914 at Cincinnati, Ohio to David and Dora Neumark.[233] He married Ruth Schmerler ca. 1938, she was born 15 May 1914 at New York to Elias and Bertha Schmerler. Immanuel Kant Neumark died 2 November 1993 at Miami, Florida.[234] Ruth Neumark died 20 January 2002 at Deerfield Beach, Broward, Florida.[235]

Discussion

In the 1930 Federal Census, Immanuel Kant age 15 was living with his mother Dora Neumark, a widow, in the Bronx, New York at 66 West Gun Hill Road.[236] Immanuel graduated from the City College of New York in 1933 with a B.S. and was listed as cum laude in the college yearbook *The Microcosm*; his photograph was included in the yearbook with the information that he spoke fluent German.[237] He was considered a genius and graduated from high school at age 14. He received his master's degree at age 20 and became a member of Phi Beta Kappa.

I estimate that Immanuel Kant married Ruth Schmerler in New York ca. 1938. Immanuel and Ruth were married and listed in the 1938 City Directory for Washington, D.C.[238] By the 1940 Federal Census, Immanuel and Ruth were still living in Washington, D.C. with their young daughter Lucyy. Immanuel was employed as a statistical clerk for the U.S. Social Security Board and Ruth was employed as an editorial clerk for the W.P.A. They lived on Kenyon Street N.W.[239] Relatives reported that Immanuel was also a talented musician and played the organ, guitar and accordian.

Children of Immanuel Kant Neumark and Ruth Schmerler:

i. Lucyy[6] Neumark born 19 March 1939 at Washington, D.C.; Lucyy Bate née Neumark died 13 October 1993 at Cambridge, Massachusetts.[240] She was a writer of children's books and a playwright.

ii. Elisabeth Neumark born 17 August 1946 at New York; Elisabeth Turner née Neumark died 21 March 2000 at New York.[241]

Descendants of Benjamin Turnheim

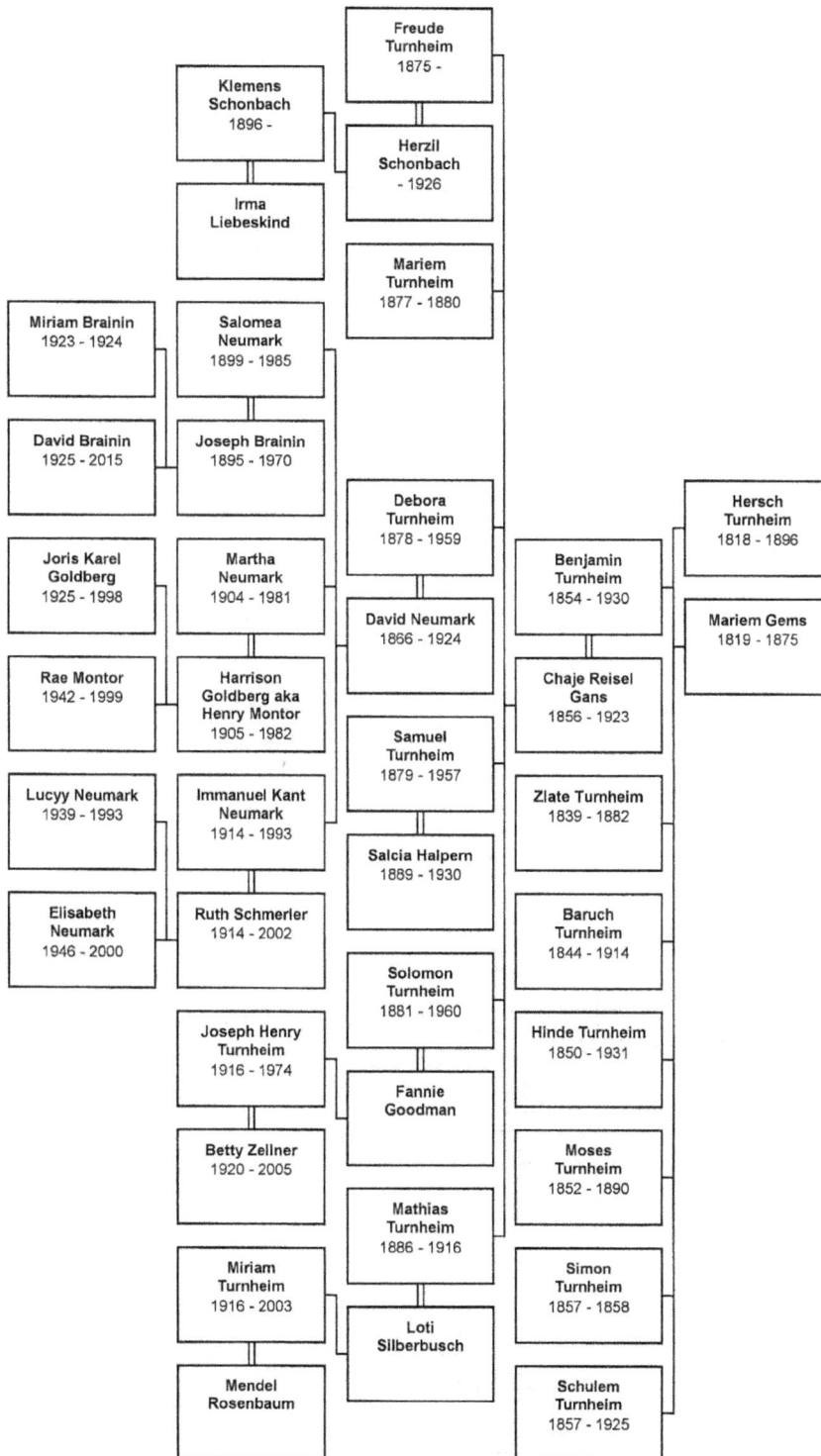

Freude Turnheim
1875 -

Klemens Schonbach
1896 -

Herzil Schonbach
- 1926

Irma Liebeskind

Mariem Turnheim
1877 - 1880

Miriam Brainin
1923 - 1924

Salomea Neumark
1899 - 1985

David Brainin
1925 - 2015

Joseph Brainin
1895 - 1970

Debora Turnheim
1878 - 1959

Benjamin Turnheim
1854 - 1930

Hersch Turnheim
1818 - 1896

Joris Karel Goldberg
1925 - 1998

Martha Neumark
1904 - 1981

David Neumark
1866 - 1924

Mariem Gems
1819 - 1875

Rae Montor
1942 - 1999

Harrison Goldberg aka Henry Montor
1905 - 1982

Chaje Reisel Gans
1856 - 1923

Samuel Turnheim
1879 - 1957

Lucyy Neumark
1939 - 1993

Immanuel Kant Neumark
1914 - 1993

Zlate Turnheim
1839 - 1882

Salcia Halpern
1889 - 1930

Elisabeth Neumark
1946 - 2000

Ruth Schmerler
1914 - 2002

Baruch Turnheim
1844 - 1914

Solomon Turnheim
1881 - 1960

Joseph Henry Turnheim
1916 - 1974

Hinde Turnheim
1850 - 1931

Fannie Goodman

Betty Zellner
1920 - 2005

Moses Turnheim
1852 - 1890

Mathias Turnheim
1886 - 1916

Miriam Turnheim
1916 - 2003

Simon Turnheim
1857 - 1858

Loti Silberbusch

Mendel Rosenbaum

Schulem Turnheim
1857 - 1925

Descendants of Solomon Turnheim

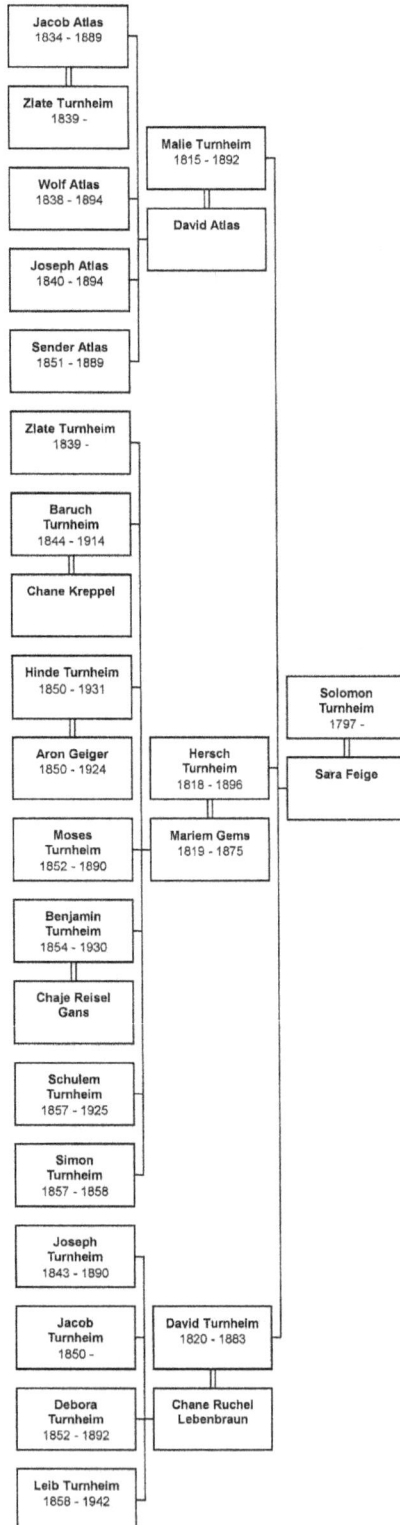

Jacob Atlas 1834 - 1889		
Zlate Turnheim 1839 -	**Malie Turnheim** 1815 - 1892	
Wolf Atlas 1838 - 1894	**David Atlas**	
Joseph Atlas 1840 - 1894		
Sender Atlas 1851 - 1889		
Zlate Turnheim 1839 -		
Baruch Turnheim 1844 - 1914		
Chane Kreppel		
Hinde Turnheim 1850 - 1931		**Solomon Turnheim** 1797 -
Aron Geiger 1850 - 1924	**Hersch Turnheim** 1818 - 1896	**Sara Feige**
Moses Turnheim 1852 - 1890	**Mariem Gems** 1819 - 1875	
Benjamin Turnheim 1854 - 1930		
Chaje Reisel Gans		
Schulem Turnheim 1857 - 1925		
Simon Turnheim 1857 - 1858		
Joseph Turnheim 1843 - 1890		
Jacob Turnheim 1850 -	**David Turnheim** 1820 - 1883	
Debora Turnheim 1852 - 1892	**Chane Ruchel Lebenbraun**	
Leib Turnheim 1858 - 1942		

Endnotes

1   Alexander Beider. *A Dictionary of Jewish Surnames from Galicia.* (Bergenfield, New Jersey: Avotaynu) 2004. p.541.

2   Virtual Jewish World: Jaroslaw, Poland. (www.jewishvirtuallibrary.org).

3   Przemysl Archive, Fond 1924. Przemysl Marriages 1790–96, 99–1803, 5–10, 13–28, 30, 32, 33, 35, 36, 38–48. 1836 Marriage 15 June 1836. Hersch Turnheim (misspelled Furnheim) age 18 with Mariem Gems age 17. Akta 1. Father of the groom was Solomon Turnheim and wife Rivka from Jaroslaw; father of the bride was Gronem Gems from Przemysl.

4   Przemysl Archive. Fond 154. Jaroslaw Deaths 1877–81, 83–87. Death 1883. David Turnheim, age 62 years 11 months. Father: Solomon Turnheim, Mother Sara Feige. Akta 18.

5   Przemysl Archive. Fond 154. Jaroslaw Deaths 1877–81, 83–87, 89–1900. Death 1892. Malie Atlas, age 77 years. Father: Solomon Turnheim, Mother Sara Feige. Akta 155.

6   Przemysl Archive. Fond 1924. Przemysl Births 1789–1827,1853–1900. Birth 1857. Schulem Turnheim. Father Hersch Turnheim, Mother Miriam. Akta 209.

7   Przemysl Archive. Fond 154. Jaroslaw Deaths 1889–1900. Death 1892. Malie Atlas nee Turnheim. Akta 155. Malie's parents were Solomon and Sara Feige Turnheim

8   Przemysl Archive. Fond 154. Jaroslaw Deaths 1889–1900. Death 1889. David Atlas. Akta 53. David's parents were Sender and Feige Atlas.

9   Przemysl Archive. Fond 1924. Przemysl Marriages 1863–1899. Marriage 1882. Jacob Atlas and Zlate Turnheim. Akta 3.

10   Przemysl Archive. Fond 154. Jaroslaw Deaths 1877–81, 83–87, 89–1900. 1894 Death. Wolf Atlass, age 55 years, 6 months. Parents Dawid and Malie Atlass. Akta 7.

11   Ibid., 1894 Death. Joseph Atlass, age 54 years. Parents Dawid and Malie Atlass. Akta 25.

12   Ibid., 1889 Death. Sender Atlass, age 38 years. Parents Dawid and Malie Atlass. Akta 18.

13   Przemysl Archive, Poland. Fond 1924. Przemysl Marriages 1789–96, 98–1803, 5–10, 13–28, 32,33, 35, 36. Marriage 1836, Akta 1. Hersch Turnheim and Mariem Gems. (www.jri-poland.org).

14   Ibid., Fond 1924, Births 1789–1827, 53–1900. Birth: Solomon Turnheim. 1881. Akta 330. Father: Benjamin Turnheim, Mother: Chaje Reisel Turnheim.

15   Przemysl Archive. Fond 1924. Przemysl Births 1789–1827, 53–1900. Birth: Ernest vel Chuma Dawid Turnheim. Birth 1896. Akta 169. Father: Szulim Turnheim, Mother: Lea Turnheim.

16   Przemysl Archive. Fond 1924. Przemysl Marriages 1798–1803. Marriage 1802 Gronem Gems and Hinde Marberg. Akta 10.

17   Alexander Beider. A Dictionary of Jewish Surnames from Galicia. Avotaynu 2004 (Bergenfield: New Jersey) p. 212

18   Ibid., p.368.

19   Przemysl Archive, Poland. Fond 1924. Przemysl Deaths 1790–1899. Death 1847 Akta 64. Hinde Gems (www.jri-poland.org)

20   Przemysl Archive, Poland. Fond 1924. Przemysl Deaths 1790–1899. Death 1846 Akta 106. Gronem Gans (www.jri-poland.org)

21   Przemysl Archive, Poland. Fond 1924. Przemysl Deaths 1790–1899. Death 1875 Page 197. Marjem Tornheim (www.jri-poland.org)

22   Przemysl Cemetery List, Przemysl, Poland.

23   The *hallel* refers to Psalms 113–118 from the Book of Psalms, first chanted by the Prophets as prayers to G-d for thanksgiving and redemption from misfortune. The prayers end with *Hallelujah.* jewishvirtuallibrary.org.

24   Przemysl Archive. Fond 154. Jaroslaw Deaths 1877–81, 83–87,89–1900. Death 1883 David Turnheim. Akta 18.

25   Przemysl Archive. Fond 154. Jaroslaw Deaths 1877–81, 83–87,89–1900. Death 1889 Chane Ruchel Turnheim. Akta 49.

26   Przemysl Archive. Fond 1924. Przemysl Marriages 1863–99. Marriage 2 January 1866 Jozef Turnheim and Ruchel Glanz. Akta 29.

27   Przemysl Archive. Fond 154. Jaroslaw Deaths. 1877–81, 83–87, 89–1900, 02–09. Death 1909 Tillie Turnheim, Akta 42.

28   Przemysl Archive. Fond 154. Jaroslaw Marriages. 1877–81, 83–86. Marriage 1884 Debora Turnheim and Leib Tirk. Akta 15.

29   Przemysl Archive. Fond 1924. Przemysl Deaths. 1790–1899. Death 1892. Debora Tirk. Akta 298.

30   Krakow Archive, Tarnow, Fond 276. Tarnow Marriages 1870–1938. Akta 67. Marriage 1885 Leib Turnheim and Ester Handgriff.

31   Krakow Archive. Fond 276. Tarnow Marriages 1876–1914. 1906 Marriage. Sali Francziska Turnheim with Chaim Schlachet. Akta 72.

32   Krakow Archive. Tarnow Branch. Fond 188, 190, 258, 260, 449. Tarnow Schools 1873–1915. Chune Turnheim date of birth 27 July 1889. Father: Leib Turnheim.

33   JewishGen.org. JewishGen Yizkor Book Necrology Database-Krakow. Chuna Turnheim and family, Tarnow.

34   Yad Vashem.org. The Central Database of Shoah Victims' Names. Page of Testimony for Edward Turnheim.POT. Yosef Kurenitz.

35   Krakow Archive. Tarnow Branch. Fond 188, 190, 258, 260, 449. Tarnow Schools 1873–1915. Jozef Turnheim date of birth 8 January 1899. Father: Leib Turnheim.

36   Yad Vashem.org. The Central Database of Shoah Victims' Names. Solomon Turnheim. The Tarnow Memorial Book v.2. printed in Tel Aviv, Israel, 1968.

37   JewishGen.org. Viewmate. Translations by Alejandro Landman, Jonathan Michael Wien, Suzan Wynne, Henry Gruder.

38   Krakow Archive Tarnow Branch. Tarnow Deaths 1877–1903. Not yet on-line. Death 1929 Leon Turnheim. Akta 191.

39   Krakow Archive Tarnow Branch. Tarnow Deaths 1877–1903. Not yet on-line. Death 1932 Estera Turnheim. Akta 95.

40   Krakow Archive Tarnow Branch. Fonds 188,190,258,260,449. Tarnow Schools 1873–1915. Chune Turnheim, Josef Turnheim. www. jri-poland.org.

41   JewishGen.org. Polish Medical Questionnaires. Salamon Schlachet, a physician, was listed. His birthdate was 22 July, 1911 and his maternal grandparents were Leon Turnheim and Esther Handgriff. His paternal grandparents were Meier Nathan Schlachet and Ester Klein.

42   Yad Vashem.org. The Central Database of Shoah Victims' Names. Medical Dr. Schlachet, Salamon. Item: 7074450.

43   Tarnow, Malopolskie, Poland. (en.wikipedia.org/wiki/Tarnow#1939_invasion_of_Poland).

44   Przemysl Archive. Fond 1924. Przemysl Marriages 1790–1899. Marriage 1882. Zlate Turnheim with Jacob Atlass. Jacob's age was 47 years 6 months and Zlate's age was 42 years 3 months. Akta 3.

45   Przemysl Archive. Fond 1924. Przemysl Births 1853–1900. 1856 Birth Schie Atlas. Akta 102.

46   Przemysl Archive. Fond 1924. Przemysl Births 1853–1900. 1859 Birth Feige Atlas. Akta 229.

47   Przemysl Archive. Fond 1924. Przemysl Marriages 1863–99. 1882 Marriage Feige Atlas and Israel Angerman. Akta 6.

48   Przemysl Archive. Fond 1924. Przemysl Births 1853–1900. 1883 Birth: Ester Angerman, Akta 81.

49   Przemysl Archive. Fond 1924. Przemysl Births 1853–1900. 1885 Birth: Freude Angerman. Akta 238.

50   Przemysl Archive. Fond 1924. Przemysl Births 1853–1900. 1865 Birth: Josef Atlas. Akta 165.

51   Rzeszow Archive. Fond 533. Rzeszow Marriages 1896–1913. Marriage 1896. Jozef Atlas and Malcia Gleicher. Akta 63.

52   Przemysl Archive. Fond 1924. Przemysl Births 1863–1899. Birth: Rebeka Atlas. Akta 641.

53   Przemysl Archive. Fond 1924. Przemysl Births 1853–1900. Birth 1875 Marim Atlas. Akta 54.

54   Przemysl Archive. Fond 1924. Przemysl Marriages 1789–1899. Marriage 1899. Maryem Atlas and Szymon Mandel.

55 Suzan Wynne. *The Galitzianers: the Jews of Galicia 1772–1918.* (Kensington, MD: Suzan Wynne), 2006. pp. 55–62.

56 AGAD Archive. Fond 300. Drohobycz Marriages 1877/1913. Marriage 1887. Baruch Turnheim and Chane Kreppel. Akta 24.

57 AGAD Archive. Fond 300. Drohobycz Marriages 1877/1913. Marriage 1900. Etel Turnheim and Moses David Schindler. Akta 34.

58 AGAD Archive. Fond 300. Drohobycz Deaths 1852/1913. Death 1896. Rysche Turnheim. Akta 40.

59 AGAD Archive. Fond 300. Drohobycz Births 1877–1913. Birth 1879 Marjem Turnheim. Akta 285.

60 AGAD Archive. Fond 300. Drohobycz Deaths 1914, 15. Death Baruch Turnheim. Age 70. Akta 163.

61 AGAD Archive. Fond 300. Drohobycz Deaths 1852/1913.1895 Death of Chana Turnheim. Age 54 years, 8 months. Akta 264.

62 AGAD Archive. Fond 300. Drohobcyz Deaths 1852/1913. 1904 Death Leizor Kreppel. Akta 310.

63 AGAD Archive. Fond 300. Drohobcyz Deaths 1852/1913. 1908 Death. Israel Ber Kreppel. Akta 9.

64 AGAD Archive. Fond 300. Drohobycz Deaths 1852/1913. 1905 Death. Munisch Kreppel.Akta 300.

65 Przemysl Archive. Fond 1924. Przemysl Births 1789–1827, 53–1900. Birth 1871. Naftale Tornheim. Akta 69.

66 Przemysl Archive. Fond 1924. Przemysl Deaths 1790–1899. Death 1877. Naftali Geiger. Akta 79.

67 Weiner Stadt-und Landesarchiv, Wien. Email dated 25 March 2011 from Dr. Michaela Laichmann, MAS. Records from the Vienna vital records archive indicated that Hinde Heiger (Geiger) nee Turnheim was born 1 January 1850 in Przemysl. She died 11 October 1931 inVienna.

68 Weiner Stadt und Landesarchiv, Vienna. Totenbeschaubefund 9676_1924. Death record: Aron Geiger. He was born 1850 in Blazowa and he married 1868. He died 17 August 1924 and was buried 19 August 1924 at the Weiner Zentralfriedhof Cemetery, Vienna. Gate 4, group 10, row 11, grave 66. Aron Geiger was listed as a businessman.

69 Wolf-Erich Eckstein email dated 14 June 2011 from the IKG, Vienna. Mr. Eckstein researched the birth and death information for Hinde Geiger nee Turnheim. She was born 1 Jan 1850 in Przemysl and she died 11 Oct 1931. She was buried 12 Oct 1931 at the Weiner Zentralfriedhof cemetery, Vienna at location gate 4, group 10, row 11, grave 65.

70 Przemysl Archive. Fond 1924. Przemysl Deaths 1790–1899. 1877 Death: Chana Turnheim. Age 7 years. Akta 212.

71 Yad Vashem.org. Central Database of Shoah Victim's Names. Edka Turnheim nee Schmidt. POT submitted by Ester Schmidt Yardeni.

72 JewishGen.org. Online Worldwide Burial Registry: Lwow. Jozef Thurnheim died 15 July 1942, buried at Przemysl New Jewish Cemetery.

73 Przemysl Archive. Fond 1924. Przemysl Births 1789–1827, 53–1900. 1885 Birth: Ester Turnheim. Akta 265. Notation on birth record indicated that Ester died 1895.

74 Przemysl Archive. Fond 1924. Przemysl Births 1789–1827, 53–1900. 1854 Birth: Benjamin Tornheim. Akta 138.

75 Przemysl Archive. Fond 1924. Przemysl Births 1789–1827, 53–1900. 1856 Birth: Chaje Reisel Gans. Parents Meilech Gans and Sara Riwka Feldstein.

76 See photo of Benjamin Turnheim's grave in Przemysl Cemetery.

77 JewishGen.org. 1891 Galicia Business Directory. B. Turnheim, Przemysl.

78 GenealogyIndexer.org. Benjamin Turnheim was listed in the 1896 Galicia Business Directory under Korzenne Handle or Spice Dealer.

79 JewishGen.org. www.jewishgen.org/Yizkor/przemysl/przo81.html.

80 Przemysl Archive. Fond 1924. Przemysl Births: 1789–1827, 53–1900. 1857 Twin Births: Simon and Schulem Turnheim. Akta 208 and Akta 209.

81 Przemysl Archive. Fond 1924. Przemysl Deaths. 1790–1899. 1858 Death: Simon Turnheim, 5 months. Page 69.

82   AGAD Archive. Fond 300. Lviv Marriages 1870–1899. 1879 Marriage Szulim Turnheim and Sobel Pilpel. Akta 52.
83   AGAD ARchive. Fond 300. Drohobycz Marriages 1877/1913. 1887 Marriage Szulim Ozer Turnheim and Laje Turnheim. Akta 25.
84   AGAD Archive. Fond 300. Lviv AGAD Births 1877–99. Birth. 1880. Marya Turnheim. Father: Szulem Turnheim. Mother Sabina Pilpel. Akta 449.
85   AGAD Archive. Fond 300. Lviv AGAD Births 1877–99. Birth 1881. Kelman Jozef. Father: Szulem Turnheim. Mother: Sabina Pilpel. Akta 1025.
86   JewishGen.org. Online Worldwide Burial Registry. Sigmund Salomon Turnheim was buried 8 Nov 1909 at the Weiner Zentralfriedhof Cemetery, Vienna. He was buried in the same grave as his father Solomon aka Schulem Turnheim, both at grave location T1, group 9, row 33, grave 084A. Sigmund Salomon's occupation was schmiedegehilfe (blacksmith's assistant).
87   AGAD Archive. Fond 300. Drohobycz Marriages 1877/1913. 1887 Marriage Schulem Turnheim with Lea Turnheim. Akta 165.
88   Personal correspondence 24 Mar 2016 with Fritz Neubauer regarding Freida Prisand.
89   Przemysl Archive. Fond 1924. Przemysl Births. 1789–1827, 53–1900. 1894 Birth: Malka Elizbieta. Father; Schulem Turnheim . Mother: Lea Turnheim. Akta 432.
90   Przemysl Archive. Fond 1924. Przemysl Deaths 1790–1899. 1896 Death: Malka Elizbieta. Akta 197.
91   Przemysl Archive. Fond 1924. Przemysl Births. 1789–1827, 53–1900. 1896 Birth: Ernst Chuna Dawid Turnheim. Father: Szulim Turnheim. Mother Lea Turnheim. Akta 169.
92   Yad Vashem.org. Central Database of Shoah Victims' Names. Maria Turnheim. Page of Testimony by Metza Torenheim.
93   Yad Vashem.org. Central Database of Shoah Victims' Names. Maria Turnheim. She was born and residing at Lwow however she was on the list of murdered Jews from Austria as she was in Vienna during the war.
94   Weiner Stadt-und Landesarchiv, Wien, Austria. Email mailed 25 March 2011 from Dr. Michaela Laichmann, MAS. This information contained the death date for Schulem Turnheim on 29 August 1925 in Vienna and also confirmed his birthdate as 7 December 1857 in Przemysl. He was 68 years of age when he died.
95   Przemysl Archive. Fond 1924. Przemysl Marriages 1790…1899. 1866 Marriage: Josef Turnheim, age 23 and Rachel Glanz age 20 years. Akta 29.
96   Przemysl Archive. Fond 1924. Przemysl Births 1789–1827, 53–1900. 1864 Birth: Freude Turnheim. Akta 140. Father: Josef Turnheim. Mother: Rachel Glanz.
97   Przemysl Archive. Fond 1924. Przemysl Births 1789–1827, 53–1900. 1867 Birth: Tile Turnheim. Akta 94. Father: Josef Turnheim. Mother: Rachel Glanz.
98   Przemysl Archive. Fond 154. Jaroslaw Deaths 1877–81, 83–87, 89–1900, 02–09, 13–18, 20, 22, 23, 28–34. Death 1909 Tillie Turnheim. Akta 42
99   Przemysl Archive. Fond 154. Jaroslaw Deaths. Death: 1890. Josef Turnheim. Akta 65.
100 Przemysl Archive. Fond 154. Jaroslaw Births., Birth: 1891. David Turnheim. Akta 170.
101 Przemysl Archive. Fond 154. Jaroslaw Births, Birth: 1900. Moritz Turnheim. Akta 194.
102 Przemysl Archive. Fond 154. Jaroslaw Deaths. Death: 1894. Isidor Turnheim. Akta 111.
103 Przemysl Archive. Jaroslaw Births. Birth: 1895. Anna Turnheim. Akta 43
104 Przemysl Archive. Fond 154. Jaroslaw Marriages 1877–81, 83–86, 89–1906. 1884 Marriage Dobra Turnheim age 32 with Leib Tirk age 37. Akta 15.
105 Przemysl Archive. Fond 1924. Przemysl Deaths 1790–1899. 1892 Death Dobra Tirk. Akta 298.
106 Przemysl Archive. Fond 154. Jaroslaw Births 1877–81, 83–87, 89–91, 93–1908. Birth 1878. Betty Tirk. Akta 16.
107 Ibid., Birth 1879. Sigmund Tirk. Akta 54.
108 Przemysl Archive. Fond 154. Jaroslaw Deaths. 1877–81, 83–87, 89–1900, 02–08. Death 1880. Alexander Tirk. Akta 98.

109 Przemysl Archive. Fond 154. Jaroslaw Births 1877–81, 83–87, 89–91. 1891 Birth David Turnheim. Akta 170.

110 Jewish Gen.org. Holocaust Database. Polish Medical Questionnaires. David Turnheim : date of death 25 May, 1942. See Yad Vashem: The Central Database of Shoah Victims' Names. Item ID 7066001. Genealogyindexer.org. Listing of David Turnheim in the 1923 and 1924 Polish Officers Handbooks. Genealogyindexer.org. Listing of David Turnheim in the 1938 and 1939 Polish Medical Directories

111 Jewish Gen.org. Holocaust Database. Polish Medical Questionnaires. David Turnheim : date of death 25 May, 1942. See Yad Vashem: The Central Database of Shoah Victims' Names. Item ID 7066001.

112 Chabad.org. Hillel Zaltzman. Starvation in Wartime Samarkand.

113 YadVashem.org. World Jewish Congress. List of Jewish refugees from Poland living in the Soviet Union listed August 1943.

114 Genealogyindexer.org. Listing of David Turnheim in the 1923 and 1924 Polish Officers Handbooks.

115 Genealogyindexer.org. Listing of David Turnheim in the 1938 and 1939 Polish Medical Directories

116 Przemysl Archive. Fond 1924. Przemysl Births 1853–1900. Birth 1866. Leib Turnheim. Akta 17.

117 AGAD Archive. Fond 300. Lwow Marriage 1899.Marriage Leon Turnheim and Antonian Kalmus, akta 185.

118 AGAD Archive. Fond 300. Drohobycz Births 1877–1913, Marriages 1877/1913. 1900 Marriage. Etel Turnheim and Moses Dawid Schindler. Akta 34.

119 AGAD Archive. Fond 300. Lviv. Births 1863–76, 1900, 01. Birth: 1901. Josef Schindler. Akta 1641.

120 AGAD ARchive. Fond 300. Lviv Births and Marriages 1902, 03. Birth: 1902. Joachim Schindler. Akta 1718.

121 Przemysl Archive. Fond 1924. Przemysl Births 1789–1900. Birth 1875: Freude Turnheim, Akta 142.

122 Przemysl Archive. Fond 1924. Przemysl Marriages 1790–96, 99–1803, 5–10, 13–28, 30, 32, 33, 35, 36, 38–48, 53, 55, 56, 58, 59, 61, 63–99. Marriage 1895. Freida Turnheim age 20 and Herzil Schonbach age 33 years 8 months. Akta 33.

123 Photo of the headstone of Henryk Schonbach in Przemysl Cemetery by Domi Grossman.

124 Przemysl Archive. Fond 1924. Przemysl Births 1789–1827, 53–1900. Birth 1896: Klemens Schonbach, Akta 251.

125 Krakow Archive. Krakow Progressive Marriages 1919–1934. Marriage 1925 Klemens Schonbach and Irma Liebeskind, Akta 731.

126 JewishGen.org. Pinkas HaNitzolim I-Register of Jewish Survivors, Krakow Committee List. pp. 142–143.

127 Przemysl Archive. Fond 1924. Przemysl Births 1789–1827, 53–1900. Birth 1878. Debora Turnheim. Akta 125.

128 Ancestry.com. New York Naturalization Records 1882–1944. Salomea Neumark Brainin. Birthdate: 11 Sept 1899, Przemysl, Poland. Date of petition: 17 Dec 1931.

129 Ancestry.com. Berlin, Germany Births 1874–1906. Birth 3 May 1904 Martha Neumark. Note the discrepancy of day of birth with other records.

130 Ancestry.com. US WWII Draft Cards for Young Men 1940–1947. Birthdate Immanuel Kant Neumark. 23 April 1914 at Cincinnati.

131 Przemysl Archive. Fond 1924. Przemysl Marriages 1790–1899. Marriage 1898. Debora Turnheim and David Neumark. Akta 38.

132 de.wikipedia.org/wiki/David_Neumark.

133 Wikipedia.org. Halacha translated as "The Way" is Jewish law based on the Talmud as well as written and oral laws that prescribe how Jews should behave encompassing civil, criminal and religious sections.

134 AmericanJewishArchive.org. Martha Neumark Montor. Papa was a Philosopher. Jacob Rader Marcus Center. David Neumark papers. P.10.

135 Newspapers.com. *Wisconsin Jewish Chronicle.* 19 December 1924. Obituary. Prof. David Neumark Hebrew Scholar Dies.

136 Ancestry.com. New York Passenger Lists 1820–1957. Ship: President Lincoln leaving Cauxhaven and arrival in New York on 29 November 1907. David Neumark, his wife Dora and their two children Salomea and Marta.

137 Newspapers.com. *The Wisconsin Jewish Cronicle*. 19 December 1924. Obituary of Professor David Neumark.

138 Ancestry.com. 1930 United States Federal Census. Bronx, New York. Enumeration District 3-677.

139 AmericanJewishArchives.org. Martha Neumark Montor. Papa was a Philosopher. Jacob Rader Marcus Center. Cincinnati, Ohio. David Neumark papers.pp. 7–8.

140 Ancestry.com. 1910 United States Federal Census. Cincinnati Ward 9, Hamilton, Ohio.Enumeration District 108.

141 Ancestry.com. New York Passenger Lists 1820–1957. S.S. Rheim. David Neumark.

142 Ancestry.com. 1920 United States Federal Census. Cincinnati Ward 13. Hamilton, Ohio. Enumeration District 225.

143 Ancestry.com. Ohio Deaths 1908–1932. Department of Health. Death 15 December 1924. David Neumark. Volume 4610, page 6175, certificate 66360.

144 Ancestry.com.1930 United States Federal Census. The Bronx. Enumeration District 3-684.

145 www. Ancestry.com. 1940 United States Federal Census. New York, New York. Dora Neumark. Enumeration District: 31–719.

146 FindAGrave.com. Death 14 July 1959 Dora Neumark.

147 Ancestry.com. U.S. Passport Applications, 1795–1925. Roll 2279. 1923. Certificate 297348. Issued to Dora Neumark.

148 Ancestry.com. New York, Passenger Lists 1820–1957. Dora Neumark. Ship: Resolute. Sailing from Hamburg 21 August 1923.

149 Przemysl Archive. Fond 1924. Przemysl Births 1789–1827, 53–1900. Birth 1879: Samuel Turnheim. Akta 310.

150 Przemysl Cemetery List, Przemysl, Poland. 1957 Death Samuel Thurnheim.

151 AGAD Archive. Fond 300. Stanislawow Marriages 1889-1912. Marriage 1 November 1908. Samuel Turnheim and Salcia Elza Halpern. Akta 105. www.jri-pl.org.

152 JewishGen.org. www.jewishgen.org/Yizkor/przemysl/prz08.1html#Page90.

153 JewishGen.org. Przemysl Memorial Book. Translation from sefer Przemysl. Published in Israel by Irgun Yotzei, 1964. Dr. Arie Menczer, Editor. Part III. Przemysl Jews 1918-1939. Chapter 7. The Jewish Health Institutions in Przemysl. The Jewish Hospital.

154 GenealogigyIndexer.org. 1914 Przemysl Calendar for Physicians. Dr. Salomon Turnheim.

155 Genealogyindexer. Org. Multiple listings for Dr. Samuel Turnheim.

156 Ibid., Bnai Brith Membership Dr. Samuel Turnheim.

157 AGAD Archive. Fond 300. Ivano-Frankivsk. Stanislawow Marriages 1872-76, 89-1912. Marriage: 1908. Samuel Turnheim and Salcia Elza Halpern. Akta 105.

158 AGAD Archive. Fond 300. Stanislawow Births 1877–1904. Birth 10 June 1889 Salcia Elza Halpern. **www.jri-pl**. org.

159 See image of matsevahs at Przemysl Cemetery for Dr. Samuel Thurnheim (Turnheim) and Elza Thurnheim.

160 Przemysl Archive. Fond 1924. Przemysl Births 1789–1827, 53–1900. Birth: 1881. Salomon Turnheim. Akta 330.

161 Ancestry.com. Kentucky Birth Index 1911–2000. Birth 13 Feb 1916. Joseph Henry Turnheim.

162 JewishGen.org. Yizkor Book Przemysl. Chapter Three: Political Movements in the Jewish Street. History of the Zionist Movement in Przemysl Until the First World War. P. 96.

163 Ancestry.com. Kentucky Naturalization Records 1906 –1991. Declaration of Intention: Solomon Turnheim. Date: 10 March 1914.

164 Ancestry.com. U.S. Social Security Death Index 1935-2014. Fanny Turnheim Death: 30 March 1976, Louisville, Kentucky.
165 Ancestry.com. Kentucky Death Index 1911-2000. Solomon Turnheim. Death: 28 Jan 1960, Louisville, Kentucky.
166 Przemysl Archive. Fond 1924. Przemysl Births. Birth 1886: Mathias Turnheim. Akta 66.
167 Geni.com. www.geni.com/people/Loti_Turnheim. Tree managed by Ilan Rotem.
168 JewishGen.org. My ViewMate. Translations provided by Yitschok Tzvi Margareten and Fredel Fruhman. 21 December 2020.
169 JewishGen.org. My ViewMate. Translations provided by Yitschok Tzvi Margareten, Odeda Zlotnick and Fredel Fruhman. 21 December 2020. The Hebrew idiom "A stone shall scream from the wall" is used to express feelings of shock, horror or outrage so great that they would even make stones scream.
170 JewishGen.org. Lodz Ghetto List. Friede Prisand. Born 11 Aug 1889, registered 31 May 1942, occupation Farmacy. Transported to the Lodz Ghetto from Vienna 23 Oct 1941.
171 JewishGen.org. Online Worldwide Burial Registry- Austria. Burial record for Salomon Turnheim..
172 JewishGen.org. Vienna Marriages. 1925. Bride: Frieda Turnheim, Groom: Zallel W. Prisand. Alsergrund Synagogue, Vienna, Austria. Number 46.
173 YadVashem.org.
174 Personal papers of Elizabeth Lifschitz. Affidavit of Support for Freida Prisand nee Turnheim. 1938.
175 YadVashem.org.
176 YadVashem.org.
177 Personal correspondence from Fritz Neubauer, including Freida Prisand's last letter from the Lodz Ghetto.
178 JewishGen.org. Last Letters from the Lodz Ghetto. Freida Prisand.
179 JewishGen.org. Lodz-Names: A record of the 240,000 Inhabitants of the Lodz Ghetto.
180 Ancestry.com. Kentucky Birth Index 1911-2000. Birth 13 February 1916 Joseph H. Turnheim.
181 Ancestry.com. Kentucky Death Index 1911-2000. Joseph Henry Turnheim . Death: 25 June 1974, Louisville, Kentucky.
182 Ancestry.com. Find a Grave. Betty Zellner Birth: 20 May 1920. Betty Turnheim Death: 8 July 2005.
183 Geni.com. Miriam Turnheim family information supplied by her son Ilan Rotem.
184 Przemysl Archive. Fond 1924. Przemysl Births 1789-1900. Birth: 1899. Salomea Neumark. Akta 481.
185 Ancestry.com. Hamburg Passenger Lists, 1850-1934. Salomea Neumark. Age 8. Microfilm K_1803.
186 Ancestry.com. New York, Passsenger Lists, 1820-1957.
187 Ancestry.com. U.S. School Yearbooks, 1880-2012.
188 Ancestry.com. New York, New York Marriage Index 1866-1937. 3 October 1921. Marriage Salomea Neumark and Joseph Brainin. Certificate 900.
189 Ancestry.com. U.S. Social Security Index.
190 Ancestry.com. UK, WWI Service Medal and Award Rolls, 1914-1920. Joseph Brainin. From the National Archives of the U.K., Kew, Surry, England.
191 Jewish Legion. Wikipedia.org/wiki/Jewish_Legion.
192 Ancestry.com. Dionne-Krosnick Family Tree. Reuben Brainin 1862–1939. Outline of Reuben Brainin life events and family.
193 Ancestry.com. 1930 United States Federal Census. Joseph Brainin. Bronx. 3405 Putnam Place. Enumeration District 3-677. Ward. A.D.8. Tract 423. Block E.
194 Ancestry.com. New York, Naturalization Records, 1882–1944 for Salomea Neumark Brainin.
195 Ancestry.com. 1940 United States Federal Census. E.D. 31-793. 562 West End Avenue. Joseph Brainin.
196 Ancestry.com. U.S. World War II Registration Cards 1942. Joseph Brainin. He listed that he was self-employed with his own business.
197 Ancestry.com. List or Manifest of Alien Passengers Applying for Admission to the U.S., Border Crossings from Canada to U.S., 1895–1956.Joseph Brainin.

198 Ancestry.com. Canadian Passenger Lists, 1865–1935. Joseph Brainin. Ship: Andania. Date of arrival: 18 November 1929.

199 Ancestry.com. U.S. Social Security Death index, 1935–2014. Death: February 1970. Joseph Brainin. Last residence: New York City.

200 Ancestry.com. U.S. Social Security Death Index, 1935–2014. Death: March 1985. Salomea Brainin.

201 Ancestry.com. U.S. Obituary Collection, 1930–current. David N. Brainin.

202 Ancestry.com. Cook County Illinois Marriage Index 1935–1960.

203 www. Ancestry.com. U.S. Social Security Death Index 1935–2014. Death: Zalman Alper, 1 Nov 2008 at Chicago, Ill.

204 Ancestry.com. U.S., Social Security Death Index, 1935–2014. Birth: Martha Montor 5 May 1904; Death: Martha Montor 21 Sept 1981 at New York.

205 JewishGen.org. Online Worldwide Burial Registry. Martha Montor.

206 Ancestry.com. Indiana Marriage Index 1800–1941. Marriage Harrison Goldberg and Martha Neumark 16 Sept 1924.

207 Ancestry.com. U.S., School Yearbooks, 1880–2012.

208 Ancestry.com. U.S. 1920 Federal Census. Ohio, Hamilton County, Cincinnati. Ward. 13, Enumeration District 225. House Number 836, Rockdale Avenue East. David Neumark family.

209 Ancestry.com. U.S., School Yearbooks 1880–2012. Martha Newmark, B.A. 1924.

210 Ancestry.com. The Cincinnatian Yearbook, 1922. Martha Newmark.

211 Ancestry.com. Indiana, Marriage Index, 1800–1941. Marion County, Indiana. Index to Marriage Record 1920–1925.

212 Ancestry.com. U.S. WWII Draft Cards Young Men, 1940–1947. Henry Montor. Birthdate: 27 December 1905 Birthplace: St. Johns, N.B. Canada. He was working for the United Appeal at 342 Madison Avenue, N.Y.C.

213 Ancestry.com. U.S., Social Security Death Index, 1935–2014.

214 Ancestry.com. 1930 United States Federal Census. New York. Bronx. Enumeration District 3-677.

215 Ancestry.com. 1940 United States federal Census. New York, Queens. Enumeration District 41-820.

216 Ancestry.com. New York, Passenger Lists 1820–1957. 1935. Henry Montor, age 30, passport 242701 by virtue of his father's citizenship. Arriving in New York, 23 December 1935.

217 Ancestry.com. U.S. Departing Passenger and Crew Lists, 1914-1962. Henry Montor was age 43 and was living in Bayside, L.I., New York.

218 Ancestry.com. New York Passenger Lists 1820-1957. Henry Montor had passport 18927 and was listed as a U.S. citizen. He was residing in Bayside, L.I., New York.

219 Ancestry.com. U.S., Departing Passenger and Crew Lists 1914-1962. Henry Montor, listed as an executive, age 46 and living in Bayside.

220 Ancestry.com. U.S. Social Security Death Index, 1935-2014. Death: Henry Montor, April 1982.

221 Newspapers.com._ *Times-Advocate* (Escondido, California). Obituary Henry Montor. 16 April 1982. p. 20.

222 Newspapers.com._ *The Des Moines Register*, 24 December 1920; also the Santa Ana California Register, 23 December 1920.

223 Pamela S. Nadell. *Women Who Would be Rabbis: A History of Women's Ordination, 1889-1985*. Beacon Press, Boston. 1998. p. 62.

224 Ibid., p. 71.

225 Ibid., p. 72.

226 Ibid., p. 102.

227 Ibid., p. 103.

228 Ibid., p.104.

229 U.S. Find a Grave Index. www.findagrave.com/cgi-bin/fg.cgi. Death Martha N. Montor 21 Sept 1981.

230 AmericanJewishArchives.org. Martha Neumark. Papa was a Philosopher. Jacob Rader Marcus Center. Cincinnati, Ohio. David Neumark papers.

231 Ancestry.com. Massachusetts Death Index, 1970–2003. Death Rae Montor 13 Sept 1999 at Oak Bluffs, Massachusetts.

232 Ancestry.com. U.S. Social Security Death Index, 1935–2014. Death Joris Karel Montor 13 March 1998 at Severna Park, Maryland.

233 Ancestry.com. Ohio Birth Index, 1908–1964. Birth: Immanuel Neumark 23 April 1914, Ohio.

234 Ancestry.com. U.S., Social Security Death Index, 1935–2014. Immanuel Neumark.

235 Ancestry.com. U.S., Social Security Death Index, 1935–2014. Ruth Neumark.

236 Ancestry.com. 1930 Federal Census. Bronx, New York. Dora Neumark and Immanuel Neumark.

237 Ancestry.com. U.S. School Yearbooks, 1880–2012. Immanuel Neumark graduated 1933.

238 Ancestry.com. U.S. City Directories 1822–1995.1938. Washington, D.C. City Directory. Immanuel and Ruth Neumark. Address: 2121 H NW. Washington, D.C.

239 Ancestry. Com. 1940 Federal Census. Washington, D.C. Enumeration District 420. Immanuel Neumark.

240 US Social Security Death Index, 1935–2014; Lucyy N. Bate.

241 US Social Security Death Index, 1935–2014; Elisabeth N. Turner.

Chapter Six

Chaskel Geiger and Esther Mamlock

Early Years

Chaskel aka Charles Geiger was the first child born to Aron Geiger and Hinde Turnheim. He was born 18 May 1868 at Przemyśl, Podkarpackie, Poland. He died 1955 in Manhattan, New York. His siblings were: Naftali (1871–1877), Abraham (1872–1946), Israel (1874–1933), Mariem (1880–1946), Freude (1882–d. before 1924), my grandmother Mindla (1887–1960). Chaskel was the name written on his birth record and was an Eastern European Jewish kinnui for Ezekiel (the prophet).

My main sources for memories for Charles Geiger came from interviews that I had with his granddaughter Carol Lebeaux prior to her death, his grandson Alan Rolland's wife Mickey Rolland, his great-granddaughter Cathy Cohen and information obtained from Liz Lifschitz, his niece once removed. I personally recalled Charles Geiger during his senior years and the respect for Charles by my mother and grandmother. Charles differed from his parents by being less reli-

Chaskel Geiger birth record

giously orthodox, perhaps being influenced by the *Haskalah* movement. Charles Geiger was certainly not as religious as his younger brother Abraham who became a rabbi. Charles was said to be a mischievous youngster who once cut off his brother Abraham's payeses while his brother Abraham was sleeping. Charles also smeared garlic on the family mezuzah fastened to the door so that when Abraham put his hand to kiss it, he would taste the garlic. Carol told me she recalled that Charles would giggle while conducting the Passover seder at his apartment in Manhattan. She added "maybe he was fudging on the Hebrew, making it up when he couldn't read it." She told me that "he rebelled against the strict religion of the old country and was a sort of maverick. Perhaps he saw an in-joke on himself posing as a traditional patriarch of the family." There were other more serious characteristics of Charles that will be discussed later in this chapter.

Immigration and Naturalization

Charles may have immigrated to the USA to avoid conscription in the Austrian-Hungarian army as it required a 20-year commitment for service for men between ages 16 to 36. He was also ambitious and wanted to find greater opportunities in Amer-

Charles Geiger, *S.S. Suevia* ca. 1886

ica, perhaps listening to stories about the Golden Land of America. Charles Geiger was the first in his family to immigrate to the USA and New York City on August 2, 1886 at age 18 on the ship *S.S.Suevia* leaving from Hamburg and LeHavre. His occupation was merchant and his stated destination was Cincinnati. The *S.S.Suevia* was a passenger steamship built 1874 for the Hamburg America Company for transatlantic crossings between Hamburg Germany and New York City. It had 100 first class, 70 second class and 600 third class passengers. Charles arrived at Castle Garden as that was the port where immigrants disembarked between 1855 to 1890 prior to Ellis Island. He was virtually penniless and he decided to remain in New York. He began life in New York City with only a few dollars and worked as a peddler pushing a cart on the Lower East Side selling small wood products such as picture frames, boxes, mirrors, then larger items such as end tables according to information from his granddaughter Carol. He eventually made enough money to go into the furniture business with a partner, Mr. Braverman.[1]

Charles Geiger was naturalized on 7 March 1891 at the Superior Court of New York County.[2] His naturalization papers listed his occupation as furniture dealer. His address was 1471 First Avenue. The witness to his naturalization was M. Neuwirth, a peddler.

Charles Geiger, Naturalization

Marriage and Children

Charles wanted to be able to provide for a wife and children and worked hard until he was in a stronger financial position. This took eight years from the time he first immigrated. Charles met his wife Esther Mamlock at Manhattan, New

Charles Geiger, Marriage Certificate, 1894

York and they were married 6 March 1894. Relatives informed me that their marriage was arranged. Their marriage record was obtained from the New York City Municipal Archives.[3] On this record, Charles was living at 6 Attorney Street, he listed his parents Aaron Geiger and Hinde Turnheim. Esther Mamlock was living at 161 Park Row and her parents were Meyer Mamlock and Caroline Sobel. Esther Mamlock was born in New York 14 April 1868 at New York City.[4] She died 10 January 1944 at New York City.[5] Charles and Esther Geiger had three children: Marion Geiger (1895–1991); Minna Geiger (1896–1983); Milton Geiger (1902–1959).

Charles Geiger ca. 1902

The American Dream

Charles rose from being a pushcart peddler to becoming a prosperous merchant of furniture from the time of his immigration in 1886 to 1900. He was in the

Esther Mamlock ca. 1902

1900 Federal Census for New York City and the family consisted of Charles, Esther, Miriam, Minna aka Minnie and a servant named Annie Kanengeser.[6] They were living at 230 East Broadway in Manhattan and Charles was listed as having a furniture business. The 1900 census indicated that he was naturalized. Charles Geiger gave his birthdate as May 1870 and Esther gave her birthdate as April 1869.

It is also interesting to see in this 1900 census that at the same address Michael Price with his wife Minnie and widowed mother-in-law Carolina Mamlock lived in a nearby apartment. Esther's sister Minnie Price née Mamlock was born ca. 1866 at New York. She married Michael Price 14 June 1891 at Manhattan.[7] Michael Price was born 1861 at Austria. He immigrated 1886, was naturalized and worked as a jeweler.[8] A huge change for Charles and his family occurred when Minnie Price became widowed after her husband Michael Price died 6 June 1904.[9] Minnie Price moved in with Charles Geiger and his family by 1905, remaining with them for many years until the death of her sister Esther Geiger in 1944. Charles Geiger was listed in the 1900–1901 NYC Telephone Directory as Chas. Geiger Furniture at 71 and 98 Essex Street, Manhattan and his home address was 280 East Broadway.

More members were added to the Charles Geiger family as indicated on the 1905 New York State Census. The family consisted of Charles, Esther, their children Marion, Minnie, Milton, Esther's widowed sister Minnie Price, Charles' sister Mina Geiger (my grandmother Minnie), also a live-in maid Rose Kessler. Their address was 327 East 68th Street in Manhattan.[10] Charles was financially successful and could now afford to live in that upscale upper east side neighborhood. I speculate that Charles never met his youngest sister Minnie until she arrived at Ellis Island 1 November 1904, as he left home in 1886 and my grandmother was born in 1887. I think their meeting must have been very emotional for both. Minnie then lived with his family until ca.1908 when she moved in with her sister Miriem and brother-in-law Getzel Holoszycer.

In the 1905 Manhattan Telephone Directory, Charles Geiger's business was a furniture store on Grand Street listed as Geiger and Braverman. In the 1910 Federal Census, the family now consisted of Charles, Esther, Marion, Minnie, Milton, Minnie Price (the widowed sister-in-law), Julie Waterman (a widowed cousin of Esther) and a 22-year-old servant, Bertha Valesk.[11] They were still residing at 327 East 68th Street in Manhattan. Charles was listed as a furniture merchant and an employer. Other families living at the same address also had servants and were either professionals or business owners. He was financially quite successful; his daughters attended private schools and he had servants and a chauffeur. Charles made a trip during the summer 1910 to Europe. He departed from Bremen, Germany 6 August 1910 on the *S.S. Bremen* and arrived at New York 16 August 1910.[12]

In the 1913 NYC Trow Directory, his store was listed as Geiger and Braverman Furniture at 49 West 23rd Street in Manhattan and his home was at 2094 Fifth Avenue, Manhattan in a prosperous neighborhood. In the 1915 New York State Census, Charles Geiger and his family lived at 2094 Fifth Avenue in Manhattan.[13] He had a live-in maid and a live-in cook. His family consisted of his wife Esther, his children Marion, Minna, and Milton as well as his sister-in-law Minnie Price. Charles simply listed his occupation as "furniture." His granddaughter Carol told me that he owned a large furniture store in Manhattan.

In the 1920 Federal Census, Charles, Esther, daughter Marion, son Milton and sister-in-law Minnie Price were living at 602 West 157th Street, Manhattan.[14] His daughter Minna was no longer living with her parents as she married Albert Rolland in 1919. Charles was listed as a retail furniture dealer and his son Milton, age 17, worked for him as a furniture salesman. Marion was age 25, living with her parents and was single. Minnie Price, his sister-in-law, lived with them.

Charles Geiger ca.1915

By the 1925 New York State Census, Charles Geiger, his wife Esther, and his sister-in-law Minnie Price were living at 302 West 92nd Street, Manhattan.[15] Charles and Esther's children were not living with them as they were all married. Charles was still working as a furniture dealer. Charles Geiger was on the ship manifest for the *RMS Mauretania* that departed from Cherbourg, France. He arrived at New York 12 August 1927.[16] Charles made a trip from New York to Vienna in 1927.[17] The purpose of his trip was to visit his widowed mother Hinde, his brother Abraham Geiger and Abraham's wife and children. I have a family photograph of Charles sitting with his family in 1927 taken at Vienna.

Charles, Esther, and Minnie Price made another trip on the Hamburg America Line ship *S.S. Resolute* that departed from Cherbourg, France on 14 August 1929 and arrived at New York on 22 August 1929. Their address was 340 Riverside Drive, Manhattan.[18] This trip was made two months prior to the devastating stock market crash on 27 October 1929.

Standing (L to R) Minna, Charles, Esther. Sitting, Marion ca. 1920

Charles traded in stocks in addition to managing a furniture store. However, when the 1929 stock market crash came, Charles lost everything, including his large furniture store off Fifth Avenue and 23rd. Street. He told his granddaughter Carol Lebeaux that up until then he felt he was a very arrogant man but became a better person and gained humility after his financial losses. Charles decided to educate himself to learn about the stock market as an investor. He became quite skilled at trading and investing and put in less time at his furniture business. Mickey Rolland recalled that Charles would stay all day at the brokerage house and watch the stock prices go up and down. He could recite the symbols and the prices of stocks verbatim. Charles was able to live an upper middle-class lifestyle from his investing acumen. This ability to profit from stocks took him all the way through retirement until his death.

His granddaughter Carol Lebeaux recalled that he was very lively and full of personality. Charles was considered by other family members to be warm, affectionate, and with a terrific sense of humor. Charles used to say that he sold Jewish newlyweds bedroom suites and he jokingly told them "I stand behind every bedroom suite that I sell"!

Sitting (L to R) Charles, Hinde, Abraham, Sprinza. Standing (L to R) Mina, Stella, Rose, Max, unknown relative, Josef, Esther, Vienna 1927.

Portrait Charles Geiger ca.1945

Charles Geiger ca. 1945

Charles Geiger ca. 1930

In the Federal 1930 census, the family consisted of Charles, Esther, and his sister-in-law Minnie Price. Their address was still 340 Riverside Drive, Manhattan.[19] By that time, his daughter Marion was married to Eugene Messner in 1920 and his son Milton was married to Dorothy Ducker in 1925. His children were married and no longer living with their parents. Charles put his occupation as retired, at age 61 however he was self-employed as an active stock investor. His former business partner, Solomon Braverman, was also living at the same address in the next apartment and they remained friends. Mr. Braverman also listed his occupation as retired and was from Odessa, Russia. Families living at this address were business owners, retired or professionals and most families had live-in maids.

By the 1940 Federal Census, Charles and Esther Geiger moved to 585 West End Avenue in Manhattan.[20] Charles indicated on the 1940 Federal Census that the highest grade that he completed was the eighth grade. He continued as an active investor in the stock market for many years. I noted that Minnie Price was no longer living with Charles and Esther on this census.

Death

Charles Geiger died 24 April 1955 at age 87, his residence still at 585 West End Avenue, Manhattan.[21] The age on his death certificate was given as 85 but that was because Charles and his family estimated his actual birthdate as they did not have his actual birth record. This was the case with many immigrants. His death was due to natural causes. Charles was a widower; he was predeceased by his wife Esther who died 10 January 1944.[22] Most photographs of Charles show him smoking a cigar. Charles visited with my family and his sister Minnie Weiss née Geiger several times while we were living in Brooklyn. I personally recall visiting my great uncle Charles prior to his death when I was age 12. My impressions were of a dark apartment, with heavy drapes and mahogany furniture. People took turns saying their farewells to Charles, something like the movie *The Godfather*. He was buried at Mt. Neboh Cemetery, Glendale, Queens, New York in a family plot that he purchased for himself and his family from The First Galician Society in 1923 that was a *landsmanschaften*. Many Jewish immigrants such as Charles joined *landsmanschaften* that were organizations based on common geographic origins in the "old country" and were established in the USA as dues paying social networks to help members with financial needs such as medical care and purchasing burial plots.[23]

It is noteworthy that Charles did not want to be buried next to his wife Esther. He told his granddaughter Carol Lebeaux that he arranged to be buried in a different cemetery from his wife. He said that his wife had refused to sleep with him in life, so he did not want to be next to her in death. Their marriage had degenerated over the years, when his sister-in-law Minnie Price moved in with

פ״נ הצלקאל בר אהרן הלוי

BELOVED FATHER
CHARLES GEIGER
DIED APRIL 24, 1955
AGE 85 YEARS

Charles Geiger Matsevah, Mt Neboh Cemetery, New York

Mt. Neboh Weiss Geiger Plot

the family after she was widowed in 1904. His wife Esther and her sister Minnie shared a bedroom and Charles was moved into a guest bedroom. After having their three children, affection in their marriage gradually deteriorated. Esther and Minnie would spend all day in the kitchen baking bread and cooking. Carol observed that when one scolded a child, the other did the same. Carol also reported that Minnie Price had severe leg cramps that were intolerable. She committed suicide 25 May 1946 by jumping out of a window.[24] According to Carol, Minnie left a note saying that she could not tolerate her leg pains any longer.

Levite or Not

Since Charles was not orthodox nor especially religious, I compared the matzevot of four known direct line male Geiger descendants with Charles Geiger's matsevah. His was the only matsevah with the HaLevi after his name, indicating he was a Levite. Levites are the male descendants of Levi who was the third son of Jacob and the grandson of the patriarch Abraham. Moses and his siblings Miriam and Aaron were also descendants from the tribe of Levi; the Kohanim were a special subgroup designated as priests within the tribe of Levi. Levites were set apart from the rest of the Israelite tribes for spiritual service in fulfillment of G-d's will.[25] Often Levite descent is based on oral tradition passed down from generation to generation.

I compared Charles' matsevah with the following matsevot: Aron Geiger (Charles' father); Yehezkiel Geiger (Charles' first cousin); Abraham Geiger (Charles' brother); Chaim Yehuda Geiger (Charles' uncle). Those were all religiously orthodox and direct male descendants of the Geiger family. None of those matsevot contained the designation for HaLevi or Kohanim except for Charles Geiger's matsevah indicating Levite. Moreover, a descendant of Yehezkiel Geiger told me that he was an Yisraelite, not a Levite or Kohanim. I sent a question to www.jewishgen.org concerning this inconsistency for why Charles' matsevah was the only Geiger matsevah found with the designation Levite. My question was forwarded to an on-line discussion group of people who descend from various rabbinical lineages. Many were authorities on designations for Kohanim, Levite and Yisraelite.

Replies were not conclusive one way or another however several theories were presented. Could Charles Geiger differ from the rest of the family by having another biological father? I ruled this theory out because I saw Charles Geiger's original birth records that came directly from the Przemyśl Archive and noted that Chaskel aka Charles was born to Aron Geiger and Hinde Turnheim.

Another theory presented by the on-line discussion group was that the designation Levite could have been an error on Charles Geiger's matsevah since there were no known Kohanim or Levite traditions in the Geiger family and Charle's matsevah was the only one in the Geiger group with the designation HaLevi.[26] Another possibility was not all Jews who were Levite are indicated as such on their matsevah so the lack of the designation may not be significant, however it was a conspicuous omission on all four matsevot. Charles' daughter Marion Messner provided the information for his death certificate, and she probably arranged his funeral and matsevah. I entertained another possibility that the monument company asked Marion if Charles was a Cohen, Levite or Yisraelite, Marion may have simply guessed Levite and so that designation was carved on his stone marker. My hypothesis is the HaLevi designation was an error and therefore Charles was most likely in the Yisraelite group that includes all male Jews who were not designated as Levites or Kohanim. Please read the DNA section at the end of this chapter.

Benefactor to Many

Charles Geiger was quite close to his youngest sister Minnie Geiger, my grandmother, and the evidence is as follows: the ship manifest for my grandmother Minnie had information that Charles paid for her passage for her immigration to New York in 1904. On her manifest, it was also reported that she was going to join her brother Mr. Charles Geiger at 305 and 307 Grand Street, Manhattan; she was discharged to her brother who met her at Ellis Island. My great uncle Charles was therefore responsible for my grandmother leaving Błażowa, Poland for America. It was probably my great uncle Charles who paid for the lavish wedding for my grandparents Minnie Geiger and Oscar Weiss in 1911. Our family has several photos of their wedding with perhaps 200 guests in formal dress attending the reception at the Lexington Hotel at New York City.

I have a family movie showing Charles visiting with my parents and my grandmother in 1948 (his sister Minnie) taken at our home at Canarsie, Brooklyn, New York. This visit was to help celebrate my 5th birthday. Charles was smoking cigars and he was affectionate with my family and Minnie. He was 80 years old at the time and appeared frail.

Charles Geiger assisted his younger siblings to immigrate to the United States and helped them to build their lives as new citizens. His love, loyalty, and generosity will be elucidated in the chapters written about each sibling. The following are some examples how Charles helped family and other Jews.

When Charles learned that his niece, Pearl Holly, wanted to go to medical school but did not have the funds, he generously gave her the money to do so. He was reportedly careful with money but gave generously to his relatives and to certain Jewish causes when there was an opportunity to benefit future generations, for the future good of many people. His generosity was not for anything trivial or frivolous.

Charles provided well for his family however he did not forget poor Jewish children who needed help. He became involved with the Downtown Talmud Torah, an elementary and secondary school afternoon Hebrew day school located in the Lower East Side of New York City. This school was founded 1892 and was considered a pioneer in modern Jewish education in the United States, advocating integration between Judaism and Americanization. The school provided thousands of poor and orphaned Jewish children a Jewish education free of charge and functioned until 1970. Charles was a benefactor and he served on the Board of Directors for many years.[27]

Charles made immigration to the USA a reality for my grandmother Minnie Geiger. He also ensured that she begin married life to a good man (my grandfather Oscar Weiss) and provided her with a huge wedding. Charles also granted his sister Minnie Weiss née Geiger one-half interest and title in the cemetery plot at Mt. Neboh Cemetery, Queens County, New York that he purchased from the First Galician Society on 29 March 1923. This document was signed on 23 January 1948.[28] The remaining interest and title of the family plot was later granted to my mother by Charles's daughter Marion. This family plot, Weiss-Geiger, is where Charles Geiger was ultimately laid to rest and where my grandparents, my parents and my brother are also buried. This was another example of the close relationship shared by my grandmother and her brother Charles. Prior to his death, my grandmother Minnie would frequently visit Charles to help him during his illness. Please see the chapter *Minnie Geiger and Oscar Weiss*.

Charles Geiger was a witness for the 1893 naturalization of Leon Sobel who was Esther Mamlock's first cousin on her Sobel lineage.[29] In the 1900 Federal Census Leon Sobel was living at 1487 First Avenue, Manhattan and working in the furniture business.[30] Charles and Esther also helped their daughter-in-law Dorothy Geiger raise their grandson Richard Geiger by providing financial and emotional support after Dorothy's divorce from Milton. Charles provided the funds for his sister Mariem and her family to immigrate to the USA; she indicated on the ship manifest that her destination was to her brother Charles Geiger.

Please see the chapter *Mariem Geiger and Getzel Holoszycer*. Charles Geiger assisted his younger brother Israel Geiger with immigration to the USA and employment in New York and in Chicago. Charles put family first to the extent that he was able and was an example for all to follow. Please see the chapter *Israel Geiger and Esther Perlberg*.

Charles as Family Rescuer during the Holocaust

Charles's granddaughter Carol Lebeaux wrote me a letter after she learned about the good deeds he performed. She reflected that descendants knew they had a relative who helped them but did not know it was Charles Geiger. She wrote "can you estimate how many people owe so much to Charles Geiger? We can't count all the generations of offspring from the families he saved."[31] My cousin Liz L. told me about Charles Geiger's incredible rescue efforts that grew from his love for his family during the outbreak of WWII. Liz informed me about his rescue of his brother Abraham Geiger and family who lived in Vienna, Austria which was increasingly dangerous for Jews. Liz fortunately saved the letters written by Charles to her parents George and Pearl Bronz who were also instrumental in that rescue. Charles was the moving force behind their rescue efforts. Please see the chapters *Mariem Geiger and Getzel Holoszycer; Abraham Yitzak Geiger and Sprynca Stark*.

Background

Adolf Hitler became head of the National Socialist party in Germany then rose to become Chancellor of Germany in 1933. This party became known as the Nazi party. Soon after President Paul von Hindenburg's death in 1934, Hitler assumed twin titles for Fuhrer (leader) and Chancellor. He remained dictator of Germany until 1945, when he committed suicide upon being defeated by the Allied Powers. The financial hardship of the Great Depression accelerated Hitler's rise to power. Hitler's "new order" called for targeted extermination of minority people, especially the Jews of Europe. The Jews were blamed for the huge economic upheaval during the 1920s and 1930s. Jews were scapegoated and accused of being inferior to the "Aryan" race. It was not long before anti-Semitism led to violence and mass murder. Hitler annexed Austria in 1938 along with other German speaking areas, then on September 1, 1939 he invaded Poland. Two days later Britain and France declared war on Germany. WWII began followed by the horrors of the Shoah. Millions of people were killed in battles between the

Allied and Axis Powers throughout the years from 1939–1945. The total number of deaths reached 50–80 million including the systematic genocide of 6 million Jews.

Charles understood what was happening in Europe as he heard/read about Kristallnacht in Berlin that took place 9 November 1938 and lasted for two days. This was an anti-Semitic rampage in Nazi Germany where 91 Jews were murdered, and 267 synagogues were destroyed. Charles knew that it was imperative to try to get his relatives who remained in Europe to the safety of the United States. He began a campaign to enlist all the help he could both politically and financially to help his Geiger relatives escape from the Nazis. He saw the handwriting on the wall that the situation in Europe would not improve for the Jews.

Redoubled Efforts

When Charles realized that his efforts alone did not result in securing the necessary affidavits for relatives to enter the United States, he then enlisted his niece Pearl (his sister Mariem's daughter) and Pearl's husband George Bronz for their political connections in Washington, D.C. George Bronz was working as the chief legal advisor in the US Department of the Interior, Office of the Solicitor. Their daughter Liz fortunately saved the personal letters written by Charles Geiger to her parents begging their help for obtaining affidavits and safe passage for Geiger relatives to the safety of the United States. Please see Appendices for the letters.

The earliest saved letter written by Charles was dated 5 December 1938 after Kristallnacht and addressed to Pearl and George. He asked for their help in getting affidavits for the Geiger relatives in Europe so that they could be admitted into the United States. Charles wrote that he had 13 individuals to "take care of" and he had succeeded in sending 5 affidavits however he was at "the ropes end." He apparently helped his nephew Markus aka Max Geiger obtain an affidavit and he gave the address for Markus as Darwingasse 35, Vienna. He asked George Bronz for help in getting affidavits for the rest of Markus Geiger's family to include his wife Ruchla Geiger and their children Clara and Susi.[32] Charles stated that it was "very urgent that the rest of his (Markus Geiger) family get affidavits so that they at least get out of Vienna…even those of them who have affidavits cannot get here for a long time but at least it helps them a lot. Please do all you possible can to help me in this matter as it almost drive me crazi." He signed the letter "hope and pray you will succeed, Uncle Chas."

In another letter to Pearl and George dated 13 July 1939 written by Charles, he reported that his brother, Abraham Geiger, was living in London.[33] He wrote "I received a letter from my brother Abraham in London stating that his son Josef and wife must leave Milano Italy shortly or be deported back to Germany." Charles mentioned the quota by the USA government for limiting Jews to enter and although Josef and his wife had affidavits, it could take years for them to be admitted into the US. Abraham had been trying to get Josef to London where he had a good job waiting, however the Jewish Committee in London wanted assurance that Josef and his wife would not become public charges. Charles asked George to put a statement in an affidavit that Josef and his wife would be financially supported while they were in England until they could enter the US. He gave George the affidavit reference number to send this assurance to the Jewish Committee in London. Charles wrote to George that the assurance was only a matter of form and that he, Charles, would take full responsibility for their support. He dramatically added, "I will keep you free from any obligation as to their support etc. You practically risk nothing outside of helping a near relative from going back to hell."

Charles wrote another letter 17 July 1941 addressed to Pearl and George, where he discussed sending them furniture and carpets at wholesale prices.[34] He added that he was gathering dates for the affidavit of support for Josef and Erma Geiger and asked George for a copy of the form dated 6 July 1941 for his own records. A discussion of the actual papers submitted by George Bronz on behalf of the Geigers can be found in the chapter for *Mariem Geiger and Getzel Holosczycer*. A discussion of the rescue attempts for a Turnheim cousin Freida Prisand can be read in the *Turnheim Family* chapter. A discussion of the Geigers who were rescued by Charles Geiger, Pearl and George Bronz can be found in the chapter *Abraham Yitzak Geiger and Sprynca Stark*. Except for Freida Prisand, most relatives were rescued from death by the Nazis due to Charles Geiger's determination to save them with valuable assistance provided by Pearl and George Bronz.

Esther Mamlock and Her Family

Esther was born 14 April 1869 at New York City; her parents were Meyer Mamlock and Carolina Sobel.[35] Esther Geiger née Mamlock died 10 January 1944 at Manhattan, New York.[36] Esther was interred at the Price-Geiger Mausoleum in Bayside Cemetery, Ozone Park, Queens, New York. Charles Geiger and Esther Mamlock were married at Manhattan, New York on 6 March 1894.[37] Esther's siblings were Minnie and Julius. Condolences on the passing of Esther Geiger were announced in the *New York Times* obituaries from the Sobel Society of which Esther had been a member, from the Home and Hospital of the Daughters of Jacob, from the Downtown Talmud Torah and from the Sisterhood of Congregation B'nai Jeshurun. I noted that the Sobel Society listed a Dr. William Tuck as President and Larry Sobel as Secretary, who were Esther's maternal relatives.[38]

Esther's father Meyer Mamlock was born 12 February 1832 at Kochwien, Posen, Germany; he died 9 June 1897 at New York.[39] Meyer Mamlock immigrated from Germany and arrived 6 July 1865 at New York. In the 1870 United States Federal Census Meyer became Max Mamlock; his family consisted of wife Caroline, son Julius age 10; daughter Mary age 4 whose name changed to Minnie; and daughter Lillian age 2 whose name later changed to Esther. His occupation was retail clothing.[40] His children were all born at New York. Meyer became a naturalized citizen 29 January 1885.[41] His address was 213 East Broadway and he was a merchant. Meyer Mamlock applied for a United States passport 26 April 1892 for himself and his wife. His occupation was merchant.[42]

Esther's mother Carolina Mamlock née Sobel was born June 1830, Germany and died 3 May 1901 at New York. Carolina's father was Nathan Sobel, born 1799 at Posen, Sasle Holzland-Kreis, Germany to Elias Sobel and Bertha; he died 1891 at New York.[43] Nathan Sobel was married 1817 to Handel Tuck. Handel was born 1800 and died 1894 at New York. Nathan Sobel immigrated to the United States 4 October 1859 on the *S.S. Teutonia* from Hamburg, Germany.[44] Nathan and Handel had the following children: Hannah Johanna (1825–1931); Ernestina (1829–1929); Carolina (June 1830–3 May 1901); Elias (1836–1914); Nancy Nannie (1841–1897); Jacob (1841–1920).[45] Based on the 1910 Federal Census, Frederick Sobel was another child born to Nathan Sobel and Handel Tuck. He was in the same generation as his siblings and lived next door to his brother Elias Sobel.[46] I found Frederick Sobel in the 1870 Federal Census listed as age 30, married to Sarah, with their son Samuel. He was born in Germany and his age was 30, thus born 1840.[47] Elias Sobel was also living nearby; he was born in Germany and was listed on the same 1870 United States Federal Census.

Esther Mamlock's sister Minnie Price née Mamlock was born 23 March 1867 at New York City. She died 25 May 1946 at New York City. She was interred in the Price-Geiger Mausoleum at Bayside Cemetery, Ozone Park, Queens, New York.[48] Minnie married Michael Price 14 June 1891 at Manhattan, New York.[49] The following information was obtained from the 1900 United States Census. Michael Price was born April 1861 at Austria, immigrated to the United States

1886 and he became a naturalized citizen. His occupation was jewelry dealer. Michael Price age 39, with his wife Minnie age 34 and mother in law Carolina Mamlock age 70 were residing at 232 East Broadway, Manhattan, New York. Charles Geiger with his wife Esther and his children Miriam, Minnie and a servant resided in an adjoining building at 230 East Broadway.[50] Michael Price died 6 June 1904 at Manhattan, New York.[51] There was no issue.

Esther Mamlock's brother Julius Mamluck was born 4 November 1860 at New York. Mamluck was an alternate spelling of Mamlock. He died 5 August 1939 at Queens County, New York.[52] He married Effie Brull 22 March 1887 at Manhattan, New York.[53] Julius applied for a birth certificate at age 27 to provide evidence that he was an American citizen by birth.[54] His wife was Effie Mamluck née Brull and his son was Solomon aka Solon Mamluck. Effie was born ca. 1865 and died 31 December 1945 at Manhattan, New York.[55] A 1900 United States Federal Census shows Julius Mamluck, Effie, sons Solon and Mark, daughter Hattie and mother in law Johanna Bruel residing at 62 East 122 Street, Manhattan.[56] Julius stated that his occupation was Property Receivatress. This was an old term that referred to Receivership; this is a court appointed neutral person called a receiver to manage and protect the assets of an insolvent business or person until final disposition or sale of the assets and distribution to creditors.[57]

In the 1905 New York State Census Julius Mamluck and his family were residing at 258 West 113 Street and his occupation was now dealer in precious stones.[58] By the 1910 United States Federal Census Julius and his family lived at the same address 258 West 113 Street in Manhattan. His occupation was importer of stones.[59] Their new address was 251 West 92 Street, Manhattan, New York as seen on the 1915 New York State Census. Julius was an importer of diamonds and both sons were precious stone salesmen.[60] Julius Mamluck, his wife Effie and his son Mark Mamluck applied for passports 29 June 1922. Their travel was a business trip to Holland, France, the British Isles and Germany as importers.[61] Julius Mamluck made frequent trips to Europe. His obituary listed his wife Effie, sons Mark and Sol, daughter Hattie Collins, his sisters Minnie Price and Esther Geiger.[62] He was interred at Bayside Cemetery, Ozone Park, New York.[63]

Children of Charles Geiger and Esther Mamlock

Marion Geiger

Marion Geiger was born 10 January 1895, the first of three children born to Charles Geiger and Esther Mamlock.[64] There is another birthdate given for Marion from a different record source as 9 May 1895.[65] My mother Sylvia recalled that Marion was a refined, kind, and beautiful lady with striking blue eyes. She played the piano extremely well and had a wonderful singing voice. She met her future husband Eugene Messner while selling WWI war bonds and they soon fell in love. Their marriage was delayed until after WWI ended as Eugene was deployed overseas to fight in France. Marion married Eugene Messner on 12 October 1920 at the Ritz Carlton Hotel, New York City.[66]

By 1945, the Messners were living at 1235 Park Avenue in Manhattan.[67] Marion loved reading and the opera. She memorized every word of every opera. She was an active volunteer for tutoring underprivileged children in reading and math education. Even in her 80s she also volunteered at the Gutman Institute for Breast Cancer Detection interviewing patients to take their histories. Marion's daughter Carol described how her mother had a beautiful soprano voice and knew many opera arias by heart. She frequently attended operas and memorized the entire scores. Carol described her mother Marion as being modest, honest, gentle, and straightforward. Marion Messner died on 3 December 1991 in Manhattan at the advanced age of 96 years.[68] She remained alert and active until her death. She was buried at Salem Fields Cemetery, Brooklyn, New York.[69]

Marion Messner

Eugene Messner

Prior to her death, Marion wrote an autobiography in 1985 describing her life. Marion wrote how she always loved music. After she graduated from high school, she became a piano teacher at the New York Conservatory of Music. Marion aspired to become an opera singer and took singing lessons. She later joined a choral group in New York and wrote: "The highlight of my choral experience was singing the Beethoven 9th with Toscanini conducting at Carnegie Hall."[70] Her musical ability and appreciation was passed down to her children and grandchildren. Children of Marion Geiger and Eugene Messner were Arnold (1922–2017) and Carol (1924–2017).

Eugene Messner, his Parents and Siblings

Eugene Messner was born 27 April 1893 at New York City, the second of three sons born to Emil Messner and Betty Shuster. His older brother was Julian and his younger brother was Harold.[71] Eugene died 2 October 1965 at Manhattan.[72] He was buried at Salem Fields Cemetery, Brooklyn, New York.[73] Eugene worked in his father's lace manufacturing company Loomskill Textiles and then assumed leadership of the company after the death of his father. Eugene Messner entered the U.S. Army during WWI on 28 August 1917 and he served overseas from January 2018 to February 1919. He became a Sgt.1st Class and was honorably discharged 18 March 1919.[74] The 1920 United States Federal Census indicated Eugene lived with his widowed mother Betty and his siblings Julian and Harold. Eugene was an importer of cotton fabrics; Julian was a manager in a publishing house and Harold was a salesman of silk textiles.[75]

That same year, Eugene married Marion Geiger, 12 October 1920 at the Ritz Carlton Hotel, Manhattan, New York. Eugene listed his occupation as manager.[76] On the 1925 New York State Census Eugene, Marion with their children Arnold and Carol lived at 203 West 81 Street, Manhattan. Eugene was a salesman.[77] The family moved out of New York City by 1930 to Croton on Hudson, Westchester County, New York. They rented a private house at 263 Mt. Airy Street. Their daughter Carol told me her family moved to the country so their children could attend a wonderful private school.[78] Eugene and his family returned to Manhattan by 1940 and lived at 105 West 72 Street, Manhattan, New York. He was a textile salesman.[79] Eugene registered for the 1942 WWII draft (the old man's draft). His address was 105 West 72 Street, Manhattan.[80]

Eugene's father Emil Messner was born 15 May 1851 at Kassel, Germany. He immigrated from Germany and arrived at the port of New York 8 May 1869 on the German ship *S.S. Union* from Bremen, Germany.[81] The ship manifest indicated he was from Kassel, Germany, age 18, travelled second class and was a merchant. Emil made another trip to the United States from Hamburg, Germany, on the *S.S. Hammonia*, arrived at New York 26 June 1873. He was age 22 and a merchant.[82] A passport application made by Emil's son Harold Hans Messner provided an interesting fact that Emil Messner was born at Kassel, Germany and lived in both New York City and Leavenworth, Kansas.[83] I decided to check out the Kansas information. Emil Messner was on the 1870 United States Federal Census for Leavenworth, Kansas. He was age 19 and a store clerk.[84] Emil was also listed on a city directory for Leavenworth, Kansas with the occupation of clerk.[85]

Emil Messner moved to New York City from Kansas between 1870 and 1880. The 1880 United States Federal Census listed Emil Messner, single, age 27, from Prussia, a boarder, who lived at 71 East Fourth Street in Manhattan, New York. He worked as an office clerk.[86] Emil Messner married Betty Shuster 14 December 1884 at New York.[87] The 1900 United States Federal Census listed Emil Messner as a silk manufacturer. He resided at 254 West 139th Street, Manhattan, New York with his wife Betty and three sons Julian, Eugene, and Harold.[88] By 1905 Emil was a waist manufacturer and an employer. His son Julian worked as a bank clerk.[89] The 1910 United States Census listed Emil Messner as a real estate broker, Julian was a stockbroker and Eugene worked as a clerk in a broker's office.[90] Emil died 8 February 1913 at Manhattan, New York and he was buried in Salem Fields Cemetery at Brooklyn, New York.[91]

Eugene's younger brother Harold Hans Messner was born 14 May 1896 at New York; died 8 May 1990 at New York.[92] He married Sally Altman on 25 August 1931 at Manhattan.[93] Sally Altman was born 10 September 1899 and she died 3 May 2003 at New York.[94] The 1940 Federal Census listed Harold Messner as an insurance salesman and Sally as a secretary for an accounting firm. They lived at 123 West 93 Street, Manhattan, New York.[95] Harold completed his WWII draft registration. His employer was Massachusetts Mutual Life Insurance. He listed his brother Julian Messner as someone who will always know his address.[96] They had no issue.

Eugene's older brother Julian Messner was born 25 September 1885 at New York, died 8 February 1948 at his apartment in the Hotel Delmonico, New York.[97] Julian Messner registered for the WWI draft on 12 September 1918. The local draft board was at Columbia University where Julian was an undergraduate. He was employed by Boni and Liveright, publishers at 105 West 40 Street.[98] Julian applied for a passport, and it was issued 20 April 1922. He was living at 533 West 112 Street at Manhattan and his occupation was publisher. His travel destination was to France and the British Isles.[99] Julian Messner married Kathryn G. Karn 10 May 1929 at Manhattan.[100] He was 44 and she was 27. Kathryn aka Kitty was born 25 November 1902 at Chicago, Illinois.[101] The 1940 Federal Census for Manhattan listed the address for Julian and Kathryn Messner at the Wyndham Hotel located at 42 West 58 Street. His occupation was book publisher.[102] Julian and Kathryn Messner founded the publishing house Julian Messner, Inc. in 1933. Julian Messner Inc. was a successful publisher that published many best-selling books by authors John Erskine, Charles Beard, Francis Parkinson Keyes, Lillian Hellman, and Grace Metalious. Metalious wrote the novel *Peyton Place* that was considered scandalous at the time it was published in 1956.[103] Julian Messner created the Julian Messner Award for the best book promoting racial or religious tolerance in America with a significant cash award. Julian and Kathryn divorced 1944. After Julian's death in 1948, Kathryn became president and editor-in-chief of their publishing house. Kathryn Messner died August 1964 at West Long Branch, New Jersey.[104] They had no issue.

Julian registered for the WWII draft in 1942. His business address was 8 West 40 Street, New York. He listed his brother Harold Messner as the person who will always know his address.[105] When Julian died 1948, there was a laudatory obituary published by the *New York Times* that provided many details about his 30-year career as a successful book publisher.

Eugene Messner's mother Betty Shuster was born 28 June 1858 at New York to Arnold David Shuster and Johanna Schwab. Betty Messner née Shuster died 8 October 1936 at Manhattan, New York and she was buried at Salem Fields Cemetery, Brooklyn, New York.[106] Betty Shuster was listed on the 1880 United States Federal Census with her parents. They were living at 99 West Third Street, Manhattan, New York. Betty was 21 and lived

Self-Portrait Arnold D. Shuster

at home. Her father Arnold Shuster was age 68 and retired. Her mother Johanna was age 60 and keeping house.[107] Her father, Arnold David Shuster, was born 29 December 1812 at Moenchsroth, Bavaria, Germany to parents Johann Adolph Schuster and Anna Catharina Himmerich from Prussia. I discovered that many Jews from Moenchsroth and the surrounding region were buried in the Schopfloch Cemetery in Bavaria.[108]

Betty's father Arnold David Shuster immigrated to the United States ca. 1854 and was naturalized by the Superior Court in New York 8 September 1859.[109] The 1860 United States Federal Census for New York City listed Arnold Shuster, age 48; his wife Johanna, age 37 and their daughter Elizabeth, age 2. His occupation was cigar maker and both he and his wife were born at Bavaria.[110] Arnold David Shuster died 2 August 1890 at New York and was buried in the Salem Fields Cemetery, Brooklyn, New York.[111] He was married to Johanna Schwab, born ca. 1820, at Bavaria, Germany. She died 24 February 1882 and was buried at the Salem Fields Cemetery. [112]Arnold Shuster was a talented artist who specialized in portraits. His biography was in *Who's Who in American Art, 19th Century edition*; he was listed as a lithographer and artist for porcelain.[113] He studied art at the Academy of Fine Arts, Munich, Germany. Arnold was one of ten brothers and he created a lithograph including himself with his brothers. The names of his brothers remain unknown. Arnold Shuster painted his own self-portrait that was inherited by his great-granddaughter Carol Lebeaux. Photographs of his self-portrait and lithograph are included on the FindaGrave memorial page including a biography for Arnold D. Shuster. While living in New York City, Arnold worked as a tobacconist, cigarmaker and cigar salesman as noted from his annual U.S. IRS tax records during 1862 to 1865.[114]

*

Arnold Shuster and his brothers

Minna Geiger

Minna Geiger was born 3 September 1896 in New York City.[115] She was the second of three children born to Charles Geiger and Esther Mamlock. Minna Geiger married Albert M. Rolland on 17 June 1919 at New York City.[116] She lived at 602 West 157th Street, Manhattan with her family.[117] Minna was 22 years of age and Albert was 28 years of age and he was listed as an importer. Albert was a French Jew, born in Paris, France. His parent's names were Jules Rolland and Hattie Metzger. While living in France, Albert's father changed the family name from Rosenberg to Rolland. Minna and Albert were married at the Ritz Carlton Hotel, by the same rabbi, Rudolph Grossman, who also officiated at the marriage for her sister Marion and Eugene. Minna was an attractive lady with expressive brown eyes. She became an interior decorator as she had a wonderful sense of color and design. Tragedy struck when Albert Rolland committed suicide by gunshot on 15 August 1930 after the stock market crash October 1929. He was heavily invested in stocks and bonds.[118] He was interred in a mausoleum at Mt. Kisco, New York. Minna and Albert Rolland had two children: Margot Rolland (1921–1983) and Alan Rolland (1925–2004).

Standing (LtoR) Shelley, Margot, Minna, Alan, Maxine, Wedding, 1955

Two years after her husband Albert's suicide Minna married Jesse Daniel Gidding on 3 July 1932 at Somerville, New Jersey.[119] Jesse Gidding was first married to Irene J. Rosenberg 25 June 1929 at Detroit, Michigan.[120] Jesse was divorced from his first wife Irene sometime after 1930.[121] They had a daughter. Jesse was described by Carol as being tall, strong, and athletic. Although he was a confident swimmer, he drowned on 11 August 1953 while caught in an undertow swimming in the ocean at Westhampton Beach, Suffolk County, New York.[122] According to his obituary he was a partner with his brother Leonard Gidding as manufacturers for children's wear.[123] Minna Geiger did not marry again after the loss of her second husband. Minna Gidding died September 1983 in New York.[124]

Milton Geiger

Milton was the third of three children born to Charles Geiger and Esther Mamlock. He was born 27 April 1902 at Manhattan.[125] Charles and Esther Geiger were living at 215 East Broadway, Manhattan when Milton was born; Charles was listed as a merchant. Carol Lebeaux remembered Milton very well and she described him as charming and a playboy, in fact as a young man he was often in trouble. Carol thought that his parents indulged and rescued him every time. Milton Geiger and Dorothy Ducker were married on 5 March 1925 at the Astor Hotel.[126] On their marriage certificate Milton was listed as age 23, single and a salesman. Dorothy was age 20. Dorothy was born

Marion and Minna Geiger ca. 1899

Minna Gidding and Alan Rolland

5 February 1905, at Brooklyn, New York to Solomon Ducker and Rachel Bell Fedigreen.[127]

Milton and Dorothy had one child, a son Richard, born 23 November 1925.[128] Milton and his wife Dorothy divorced after the birth of their son, however on the 1930 Federal Census Milton Geiger was listed as still living with his wife and son Richard, age four.[129] The family address was 90 Riverside Drive, Manhattan. His occupation was a stock and bonds salesman. After their divorce Milton moved to Minneapolis and worked as a furniture salesman. Dorothy found employment in an upscale fashion boutique called *Martha* at Manhattan, New York. Charles and Esther Geiger helped their daughter-in-law Dorothy raise their grandson Richard Geiger. Dorothy Geiger died 25 June 1991 at Hallandale, Dade County, Florida. She was interred at Beth David Memorial Gardens, Hollywood, Florida.[130]

While living at Minneapolis, Milton married Alma Petrine Holm-Reischl on 12 January 1937 at Carver, Minnesota.[131] Alma was born 23 May 1911. Her parents were Martin and Julie (Arnstad) Holm who were both born in Norway. Alma's first husband was Frank Reischl; they married on 7 November 1928 at Hennepin, Minnesota.[132] They had a daughter, Gloria Jean born 13 May 1929 at

Milton Geiger

Milton and Alma

Minnesota.[133] Alma and Frank Reischl subsequently divorced 5 February 1936. Although Milton never legally adopted Gloria Jean, he raised her as his own child. Gloria Jean married Richard Vernon Ebner, and they had two sons: Scott Alan, who is still living and Rickie Lee, status unknown. Gloria Jean Ebner died on 7 June 2009 at Palm Springs, California.[134]

Milton and Alma Geiger subsequently had two children: Gary Alan and Julie Ann. Milton lived at Minneapolis from 1934 until his death in 1959, at age 57. Milton died 29 November 1959 at Minneapolis, Minnesota.[135] His obituary was published by the *Minneapolis Tribune*.[136] His last address on his death certificate was 511 West 50th Street, Minneapolis.[137] Milton was described in his obituary as being a member of St. John's Lutheran church. He was survived by his wife Alma and his three children, his two daughters Julie and Gloria and son Gary as well as two grandchildren, and his sisters Mrs. Eugene Messner and Mrs. Minna Gidding.

Both Gary and Julie gave me much family history and they reported having positive memories of their father Milton Geiger. Milton was described as having a wonderful sense of humor, was warm, social and was a top furniture salesman. He died of lung cancer and there was a long procession for his funeral as he was so well regarded. Milton made attempts to be involved in his son Richard's life, however that relationship remained strained and distant.

Grandchildren of Charles Geiger and Esther Mamlock

Arnold Emil Messner

Arnold was the first of two children born to Eugene Messner and Marion Geiger on 19 March 1922 at Manhattan.[138] He died 1 June 2017 at New Jersey and was buried next to his wife Barbara at Beth Moses Cemetery, Farmingdale, New York.[139] Most of this information about Arnold was based on the 29 September 2012 audio interview with Arnold's son Stephen. Stephen kindly provided me with a transcript of the interview. Arnold went to the progressive private school Hessian Hills at Croton-on-Hudson. He then went to the private City and Country School at Manhattan. He was admitted to the New York City High School of Music and Art as a music major for the piano. He also met his future wife Barbara while a student at that high school. Arnold transferred his focus from being a musician to studying voice. When Arnold graduated from high school, he was selected to be the class valedictorian. He graduated from Oberlin College in 1947 majoring in Music and Modern Languages. He received his Ph.D. in Romance Philology from Columbia University during the 1960s.[140] Arnold became a linguist and was fluent in French, German, Spanish, Italian. He also understood Latin and became conversational in Russian. He was a language teacher employed first at Scarsdale High School in New York and then at Great Neck High School, New York for many years.

Arnold registered for the WWII draft in 1942 at age 20 and lived at 105 West 72 Street, Manhattan.[141] During WWII, when Arnold was about to begin Oberlin College, he decided to apply for the Army Reserve Corps so that he could continue with his education until his college was called to active duty.[142] He was sworn into the Army Reserve Corps at Cleveland, Ohio August 1942. His college was called to active duty in May 1943. While at Oberlin, Arnold took theory, voice lessons, eurythmics (developing rhythmic body movements to musical improvisation) and he sang in a choir. Arnold took the Army Intelligence Test and did very well, scoring in the 140s. Arnold was interviewed by army intelligence as they were looking for people who majored either in engineering or foreign languages. They chose Arnold due to his linguistic ability and sent him to Camp Ritchie, the Army intelligence camp at Maryland. Arnold took a specialized course in German, so that he could interrogate German prisoners.

He was promoted to master sergeant and was sent to Camp Sacks at Rockland County, New York. His destination was Southampton, England then London. English fog prevented their plane from flying to France, but eventually Arnold landed at Le Bourget airfield in November 1944. He went to Paris and during that time he shipped back a Nazi flag and a Nazi pistol to his fiancée Barbara, however she threw them out as she was so disgusted to see them. Arnold was at army intelligence headquarters at Le Lavigne, France then was moved to Bad Schwalbach, Germany. He was assigned to interview

Arnold Messner ca.1942

German prisoners, who all "swore they had nothing to do with Nazism." From there, Arnold was transferred to Ansbach, Bavaria and during September 1945 he was assigned to translate classified German documents that included descriptions of the bombs the Germans used during the Blitz in London and the rockets they used later during the war. In November 1945, he was transferred to Wright Field at Dayton, Ohio. By March 1946 he was eligible for discharge, and subsequently married his fiancée Barbara Reese at New York, 2 May 1946.[143]

Arnold and Barbara returned to Oberlin to complete the senior year,[144] then returned to New York where he studied Russian under a special government program at Columbia University. Arnold was recommended for continued studies at Brown University. He taught there part-time and studied for his master's degree on the French writer Chateaubriand. After Brown, Arnold and Barbara returned to New York. He worked as a proofreader for Seventeen Magazine. He obtained a teaching position at the Darrow School in upstate New York where his wife worked as a secretary. Barbara became pregnant and they decided to move nearer to New York City. Arnold was hired as a French teacher for Scarsdale High School. Arnold spoke about how he always loved languages and teaching. He appreciated that his parents did not try to persuade him or force him to change his career path to earn more money.

Arnold and Barbara

Arnold found another teaching position at Great Neck South Middle School teaching French and Spanish. After teaching at Great Neck for two years, his Army Reserve Unit was called back to active duty when the Berlin Wall went up 1961. Congress passed a ruling that reservists who were called back to active duty were not deployed overseas. Arnold spent his 10 months of active duty at Ft. Gordon, near Augusta, Georgia. During his time in the Army, Arnold became a second lieutenant, promoted to 1st lieutenant and then to captain. The superintendent of Great Neck School District gave tenure to any teacher who was called up to active duty. Arnold transferred as a language teacher from the Junior High teaching position to the High School at the Great Neck schools.

During 1985, his last year teaching, his wife Barbara developed breast cancer and Arnold became her caregiver until she died in 1986. After her death, Arnold lived alone for several years and during that time he became involved in two motor vehicle accidents. He subsequently stopped driving. He also could not physically manage independently where he was living. His children helped him relocate to an assisted living facility where he could safely live. Arnold and Barbara had two children: Stephen and Nancy, both are still living.

Arnold had a wonderful baritone voice and he loved to sing in public. His sister Carol Lebeaux enjoyed telling amusing Arnold stories. She recounted an incident where a stranger heard Arnold sing and gave him his card, asking Arnold to audition. The name on the card was Burl Ives however Arnold never followed up. When Arnold was engaged to Barbara, they celebrated at the Village Vanguard where Burl Ives performed. He recognized Arnold and sat down at their table, telling Arnold he should have auditioned.

Arnold was considered frugal by his family and friends; he preferred to walk or ride a bus rather than take a taxi. One day, he visited his mother and Carol. They asked him if he would like to join them for lunch. Arnold declined saying that he already had lunch. His mother and Carol questioned him where he had lunch and Arnold replied, "I went to a wedding at the Ritz." They asked him whose wedding and Arnold answered that he didn't know, that he would mix with the crowd and eat the appetizers served; in fact he once carried a shopping bag to take home some of the appetizers but he was caught. He apparently made the rounds to hotel weddings and acted like he was an invited guest, commenting on how good the appetizers were to other guests so was never suspected as being a wedding crasher.

Carol recalled the story of how Arnold was eating a bagel and coffee in a restaurant and hung up his coat. When he was through and ready to leave, he realized that another man mistakenly took his coat, so Arnold took the man's coat which was hanging next to him. A month later, he noticed a fellow bus passenger wearing something familiar. He said, "Excuse me, but I think you have my coat." The gentleman said "Well, the one you're wearing looks like mine." Riding crosstown, they exchanged coats. Arnold later commented "I actually liked the one owned by that other guy better."[145]

Arnold admitted that he had no religious upbringing and he thought that was true of his parents; he never had a bar mitzvah and his family never went to temple. He said "I was aware of being Jewish and not at all ashamed of it or unhappy about it, but we just had a real absence of religious upbringing. My wife has had a religious upbringing, not that her parents were very religious, but she was quite spiritual and she went to Sunday School and I think was confirmed and got us going to temple fairly regularly...we joined Temple Beth El in Great Neck and we had many pleasant years there. And I have still been a member of Beth El since then."

Barbara Reese

Barbara Reese was born 5 February 1924 at New York to Harry Reese and Blanche Schaumburger.[146] Barbara had one sibling, a brother Howard Charles Reese, who was born 17 April 1918 in New York and died 29 July 2006. Barbara's mother Blanche Schaumburger was born 31 July 1895 and died February 1965. Barbara's father Harry Reese was born ca. 1892 in Russia. Harry was a salesman, had three years of college and then was an exporter of food products. Blanche and Harry Reese were married at Manhattan 3 June 1917.[147] Harry died 1964 and Blanche died February 1965. Both Harry and Blanche Reese are buried at Mt. Zion Cemetery in Maspeth, New York.

Barbara's maternal grandparents were Charles Schaumburger, born 1 July 1866 in Eppemood, Germany. He immigrated to the United States in 1885 and was naturalized as a citizen in 1890. He married Rebecca Lindeman on 4 October 1892 at New York.[148] Charles and Rebecca Schaumburger had three children: Blanche born 1895; Leo born 30 August 1896; Norman was born 11 May 1903, died 31 May 1986 in New York. Charles Schaumburger listed his occupation as confectioner and apparently had a confectionery business, employing his sons. In the 1940 Federal Census Charles was listed as a candy wholesaler and manager of his business. His sons Leon and Norman both worked in their father's candy wholesale business.[149]

Barbara graduated from Music and Art High School as a music major and was admitted to the Oberlin Conservatory of Music for piano. After the start of WWII, she returned to New York and completed her BA degree at Hunter College in 1944. Barbara worked as a secretary to Frank Stanton, the president of CBS, in the 1940s. She later worked part-time as a medical secretary/administrator from 1961 until a few months before her death on 28 July 1986.

Carol June Messner

Carol was the second of two children born to Marion Geiger and Eugene Messner. Carol Lebeaux told me that she was named after her great-grandmother Caroline Sobel. Carol was born 15 June 1924 at New York City.[150] She died 9 March 2017 at Worcester, Massachusetts and was buried in Mountain View Cemetery at Shrewsbury, Massachusetts. I was fortunate to become acquainted with Carol not only as a cousin but also as a friend over a period of ten years prior to her death. I interviewed Carol on June 2011 with a video camera. We often e-mailed back and forth about genealogy and Carol's recollections of her life and her family proved to be invaluable. My husband and I visited her house at Shrewsbury, Massachusetts and she visited us at Bedford, New Hampshire. Carol and her son Roy joined us for a family reunion of Geiger cousins during June 2013. Carol was very curious about the Shuster side of her family and I assisted her with her genealogical research. She was a gifted artist and she felt that she inherited her artistic talent from her paternal great-grandfather Arnold David Shuster (29 December 1812–2 August 1890). Carol was proud to have Arnold Shuster as an important visual artist in her family and noted that he was a portrait artist listed in *Who's Who in American Art* in the 19th Century edition.

Carol and I shared a common background in another respect, we both went to the High School of Music and Art in Manhattan as art majors, although at different years. We were both interested in family history and in art. Carol was a prolific visual artist throughout her long life up until her death. When Carol spoke of her past experiences, she lit up the room with her joy of life, sense of humor, intelligence, kindness, and sincerity. She especially loved her children, her parents, and her brother Arnold and his family. Carol also enjoyed dressing up in costumes, whether as a gypsy palm-reader or at a Renaissance Fair while conducting her art business. Besides her considerable art talent in silk screening and as a silhouette artist, she was at heart an entertainer. Carol shared a special close relationship with her grandfather Charles Geiger.

Carol recalled that her family moved to Croton-on-Hudson by the time she was four years so that Carol and Arnold could attend a private progressive grade school called Hessian Hills School. Despite having household help at Croton-on-Hudson, Carol recalled that her mother Marion would shovel coal into their house furnace, put chains on the tires in adverse weather conditions and do many household repairs because Carol's father Eugene was away in Manhattan during the work week. When Carol was age nine her family moved back to Manhattan, leaving behind the idyllic country setting at Croton-on-Hudson. Carol described the apartment as being "dark and dismal." During the Depression years many people heard things were better under Communism because they thought everyone would be treated equally and that poverty would be eradicated. During her grade school years, Carol and her brother went to City and Country School, a progressive private school in Manhattan, New York.

While at the City and Country School, Carol wrote a true story that described how Carol and her best friend Judy Churchill Skinner became concerned about the deplorable conditions of New York City work horses in 1934. This story was titled "Our Year of the Horse 1934." The book is about Carol's recollections of the actions taken with her friend Judy, as precocious ten-year old children who became animal rights activists. They took it upon themselves to monitor the health and safety of the local NYC work horses in 1934 and bring their concerns and observations to the attention of city authorities. This charming short book was unpublished and was dedicated by Carol to her friend Judy.

Carol and her family later moved to 105 West 72nd Street and then to 1235 Park Avenue at 96th Street. Carol went to the High School of Music and Art, following the footsteps of her brother Arnold. She graduated from Music and Art High School as an art major, then enrolled at Barnard College. She was a college student during WWII. She recalled how everyone was fearful that New York City could be bombed. There were frequent brownouts and the city was always so dark at night. Consumer products were rationed, such as butter and gasoline. The newspapers described Hitler's armies taking over many European countries. People did not know about the Jews in Europe being persecuted and murdered until after 1938.

While Carol was at Barnard, a fund raiser was proposed for the Red Cross and students were asked if anyone could read palms. Carol volunteered as she read various books on palm reading. She dressed as a gypsy and charged a dime per reading, doing 100 readings that day. She was friends with Marlon Brando's sister who invited Carol to her wedding. Wally Cox, an actor and comedian, was at the wedding and he also read palms while making people laugh. Carol got the idea that if she could read palms and entertain people then she could find work and charge more money, so she went to her favorite night club at 1 Fifth Avenue at 8th Street and convinced the manager to employ her as a palm reader. That began her successful career as a palm reader/entertainer. During her career she met many celebrities such as Frank Sinatra, Yvonne de Carlo, Al Capp, Ava Gardner. Carol worked in various nightclubs in Chicago, Miami, Palm Beach as well as New York. Carol loved what she was doing and made "a lot of money" for that time.

She worked as a palm reader at the Little Club on East 55th Street in Manhattan, when she sat with a man who wanted to know if he had talent and asked her if he should quit his job with the Blumenthal Button Company. She read his palm telling him that he did have both artistic and writing talent. She later learned that he was "pulling her leg" and that he was Al Capp, who was the cartoonist and writer for the cartoon series "Lil Abner." Carol was also interviewed by Dave

Carol as a model

Carol as silhouette artist 2011

Garroway on his NBC Today show and this served to further publicize her palm reader/entertainer abilities.

Carol, who was a natural beauty, also worked during 1945 as a model with the Harry Conover Modeling Agency. She became a glamorous model featured on the covers of many popular magazines however she did not see a paycheck. Carol described how modelling was a "racket," that would attract girls from out of town who only lasted a short time and who never got paid. When Carol's father Eugene learned that the agency was not paying her, he went directly to the head of the agency threatening to sue them unless they immediately paid her, which they did. When I told Carol how beautiful she was as a model, she modestly replied "it was an accident of birth, I had nothing to do with it."

In 1947 Carol purchased a small kiln and created a line of ceramic jewelry. She sold her jewelry to upscale stores on Fifth Avenue during the Korean War. She described using bright colors and unique motifs including images from Egyptian hieroglyphics. Carol also had musical ability and she learned to play the guitar and recorder. Carol had to give up making ceramic jewelry when she developed a severe allergy to the material. She then experimented with linoleum block printing and learned silk-screen printing. In time, Carol was taking orders from colleges, banks, insurance companies for unique linen calendars to give as gifts to their valued customers and donors. Carol took up portraiture and she became a much sought-after silhouette artist, travelling to craft festivals and fund raisers. Carol regaled us with her silhouettes of us during our Geiger family reunion.

Carol first married Alexander Jack Goldfarb in 1945. He was born 28 February 1924 in New York City, he died 18 November 1995 at Brooklyn, New York.[151] His family was listed on the 1930 Federal Census, and they lived at 117 West 13th Street in Manhattan.[152] Carol and Alexander's marriage was brief, and they divorced with no issue.

Carol next married Irving Wernick 11 May 1948 at Chicago, Illinois.[153] Irving Wernick was born November 1923 at Brooklyn, New York to parents Abraham and Rosa Wernick; his sister was Eleanor Wernick born 1921. Irving was discovered as a talented artist while drawing portraits at Washington Square in Manhattan, New York. He won a scholarship to the High School of Music and Art, and he graduated with a university entrance diploma. From 1941 to 1943 he studied at the Art School of the National Academy of Design then he enlisted in the Navy where he served from 1943–46. Following the war, he went on to Cornell University where he studied art history.[154]

Carol and Irving divorced soon after the birth of their daughter Annie in 1948. After their divorce, Irving travelled to Florence to study at the Academy of Fine Arts and it was there that he met his second wife, Doreen M. Kennedy. They returned to London and were married during 1953 at Pancras, London, UK.[155] Irving continued with his art studies at the Slade School of Fine Arts, London from 1952–55. Irving and Doreen had two children Jane and William. He lived in London at 8 Mall Studios, Tasker Road, London until his death. The Slade School of Fine Arts organized the Irving Wernick Art Scholarship award August 2015.

Carol and Maxim Lebeaux with Arnold and Barbara Messner ca.1955

After her divorce from Irving Wernick, Carol met Craig Rowan, a veterinarian, who subsequently moved to Idaho. Carol travelled with her young daughter Annie to visit him in Weiser, Idaho. While in Idaho, Carol met his veterinarian business partner Maxim Lebeaux and they fell in love. Carol and Maxim married 1 April 1951 at Manhattan, New York.[156] Soon after their marriage, Maxim adopted Annie. Carol became Maxim's business partner in their veterinary practice and animal hospital at Leominster, Massachusetts for many years until their divorce in 1966. Carol and Maxim had two children, Annie, and Roy, both are still living.

Maxim I. Lebeaux was born 28 January 1922 in Worcester, Massachusetts to Alexander Lebeaux (1881–1953) and Katie Peacol (1883–1965). After graduating from Shrewsbury High School in Massachusetts, Maxim studied at the University of Massachusetts at Amherst, Massachusetts. He enlisted in the Army on 28 May 1943 and was discharged 10 February 1946.[157] Maxim was also a Mason as indicated by his membership card dated 1954 for Wilder Lodge in Leominster, Massachusetts, listing his occupation as veterinarian.[158] The original name of Lebeaux was Leibowitz or Leibovici as his ancestors were from Romania. Maxim developed diabetes and heart ailments. He died at 56 years on 15 May 1978 in Boston, Massachusetts.[159]

Margot Ellen Rolland

Margot was the first of two children born 8 January 1921 at New York to Minna Geiger and Albert Jules Rolland.[160] Margot married Shelley Bortin Lashman 22 July 1944 in Manhattan.[161] They had four children: Karen, Gail, Mitchell, and Chris, all still living. Margot later divorced Shelley, retaining her maiden name. Margot died 24 March 1998 at Silver Spring, Maryland.[162] Margot's husband Shelley B. Lashman was the first child born 18 August 1917 at Camden, New Jersey to William and Anna Lashman.[163] He graduated from college and achieved the rank of Captain in the U.S. Navy.[164] Shelley Lashman died 16 December 2013.[165]

Alan Rolland

Alan was the second of two children born 13 February 1925 at New York to Minna Geiger and Albert Rolland.[166] He married Maxine Rosenberg 18 February 1955 at New York. Maxine was born 17 January 1930. Her father was Julius Rosenberg born April 1896 at Austria; he died 20 February 1970. Her mother was Frances Irene Perlow born in the U.S. 8 January 1900; she died October 11, 1965. Maxine aka Mickey described her late husband Alan as a person with a great sense of humor, who was a "great father and grandfather and loved by many, especially my mother." Alan was also a wonderful tennis player who used to say: "it's not whether you win or lose—it's how you play the game."[167] Alan and Maxine had two children: Ann and Joan. They are both still living. Alan Rolland died 11 May 2004 at Tampa, Florida.[168] Alan Rolland's widow Maxine aka Mickey was extremely helpful and she provided me with much information about her family including family photographs. She is still living.

Richard Saul Geiger

Richard S. Geiger was born 23 November 1925 at New York to Milton Geiger and Dorothy Ducker.[169] Milton left the family and moved out of state following his divorce with Dorothy. Richard was raised by his mother Dorothy and his grandparents Charles and Esther Geiger. Richard registered for the WWII draft 23 November 1943 in New York City while he was a student at Olivet College.[170] He enlisted in the Army 18 July 1944 and had one year of college.[171] Richard graduated from Olivet College, Michigan in 1948 after he was discharged from

Richard Geiger

Left, Alan Rolland, Right, Richard Geiger

the army during WWII. He fought in Northern Italy during 1944–1945. After his college graduation, he married Judith Lynn Spiegel on 21 August 1949 at the Hampshire House in New York City.[172] Judith was the daughter of Emanuel Spiegel and Freida aka Fritzi.[173] Richard's cousin Alan Rolland was his best man. The marriage announcement stated that Richard served for two and a half years with the Army and held a second lieutenant's commission in the Reserve Corps.

Richard became a land developer in Englewood and Englewood Cliffs, New Jersey. He continued as a builder of homes in Hollywood, Florida. He owned a movie theater and was vice-president of an investment company until his death. He was the building chairman for Temple Sinai in Tenafly, New Jersey from 1957–1960. He received a plaque in gratitude for his work in coordinating the building of the temple. After he had a heart attack at age 44 years in Florida, he became less active and outgoing. He was residing at Hollywood, Florida where he died 22 July 1988 at age 62.[174] He was interred at Beth David Cemetery, Hollywood, Florida.

Judith Lynn Spiegel

Judith Lynn Spiegel was born 15 September 1930 at New York City to Frieda Cohn and Emanuel M. Spiegel.[175] Her parents obtained a marriage license 13 September 1928[176] and married 10 October 1928 at Manhattan, New York.[177] The Spiegel family consisting of Judith, Freida (later known as Fritzi) and Emanuel were listed on the 1940 Federal Census living at Brooklyn, New York.[178] Emanuel Spiegel was an attorney in private practice. Judith Spiegel and Richard S. Geiger obtained their marriage license 5 August 1949 at Manhattan, New York.[179] According to family records, their marriage was 21 August 1949. Fifteen years after the death of her husband Richard, Judith Lynn Geiger married Charles Veil. Richard Geiger and Judith Spiegel had two children: Cathy Ellen, who is still living and Robert Stephen Geiger (1950–2004). Judith Geiger-Veil died 2 August 2004 at Broward County, Florida. She was residing at Hollywood, Florida.[180]

Judith Spiegel

Robert Stephen Geiger

Robert Stephen Geiger was born 25 October 1950 at New York City to parents Richard Geiger and Judith Spiegel. He died 6 February 2004 at Miami, Florida.[181] Robert Stephen Geiger graduated from Hobart and William Smith Colleges at Geneva, New York. He also graduated from the Levin Law School, University of Florida. Robert was a well-respected corporate and real estate attorney in Miami, Florida. He founded the law firms Geiger, Kuperstein, Riggs and Freud, also Levine and Geiger. His first marriage was to Francine Klebanoff, August 1972 at Tenafly, New Jersey.[182] They were divorced 29 January 1979 at Miami-Dade, Florida.[183] His second marriage was to Donna Kolikoff on 7 October 1979 at Florida.[184] Their marriage ended in divorce. Donna and Robert had a son, Adam Scott, who is still living.

Gary Alan Geiger

Gary Alan Geiger was the first of two children born to Milton Geiger and Alma Petrine Holm-Reischl. Gary was born 12 September 1939 at Hennepin, Minnesota.[185] I learned that Gary had several careers, first as a sales manager, then working for many years as a security analyst for the Internal Revenue Service. However he especially enjoyed his part-time career as an entertainer, and he was a successful

Robert Stephen Geiger

Gary Geiger

D.J. working at weddings and other events at Atlanta, Georgia. While residing at Plantation, a retirement community in Leesburg, Florida, Gary became a Master of Ceremonies for many community events both in and outside his retirement community as well as an announcer for countless soft ball league games. He was known as the *Voice of Plantation,* and he was voted as Best of the Best Emcees by the Daily Commercial newspaper survey. He also did voiceovers for cable TV in Atlanta, Georgia. He was an Army veteran. Gary married Jaqueline Ulrich 3 June 1961 at Hennepin, Minnesota.[186] They divorced December 1978. Gary and Jacqueline had three children, all still living: Theresa Ann Geiger, Gary Michael Geiger, David Alan Geiger. Gary's second marriage was to Corriene Seider August 1979; the marriage ended in divorce December 1983. Gary married Margery Speckin Defaut 18 August 1984 at Waukesha, Wisconsin.[187] While living at Atlanta, Georgia, Gary with his wife Margery became business partners for their D.J. business "Two Frogs on Horseback" for 20 years. Gary had a wonderful sense of humor and a sparkling personality. He loved his family and was proud of their accomplishments. Gary Geiger died 30 May 2019 at Tavares Hospice House, Tavares, Florida. Margery Geiger is still living.

Julie Ann Geiger

Julie Ann Geiger is the second of two children born to Milton Mark Geiger and Alma Petrine Holm. She is still living.

Locating Relatives

No one in the family knew what happened to Milton Geiger's descendants or where they were. I decided to try to find them. I was eventually successful and immediately put Milton's descendants from his first wife Dorothy in touch with descendants from his second wife Alma. This was a mitzvah and happy result of my family research. They all wanted to know about each other and were extremely grateful to me. It was quite an emotional experience to hear how Gary expressed his shock and sadness that he never knew that he had a half-brother Richard Geiger. Gary's father Milton never told him about his Jewish heritage or about his grandfather Charles Geiger. Gary's sister Julie was also over-whelmed by this discovery. Both were happy and grateful to learn of their Geiger relatives. Their Geiger relatives were also pleased and amazed to meet their "lost cousins."

For my investigation I used a combination of finding vital records as well as online telephone directories. I first sent for Richard Geiger's death record in Florida and found that his wife was Judith Spiegel, with Richard's birth information and his mother's name. I then used Intelius to look up Judith Geiger and found her as being related to Richard Geiger and to Charles Veil, residing at Hollywood, Florida. I called the telephone number and spoke with Charles Veil, Judith's second husband, who told me Judith was deceased, however he gave me the name and telephone number for her daughter Cathy. I spoke with Cathy by telephone, introducing myself and telling her of my genealogical research. Cathy knew nothing about her grandfather Milton or his second family. She said her father Richard Geiger never discussed him. My husband and I visited with Cathy and her husband 2011 at Hollywood, Florida. Cathy was happy to learn she had more family and she provided valuable family information and photographs.

I searched Ancestry to find information about Milton Geiger, his second wife Alma and their children Gary and Julie. I did not know where Milton's children Gary or Julie were located, so I again went into vital records for Gary Geiger, piecing together where he moved to several states. By using telephone directories, I found he was living in a retirement community in Florida. I made telephone contact with Gary. My sudden information about his family and our relationship was both a shock and a pleasant surprise for Gary![188] Gary then gave me his sister Julie's telephone number in Minnesota. Julie was also both surprised and delighted to discover the rest of the family. Milton's descendants did not know about each other and Cathy told me she thought that she had no relatives. Cathy and Gary learned that they were uncle and niece. I was delighted to find our Geiger relatives. I hope Charles, Milton and Richard somehow know that their family came together after all. Since then, those descendants have been in frequent contact with one another in Florida.

The DNA Key

Jews from Eastern Europe generally did not acquire surnames prior to the 18th century until the Napoleonic Era during the late 18th–early 19th centuries. Hereditary surnames were mandated for tax collection and for military recruitment in the Austro-Hungarian Monarchy (1787), in the German states (1790) and in the Russian Empire (1804). It has been difficult to find vital records prior to the mid-1700s. The name Geiger in German means violinist or fiddler, perhaps the original Geiger name was based on this occupation. I reasoned clues for origins and migrations may be deduced through genetic testing and analysis in addition to the paper trail or lack thereof.

I wanted to go further back in time to trace direct patrilineal descent however at the beginning of my research all my known Geiger male ancestors were deceased. I needed to locate a living male Geiger relative who was a direct descendant of Charles Geiger. This finally happened when I located Charles Geiger's grandson Gary Geiger who was still living at the time of my DNA research. He graciously agreed to do both Y-DNA and autosomal testing through www.familytreedna.com. I hoped to understand the genetic origins of the male Geiger descendants for knowledge of their past migrations and ancestry through the centuries. The Y-DNA is passed down only from father to son thus Gary became the missing Geiger link. The Y-chromosome is unique in that it does not undergo a process of recombination; all other chromosome pairs recombine and exchange genetic material. Every male has genetic information on his Y-chromosome that is basically the same as his ancient male ancestors except for occasional mutations.

DNA tests analyze genetic material for haplotypes then categorize results by using a set of numbers or letters for the purpose of determining genetic relationships within a specific time frame of genealogical interest. A haplogroup is a group of similar and related descendant haplotypes that share a common ancestor, as defined by a unique event polymorphism at a specific locus in their DNA sequence, basically a type of mutation.[189] People within a haplogroup share similar numbers of short tandem repeats (STRs) and types of mutations called single nucleotide polymorphisms (SNPs). Haplogroup branches are assigned alphanumeric designators by geneticists. The International Society of genetic Genealogy (ISOGG) diagramed male Y-DNA haplogroups on a Phylogenetic Tree. Y-DNA haplogroups share numerous mutations unique to each haplogroup.

Based on the genetic tests of Gary's Y-DNA, his haplogroup was found to be E-M35 or E1b1b1, also known as E-L117. This haplogroup comprises a significant percentage of the Y-DNA found in tested Ashkenazi Jewish men (18%–20%) and is also found in tested Sephardic Jewish men (8%–30%).[190] The haplogroup E-L117 is one of the major founding lineages of the Jewish male population, transmitted by Jews who migrated to Europe from the Middle East and were later absorbed within the Jewish Ashkenazi or Sephardic populations.[191] Few Jewish families have been able to trace their family lines beyond the 18th century unless they were from prestigious/rabbinical families. A Y-DNA study indicated the E-L117 haplogroup was found in all documented and genetically tested patrilineal descendants of a prominent Hasidic rabbinical lineage from the Ukraine and Bessarabia, the Savran-Bendery Hasidic dynasty that developed into the Wertheim-Giterman Hasidic dynasty. This dynasty originated in the mid eighteenth century in Bessarabia and the Ukraine.[192] There were many marriage connections of this dynasty with other prominent rabbinical lineages throughout Europe and the Russian Empire including the Spira/Shapira/Shapiro rabbinical lineage tracing descent from Rashi.[193] Various Jewish subclades within the E1b1b1 haplogroup were first researched by genetic genealogists in 2010. They were found to originate in the Middle East; their emergence at estimated time periods coincided with historic Jewish events in that region.[194]

Distant Ancient Ancestors

The beginnings of modern man, *Homo sapiens,* emerged ca. 200,000 years ago in Africa. Some groups migrated away from their homelands in East and sub-Saharan Africa to the Near East where burial sites in Israel, Skhul and Qafzeh were discovered by archeologists and were dated respectively between 90,000 and 130,000 years old.[195] Genetic anthropology studies in the Middle East included Canaanite/Bronze Age Levantine populations. This period gave rise to Semitic-speaking populations from the Levant, Mesopotamia, the Arabian Peninsula and Horn of Africa. Speakers of East Semitic populations included people of the Akkadian Empire, Assyria, and Babylonia. Central Semitic populations were the Northwest Semitic languages and Arabic. Speakers of Northwest Semitic included the Canaanites, the Phoenicians, the Hebrews, and the Arameans. South Semitic populations included speakers of Modern South Arabian languages and Ethiopian Semitic languages. Records of Semitic languages began appearing in the late fourth millennium BCE. Between the 13th and 11th centuries BCE Canaanite speaking populations rose in an area corresponding to modern Israel, Jordan, Palestinian territories, and the Sinai Peninsula. Those were the lands of the Edomites, Moabites, Hebrews (Israelites/Judaeans/Samaritans), Ammonites and Amalekites.[196]

A major Y-DNA haplogroup, E-M215 also known as E1b1b emerged in East Africa ca. 22,400 years ago. The subclade E-M35 known as E1b1b1 emerged 22,400 years ago in North Africa with low frequencies in Egypt, Tunisia, Algeria, and Morocco. The E-M35 project in www.familytreedna.com further analyzed Gary Geiger's Y-DNA results to be within the subclade E1b1b1b2 also known as E-Z830. This is a recently discovered subclade that includes four distinct clusters of Z830 carriers, two of which are exclusively Jewish in origin. A study by M.F. Hammer et. al. supported the hypothesis that paternal gene pools of Jewish communities in Europe, North Africa, and the Middle East descend from a common Middle Eastern population.[197] Statistical evidence supported the hypothesis that Diaspora Jews from Europe, Northwest Africa, and the Near East genetically resembled each other more closely than they resembled their non-Jewish neighbors; they were less genetically divergent from each other than any other group of populations studied. The study concluded that a common Middle Eastern source population several thousand years ago predated contemporary Jewish populations.

Gary's Subclade

Gary allowed further testing to refine his Y-DNA results for more accurate time estimates when his subclade emerged. Results of Y-DNA testing indicated Gary's subclade was E-PF 1952. This subclade is called a Jewish cluster because it is composed mainly of Jewish males with ancient origins in the Middle East.[198] The approximate time that his E-PF 1952 subclade originated was during the Intermediate Bronze Age (2000–1500 BCE) estimated at ca. 4200 years before the present.[199] The Intermediate Bronze Age in Mesopotamia produced innovations such as metallurgy and bronze manufacture, the potter's wheel, proto-writing, written law codes, foundations for city and nation governments as well as astronomy, mathematics, and astrology.[200]

Gary Geiger's Y-DNA subclade E-PF 1952 was ancient and emerged from a prehistoric past. Gary Geiger was one of 47 matches within www.familytreedna.org found to be in the subclade E-PF 1952. Some matches were able to trace their ancestors through family trees and records to Germany, Poland, the Ukraine, Hungary, Belarus although several matches did not know their ancestors' origins. Earliest ancestor dates given by the matches were mainly from the 19th century, several from the 18th century and one from the 17th century. Some of the surnames in the subclade E-PF 1952 matched with Gary Geiger were Dreyer, Einstein (a direct descendant from the family of Albert Einstein), Herzfeld, Jacobs, Loewenstein, Nussbaum, Kuehnert, Stein, Zlot, Mathes, Wishnic, Leshok, Schorr, Heltzer, Blumberg, Arkin.[201]

Hebrew Origins

The subclade E-PF 1952 emerged in the Middle East during the time a new culture formed, designated the Ivriim or Habiru, and was in sharp contrast with other populations such as the Philistines and Canaanites. It should be mentioned that in Genesis 14:13 Abraham was named *Avram Ha-Ivri*, translated as Abram the Hebrew. Many scholars think the Habiru or Hebrews branched off from

Canaanite society; having lived in the land of Canaan. Archeologists who studied the culture of those ancient Hebrews were struck that the sites were devoid of pig bones, and they also found archaeological evidence that the Hebrews practiced circumcision and prohibited intermarriage with other cultures. The new Hebrew culture emphasized monotheism, moral and ethical behavior, prohibition of human sacrifice, and the importance of family history and genealogy. The dramatic transformation of a Hebrew culture happened suddenly within the span of a few generations; there was no sign of a violent invasion or infiltration by another ethnic group. The change appeared to be a revolution of belief and lifestyle. These first Hebrews lived in the highlands of the Judean hills and in the hills of Samaria.[202] They were Semitic speaking and semi-nomadic.

When there was a drought and crops destroyed, Joseph and other Hebrews left Canaan 1600 BCE to enter Egypt for improved conditions. The Jews who went to Egypt became enslaved by the pharaoh for 400 years until Moses the liberator led the Israelites out of Egypt 1200 BCE., back to the land of Canaan. The book of Exodus described their exodus from slavery, the revelation of the Mosaic Code of Law and the forty years of wandering in the Sinai. The Hebrews were now referred to as the People of Israel.[203]

Archaeological evidence was discovered that established the presence of the Israelites in the Middle East. The Merneptah Stele, 1208 BCE found in Thebes, Egypt referred to a people, Israel in Canaan being laid to waste by the Pharoah Merneptah. Archaeological ruins located at Tel, Dan in Israel were dated 797–776 BCE during the reign of the first king of the Northern Kingdom of Israel, King Jeroboam ben Nevat. A stele from the Assyrian ruler Shalmaneser III 825 BCE depicts King Jehu of the House of Omri, from the Northern Kingdom of Israel paying homage with tribute to King Shalmaneser III. A stele of king Mesha of Moab 840 BCE referred to Omri, Kingdom of Israel conquest of the Moabites. An inscription known as the Shiloah Inscription was found in the Siloam Tunnel at Jerusalem dated 8th century BCE and described how the tunnel was engineered by order of the Israelite King Hezekiah. The Shebna Inscription from the 7th century BCE described the contents of the tomb for the royal steward Shebna who served under King Hezekiah of Israel.[204]

King Nebuchadnezzar of Babylon besieged Jerusalem 605 BCE with subsequent demands to the Hebrew kings for tribute. After he deemed the tribute to be insufficient, he destroyed much of Jerusalem during 597 BCE and then destroyed King Solomon's Temple 587 BCE, known as the First Temple (completed 957 BCE). The Babylonians began a series of deportations of Israelites from Jerusalem to Babylon 597 BCE, 587 BCE and 582 BCE. This began the exile of Jews from the Kingdom of Judah. The Babylonian exile became known as the beginning of the Jewish Diaspora. After the fall of Babylon to the Persian king Cyrus the Great in 539 BCE, Cyrus allowed exiled Jews to return to Judah in 538 BCE however many Jews continued to live outside Eretz Israel. The Israelite refugees continued to live in Egypt and Babylon, also in northern Israel, Lebanon, the Achaemenid Empire (Persia) and Syria. The Jews that did return to Jerusalem laid the foundations for the Second Temple.[205] Babylon became one of many metaphors for the Jewish diaspora prior to the destruction of the Second Temple in 70 AD.

Although the ancient Israelites battled world powers such as Egypt, Babylon, and Assyria, it was the Romans who destroyed their Second Temple at Jerusalem in 70 CE scattering them from their homeland in another diaspora. This event started a rebellion against Roman rule by the Israelite Zealots 66–3 CE where they made their tragic last stand at Masada. After the destruction of the temple, another uprising by Jews against Roman rule continued during the Bar Kokhba revolt 132–135 CE; this led to many Jews being taken to Rome as slaves. There were as many as 50,000 Jews in and around Rome by the first century CE, who were initially scorned for their poverty and slave status. Eventually many of those slaves gained their freedom and continued to live in Rome as citizens.[206] Jews that remained in Italy built thriving communities in Rome, Genoa, Sicily, Florence, Venice, and Pisa.

Jewish Populations in Europe

After the fall of the Roman Empire, Jews in Europe migrated from Italy during the 4th century through the 10th century giving rise to Jewish populations in Germanic lands, Gaul (France) and Spain. By the sixth and seventh centuries Jews were found in Marseilles, Cologne, Mainz, Worms and Speyer employed as bankers, money lenders and merchants trading in swords, furs, spices, fragrances.[207] Mainz especially became a center of Jewish erudition, and a Yeshiva was founded in the 10th century by Gershom ben Judah attracting Jews from all over Europe including the biblical scholar Rabbi Shlomo Yitzchak known as Rashi (1040–1105).

The First Crusade began a period of massacres of Jews in Germanic lands from 1096–1349. By the 12th and 13th centuries CE, Jews were expelled from many countries in Western Europe such as England and France but were granted charters by Polish kings to settle in Poland and Lithuania for the purpose of managing estates, operate taverns, engage in money lending and other ventures prohibited to Christians by the Church. The Ashkenazi Jewish population expanded rapidly in Eastern Europe growing from about 15,000–25,000 people in the 13th–15th centuries to two million by 1800 and then eight million by 1939.[208]

Jews had a continuous living history for four thousand years. They have been a spiritual and intellectual force through the ages despite persecution and adversity. They preserved their ethnic identity while living among different peoples and cultures. They expressed their ideas not only in their own language but in practically all the major languages of the world.[209] Through the passage of time and different locations, names also changed as well as physical appearances and traits. Y-DNA testing confirmed that Jewish ancestral roots for my male Geiger lineage originated in the Middle East thousands of years ago. Their odyssey ended in Poland and Eastern Europe. Thanks to Charles Geiger's influence, persistence, love, and beneficence other Geiger descendants were also able to immigrate to the United States of America from Europe before and during the Shoah. Charles Geiger was a righteous man who observed basic Jewish ethical traditions such as *what is hateful to you, do not do to your neighbor.* He was immersed in *tzedakah meaning righteousness to do the right thing through acts of human kindness.*

Descendants of Chaskel Geiger

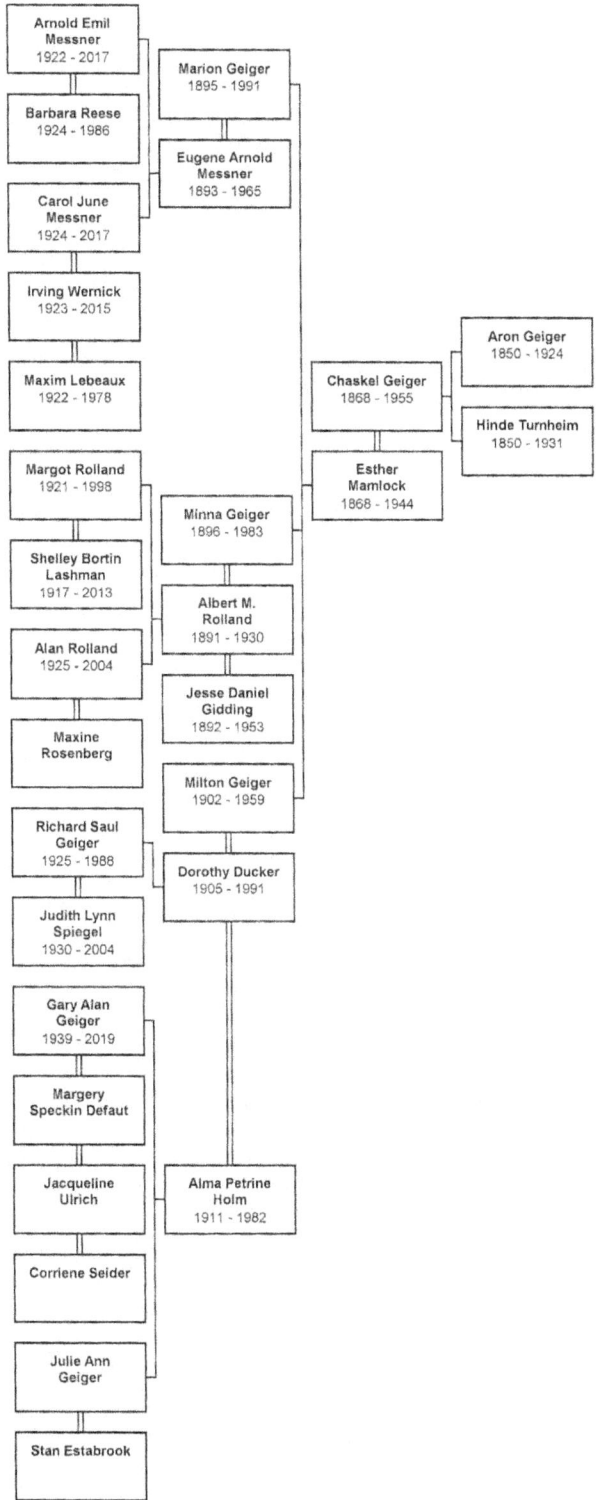

Name	Dates
Arnold Emil Messner	1922 - 2017
Barbara Reese	1924 - 1986
Carol June Messner	1924 - 2017
Irving Wernick	1923 - 2015
Maxim Lebeaux	1922 - 1978
Margot Rolland	1921 - 1998
Shelley Bortin Lashman	1917 - 2013
Alan Rolland	1925 - 2004
Maxine Rosenberg	
Richard Saul Geiger	1925 - 1988
Judith Lynn Spiegel	1930 - 2004
Gary Alan Geiger	1939 - 2019
Margery Speckin Defaut	
Jacqueline Ulrich	
Corriene Seider	
Julie Ann Geiger	
Stan Estabrook	
Marion Geiger	1895 - 1991
Eugene Arnold Messner	1893 - 1965
Minna Geiger	1896 - 1983
Albert M. Rolland	1891 - 1930
Jesse Daniel Gidding	1892 - 1953
Milton Geiger	1902 - 1959
Dorothy Ducker	1905 - 1991
Alma Petrine Holm	1911 - 1982
Chaskel Geiger	1868 - 1955
Esther Mamlock	1868 - 1944
Aron Geiger	1850 - 1924
Hinde Turnheim	1850 - 1931

Endnotes

1   Ancestry.com. New York City Directory 1898. Geiger and Braverman. 71 Essex Street.

2   Ancestry.com. New York, Naturalization Petitions, 1794–1906. Superior Court, New York County. 7 March 1891. Bundle Number 466. Naturalization of Charles Geiger.

3   City of New York, Municipal Archives. Manhattan. Marriage Records. Certificate Number 2970. Charles Geiger and Esther Mamluck. Date: 6 March 1894.

4   Ancestry.com. New York Passenger Lists 1820–1957. S.S.Resolute arriving in New York 22 August 1929 from Cherbourg, France. Line 30. Esther Geiger. Birthdate listed as 14 April 1868.

5   Ancestry.com. New York, New York Death Index 1862-1948.

6   Ancestry.com. 1900 Federal Census. Manhattan, New York. Enumeration District 79. Address: 230 East Broadway. Charles Geiger, Esther, Marion, Minnie.

7   Ancestry.com. New York, New York, Extracted Marriage Index, 1866–1937. Marriage: Minnie Mamluck and Michael Price. Date: 14 June 1891, Manhattan, New York. Certificate 7280.

8   Ancestry.com. 1900 Federal Census, Manhattan, New York. Fourth Assembly District, Enumeration District 0079.

9   Ancestry.com. New York, New York, Extracted Death Index 1862–1948. Death Michael Price 6 June 1904, Manhattan, New York.

10   Ancestry.com. New York State Census, 1905. Election District 4, Assembly District 26.

11   Ancestry.com. 1910 United States Federal Census. Manhattan Ward 19, Enumeration District 1067. 327 East 68th Street. Charles Geiger.

12   Ancestry.com. New York Passenger Lists 1820–1957. Charles Geiger. Age 42. S.S. Bremen. August 1910. Microfilm T715, roll 1535, line 20, p.6.

13   Ancestry.com. New York State Census 1915. Manhattan Assembly District 21, Election District 9.

14   Ancestry.com. 1920 United States Federal Census. Manhattan Assembly District 22, Enumeration District 1485. Charles Geiger.

15   Ancestry.com. New York State Census, 1925. Manhattan Assembly District 9-185, Election District 42.

16   New York Passenger Lists 1820-1957. 1927 Charles Geiger.

17   Ancestry.com. New York Passenger Lists 1820–1957. 1927 Charles Geiger. .

18   Ancestry.com. New York Passenger Lists 1820–1957. 1929 Charles Geiger, Esther Geiger, Minnie Price

19   Ancestry.com. 1930 United States Federal Census. Manhattan. Enumeration District 31-491. Charles Geiger.

20   Ancestry.com. 1940 United States Federal Census. Manhattan. Enumeration District 31-789. Charles Geiger.

21   The City of New York. Department of Health. Bureau of Records and Statistics. Manhattan. Charles Geiger. Death Certificate Number 156-55-109318. Date: 24 April 1955. Listed as an executive in the furniture business. Burial 25 April 1955 at Mt. Neboh Cemetery, Services at Riverside Memorial Chapel 180 West 26th Street, Manhattan.

22   Ancestry.com. New York, New York, Extracted Death index, 1862-1948. Esther Geiger. Death: 10 January 1944, Manhattan, New York. Certificate 1197.

23   Ackman and Ziff Genealogy Institute. Center for Jewish History. Landsmanshaften. (genealogy.cjh. org).

24   Ancestry.com. New York, New York, Extracted Death Index, 1862-1948. Death 25 May 1946 Minnie Price. Birth year ca. 1866. Certificate 12086.

25   The Role of the Levites. Levites constantly risked their lives for G-d's service such as carrying the sanctified vessels of the Tabernacle through the desert. They were the guards, gatekeepers and musicians of the Temple. They assisted the Kohanim with Temple functions. Levites had no ownership of land and depended on tithes and gifts of food for their sustenance. Levites were also exempt from military service

however they were required to take part in saving lives. Levites also functioned as spiritual teachers for the Israelites. (www.cohen-levi.org).

26   Ackman and Ziff Genealogy Institute. Center for Jewish History. Landsmanshaften. (genealogy.cjh. org).

27   Yivo Institute for Jewish Research. Downtown Talmud Torah. (www.yivoarchives.org/index).

28   Personal records of this writer.

29   Ancestry.com. New York, State and Federal Naturalization Records, 1794-1943. Leon Sobel, Naturalization Date: 25 Oct 1893. Witnessed by Charles Geiger.

30   Ancestry.com. 1910 United States Federal Census. Leon Sobel head. Adelina, spouse. Address: 1487 First Avenue. Immigration Year 1887. Birth: Nov 1864.

31   Personal letter from Carol Lebeaux. Dated June 2013.

32   Personal Records from Liz L. Letters written by Charles Geiger to Pearl and George Bronz. 5 December 1938. E-mailed to this writer 26 June 2010.

33   Ibid., 13 July 1939.

34   Ibid., 17 July 1941.

35   Ancestry.com. 1900 United States Federal Census. Manhattan, New York. Enumeration District 79. Esther Geiger gave her birthdate as April 1869 at New York.

36   Ibid., Death Esther Geiger. 10 January 1944. Manhattan, New York. Certificate 1197.

37   Ancestry.com. Extracted Marriage Index, 1866-1937. Marriage Charles Geiger and Esther Mamlock. 6 March 1894 at Manhattan, New York. Certificate 2970.

38   Ancestry.com. Historical Newspapers, Birth, Marriage & Death Announcements, 1851-2003. *New York Times*. 1857-current file. Esther Geiger. Obituary 12 January 1944.

39   Ancestry.com. New York, New York, Death Index, 1892–1898. Death date: 9 June 1897 at New York, New York. Meyer Mamlock. Certificate 17330.

40   Ancestry.com. 1870 United States Federal Census. Manhattan, New York. Ward 1, District 3. Max Mameluke (Mamlock).

41   Ancestry.com. New York, State and Federal Naturalization records, 1794–1943. Meyer Mamlock, Oath of Allegiance 29 January 1885, New York

42   Ancestry.com. U.S. Passport Applications, 1795–1925. Passport Issue Date: 29 April 1892. Birthdate: 12 February 1832, Kochwien Province, Posen, Germany.

43   Ancestry.com. Victoria Tauber Family Tree. Public Family Tree. .

44   Ancestry.com. New York Passenger and Crew Lists 1820–1957. Nathan Sobel arrived at New York 4 October 1859 on the S.S. Teutonia from Hamburg, Germany.

45   Ancestry.com. Altman, Cohen, Sobel, Stacy Family Tree. Public Member Trees.

46   Ancestry.com. 1910 United States Federal Census. Manhattan Ward 12, New York. Enumeration District 0558. Frederick Sobel, head. Sarah, wife.

47   Ancestry.com. 1870 United States Federal Census. Manhattan Ward 3, District 5, New York. Address: 181 Dey Street. Frederick Sobel, Sarah and child Samuel.

48   Ancestry.com. New York, New York, Extracted Death Index, 1862-1948. Death Minnie Price. 25 May 1946. Manhattan, New York. Certificate 12086.

49   Ancestry.com. New York, New York, Extracted Marriage Index, 1866-1937. Date: 14 June 1891. Manhattan, New York. Marriage Minnie Mamluck and Michael Price. Certificate 7280.

50   Ancestry.com. 1900 United States Federal Census. Manhattan, New York. Enumeration District 0079. Michael Price, Minnie, Carolina Mamlock living at 232 East Broadway, New York, New York.

51   Ancestry.com. New York, New York, Extracted Death Index, 1862–1948. Death: 6 June 1904, Michael Price. Certificate 21213.

52   Ancestry.com. New York, New York, Extracted Death Index, 1862–1948. Death Julius Mamluck. 5 August 1939. Queens County, New York. Certificate 5506.

53   Ancestry.com. New York, New York, Extracted Marriage Index 1866-1937. Marriage Date: 22 March 1887 at Manhattan, New York. Julius Mamluck and Effie Brull. Certificate 82837.

54   Ancestry.com. New York, New York, Index to Birth Certificates, 1866–1909. Name: Julius Mamluck. Birthplace: U.S. Certificate 10290.

55   Ancestry.com. New York, New York, Extracted Death Index, 1862–1948. Death Date: 31 December 1945 at Manhattan, New York. Effie Mamluck. Certificate 129.

56   Ancestry.com. 1900 United States Federal Census. Manhattan, New York. Enumeration District 860. Julius Mamluck.

57   Henry Campbell Black. Black's Law Dictionary. (St. Paul Minnesota: West Publishing Co., 1979). Pp. 1140–1141.

58   Ancestry.com. 1905 New York State Census. A.D. 21, E. D. 35. Julius Mamluck.

59   Ancestry.com. 1910 United States Federal Census. Manhattan, New York, Ward 12. Julius Mamluck.

60   Ancestry.com. 1915 New York State Census. Manhattan, New York. E.D.10. Julius Mamluck.

61   Ancestry.com. NARA. U.S. Passport Applications, 1795–1925. Roll 2048. Certificates 199350-199725. Passport Issue Date: 29 June 1922. Certificate No. 199723. Julius Mamluck.

62   Ancestry.com. Historical Newspapers, Death Announcements, 1851-2003. *New York Times* obituary 7 August 1939. Julius Mamluck.

63   FindAGrave.com. Julius Mamluck. Interred Bayside Cemetery, Ozone Park, New York.

64   Ancestry.com. Social Security Death Index listed Marion Messner née Geiger's birthdate as 10 January 1895.

65   Ancestry.com. New York City Births 1891–1902. Marion Geiger, parents Charles and Esther Geiger. It is possible that her birthdate was given later to the municipal registry and was mistakenly recorded.

66   Municipal Archives, the City of New York. Marriage Records, Manhattan. Certificate Number 29205. Eugene Arnold Messner and Marion Geiger. Date: 12 October 1920.

67   New York Public Library. Manhattan, New York. Manhattan telephone directory 1945.

68   Ancestry.com. Social Security Death Index. Manhattan. Marion Messner. Date of Death: 3 December 1991.

69   Ancestry.com. Global, Find a Grave Index for Burials at Sea and other Select Burial Locations,1300s-Current. Marion Messner. Death Date: 1991. Burial: Salem Fields Cemetery, Brooklyn, New York.

70   Autobiography written by Marion Messner in 1985. Copy sent by Steve Messner, July 2018.

71   Ancestry.com. Social Security Death Index. Eugene Messner. Birthdate listed as 27 April 1893, Death date in October 1965. His children provided exact death date as 2 October 1965.

72   Ancestry.com. New York Extracted Death Index 1862–1948. Death Eugene Messner 2 October 1965, New York.

73   FindAGrave.com. Global, Find a Grave Index for Burials at Sea and Other Select Burial Locations, 1300s-Current. Eugene Messner. Death: 2 October 1965. Burial: Salem Fields Cemetery, Brooklyn, New York.

74   Ancestry.com. New York Abstracts of WWI Military Service 1917–1919 for Eugene Messner.

75   Ancestry.com. 1920 United States Census. Manhattan, New York. A.D.11. Eugene Messner.

76   City of New York. Department of Health. Municipal Archives. Marriage Records for Manhattan, New York. Eugene Arnold Messner and Marion Geiger. Certificate 29205.

77   Ancestry.com. 1925 New York State Census, Manhattan, New York. E.D. 42. Eugene Messner.

78   Ancestry.com. 1930 United States Federal Census. E.D. 60-99. Croton on Hudson Village, New York. Eugene Messner.

79   Ancestry.com. 1940 United States Federal Census. E.D. 31-596. Manhattan, New York. Eugene Messner.

80   Ancestry.com. WWII Draft Registration. Eugene Messner. Serial No. 1155.

81   Ancestry.com. New York Passenger and Crew Lists, 1820–1957. Emil Messner. Date of Arrival: 8 May 1869. Ship: S.S. Union from Bremen, Germany to New York. (www.ancestry.com).

82   Ibid., Emil Messner. Date of Arrival: 26 June 1873. Ship: S.S. Hammonia from Hamburg, Germany to New York.

83   Ancestry.com. U.S. Passport Applications, 1795-1925. Harold Hans Messner. Passport issued 6 July 1923. Certificate 320532.

84   Ancestry.com. 1870 United States Federal Census. Ward 4. Leavenworth, Kansas. Emil Messner. Store clerk.

85   Ancestry.com. U.S. City Directories, 1822–1995. 1870 City Directory for Leavenworth, Kansas. Emil Messner.

86   Ancestry.com. 1880 United States Federal Census. E.D. 267. New York County, New York. Emil Messner.

87   Ancestry. New York, New York, Extracted Marriage Index, 1866–1937. Marriage Emil Messner and Betty Shuster, 14 December 1884 at Manhattan, New York. Cert. 40376

88   Ancestry.com. 1900 United States Federal Census. E.D. 621. Manhattan, New York. Emil Messner.

89   Ancestry. Com. New York, State Census, 1905. Manhattan, New York. Assembly District 23, Election District 20. Emil Messner.

90   Ancestry.com. 1910 United States Census. Ward 12, Manhattan, New York. Emil Messner.

91   FindAGrave.com. Global, Find a Grave Index for Burials at Sea and Other Select Burial Locations, 1300's–Current. Death Record: Emil Messner. Death date 8 February 1913.

92   Ancestry.com. United States Social Security Death Index, 1935-2014. Death: 8 May 1990. Harold H. Messner.

93   Ancestry.com. New York Extracted Marriage Index 1866–1937. Marriage: Harold Messner and Sally Altman on 25 August 1931. Certificate 20054.

94   Ancestry.com. U.S. Social Security Death Index, 1935–2014. Death: 3 May 2003. Sally A. Messner.

95   Ancestry.com. 1940 United States Federal Census. E.D. 31-527. Harold Messner. New York, New York.

96   Ancestry.com. U.S. World War II Draft Registration Cards, 1942. Harold Messner. New York City, New York.

97   Ancestry.com. New York Extracted Death Index 1862-1948. Betty Shuster Messner Death 8 October 1936 Manhattan. Certificate 21945.

98   Ancestry.com. WWI, Draft Registration cards 1917–1918. Julian Messner.

99   Ancestry.com. U.S. Passport Applications 1795-1925. Julian Messner. Passport Issue Date 20 April 1922. Certificate 150335.

100 Ancestry.com. New York City Marriage License Indexes 1907–2018. Marriage Julian Messner and Kathryn G. Karn 10 May 1929. Certificate 10786.

101 Ancestry.com. New York State Passenger and Crew Lists 1917-1967. Kathryn G. Messner, Birth 25 Nov 1902, Chicago.

102 Ancestry.com. 1940 United States Federal Census. E.D. 31-1382. Julian Messner.

103 Ancestry.com. All Historical Newspapers, Birth, Marriage and Death Announcements, 1851-2003. *New York Times*. Obituary for Julian Messner, 9 February 1948.

104 Newspapers.com. *The Daily Record* (Long Branch, New Jersey). Kathryn Messner. Obituary 5 August 1964. p.4.

105 Ancestry.com. U.S. World War II Draft Registration Cards, 1942. Julian Messner.

106 Ancestry.com. Global, Find A Grave Index for Burials at Sea and other Select Burial Locations, 1300's – Current. Betty Messner. Birth: 28 June 1858. Death: 8 October 1936. Burial Salem Fields Cemetery, Brooklyn, New York.

107 Ancestry.com. 1880 United States Federal Census. E.D. 162. Manhattan, New York. Arnold Shuster.

108 Email received 27 February 2014 from franluebke @ wi.rr.com. Moenchsroth Records.

109 Ancestry.com. New York, State and Federal Naturalization Records, 1794-1943. Arnold D. Shuster. Oath Date: 8 September 1859, New York.

110 Ancestry.com. 1860 United States Federal Census. Ward 14, District 2. New York. Arnold Shuster.

111 Ancestry.com. U.S. Find a Grave Index, 1600's-Current. Arnold D. Shuster born 1812 and died 1890. Salem Fields Cemetery, Brooklyn, New York.

112 FindAGrave.com. U.S. Find a Grave Index, 1600's-Current. Johanna Schuster. Death: 24 February 1882. Salem Fields Cemetery, Brooklyn, New York.

113 George C. Groce and David H. Wallace. The New York Historical Society's *Dictionary of Artists in America, 1564–860*. New Haven: Yale University Press, 1957. Ancestry.com. *Biography and Genealogy Master Index.*

114 Ancestry.com. U.S. IRS Tax Assessment Lists, 1862–1918. Arnold D. Shuster. Tax Years 1862-1865. New York.

115 Ancestry.com. U.S. Social Security Death Index. Minna Gidding born 3 September 1896; died September 1983 in New York City.

116 Municipal Archives, New York City. Marriage Certificate Number 16728. 17 June 1919. Albert M. Rolland and Minna Geiger.

117 Municipal Archives. New York City. Marriage Records, Manhattan. Certificate 16728. Date of Marriage: 17 June 1919, Albert M. Rolland and Minna Geiger.

118 Ancestry.com. New York, New York Death Index 1862-1948. Death Certificate 19535. Albert M. Rolland died 15 August 1930 in Manhattan, New York.

119 Ancestry.com. New Jersey Marriage Index 1901–2016. Bride Index 1930-1935 E-K. Minna Geiger married Jesse Gidding 1932.

120 Ancestry. Michigan Marriage Records 1867–1952. Marriage 25 June 1929 at Detroit, Michigan. Jesse D. Gidding and Irene Rosenberg. Certificate 365662.

121 Ancestry.com. 1930 Federal Census, Manhattan, New York. District 0424. Jesse D. Gidding with his wife Irene.

122 Ancestry.com. Social Security Death Index 1935–Current. Death of Jesse D. Gidding 11 Aug 1953, New York.

123 Newspapers.com. *The Courier-News* (Bridgewater, New Jersey). Date: 13 August 1953, p. 30. Obituary Jesse D. Gidding.

124 Ancestry.com. U.S., Social Security Death Index, 1935-Current. Death of Minna Gidding in September 1983.

125 Ancestry.com. City of New York. Department of Health. Bureau of Vital Records and Statistics. Special Certificate 19931. Milton Geiger. Birth 27 April 1902 to parents Charles Geiger and Esther Mamluck. This record was a delayed registration of Milton Geiger's birth. The record was issued 23 July 1942. An abstract of evidence was recorded: the 1905 New York State census listing Milton and his parents also a record of when Milton Geiger entered school in September 1908, date of birth given 27 April 1902.

126 Municipal Archives, New York City, Marriage Records. Manhattan. Certificate Number 6810. Milton M. Geiger and Dorothy A. Ducker. 5 March 1925.

127 Ancestry.com. New York, New York Index to Birth Certificates 1866–1909. Birth of Dorothy Annette Ducker 5 February 1905. Kings County, New York.

128 Ancestry.com. State of Florida. Office of Vital Statistics. Death Certificate 070477. Richard Geiger. Date of Birth: 23 November 1925. Date of Death: 22 July 1988.

129 Ancestry.com. 1930 Federal Census. Manhattan. Enumeration District 31-416. Address: 90 Riverside Drive.

130 Ancestry.com. Florida Death Index 1877–1998. Dorothy D. Geiger. Death: 25 June 1991. Florida.

131 Ancestry.com. Minnesota Marriages Index, 1849–1950. Marriage: Milton M. Geiger and Alma Holm Reischl on 12 January 1937, Carver, Minnesota. FHL Film Number 1434895.

132 Minnesota Official Marriage System 1850-2019. Marriage: 7 November 1928. Alma Petrine Holm and Frank Reischl. Hennepin, Minnesota. (moms.mn.gov.)

133 Ancestry.com. Minnesota, Birth Index, 1900-1934. Gloria Jean Rieschl. Birth: 13 May 1929. Hennepin, Minnesota. Certificate 1929-35575.

134 Ancestry.com. All U.S. Social Security Death Index 1935–2014. Gloria Jean Ebner. Birth: 13 May 1929. Death: 7 June 2009, Palm Springs, California.

135 Vital Statistics, Minnesota Department of Health. Death Certificate Number 26915. 29 November 1959. Milton M. Geiger.

136 St. Paul, Minnesota. Minnesota Historical Society. *Minneapolis Tribune.* 1 December 1959. Obituaries, p.25. Milton M. Geiger.

137 St. Paul, Minnesota. Minnesota Historical Society. Minnesota Department of Health. Section of Vital Statistics. Milton M. Geiger. Death Certificate Number 5800. Death 29 November 1959.

138 New York, New York Birth Index 1910–1965. Arnold E. Messner. Birth: 19 March 1922. Manhattan, New York.

139 Ancestry.com. New Jersey Death Index 1901–2017. Arnold Messner. Birth: 19 March 1922 at New York; Death: 1 June 2017 at New Jersey.

140 Wikipedia.org. Philology is the study of language in oral and written historical sources to establish their authenticity and meaning.

141 Ancestry.com. U.S. WWII Draft Cards Young Men, 1940–1947. Arnold Messner.

142 Ancestry.com. U.S. World War II Army Enlistment Records 1938–1946. Arnold E. Messner. Military Service 24 Aug 1942, Cleveland, Ohio. Reserve Corps on active duty.

143 New York City Municipal Archives. Marriage Indexes 1907–1995. Marriage Arnold E. Messner and Barbara Reese, 26 April 1946, Manhattan. Certificate 13383. Note the discrepancy of the marriage date as recalled by Arnold Messner and his family with the date on the marriage certificate.

144 Ancestry.com. U.S., School Yearbooks, 1900–1990. Oberlin College Year Book 1947. Arnold Emil Messner.

145 Cindy Adams. New York Post article Celebs Who Gamble. 26 February 2010. Forwarded by Carol Lebeaux.

146 Ancestry.com. New York, New York Birth Index 1910–1965. Barbara Reese. Birth: 5 February 1924. Bronx, New York. Certificate 1811.

147 ItalianGen.org. Marriages in Manhattan. Harry Reese married to Blanche Schaumburger, 3 June 1917. Certificate 18145.

148 ItalianGen.org. Marriages in Manhattan. Charles Schaumburger married to Rebecca Lindeman, 4 October 1892. Certificate 12198.

149 Ancestry.com. 1940 United States Federal Census. Bronx, New York. E.D. 3-1489. Charles Schaumburger. Address: 1924 University Avenue. Bronx, New York.

150 Ancestry.com. New York, New York Birth Index 1910-1965. Carol J. Messner. Birth: 15 June 1924. Manhattan, New York.

151 Ancestry.com. U.S. Social Security Applications and Claims Index 1936–2007: Alex Goldfarb.

152 Ancestry.com. Federal Census 1930, Manhattan, New York. Enumeration District 31-25A, 10th Assembly District.

153 Ancestry.com. Cook County, Illinois. Genealogy Records: Marriage of Irving Wernick with Carol June Messner, 11 May 1948. File 2027362.

154 Slade School of Fine Arts, London, UK. Announcement of the Irving Wernick Scholarship, August 2015. In memory of Slade alumnus Irving Wernick.

155 Ancestry.com. England and Wales Civil Registration Marriage Index 1837–2005. Volume 5D, page 1024.

156 Ancestry.com. New York City Municipal Archives. Marriage Indexes 1907–1995. Marriage: 1951, Manhattan. Maxim I. Lebeaux to Carol J. Wernick, certificate 4997.

157 Ancestry.com. U.S. Department of Veterans Affairs BIRLS Death File, 1850–2010. Maxim Lebeaux.

158 Ancestry.com. All Society and Employment Directories. Massachusetts, Mason Membership Cards, 1773–1990. New England Historic Genealogical Society, Boston, Massachusetts. Maxim Ian Lebeaux.

159 Ancestry.com. Massachusetts Death Index, 1970–2003. Maxim I. Lebeaux, death 15 May 1978, Boston. Certificate 003627.

160 Ancestry.com. U.S. Social Security Applications and Claims Index 1936–2007. Margot Ellen Rolland. Birthdate: 8 January 1921; Death Date: 24 March 1998.

161 Ancestry.com. New York City Municipal Archives, New York. Marriage: Margot E. Rolland and Shelley B. Lashman, 22 July 1944, New York. License 19300.

162 Ancestry.com. All Society and Employment Directories. Massachusetts, Mason Membership Cards, 1773-1990. New England Historic Genealogical Society, Boston, Massachusetts. Maxim Ian Lebeaux.

163 Ancestry.com. 1940 Federal Census: Camden, New Jersey. Shelley Lashman, age 23.

164 Navy Department Library. Navy Register: Officers of the U.S. Naval Reserve; Year 1967. Ancestry.com. Navy and Marine Corps Registries 1814–1992).

165 Ancestry.com. U.S. Obituary Collection, 1930–2017. Shelley Lashman; Death 16 December 2013. Obituary: Brigantine, New Jersey, 19 December 2013.

166 Ancestry.com. New York, New York, Birth Index 1910-1965. Alan Rolland. Birth 13 February 1925, Manhattan, New York.

167 Telephone interview with Maxine Rolland, 30 November 2011.

168 Ancestry.com. U.S. Social Security Applications and Claims Index. 1936–2007. Death: Alan Rolland, 11 May 2004.

169 Ancestry.com. Florida Death Index, 1877-1998. Richard Geiger. Birthdate: 23 November 1925. Death: 22 July 1988, Broward County, Florida. Also note that the Social Security Death Index has a Richard W. Geiger with the same date of death as 22 July 1988, however the birthdate given is 23 November 1924.

170 Ancestry.com. U.S. World War II Draft Cards Young Men, 1940–1947. Richard Saul Geiger. Date: 23 November 1943.

171 Ancestry.com. U.S., World War II Army Enlistment Records, 1938–1946. Richard S. Geiger. Service Number 42074842. Enlistment Place: New York City, New York.

172 Ancestry.com. All Historical Newspapers Birth, Marriage and Death Announcements, 1851–2003. Marriage Announcements. New York Times. 22 August 1949. Judith Spiegel Wed to Richard S. Geiger.

173 Ancestry.com. 1940 Federal Census. Kings County, New York. ED 24-300. Emanuel Spiegel. Address: 1439 East 15th Street, Brooklyn.

174 Ancestry.com. U.S. World War II Draft Cards Young Men, 1940-1947. Richard Saul Geiger. Date: 23 November 1943.

175 Ancestry.com. New York, New York. Birth Index 1910–1965. Birth: 15 September 1930. Judith Spiegel.

176 Ancestry.com. New York, New York. Marriage License Indexes, 1907–2018. Marriage License: 13 September 1928. Emanuel M. Spiegel and Frieda Cohn. No. 22783.

177 Ancestry.com. New York, New York. Extracted Marriage Index. 1866–1937. Marriage Date: 10 October 1928. Emanuel M. Spiegel and Freida Cohn. Np. 24049.

178 Ancestry.com. 1940 United States Federal Census. E.D. 24-300. Address: 1437 E. 15th Street. Kings County. Emanuel M. Spiegel.

179 Ancestry.com. New York, New York, Marriage License Indexes, 1907–2018. Marriage License: 5 August 1949. Judith L. Spiegel and Richard S. Geiger. License No. 20539.

180 Ancestry.com. All U.S. Social Security Death Index 1935–2014. Judith Geiger. Death: 2 August 2004, Hollywood, Florida.

181 Ancestry.com. U.S., Social Security Death Index, 1935–2014. Robert S. Geiger. Birth: 25 October 1950. Death: 6 February 2004.

182 Ancestry.com. New Jersey Marriage Index 1901–2016. Marriage Date: August 1972. Tenafly, New Jersey. Robert S. Geiger and Francine Klebanoff.

183 Ancestry.com. Florida, Divorce Index, 1927–2001. Divorce Date: 29 January 1979. Miami, Florida. Robert Stephen Geiger and Francine. Cert. 001648.

184 Ancestry.com. Florida, Marriage Indexes, 1822–1875, 1927–2001. Marriage date: 7 October 1979. Robert S. Geiger and Donna L. Kolikof. Miami, Florida. Cert. 077887.

185 Ancestry.com. Minnesota Birth Index 1935–2000. Birth: 12 September 1939, Hennepin, Minnesota. Gary Alan Geiger.

186 Ancestry.com. Minnesota Marriage Index 1958–2001. Marriage Date: 3 June 1961, Hennepin, Minnesota. Gary Alan Geiger and Jaqueline Ulrich.

187 Ancestry.com, Wisconsin Marriage Index 1973–1997. Marriage: 18 August 1984, Waukesha, Wisconsin. Gary Alan Geiger and Margery Defaut Speckin. Certificate 018657.

188 Telephone interview with Gary Geiger 6 November 2011.

189 Blaine T. Bettinger and Debbie Parker Wayne. *Genetic Genealogy in Practice.* (Arlington, Virginia: National Genealogical Society), 2016. Pp.1–42.

190 Jeffrey Mark Paull and Jeffrey Briskman. "Connecting to the Wertheim-Giterman Rabbinical Lineage Through Y-DNA." *Avotaynu.* Volume XXX, No. 3. Fall, 2014. Pp.46–53.

191 A.A. Aliev. Origin of "Jewish" Clusters of E1b1b1 (M35) haplogroup. *The Russian Journal of Genetic Genealogy*; 1(1):47-49, 2010. (ru.jjgg.org).

192 Jeffrey Mark Paull and Jeffrey Briskman. "Connecting to the Wertheim-Giterman Rabbinical Lineage Through Y-DNA." *Avotaynu.* Volume XXX, no.3, Fall 2014. Pp. 51–52.

193 e1b1b1-m35.blogspot.com/2015/06/e1b1b1-l117-chassidic-rabbinical.html.

194 A.A. Aliev. Origin of Jewish Clusters of E1b1b1 (M35) haplogroup. *The Russian Journal of Genetic Genealogy*; 1 (1): 48–49, 2010. (ru.rjgg.org.)

195 Emma Groeneveld. Early Human Migration. Ancient History Encyclopedia. 15 May 2017. (www.ancient.eu/article/1070/early-human-migration/).

196 Ancient Semitic-speaking peoples. (en.wikipedia.org/wiki/Ancient_Semitic-speaking_peoples).

197 M.F. Hammer, A.J.Redd, E.T. Wood, M.R. Bonner, H. Jarjanazi, T.Karafet, S. Santachiara-Benerecetti, A.Oppenheim, M.A. Jobling, T.Jenkins, H. Ostrer, and B.Bonne-Tamir. "Jewish and Middle Eastern non-Jewish populations share a common pool of Y-chromosome biallelic haplotypes." *Proceedings of the National Academy of Sciences of the United States of America.* 2000 June 6, 97 (12) pp. 6769–6774.

198 www.haplozone.net/e3b/project/cluster/4. Cluster Analysis. Cluster Name: E-PF 1952. Formerly known as cluster E-Z830-B- Jewish Cluster.

199 Aaron R. Brown. Email 23 March 2019. ISOGG. Estimate age of E-PF1952 as 4200 BCE.

200 Wikipedia.org. The Bronze Age.

201 www.haplozone.net/e3b/project/cluster4. Chart of member haplotypes with genetic matches to Gary Geiger for Cluster E-PF 1952.

202 Wikipedia. History of Ancient Israel and Judah. www.wikipedia.com. Also see Israel Finkelstein and Neil Asher Silberman. *The Bible Unearthed.* 2001.

203 Max I. Dimont. *Jews, God and History.* (New York: New American Library 1962). Pp.33–43.

204 www.academia.edu./Documents/in/Archaeology_of_Ancient_Israel.

205 Babylonian Captivity. (en.wikipedia.org/wiki/Babylonian_captivity).

206 iogg.info/11/coffman.htm.

207 Jon Entine. *Abraham's Children.* New York: Grand Central Publishing, 2007. Pp. 203–204.

208 Ellen Levy-Coffman. "A Mosaic of People: the Jewish Story and a Reassessment of the DNA Evidence." *Journal of Genetic Genealogy.* 2005. V.1, pp.12–33.

209 Max I. Dimont. *Jews, God and History.* (New York: New American Library 1962). Pp.15–16.

Chapter Seven

Abraham Yitzak Geiger and Sprynca Stark

Beginning

After the birth of Charles Geiger, the second child born to Aron and Hinde Geiger was Naftale Geiger (1871–1877) who died before reaching adulthood. Abraham Yitzak Geiger was the third child born 19 November 1872 at Przemyśl, Podkarpackie, Poland to Aron Geiger and Hinde Turnheim.[1] His bris was on 26 November 1872. The house number listed on his birth record was number 153, a different house number from the birth record of his older brother Chaskel Geiger. Rabbi Schmelkes officiated and Dwore Mark was the midwife. The relatives listed as godparents (*Patrini*) were Hinde Turnheim's brother Benjamin Turnheim and his wife Chaje Reisel Gans. Abraham's birth was considered *legitimi* because by 1872 his parents paid whatever marriage tax was due, registered their marriage with municipal authorities and with the official rabbinate thus legitimizing their offspring.

His Connection with the Blozhova Rabbi

Abraham Yitzak Geiger followed the Geiger rabbinical tradition by becoming an Orthodox and Hasidic Rabbi. He should not be confused with the German

Birth record for Abraham Geiger, 1872 Przemyśl, Poland

born Rabbi Abraham Geiger who modernized Judaism and led the way to the Reform Jewish movement. The latter Abraham Geiger was born 24 May 1810 at Frankfurt, Germany and died 23 October 1874 at Berlin, Germany.[2] By contrast, my great uncle Rabbi Abraham Geiger was raised in an Orthodox and Hasidic home and adhered to traditional Judaism. While living at Błażowa, Podkarpackie, Poland he studied with noted Hasidic rabbis descended from the Dinov rabbinical dynasty. Błażowa became known for their Hasidic dynasty of rabbis, namely Grand Rabbi Tzvi Elimelech Spira (1841–1924) who became the Blozhova (Yiddish) rabbi. In addition, Abraham Geiger also became a *mohel* and the *gabbai* to the Grand Rabbi Tzvi Elimelech Spira of Blozhov (Błażowa). Rabbi Abraham Geiger was listed as the *mohel* during the year 1935 in the Virtual Shtetl History of Błażowa.[3] The *mohel* is trained in the *brit milah* or covenant of circumcision when the Jewish male baby is 8 days old. The *gabbai* or shamash ensures the synagogue services run smoothly and is the personal assistant to the head rabbi.

Family Background and Influence of the Bluzhover Rabbi

Rabbi Tzvi Elimelech Spira (1783–1841) of Dinov (Dynów), Podkarpackie, Poland was a renowned scholar and nephew of Rebbe Elimelech of Lizhensk.[4] Rabbi Tzvi Elimelech Spira was best known for his mystical work *Bnei Yissaschar*; he was the son of Pesach and Ita Langsam. When Rabbi Tzvi Elimelech was drafted in the army, a miracle was reported. The wagon he was riding in overturned on a bridge and all the draftees died in the river; he was the lone survivor. To avoid being taken by the army once again, the family changed their surname from Langsam to Spira. He became the patriarch of the Hasidic dynasties of Dinov, Munkacs, and Błażowa.[5] His son was Rabbi David Spira (1804–1874) of Dynów, the author of *Tsemah David*. He had a son, Rabbi Tzvi Elimelech Spira (1841–1924), who was named after his grandfather and became known as the Grand Rabbi Tzvi Elimelech Spira of Błażowa. He was the author of *Tzvi Latzaddik*, a work that included important Hasidic teachings and responsa. He was the main spiritual influence for my Geiger rabbinical ancestors who lived in Błażowa.

Grand Rabbi Tzvi Elimelech Spira married Sara Horowitz, the daughter of Rabbi Moshe Horowitz of Rozwadów, Podkarpackie, Poland. They had twelve children however only three survived to adulthood. They were his first-born Rabbi Yehoshua Spira (1862–1932) of Rozwadów, Podkaropackie, Poland; a son Rabbi Yosef who died during the lifetime of his father and a daughter, the Rebbetzin Alta Malka. Grand Rabbi Tzvi Elimelech Spira became the rabbi for Rozwadów and Błażowa until WWI when he fled to Budapest. After WWI ended, he settled in Przemyśl and Reisha (Rzeszów) where he died in 1924. His son Rabbi Yehoshua Spira was buried next to the grave of his father at Rzeszów in 1932. [6]

When Grand Rabbi Tzvi Elimelech Spira moved to Rzeszów after WWI, his house was in a section of Rzeszów called "Di Walia" and this place became a center for the Hasidim of Błażowa who lived in Rzeszów. A congregant noted that his Torah sermons were clear and despite their depth, all could understand his way of thinking. He recalled how the rabbi's prayers touched the hearts of all who listened focusing more on supplications and entreaties rather than on song. The rabbi recited the Musaf of Rosh Hashana and congregants were moved by the devotion and sweetness of his prayers.[7] Hundreds of Hasidim from other Hasidic dynasties such as Sanz, Belz, Sadigora joined his congregation at Rzeszów. He devoted much of his time to young scholars and guided them in Torah and Hasidism.

Other Respected Rabbis of Błażowa

Rabbi Yehoshua Spira, the son of Rabbi Tzvi Elimelech Spira married Miriam Mariles who died giving birth to their son Meir (1884–1941). Rabbi Yehoshua Spira then married Tzipora Dachner. His son from his second marriage was named Yisrael Spira (1889–1989). Both Rabbi Meir Spira and Rabbi Yisrael Spira were therefore half-brothers from the two wives of their father Rabbi Yehoshua Spira. During WWI Rabbi Meir Spira became the head of the Rabbinical Court at Błażowa. He had in his possession the manuscripts from his grandfather Grand Rabbi Tzvi Elimelech of Błażowa. Rabbi Meir was murdered by the Nazis but before his death, he went to a gentile neighbor who lived next door who agreed to hide the manuscripts. Rabbi Meir promised the neighbor that if the papers were sent to an address in the USA after the war, the gentile would be well paid for this deed. The writings were buried in the ground for several years; they did not become faded or damaged and finally arrived safely to their destination.[8]

Rabbi Yisroel Spira of Bluzhov suffered greatly before he arrived in the United States. He witnessed the Nazis murder his only daughter, his son-in-law, and his granddaughter as well as his wife Perel. He was transferred from one concentration camp to another doing backbreaking work and was selected several times for death, yet he was always saved at the last minute by a series of miracles. He arrived in the United States as a last survivor of the rabbinical Spira dynasty of Błażowa. While living in New York, he received the manuscripts of Grand Rabbi Tzvi Elimelech Spira.[9] Rabbi Yisroel Spira immigrated to New York in 1946 and he saw the Statue of Liberty. A Yiddish speaking American soldier translated the words of Emma Lazarus written on the statue from English to Yiddish. "The rabbi listened intently and wiped a tear from his eye. There he was, the lone survivor of his family; his beard was burnt off, his head and body still covered with open wounds from beatings with truncheons, iron rods, and boots. He was a lonely man at the portals of freedom. He placed his hand on the soldier's shoulder and said, "My friend, the words you have just translated to me are indeed beautiful. We, the few survivors coming to these shores, are indeed poor, tired, and yearning for freedom. But there are no longer masses. We are remnants, a trickle of broken individuals who search for a few moments of peace in this world, who hope to find a few relatives on these shores. For we survived…"[10]

Family Memories of Rabbi Abraham Geiger

Rabbi Geiger's granddaughter Clara Chopp recalled her grandfather Rabbi Abraham Geiger as being fascinating and witty as well as pious, who wore his long coat in the manner of Hasidim. Rabbi Geiger's great-granddaughter Debra recalled hearing from other relatives how his eyes would shine with reverence and love when discussing the Bluzhover Rabbi. Rabbi Geiger sang so beautifully that he often served as a cantor as well as a rabbi. My mother gave me a coin for "luck" that she said was blessed by a famous rabbi. I now believe that the coin was blessed by Grand Rabbi Tzvi Elimelech Spira who was so closely affiliated with my ancestor Rabbi Abraham Geiger. Abraham gave the coin to my mother after he immigrated to the United States. My aunt Martha Cantor also recalled Abraham singing, enjoying beer and eating herring when visiting their home. She could not understand why he ate food with his hands rather than with the silverware and plates provided. She did not realize that because her home was not completely kosher and thus not in keeping with the laws of kashrut Abraham had no choice other than using his hands for eating her food.

The Early Married Life of Abraham Geiger and Sprynca Stark

Abraham Geiger married Sprynca aka Sprinza Stark, who was born 8 June 1870 at Kańczuga, Podkarpackie, Poland.[11] Her birth record was obtained from the Przemyśl Archive.[12] Sprynca's parents were Moses and Sara Stark; Sprynca had two siblings: Ruchel born 1861 and Berl born 1864 both at Kańczuga. The name Sprynca derives from Shprintse, a name borrowed by Ashkenazi Jews from the German noun for female sparrowhawk.[13] There was another name on Sprinza's birth record under the column for patrini indicating a godparent. The name was

Freide Feldman. Freide was married to Leiser Feldman, and her birth surname was Krameisen.[14] There was possibly a family relationship with the Stark family in Kańczuga.

Abraham and Sprinza were married July 1894 at Kańczuga.[15] Kańczuga is about 22 miles SE of Rzeszów and 26 miles NW of Błażowa. The Jewish population of Kańczuga in 1896 was 949, comprising most of the total population. There is no Jewish presence there today. A traveler, Robert Bernheim, took photos of Kańczuga and wrote about his trip in 1996.[16] He noted there was a Bluzhover shul in Kańczuga that once existed between two houses. Now, over a century later, it is an empty lot. This location may have been Rabbi Abraham Geiger's shul when he was first married and established as a rabbi at Kańczuga. Abraham and his family moved from Kańczuga to Błażowa by 1898 and lived there at least until 1902 through the births of their three additional children.

The Geigers Move to Vienna

Sometime before or during WWI, Aron and Hinde Geiger joined their son Abraham and his family during their move from Poland to Vienna, Austria. Vienna was considered at the time to be a safe-haven from the battlegrounds of WWI. Abraham, his family, and his parents settled in the predominantly Jewish Leopoldstadt district (District II) at Vienna, where many ultra-religious orthodox and Hasidic Jews lived. Abraham Geiger continued his work as a rabbi and as a mohel in Vienna. According to his descendants he had a shul in Leopoldstadt. A photograph owned by Geiger descendants shows Rabbi Abraham Geiger at work in Vienna as a *mohel* with his father Rabbi Aron Geiger as *sandek*. The photograph was taken prior to 1924 and the original is in the IKG (Israelitische Kultus Gemeinde Wien) archives at Vienna. (*See Chapter 3 image bottom of p. 42.*)

Rabbi Abraham Geiger with pipe

Population censuses were taken by the Austrian government for Vienna in 1910 and 1934. Jews numbered 175,294 of a total population of 2,031,420 (8.6%) in 1910. The Jewish population in Vienna was 9.1% of the total population during 1934.[17] After WWII another census was taken 1951 and there were approximately 9,000 remaining Jews in Vienna out of 1,616,128 total population (0.6%).[18] A study was taken in 1934 listing occupations of Jews in Vienna. Jews comprised significant percentages for: physicians 51%; lawyers 85%; furniture tradesmen 85%; wine dealers 73%; pharmacists 31%; bakers 60%; shoemakers 70%; café operators 40%; textiles 73%; milliners 34% with lower percentages in other assorted trades.[19]

Abraham and Sprynca's Exodus from Vienna

The Nazi regime enacted the Nuremberg Race Laws in 1935. The laws considered Germans to be members of a supposedly superior "Aryan" race. In contrast, Jews, Roma (also called Gypsies), and Black people were considered inferior to all other races and could not be full citizens of Germany nor could they marry or have sexual relations with Germans. They had no political rights. According to the Nuremberg Laws a person with three or four Jewish grandparents was considered a Jew. If a person had one or two Jewish grandparents that person was *Mischlinge* (mixed race) and was neither German nor Jewish. Subsequent laws

Birth record Sprinza Stark, 1870 Kańczuga

were passed targeting Jews such as changing one's given name to conform to government approved names for Jews; passports were invalidated for German Jews unless they were stamped with the letter "J". During 1941 all Jews in Nazi Germany were required to wear a yellow Star of David badge sewn on their clothes.[20]

When Hitler and Nazi Germany annexed Austria including Vienna on 12 March 1938, known as the *Anschluss*, anti-Semitic rhetoric escalated to violence during 9–10 November 1938. This was a pogrom against Jews known as *Kristallnacht* or Night of Broken Glass. Jewish synagogues, homes, schools, and businesses were torched and almost 100 Jews were murdered. A short time later Jews were systematically chosen for extermination and genocide. Abraham Geiger's shul in Vienna was destroyed by the Nazis including their many books and Torah scrolls. Abraham and Sprinza Geiger managed to escape from Vienna to Antwerp, then arrived at London where they re-united with their son Josef and daughter-in-law Esther who were already settled in London. There was a UK record for Abraham Geiger indicating that Abraham and Sprinza were living in London by November 1939. Their address at London was 15 Russel Parade, N.W.11. They were registered with the London police as aliens 22 November 1939 and were exempt from internment due to refugee status.[21]

Abraham and Sprinza were eventually able to obtain visas from the US Consulate in England on 16 August 1940. This enabled them to travel by ship on the *S.S. Antonia* departing from Liverpool on 18 September 1940 to Quebec, Canada. They arrived at Quebec on 27 Sept 1940.[22] The *S.S. Antonia* was built 1922 by Vickers Limited of Barrow-in-Furness, UK originally for the Cunard White Star Company.[23] The ship held 500 cabin and 1200 third class passengers. The Geigers continued by train on the Central Vermont Railroad (CVRR) from Montreal, Quebec, Canada crossing the Canadian border to St. Albans, Vermont. They continued their journey from Vermont to New York City.

Abraham and Sprinza Geiger, 1927

As WWII was becoming a global reality, there was a flurry of correspondence between Charles Geiger and George Bronz to get Abraham and his family from Europe to the safety of the USA. Please see Appendix A Geiger and Bronz Letters and refer to the chapters *Charles Geiger and Esther Mamlock* also *Mariem Geiger and Getzel Holoszycer*. Once settled in New York, Abraham wrote a letter to his niece Pearl's husband attorney George Bronz on 30 October 1940 asking him to renew affidavits made two years ago for Abraham's son Joseph Geiger and daughter-in-law Esther.[24] Abraham Geiger wrote: "I am enclosing the forms for affidavits for my son Joseph. You made this affidavit two years ago and the American Counsel in London demand a renewal of same." He provided the birthdates and address for Joseph and Esther Geiger at 16 Courtleigh, Bridge Lane, London N.W.11. He added: "I would appreciate it very much if you would be so kind as to take care of same immediately because of the terrible situation there and I would like to take them out as soon as possible." He also provided George Bronz with addresses for all his children to immigrate to the U.S. with needed affidavits. Among the affidavits written by George Bronz addressed to the United States Government in Washington, D.C. was the Affidavit of Support for another relative, Frieda Prisand née Turnheim, who was a cousin of George's wife Pearl. For further information please refer to the chapter on the *Turnheim Family*.

Borders Closed for Immigration to the USA During WWII

Many seeking safety from persecution during the 1930s and 1940s found their efforts blocked by the American government's restrictive immigration quotas and complicated requirements for obtaining visas. Public opinion was against increased immigration due to economic concerns and national security. The United States had no refugee policy during the war. Strict quotas limited the number of people who could immigrate to the USA. Though at least 110,000 Jewish refugees escaped to the United States from Nazi held territories between 1933 to 1941, hundreds of thousands more applied for immigration and were denied.

Quotas were influenced by proponents of eugenics, slanted towards "desirable" immigrants from northern and western Europe. Immigrants considered less "racially desirable" included southern and eastern European Jews. People born in Africa and Asia were entirely barred from immigrating to the United States on racial grounds. Potential immigrants such as the Geigers had to gather documents for obtaining an American immigration visa. The process included first registering with the consulate and be placed on a waiting list. The next step was to gather all necessary documents for obtaining a visa such as identity paperwork, police certificates, exit and transit permissions including a financial affidavit. The visa had expiration dates, and everything had to come together at the same time. Immigrants needed to find an American sponsor with financial resources to guarantee they would not become a burden on the state. Immigrants also had to have a valid ship ticket prior to obtaining a visa. This was a problem during the war since many passenger lines stopped crossing the Atlantic due to German submarine torpedos of passenger vessels.

Refugees faced a crisis during 1938 as there was increased competition for visas, affidavits, and travel options. During June 1939 refugees in Germany faced a waiting list of 309,782 with only 27,370 people receiving visas by the end of the year. The following year 1940 had 27,355 people receiving visas. Although more than 50% of all immigrants to the United States identified themselves as Jewish many refugees selected a different category as "German" or they did not consider themselves Jewish even if the Nazis did.

The American public was mainly opposed to changing immigration laws. They feared that the Germans would be sending spies among the immigrants. The State Department denied visas to immigrants with close family still in Nazi held territory. Some private Jewish and Christian organizations gave assistance to thousands of prospective immigrants in the forms of food, clothing, transit fare, employment, and affidavits for those without family in the United States. The State Department required additional paperwork including a second financial affidavit in July 1941. After this date immigration from Nazi held territory was impossible. Between 1938 and 1941 self-identified Jewish refugees numbering 123,868 immigrated to the United States. The hundreds of thousands who applied but who were unsuccessful in obtaining visas were trapped in Europe and systematically murdered during the Holocaust.[25]

Naturalization

A year after Abraham and Sprinza Geiger arrived at St. Albans, Vermont from Quebec, Canada, Abraham then applied for U.S. naturalization. He obtained his Certificate of Arrival on 29 September 1941 from the U.S. District Court at Brooklyn, New York.[26] He also completed his Petition for Naturalization 29 September 1941 declaring his intention to become a citizen of the United States.[27] In addition, he filed his Declaration of Intention for naturalization on 29 September 1941. On both his petition and declaration, he stated that he emigrated from Montreal, Canada to St. Albans, Vermont by train.[28] Five years later he took his Oath of Allegiance on 21 January 1946. His two witnesses were Willy Wolfgang Apfel and Abraham's daughter Stella Steinbock, both testifying they knew

TRIPLICATE
(To be given to declarant when originally issued; to be made a part of the petition for naturalization when petition is filed; and to be retained as part of the petition in the records of the court)

UNITED STATES OF AMERICA

318009

DECLARATION OF INTENTION   No.
(Invalid for all purposes seven years after the date hereof)

In the .... Court
of .... at ....

(1) My full, true, and correct name is **ABRAHAM GEIGER** ....
(2) My present place of residence is **201 East Broadway, NY NY NY** (3) My occupation is **Rabbi**
(4) I am **68** years old. (5) I was born on **November 19, 1872** in **Przemysl, Austria**
(6) My personal description is as follows: Sex **male**, color **white**, complexion **medium**, color of eyes **gray**, color of hair **gray**, height **5** feet **4** inches, weight **180** pounds, visible distinctive marks **none**
race **white**, present nationality **Austria**
(7) I am **married**; the name of my wife or husband is **Sprince** ... we were married on **7-1894**
at **Kanczugal Austria** ; he or she was born at **Kanczugal Austria**
on **June 8, 1870** and entered the United States at **St. Albans, Vt.**
on **September 28, 1940** permanent residence in the United States, and now resides at **201 E. Broadway, New York, NY**
(8) I have **4** children, and the name, sex, date and place of birth, and present place of residence of each of said children who is living are as follows:
Minna(f) July 1897; born in Austria; resides at Palestine; Marcus(m) Feb. 1898; resides at France; Joseph(m) March 1899; resides at London England; Sally(f) January 1901; resides at Bklyn, NY; last three born at Austria-Poland
(9) My last place of foreign residence was **London England**
Montreal Canada (11) My lawful entry for permanent residence in the United States was
at **St. Albans, NY** under the name of **Abraham Geiger**
on **September 28, 1940** on the **28 G.V.R.R.**
(12) Since my lawful entry for permanent residence I have **not** been absent from the United States, for a period or periods of 6 months or longer, as follows:

DEPARTED FROM THE UNITED STATES			RETURNED TO THE UNITED STATES		
PORT	DATE (Month, day, year)	VESSEL OR OTHER MEANS OF CONVEYANCE	PORT	DATE (Month, day, year)	VESSEL OR OTHER MEANS OF CONVEYANCE

(13) I have **not** heretofore made a declaration of intention: No. .... on .... at .... in the ....
(14) It is my intention in good faith to become a citizen of the United States and to reside permanently therein. (15) I will, before being admitted to citizenship, renounce absolutely and forever all allegiance and fidelity to any foreign prince, potentate, state, or sovereignty of whom or which at the time of admission to citizenship I may be a subject or citizen. (16) I am not an anarchist; nor a believer in the unlawful damage, injury, or destruction of property, or sabotage; nor a disbeliever in or opposed to organized government nor a member of or affiliated with any organization or body of persons teaching disbelief in or opposition to organized government. (17) I certify that the photograph affixed to the duplicate and triplicate hereof is a likeness of me and was signed by me.
I do swear (affirm) that the statements I have made and the intentions I have expressed in this declaration of intention subscribed by me are true to the best of my knowledge and belief; SO HELP ME GOD.

Abraham Geiger

Subscribed and sworn to (affirmed) before me in the form of oath shown above in the office of the Clerk of said Court at **Brooklyn, NY**
this **29** day of **September** anno Domini **1941**. I hereby certify that
Certificate No. **2-874035** from the Commissioner of Immigration and Naturalization, showing the lawful entry for permanent residence of the declarant above named, on the date stated in this declaration of intention, has been received by me, and that the photograph affixed to the duplicate and triplicate hereof is a likeness of the declarant.

[SEAL]

Deputy Clerk of the **US DISTRICT** Court

By .... Deputy Clerk

Abraham Geiger

Form N-315
U. S. DEPARTMENT OF JUSTICE
IMMIGRATION AND NATURALIZATION SERVICE
(Edition of 1-43-41)

16—19113   U. S. GOVERNMENT PRINTING OFFICE

Rabbi Abraham Geiger Declaration, 1941 New York

Abraham Geiger in the United States since 1 October 1940. His naturalization as a United States citizen was granted.[29] Sprinza Geiger died the year before she could take her Oath of Allegiance.

Sprinza Geiger

Abraham and Sprinza Geiger in America

Abraham and Sprinza Geiger first settled at New York City during October 1940 with the help of relatives such as Abraham's brother Charles Geiger, their daughter Stella and son-in-law Morris Steinboch. They resided at 212 East Broadway in Manhattan. Abraham continued his work as a rabbi in New York at his own shul and Hebrew school located at 156 Henry Street at Manhattan, *Agudas Anshei Mamud u 'Bais Vaad Lachachomin*.[30] Rabbi Abraham Geiger died in Manhattan 28 September 1946 due to natural causes.[31] Rabbi Abraham Geiger and his congregation were known and respected as learned Torah and Talmudic scholars.

Rabbi A. Geiger

Sprinza Geiger died on 6 February 1945.[32] Both Sprinza and Abraham were buried at Beth David Cemetery, Elmont, New York at Joshua, Section H, block 5. Beth David Cemetery provided photographs of their matsevahs. Rabbi Joshua Segal translated Sprinza's matsevah:

> *Here lies a righteous, modest and prominent woman*
>
> *Who busied herself with mitzvot and good deeds*
>
> *All the days of her life. Mrs. Sprinza, rest in peace*
>
> *Daughter of Reb Moses, rest in peace*
>
> *Died 23 Shevat 5745*
>
> *May her soul be bound up in the bonds of the living*
>
> *Wife of Reb Abraham Geiger*

Sprinza Geiger Matsevah

Rabbi Abraham Geiger's Death and Will

Rabbi Abraham Geiger died 28 September 1946 of natural causes. He was living at 212 East Broadway, New York at the time of his death.[33] His son-in-law Morris Steinbock provided the information on his death certificate. Abraham's profession was rabbi, and his business was Hebrew School. His son Max Geiger gave permission for burial at Beth David Cemetery, Elmont, New York on 29 September 1946. I confirmed my great-uncle Rabbi Abraham Geiger's close connection with Grand Rabbi Tzvi Elimelech Spira of Bluzhov when I obtained a photograph of Abraham Geiger's matsevah at Beth David Cemetery in Elmont, New York; Rabbi Joshua Segal translated the Hebrew inscription. A corresponding translation was also provided by Sheindle Cohen from Viewmate at Jewishgen.org.[34]

A Memorial for A living Soul

Abraham pursued righteousness and feared G-d.

He loved humanity and was a father to orphans

All his deeds were pure and pleasant.

He died with a good name, at a ripe old age.

Our Teacher and Rabbi, Abraham son of Reb Aron, rest in peace.

Died on 3 Tishri 5707

Most of his days he served with faithful dedication

In the courtyard of the master, the Gaon of Błażowa[35]

The author of the book of Tzvi L'Tzaddik[36]

May the memory of the righteous be a blessing

May his soul be bound up in the bonds of the living

Reb Abraham Geiger

Abraham Geiger Matsevah

Death and Wills

In Ancestry.com, I came across an interesting item that was listed on the National Probate Calendar for England and Wales, Index of Wills and Administration, 1858–1966, for 25 July 1947. Apparently, Abraham Geiger made out a will when he and his wife were living in London prior to their immigration to the US. He appointed his son Josef Geiger executor since Josef was living in London. Abraham Geiger's will was scheduled for probate 25 July 1947 at London following his death 1946 in the USA. His estate consisted of £ 574.[37] After Abraham Geiger immigrated to the United States, he made another will for the remainder of his estate.

Rabbi Abraham Geiger's new will made in New York was obtained from Probate Court at Manhattan.[38] The date of this will was 24 January 1946. His son-in-law Morris Steinbock was named executor. Abraham and Sprinza Geiger's children and their addresses were listed: Max Geiger of 212 East Broadway, New York; Stella and Morris Steinbock of 146 Henry Street New York; Chaja Neumann of 154 Hayarkon Street, Tel Aviv, Palestine; Josef Geiger of 16 Courtleigh Bridge Lane, London, N.W.11, England. Rabbi Geiger left most of his estate in equal shares to his four children. He also left money to his grandchildren Clara and Susi, to his shul *Agudas Anshei Mamud u 'Bais Vaad Lachachomin*, to his son-in-law Morris Steinboch and to Chana Halberstam of 5120 Ft. Hamilton Parkway in Brooklyn, New York. Abraham also bequeathed to his son Max Geiger 25% of the war damage award made in London as compensation for the destruction of 8 cases of his personal property.

Based on this will Rabbi Abraham Geiger requested that Morris Steinbock learn Mishnaes (Mishnah) for the entire year of mourning after his death. My cousin Debra informed me that saying kaddish, the traditional mourning prayer for a deceased close relative would involve going to the shul three times a day for an entire year and there must be a minion of at least 10 men present each time. Rabbi Geiger also specified in his will that his shul engrave his name "Abraham ben Aaron and the name of my beloveth late wife Sprinza bas Moshe on the Crystal Memorial Tablet on condition that said organization will issue a receipt that they will learn Mishnaes in my memory during the entire year after my decease and will each year observe the Yarzeits of my beloveth late wife and of myself." I learned that Hasidic and orthodox tradition recommended daily study of the Mishnah during the year of mourning after the death of a close relative or friend to elevate the souls of those who departed from this world as well as elevate the soul of the living person who observed this tradition.[39]

Solving the Mystery of Chana Halberstam

Rabbi Geiger specified in his will that Mrs. Chana Halberstam observe his memory during prayer and he left her a small sum of money. I wondered about Mrs. Chana Halberstam, as that surname did not come up in my family research. I found her petition for citizenship: she was born 15 December 1882 at Błażowa.[40] She married Isaac Halberstam on 12 February 1904 at Struza, Poland. He was born August 1883 at Czechoslovakia and he was naturalized 22 March 1927 at Brooklyn, New York. Their four children were all born at Błażowa. They were: Chaim Moses born 15 March 1905, Boruch born 5 June 1909, Joseph born 10 January 1912, and Tobias born 10 June 1913.

Chana Halberstam's ship manifest agreed with the facts on her petition for naturalization. She travelled on the ship *S.S. Leviathan*, arrived 5 September 1927 at New York to join her husband Rabbi Isaac Halberstam who lived at Ft. Hamilton Parkway, Brooklyn, New York.[41] Chana travelled with her youngest son Tobias and her husband travelled with their other sons.

Chana and Isaac Halberstam were found in the 1930 and 1940 Federal Census, with their address at 5122 Ft. Hamilton Parkway, Brooklyn. Isaac was listed as a rabbi for a synagogue on both censuses. I then found Isaac Halberstam in the New York Death Index; he died 17 September 1944.[42] Following this up, I learned that both Chana (called Anna on her gravestone) and her husband Isaac Halberstam were buried at Beth David Cemetery, Elmont, New York at the same location where Abraham and Sprinza Geiger were buried: Joshua, section H, block 5. I also learned that Chana died 21 August 1950.[43] Both the Geigers and Halberstams were buried by the same burial society called Chevra Beth Hamedrash Sheiras Israel, which was roughly translated by Sheindle Cohen, as the Society of the House of Study of the Remnant of the Nation of Israel. Therefore, they all belonged to the same burial society and were probably from the same shul. My on-going question continued: was Chana a Geiger relative?

Another clue became available when I read several chapters from the Yizkor book for Rzeszów.[44] As previously mentioned, Abraham Geiger was strongly associated with Grand Rabbi Tzvi Elimelech Spira (also known as Shapira) at Błazowa. Rabbi Spira had three surviving children: Rabbi Yehoshua, Rabbi Yosef, Rebbetzin Alta Malka. The yizkor book mentioned that Rabbi Yehoshua had a son-in-law, Rabbi Yitzchak Halberstam, who left Rzeszów with his entire family to move to Brooklyn, New York.

I searched Ancestry public trees for Rabbi Yehoshua Spira and learned that Chana Halberstam was born to Rabbi Yehoshua Shapira and Tziporah Dachner. A photograph of her matsevah was obtained from the Beth David cemetery. I placed a photo of her tombstone on JewishGen.org View Mate and volunteers translated the Hebrew therefore Chana was the daughter of Rabbi Yehoshua Spira. Chana's husband Rabbi Yitzchak Halberstam's father was Rabbi Moshe Halberstam (1850–1903) who was the Rabbi of Bardejov at Slovakia. Chana Halberstam was a direct descendant of the illustrious Rabbinic Spira Dynasty of Blozhov. Chana's brother was Rabbi Israel Spira of Blozhov born 12 November 1891 at Błażowa, who died 30 October 1989 at Brooklyn, New York. Chana's father Rabbi Yehoshua Spira was born 8 June 1862 and died 19 February 1932 at Rzeszów, Poland. Chana's siblings Eliezer, Yuta, Hinde, and her mother Tziporah Dachner Spira were all murdered during the Holocaust 1941–1943.

The answer to my question about whether Chana was a Geiger relative was negative, however she was a granddaughter of the Grand Rabbi Tzvi Elimelech Spira and connected by common roots in Błażowa as well as by friendship and piety with Rabbi Abraham Geiger. She would be a person trusted implicitly by Rabbi Abraham Geiger to arrange a minion of ten adult males so the appropriate prayers could be said daily for a year upon his death. Upon reading her tombstone, I could see that she was indeed well respected, honored and a person who would inspire trust.

I am indebted to the volunteers David Barrett, David Ziants and Odeda Zlotnik through View Mate on JewishGen.org who provided the translation from the Hebrew on Chana Halberstam's tombstone:

Here lies the righteous Rabbanit (a crown upon our heads) Channah (may peace rest on her). The wife of the righteous Gaon Rabbi Yitzack Halberstam (may his memory be for a blessing). Daughter of the righteous Gaon our honored Rabbi Yehoshua, the Keren Yehoshua; the granddaughter of the holy Gaon of Rybotycze, our respected Rabbi from Blazov, the composer of the holy book Tzvi L' Tzadik. Going up in sanctity the (great) granddaughter of the knowledgeable and holy Gaon Rav Tzvi Elimelech of Dynov who wrote the Bnei Yissachar and my Rabbi Rav Shimon of Jaroslav (of blessed memory) who died 4th of Adar 5710.

Here is the acrostic poetry section as translated:

Chet: Our heart's delight is lost and dimmed the light in our eyes

Nun: Solace has distanced itself from us and there is no balm for our heartbreak

Hey: Why has the sun set before it's time?

Bet: In her righteous soul was every virtue

Tav: Perfect in her good, gentle and righteous soul

Yud: Dear and faithful to each one she encountered

Hey: Should not her heart be reknown everywhere

Vav: And she would rise whilst night to pray to the almighty, pouring out her soul

Shin: She spread an abundance of love and healed broken hearts

Ayin: Is her righteous strength not known in the Gates? (of Heaven)

May (Her) Soul be Bound Up in the Bond of Life

Children of Rabbi Abraham Geiger and Sprynca Stark

Chaja aka Mina Geiger

Chajija or Chaja was the first-born child of Rabbi Abraham and Sprynca Stark, born 21 May 1895 at Kańczuga, Podkarpackie, Poland.[45] Chaja was named after her great-grandmother, Chaja Mindel, since her grandparents Aron and Hinde Geiger were still living at the time of her birth. She was standing to the far left in the Geiger photograph of 1927. My cousin Clara C. recalled that Chaja aka Mina was married to Carl Neumann. Chajija is a Polish variant of the name Chaja, deriving from the Hebrew noun for life.[46] I was puzzled by this child as there was no mention of Chaja by relatives, however the mystery was solved when I learned that Chaja was also called Mina by her family and that they are the same person. Abraham lived at Kańczuga and worked there as a rabbi after he married Sprinza. Abraham and Sprinza with Chajija moved to Błażowa about three years later. Their next three children Max, Josef and Stella were all born at Błażowa, Podkarpackie, Poland.

Some important documents surfaced regarding Chaja (Mina) and Carl Neumann. Apparently, Chaja and Carl Neumann came to the United States in 1948 on the *S.S. Rossia* sailing from Haifa, Israel to New York.[47] They came to the United States after having lived in Tel Aviv, Israel.[48] They had visas issued in Jerusalem and were considered stateless, since Israel was still Palestine and was not yet officially an independent country.

On the ship manifest, Chaja was listed as being 53 years and her husband Carl was listed as being 67 years and was a merchant. She was born at Kańczuga, Podkarpackie, Poland. Her husband Carl Neumann was born at Vienna, Austria. Chaja Geiger married Carl Neumann at Vienna. Chaja was described as 4 feet 7 inches with brown hair and blue eyes. Her husband was 5 feet 3 inches, was bald with brown eyes. They intended to become permanent residents in the United States and they were visiting Max Geiger at 212 East Broadway in New York.

Some documents came to light for Carl Neumann. If he was 67 years in 1948 then he would be born about 1881. An index card for a Carl Neumann was found, giving his birthdate as 30 April 1880. Under the auspices of the American Joint Distribution Committee and Refugee Aid, his emigration file opened 19 October 1951 and closed 31 December 1951.[49]

Avotaynu provided another source of family information of the Geiger family when they were living in Vienna. In 1997 Avotaynu acquired lists of individuals who held Holocaust-era unclaimed Swiss bank accounts as well as Jews living in Vienna in 1938 whom the Nazis forced to complete detailed property decla-

Chaja Geiger, 1927

Chana Halberstam Matsevah

rations under penalty of imprisonment if any asset information was withheld. Those lists were later used to help find legitimate heirs for the assets.[50] In perusing this list, I came upon names of relatives with their corresponding birthdates. Here is the list of relatives with their birthdates who had unclaimed accounts in Vienna, Austria during the Holocaust:

Chaja Neumann 21 May 1895

Erna Geiger 26 October 1898

Josef Geiger 06 December 1899

Markus Geiger 08 March 1898

Rosa Geiger 06 October 1898

Mojzesz Steinbock 20 May 1904

This researcher made an inquiry to the organization Conference on Jewish Material Claims Against Germany to find out how our relatives could make a claim about those assets, without hearing a response. For those wishing to pursue this path, the organization is www.claimscon.org. or Claims Conference, the Conference on Jewish Material Claims Against Germany. Their email is: info@claimscon.org. Thus far, I was unable to find when or where Chaja and Carl Neumann died or where they were buried. I estimate Chaja Neumann must have been deceased after she arrived in the United States 1948 and before January 1959, because a cousin born January 1959 was named after her. Chaja and Carl Neumann left no issue.

Mordechai/Markus aka Max Geiger

Abraham and Sprynca Geiger's second child, Mordecai, was born 8 March 1898 at Błażowa, Podkarpackie, Poland.[51] He was born at the start of the Hebrew festival of Purim. Jewish parents would often give the name Mordechai to male children born during that holiday. Purim is an annual festival honoring the deliverance of Jews in Persia from planned genocide by the king's evil advisor Haman. The Persian Jews salvation was through the intercession by the Jewish wife Queen Esther, who was married to Persian King Achashverash (Ahasuerus).[52] Max Geiger died at Kings County, New York on 25 February 1981.[53] He married Ruchla aka Rose Ginsberg in Vienna, Austria on 31 October 1922.[54] She was born 6 October 1898 at Buczacz, Poland to parents Isidore and Schewa Ginsberg.[55] Rose died at Kings County, New

Max and Rose Geiger

York 3 September 1973.[56] Both Max and Rose Geiger were buried at Wellwood Cemetery, Farmingdale, New York.[57] At the time of his death, Max Geiger was residing at 2415 Avenue K, Brooklyn, New York with his daughter Clara and son-in-law Manny Chopp.

Vienna from the 1920s to the Anschluss in 1938

Rose's parents Isidore and Schewa Ginsberg owned a company in Vienna that manufactured paper bags. Although this company was the first one in Europe at that time according to Geiger descendants, the innovation of paper bag manufacture processing began in America during the mid-19th century by American inventors. Max Geiger became the operating director of the paper bag company after he and Rose Ginsberg married. Paper bag manufacture became increasingly profitable both in the USA and Europe as demand increased during the early 20th century. Their paper bag factory consisted of three buildings in Vienna on Gerhardusgasse 26 in the XX District known as Brigittenau. The Brigittenau District shares an island with the Leopoldstadt District. Both districts had the highest Jewish populations in Vienna prior to WWII. The Geiger family prospered becoming upper middle class in Vienna. They were able to afford spacious living quarters, household help, comfortable furnishings, season tickets to the Vienna Opera and luxury items such as furs and jewelry. All was well until….

The economic situation changed beginning with the American stock market crash of 1929 that precipitated a worldwide depression lasting through the 1930s. Businesses were failing; unemployment rates grew as companies failed. Banks had no cash on hand to pay their customers when there were runs on the banks. European countries were heavily in debt to the United States. When the U.S called for loans to be repaid this also threw foreign states into economic depression with more banks closing and unemployment continuing to rise.

The Great Depression prepared the way for the rise of Adolf Hitler in Germany. Deteriorating economic conditions in the 1930s triggered feelings of anger and hatred in people who became open to extreme solutions. Hitler had an audience for his anti-Semitic rhetoric as he blamed Jews for causing the Depression. He added fuel to the fire with propaganda that Jews were racially inferior to the Aryan German race. Soon hatred engendered violence.[58] When Hitler and the Nazis invaded Austria in 1938, they met with no resistance, in fact were welcomed by throngs of people. The Nazis immediately began to target Jewish owned businesses and wealth. Their underlying goals were to rid German territories of Jews and other populations they feared would pollute the German race, in a devastating policy of genocide.

By the end of 1938, the Nazis confiscated the entire Geiger paper bag business, consisting of three factories, as well as their residence.[59] This began with the decree issued by the Nazi government 26 April 1938 ordering Jews to report all their assets under penalty of imprisonment. Max wrote a letter to the Property Transaction Office, registration for Jewish owned property, declaring that his commercial assets on 2 April 1938 were RM 11,795. He added in a letter 13 December 1938 his entire company and assets were liquidated (seized) by the government along with any outstanding accounts for income and business taxes leaving him without any assets or means for his own subsistence.[60] Meanwhile the Gestapo arrested 30,000 wealthy Jews who were released only on conditions of complete surrender of their wealth and emigration out of German held lands.

How Max Geiger and His Family Escaped from the Nazis

Family information was emailed to me 7 June 2010 by Max Geiger's granddaughter Debra P. She shared important family history told to her by her mother Susi and her aunt Clara. The Nazi regime in Vienna under Hitler soon began to remove Jewish men from their families for deportation to labor camps or worse. A gentile employee from the paper bag factory heard this was happening to the Jews and so he hid Max within Christian cemeteries for several days. The Geigers lost no time escaping from the Nazis during December 1938 after *Kristallnacht* and after the Nazi confiscation of their business. Max and his family did not carry suitcases. They wore all their clothing in many layers with diamonds sewed into the recesses of their clothing in "places we don't talk about" as they needed to leave quickly. They packed their valuables such as art and silver in trunks which they sent to Max's brother Josef, who left Vienna before them and who was in London, England where he stored the trunks in a warehouse. Unfortunately, that warehouse was bombed and destroyed during the *Blitzkrieg* in London during WWII. In my telephone interview 2010 with Max's daughter Clara Chopp, she recalled how she saw the Nazis marching past her window in Vienna with Hitler in a car waving to cheering crowds.

The family travelled to Antwerp, Belgium since that was a neutral country at the start of WWII. While in Belgium, Max and his family held fake German passports. When the German Army began their invasion of Belgium, Max was arrested by the Flemish police and placed in jail because they thought he and his family were all German spies. Rose, Clara, and Susi were placed in a separate jail for women and were cared for by nuns. Bombs were falling everywhere; everyone was terrified they would die. Max was sent to another jail at Marseilles, France. After the Nazis invaded Belgium in May 1940 and gained control, a Nazi soldier freed Rose, Clara, and Susi from jail, thinking they were gentile Germans on the side of the Axis Powers. Max Geiger and his family reunited in Marseilles, France and they were held in a refugee camp while WWII raged on in Europe.

Es wird ersucht, diesen Akt an das zuständige Finanzamt weiterzuleiten.
===

Veränderung des Vermögens in der Zeit vom 27.

bis 12. November 1938

GEIGER Markus, Kaufmann, Wien II, Darwingasse 35/18, 40 Jahre alt.
===

An die Vermögensverkehrsstelle (Anmeldung d. Vermögens v. Juden)

Wien I.
================
Strauchgasse 1

Im Sinne der Verordnung vom 26. April 1938 und des Runderlasses vom 12. November 1938 gestatte ich mir mit Gegenwärtigem die Veränderung meines Vermögens in der Zeit vom 27. April 1938 bis 12. November 1938 anzuzeigen.- ad III. Geschäftsvermögen (Stand vom 27. IV. 1938) RM 11.795Rpf.

Inzwischen wurde die Firma, die unter kommissarischer Leitung stand liquidiert, xxxxxxxxx und verblieb mir kein Vermögen, so dass ich nicht einmal meinen Lebensunterhalt bestreiten kann. Die noch restlichen Aussenstände wurden zuGunsten der Einkommen-bezw. Erwerbsteuer beschlagnahmt.-

Wien, 13. Dezember 1938

Markus Geiger

Markus Geiger letter, 13 Dec 1938

The German army invaded France during May–June 1940. An armistice was signed by Nazi Germany with Marshal Petain's government on 22 June 1940 following the Battle of France. France was subsequently divided by a demarcation line between the German Occupied Zone in the north and the Free Zone in the south. The Free Zone was administered by Marshal Petain in Vichy. The Vichy administration lasted only until the Allies invaded North Africa 8 November 1942.[61] Marseilles was within the Free Zone.

While in a refugee camp in Marseilles, the Geiger family's only hope was to obtain visas; they were probably under extreme pressure as it was only a matter of time before the Free Zone would soon be occupied by Nazi Germany. Abraham Geiger, his wife Spyrnca, his daughter Stella and her husband Morris Steinboch were already in the USA. Meanwhile a life-saving letter was written by Charles Geiger's niece Pearl Bronz's husband George Bronz in 1941, also discussed in the chapter *Mariem Geiger and Getzel Holoszycer*, that appeared to be official with the US government seal on it. That letter impressed the bureaucrats under the Vichy French government into thinking that the President of the United States was sponsoring Max, Rose, Clara, and Susi to enter the USA. This letter was first sent to the US Consulate in Lisbon, Portugal then ended up at the US Consulate in Marseilles. The letter was sent by official diplomatic pouch and proved to be the key that enabled Max Geiger and his family to obtain immigration visas to enter the USA. George Bronz also sent an affidavit testifying that he was willing to financially support Max Geiger and his family in the USA.

The Geiger's uncertain future improved when their visas were issued at Marseilles on 11 June 1941. They were listed on the ship manifest for a cargo steamship *S.S. Navemar* departing from Seville, Spain. The situation was becoming critical for them to get out of Europe as soon as they could book passage. Their search for passage must have been desperate as time was running out since few ships would risk being torpedoed by German submarines in the Atlantic Ocean. Max and his family were among the last group of Jews to enter the USA before the government closed the quota on Jewish refugees July 1941. After that date ships carrying Jews were turned away from American ports thus sending Jews back to Europe to their tragic fates.

The *S.S. Navemar* was built 1921 in England and was Norwegian-owned until 1927 then became Spanish-owned. It was steam driven with capacity for 28 passengers and 36 crew. In 1941, the American Jewish Joint Distribution Committee sought to rescue Jewish refugees from Nazi persecution especially since many refugees held visas due to expire. The Joint's agents directed the refugees to

Seville, Spain where the *S.S. Navemar* was privately chartered to make the transatlantic crossing to the US. Tickets for the few passenger cabins sold at exorbitant prices. The captain of the *S.S. Navemar* vacated his cabin charging $2,000 to whoever could pay this and fit into the tight space.[62] They departed from Seville, Spain on 7 August 1941 and did not arrive at New York until 12 September 1941.[63] Max Geiger and family indicated on the manifest they were joining Max's father Abraham Geiger who lived at 212 East Broadway, Manhattan.

The *S.S. Navemar* first called at Lisbon, Portugal so that visas due to expire could be extended by the American consulate. The ship made another call at Havana, Cuba; some passengers and crew members abandoned the ship to take their chances in Havana because of the intolerable living conditions onboard the ship. Passengers contracted typhus and 6 died during the seven-week ordeal.

LIST OR MANIFEST OF ALIEN PASSENGERS FOR THE UNITED

S.S. NAVEMAR   Passengers sailing from Seville   August 7, 1941

Marcus Geiger Family Navemar, 1941

Bodies were buried at sea. The ship was reported by Victor Bienstock in Havana to be a "nightmare" with tiers of bunks rising on all sides. He wrote "old men and women were gasping for breath in the insufferable heat lying motionless on their bunks while children tossed and cried."[64] The final port of call was at New York on 12 September 1941.

The ship was severely over-crowded with 1,250 Jewish passengers including 6 oxen for food. This was one of the last ships carrying Jews to the US before the U.S. government started turning ships back to Europe. As the ship came into port, sailors were busily painting the outside of the ship so it would look somewhat presentable coming to the US to pass inspection. When the ship arrived at New York, there were 769 passengers mainly Jewish refugees. The ship was described as filthy, overcrowded, and disease ridden. The refugees from the *S.S. Navemar* later tried to sue the ship owners for damages however on 23 January 1942 an Italian submarine *Barbarigo* torpedoed the freighter and sank her in the Straits of Gibraltar.

The crew split up the men and women; women remained with their children. Ship passengers included a *shochet*, a Kosher butcher, to kill the cattle on board to feed the 1,250 people. However, there was an outbreak of a cattle disease that killed all the cattle and the cattle had to be thrown overboard. The passengers were de-loused by pouring gasoline all over themselves. Newspaper journalists reported the ship should be named "Nevermore." During my interview with Susi Kleiman née Geiger 2010 she recalled additional details about her journey with her family on the *S.S. Navemar*. There was a severe lack of water and food during the entire voyage. Her parents resorted to giving her worms to eat to stay alive. She was skeletal in appearance when she arrived in New York. She also recalled there was much emotion of joy and excitement when passengers first saw the Statue of Liberty.

She told me that her grandfather Rabbi Abraham Geiger had a shul in Vienna and that her father Max and his brother Josef tried to save the holy sefer torah scrolls and books when the Nazis came, however the Nazis burned down the shul and all the scrolls and books were lost. Susi said that she kept certain documents about her family in her safe as well as family photographs. She recalled having seen the photograph of her great-grandfather Aron Geiger with her grandfather Rabbi Abraham Geiger together as they officiated at a bris in Vienna.

Naturalization

Markus Geiger's Certificate of Arrival was issued 2 December 1941. He reported that he travelled on the ship *S.S. Navemar*, arriving at New York 12 September 1941.[65] Markus changed his name to Max Geiger on his Declaration of Intention. Max Geiger stated that he was living at 5 Hester Street, New York and his occupation was diamond cutter. His Declaration of Intention for Naturalization was made 1 April 1942 and it included a photograph of Max Geiger.[66] On his Petition for Naturalization made five years later, Max Geiger's personal description was 5'8", weight 160 lbs., gray hair, brown eyes. His address was 212 East Broadway, New York and his occupation was diamond broker. His wife was listed as Rosa, born 10 June 1898 at Beckaur (misspelling for Buczacz), Poland. Their daughters were Clara born 8 July 1926 and Susi born 9 April 1931. Both children were born at Vienna. The two witnesses on his Petition for Naturalization were Esriel (misspelling for Israel or Azrial) Anfel, a diamond broker at 2 Suffolk Street and Willy Apfel, a dealer in zippers, also at 2 Suffolk Street. They attested that they have known Max Geiger since 1 January 1942. The date of the Petition for Naturalization was 2 January 1947.[67] The Oath of Allegiance was made by Max Geiger on 3 February 1947 and was granted, thereby completing the naturalization process for Max Geiger.[68]

Sleeping in *Navemar* Lifeboats

TRIPLICATE
(To be given to declarant when originally issued; to be made a part of the petition for naturalization when petition is filed; and to be retained as part of the petition in the records of the court.)

UNITED STATES OF AMERICA

No. 51720

DECLARATION OF INTENTION
(Invalid for all purposes seven years after the date hereof)

STATE OF NEW YORK
SOUTHERN DISTRICT OF NEW YORK } ss: In the _____ DISTRICT _____ Court
of UNITED STATES NEW YORK, N.Y.

(1) My full, true, and correct name is MAX GEIGER formerly Markus Geiger

(2) My present place of residence is 5 Hester St. New York NY, NY (3) My occupation is diamond cutter

(4) I am 44 years old. (5) I was born on March 8, 1898, in Blazova, Poland

(6) My personal description is as follows: Sex male, color white, complexion dark, color of eyes brown, color of hair grey, height 5 feet 8 inches, weight 160 pounds, visible distinctive marks none

race white, present nationality Poland

(7) I am married; the name of my wife or husband is Roza; we were married on 10/31/22 at Vienna, Austria; he or she was born at Beckach, Poland on June 10, 1898; and entered the United States at New York, NY on September 12, 1941 for permanent residence in the United States, and now resides at 5 Hester St. NY, NY, NY

(8) I have 2 children; and the name, sex, date and place of birth, and present place of residence of each of said children who is living, are as follows: Clara-f, July 8, 1926; Suzi-f, April 9, 1931; both born Austria and residing at New York, NY

(9) My last place of foreign residence was Marseille, France (10) I emigrated to the United States from Sevilla, Spain (11) My lawful entry for permanent residence was at New York, NY under the name of Markus Geiger on September 12, 1941, on the Maxmus Nevemer

(12) Since my lawful entry for permanent residence I have not been absent from the United States, for a period or periods of 6 months or longer, as follows:

DEPARTED FROM THE UNITED STATES			RETURNED TO THE UNITED STATES		
PORT	DATE (Month, day, year)	VESSEL OR OTHER MEANS OF CONVEYANCE	PORT	DATE (Month, day, year)	VESSEL OR OTHER MEANS OF CONVEYANCE

(13) I have not heretofore made declaration of intention: No. _____, on _____ at _____ in the _____

(14) It is my intention in good faith to become a citizen of the United States and to reside permanently therein. (15) I will, before being admitted to citizenship, renounce absolutely and forever all allegiance and fidelity to any foreign prince, potentate, state, or sovereignty of whom or which at the time of admission to citizenship I may be a subject or citizen. (16) I am not an anarchist; nor a believer in the unlawful damage, injury, or destruction of property, or sabotage; nor a disbeliever in or opposed to organized government; nor a member of or affiliated with any organization or body of persons teaching disbelief in or opposition to organized government. (17) I certify that the photograph affixed to the duplicate and triplicate hereof is a likeness of me and was signed by me.
I do swear (affirm) that the statements I have made and the intentions I have expressed in this declaration of intention subscribed by me are true to the best of my knowledge and belief: SO HELP ME GOD.

Max Geiger
(Original and true signature of declarant without abbreviation, also other name if used)

Subscribed and sworn to (affirmed) before me in the form of oath shown above in the office of the Clerk of said Court, at New York, NY this 1 day of April, anno Domini 19 42. I hereby certify that Certification No. 2-941296 from the Commissioner of Immigration and Naturalization, showing the lawful entry for permanent residence of the declarant above named on the date stated in this declaration of intention, has been received by me, and that the photograph affixed to the duplicate and triplicate hereof is a likeness of the declarant.

[SEAL]

GEORGE J.H. FOLLMER
Clerk of the _____ N.Y. DISTRICT _____ Court

By _____ Deputy Clerk.

[Signature: Max Geiger]

Form N-315
U. S. DEPARTMENT OF JUSTICE
IMMIGRATION AND NATURALIZATION SERVICE
(Edition of 1-13-41)

e16—19119   U. S. GOVERNMENT PRINTING OFFICE

Markus Geiger Declaration, 1942

Max and His Family in New York City

Max Geiger and his family first lived at 5 Hester Street in the Lower East Side of Manhattan. Max's wife Rose obtained a job working in an umbrella factory and it was probably the same umbrella factory owned by my grandparents Minnie and Oscar Weiss. However, a short time later, Rose left the factory because the concept of employment was foreign to Rose. She came from a wealthy family in Vienna and lived in a mansion with many bedrooms, servants and nannies before the Nazis confiscated everything. Their daughter Susi recalled playing on the streets of New York with people calling her as a "greener" meaning a newly arrived immigrant. People took pity on her emaciated appearance and would sometimes give her pastry treats.

Max Geiger found employment at New York first as a diamond cutter and later as a diamond broker. I recall how my grandmother Minnie Weiss née Geiger took me to the diamond exchange on 47th Street. She seemed to be quite familiar with certain dealers there. I recall that she introduced me to Max Geiger, who was a diamond broker. Max probably learned this trade during the time he lived in Antwerp. Max's in-laws, Schewa and Isidore Ginsberg, remained in Vienna thinking that the Nazis would not bother with such old people, however they were sadly mistaken about the barbarism of the Third Reich. They were deported to the death camp at Auschwitz. This certainly would have been the same fate for Max Geiger and his family had they remained in Vienna.

Debra P., Max Geiger's granddaughter, wrote me a very moving e-mail: *I have papers showing what his (Charles Geiger) finances were and proof that he could put up 500.00 per person to sponsor them (Max Geiger and his family) and bring them here. He showed receipts of furniture he bought to put in the apartment he had obtained for them, the linens, towels and dishes…If it wasn't for Uncle Charlie, this end of the family would have disappeared as if we never existed. My Auntie Clara, who is now the only one left alive from our end of the family, now has something like 50 great-grandchildren, all very religious. They would not be in existence if not for Uncle Charlie.*[69]

Death

I obtained Max Geiger's death certificate from the New York City Municipal Archives.[70] Max Geiger died 25 February 1981 of natural causes at Maimonides Medical Center, Brooklyn, New York. His wife Rose died 1973. His occupation listed was broker. Both Max and Rose were buried at Wellwood Cemetery, Pinelawn, New York. His address in Brooklyn was listed on the certificate and the informant for the information was his daughter Clara Chopp. I looked up her address and sure enough, it was the same address as listed on the certificate. I called and could not leave a message as there was no answering machine. I also tried calling the other Chopp names listed in the telephone directory but also could not leave a message due to no answering machines. I finally wrote a letter on 26 April 2010 to those names: Alan, Martin, and Mordechio Chopp about how I was related and how I wanted to speak to Clara about my genealogical research on the Geiger family. I enclosed a copy of the ship manifest *S.S. Navemar*.

In a few days, Clara called to discuss our Geiger family and her recollections while living in Vienna. She mentioned that she was age 84 and still working. She took over her husband's business of making specialty folding paper boxes, started by her late husband, Emanuel aka Manny Chopp. Clara recalled she never met her great-grandfather Aron Geiger as he died prior to her own birth. Clara remembered her grandfather Rabbi Abraham Geiger wearing a long coat in the Hasidic manner. She said that he was pious, also fascinating, brilliant, witty and would sing rhyming songs. She said that he had a good voice like a cantor. Clara added that her father Max Geiger became a diamond broker when he was in the USA.

She recalled hearing about a distant Geiger cousin from Błażowa, Oscar Geiger. He immigrated to the United States with his wife in 1941; they had a daughter named Helen. (Please refer to the chapter on *Yechezkeil Geiger and Fradal Landesman*). Clara and Emanuel aka Manny continued the tradition of orthodox Judaism and passed down this legacy to their children and grandchildren. Clara also gave me her sister Susi's telephone number and the telephone numbers of her children. Clara thought that her uncle Josef Geiger immigrated to the United States in 1946.

Josef Geiger

Abraham Geiger and Sprinza's third child was Josef Geiger; his name was based on the biblical Yosef, who was the first son of Jacob and Rachel.[71] Josef was born 6 December 1899 at Błażowa, Podkarpackie, Poland to Abraham and Sprnyca Geiger.[72] He married Esther Schonfeld. She was born 26 October 1898 at Bucharest, Romania.[73] She died 8 July 1959 at London.[74] Descendants of Max Geiger told me that after Josef's first wife died, Josef married a woman from Switzerland who owned businesses including a bank at Zurich. The only information was that her given name was Elsa and her surname sounded like "Moderna". I contacted the Jewish Community in Switzerland and at Zurich, however nothing turned up.[75] I then contacted a genealogy researcher in Israel named Brenda Habshush who helped me in the past.

Brenda knew an Israeli citizen named Rachel Shapiro who could be of help and told Rachel that I was searching for information about my cousin Josef Geiger. Rachel recalled meeting Josef Geiger in Israel and she recalled hearing he had a brother named Max. Indeed, Rachel's husband Moshe assisted Josef in arranging for his own burial at Jerusalem. With additional research I was able to confirm that Josef Geiger married Elsie Monderer October 1960 at Hendon, Middlesex, London.[76]

Rachel confirmed that Josef's wife was Elsa Monderer, who had a daughter from a prior marriage named Giti. I tried to contact Giti many times with the telephone number given to me by Rachel and left messages however with no response. I had research contacts living at New York City, who find "lost" relatives who lived in Israel. Those contacts wished to remain anonymous. They found that Josef Geiger entered Israel November 1989 only days before he died. They also confirmed Josef's birth date and death date, as well as the names of his parents Abraham and Sprinza Geiger. Brenda contacted the secretary for the Chevra Kadisha at Jerusalem and learned that Josef Geiger passed away on 18 November 1989 at Jerusalem. He was buried at grave "tet," row A, plot "aleph," area "yud-aleph" at the cemetery Har Hamenuchot, Jerusalem, Israel near the Givat Shaul entrance to Jerusalem.[77] I wrote to a Geiger cousin, Martin, who lives in Israel about Josef Geiger. (See the chapter *Yechezkiel Geiger and Fradal Landesman*). Martin offered to visit the cemetery to find Josef Geiger's grave. He translated the Hebrew inscription as:

> *Here is buried Yoseph Aryeh son of Abraham Geiger from Blozev-Zurich*
>
> *Died Kaf (20) Cheshvan 5750*

He added that there were an additional 8 sentences from different parts of the scriptures that he did not translate. Martin noted that there were small stones left on Josef's grave indicating that people visited the grave.[78]

How Josef Geiger and Esther Schonfeld Escaped from Nazi Germany

Josef and Estera aka Esther Geiger managed to leave Vienna after the Anschluss and Kristallnacht however they were detained at Milan, Italy in 1939 and placed in an Italian refugee camp since Italy and Germany signed a pact May 1939 for mutual military alliance. Josef and his wife were at great risk of being returned to Germany unless they could quickly obtain visas to enter England, with the purpose of staying there until the quota for immigration to the USA was lifted. Charles Geiger was instrumental in writing letters to his niece Pearl and her husband George Bronz, asking them for their help in obtaining affidavits for Josef and Esther to enter the United States. Due to the American quota for refugees, George Bronz also sent an affidavit to the London German Jewish Committee to approve the immigration of Josef and Esther Geiger to England, with the assurance they would not be a financial burden to the London German Jewish community. They were successful in obtaining visas for immigration to the UK and entered England sometime between 1939–1940. Their address in England was given by Abraham Geiger in a letter addressed to George Bronz, as being 16 Courtleigh, Bridge Lane, Golder's Green, London, England.

British Citizenship

Josef and Esther were finally able to obtain immigration visas to the USA once the quota was lifted, in 1946. Their ship was a magnificent ocean liner, *Queen Elizabeth*, and they sailed tourist class from the port of Southampton on 6 November 1946 arriving in New York, on 11 November 1946.[79] Their visas were issued in London on 30 July 1946. Josef listed his occupation as manager. He stated he was going to join his brother Markus Geiger in New York, living at 212 East Broadway, New York City. Josef's physical description was 5 feet 11 inches with brown hair and grey eyes.

Josef and Esther Geiger, 1927

The next voyage for Josef Geiger was on the *Queen Mary* that departed from Southampton, England on 17 February 1951 and arrived in New York on 22 February 1951, his destination was 212 East Broadway. In another ship manifest both Josef and Esther Geiger were passengers on the ship the *Queen Mary* in cabin class, that departed from Southampton, England on 19 February 1952 and arrived in New York 14 February 1952; their nationality was listed as British. Their destination was 212 East Broadway, New York. Josef and Esther Geiger were passengers listed on the ship manifest for the *Queen Elizabeth* that departed from Southampton, England on 25 February 1954 and arrived in New York on 02 March 1954. Their destination was 212 East Broadway, NY to Max Geiger.[80] Josef and Esther Geiger took a flight on Pan American World Airways from London to New York on 10 December 1955. Josef and Esther frequently travelled to New York from England 1946 through 1959 on luxurious ships or by airline to visit his brother Max Geiger. Since Josef and his wife were British citizens they always returned to the UK. Josef and Esther Geiger left no issue.

Information gathered from www.ancestry.com England and Wales National Probate Calendar, 1858–1966 contained information that Esther Geiger died 8 July 1959 in London. She resided at 16 Courtleigh Court, Bridge Lane, London adjacent to Golder's Green.[81] Her estate amounted to £ 2026 and was bequeathed to her husband Josef Geiger who was a company director. The UK Death Records from JewishGen.org, indicated Esther aka Estera Geiger was buried 9 July 1959 at the Enfield Jewish Cemetery in London. Information was provided by the Adath Yisroel Burial Society, an orthodox Jewish organization.[82]

Szejwa Golda aka Stella Geiger

Stella was born 11 July 1902 at Błażowa, Poland.[83] She was Abraham and Sprinza's fourth and last child. Her Hebrew name Szejwa was based on the biblical Tsivye referring to the mother of Yehoash, the King of Judah; her name was also derived from the Hebrew noun for deer or gazelle.[84] She was known as Stella by her family. She died 7 November 1989 at Miami, Florida.[85] She married Morris Steinboch 29 November 1931 at Vienna.[86] Morris Steinboch was a manager, employed 1931–1938 at the paperbag manufacturing business in Vienna that was owned by Stella's brother Max Geiger. Her husband Morris was born 20 May 1904 at Tarnów, Poland. He died 28 August 1986 at Miami, Florida.[87] They had no issue.

Stella and Morris Steinboch left Vienna soon after the *Anschluss* to stay with Morris Steinboch's brother Josef Steinboch at Antwerp, Belgium. I found the ship manifest for Stella and Moses aka Morris as passengers on the *S.S.Pennland* that sailed from Antwerp, Belgium on 26 April 1940 and arrived at New York on 16 May 1940. Their last address was at Antwerp, Belgium and they listed Josef Steinbock, Morris Steinboch's brother, who lived in Antwerp as a reference, his address was 10 Oosten Street, Antwerp, Belgium.[88] Belgium was a neutral country during WWII until it was occupied by the Nazi Army 28 May 1940. Stella and Morris's visas were issued 8 April 1940 from Antwerp. Their destination was to New York, to their uncle Charles Geiger at 585 West End Avenue, New York City. Morris listed his occupation as merchant on the ship manifest. Sponsors assisting Morris and Stella for obtaining visas were probably Charles Geiger and George Bronz.

Morris Steinboch wrote a distressed letter 27 September 1941 to George Bronz to help his brother Josef Steinboch and wife Melanie obtain visas from Marseilles for immigration to the USA. I did not locate Josef Steinboch in any database; his fate remains unknown. Josef's wife was Melanie Steinboch née Ullmann. I located her on a ship manifest for the *S.S. Thome* that departed from Lisbon, Portugal 25 September 1942 and arrived at Baltimore, Maryland 8 October 1942.[89] She indicated she was age 47, married, travelling by herself and her husband was Josef Steinbock. Her last residence was Marseilles, France. She was going to her brother Maurice Ullmann living in Manhattan, New York. I also found a death record for Melanie Steinbock; she died 12 January 1944 at Kings County, New York.[90]

Morris and Stella Steinbock lived in Manhattan at 146 Henry Street, New York. Both Stella and Morris applied for naturalization, and both were naturalized on the same day 23 August 1945 by the U.S. District Court in New York City.[91] I obtained a copy of Stella Steinboch's Petition for Naturalization, the Certificate of Arrival and Oath of Allegiance, dated 23 August 1945. Her photo on her Petition was dated 10 December 1940.[92] Stella Steinboch indicated on her Petition for Naturalization that her occupation was diamond cutter. She probably learned the trade of diamond cutter when they lived in Antwerp since Antwerp was a diamond center.

Morris Steinboch at Oscar Weiss Umbrella Factory

U. S. DEPARTMENT OF ~~JUSTICE~~ LABOR
IMMIGRATION AND NATURALIZATION SERVICE

No. 2 776366

CERTIFICATE OF ARRIVAL

I HEREBY CERTIFY that the immigration records show that the alien named below arrived at the port, on the date, and in the manner shown, and was lawfully admitted to the United States of America for permanent residence.

Name:
Port of entry: Schejwa (Szejwa) Steinbock
Date: New York, N. Y.
Manner of arrival: May 16, 1940
                    SS Pennland

I FURTHER CERTIFY that this certificate of arrival is issued under authority of, and in conformity with, the provisions of the Act of June 29, 1906, as amended, solely for the use of the alien herein named and only for naturalization purposes.

IN WITNESS WHEREOF, this certificate of arrival is issued

OCT 21 1940

IMMIGRANT IDENTIFICATION CARD ISSUED

Form 161

                                        JAMES L. HOUGHTELING
                                        Commissioner.

(10) My last foreign residence was **Antwerp, Belgium** .... I emigrated to the United States of America from **Antwerp, Belgium** .... My lawful entry (arrival) for permanent residence in the United States was at **New York, N. Y.**, under the name of **Schejwa (Szejwa) Steinbock** on **May 16, 1940**, on the vessel **Pennland** as shown by the certificate of my arrival.

(11) I am not an anarchist. I am not a polygamist nor a believer in the practice of polygamy. I declare that it is my intention in good faith to become a citizen of the United States of America; that I will, before being admitted to citizenship, renounce absolutely and forever all allegiance and fidelity to any foreign prince, potentate, state, or sovereignty, of whom or of which I may be at the time of admission to citizenship a citizen or subject; and that it is my intention to reside permanently in the United States.

I do swear (affirm) that I know the contents of this declaration of intention subscribed by me; that the same are true to the best of my own knowledge, except as to matters therein stated to be alleged upon information and belief, and that as to those matters I believe them to be true; that this declaration was signed by me with my full, true name; and that the photograph affixed to the duplicate and triplicate of this declaration of intention is a likeness of me; SO HELP ME GOD.

Subscribed and sworn to (affirmed) before me in the form of oath shown above in the office of Clerk of said Court at **New York, N. Y.** this **10** day of **December** anno Domini, 19 **40** I hereby certify that Certification No. **2-776366** from the Commissioner of Immigration and Naturalization, showing the lawful entry for permanent residence of the declarant above named on the date stated in this declaration of intention, has been received by me, and that the photograph affixed to the duplicate and triplicate hereof is a likeness of the declarant.

GEORGE J. H. FULLMER

[SEAL]

By .... Court. Clerk.

Form 2202-L-B
U. S. DEPARTMENT OF JUSTICE
IMMIGRATION AND NATURALIZATION SERVICE
(Edition 4-26-40)

No. 715576

Stella Steinboch Certificate of Arrival

TRIPLICATE
(To be given to declarant when originally issued; to be made a part of the petition for naturalization when petition is filed; and to be retained as part of the petition in the records of the court)

No. 476508

HFL

UNITED STATES OF AMERICA

DECLARATION OF INTENTION
(Invalid for all purposes seven years after the date hereof)

In the .... DISTRICT .... Court

ss:

of .... UNITED STATES .... at NEW YORK, N.

(1) My full name is ...... **MORRIS STEINBOSK** ......

(2) My place of residence is ...**20 W. 22 St. New York, NY**... (3) My occupation is ...**Cutter-Umbrellas**...

(4) I was born at **Tarnow, Poland**, on **May 20, 1904** my age is ...**36** years. (5) My nationality is **Poland**

(6) My personal description is:

Race ...**Hebrew**; sex ...**male**; color ......**white**; complexion ...**dark**...; color of eyes ...**brown**; color of hair ...**brown**...; height ...**5**... feet, ...**7**... inches; weight ...**175**... pounds; visible distinctive marks ....**none**.................... (7) I have ...**not**... heretofore made a declaration of intention:

Number ...., on ...., at ....

(8) I am .... married. The name of my wife or husband is ...... **Schejwa** ....; (s)he resides at ...... **20 W. 22 St. New York, NY** were married at **Vienna, Austria** on **November 29, 1931**; (s)he was born at **Blajowa, Poland**, on **July 11, 1902**; entered the United States at ...... **New York, NY** ......, on ...**May 16, 1940**..., for permanent residence therein. (9) I have ...**no**... children, and the name, date, and place of birth and place of residence of each of said children are as follows: ......

(10) My last foreign residence was ......**Antwerp, Belgium**............ I emigrated to the United States of America from ......**Antwerp, Belgium**... My lawful entry (arrival) for permanent residence in the United States was at ....**New York, NY**..., under the name of ...... **Mojsesz Steinbok (Steinbock)** on ...**May 15, 1940**... on the vessel ...**Penland**... as shown by the certificate of my arrival.

(11) I am not an anarchist. I am not a polygamist nor a believer in the practice of polygamy. I declare that it is my intention in good faith to become a citizen of the United States of America; that I will, before being admitted to citizenship, renounce absolutely and forever all allegiance and fidelity to any foreign prince, potentate, state, or sovereignty, of whom or of which I may be at the time of admission to citizenship a citizen or subject; and that it is my intention to reside permanently in the United States.

I do swear (affirm) that I know the contents of this declaration of intention subscribed by me; that the same are true to the best of my own knowledge, except as to matters therein stated to be alleged upon information and belief, and that as to those matters I believe them to be true; that this declaration was signed by me with my full, true name; and that the photograph affixed to the duplicate and triplicate of this declaration of intention is a likeness of me; SO HELP ME GOD.

Morris Steinbock
(original signature of declarant without abbreviation, also other name, if used)

Subscribed and sworn to (affirmed) before me in the form of oath shown above in the office of Clerk of said Court at ......**New York, NY**...... this ......**5**... day of ....**December** anno Domini, 19...**40** I hereby certify that Certification No. **2-780534**.... from the Commissioner of Immigration and Naturalization, showing the lawful entry for permanent residence of the declarant above named on the date stated in this declaration of intention, has been received by me, and that the photograph affixed to the duplicate and triplicate hereof is a likeness of the declarant.

.... **GEORGE J.H. FOLLMER** .... DISTRICT .... Court.

[SEAL]

By .... Deputy Clerk.

Form 2202-L-B
U. S. DEPARTMENT OF JUSTICE
IMMIGRATION AND NATURALIZATION SERVICE
(Edition 4-26-40)

U. S. GOVERNMENT PRINTING OFFICE

Nº 690915

Morris Steinbock

Morris Steinboch Declaration

I also obtained a copy of Morris Steinboch's Declaration of Intention with his photo.[93] Morris Steinboch gave an address for his residence as 20 W. 22 St., New York. He gave his occupation as Cutter-Umbrellas. This address was familiar to me as it was the umbrella manufacturing business owned by my grandparents Oscar and Minnie Weiss née Geiger. I have a rare photo taken at the site of their business that included my grandparents and my mother Sylvia with all their employees. I previously did not carefully examine the photo however with this new information I quickly matched the photo of Morris Steinboch on his Declaration of Intention as the same man who stood behind my grandparents in the photo of the umbrella factory. It was obvious that he was employed there.

The Archives in Vienna

I wrote to the Osterreichisches Staatarchiv (archives at Vienna, Austria) for information about my Geiger relatives. Vital information for Morris and Stella Steinboch was confirmed in the records sent to me 26 July 2010 from the archive in a huge correspondence file. The records from the Fonds Zur Hilfeleistung an Politisch (Hilfsfonds) were included in the package from the Austria State Archives, Vienna, Austria.[94] The archive records indicated that during 1964 Stella and Morris Steinboch learned of restitution for persecuted Jews during WWII by the organization, Fonds zur Hilfeleistung an Politisch Verfolgte (Hilfsfonds) in Vienna. This organization awarded financial restitution to victims of the Holocaust for their pain, suffering and medical conditions. Stella and Morris Steinboch were awarded monetary restitution over the years from 1965 through the 1980.[95] Their address during 1938 in Vienna was given as Wintergasse 29 in District XX.

Based on the correspondence file sent by Hilfsfonds, they lived at 146 Henry Street, Manhattan, New York from May 1940 to September 1959. They moved from New York September 1959 to Florida and lived at 1770 Meridian Avenue, Miami Beach, Florida, also at 1420 Pennsylvania Avenue, Miami Beach, Florida.

While living in Florida, Morris worked part-time at the Tarleton Hotel on Collins Avenue, Miami Beach as seen by his 1975 W-2 form. Morris petitioned Hilfsfonds to grant him additional funds 7 September 1978: *"As already written, I had operated in District XX Gerhardusgasse 26, a paperbag manufacturing factory in the years 1931 to 1938. The factory was confiscated. I had no schilling indemnity besides I have an ulcer and am always under medical care. This ulcer justifies an increase."* Stella also wrote to Hilfsfonds 3 August 1978: *"As already written, I suffer from angina pectoris and am under medical treatment. My illness has become aggravated and I will probably need a pacemaker to feel better. I have only a small budget and will need additional financial assistance.*"[96] Their requests were under consideration by Hilfsfonds officials.

Debra P. recalled that after her tanta (aunt) Stella Steinboch arrived in New York, she set out to Washington D.C. to find other relatives she knew, probably her cousins George and Pearl Bronz who lived in Washington D.C. Stella would have difficulty at that time as she spoke little English.

Grandchildren of Rabbi Abraham Geiger and Sprynca Stark

Clara Geiger was the first child born 8 July 1926 at Vienna, Austria to Max and Rose Geiger née Ginsberg. She married Emanuel aka Manny Chopp 23 May 1947 at Manhattan.[97] Manny was born to Nathan Chopp and Sali Tuchman 21 June 1917 at Poland.[98] Manny's father Nathan Chopp was naturalized by the U.S. District Court in Brooklyn, New York 27 December 1943.[99] Nathan and Sali, including their six children Manny, Herman, Freddy, Joseph, Rose and Helen indicated they were born in Poland.[100] Manny Chopp died 24 February 2007 at New York, and he was buried at Beth David Cemetery, Elmont, New York.[101] Clara and Manny Chopp had the following children: Avraham Yitzak, Moishe, and Joshua. Clara and her children are still living.

Susi Geiger was the second child born 9 April 1931 at Vienna, Austria to Max and Rose Geiger. She married Benjamin David Kleiman 12 May 1949 at Manhattan, New York.[102] He was born 18 December 1928 at New York to Louis and Esther Kleiman.[103] His date of birth was also found in the New York Birth Index.[104] Benjamin David's father Louis Kleiman was born in Russia and immigrated to the U.S. 1912; his mother Esther was also born in Russia and immigrated 1913.[105] Benjamin Kleiman died 28 May 2010 at Jamesburg, Middlesex County, New Jersey.[106] Susi Kleiman died 18 June 2013 at New Jersey.[107] Susi and Benjamin Kleiman had the following children: Sheva Sprintzer, Devora Frimi, and Mindy Bela. They are still living.

I learned from Sheindle Cohen, another genealogical researcher, of a new website organized by Rabbi Baruch Amsel. This website is a compilation of over 1,681 rabbis buried in North America. Relatives and friends of the rabbis contributed to the website with relevant photographs, burial, and biographical information. I became one of the contributors and donated information for Rabbi Avroham Yitzchok Geiger to the website kevarim.com/rabbi-avroham-yitzchok-geiger/. Rabbi Avroham Yitzchok Geiger was remembered as a righteous man who transmitted the spirit and practice of orthodox Judaism to his family and many others.

Descendants of Abraham Geiger

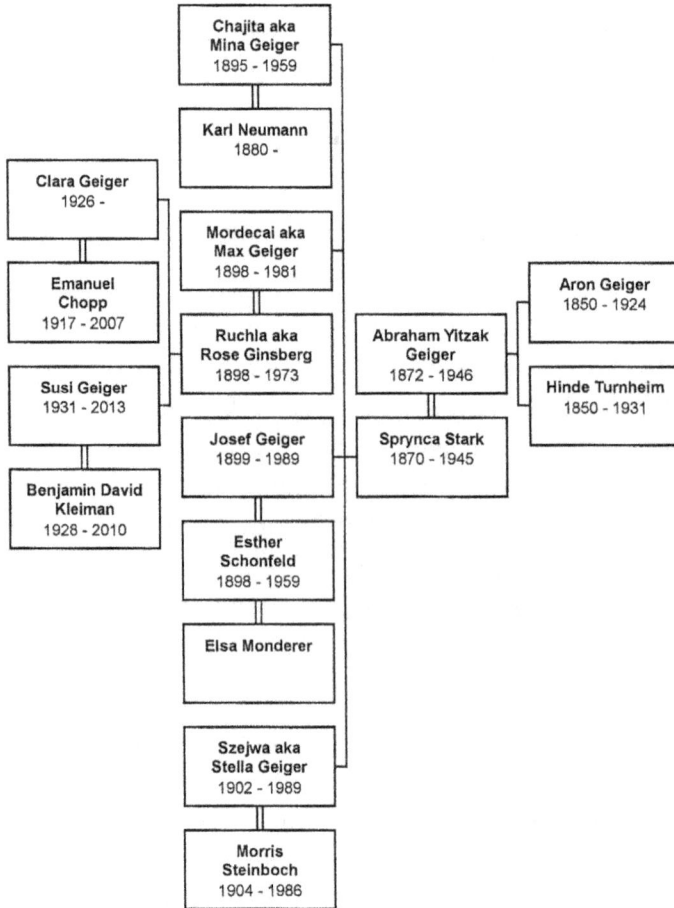

```
                                    ┌──────────────────┐
                                    │  Chajita aka     │
                                    │  Mina Geiger     │
                                    │  1895 - 1959     │
                                    └──────────────────┘
                                    ┌──────────────────┐
                                    │  Karl Neumann    │
                                    │  1880 -          │
                                    └──────────────────┘
      ┌──────────────────┐          ┌──────────────────┐
      │  Clara Geiger    │          │  Mordecai aka    │
      │  1926 -          │          │  Max Geiger      │
      └──────────────────┘          │  1898 - 1981     │
      ┌──────────────────┐          └──────────────────┘          ┌──────────────────┐
      │  Emanuel         │          ┌──────────────────┐          │  Aron Geiger     │
      │  Chopp           │          │  Ruchla aka      │  ┌──────────────────┐ │  1850 - 1924     │
      │  1917 - 2007     │          │  Rose Ginsberg   │  │ Abraham Yitzak  │ └──────────────────┘
      └──────────────────┘          │  1898 - 1973     │  │ Geiger          │
      ┌──────────────────┐          └──────────────────┘  │ 1872 - 1946     │ ┌──────────────────┐
      │  Susi Geiger     │          ┌──────────────────┐  └──────────────────┘ │ Hinde Turnheim   │
      │  1931 - 2013     │          │  Josef Geiger    │  ┌──────────────────┐ │ 1850 - 1931      │
      └──────────────────┘          │  1899 - 1989     │  │ Sprynca Stark   │ └──────────────────┘
      ┌──────────────────┐          └──────────────────┘  │ 1870 - 1945     │
      │ Benjamin David   │          ┌──────────────────┐  └──────────────────┘
      │ Kleiman          │          │  Esther          │
      │ 1928 - 2010      │          │  Schonfeld       │
      └──────────────────┘          │  1898 - 1959     │
                                    └──────────────────┘
                                    ┌──────────────────┐
                                    │  Elsa Monderer   │
                                    └──────────────────┘
                                    ┌──────────────────┐
                                    │  Szejwa aka      │
                                    │  Stella Geiger   │
                                    │  1902 - 1989     │
                                    └──────────────────┘
                                    ┌──────────────────┐
                                    │  Morris          │
                                    │  Steinboch       │
                                    │  1904 - 1986     │
                                    └──────────────────┘
```

Endnotes

1   Przemyśl Archives, Poland. Fond 1924. Przemyśl Births 1789–1827, 1853-1900. Akta 255.

2   www.jewishvirtuallibrary.org/abraham-geiger. Rabbi Abraham Geiger advocated that Judaism become a modern religion of reason and science. This became known as Reform Judaism with innovations for prayers and sermons to be in the vernacular as well as in Hebrew.

3   www.sztetl.org.pl/en/artcle/blazowa/2,location/ Błażowa Rabbis. Abraham Geiger, mohel. 1935.

4   See Wikipedia: Elimelech Weisblum of Lizhensk. He was born 1717 at Tykicin, Poland and he died 11 March 1787 at Lezajsk, Poland. He was a founding rabbi of the Hasidic movement in Galicia and was the author of *Noam Elimelech*.

5   Geni.com. Moishe Miller. R'Tzvi Elimelech Spira of Dynov (Langsam) Family.

6   See Wikipedia: Dinov (Hasidic Dynasty). Dinov is the Yiddish name of Dynow in southern Poland, once the historic region of Galicia.

7   JewishGen.org. *Yizkor Book of Rzeszow*. p. 115.

8   Ibid., pp.115–131.

9   JewishGen.org. Yizkor Book Project. Rzeszow, Poland. Pp. 115-120.

10   *Eliach, Yaffa*. Hasidic Tales of the Holocaust. New York: Vantage Books (1988). 195.

11   Ancestry.com. Border Crossings from Canada to the United States 1895-1956. Roll M 1464 St. Albans, Vermont 1895–1954. *S.S. Antonia* leaving Liverpool 18 September 1940, arriving Quebec 27 September 1940. Abraham and Sprince Geiger passports issued in England, 16 August 1940.

12   Przemysl Archive. Kanczuga. Fond 1731. Aktu 58. 8 June 1870. Birth Shprinza Stark. House Number 289.

13   Beider, Alexander. *A Dictionary of Ashkenazic Given Names*. Bergenfield, New Jersey: Avotaynu (2001), pp. 570–571.

14   Przemysl Archive. Fond 1731. Kanczuga Birth Records 1851–91. Birth: Boruch Feldman 1858 born to Leizer Feldman and Frade Krameisen.

15   FamilySearch.org. Abraham Geiger. Petition for Naturalization. U.S. District Court of Southern District, New York. Petition No. 529015. Date: 10 October 1945. Marriage Date: July 1894 in Kanczuga, Poland.

16   kehilalinks.jewishgen.org/kolbuszowa/kanczuga/kanczuga8.jpg. Photos of Kanczuga by Robert Bernheim.

17   *Austrian History Yearbook V. XI*. Vienna: Censuses 1910 and 1934. Berghahn Books. (Houston, Texas: Rice University Press, 1975).

18   Statistics of Austria. Census of 1951. www.archiv.wien.at.

19   wikipedia.org. History of the Jews in Vienna.

20   encyclopedia.ushmm.org/the-nuremberg-race-laws.

21   Ancestry.com. UK WWII Alien Internees 1939–1945. Abraham Geiger. 201-250-225 Dead Index. 1941–1947. Gabel-Gohrt.

22   Ancestry.com. Border Crossings from Canada to the U.S. 1895–1956. Roll M 1464, St. Albans Vermont 1895-1954. Abraham Geiger and Sprince Geiger, S.S. Antonia leaving Liverpool 18 Sept 1940.

23   www.clydemaritime.co.uk/troon_shipbreaking/s-s-antonia/

24   Abraham Geiger's personal letter to George Bronz, from the private collection of Elizabeth L. Dated 30 Oct 1940.

25   Immigration to the United States 1933–1941. The Holocaust Encyclopedia. United States Holocaust Memorial Museum. (encyclopedia.ushmm.org/content/en/article/immigration-to-the-united-states-1933-41).

26   Family Search.org. Southern District Court. U.S. District Court Naturalizations 1824-1946.

27   Ibid., Abraham Geiger Petition for Naturalization, No. 529015.

28   Ibid., Abraham Geiger Declaration of Intention, No. 318009.

29   Ibid., Abraham Geiger 21 January 1946 Oath of Allegiance, No. 6584227.

30   The Synagogues of New York City. Former Synagogue List Manhattan. 156 Henry Street. Agudas An-shei Mamud u'Bais Vaad Lachachomim. The Museum of Family History. Education and Research Center. (postmaster@museumoffamilyhistory.com.).

31   City of New York, Department of Health. Bureau of Records and Statistics. Abraham Geiger. Death Certificate 20576.

32   Ancestry.com. New York Death Index 1862–1948. Manhattan. Sprince Geiger Death Certificate number 3271.

33   New York City, Department of Health, Bureau of Vital Records. Death 28 September 1946. Abraham Geiger. Death Certificate 20576.

34   Email correspondence with Sheindle Cohen, 9 Dec 2016.

35   Gaon is an honorary title given to a Jewish scholar noted for wisdom and knowledge of the Talmud.

36   This was a reference to the famous Blazowa Rebbe Tzvi Elimelech Spira of Blazowa (1841–1924) who was also called the Tzvi Latzaddik in reference to his book. He was also known as the Bluzower Rebbe.

37   Ancestry.com. England & Wales, National Probate Calendar, Index of wills and Administrations, 1858–1966. Administration 25 July 1947 to Josef Geiger manager. P. 469.

38   Probate Court, New York City, Manhattan. Obtained by researcher David Priever.

39   www.chabad.org

40   U.S. Naturalization Records- Original Documents, 1790–1974. District Court, Eastern District., number 146758. Date: 4 August 1930.

41   New York, Passenger Lists, 1820-1957. Chana Halberstam, 1927, New York. S.S. Leviathan. Departing Cherbourg, France 30 August 1927, arriving New York 5 September 1927. Microfilm Serial: T715; Microfilm Roll: Roll 4121; Line 4; page 79.

42   New York Death Index 1862–1948.

43   Ancestry. Com. New York, New York Death Index 1949–1965. Chana Halberstam. Died 21 Aug 1950. Cert. 1553.

44   JewishGen.org. Rabbi Moshe Kamelhar. *Hassidic Courts; Shlomo Tal The Rabbi of Blazowa and His Dynasty. Rzeszow Community Memorial Book,* edited M. Yari-Wold. Translated by Jerrold Landau. Published Tel Aviv, 1967. Pp. 115–116.

45   Przemyśl Archive. Kanczuga Birth Records. Fond 1731. Akta 25. Birth 21 May 1895. Chajia Geiger.

46   Beider, Alexander. *A Dictionary of Ashkenazic Given Names.* Bergenfield, New Jersey: Avotaynu (2001). P. 525.

47   Ancestry.com. New York, Passenger Lists 1820–1957. Chaja and Karel Neumann were listed as passengers on the S.S.Rossia, leaving Haifa 26 February 1948 and arriving in New York 18 March 1948.

48   Private email from David P., a genealogist living in New York, who found an estate file for Abraham Geiger and Will Liber 1826, page 475, with names and addresses of Chaja Neumann at 154 Hayarkon Street, Tel Aviv as well as Max Geiger at 212 East Broadway, New Yor; Stella Steinbock at 145 Henry Street, New York; Josef Geiger at 16 Courtleigh Bridge Court, London. The executor of the estate was Morris Steinbock, husband of Stella.

49   Ancestry.com. Munich, Vienna and Barcelona Jewish Displaced Persons and Refugee Cards, 1943–1959.

50   www.avotaynu.com/holocaustlist/aboutavotaynu.htm. 2006. *Avotaynu.*

51   Ibid.

52   Ibid., pp.381–83.

53   The City of New York, Department of Health, Bureau of Vital Records. Certificate Number 156-81 303221. Max Geiger, died 25 February 1981. Max died in Maimonides Medical Center and he lived at 2415 Avenue K, Brooklyn, New York. His occupation was listed as a broker.

54   United States Petition for Naturalization, Southern District Court. Number 551588. Max Geiger, occupation listed as a diamond broker.

55   Petition for Naturalization for Max Geiger lists Rose Geiger's birth as 10 June, 1898.

56   United States Social Security Death Index. Rose Geiger, born 6 October 1898, died in Brooklyn, New

York in September, 1973. Interment search for Wellwood Cemetery at Farmingdale, NY indicates her date of death was 3 Sept 1973.

57   Wellwood cemetery internment search. Both Max and Rose Geiger were buried at section Society Cong Sharis Adath Israel Menhag Sefard block 48. Max was at row 5, grave 4R; Rose was at row 6, grave 7L.

58   encyclopedia.ushmm.org/content/en/article/the -great-depression.

59   Susi Kleiman, personal emails to this writer, December 2011.

60   German translations were provided by Marcel Herbst, Zipora Neustadt and Jonathan Michael Wien through ViewMate at www.jewishgen.org.

61   Zone Libre. (en.wikipedia.org/wiki/Zone_libre.)

62   *S.S. Navemar.* (en.wikipedia.org/wiki/SS_Navemar.)

63   Ancestry.com. New York Passenger List. *S.S. Navemar*, leaving Seville, Spain 7 August 1941 arriving New York 12 September 1941. Passengers: Markus, Ruchla, Klara, Susi Geiger.

64   *The Royal Gazette*, Bermuda. Published 6 Oct 2012. Eye witness reportof the Navemar at Havana by Victor Bienstock.

65   United States Department of Justice, Immigration and Naturalization Service. Number 2 941296. Markus Geiger arriving in the port of New York on 12 September 1941 on the *S.S. Navemar.*

66   U.S. District Court at Southern District, New York. Max Geiger. Declaration of Intention. 1 April 1942. Cert. 547720.

67   U.S. District Court at Court of Southern District, New York. Max Geiger. Petition for Naturalization. 2 Jan 1947. Cert. 551588.

68   Ibid., Oath of Allegiance, granted, Cert. 6703113.

69   Debra P., e-mail sent 30 June 2013.

70   The City of New York. Department of Health. Bureau of Vital Records. Death Certificate Max Geiger. Death: 25 February 1981. Maimonides Medical Center, Brooklyn, New York. Death due to natural causes. Cert. No. 303221.

71   Beider, Alexander. *A Dictionary of Ashkenazic Given Names.* Bergenfield, New Jersey: Avotaynu (2001), p. 455.

72   See personal letter dated 30 October 1940 written by Abraham Geiger to George Bronz concerning affidavits for his son Josef Geiger born 6 December 1899 in Blazowa, Poland. Josef Geiger was living in London at 16 Courtleigh, Bridge Lane, Golder's Green with his wife Esther and Abraham Geiger was also requesting affidavits for her.

73   See note written by George Bronz indicating Esther's birthdate as 26 October 1898 in Bucharest, Roumania.

74   JewishGen.org. UK Death Records. Estera Geiger was buried in the Enfield Cemetery in London, through the Adath Yisroel Burial Society.

75   Contact has been made with the Israelitische Culrusgemeinde Zurich (ICZ) for information concerning Josef Geiger after 1959 as family members thought that Josef had married a woman named Elsa from Zurich, who owned businesses in Zurich.

76   Ancestry.com. England and Wales, Civil Registration Marriage Index 1916–2005. Volume 5e, page 926. Oct 1960. Elsie Monderer and Josef Geiger.

77   Personal email from Brenda H. dated 16 November 2014. Josef Geiger was buried at Givat Shaul, Grave "tet", Row A, Plot "aleph", area "yud-aleph", Har Hamenuchot Cemetery, Jerusalem, Israel.

78   Personal email, Martin Bialik, regarding Josef Geiger, 4 Aug 2019.

79   Ancestry.com. New York Passenger Lists. Josef and Estera Geiger. S.S.Queen Elizabeth. Leaving Southampton England to New York, 6 November 1946 and arriving in New York 11 November 1946.

80   Ibid., Josef and Estera Geiger. *S.S. Queen Elizabeth.* Leaving Southampton England 25 February 1954 and arriving at New York 2 March 1954.

81   Ancestry.com. England and Wales, National Probate Calendar, 1858–1966. Estera Geiger.

82   JewishGen.org. UK Death Records. Estera Geiger, buried Enfield Cemetery, London, UK. Plot H-19-1. Adath Yisroel Burial Society.

83   Vienna Archives. Hilfsfonds documents pertaining to Stella Steinboch nee Geiger. Birthdate: 11 July 1902 in Blazowa, Poland.

84   Beider, Alexander. *A Dictionary of Ashkenazic Given Names*. Bergenfield, New Jersey: Avotaynu (2001), p. 593. The Polish spelling of a name based on Tsivye is Czywa, that is phonetically close to Szejwa.

85   Ancestry.com. U.S. Social Security Index Death Index 1935–2014. Death: November 1989. Stella Steinboch. Miami, Florida.

86   FamilySearch.org. New York, Southern District, U.S. District Court Naturalization Records 1824-1946. Petition for Naturalization, Stella Steinboch, No. 521907, 1940.

87   Ancestry.com. U.S. Social Security Death Index 1935–2014. Death: August 1986. Morris Steinboch. Miami, Florida.

88   Ancestry.com. New York, U.S., Arriving Passenger and Crew Lists, 1820–1957. *S.S. Pennland*. Departing Antwerp 26 April 1940, Arriving New York 16 May 1940.

89   Ancestry.com. Baltimore, Passenger Lists, 1820–1964. Melanie Steinbock. *S.S. Thome*. Departing Lisbon, Portugal 25 September 1942; Arrival Baltimore, Maryland 8 October 1942.

90   Ancestry.com. New York, New York, U.S., Extracted Death Index, 1862–1948. Melanie Steinbock. Death: 12 January 1944. Kings County, New York. Cert. 1263.

91   Ancestry.com. New York, Index to Petitions for Naturalization filed in New York City, 1792–1989. Stella Steinbock, Petition No. 521907 and Morris Steinbock, Petition No. 521908. Their address was listed as 146 Henry Street, New York.

92   FamilySearch.org. New York, Southern District, U.S. District Court Naturalization Records, 1824–1946, Petitions for Naturalization and Petition Evidence 1945 box 1046, no. 521737-521950.

93   FamilySearch.org. New York, Southern District, U.S. District Court Naturalization Records, 1824-1946.

94   Osterreichisches Staatarchiv. Vienna, Austria. Hilfsfonds: Fonds Zur Hilfeleistung an Politisch Verfolgte. Files: Stella Steinboch. Morris Steinboch. Sent July 2010.

95   Osterreichisches Staatarchiv. Address: Nottendorfer Gasse 2, Wien, Austria. Those archives contained files and correspondence dealing with Jewish property and funds for the politically persecuted during WWII. Files for Stella and Morris Steinboch, Markus Geiger and Oscar Geiger were mailed to this writer with documentation indicating evidence of trauma and illness. Some monetary restitution was provided to our relatives by the Hilfsfonds organization.

96   Hilfsfonds. 14 August 1978. Dr. Georg Weis in response to a request by Stella Steinboch.

97   Ancestry.com. New York, New York Marriage License Indexes, 1907–2018. Marriage License 15387. Manny Chopp and Clara Geiger.

98   Ancestry.com. U.S. Social Security Applications and Claims Index, 1936-2007.

99   Ancestry.com. U.S. Naturalization Records Indexes, 1794–1995. Number 5729765. Nathan Chopp.

100   Ancestry.com. 1940 Federal Census, Brooklyn, New York. Enumeration District 24-2811. Manny Chopp.

101   Ancestry.com. U.S. Social Security Applications and Claims Index, 1936–2007. Manny Chopp.

102   Ancestry.com. New York City Municipal Archives. New York, New York. Marriage License Indexes, 1907-2018. Marriage License 11636. Benjamin D. Kleiman and Susi Geiger.

103   Ancestry.com. 1930 Federal Census, Brooklyn, New York. Enumeration District 1230. Dave Kleiman, age 2.

104   Ancestry.com. New York, New York Birth Index, 1910–1965.

105   Ancestry.com. 1920 Federal Census, Brooklyn, New York. Enumeration District 73. Louis and Esther Kleiman.

106   U.S. Social Security Death Index, 1935–2014. Benjamin Kleiman. (www.ancestry.com).

107   Ancestry.com. New Jersey Death Index 1901–2017. Death: Susi Kleiman 18 June 2013.

Chapter Eight

Israel Geiger and Esther Perlberg

Beginnings

Israel aka Isidore was the fourth child born to Aron Geiger and Hinde Turnheim 16 January 1874 at Przemyśl, Podkarpackie, Poland. I obtained his birth record from the Przemyśl Archives in Poland and noted that his grandfather Solomon David Geiger was listed as the *sandek* for the *bris*.[1] There was a six-year age difference between Israel and his older brother Chaskel. Israel was either about to become a *bar mitzvah* or had just completed his coming-of-age Judaic ritual when Chaskel left home to immigrate to the United States. I speculate that Israel longed to do the same, however his parents probably refused to even consider this as an option for Israel due to his age. While living at Przemyśl Israel found work as a cigarmaker and he prudently saved money for his planned trip and immigration. His occupation was stated on the ship manifest as cigarmaker when he finally journeyed from Poland to Hamburg, Germany and subsequently immigrated to the United States.

Birth record for Israel Geiger

№ 943

№ 1045

Verzeichniss

der Personen, welche zur Auswanderung nach _Nord Amerika_ via _Liverpool_ durch Unterzeichneten engagirt sind, und mit dem Dampf-/Segel- Schiffe _Panther_ Capitain _Leggott_ unter _englischer_ Flagge nach _Hull_ befördert werden.

Abgang des Schiffes den _24. Juni_ 1890

	Zuname	Vornamen	Geschlecht männlich	Geschlecht weiblich	Alter	Bisheriger Wohnort	Im Staate resp. in der Provinz	Bisheriger Stand oder Beruf	Ziel der Auswanderung (Ort und Land bei anzugeben)	Zahl der Personen	Davon sind: Erwachsene und Kinder über 10 Jahre	Davon sind: Kinder unter 10 Jahr	Davon sind: Kinder unter 1 Jahr
1.	Kossowoi	Sophie		1	43					1	1		
2.	Rachliz	Feige		1	40	Kiew	Russland			1	1		
3.	do	Chaie		1	16					1	1		
4.	do	Kalmen	1		14					1	1		
5.	Kaufman	Mordche	1		35	Lachowitz	do	Fündler		1	1		
6.	Rosenberg	Moses	1		40			do		1	1		
7.	Zelinak	Georg	1		25	Gyopolotz	Ungarn	Arbeit		1	1		
8.	Rindokas	Rosa		1	22	Wainutte	Russland			1	1		
9.	Brewer	Leiser	1		39	Kremenetz	do	Tischler		1	1		
10.	Horowitz	Schlome	1		15	Minsk	do			1	1		
11.	Brauer	Jochem	1		28	Kowno	do			1	1		
12.	Lasdan	Schimen	1		39	do	do			1	1		
13.	Handman	Moses	1		29	Schmilewitz	do			1	1		
14.	Brauer	Pesche		1	32					1	1		
15.	do	Freide		1	9	Kowno	do			1		1	
16.	do	Hillel	1		8					1		1	
17.	Spirian	Josul	1		40	do	do			1	1		
18.	Scheldin	Eilias	1		30	Minsk	do			1	1		
19.	Rosenblum	Scholem	1		24	Makowa	do	Fündler		1	1		
20.	Weitzman	Rische		1	17	Gwzd	do			1	1		
21.	Kitaj	Keile		1	17	do	do			1	1		
22.	Hurwitz	Leib	1		24	Olschan	do	Schlosser		1	1		
23.	Gerstenkern	Feige		1	40					1	1		
24.	do	Faiwel	1		9					1		1	
25.	do	Gmendel		1	7					1		1	
26.	do	Pipre		1	6	Plock	do			1		1	
27.	do	Taube		1	3					1		1	
28.	do	Simche	1		4M					1			1
29.	do	Chaie		1	4M					1			1
30.	Schimernitzk	Mosche	1		18			Schneider		1	1		
31.	do	Chaie		1	17	Olschan	do			1	1		
32.	Geiger	Israel	1		17	Przemysl	Galizien	Kaufmann		1	1		
			18	14						32	23	7	2

Immigration record for Israel Geiger

Immigration

Chaskel Geiger as the big brother helped Israel secure passage and employment in New York. My search for Israel Geiger in immigration records led me to the Hamburg passenger lists. Israel Geiger departed 24 June 1890 on the ship *S.S. Panther* from Hamburg, Germany to arrive at Hull, England with a destination to North America via Liverpool. He stated that he was 17 years and resided in Przemyśl, Galicia.[2] The *S.S. Panther* was built 1861 at Hull, U.K. and was a steamship holding 149 passengers. Israel Geiger listed his occupation as cigarmaker (German word was *zigarrenmacher*). Records for the *S.S. Panther* were not among the list of ships that arrived at New York 1890–1891 with immigrants from Austria, Poland, and Galicia.[3] After his arrival at New York, Israel was employed by his older brother Charles Geiger in the retail furniture business, a trade that provided Israel with continuous employment in the USA.

Marriage

Israel aka Isidore Geiger met Esther Perlberg on the Lower East Side in New York City. They were married 27 November 1898 as noted on their marriage certificate obtained from the Municipal Archives at New York City.[4] Their marriage record contained the following information: his parents were Aron Geiger and Hinde Turnheim. He lived at 66 Orchard Street in Manhattan. Esther's parents were Elias Perlberg and Sarah Malter. Esther lived at 611 East 6th Street at Manhattan. As was the case for most immigrants at that time, reporting one's age was usually approximate because their birth records were not available to them, memories often faded and so there were often age discrepancies.

The 1900 United States Federal Census listed Isidore Geiger, his wife Esta, and their infant daughter Jennie at 528 East 6th Street in Manhattan.5 In the next apartment at that same address lived Esther's mother Sarah Perlberg, a widow, with two sons and a daughter: Meyer age 22; Abraham age 19; and Ella age 12. All were listed as having been born in Austria except for Ella, who was born at Cincinnati, Ohio. Meyer's occupation was simply "butter," either making butter or selling butter and Abraham's occupation was a stock clerk. Isidore's occupation was listed as a salesman. Both Isidore and Esther stated they were born in Austria.

Isidore and Esther had two children born at New York City followed by a third child born in Chicago. Their daughter Jennie Geiger was born 7 September 1899 at New York City. Although no birth record has been found, her birth

Esther Perlberg age 21

month and year was recorded on the 1900 United States Federal Census for Manhattan.[6] Their son Elias (later named Eli) Geiger was born 30 April 1901 at New York City.[7] Elias was named after Esther's deceased father Elias Perlberg. Sometime between 1901 and 1904, Isidore and Esther with their children Jenny and Eli moved to Chicago, Illinois Their third child, Harry, was born 11 December 1908 at Chicago.[8]

Esther Geiger née Perlberg: Her Parents and Siblings

Immigration

Esther Perlberg (1874–1931) was born 22 November 1874 at Żabno, Małopolskie, Poland to Elias Perlberg and Zurtel Malter.[9] Her dates of birth and death were inscribed on her matsevah in Chicago, however since Esther immigrated 1885 with her parents and siblings to the USA at age 9, then her birth year was probably 1876. Esther's mother was named Zurtel (1850–1925), a female name used in 19th century Galicia as a kinnui for Sarah.[10] Zurtel later became known as Sarah in the USA. Based on her reported age of 35 years on her immigration record, she was born ca.1850 in Żabno, Poland. She immigrated to the USA with

Zurtel Perlberg Manifest 1885

their children Esther, Chaje, Meyer and Abraham on the *S.S. Rugia*. The ship departed from Hamburg 26 August 1885 and arrived at New York 7 September 1885.[11] Her husband Elias Perlberg (1846–1887) immigrated two years earlier from Hamburg, Germany on the *S.S.Rhaetia* and he arrived in New York 11 June 1883.[12] His birth year was ca.1846 according to his reported age of 37 years on the ship manifest.

Zurtel's parents were Aaron Malter and Sheindel from Żabno. My cousin Evelyn posted a photograph and death record for Aaron Malter (1831–1904) on the Joseph and Dora Bandes Family Tree at www.ancestry.com. Aaron Malter was listed in the 1891 Galicia Business Directory as a (*gastwirthe und gasthofe*) guesthouse/innkeeper at Żabno.[13] According to information on his death certificate concerning the number of years in the U.S., I estimate that Aaron Malter immigrated ca. 1898 from Galicia. He died 18 July 1904 at 205 Manhattan Avenue, Brooklyn, New York.[14] The 1900 United States Census indicated that he was a widower and lived with his daughter Lena and her husband Max Wigdor at 466 Grand Street in Brooklyn, New York.[15]

Both Elias Perlberg and Zurtel aka Sarah Malter were from Żabno, Małopolskie, Poland. This was a town 9 miles NW of Tarnów and 43 miles E of Kraków, Małopolskie, Poland. The Jewish population of Żabno in 1890 was 696 and was more than half the total population. I found a list of Jewish surnames from Żabno; Perlberg and Malter were on that list.[16] Jews lived in Żabno since 1675 when they received the right to settle and trade. By 1692 they received rights for money lending, arenda arrangements for leasing land, land purchase, building houses, construction for a synagogue and a cemetery. Jews were always an important part of the local Żabno community until WWII.[17] Before WWI Żabno was in the Tarnów District, Galicia and considered part of the Austro-Hungarian Empire hence Osterreich. I located a birth record for their child, Hirsch Perlberg, born 9 November 1882 to parents

Aaron Malter

Elias Perlberg and Zurtel Malter at Tarnowiec, a small village within Tarnów, Małopolskie, Poland.[18] Hirsch Perlberg probably died sometime after birth because no other records with his name were found.

Elias Perlberg and Zurtel Malter with their four children Esther, Chaje, Meyer and Abram made their momentous decision to emigrate from Galicia to the United States. The lure of immigration to the new unknown land of freedom with limitless possibilities was fed by glowing reports of success and where all men were treated equally before the law. Steamship agents stirred the imagination by spreading Yiddish leaflets with stories of wealth and freedom.[19]

Men often immigrated first then sent for their families. After Elias became acclimated to the USA, he sent for his wife and children. Zurtel indicated their last residence was Żabno, Osterreich. Elias, Zurtel and their children re-united at New York and they decided to continue their journey westward to Cincinnati, Ohio.

Life in Cincinnati, Ohio

By 1886 Elias was listed on the Cincinnati City Directory as a Clothing Renovator.[20] Elias and Sarah Perlberg had two more children born at Cincinnati: Benjamin, born July 1886 and Ella, born May 1888.[21] Elias died an early death as indicated on the Cincinnati City Directory of 1890 listing Sarah Perlberg as a widow and her daughter Esther who worked as a wrapper at age 16.[22] The teenager Esther appeared to be the sole support for her family. Her baby sister Ella was probably named for their deceased father Elias.

I initially could not locate any death information for Elias Perlberg on the usual websites. I found the organization Jewish Cemeteries of Greater Cincinnati. I emailed this organization an inquiry about death information for Elias Perlberg. A researcher, Alter Raubvogel, responded to my request. He discovered old hand-written death records that were not digitized or on-line for Elias Perlberg and his daughter Hannah (born Chaje). He emailed me that information including photographs of Elias's gravestone and records. Elias Perlberg (misspelled as Pelberg in the records) died 22 November 1887, age 41 and his daughter Hannah died 29 October 1887, age 12.[23] Both were buried in the Old Grounds Jewish Cemetery, Cincinnati, Ohio. Elias was buried in row 34, grave 27 and Hannah was buried in row 35, grave 24. Sarah Perlberg delivered her daughter Ella, May 1888, several months after the deaths of both her husband Elias and her daughter Hannah. Sarah Perlberg as a young widow with five children decided to move to New York City sometime between 1888 and 1898. Her motivation was to join her family members.

The Perlbergs in New York

Sarah Perlberg née Malter had a sister Lena Malter married to Max Wigdor and they immigrated to Brooklyn, New York during 1892; their father Aaron Malter immigrated ca. 1897 or 1898 and he lived in Brooklyn with the Wigdors.[24] The New York State Census for 1905 indicated Sarah Perlberg and her children Abraham, Benjamin and Ella lived at 528 East 6th Street at Manhattan.[25] They lived in an apartment next door to Isidore Geiger with his wife Esther and their daughter Jenny.[26] By the 1910 United States Federal Census for New York, Sarah age 55 and her children Abe, Bennie, and Ella lived at 167 Manhattan Avenue, in Brooklyn, New York. Both Bennie and Ella were born at Cincinnati, Ohio; Abe was born in Galicia, within the Austro-Hungarian Empire, most likely Żabno.[27] Sarah indicated on that census that she had seven children born and five children living. Her two deceased children were probably Hirsch and Hannah. Her five surviving children were Esther, Meyer, Abe, Ben, and Ella.

On the 1915 New York State Census, Kings County, New York, Assembly District 13 Sarah Perlberg lived in an apartment at 184 Meyer Street, Brooklyn, New York with her three children Abraham, Benjamin, and Ella.[28] I noted the occupation listed for Benjamin Perlberg was teamster. Ella worked as a stenographer and Abraham was in neckwear. Sarah Perlberg died 13 March 1925.[29] She was buried 15 March 1925 at Mount Zion Cemetery, Queens County, New York under the *landsmanschaften* ZABNO at the same grave location as her father Aaron Malter, 16L-6-249.[30]

Children of Elias Perlberg and Sarah Malter

Meyer Perlberg

Meyer Perlberg was born 2 May 1878 at Żabno, Małopolskie, Poland to Elias Perlberg and Sarah Malter. After he immigrated to the United States of America, he applied for naturalization and gave his immigration date as 1886. He obtained naturalization on 15 July 1903 by the Supreme Court of New York County. His listed occupation was cutter for the clothing or textile industry.[31] The cutter was considered as skilled labor, crucial to the quality of the finished product in the emerging ready-to wear clothing industry.[32] Meyer married Barbara Straks 7 February 1904 at Manhattan.[33]

The 1905 New York State Census listed Meyer Perlberg, his wife Barbara, and their infant son Elijah.[34] The 1910 United States Federal Census included Meyer Perlberg, age 31, wife Barbara age 28, children Elijah age 5, Jennie age 3 and Martha age 9 months. Meyer worked as a cutter in the waists industry. The term *waists* referred to a type of closefitting blouse with stand-up collars and long sleeves.[35] His draft registration for WWI was dated 12 September 1918; he indicated that he was a pattern maker at Solomon and Metzler at 33 East 33rd. Street, Manhattan.[36] The 1920 United States Federal Census listed Meyer, his wife Barbara with their children Elijah, Jennie, Martha, and Maurice. They lived at 1586 St. Mark's Avenue, Brooklyn, New York. Meyer was employed by a manufacturer of ladies' waists.[37]

The 1930 United States Federal Census included Meyer, 51 working as a pattern maker for dresses. This census listed his wife Barbara, 47 and their children Elijah, 25; Jeanne, 23; Martha, 20; Murray, 19; and Sylvia, 9. They were living at 586 East 4th Street, Brooklyn.[38] The 1940 United States Federal Census included information that all their children left home except for Sylvia. Meyer's occupation was salesman for a general store.[39] Meyer Perlberg died 9 March 1955 at Miami, Dade, Florida.[40] He was buried 13 March 1955 at Mt. Zion Cemetery, Maspeth, New York.[41] Barbara died 27 December 1963 at New York.[42] She was buried 29 December 1963 at Mt. Zion Cemetery, Maspeth, New York.[43] Their graves are at 17R-Road-2-28A1, Mt. Zion Cemetery.

Abraham Perlberg

Abraham Perlberg was born 15 October 1881 at Żabno, Małopolskie, Poland to Elias Perlberg and Sarah Malter.[44] In the 1910 United States Federal Census, he lived with his mother Sarah, brother Ben and sister Ella at Manhattan Avenue, Brooklyn, New York. He worked as a store cleaner.[45] Abraham married Frances Unger 18 May 1920 at Brooklyn, New York.[46] The 1930 United States Federal Census listed Abraham Perlberg and his wife Frances living on South 2nd Street, Brooklyn, New York. He was the proprietor of a dry goods store. He had alien status and was not naturalized.[47] Abraham Perlberg died 24 September 1937 at Queens, New York and was buried 26 September 1937 at Beth David Cemetery, Queens, New York. His occupation was described as general merchandise store. His wife Frances was the executor.[48] They had no issue.

Benjamin Perlberg

Benjamin Perlberg was born 11 July 1886 at Cincinnati, Ohio. His birth date was on his application for a seaman's protection certificate on 15 August 1919.[49] His address was 207 Manhattan Avenue, Brooklyn, New York. Affidavits were usually attached with this application, that consisted of a birth certificate, photograph, thumb print and identifying information. This document served as a seaman's passport to protect him from being pressed into a foreign service, especially during periods of war. Benjamin Perlberg was employed as a ship fireman and crew member. I found a record that he served as a crew member on the ship *Albert Ballin* that departed from Hamburg and arrived at New York 7 October 1923. This ship was an ocean liner that was launched 1923 and was owned by the Hamburg-America line.[50] Benjamin Perlberg died 21 February 1926 at 207 Manhattan Avenue, Brooklyn, New York. The direct cause of death was chronic myocarditis. The executor of his estate was his brother Meyer Perlberg.[51] Benjamin was single and had no issue.

Benjamin Perlberg

Ella Perlberg

Ella Perlberg was born May 1888 at Cincinnati, Ohio. She moved to New York with her mother and siblings, then lived at Brooklyn, New York by 1910. She was single according to the 1915 New York State Census and worked as a stenographer. She married Joseph Brounfield 11 February 1916 at Brooklyn, New York.[52] Joseph Brounfield aka Brownfield was born 15 September 1891 and died February 1969 at Jamaica, Queens, New York.[53]

By the 1920 United States Federal Census their surname changed to Brownfield. Ella and Joe Brownfield were living at 194 Rodney Street, Brooklyn, New York. Joe Brownfield was a travelling salesman for a food company. On the 1940 United States Federal Census for Queens County, New York, Ella, and Joe Brownfield stated they lived at Chicago, Illinois during 1935. Their address in New York was 90–23 149th Street, Queens, New York. Joe was working as a salesman for imported goods.[54] Ella Brownfield died 20 August 1961 at Queens, New York.[55] They had no issue.

Naturalization of Isidore Geiger

My lengthy search for Isidore Geiger's naturalization ended at the Clerk of the Circuit Court at Cook County, Chicago, Illinois. The court mailed me copies of Isidore's naturalization papers. Isidore Geiger's Petition for Naturalization contained information that he came to the United States while still a minor (under age 18) on 1 January 1892. Isidore Geiger was listed on the passenger manifest for the *S.S. Panther,* that departed from Hamburg, Germany on 24 June 1890.[56] Isidore reported that he arrived at New York from London, England. He testified in 1904 that he lived in the United States for 12 years, if the year when he first arrived in the USA was 1892.

Isidore Geiger was naturalized on 28 October 1904 when he made his Oath of Renunciation and Allegiance at the Superior Court of Cook County, State of Illinois. He resided at 674 West 14th Street, Chicago, Illinois.[57] His occupation was salesman. There were two witnesses on Isidore's naturalization application: Harry Lustgarten, a cigarmaker who lived at 369 Blue Island Avenue, Chicago, then later lived at 258 West 14th Street, Chicago.[58] The other witness, Isaac Scheuer, was also a cigarmaker who lived at 673 W. 14th Street, Chicago.[59] The connection between Israel aka Isidore and his two witnesses appeared to be the occupation of cigarmaker. His witnesses stated that they were acquainted with Isidore since 1892. Although Israel was a cigarmaker while living at Przemyśl, he found new employment in the USA as a furniture salesman in Chicago by the time he was naturalized.[60]

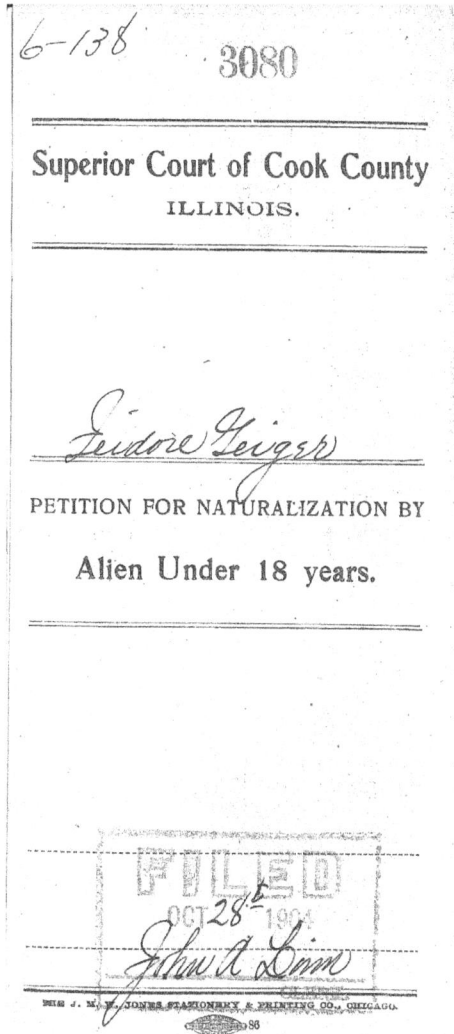

6-138   3080

Superior Court of Cook County
ILLINOIS.

Isidore Geiger

PETITION FOR NATURALIZATION BY

Alien Under 18 years.

FILED
OCT 28th 1904
John A. Linn

THE J. M. W. JONES STATIONERY & PRINTING CO., CHICAGO.

Isidore Geiger Naturalization

PETITION BY ALIEN WHO ARRIVED IN THE UNITED STATES UNDER 18 YEARS OF AGE. (Minor)

United States of America,
STATE OF ILLINOIS, } ss.
COOK COUNTY.

TO THE HONORABLE THE JUDGES OF THE SUPERIOR COURT OF COOK COUNTY, IN THE STATE OF ILLINOIS:

Your petitioner, *Isidor Geiger*
respectfully represents unto your honors and upon his oath states that he resides at No.
674 W 14 th St
in the city of *Chicago* county of Cook
and state of Illinois; that he was born in the *Hagarn* *in* *Austria* of
on or about the *15* day of *Feb,* A. D. 18 *74*;
that on or about the *1* day of *Jany* A. D. 18 *92*
he arrived in the United States at the city of *New York*,
from *London* in *England* and has since
then continuously resided in the United States of America; that he has resided continuously for
17 years last past in the state of Illinois and during that period has followed
the occupation of *Salesman*;
that he has never been convicted of a felony or other crime or misdemeanor involving moral turpitude (but this statement has no reference to purely political offenses not involving moral turpitude); that it is now and has been for two years next preceding the making of this application, continuously, his intention to become a citizen of the United States of America; that he is well disposed to the good order and happiness of the United States and attached to the principles of the Constitution thereof; that he now and hereby expressly renounces all hereditary titles, if any, heretofore borne by him, and every membership to which he is entitled, if any, in any and every order of nobility in the kingdom, state or country from which he came; that he has not violated any of the provisions of an Act of the Congress of the United States, entitled "An Act to Regulate the Immigration of Aliens into the United States," approved March 3, 1903; that he is not a disbeliever in or opposed to all organized government; that he is not a member of or affiliated with any organization entertaining and teaching disbelief in or opposition to all organized government; that he does not advocate or teach it as a duty, necessity or propriety to assault or kill any officer or officers, either specific individuals or officers generally, of the United States or of any other organized government because of the official character of such officer or officers, neither does he belong to any organization that advocates or teaches the assaulting or killing of any such officer or officers to be a duty or a necessity or to be proper; and that he is now an alien friend and a subject of *Emperor of Austria*, but desires to become a citizen of the United States of America and agrees if granted such citizenship to assume all the responsibilities thereof;

WHEREFORE your petitioner prays that his fitness and qualifications in this behalf may be inquired into by this honorable court, that he may be naturalized and be admitted to all the rights, privileges and immunities of citizenship as a naturalized citizen of the United States and that a certificate of his naturalization may be issued to him by this honorable court.

Isidor Geiger
Petitioner.

STATE OF ILLINOIS, } ss.
COOK COUNTY.

Isidor Geiger
being duly sworn, upon his oath says that the statements made in the foregoing petition by him subscribed are true.

Subscribed and sworn to before me, this *Isidor Geiger*
28 day of *Oct* A. D. 190.
John A. Linn
Clerk of the Superior Court of Cook County.

NOTE.—It is the duty of the clerk to permit no one to subscribe and swear to this petition without knowing the contents.

Isidore Geiger Naturalization

Israel aka Isidore Geiger WWI Draft Registration

Isidore Geiger completed his WWI Draft Registration Card on 12 September 1918 at New York. He listed his birth date as 5 January 1875, he was 43 years of age, a naturalized U.S. citizen, and his present occupation was shipping clerk for his brother Charles Geiger's company Geiger and Braverman at 49 W. 23rd Street in Manhattan, New York. He listed his nearest relative as Esther Geiger, who lived in Chicago, Illinois. Isidore Geiger lived in the Bronx, New York. I noted that he and his wife Esther were living apart, Isidore in New York and Esther in Chicago.[61] Perhaps Charles Geiger was short-handed due to WWI and needed Isidore to work for him temporarily as a shipping clerk.

Life in Chi-Town

Isidore and Esther Geiger were listed in the 1900 United States Federal Census for Manhattan, New York with their daughter Jennie however they were not listed in the 1905 New York State Census.[62] It is reasonable to assume that they moved from New York to Chicago after the birth of their second child Eli born April 1901 at Manhattan and prior to Isidore's naturalization in Chicago during October 1904. They continued to reside in Chicago by the time their third child Harry was born at Chicago 11 December 1908.[63]

By 1910 Israel aka Isidore Geiger and family lived in Chicago at 819 South Irving Avenue.[64] In the 1910 United States Federal Census, Isidore stated that he arrived in the USA 1891. He was working as a manager in a retail furniture store. Both Isidore and Esther were married for 11 years. Information given for this census indicated their children Jennie and Eli were born at New York and their youngest child Harry was born 1909 at Chicago.

Jewish immigrants such as Isidore and Esther settled in Chicago in the Maxwell Street and Lawndale neighborhoods. Yiddish was the lingua franca, with stores and pushcarts reminiscent of the Lower East Side in New York City. The Jews worked mainly as merchants, peddlers, and factory workers. There was an extensive outdoor market with 40 synagogues resembling a European shtetl. Isidore and his family first lived in this neighborhood, then changed addresses at least every ten years as reflected by the United States Federal Censuses. They moved to slightly more upscale areas within the city of Chicago, towards the Southside of the city and ever closer to Lakeshore Drive. With each move, the family became more assimilated into American culture speaking English rather than Yiddish. Children were educated and encouraged to seek employment as professionals or in business. There were 275,000 Jews in Chicago by 1930 making it the third largest Jewish population after New York City and Warsaw.[65]

By the 1920 United States Federal Census Isidore and his family lived at 4431 Calumet Avenue in Southside Chicago; their daughter Jennie, 20 worked as an office manager. Isidore was listed as a manager of a furniture store.[66] Isidore stated that he immigrated in 1885, at approximately 11 years of age and was naturalized in 1902 (it was 1904). Esther stated that she immigrated 1890 (it was 1885) and was naturalized in 1898. Eli was age 18 and Harry was age 11.

In the 1930 United States Federal Census for Chicago, Cook County, Illinois, Isidore with his wife Esther and sons Eli and Harry lived on 7007 Chappell Avenue.[67] This address was in the South Shore of Chicago near the prestigious Lake Shore Drive. Their daughter Jennie was now married to Francis Richard Glenner in 1925. On this census, Isidore's date of immigration to the USA was given as 1890 and Esther's date of immigration was 1896. Isidore gave his occupation as a furniture salesman. Eli, age 28, worked as a real estate salesman and Harry, age 21, was employed as a clerk in an insurance company; both sons lived with their parents.

(LtoR) Esther, Isidore, Jennie, Harry Geiger, ca. 1918

Journey to Europe

A ship manifest listed Isidore Geiger as a US citizen, on the *S.S. General Von Steuben*. The ship departed from Boulogne, France on 18 December 1931 and arrived at New York on 27 December 1931.[68] Isidore was issued a passport 15 September 1931, just a month after the death of his wife Esther on 12 August 1931.[69] Isidore probably observed the Jewish tradition of mourning for 30 days after

Isidore and Esther Geiger, ca. 1930

Esther's death and burial known as *sheloshim*. My theory is that Isidore learned that his mother Hinde was dying in Vienna and he wanted to see her as soon as possible. Although no manifest was located for Isidore Geiger's passage to Europe from the USA during September–October 1931, Isidore probably managed to visit his mother Hinde Geiger before her death 11 October 1931 at Vienna, Austria. Isidore Geiger suffered two personal losses that year, the deaths of both his wife and his mother.

Deaths

Esther Geiger died 12 August 1931 at Chicago, Illinois and was buried 14 August 1931 at Mt. Isaiah cemetery, Chicago.[70] Esther's obituary listed her surviving

family members, her husband Isidore, children Mrs. Jennie Glenner, Eli and Harry Geiger and her siblings Abraham and Meyer Perlberg and Mrs. Ella Brownfield.[71]

In the Illinois Deaths and Stillbirths Index, 1916–1947, Isidore Geiger's birth date was given as 5 January 1876 in Austria and his death was 29 April 1933 in Chicago.[72] He was buried on 1 May 1933 at

Isidore and Esther Geiger matsevah

Mt. Isaiah Cemetery, Chicago adjoining his wife's grave. Isidore's death certificate from Chicago, Cook County gave his cause of death as a coronary thrombosis on 29 April 1933. My husband Michael and I visited the graves of Isidore and Esther at the Mt. Isaiah Cemetery, renamed Rosemont Park Cemetery when we were in Chicago for the 2008 International Association of Jewish Genealogical Societies conference.[73] At the time of his death, he was living at 7039 Grandon Avenue with his son Eli Geiger. Eli was the informant for the death information. Isidore was listed as a widower. His occupation was merchant for retail furniture with 34 years of experience working at that trade.

Children of Isidore Geiger and Esther Perlberg

Jennie Geiger

Jennie was the first-born child of Isidore and Esther Geiger, born 7 September 1899 at New York City.[74] She was raised in Chicago, worked as an office manager, and married Francis Richard Glenner at Chicago on 19 April 1925.[75] My cousin Evelyn, Isidore and Esther's great-granddaughter, sent me a copy of the newspaper engagement announcement photograph for Jennie Geiger. Evelyn also found the wedding invitation sent by Isidore and Esther Geiger for the marriage of their daughter Jennie to Francis R. Glenner on 19th of April 1925 at the Windermere Hotel East in Chicago. Those documents provided the marriage date, especially important because neither I nor my cousin could find their marriage listed in any database. They were married at the luxurious Hotel Windermere East, later converted 1981 to apartments and placed on the National Register of Historic Places.[76] Their engagement announcement mentioned that the couple will reside in New York. Soon after they were married, they moved to Brooklyn, New York probably due to an employment opportunity for Francis.[77]

Jennie's husband Isidore aka Francis Richard Glenner was born 31 October 1895 at Chicago.[78] His father Jacob Glenner was born April 1856 at Poland and died 29 September 1943 at Chicago, Illinois.[79] Francis Richard Glenner's grandfather was Philip Goliner, therefore the original name for Glenner was Goliner. Francis Richard Glenner's mother was Sarah Mary Joseph, born 15 March 1861 at Koenigsberg, Germany; she died 10 June 1929 at Chicago, Illinois. Sarah Mary Joseph's parents were Louis Gedalia Joseph (1821–1874) and Rosa Lewis Citron (1807–1909). Jacob Glenner and Sarah Mary Joseph married 19 October 1879 at Manhattan.[80] Jacob Glenner and family moved to Chicago after their first child Esther was born 1881 at New York. Jacob and Sarah Mary Glenner's subsequent children were all born at Chicago: Lillian b. 1883; Louis b. 1884; Goldie b.1886;

Phoebe (1888–1982); Benjamin b. 1891; Mortimer b.1893; Isidore aka Francis Richard (1895–1980); Evelyn b. 1898; Sidney b. 1900; Adelaide b. 1902; Robert b. 1909.[81]

Francis Richard Glenner completed a draft registration card for WWI during 1917. He worked for Dr. Leman, and financially supported his parents and a brother.[82] My cousin Jeanne recalled that her father Francis changed his given name from Isidore to Francis Richard to avoid anti-Semitic discrimination when he worked as a chemical engineer. He was trained as a chemist and he formed a company, Homogeneous Equipment Company located at Downingtown, Pennsylvania; the company manufactured lead-lined steel pipes. I met Jennie and Francis when they lived in Pennsylvania and recalled that Francis told me he held a patent for rust proofing metal. He also taught chemistry at Temple University, Philadelphia. Francis Glenner died 4 November 1980 at Oakland, Alameda, Cal-

Francis Glenner

Mr. and Mrs. I. Geiger of 62u Champlain avenue announce the engagement of their daughter, Jennie,

Steffens Photo

MISS JENNIE GEIGER

to Francis R. Glenner, son of Mr. and Mrs. Jacob Glenner. The marriage will take place in spring, and the couple will reside in New York.

Jennie Geiger engagement announcement

ifornia.[83] Jennie Glenner died 6 days later, 10 November 1980 at Oakland, Alameda, California.[84] Francis and Jennie Glenner had two children: George Glenner (1927–1995) and Jeanne Glenner who is still living.

Eli Geiger

Eli Geiger soldier

Eli was the second child born to Isidore and Esther Geiger on 30 April 1901, at New York City.[85] Eli lived with his parents Isidore and Esther until their respective deaths. He registered for the draft February 1942 listing his sister Jennie Glenner as someone "who will always know your address." He worked for a company in Chicago.[86] Eli then served in the Army during WWII and was promoted to Captain. His military service began 9 July 1942 and ended on 14 May 1945.[87] Eli remained single until he married relatively late in life; he married Dorothy Taman, December 1969 at Dade County, Florida.[88] Eli died 26 January 1979 while hospitalized at the Downey Veterans Administration Hospital, North Chicago, Illinois.[89] The database Jewish On-line Worldwide Burial Records from www.jewishgen.org. provided this additional information; Eli Geiger was buried 30 January 1979 at Wood National Military Cemetery at Milwaukee, Wisconsin, Section A Row O Site 676.

Eli's obituary provided the information that he was a real estate broker for more than 30 years and was retired. His address in Chicago was 4750 N. Clarendon Avenue. Survivors were his wife Dorothy, his brother (Harry Geiger) and sister (Jennie Glenner).[90] Dorothy Taman was born 18 July 1918 in Chicago, Cook County, Illinois to parents Benjamin Taman and Elsie Robeek; she died 14 May 2008 at Chicago.[91] Eli and Dorothy left no issue.

Harry Geiger

Harry was the third and youngest child born to Isidore and Esther Geiger. He was born 11 December 1908 at Chicago, Illinois.[92] The following information was obtained from his application for WWII compensation for honorably discharged veterans in the Commonwealth of Pennsylvania in 1960.[93] Harry enlisted in the Army 12 August 1942 and served overseas 19 May 1943. He returned to the United States on 19 September 1945. His separation date from the Army was on 13 April 1946 at Camp Grant, Illinois.

There was an engagement announcement in the *Chicago Tribune* for Harry Geiger son of the late Mr. and Mrs. Isidore Geiger of Chicago, engaged to marry Betty Louise Newmann, daughter of Mr. and Mrs. Edward Newmann of Hyde Park Blvd, Chicago, Illinois. The wedding was to take place 14 June 1952.[94] Their marriage took place several days earlier, on 6 June 1952 in Chicago, Illinois.[95] My cousin Jeanne told me that Harry and Betty divorced after ten years of marriage. I found a death record for Betty Geiger, maiden name Newman, age 71, who died 26 May 1993 at Chicago.[96] If this was the same Betty Louise Newmann who married Harry Geiger, then there was a fourteen-year age difference when they married. They left no issue.

Harry's death information was obtained from the California Death Index, 1940–1997.[97] Harry Geiger resided at San Diego, California where he died 10 February 1987.[98]

Children of Jennie Glenner and Francis Richard Glenner

George Glenner

George Glenner was the first of two children born to Francis and Jennie Glenner. He was born at Brooklyn, New York, on 17 September 1927.[99] George enlisted at age 18 during the WWII draft. He lived at Merion, Pennsylvania with his parents.[100] He graduated from Johns Hopkins University School of Medicine where he received his medical degree in 1953. He enlisted and was accepted as a trained health provider by the United States Public Health service from 1955 until his release date 1982.[101] George continued his training in surgery and pathology at Mount Sinai Hospital in New York and at the Mallory Institute in Boston City Hospital.

Dr. George Glenner became one of the earliest Alzheimer researchers during the 1960s to examine amyloid functions in the brain. He was known for his ground-breaking publications during 1984 in which he analyzed and identified

(LtoR) George, Harry, Jennie, Francis Glenner, Jeanne

the molecular structure of the beta-amyloid protein linked to Alzheimer's disease.[102] He also compared a unique cerebrovascular amyloid protein in the brains of Alzheimer patients with Down's syndrome.[103] He contributed to the New England Journal of Medicine with his research on amyloid deposits and amyloidosis.[104] The president of the National Alzheimer's Association praised Dr. George Glenner for being a pioneer in Alzheimer's research who provided a medical breakthrough for others working towards a cure for Alzheimer's Disease.[105]

Dr. George Glenner worked at the National Institute of Health in Bethesda, Maryland 1958–1980 as chief of molecular pathology and Chairman of the Department of Medicine and Physiology at the Foundation for Advanced Education in the Sciences at the National Institutes of Health. In 1982 the University of California at San Diego appointed George Glenner as an attending physician at the medical school and as research pathologist in the Department of Pathology at UCSD School of Medicine.[106] A recent letter by Dr. Marchesi from Yale University was published in the Wall Street Journal, where he stated "George Glenner's discovery of amyloid peptides reported in 1984, and the resulting recombinant DNA applications of them have unleashed a flood of information and insights that remain to be exploited."[107]

A complete archive of Dr. George Glenner's papers and research dating from 1932–1995 may be found at the UC San Diego Library Special Collections.[108]

Dr. George Glenner with his second wife Joy founded the first Alzheimer's Family Center in 1982 for providing day care and respite for Alzheimer's patients. They also founded the Alzheimer's School of Dementia Care in 1987 which provided training for Certified Nursing Assistants and other health care workers. The mission statement of the George G. Glenner Alzheimer's Family Centers in California was to provide compassionate care and education for those suffering from Alzheimer's disease and their loved ones.[109]

George and Jeanne Glenner

Dr. George Glenner was a member of the National Alzheimer's Association Board of Directors and of the Medical/Scientific Advisory Board. He served as Medical Advisor to the Alzheimer's Association in San Diego and he was Chairman of California State Alzheimer's Disease Task Force. He was named San Diego Citizen of the Year in 1985.

George's first wife was Joyce Saunders; she was born to parents Cyril and Lillian Saunders at Ashton Upon Mersey, Cheshire, England on 25 October 1929.[110] George married Joyce 1954 at Manhattan, New York after completing medical school.[111] They had three children: a son Jonathan and two daughters Amanda and Sarah; all are still living. The final divorce decree between George and Joyce was issued August 1979. Joyce Glenner died 31 October 2010 at Silver Spring, Maryland.[112] George married Joy Arlene Sharp Stone on 15 August 1979 at Arlington, Virginia.[113] Joy was divorced from her first husband March 1977. She had a daughter from her prior marriage, Shelley, who became George Glenner's stepdaughter. They moved to San Diego where George continued his research with Alzheimer's disease. George and Joy Glenner were married for fifteen years until his death 12 July 1995 at Rancho Santa Fe, California.[114] He was interred in Lakeview Mausoleum Bay 1 Crypt 72B at El Camino Memorial Park in San Diego.[115] Dr. George Glenner died at age 67 of a rare disease, systemic senile amyloidosis, where the amyloid protein can block the blood vessels of the heart.[116] The amyloidosis to which he succumbed caused the waxy protein to build up in organs, blood vessels and tissue; affecting almost all organs except the brain.[117] Joy Glenner and her daughter Shelley are still living.

Jeanne Glenner, the second child born to Jennie and Francis Glenner is still living. My husband Mike and I visited Jeanne and her husband Henry 2010 in San Diego, and she shared her family photographs and her recollections of her Geiger family history. I learned that Jeanne and her husband Henry were active docents at the Museum of Natural History in San Diego, and she was an accomplished violinist. Jeanne also participated in my DNA study on our Geiger lineage by submitting her autosomal DNA to www.familytreedna.com.

Descendants of Israel Geiger

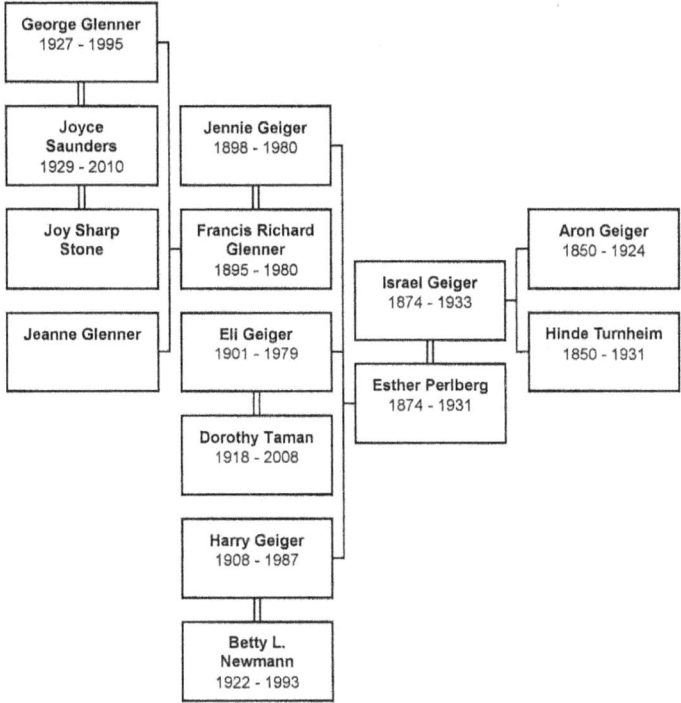

```
George Glenner
1927 - 1995

Joyce
Saunders
1929 - 2010                Jennie Geiger
                           1898 - 1980

Joy Sharp                  Francis Richard                              Aron Geiger
Stone                      Glenner                                      1850 - 1924
                           1895 - 1980      Israel Geiger
                                            1874 - 1933
Jeanne Glenner             Eli Geiger                                   Hinde Turnheim
                           1901 - 1979                                  1850 - 1931
                                            Esther Perlberg
                           Dorothy Taman    1874 - 1931
                           1918 - 2008

                           Harry Geiger
                           1908 - 1987

                           Betty L.
                           Newmann
                           1922 - 1993
```

Descendants of Aaron Malter

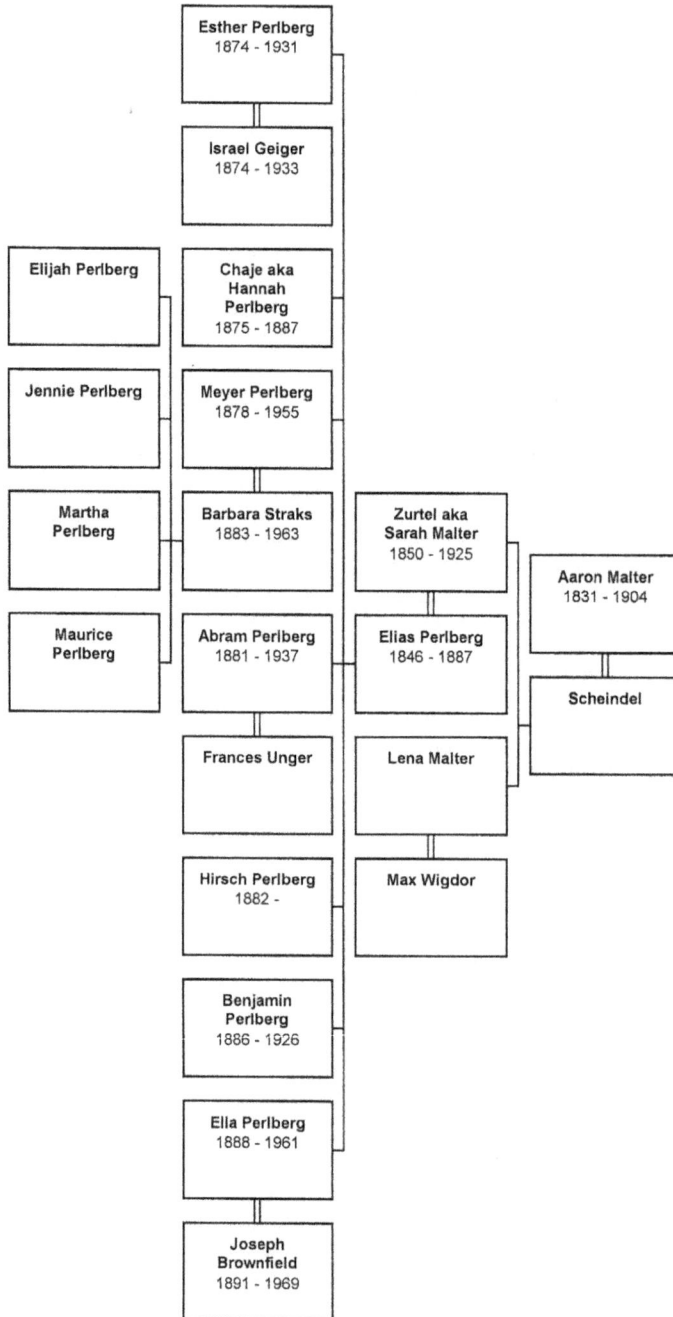

```
                                    ┌─────────────────┐
                                    │ Esther Perlberg │
                                    │   1874 - 1931   │
                                    └─────────────────┘
                                    ┌─────────────────┐
                                    │  Israel Geiger  │
                                    │   1874 - 1933   │
                                    └─────────────────┘
        ┌─────────────────┐         ┌─────────────────┐
        │ Elijah Perlberg │         │   Chaje aka     │
        │                 │         │    Hannah       │
        │                 │         │    Perlberg     │
        │                 │         │   1875 - 1887   │
        └─────────────────┘         └─────────────────┘
        ┌─────────────────┐         ┌─────────────────┐
        │ Jennie Perlberg │         │ Meyer Perlberg  │
        │                 │         │   1878 - 1955   │
        └─────────────────┘         └─────────────────┘
        ┌─────────────────┐  ┌─────────────────┐  ┌─────────────────┐  ┌─────────────────┐
        │     Martha      │  │ Barbara Straks  │  │   Zurtel aka    │  │   Aaron Malter  │
        │    Perlberg     │  │   1883 - 1963   │  │  Sarah Malter   │  │   1831 - 1904   │
        │                 │  │                 │  │   1850 - 1925   │  │                 │
        └─────────────────┘  └─────────────────┘  └─────────────────┘  └─────────────────┘
        ┌─────────────────┐  ┌─────────────────┐  ┌─────────────────┐  ┌─────────────────┐
        │    Maurice      │  │ Abram Perlberg  │  │ Elias Perlberg  │  │    Scheindel    │
        │    Perlberg     │  │   1881 - 1937   │  │   1846 - 1887   │  │                 │
        └─────────────────┘  └─────────────────┘  └─────────────────┘  └─────────────────┘
                             ┌─────────────────┐  ┌─────────────────┐
                             │  Frances Unger  │  │   Lena Malter   │
                             └─────────────────┘  └─────────────────┘
                             ┌─────────────────┐  ┌─────────────────┐
                             │ Hirsch Perlberg │  │   Max Wigdor    │
                             │     1882 -      │  │                 │
                             └─────────────────┘  └─────────────────┘
                             ┌─────────────────┐
                             │    Benjamin     │
                             │    Perlberg     │
                             │   1886 - 1926   │
                             └─────────────────┘
                             ┌─────────────────┐
                             │  Ella Perlberg  │
                             │   1888 - 1961   │
                             └─────────────────┘
                             ┌─────────────────┐
                             │     Joseph      │
                             │   Brownfield    │
                             │   1891 - 1969   │
                             └─────────────────┘
```

Endnotes

1   www.jri-poland.org. Przemysl Archives, Poland. Fond 1924. Przemysl Births 1789-1827, 53-1900. Birth Record Israel Geiger, 16 January 1874, Akta 7. Solomon David Geiger was listed on the record as the sandek.

2   Ancestry.com. Hamburg Passenger Lists 1850–1934. S.S. Panther. Date: 24 June 1890. Israel Geiger.

3   www.jewishgen.org/databases/USA/1890ny.htm. Index of 1890–1891 NY Immigrants from Austria, Poland and Galicia. Compiled by Dr. Howard M. Relles.

4   New York, New York City Municipal Archives. Marriage Certificate 18221. Date: 27 November 1898. Isidor Geiger age 24 and Esther Perlberg age 21.

5   Ancestry.com. Federal Census 1900, Manhattan, District 1, Enumeration District 232. Address: 528 East 6th Street. Isidor Geiger. The Perlbergs were living next door to Isidore Geiger and his family.

6   Ancestry.com. Federal Census 1900, Manhattan. Enumeration District 232. 6th Street. Isidore Geiger, Esta, Jenny.

7   New York City Department of Records, Municipal Archives. Certificate 33288. Elias Geiger. Birth: 30 April 1901. Address: 528 6th Street, New York. Father: Isidore Geiger. Mother: Esther Perlberg.

8   Ancestry.com. Pennsylvania, Veteran Compensation Application Files, WWII, 1950–1959. Harry Geiger. Birth: 11 December 1908, Chicago, Illinois.

9   Ancestry.com. Hamburg Passenger Lists, 1 July 1885–31 Dec 1885. Ship: *Rugia* leaving Hamburg 26 August 1885, arriving in New York 7 September 1885. Sarah Perlberg indicated they came from Zabno, Austria.

10   Alexander Beider. *A Dictionary of Ashkenazic Names.* p. 577.

11   Ancestry.com. Hamburg State Archives, Hamburg Passenger Lists, 1850-1934. Zurtel Perlberg travelled with her children Esther, Chaie, Meyer, Abram. *S.S. Rugia.*

12   Ancestry.com. New York Passenger and Crew Lists including Castle Garden and Ellis Island, 1820-1957. Elias Perlberg Immigration 1883. S.S. Rhaetia.

13   JewishGen.org. 1891 Galicia Business Directory. Aaron Malter. Business: guesthouse/innkeeper in Zabno..

14   Ancestry.com. New York, New York, U.S., Index to Death Certificates, 1862–1948. Aaron Malter Death 18 July 1904. Brooklyn, New York, Certificate 14747.

15   Ancestry.com. 1900 United States Federal Census. Kings County, Ward 15, District 0208. Aron Malter, father-in-law, lived at 466 Grand Street, with Max and Lena Wigdor.

16   www.jri-poland.org/psa/zabno_surn.htm.

17   www.bloodandfrogs.com/compendium/poland/lesser-poland/zabno.

18   www.jri-poland.org. Krakow Archive. Fond 276. Tarnow Branch. Tarnow Births 1870-1914. Birth: 9 November 1882. Hirsch Perlberg, akta 421, p.8, sygnatura 33/276/7.

19   Irving Howe. *World of Our Fathers.* (New York: New York University Press, 2005). pp. 36–39.

20   Ancestry.com. U.S. City Directories, 1822-1995, Cincinnati, Ohio City Directory 1886. Elias Perlberg, clothing renovator. 2nd and Broadway.

21   Ancestry.com. 1900 United States Federal Census. Manhattan, New York. Ella Perlberg. Birth: May 1888, Cincinnati. Address: 528 6th Street. Enumeration District 23a.

22   Ancestry.com. U.S. City Directories, 1822-1995, Cincinnati, Ohio City Directory 1890. Esther Perlberg, wrapper. Sarah Perlberg, widow. 348 W. 5th Street.

23   Alter Raubvogel. Email 28 January 2019. Jewish Cemeteries of Greater Cincinnati. Hamilton County, Ohio Burial Records Volume 15- Walnut Hills United Jewish Cemetery 1850-2002. Elias Perlberg buried in Old Grounds Cemetery, Row 34, grave 27. Hannah Perlberg buried in Old Grounds Cemetery, Row 35, grave 24. (www.jcemcin.org).

24   1900 United States Federal Census, Kings County, New York, enumeration district 208, ward 15. Max Wigdor, Lena Wigdor, children Myer and Benjamin and father-in-law Aron Malter.

25   Ancestry.com. New York State Census 1905, election district A.D.10, 10 E.D. 528 6th Street.

26   Ibid.

27   Ancestry.com. United States Federal Census 1910. Brooklyn, New York, enumeration district 331.

28   Ancestry.com. New York State Census 1915, Election District 14, Assembly District 13, Kings County. Sarah Perlberg, children Abraham, Benjamin and Ella.

29   Ancestry.com. New York, New York Extracted Death Index 1862–1948. Sarah Perlberg, age 74, died 13 March, Kings County, New York.

30   FindAGrave.com. Sarah Perlberg. Died March 1925. Mt. Zion Cemetery. Zabno Society. 16L-6-249. Slso see Mt. Zion Cemetery, internment search.

31   Ancestry.com. U.S. Naturalization Record. Indexes 1791–1992. V.225, Record 46. Meyer Perlberg.)

32   americanhistory.si.edu/sweatshops/history-1880-1940. Cloth cutting devices was the next important breakthrough after the sewing machine. By the 1890s cutters could slice through stacks of cloth using electrically driven blades around pattern pieces. Also see www.textileschool.com/465/importance-of-cutting-room.

33   New York, New York Extracted marriage Index 1866–1937. Marriage Meyer Perlberg with Barbara Straks, 7 Feb 1904, cert. 4354.

34   Ancestry.com. New York, State Census 1905. Manhattan, New York. Assembly District 23, Election District 37. Address 504 W. 168th Street. Meyer Perlberg.

35   Ancestry.com. 1910 United States Federal Census. Brooklyn, New York. Ward 24. Address 1586 St. Marks Avenue, Brooklyn, NY.

36   Ancestry.com. WWI Draft Registration Cards 1917–1918. Brooklyn, New York, Division 84. Meyer Perlberg.

37   Ancestry.com. 1920 United States Federal Census. Brooklyn, New York. Assembly district 23.

38   Ancestry.com. 1930 United States Federal Census. Brooklyn, New York. Enumeration district 0884.

39   Ancestry.com. 1940 United States Federal Census. Brooklyn, New York. Enumeration district 24-2524.

40   Newspapers.com. Obituary. Meyer Perlberg. 11 March 1955. *The Miami News*, Miami, Florida. Date of death 9 March 1955.

41   www.mtzioncemetery.com Interment search Meyer Perlberg. Buried 13 March 1955, Mt. Zion Cemetery, Maspeth, New York, Ceres Union, 17R-Road-2-28A1.

42   Ancestry.com. Information from the Lipscomb-Strahs Family, Public Trees.

43   www.mtzioncemetery.com Interment search Barbara Perlberg. Buried 29 December 1963 at the same location as Meyer Perlberg.

44   Ancestry.com. New York, New York Index to Death Certificates, 1862–1948. Abe Perlberg. Birth: 15 October 1881, Austria. Death: 24 September 1937. Died at Queens, New York. Burial: Beth David Cemetery, Queens, New York.

45   Ancestry.com. 1910 United States Federal Census. Enumeration District 331, Brooklyn, New York. Abe Perlberg age 28.

46   Ancestry.com. New York, New York. Marriage License Indexes, 1907–2018. Marriage Abe Perlberg to Frances Unger 18 May 1920. Cert. 7691.

47   Ancestry.com. 1930 United States Federal Census. Brooklyn, New York. Enumeration District 0201. Abraham Perlberg.

48   Ancestry.com. New York, New York Index to Death Certificates 1862-1948. Death Certificate Abe Perlberg, cert. 6731.

49   Ancestry.com. U.S., Applications for Seaman's Protection Certificates, 1916-1940. Benjamin Perlberg.

50   Ancestry.com. New York, Passenger and Crew Lists 1820–1957. Benjamin Perlberg. Manifest of Aliens Employed on the Vessel as Members of Crew.

51   New York, New York, Index to Death Certificates 1862–1948. Death: Benjamin Perlberg, died 21 Feb 1926. Cert. 4085.

52   New York, New York, Marriage License Indexes, 1907–2018. Ella Perlberg married Joseph Brounfield 11 Feb 1919. Brooklyn, New York. License 2128.

53   Ancestry.com. U.S. Social Security Death Index, 1935–2014. Joseph Brownfield. Death February 1969, Jamaica, Queens, New York.

54   Ancestry.com. 1940 United States Federal Census. Queens, New York. Enumeration District 41-1191A. Joseph Brownfield, Ella Brownfield.

55   Ancestry.com. New York, New York, Death Index, 1949–1965. Death: 20 August 1961. Ella Brownfield. Certificate 9762. .

56   Ancestry.com. Hamburg Passenger Lists, 1850–1934. Immigration of Israel Geiger age 17, departure 24 June 1890 from Hamburg via Liverpool to North America. Ship: Panther

57   National Archives and Records Administration (NARA), Washington, D.C. Naturalization Service District 9, 1840–1950 (M1285), Microfilm Serial M 1285, Microfilm Roll 63. Also in Ancestry.com U.S.Naturalization Record Indexes 1791-1992. Court District: Illinois, Indiana, Wisconsin, Iowa. Isidore Geiger date of birth 15 Feb 1874, date of arrival 1 Jan 1892 New York, Date of Action 28 Oct 1904.

58   Ancestry.com. 1900 United States Federal Census. Chicago, Illinois. Ward 7. Harry Lustgarten.

59   Ancestry.com. 1920 United States Federal Census. Chicago, Illinois. Ward 15. Isaac Scheuer.

60   Cook County, Illinois. Superior Court. Clerk of the Circuit Court. Cook County, Illinois. Petition 3080 Petition for Naturalization by Alien Under 18 Years. Isidore Geiger. Oath of Allegiance: 28 October 1904.

61   Ancestry.com. U.S. World War I Draft Registration Cards, 1917–1918. New York, Bronx. Isidore Geiger.

62   Ancestry.com. 1900 United States Federal Census. Manhattan, New York. Enumeration District 0232. Isidor Geiger. Address: 528 6th Street.

63   Ancestry.com. Pennsylvania, Veteran Compensation Files, WWII, 1950-1959. Harry Geiger. Birth Date: 11 Dec 1908. Birth Place: Chicago, Illinois.

64   1910 United States Federal Census. Chicago Ward 20, Cook County, Illinois. Enumeration District 0898. Name: Isadore Geiger, age 34, born in Austria, manager retail furniture store. His wife was Esther, age 34, children Jennie age 10, Eli age 8, Harry age 1 and 4 months.

65   en.wikipedia.org/wiki/History_of_the_Jews_in_Chicago.

66   1920 United States Federal Census. Chicago Ward 3. Cook County, Illinois. Enumeration District 175. Name: Isador Geiger, age 45, wife Esther age 45, children Jennie age 20, Eli age 18, Harry age 11. Address: 4431 Calumet Avenue.

67   1930 United States Federal Census. Chicago Ward 7. Cook County, Illinois. Enumeration District 0271. Address: 7007 Chappel Avenue. Isadore Geiger, age 54, furniture salesman, wife Esther age 54, children Eli, age 28 real estate salesman, Harry age 21 clerk for insurance company.

68   Ancestry.com. New York Passenger Lists, 1820–1957. From the Records of the Immigration and Naturalization Service, 1787-2004. National Archives, Washington, D.C. Ship Name: General Von Steuben, leaving Boulogne sur Mer, France on 18 December 1931 and arriving in New York 27 December 1931. Isidore's passport was number 440021 issued 15 September 1931.

69   Ancestry.com. Illinois Deaths and Stillbirths Index 1916–1947. Ester Geiger death date: 12 August 1931, Chicago, Cook County, Illinois. Burial Mt. Isaiah. Spouse Name: Isidore.

70   Ancestry.com. Illinois Deaths and Stillbirths Index 1916–1947. Death: 12 August 1931, Chicago, Illinois. Ester Geiger née Perlberg. Burial 14 August 1931, Mt. Isaiah Cemetery, Chicago, Illinois. FHL film no. 1893069.

71   Ancestry.com. Historical Newspapers. Birth, Marriage and Death Announcements, 1851–2003. Obituary, Chicago, Il. 1931 *Chicago Daily Tribune* (1872-1963). Name: Esther Geiger.

72   State of Illinois. Department of Public Health Division of Vital Records. Death Certificate Number 11765. Name: Isidore Geiger, age 57. Date of Birth: 5 January 1876. Isidore Geiger, a widower, died 29 April 1933 in Chicago, IL. Address: 7039 Grandon Avenue, Chicago. Occupation: merchant retail furniture. Father: Aaron Geiger. Informant was son Eli Geiger, also living at 7039 Grandon Avenue. Cause of death: coronary thrombosis.

73   Cemetery Association Map, Isaiah Israel. Isidore and Esther buried in Section B, Lot 61.

74　1900 Federal Census of the United States. Manhattan. Enumeration District 232. Address: 528 East 6th Street. Isidore Geiger age 26, Esther age 24 and daughter Jenny born in New York, September 1899. Isidore's occupation was salesman.

75　Personal Papers from cousin Evelyn M. Copy of the wedding invitation for Jennie and Francis Glenner, wedding date 19 April, 1925, at the Windermere Hotel East in Chicago, Illinois. Also, Evelyn sent me a copy of the engagement photo and announcement in a Chicago newspaper for Jennie Geiger and Francis R. Glenner.

76　The Hotel Windermere was originally built 1892 for the Chicago Columbian Exposition. It was rebuilt 1924 as two adjoining buildings with a connecting tunnel. Guests included John Rockefeller and Philip Roth. (en.wikipedia-org/wiki/Hotel_Windermere_Chicago.

77　1930 United States Federal Census, Enumeration District 24-1265. Address: 1569 Ocean Avenue, Brooklyn, New York. Francis Glenner was age 34, Jennie was age 30 and their son George was age 2. Francis's occupation was chemical engineer. George was listed as having been born in New York.

78　Ancestry.com. World War I Draft Registration Cards, 1917–1918. Francis Richard Glenner, date of birth: 31 October 1895 in Chicago, Illinois. Francis indicated that he supported his parents and one brother. Also, in the U.S. World War II Draft Registration Cards, 1942; Francis gave his same birthdate 31 Oct 1895 and he was now age 46, married to Jennie, was self-employed and residing at 605 Price Street, West Chester, Pennsylvania. His place of business was 115 E. Lancaster Avenue, Downingtown, Pennsylvania.

79　Ancestry.com. The Joseph and Dora Bandes Family Tree.

80　Ancestry.com. See Family Tree Joseph and Dora Bandes Family Tree for details. Francis had eleven siblings: Esther, Lillian, Louis, Goldie, Phoebe, Benjamin, Mortimer, Evelyn, Sidney, Adelaide, Robert. Francis was the 8th child of twelve children.

81　Ancestry.com. Family Tree of Joseph and Dora Bandes. Owner: Evelyn Bandes Mast.

82　Ancestry.com. U.S. World War I Draft Registration Cards 1917–1918. Francis Richard Glenner.

83　Ancestry.com. U.S. Social Security Death Index 1935–2014. Francis R. Glenner born 31 Oct 1895. Death Nov 1980 in Oakland, Alameda, California.

84　Ancestry.com. U.S., Social Security Death Index, 1935–2014. Jennie Glenner, born 7 September 1899, died November 1980 in Oakland, Alameda County, California. Jennie Glenner was also listed in the California Death Index, 1940-1997. She was born in Illinois, died 10 November 1980. Her mother's maiden name was listed as Malter and her father's surname was Geiger.

85　Ancestry.com. New York, New York Birth Index, 1878–1909. Certificate 33288. Birth: Elias Geiger. Residence: 528 6th Street, New York, New York. Parents: Isidore Geiger and Esther Perlberg.

86　Ancestry.com. U.S., World War II Draft Cards Young Men, 1940–1947. Eli Geiger.

87　Ancestry.com. U.S. Veterans Gravesites, ca. 1775–2006.

88　Ancestry.com. Florida Marriage Collection, 1822-1875 and 1927–2001. Eli Geiger, marriage date December 1969 in Dade County. Volume 2853, certificate number 65400. Also see Dorothy Taman marriage index December 1969 in Dade County, Florida, Volume 2853, certificate number 65400.

89　JewishGen.org. JewishGen Online Worldwide Burial Registry. USA- Wisconsin Burial Record.

90　Ancestry.com. Obituaries. *Chicago Tribune.* 29 January 1979. Eli Geiger.

91　Ancestry.com. U.S. Social Security Death Index.

92　FamilySearch.org. Illinois, Cook County, Birth Certificates, 1871–1949. Harry Geiger born 11 Dec 1908, Chicago, Illinois.

93　Ancestry.com. Pennsylvania, Veteran Compensation Application Files, WWII, 1950–1959.

94　Ancestry.com. Historical Newspapers, Birth, Marriage and Death Announcements, 1851–2003.

95　Ancestry.com. Cook County, Illinois Marriage Index, 1930–1960. Marriage Date: 6 June 1952. Harry Geiger and Betty Louise Newmann. Cook County Clerk. File: 2229741.

96　Ancestry.com. *Chicago Tribune,* Obituary Index, 1988–1997.

97　Ancestry.com. California Death Index, 1940–1997. Harry Geiger. Death Date: 10 February 1987, San Diego. Birth Date: 11 December 1908 Illinois. Mother's maiden name: Perlberg.

98   FamilySearch.org. U.S. Social Security Death Index, 1935-2014. Harry Geiger. Birth: 11 December 1908. Death: February 1987, San Diego.

99   Ancestry.com. U.S, Social Security Death Index, 1935–2014. George G. Glenner. Birth: 17 September 1927. Death: 12 July 1995 in Rancho Santa Fe, San Diego, California.

100 Ancestry.com. U.S. World War II Draft Cards Young Men 1940–1947. George Geiger Glenner. Registration date 1945.

101 Ancestry.com. U.S. Department of Veterans Affairs BIRLS Death File, 1850–2010. George Glenner.

102 George Glenner and Cecilia Wong. The Amyloid Deposits in Alzheimer's Disease: Their Nature and Pathogenesis. *Vito Quaranta*, 1984.

103 George Glenner. Alzheimer's Disease and Down's Syndrome: Sharing of a Unique Cerebrovascular Amyloid Fibril Protein. *Biochemical and Biophysical Research Communications*. Vol. 122, no. 3, 1984. pp. 1131–1135,

104 George Glenner. Amyloid Deposits and Amyloidosis: the Fibrilloses. *New England Journal of Medicine*. 1980. Vol. 302, no. 23, pp.1283–1292.

105 Wolfgang Saxon. Dr. George G. Glenner, 67, Dies; Researched Alzheimer's Disease. 14 July 1995. (www.nytimes.com/1995/07/14/obituaries/dr-george-g-glenner-6).

106 www.alzheimerhelp.org./index.php?option=com_content&view=article&id=2&Itemid=2

107 Vincent T. Marchesi. Amyloid and Alzheimer's: Round II. Wall Street Journal. 26 June 2015, p. A12

108 George Glenner Papers, 1932–1995 (MSS 389). (library.ucsd.edu/research-and-collections/collections/special-collections-and-archives/services/index.html.

109 www.alzheimerhelp.org/index.

110 Joyce Saunders Glenner. *Washington Post*. Obituary. Date of Birth: 25 October 1929. Date of Death: 31 October 2010 in Silver Spring, Maryland.

111 New York, New York, Marriage Licenses 1907–1995. George Glenner and Joyce Saunders, Cert. 11246.

112 Ancestry.com. U.S. Social Security Death Index, 1935–2014. Death: 31 October 2010. Joyce S. Glenner.

113 Ancestry.com. See Joseph and Dora Bandes Family Tree. Also see Virginia Marriage Records, 1936–2014 for marriage 15 August 1979: George Geiger Glenner with Joy Arlene Sharp Stone.

114 Ancestry.com. U.S. Social security Death Index, 1935–2014. George G. Glenner. Death: 12 July 1995, Rancho Santa Fe, San Diego, California.

115 Personal email 10 July 2021 from Rachel Bennett, counselor at El Camino Memorial Park.

116   www.nytimes.com/1995/07/14/obituaries/dr-george-g-glenner-6...arched-alzheimer-s-disease.html?scp=1&sq=Glenner%20obituary&st=cse

117 Newspapers.com. *Los Angeles Times*. Los Angeles, California. Obituary. 15 July 1995. Dr. George Glenner.

Chapter Nine

Mariem Geiger and Getzel Holoszycer

Beginnings

Mariem Geiger was the fifth child and the first female born to Aron Geiger and Hinde Turnheim. She was born 22 February 1880 at Przemyśl, Podkarpackie, Poland, at house number 167 where she was also named 26 February 1880.[1] Mariem was the first female child born after four males and she was the elder of her two sisters. Mariem was named for her deceased grandmother Mariem Turnheim. Mariem later became known as Manya. Her mother Hinde raised Mariem with her sisters Freude and Mindla to run their own household with knowledge of childcare, cooking, housework, sewing clothing and needlecraft. There was education in reading and writing in Yiddish, arithmetic as well as Hebrew education, although not as intensive as for her brothers. Practical life skills were taught to female children as it was assumed that young women would marry at the appropriate age and raise children.

Manya married Gershon aka Getzel Holoszycer at Błażowa, Podkarpackie, Poland on 31 March 1902.[2] This information was supplied by Manya on her 1 October 1925 Petition for U.S. Naturalization. Getzel Holoszycer was born in Kańczuga; Getzel and Manya had their Banns posted in 1902 at Kańczuga, Podkarpackie, Poland after they were engaged to announce that a marriage was

Birth record for Mariem Geiger, 1880

to take place between the named persons.[3] Banns were required for a civil marriage in Galicia. In addition to a civil registered marriage, Getzel and Manya were probably married in an orthodox Jewish marriage ceremony under a *chuppah* or wedding canopy.

The marriage between Manya and Getzel may have been arranged by Manya's older brother Rabbi Abraham Geiger who married Sprynca Stark from Kańczuga 1894. He lived at Kańczuga for the first several years of his marriage working as a rabbi. He would have been well acquainted with Hasidic families from that town who had potential husbands for his sister. Getzel's sister Freda claimed that her family were direct descendants of an important Hasidic rabbinic dynasty.[4] This was the dynasty started by Rabbi Elimelech Weisblum of Lizhensk (1717–1787) who was a great spiritual leader and one of the major rabbinic founders of the Hasidic movement. Therefore, Getzel's family had *yichus*, Yiddish for an excellent lineage or family background. The Geigers were quite orthodox and Hasidic, and probably viewed the marriage of Mariem with Getzel as a favorable match.[5] Getzel's surname was spelled on most archival records as Holoszycer, however I also found several permutations for the written name such as Holszitzer, Holloschutzer, Holschitz, Holoshitzer, Holeschuetzer, Holiszicer, Holszitzer.

Kańczuga, Podkarpackie, Poland

Jews were present in Kańczuga from 1597 until their annihilation by the Nazis. By the second half of the 19th century the Jewish community numbered 1,000 and was 40% of the total population of Kańczuga. Although economic conditions deteriorated after WWI, Jewish social and cultural life continued with the inclusion of Zionist and Agudat Israel organizations. Jewish life in Kańczuga and elsewhere abruptly ended during WWII, when the Nazis deported the Jews of Kańczuga 1 August 1942, after first murdering the elderly and weak in the nearby forest. They selected 150 young adults for labor camps and the rest were deported to Bełżec for extermination.[6]

Prior to 1942 Jews from Kańczuga were buried in the Siedleczka Cemetery located 1.5 miles west of the town. This cemetery was difficult to access and was in poor condition; many gravestones were removed and used to pave roads although some remained. The Siedleczka Cemetery Project began 2008 with a memorial for the Jews who were murdered in 1942. A second cemetery restoration began 2019 through the efforts of Patryk Czerwony; to cut back the overgrowth, to clean and repair the cemetery.[7]

Philip Trauring formed the website www.kanczuga.org where I obtained much information. Jews from Kańczuga who immigrated to New York prior to WWI formed a *landsmanshaft* in 1902 and named it the First Kancziger Aid Society. The purpose of the society was to help the sick and the destitute from Kańczuga as well provide cemetery plots where members of the society could be buried. Cemetery plots funded by the First Kancziger Society were established at the Mt. Zion Cemetery, Queens, New York and at Mt. Lebanon Cemetery, Iselin, New Jersey. Manya and Getzel Holly (Holoszycer) were buried in the First Kancziger section at Mt. Zion Cemetery.[8]

Although the organizations www.jri-poland.org and www.geshergalicia.org indexed many records from Kańczuga the actual record scans were not always available to view on their websites. I discovered a goldmine of Jewish vital records from Kańczuga scanned from the Przemyśl archive Fond 1731 and placed on the website www.kanczuga.org with permission from www.szukawarchiwach. pl. The records date from 1851 to 1942. An individual must know approximate years to research and specify the type of vital record sought, then scroll through the scans until the desired name is found.[9] This website www.kanczuga.org facilitated my research for finding Holoszycer and Wald records. I previously obtained scans of several vital records for the surname Holoszycer, Fond 1731 at the Przemyśl Archive 2012 from Polish researcher Krzysztof Malczewski.

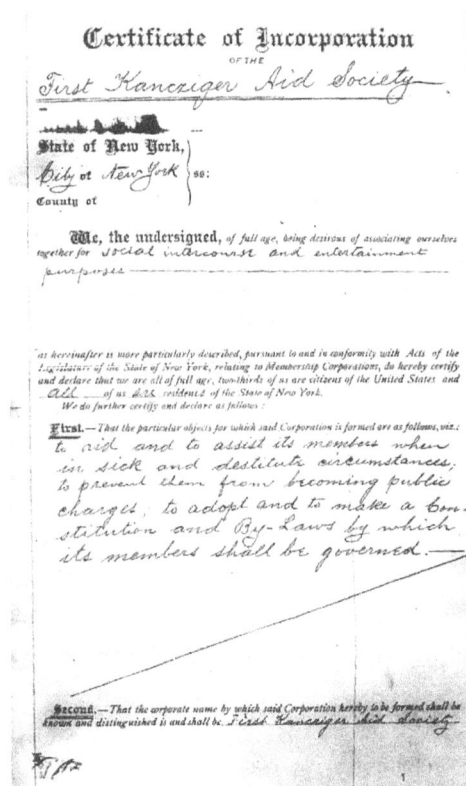

First Kancziger Aid Society p. 1

The Holoszycer Family from Kańczuga, Podkarpackie, Poland

Please refer to the *Descendants of Isak Holoszycer Family Tree.* Isak Holoszycer was born 1819 at Kańczuga to Jakob and Chane Holoszycer. He died 2 December 1890 at Kańczuga.[10] Izak Holoszycer married Pessel Frommer 11 September 1870 at Kańczuga.[11] He was age 51 and she was age 50. This was a civil marriage since their first child was Amalie, born 1843, therefore their religious marriage was probably ca. 1842. Izak and Pessel Holoszycer had the following children: Amalie (1843–ca. 1905); Jakob (1850–); Mechel (1858–); Chane (1861–1905). According to the death record for their child Chane in 1905, Izak and Pessel Holoszycer were proprietors of a bakery in Kańczuga.[12]

Children of Jakob Holoszycer and Esther Jacobes

Jakob Holoszycer was born 1850 at Kańczuga to Izak and Pessel Holoszycer. He married Ester Jakobes ca. 1870 at Kańczuga. She was born 17 June 1851 at Kańczuga and was the daughter of Lazer Jacobes and Sime. Jakob and Ester Holoszycer had the following children: Marcus (1871–); Freide (1872–1933); Getzel (1876–1933); Moses (1879–); Ryka Marjem (1882–1883); Efroim (1884–1887); Sime (1887–); Isaac (1890–1890).

Freide[3] Holoszycer (Jakob[2], Isaac[1]Holoszycer) was the second of eight children born to Jakob Holoszycer and Ester Jacobes. Freide was born 23 December 1872 at Kańczuga.[13] Her mother, Ester Jacobes, was born 17 June 1851 to Lazer and Sime Jacobes at Kanczuga.[14] Freide Holoszycer married Chaim Wald 26 December 1896 at Rzeszów, Podkarpackie, Poland.[15] Chaim Wald died 1923 at Rzeszów, Podkarpackie, Poland.[16] Their marriage record listed Chaim Wald, age 26 married to Freide Holoszycer, age 24.[17] This would make Chaim's birth year ca.1870. Chaim's parents were Josef Wald and Teme Sara Klinger. Josef Wald was born 1838 at Rzeszów; died 1870 at Rzeszów.[18] Teme Sara Klinger was

Birth record of Freide Holoszycer

born 1845 at Sędziszów, Malopolski, Podkarpackie; died 1903 at Rzeszów.[19] She was the daughter of Benzion Klinger and Ruchel Futersak. According to Chaim and Freide Wald's son Moshe Wald, ancestors of either the Klinger or Futersak family had an oral history they came to Poland as exiles from Spain. After Freide Wald née Holoszycer became a widow, she decided to emigrate from Poland to Palestine with her daughter Ester. However, Freide became ill and died 1933 at Kraków, Poland.[20]

Children of Freide Holoszycer and Chaim Wald

Chaim Wald and Freide Holoszycer had four children: Moshe Yaari Wald, Meir Yaari Wald, Tobias Lazar Wald, and Esther Wald. When the children became adults, they immigrated to Palestine and made valuable contributions to the young country of Israel. Chaim Wald and his family were found in the 1910 Rzeszów Census with their birth years recorded.[21] They were living in Rzeszów at 8 Krola Kazimierza, on the same street during the same time when my great-grandparents Aron and Hinde Geiger resided there.[22]

Chaim Wald   Freide Holoszycer

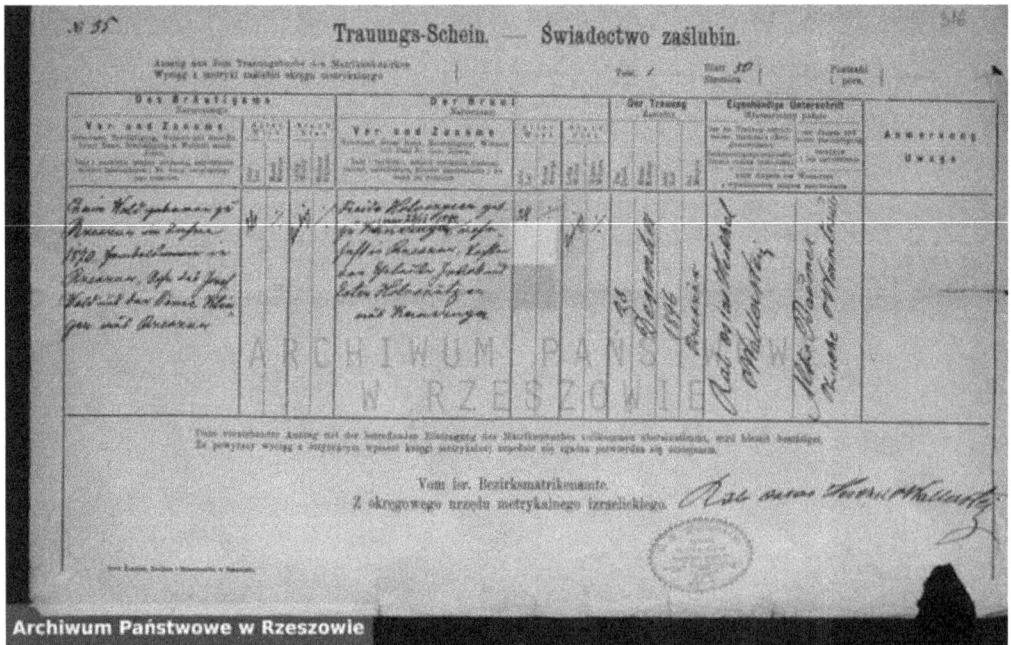

Marriage record of Chaim Wald and Friede Holoszycer, 1896

Dr. Moshe Yaari Wald discussed how his parents and siblings dreamt about making Aliyah to Palestine (before Israel was established as a new nation 14 May 1948). His father Chaim Wald wanted his children to precede him there. However, Chaim Wald died at the age of 50 in 1923 in Poland before he was able to travel to Palestine. Moshe Yaari Wald recalled that his paternal grandfather was Josef Dembitzer and on account of religious marriage not recognized by civil law, Josef received the surname Wald from his mother's surname. The name Yaari in Hebrew translates *from the forest.* The surname Wald is German for *forest.*

Moshe Yaari Wald

Moshe Yaari Wald (1895–1983) was the first of four children born 23 February 1895 at Kańczuga, Podkarpackie, Poland to Chaim Wald and Freide Holoszycer.[23] Moshe Yaari Wald took his examinations for his doctoral degree 1918 in Vienna during the decline of the Austro-Hungarian Monarchy. He witnessed angry mobs of people revolting against authority in Vienna and decided to return to his parents at Rzeszów. Anarchy reigned and there was no longer any security. He wrote: "Jew-hatred which had been kept concealed in times of peace, was now allowed free and open expression. Jews were beaten in the streets and on the roads." Riots at Rzeszów and surrounding towns broke out against the Jews on 3 May 1919 and soon became a pogrom with bloodshed and the destruction of property. After the pogrom died down, there were years of relative tranquility.[24]

Dr. Moshe Yaari Wald immigrated to Israel sometime after the death of his father Chaim Wald. He became highly regarded as a scholar, educator and was appointed Minister of Education in Israel. He resided at Tel Aviv, Israel. Dr. Wald wrote many chapters in the Rzeszów Yizkor book, such as *My Father Chaim Wald; A Portrait of Rzeszow at the Beginning of the 20th Century; The Goldsmiths of Rzeszow; During the Interregnum.* [25] Dr. Moshe Yaari Wald married Chaya Rivka Horowitz. She was born 1898 at Rzeszów to Alter Josef Horowitz and Feiga Leia Horowitz; she had two siblings: Shlomo Horowitz and Leonora Libe Horowitz. Chaya Rifka died 29 December 1966 at Israel. Moshe Yaari Wald and Chaya Rivka Horowitz had one child, Chava, later known as Carmela Unterbach. She had two sons, Eviathar Eldar and Aminadav Eldar.[26] Dr. Moshe Yaari Wald died 1983 in Israel.

Meir Yaari Wald (1897–1987) was the second of four children born 24 April 1897 to Freide Holoszycer and Chaim Wald at Kańczuga, Podkarpackie, Poland.[27] He died 21 February 1987 in Israel. While in Israel he changed his name to Meir Yaari.[28] He made Aliyah to Palestine in 1920 and joined the Kinneret moshava; he also worked as a laborer and paved roads in Palestine. During 1927 he founded Kibbutz Artzi and in 1929 he was among the founders of kibbutz Merhavia, where he lived until his death. The former Fourth Prime Minister of Israel, Golda Meir (1898–1978), made aliyah to Israel with her husband Morris 1921 and joined the same Merhavia kibbutz. They lived on the kibbutz for two years prior to Golda becoming an Israeli politician.

Meir Yaari was an Israeli politician, a social activist, and an educator. In 1948 he co-founded the Mapam political party. The Mapam party was originally Marxist-Zionist and socialistic with a radically different policy towards Arab civilians from the policy pursued by the former First Prime Minister of Israel, David Ben-Gurion. Mapam under Meir Yaari's leadership advocated for Jewish-Arab coexistence, opposed destruction of Arab houses, opposed Jewish settlements on Arab land and was in favor of Arab refugee rights to return to their homes after war.

Meir Yaari held his position as leader of the Mapam party in the Knesset from 1949 to 1974.[29] Under Meir Yaari the Mapam party in 1949 held 19 seats in the Knesset; in 1974 they held 7 seats. Meir Yaari implemented a project, Act Beyond Borders, that promoted reconciliation between Israelis and Palestinians through education.[30] Meir Yaari married Anda Karp (1902–1993). They had three children: Chaim Menachem Yaari (1941–1964), another son Avik and a daughter Rachel Yaari Groll. Avik had three daughters, Naomi, Zohar and Litral. Rachel had a daughter Iony and a son, Yedidya Yaari, who became a Major General in the Israeli Defense Forces and was Commander of the Israeli Navy 1965–2004, now re-

Meir Yaari in Israel

Meir Yaari

ח"כ מאיר יערי   Meir Yaari

Yedidya Yaari

tired. Meir Yaari wrote chapters in the Rzeszów Yizkor book: *A Heritage from a Reisha Home; The Birth of Hashomer Hatzair.*[31] His many publications were written in Hebrew, such as *The Trials and Tribulations of Our Generation* and *The Struggle for Liberated Labor.* He was appointed as a delegate to many Zionist Congresses.

Both Moshe Yaari Wald and his brother Meir Yaari shared their family memories through their chapters in the Yizkor Book of Rzeszów. Their mother, Freida Holoszycer, was a descendant of the Hassidic rabbinical dynasty that began with Rabbi Elimelech Weisblum of Lizhensk. Two surnames, Hausman and Dembitzer were mentioned in the chapter *My Father Chaim Wald* by Dr. Moshe Yaari Wald. Dr. Wald wrote: "At the age of 18, he (reb Chaim the son of Reb Yosel Dembitzer and Tema Wald) married Freida the daughter of Reb Yacov Holeshitzer and Esther née Hausman from the town of Kańczuga. This was a wide-branched family, whose roots were in the towns of Przeborsk, Dinów, Błażowa, Pruchnik, Leżajsk and Sieniawa. My mother took pride during my youth that among her relatives there were rabbinical judges, and that she was related to the family of Rabbi Elimelech of Leżajsk (Lizhensk)…".[32] Although the surnames Dembitzer and Hausman were not found among my record research related with the Holoszycer or Wald families, it is possible the names Dembitzer and Hausman pre-dated written records, did not survive, or have not yet been found.

Tobias Lazar Wald was the third of four children born 1907 at Rzeszów, Podkarpackie, Poland to Freida Holoszycer and Chaim Wald.[33] He married Faiga Mindel Amster 1932 at Sanok, Podkarpackie, Poland. She was born 1911 at Sanok to Yakov Amster and Chaya Sara Amster.[34] Faiga's parents Yakov and Chaya Sara Amster were both murdered during the Shoah.[35] Tobias aka Tuvia and Faiga aka Tziporah had two sons, Giora, Jacob and a daughter Shulamit.

Ester Wald was the last of four children born 1911 at Rzeszów, Podkarpackie, Poland to Freida Holoszycer and Chaim Wald.[36] After her mother Freida's death in 1933, Ester continued her journey to Palestine where she became a nurse in a hospital for contagious diseases at Jaffa. Esther Wald received her Nurse Certification at Israel 20 December 1937.[37] There were many terrorist uprisings and Ester's two close friends were murdered by Arab rioters.

Ester later immigrated to the United States in 1943.[38] Esther travelled from Palestine on the *S.S..El Nil.* This ship departed from Port Said, Egypt 26 March 1943 and arrived at New York 10 June 1943. She indicated that her destination was to her uncle Moses Haller at Fort Hamilton Parkway, Brooklyn, New York.[39]

She returned to Palestine after WII ended, then took passage on the ship *Marine Carp* that departed from Haifa, Palestine 26 July 1947 and arrived at New York 8 Aug 1947. Her occupation was nurse, age 36, going to visit her uncle M. Halle at 6501 Ft. Hamilton Parkway, Brooklyn, New York. Esther last resided with her brother Moshe (Yaari) Wald at 25 Beth Josef Street, Tel Aviv in Palestine.[40] My cousin Harry Holly z"l recalled Esther worked as a nurse at a hospital in Manhattan, New York.

The Family of Mariem Geiger and Getzel Holoszycer

Getzel[3] **Holoszycer** (Jakob[2], Isaac[1]Holoszycer) was the third of eight children born 21 December 1876 at Kańczuga, Podkarpackie, Poland to Jakob Holoszycer and Ester Jacobes.[41] He died 27 October 1933 at Kings County, New York.[42] Getzel's father, Jakob Holoszycer, was born 1850 at Kańczuga to Isak Holoszycer (ca.1819–ca.1890) and Pessel Frommer (ca. 1818–ca. 1888). Getzel's mother, Ester Jacobes, was born 17 June 1851 at Kańczuga to Lazer Jacobes and Sime Jacobes.[43]

Archiwum Państwowe w Przemyślu

Birth record of Getzel Holoszycer, 1876

Getzel Holoszycer married Mariem Geiger 1902 at Błażowa, Podkarpackie, Poland. She was the daughter of Aron Geiger and Hinde Turnheim of Błażowa, Podkarpackie, Poland. Mariem Geiger was born 22 February 1880 at Przemyśl, Podkarpackie, Poland. Getzel and Mariem Holoszycer had a child born 1905 at Kańczuga, Symche Tobiasz. Mariem with their child renamed Mina;[4] immigrated to New York 29 October 1907 via the *S.S. Noordam*. After settling at Manhattan, New York, Getzel and Manya subsequently had three more children all born in New York: Pauline, Harry, and Esther. Getzel Holoszycer later changed his name to George Holly. See the section *Children of Mariem Geiger and Getzel Holoszycer aka Holly.*

The Immigration of Mariem Geiger and Getzel Holoszycer to New York

I had difficulty locating records for both Mariem and Getzel Holoszycer on passenger manifests and immigration records. I then decided to research naturalization records. While researching naturalization records for Mariem aka Manya Holoszycer I found new

S.S. Noordam, 1903

Manya and Mina, *S.S Noordam,* p.1

information regarding her surname. On her Petition for Citizenship, Manya described how she entered the U.S. under a different surname, Rottmann, a name I did not recognize in either her family or in Getzel's family.[44] I then realized why I had difficulty locating her in the immigration records, she was travelling under a completely different name as the wife of Aron Rottman. I speculated that Manya obtained the ticket from the Rottmanns because she lacked the necessary legal documents for immigration.

On the *S.S. Noordam* passenger manifest, Mariem travelled as Manja Rottmann, married, age 29 years with her daughter Mina Rottmann, age two.[45] She left the port of Rotterdam 19 October 1907 on the *S.S. Noordam* and arrived at New York 29 October 1907. Manya gave her last permanent residence as Przeworsk and her nearest friend or relative as Aron Rottmann, from Rzeszów, Galicia. Such information had to conform with the ticket information. She indicated that she was going to join her brother Charles Geiger at 307 Grand Street in New York. Manya also listed her place of birth as Przemyśl, her physical description was 5 ft. 2 inches with brown hair and brown eyes. Manya and her daughter Mina were held and placed on a list for detained aliens.[46] They waited for Charles Geiger to be notified of their arrival so they could be claimed and thereby discharged from the ship; they were discharged the same day. Women and children who travelled without a male family member had to wait to be escorted off the ship by their relative who lived in the USA. Probably with the help of her brother Charles Geiger, Manya was eventually reunited with her husband Getzel in New York's Lower East Side.

Life in New York

According to the 1910 Federal Census of New York Manya, Getzel and their children lived at 52 Lewis Street in the Lower East Side of New York. [47] The head of the household was Getzel Holoschitz, age 34 listed as an egg merchant with his own business, his wife Miriam (Manya) age 32, daughters Minnie aka Mina age 5 years and Pauline aka Pearl age 11 months; also living with them was my grandmother Minnie Geiger age 21 listed as a sister-in-law (she was Manya's sister), her occupation was dressmaker in a dress shop. There was also a boarder Isaac Frankel age 17 who worked as a cutter in a cloak shop. Six people were living in that household including Manya's two small children. In looking at the census of that address, neighbors over the age of 14 years were either working or were homemakers. It was a working-class environment.

Mariem Holoszycer
née Geiger, 1904

Getzel Holoszycer,
1904

(LtoR) Mariem, Minnie, baby Pearl, Mina, New York 1910

It was not unusual at that time to take in boarders for adding extra income and help a newcomer to the United States who probably did not understand English. The common language spoken by most Jewish immigrants was Yiddish. Years later as people became more assimilated, Yiddish fell by the wayside in favor of English. On this census, the stated year of immigration for Manya, Getzel and their daughter Minnie was listed as 1907.

By the 1920 Federal census, the family moved to 382 Third Street, Manhattan and Getzel Holoschitzer changed his name to the more American sounding George Holly.[48] He was listed as an operator (probably a sewing machine operator) for children's clothing. His wife was Miriam and his children were listed as Minnie age 15, Pearl age 10, Harry age 6 and Esther age 4. George was age 42 and Miriam age 40. On this census, the date for immigration was given as 1908. The neighbors in that same building were all Jewish, speaking Yiddish and the men worked in similar occupations, essentially working-class people who worked as pressers, shipping clerks, jobbers, letter carriers, dishwashers, truck drivers, sewing machine operators.

In the 1925 New York State Census, George Holly and family were living at 470 East Houston Street in Manhattan.[49] George was age 46, Miriam was age 44, Minnie was age 20, Pearl was age 16, Harry was age 12 and Esther was age 10. George was employed as a sewing machine operator in a factory; his daughter Minnie aka Mina was employed as a stenographer. The neighbors were working class people with occupations such as a barber, stenographer, clerk, and a candy maker. George, his wife Miriam and his daughter Minnie were classified as aliens as they did not yet obtain their citizenship. Their children, Pearl, Harry and Esther were automatically citizens because they were born in the United States.

Manya Holly

By the 1930 Federal census, the family moved to Brooklyn in the Coney Island section.[50] They lived at 2927 West 29th Street. George Holly was age 52 and Miriam was age 46. Their children were Mina age 22, Pearl age 20, Harry age 17 and Esther age 14. George was employed as a sewing machine operator in men's clothing and Pearl was employed as an examiner in a hospital. The rest of the family were unemployed. They paid $50 a month for their apartment, a bit high for those times. By moving to Brooklyn, the family left the Lower East Side in Manhattan for an improved environment. Their date of immigration was given as 1907. The neighbors' occupations were varied: a pharmacist, a Hebrew teacher, a roofer, store clerks, and operators. Most people living there were Jewish with Yiddish as their primary language.

Manya filed her petition for naturalization 1 April 1928 at Brooklyn, New York and stated that she entered the USA under the name Manja Rottmann on 29 October 1907. She was a resident of Kings County, New York for six months prior to 1 October 1925. Manya Holly's certificate of arrival, petition and declara-

Mania Holly, Petition 1928

No. 3732579

Name   HOLLY? Mania

residing at   2927 West 29th St B'klyn

Age 51   years.   Date of order of admission   July 25th 1933

Date certificate issued   July 25th 1933   by the

U. S. District   Court at   Brooklyn, New York

Petition No.   1295 (9)

Mania Holly

(Complete and true signature of holder)

Mania Holly, Naturalization 1933

Manya Holly matsevah

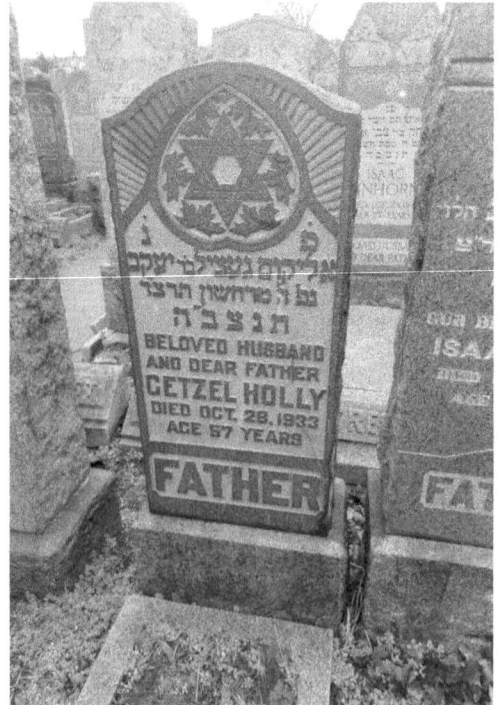

Getzel Holly matsevah

tion of intent Freitz 100 ion were accepted on 15 April 1933 by the U.S. District Court of the Eastern District, Brooklyn, New York.[51] She became a naturalized citizen 25 July 1933.

Deaths

Death certificates were obtained from the Department of Health of the City of New York. George Holly died 27 October 1933 at 2927 W. 29th Street, Coney Island, Brooklyn, New York. He was listed as being age 56, ten months and was born in Poland. His occupation was given as a tailor. His parents were listed as Jacob (Holoshitzer) and Ester Jacobitz, both from Poland. Getzel was buried in the Kańczuger Society section in Mt. Zion cemetery located at Maspeth, Queens, New York. The name spelled on cemetery records was Getzel Halley and he was buried in the Kańczuger Society section, location A15L.

Manya died 29 November 1946, at 66 years of age. She lived at 10 Monroe Street, in New York City with her single daughter Esther.[52] Their apartment was part of a huge low-income housing project in lower Manhattan. The housing project is now known as Knickerbocker Village. Manya's son Harry Holly was the informant for information provided on her death certificate however her birth date was incorrect (given as 1 March 1886), and her mother's name was Hinde instead of Mary. Manya Holly was buried 1 December 1946 at Mt. Zion Cemetery, in the Kańczuger Society location A by gate 23, near her late husband Getzel Halley aka George Holly. Her name on the cemetery records was Marion Holly.

Children of Mariem Geiger and Getzel Holoszycer

Mina Holly

Mina was the first of four children born 9 February 1905 to Manya and Getzel at Kańczuga, Podkarpackie, Poland. She was named at birth Symche Tobiasz.[53] According to Alexander Beider, Symche derives from the Hebrew word meaning joy. This name can be conferred to a male or to a female child.[54] Her second name presents a mystery since Tobiasz is usually a masculine name that derives from Tuvye.[55] Her parents soon renamed her Minnie or Mina.[56] She was a toddler age 2, and travelled with her mother when they immigrated to the United States.[57]

Mina Holly applied for citizenship on 3 June 1926 through the Southern District Court of New York. She indicated that she immigrated under the name of Mina Rottman on 29 October 1907. She stated that she was born 9 February 1905 at Kańczuga. She listed her occupation as dancer. Her last foreign residence was Cologne, Germany.[58] Mina was granted citizenship on 30 September 1930 by the U.S. District Court at Brooklyn, New York.[59]

I learned from my cousin Liz that Mina was also an artist's model. Mina associated with artistic people during her early adulthood however she also worked as a stenographer to support herself and her family. Liz told me that Mina posed as

Mina Holly Petition for Citizenship

a model for the highly regarded Social Realist artist Raphael Soyer (1899–1987). She gave me the name of the museum where I was able to view and photograph one of Soyer's paintings of *Mina* on display at the Phillips Academy Addison Gallery of American Art in Andover, Massachusetts. The other portrait of Mina is owned by the Metropolitan Museum of Art in New York City. Please see the portraits of *Mina* by Raphael Soyer, both painted 1932. Mina appeared as a pensive young adult.

My personal memories of Mina were that she was a strong, intelligent, independent individual who lived at lower Manhattan with her daughter Helen. Mina was radical to the far left of the political spectrum. She was adamant that Israel oppressed the Palestinians and unlawfully annexed their land. She clung to her socialist and leftist tendencies by being outspoken about capitalism as an unfair system that oppressed the working class. No argument could sway her to reconsider her position. Mina always expressed her empathy for the under-dog and cared deeply about people's suffering.

The following history was provided through telephone conversations during 2014 and 2015 with Mina's daughter Helen. Mina married Thomas Martin Keenan in 1940 at New York City. Thomas worked as a seaman on many ships sailing to exotic locations.[60] Helen described her father as being tall and

Portrait Mina Holly by Raphael Soyer Phillips Academy

Portrait Mina Holly, Metropolitan Museum by Raphael Soyer

blond. His height was almost 6 feet as noted on some of the ship manifests. Helen recalled that her father also had a license as sea captain. Soon after Mina and Thomas were married, they moved to Baltimore, Maryland where Helen was born the following year. The family moved from Baltimore to Cleveland, Ohio. Mina registered at Cuyahoga County, Ohio 19 September 1952 to submit evidence that she was previously naturalized 30 Sept 1930 at Brooklyn, New York. She also indicated that she lived in Cleveland, Ohio for the past two years.[61] Helen reported that when she was age 16, her parents Mina and Thomas Keenan divorced in Cleveland, Ohio 1957 due to a "mismatch" of personalities.

After the divorce, Mina and Helen returned to New York City, where they lived with Mina's sister Esther. Thomas Keenan later re-married and lived out his final years at West Palm Beach, Florida; he died 21 March 1995.[62] Mina and Helen moved to 328 East 15th Street, Manhattan, New York. Helen continued living with her mother until Mina's death at Manhattan, New York, March 1996, at 91 years of age.[63] Mina Holly and Thomas Keenan had one child, Helen. She is still living.

Pearl Holly

Pearl Holly, NYU College of Medicine

Pearl Holly was the second of four children born 6 May 1909 at New York to Manya and Getzel Holoszycer. Pearl died 2 June 1982, age 73 years, at Santa Fe, New Mexico.[64] Her obituary was published in the *New Mexican* newspaper.[65] Pearl started life in the Lower East Side, as another poor Jew. However, Pearl was extremely intelligent with scientific ability and much ambition. She worked hard to succeed academically, and she graduated from Hunter College with a B.A. in English literature in 1929. Pearl told my mother Sylvia that she needed to change her Lower East Side accent when she was in college. She went to a speech therapist who taught her to speak as if she was born and bred in England, with a very refined manner of speech that indeed helped her advance in her career.

Pearl's focus changed to a new path, to enter medical school. She graduated from New York University in 1934 with a M.S. in microbiology. She met the admission requirements for medical school and then applied to New York University College of Medicine. When she wanted to attend medical school, her uncle Charles Geiger gave her the necessary money for tuition. This was at a time when admission to medical school favored male applicants however Pearl was highly motivated and determined. She was listed in the New York University College of Medicine third year class roster in the 1937 yearbook, and she was one of three women in a class of 119. Pearl graduated from medical school 1938.[66]

She married George Bronz that same year 15 April 1938 at Alexandria, Virginia.[67] Pearl chose to intern in Gallinger Municipal Hospital at Washington, D.C. since George worked as an attorney for the Federal government in Washington,

Marriage certificate, George and Pearl Bronz

D.C. Pearl worked on the staff of George Washington Hospital for many years as an Internist and Hematologist and she became Chairperson of their Hematology Department. By 1965 Pearl set herself another goal, to specialize in psychiatry. She completed a psychiatric residency to become a psychiatrist. She began her thriving private practice as a psychiatrist and she told me that among her patients were politicians, naturally no names mentioned. Pearl retained her name Holly for her professional career. She was listed in the Biographical Directory for Fellows and Members of the American Psychiatric Association, 1977. After her husband George died, Pearl retired and moved to Santa Fe, New Mexico. Prior to her death, Pearl set up the Bronz Memorial Fund for Campus Journalism at George Washington University in 1982, in memory of her deceased son, Stephen Holly Bronz.[68] I remember Pearl as a gracious, warm, caring cousin who invited me to her house in Washington, D.C. and who went out of her way to extend her hospitality.

Pearl's husband George Bronz was born 7 July 1910 at New York to Louis Bronz and Sarah Paley. George had one sibling, Max, who was born 16 November 1907 and died 28 June 1911 at Manhattan, New York.[69] George's father Louis Bronz was an immigrant from Russia. Louis Bronz filed his Petition for Naturalization 13 June 1921. On this petition he stated that he was born 25 September 1874 at Kovna, Russia.[70] I learned that Kovno or Kovna was the Yiddish name for Kaunas in Lithuania, once part of the Russian Empire. Jews had a presence in Kaunas for many centuries and by 1897 the Jewish population was 25,448 (36% of the general population).[71] Louis stated on his Petition that he immigrated from Southampton, England on the ship *S.S. Paris* to the United States 22 July 1896 and arrived at New York on 1 August 1896. Louis took his oath of allegiance on 10 February 1922.

Louis Bronz, age 30 and Sarah Paley, age 20 married 30 December 1906 at Manhattan, New York.[72] Their marriage record contained the names for the parents of Louis: Jacob Bronz and Sarah Souber. The names for the parents of Sarah Paley were: Lazerus Paley and Frida Urdinzky. Both Louis and Sarah were born in Russia. I discovered the immigration record for Sarah Paley, her mother Frida and her sister Chane. They departed from Hamburg on 26

George Bronz, 1929

May 1901 on the ship *S.S. Graf Waldersee*.[73] When they arrived at New York 8 June 1901 they were held at Ellis Island as Aliens held for Special Inquiry because they were unaccompanied females. They were admitted to the USA 10 June 1901.[74] Frieda's occupation was dressmaker. Frieda and her two daughters Sarah and Chane were from Suwalki. This was a small region in northeastern Poland near the border with Lithuania. The capital of the region was Suwalki. At the time the family immigrated to the United States, Suwalki was under Russian rule. Jews there faced extreme anti-Semitism and persecution. There were brief episodes of prosperity and peace alternating with oppression, hunger and deprivation. Many Jews from Suwalki immigrated to the United States, Sweden, South Africa and South America.[75]

The 1910 US Federal Census contained information that Louis Bronz, his wife Sarah and their son Max lived at 1269 Second Avenue, at Manhattan, New York. Louis was proprietor of a store.[76] The 1920 U.S. Federal Census indicated that Louis, Sarah and their son George lived with Louis' nephew George Horowitz, Joseph Kavano, who was a brother-in-law and Bessy, a sister-in-law. Their address was 117 East 88th Street, Manhattan, New York. Louis listed his occupation as a mechanic.[77] The 1940 U.S. Federal Census contained information that Louis and Sarah Bronz moved to Newark, New Jersey. Their address was 268 Hawthorne Avenue, Newark. Louis worked as a machinist at a machine shop. [78] Louis Bronz died in the Bronx, New York 12 June 1949.[79] Sarah Bronz died in the Bronx, New York 15 April 1952.[80]

Cousin Liz recalled that when her father George Bronz was age thirteen, he entered and won a city-wide essay contest to become a boy mayor of NYC for one day. I found early photographs of George as an undergraduate college student at City College of New York in *The Microcosm* college yearbook for 1929. He was listed as a news editor and it was noted that he won a Frieberg Memorial Award for Oratory.[81] Years later George Bronz was also listed in the *Who's Who in World Jewry*.[82] After graduation from City College, he graduated from Columbia University Law School.

Upon becoming an attorney, George set his goal to work for the federal government. George was one of many Jews drawn to Washington, D.C. with the advent of President Franklin D. Roosevelt's New Deal. At the same time, some Jews grew aware of the growing turmoil in Europe and pleaded with the United States government to help the situation of Jews abroad. This was especially important with the rise of Hitler to power in 1933 and the barring of Jewish emigration to Palestine by the British. In the United States political currents increased against allowing Jewish refugees to enter the USA during the start of WWII. This was due to anti-Semitism and fears that Jews could be spies working for the Germans.

George completed a draft card in 1940 and listed his employer as the U.S Department of the Interior.[83] George had employment in the Department of the Interior as a chief legal counsel. He initially worked with Supreme Court Justice Felix Frankfurter and then worked directly under the United States Secretary of the Interior Harold LeClair Ickes, who was in that office from 1933 to 1946.[84] In the 1940 Federal Census Pearl and George lived at 3925 Davis Place, Washington, D.C.[85]

Harold LeClair Ickes implemented much of President Franklin D. Roosevelt's "New Deal," as the US Secretary of the Interior and Director of the Public Works Administration. He was a strong supporter for civil rights and civil liberties. During 1938 Harold Ickes proposed offering Alaska as a safe-haven for Jewish refugees from Germany and other areas of Europe who were being oppressed by the Nazis. The purpose of his plan was to bypass the restrictive immigration quotas since Alaska was not yet a state. The plan was dropped when politicians and certain Jewish groups opposed this plan as they did not want to give the impression that Jews would be taking over part of the country for settlement. President Roosevelt then imposed a limit of only 10,000 immigrants a year for five years with a maximum of only 10 percent Jews. President Roosevelt later reduced even that number.[86] When Mr. Ickes learned about the plight of Jews in Europe, he gave his full support to George Bronz's efforts to rescue relatives from the Nazis that will be described later in this chapter.

By the end of WWII, George found new employment at the U.S. Treasury Department. He was listed in the official register for Persons Occupying Administrative and Supervisory Positions in the Legislative, Executive, and Judicial Branches of the Federal Government and in the District of Columbia Government.[87] George became a specialist on international law, and he was one of the attorneys who drafted the GATT or General Agreement on Tariffs and Trade that was formed in 1947 and lasted until 1994 when it was replaced by the World Trade Organization in 1995.[88] George was a member of the United States Delegations to various international trade conferences and was Special Assistant to the General Counsel of the Treasury for International Finance and Trade 1943–1954.

George published articles in the Columbia Law Review e.g. *The Tariff Commission as a Regulatory Agency.*[89] He also published articles in the Harvard Law Review e.g. *The International Trade Organization Charter.*[90] He later went into private practice as an attorney specializing in international and tariff law and represented many corporations who were plaintiffs against government tariffs being imposed on their products. I found examples of those cases on-line, such as Ciba-Geigy Corporation v. United States when George was in private practice; his firm was Bronz and Farrell.[91] Another case was *Western Dairy Products Inc. v. United States*; once again George Bronz was counsel for the plaintiff.[92] George was a proponent for free trade. He represented the New Zealand Meat Board to lower tariffs on meat such as New Zealand lamb. His practice was going strong at the time of his death, even his name still appeared on the office door with his partners 10 years after his death. George died April 1976 at Washington, D.C.[93] Pearl Holly and George Bronz had two children, Stephen, and Elizabeth. Elizabeth is still living in Israel, with her large family.

Pearl Holly and George Bronz as Family Rescuers

It was fortuitous that Cousin Liz held on to the letters left by her parents about how they rescued the Geigers. Those papers are vitally important for our family history to learn about the impact of the horrendous era of WWII and the Shoah. The letters honor and preserve the memory of how Charles and Abraham Geiger worked together with George and Pearl Bronz to help their Geiger relatives immigrate to the safety of the United States and escape from certain torture and death at the hands of the Nazis.

Charles Geiger persuaded Pearl and George Bronz to write letters of affidavits on behalf of Geiger relatives still in Europe during the beginning of the Shoah and prior to U.S. involvement in WWII. The purpose was to make it possible for Geiger relatives

Pearl Holly Bronz

to immigrate to the U.S. during quotas. The only way they could do so was if an American citizen sponsored them by giving affidavits, with assurances the immigrants would not become a financial burden on the government. As a high-level attorney working in the federal government, George was well positioned to undertake this mission and he bravely did so. It was his letters with official government stationery from the Department of the Interior (with approval by Harold L. Ickes) that enabled Abraham Geiger's children to leave their precarious situation in Europe to enter the USA: Max Geiger, his wife Rose and their two children Clara and Susi; Josef Geiger and his wife Esther; Stella Geiger and her husband Moses Steinbock, Mina Geiger and her husband Karl Neumann, Moses Steinbock's brother's wife, and a cousin, Freida Prisand née Turnheim.

In an affidavit of support for Freida Prisand written by George Bronz in 1938, George wrote that Freida was his wife Pearl's cousin who lived in Vienna. He described his salary, his financial obligations and that he was willing and able to support Freida so she would not become a financial burden to any community in the United States. He requested the American Consul to issue her a visa.[94] His letter probably never reached the American Consul in Vienna during the *Anschluss* in Vienna. I discovered Freida Prisand's name in the Central Database of Shoah Victim's Names.[95] She was deported by the Nazis from Vienna and placed on a transport train 23 October 1941 to the Łódź Ghetto in Poland, where she remained a prisoner until she either died from starvation or illness or was murdered in an extermination camp such as Auschwitz. See the chapter *The Turnheim Family* for additional information about Freida Prisand. George was successful in getting all other individuals for whom he wrote affidavits to safety in the United States.

In another affidavit of support March 1941 George requested to have Markus aka Max Geiger, his wife Ruchla (Rose) and their children Clara and Susi who were detained in Marseilles, France to be admitted to the United States as permanent citizens. George wrote that Markus was his wife Pearl's first cousin. He also vouched for their good character and said he would ensure that no members of their family would engage in political organizations under foreign control. He stated that he was willing to maintain and support the family in the United States so they would not become a financial burden. This was written to the American consul at Marseilles; *See Appendix A.*

George realized he needed to submit proof about his employment as chief legal adviser and used the official stationery with the seal of the Department of the Interior. This letter requested by George was sent in a diplomatic pouch directly to the American consul at Marseilles, France. The letter sufficiently impressed the American consul at Marseilles and facilitated the granting of visas to the Geigers to escape from the horrors of the Shoah to safety in the United States. [96] For additional information, please refer to the chapters for *Abraham Geiger and Sprynca Stark* and *Charles Geiger and Esther Mamlock*.

George wrote to the German Jewish Aid Committee in London, England July 1938 for Josef Geiger, and his wife Ester Geiger to be permitted to enter England and live there until quota restrictions were lifted in the United States for Jewish immigration.[97] George added assurances under oath that he was able and ready to financially support Josef and Ester in both England and the United States. George referred to his prior affidavits written for Josef and Ester, that they would be his financial responsibility and not become a burden on any community.

Charles Geiger wrote an urgent letter to Pearl and George on 13 July 1939 after receiving a letter from his brother Abraham Geiger in London.[98] Time was crucial as Abraham Geiger's son Josef and his wife Ester were being held in a detention camp at Milan, Italy and unless they were able to enter England soon, they were in danger of being returned to Germany to their certain deaths by the Nazis. Charles and Abraham were also instrumental in working together to get vital information about the Geigers to George so he could properly execute the affidavits. Charles Geiger added in his letter to George that he would be the one to financially support his relatives and that George would "risk nothing outside of helping a near relative from going back to hell." George also prepared the affidavits for Abraham Geiger's daughter Stella and her husband Morris Steinbock to obtain visas from Antwerp, Belgium during April 1940.

Pearl and George rescued many members of the Geiger family who were living in Europe during the Holo-

George and Pearl Bronz

caust from certain death through George's connection with the federal government as chief legal advisor in the Department of the Interior. He persevered despite an under-current of anti-Semitism in the government and many government officials not wanting to become involved with the Jewish refugee problem during those terrible years. George and Pearl were totally dedicated to help their family members escape from the horrors of tyranny, brutality, torture, murder, and genocide during the Shoah.

Stephen Bronz

Stephen was the first of two children born to Pearl and George. He was born 5 October 1941 at Washington, D.C.[99] He tragically died in a car accident on 15 January 1971 on a road between Albuquerque and Santa Fe, New Mexico.[100] Stephen was married briefly to Ruth (last name unknown) who came from Dallas, Texas. Stephen and Ruth were separated at the time of his death.

Stephen went to Oberlin College in Ohio. I located a photo of Stephen in the Oberlin College Yearbook for Freshmen Class of 1962. Stephen became a prolific writer of American history and was a published author at a young age. His books are: *The Challenge of America, The Challenge of America from the Early Beginnings Through Reconstruction, Roots of Negro Racial Consciousness, Challenge of America: From Reconstruction to the Present with Selected Readings.* When I met Stephen, he told me that his next book was going to be a history of cowboys and that his research centered in the western part of the United States. He was intelligent, shy, polite, and determined to overcome his stutter. Stephen's fate was parallel to my brother David's fate in that they both tragically died in car accidents as young adults, both were talented, bright and they both had red hair. Prior to his death, Stephen was engaged in graduate studies at George Washington University, Washington, D.C.

Stephen Bronz

Harry Holly

Harry was the third of four children born 18 May 1912 at New York to Manya and Getzel Holoszycer. He died 14 April 2007 at Fort Lauderdale, Broward County, Florida at the age of 94 years (almost 95 years).[101] Prior to his death, Harry lived at 7208 Westwood Drive, Tamarac, Florida for many years.[102] Cousin Lisa provided information concerning her parents. Harry married Rose Nassau ca. 1942. My parents and I visited them often at their apartment when they lived in Queens, New York. Rose was born in Pennsylvania on 8 January 1911, and she died 24 July 1974 at New York at 63 years.[103] Rose Holly's obituary was in the *New York Times,*

Harry Holly

as "Loving wife of Harry. Sister of Saul. Devoted mother of Danny, Lisa and aunt of Vicki. She was kind and helpful to everyone."[104]

Lisa told me that her mother Rose grew up in Castle Shannon, a coal mining town outside of Pittsburg. Her father was a peddler who sold pots and pans door to door until he saved enough money to purchase a small food market. Rose and her family were found on the 1930 Federal Census for Castle Shannon, Pennsylvania.[105] Rose's parents were Samuel Nassau, age 52 and his wife Rebecca, age 47. Samuel was listed as a grocery merchant. Their children were: Jacob, age 24, a salesman in the grocery store; Fanny age 23, a

stenographer in a dry goods store; Isidore, age 21; Rose age 19, a stenographer in the steel mill; Saul age 16. Samuel, Rebecca and Jacob were

Harry Holly 1962

Harry Holly matsevah

born in Russia and immigrated to the U.S. in 1905. Fanny, Isidore, Rose and Saul were born in Pennsylvania.

Cousin Lisa told me that her mother Rose left Pennsylvania for New York during WWII and worked on Wall Street. Due to anti-Semitism, Rose had to conceal she was Jewish or face unemployment. While in New York, Harry, Rose, and their children lived in a comfortable apartment community at Queens, New York that had many international residents. Harry owned a business manufacturing shower parts. He had a lively intellect with many interests, including becoming adept at fashioning items from glass and making stained glass decorations. I recall that Rose also loved to create pottery on a potter's wheel. Harry's political left-wing stance moderated somewhat over the years, especially when he was running his business. Over the years, Harry suffered considerable back pain and he told me that he had some pain relief by learning to hypnotize himself.

I last spoke with Harry on the telephone 1 November 2005, two years before his death. He recalled much information from his father's side especially those cousins who immigrated to Israel and became government leaders such as Minister of Education, a founder of the Socialist party and a Major General in the Israeli army. He also knew a great deal about the Geigers and that his Uncle Abraham was a "holy man." He recalled how Charles Geiger called upon Pearl and her husband George for their political connections in getting the Geigers out from the Nazi regime. He even recalled that the Geigers had a paperbag business in Vienna prior to the war and that his cousin Freda (probably Freida Prisand née Turnheim) was very intellectual and attended Sigmund Freud's lectures at the University of Vienna.

Both Harry and Rose Holly were buried at South Florida National Cemetery, Lake Worth, Palm Beach County, Florida.[106] My cousin Dan took a photograph of Harry Holly's headstone with an inscription that he was a technical sergeant. Harry served in the Army during WWII. There was a fire in 1973 at the facility at St. Louis, Missouri that destroyed most military personnel records. After a fruitless search for his army record, I contacted the National Personnel Records Center at St. Louis, Missouri with a request for his WWII Final Pay Voucher.[107] This piece of information is often the only way to learn anything about a veteran's army record if there were no other documents. I learned much information from Harry's final payment form. He had a total of three years of active service, and he arrived back in the United States 3 July 1945. Harry was honorably discharged from the Army 25 March 1946. He enlisted in the Army at Brooklyn, New York. His home address was 10 Monroe Street, Manhattan, NY, the same address as his mother Manya. Harry and Rose had two children: Daniel and Lisa, both are still living.

Esther Holly

Esther was the last of four children born 22 March 1915 at New York to Manya Geiger and Getzel Holoszycer. She died 9 November 1981 at Sloane Kettering Hospital in New York City at 66 years.[108] After a lifetime of good health, Esther suddenly became extremely ill and cousin Liz recalled that Esther had considerable back pain over a year before her cancer was detected. Prior to her illness, Cousin Lisa added that Esther was a cheerful and athletic individual who lived her entire life in Manhattan. Her obituary was published in the *New York Times*: "Esther Holly. On Monday November 9. Beloved sister of Mina, Dr. Bronz, Harry

Ester Holly's wedding. Front Row (LtoR): George, Pearl, Stephen, Danny, Elizabeth, Helen. Back Row (LtoR): Mina, Tom, Milton, Esther, Minnie Weiss, Rose, Harry

Esther Holly 1962

and beloved aunt of Elizabeth, Helen, Lisa and Daniel."[109]

Esther was an attractive woman, who was intelligent, gentle and kind. My parents often invited her to dinners at our apartment and she enjoyed being with our family. Esther worked many years for the City of New York as an office manager. She married Milton Siegel in 1954, who was a psychologist, and an intellectual and humorous man.[110] Milton owned a coffee house in Greenwich Village that attracted intellectuals and artists. I saw how Esther and Milton loved each other but grew apart and eventually divorced sometime after 1962. Esther resumed her birth surname Holly. There was no issue.

Esther belonged to the Ethical Culture Society of New York and attended their lectures.[111] The Ethical Culture movement was developed by Felix Adler, who originally trained to be a Reform Rabbi. Their principles stress that morality is independent of theology, moral problems in modern society have not been adequately addressed by religions, and philanthropy will advance morality.

Other Holoszycer Relatives Who Immigrated from Kańczuga to the United States

Moses³ Holoszycer (Jakob², Isaac¹ Holoszycer) was the third of three children born 4 August 1879 at Kańczuga to Jakob Holoszycer and Ester Jacobes. I found a record with information about the immigration of Moses Holoszycer.[112] The ship manifest was the *S.S. Kronprinz Wilhelm* that departed from Bremen, Germany 16 May 1905 and arrived at New York on 24 May 1905. Moses was listed as age 25, single, a laborer, from Kańczuga. His destination was to his uncle Mechel Holoszycer who lived at 140 Rivington Street, New York. I noticed that Moses travelled with $300, a considerable sum of money for that era. It is possible that Moses changed his surname to Halle or Haller based on his niece Ester Wald's

1947 ship manifest with her destination to her uncle Moses Haller who lived in Brooklyn, New York.

Mechel[2] Holoszycer (Isaac[1] Holoszycer) was born 2 April 1858 at Kańczuga, Podkarpackie, Poland; he married ca. 1880 Golda Chaja Kropf, daughter of Schyja and Perl Kropf of Jarosław. Mechel immigrated from Hamburg to New York, 29 June 1888 on the ship *S.S. Prague* with his wife Golda and their three children: Ester; Lazar; David Hersch (listed as Fischel on the ship manifest).[113] Mechel (known as Michael Holschitz in New York) completed his declaration for United States citizenship 12 October 1903 at New York.[114] I also found an application for a birth certificate by Gussie (Golda) Holoshitzer from ca. 1902. She listed her spouse as Michal Holoshitzer and child Goetzel. Her maiden name was written as Knopp (Kropf). Her parents were Szyi Kropf and Perly from Jarosław. She reported having 11 children born and 10 living. Their address was Ridge Street, New York.[115] Michal Holoshitzer also applied for a birth certificate abt. 1902; listing his age as 44 years, living at Ridge Street, New York. His spouse was Gussie Holoshitzer and child was Goetzel.[116]

A genealogy researcher, Phyllis Kramer z"l, sent me her Tarnafker family tree listing her Tarnafker relatives from Kańczuga who were connected with my Holoszycer relatives through marriage. Please refer to the *Holoszycer Family Tree*.

Pincus[3] Aron Tarnafker (Amalie[2], Isaac [1]Holoszycer) was born 10 August 1869 at Kańczuga to Amalie Holoszycer and Joel Tarnafker; he died November 1967 at New York.[117] He immigrated 29 June 1888 from Hamburg, Germany on the *S.S. Prague* to New York with his uncle Mechel Holoszycer and family.[118] Pincus Aron Tarnafker married Pesel Deborah Hausman 19 November 1890 at New York.[119] Pesel born 1870 changed her name to Pauline in New York. She died 28 April 1923 in the Bronx, New York.[120] She was buried at Mokom Sholom Cemetery, Ozone Park, New York. Pincus Tarnafker and his family were listed on the 1900 United States Federal Census. They lived on Columbia Street, Manhattan, New York. His occupation was cloak presser. Their children were listed as Rose, Yetta, Isidor.[121] Pincus Aron Tarnafker was among the founding directors of the First Kancziger Aid Society incorporated 1902 at New York.[122] Pincus Tarnafker and his family were found on the 1910 United States Federal Census; they lived at 175 Attorney Street in Manhattan. His occupation was merchant of a saloon business.[123] Pincus Aron Tarnafker and Pesel Hausman had seven children all born at New York: Rose; Yetta; Irving; Frances; Mollie; Samuel; Bennie.

Descendants of Amalia Holoszycer

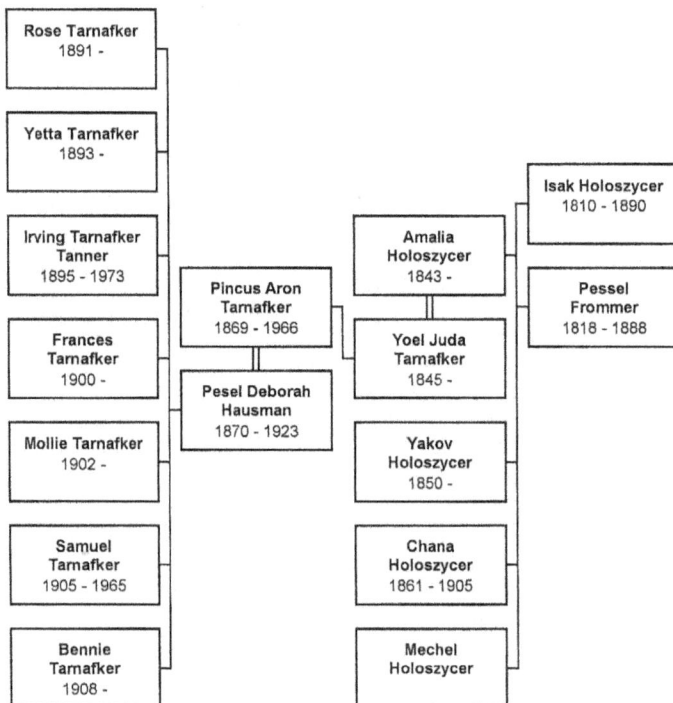

```
┌─────────────────────┐
│ Rose Tarnafker      │
│ 1891 -              │
└─────────────────────┘

┌─────────────────────┐
│ Yetta Tarnafker     │
│ 1893 -              │
└─────────────────────┘

┌─────────────────────┐                                                      ┌─────────────────────┐
│ Irving Tarnafker    │                                                      │ Isak Holoszycer     │
│ Tanner              │                                                      │ 1810 - 1890         │
│ 1895 - 1973         │          ┌─────────────────────┐                     └─────────────────────┘
└─────────────────────┘          │ Pincus Aron         │   ┌─────────────────────┐
                                  │ Tarnafker           │   │ Amalia              │
┌─────────────────────┐          │ 1869 - 1966         │   │ Holoszycer          │   ┌─────────────────────┐
│ Frances             │          └─────────────────────┘   │ 1843 -              │   │ Pessel              │
│ Tarnafker           │          ┌─────────────────────┐   └─────────────────────┘   │ Frommer             │
│ 1900 -              │          │ Pesel Deborah       │   ┌─────────────────────┐   │ 1818 - 1888         │
└─────────────────────┘          │ Hausman             │   │ Yoel Juda           │   └─────────────────────┘
                                  │ 1870 - 1923         │   │ Tarnafker           │
┌─────────────────────┐          └─────────────────────┘   │ 1845 -              │
│ Mollie Tarnafker    │                                     └─────────────────────┘
│ 1902 -              │                                     ┌─────────────────────┐
└─────────────────────┘                                     │ Yakov               │
                                                            │ Holoszycer          │
┌─────────────────────┐                                     │ 1850 -              │
│ Samuel              │                                     └─────────────────────┘
│ Tarnafker           │                                     ┌─────────────────────┐
│ 1905 - 1965         │                                     │ Chana               │
└─────────────────────┘                                     │ Holoszycer          │
                                                            │ 1861 - 1905         │
┌─────────────────────┐                                     └─────────────────────┘
│ Bennie              │                                     ┌─────────────────────┐
│ Tarnafker           │                                     │ Mechel              │
│ 1908 -              │                                     │ Holoszycer          │
└─────────────────────┘                                     └─────────────────────┘
```

Descendants of Getzel Holoszycer

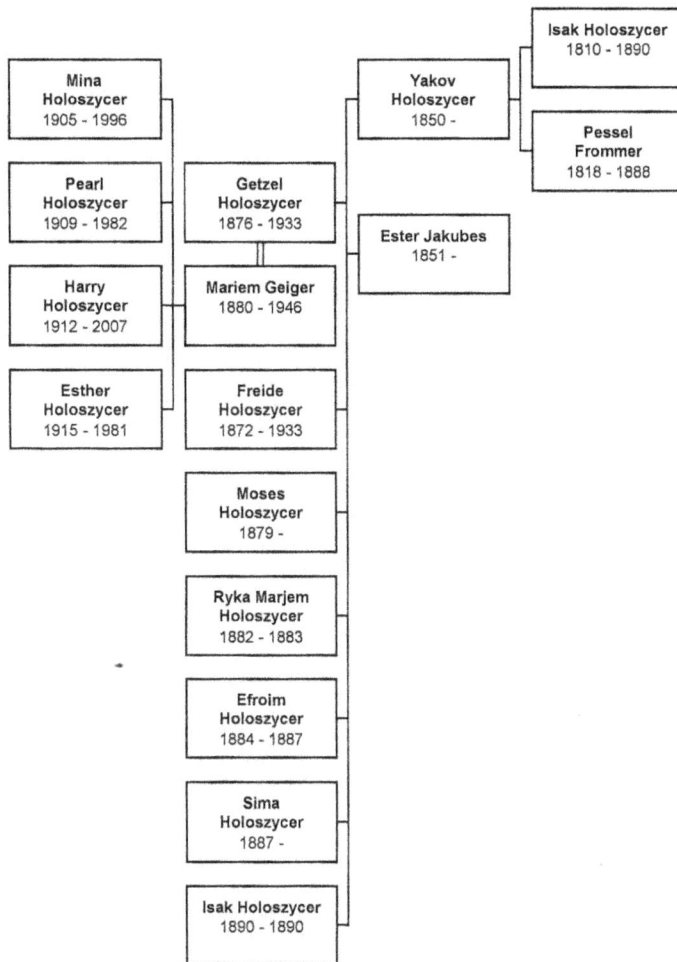

```
                                              ┌─────────────────┐
                                              │ Isak Holoszycer │
                                              │   1810 - 1890   │
                                              └─────────────────┘
┌──────────────┐            ┌──────────────┐
│     Mina     │            │    Yakov     │
│  Holoszycer  │            │  Holoszycer  │
│ 1905 - 1996  │            │    1850 -    │
└──────────────┘            └──────────────┘
                                              ┌─────────────────┐
┌──────────────┐  ┌──────────────┐            │     Pessel      │
│    Pearl     │  │    Getzel    │            │    Frommer      │
│  Holoszycer  │  │  Holoszycer  │            │   1818 - 1888   │
│ 1909 - 1982  │  │ 1876 - 1933  │            └─────────────────┘
└──────────────┘  └──────────────┘

┌──────────────┐  ┌──────────────┐            ┌──────────────┐
│    Harry     │  │ Mariem Geiger│            │ Ester Jakubes│
│  Holoszycer  │  │ 1880 - 1946  │            │    1851 -    │
│ 1912 - 2007  │  └──────────────┘            └──────────────┘
└──────────────┘

┌──────────────┐  ┌──────────────┐
│    Esther    │  │    Freide    │
│  Holoszycer  │  │  Holoszycer  │
│ 1915 - 1981  │  │ 1872 - 1933  │
└──────────────┘  └──────────────┘

                  ┌──────────────┐
                  │    Moses     │
                  │  Holoszycer  │
                  │    1879 -    │
                  └──────────────┘

                  ┌──────────────┐
                  │ Ryka Marjem  │
                  │  Holoszycer  │
                  │ 1882 - 1883  │
                  └──────────────┘

                  ┌──────────────┐
                  │    Efroim    │
                  │  Holoszycer  │
                  │ 1884 - 1887  │
                  └──────────────┘

                  ┌──────────────┐
                  │     Sima     │
                  │  Holoszycer  │
                  │    1887 -    │
                  └──────────────┘

                  ┌──────────────┐
                  │Isak Holoszycer│
                  │ 1890 - 1890  │
                  └──────────────┘
```

Descendants of Izak Holoszycer

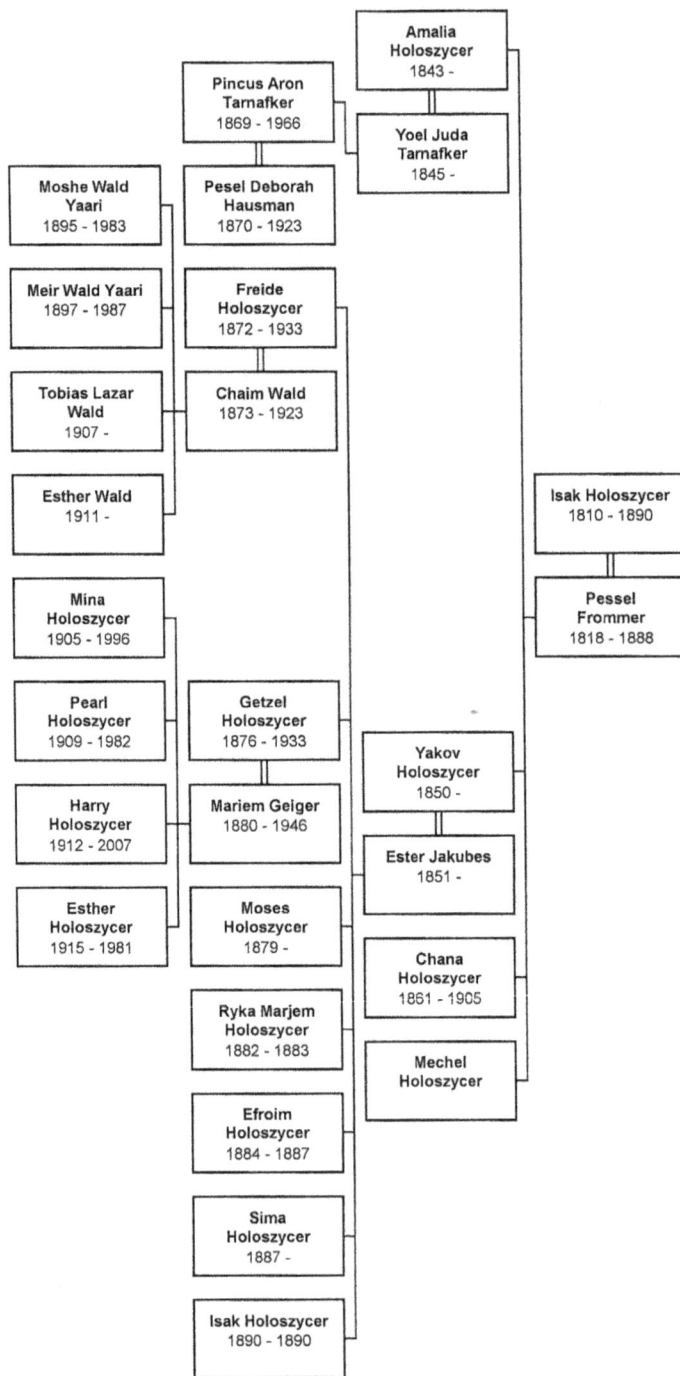

```
                                                        ┌─────────────────┐
                                                        │ Amalia          │
                                                        │ Holoszycer      │
                                                        │ 1843 -          │
                                    ┌──────────────────┐└─────────────────┘
                                    │ Pincus Aron      │
                                    │ Tarnafker        │
                                    │ 1869 - 1966      │┌─────────────────┐
                                    └──────────────────┘│ Yoel Juda       │
                                                        │ Tarnafker       │
                                                        │ 1845 -          │
                ┌─────────────────┐┌──────────────────┐└─────────────────┘
                │ Moshe Wald      ││ Pesel Deborah    │
                │ Yaari           ││ Hausman          │
                │ 1895 - 1983     ││ 1870 - 1923      │
                └─────────────────┘└──────────────────┘
                ┌─────────────────┐┌──────────────────┐
                │ Meir Wald Yaari ││ Freide           │
                │ 1897 - 1987     ││ Holoszycer       │
                └─────────────────┘│ 1872 - 1933      │
                                   └──────────────────┘
                ┌─────────────────┐┌──────────────────┐
                │ Tobias Lazar    ││ Chaim Wald       │
                │ Wald            ││ 1873 - 1923      │
                │ 1907 -          │└──────────────────┘
                └─────────────────┘                              ┌─────────────────┐
                ┌─────────────────┐                              │ Isak Holoszycer │
                │ Esther Wald     │                              │ 1810 - 1890     │
                │ 1911 -          │                              └─────────────────┘
                └─────────────────┘
                ┌─────────────────┐                              ┌─────────────────┐
                │ Mina            │                              │ Pessel          │
                │ Holoszycer      │                              │ Frommer         │
                │ 1905 - 1996     │                              │ 1818 - 1888     │
                └─────────────────┘                              └─────────────────┘
                ┌─────────────────┐┌──────────────────┐
                │ Pearl           ││ Getzel           │
                │ Holoszycer      ││ Holoszycer       │
                │ 1909 - 1982     ││ 1876 - 1933      │┌─────────────────┐
                └─────────────────┘└──────────────────┘│ Yakov           │
                                                        │ Holoszycer      │
                ┌─────────────────┐┌──────────────────┐│ 1850 -          │
                │ Harry           ││ Mariem Geiger    │└─────────────────┘
                │ Holoszycer      ││ 1880 - 1946      │
                │ 1912 - 2007     │└──────────────────┘┌─────────────────┐
                └─────────────────┘                    │ Ester Jakubes   │
                ┌─────────────────┐┌──────────────────┐│ 1851 -          │
                │ Esther          ││ Moses            │└─────────────────┘
                │ Holoszycer      ││ Holoszycer       │
                │ 1915 - 1981     ││ 1879 -           │┌─────────────────┐
                └─────────────────┘└──────────────────┘│ Chana           │
                                   ┌──────────────────┐│ Holoszycer      │
                                   │ Ryka Marjem      ││ 1861 - 1905     │
                                   │ Holoszycer       │└─────────────────┘
                                   │ 1882 - 1883      │
                                   └──────────────────┘┌─────────────────┐
                                   ┌──────────────────┐│ Mechel          │
                                   │ Efroim           ││ Holoszycer      │
                                   │ Holoszycer       │└─────────────────┘
                                   │ 1884 - 1887      │
                                   └──────────────────┘
                                   ┌──────────────────┐
                                   │ Sima             │
                                   │ Holoszycer       │
                                   │ 1887 -           │
                                   └──────────────────┘
                                   ┌──────────────────┐
                                   │ Isak Holoszycer  │
                                   │ 1890 - 1890      │
                                   └──────────────────┘
```

Endnotes

1   Przemysl Archives. Fond 1924. Przemysl Births 1789–1827, 1853–1900. Akta 59. Birth of Mariem Geiger.

2   Ancestry.com. National Archives and Records Administration. Selected U.S. Naturalization Records-Original Documents, 1790–1974 for Mania Holly. NARA Series: M1879; Roll 704; Petition No 179371-Petition No 179750.

3   Przemysl Archives. Fond 1731. Kanczuga PSA Births 1851–91, Marriages 1859-76, Banns 1896-1902, Deaths 1852–76. Akta 6. 1902. Marriage Bann for Getzel Holoszycer and Marjem Geiger.

4   Yizkor Book of Rzeszow. Dr. Moshe Yaari Wald: Chapter My Father Chaim Wald. Pp. 243–252.

5   Wikipedia.org. Elimelech Weisblum of Lizhensk. He was born 1717 in Tykocin, Poland and died 11 March 1787 in Lezajsk, Poland. Rabbi Elimelech authored the classic work Noam Elimelech that developed the Hasidic theory of the Tzaddik and shaped the role of mystical leadership. He was one of the great founding Rebbes of the Hasidic movement and was known after his hometown Lezajsk near Rzeszow in Poland.

6   Shmuel Spector, editor. *The Encyclopedia of Jewish Life Before and During the Holocaust.* (New York: New York University Press, 2001). Volume II, p. 594.

7   kanczuga.org/research/siedleczka-cemetery.

8   kanczuga.org/first-kancziger-aid-society-1902/.

9   kanczuga.org/scanned-records-kanczuga-przemysl-archives/.

10   Przemysl Archive. Fond 1731. Kanczuga. Death Izak Holoszycer 2 December 1890. Akta 35.

11   Przemysl Archive. Fond 1731. Kanczuga Marriages 1859–76. Marriage 1870. Izak Holoszycer and Pessel Frommer. Akta 43.

12   Przemysl Archive. Fond 1731. Kanczuga Deaths 1904–06. Death Chana Holoszycer 4 November 1905.

13   Przemysl Archive. Fond 1731. Kanczuga Births 1851–91. Akta 45. Birth 1872. Freide Holoszycer.

14   Przemysl Archive. Fond 1731. Kanczuga Births 1851–91. Akta 11. Birth 1851. Ester Jacobes.

15   Rzeszow Archive, Poland. Fond 533. Marriages 1896–1913. Akta 69 Marriage 1896 Chaim Wald and Friede Holoszycer.

16   Dr. Moshe Yaari Wald. My Father ChaimWald. Yizkor Book for Rzeszow, Poland. Pp. 243–252. (www.jewishgen.org/Yizkor/Rzeszow).

17   Rzeszow Archive, Lwow, Poland. Fond 533. Rzeszow Marriages 1896–1914. Akta 69. 1896 Marriage: Chaim Wald and Friede Holoszycer. (www.jri-poland.org).

18   Rzeszow Archive, Lwow, Poland. Fond 533. Rzeszow Deaths 1842–1875. Akta 7. Death: Josef Wald 1870, age 32. (www.jri-poland.org).

19   Rzeszow Archive, Poland. Fond 533. Rzeszow Deaths 1842–1939. Akta 85. Death: Teme Klinger Wald 1903. Age 58. Her parents were Benzion Klinger and Ruchel Futersak. (www.jri-poland.org).

20   www.jewishgen.org/Yizkor/rzeszow. My Father Chaim Wald by Moshe Yaari Wald. P. 252.

21   Rzeszow Archive, Poland. Fond 1. Rzeszow 1910 Census. Chaim Wald, Freide, Mojzesz, Majer, Tobiasz. Krola Kazimierza Street, apt. 8.

22   Rzeszow Archive. Fond 1. Rzeszow 1910 Census. Chaim Wald family; wife Friede, sons Mojzesz, Majer, Tobiasz.

23   Rzeszow Archive. Fond 533. Rzeszow Births 1866–1919. Akta 10. Birth: 23 February 1895 at Kanczuga. Moses Wald.

24   Moshe Yaari Wald. During the Interregnum. Pp. 132–140. (www.jewishgen.org/Yizkor/rzeszow.)

25   www.jewishgen.org/Yizkor/rzeszow. Chapters written by Moshe Yaari Wald translated from Hebrew by Jerrold Landau.

26   www.Geni.org. Family History for Moshe Wald Yaari.

27   Rzeszow Archive. Fond 1. Rzeszow 1910 Census. Birth 1897: Majer Wald, born at Kanczuga. (www.jri-poland.org).

28   Knesset Member Meir Yaari. Biography. www.knesset.gov.il.

29   www.knesset.gov.il/Mapam; Wikipedia.org. The Mapam party was dissolved in 1997. The successor to Mapam was a new party, Meretz, formed in 1992, through the alliance of three left-wing political parties: Ratz, Mapam and Shinui. The Meretz party holds four seats in the Knesset. The political agenda of Meretz is social democratic, secular, civil libertarian, anti-occupation, advocating a two-state solution and freezing construction of Israeli settlements in the West Bank.

30   www.wikipedia.org. Biography of Meir Yaari.

31   www.jewishgen.org/Yizkor/rzeszow. Chapters written by Meir Yaari translated from Hebrew by Jerrold Landau.

32   Ibid., pp. 249–250.

33   Rzeszow Archive. Fond 1. Rzeszow 1910 Census. Birth Year: 1907. Tobiasz Wald. (www.jri-poland. org). Also see
Rzeszow Archive. Fond 533. Rzeszow Births 1866–1919. Birth: 1907. Tobias Lazar Wald. Akta 53. (www. jri-poland.org).

34   Przemysl Archive. Sanok Jewish Marriages 1916–1939. Marriage: 1932. Tobias Lazar Wald and Faiga Mindel Amster. (www.jri-poland.org).

35   Central Database of Shoah Victims Names. Yakov and Chaya Sara Amster. (www.yadvashem.org).

36   Rzeszow Archive. Fond 533. Rzeszow Births 1866–1919. Akta 154. Birth 1911 at Rzeszow: Ester Wald. (www.jri-poland.org).

37   IGRA (Israel Genealogy Research Association). Esther Wald, nurse certification.

38   Ancestry.com. New York, Passenger and Crew Lists Including Castle Garden and Ellis Island), 1820–1957. Estera Wald. *S.S. El Nil.* Departed Port Said, Egypt 25 March 1943, arrived New York 10 June 1943.

39   Ancestry.com. New York Passenger and Crew Lists 1820-1957. Estera Wald age 30. Ship El Nil, arrived New York 11 June 1943

40   Ancestry.com. New York Passenger and Crew Lists Arriving at New York, 1820–1957. Estera Wald, departed from Haifa, Palestine on the Marine Carp, arrived at New York 8 Aug 1947.

41   Przemysl Archive, Poland. Fond 1731. Kanczuga Births 1851–91. Akta 49. Birth: 21 December 1876. Getzel Holoszycer. Parents Jacob Holoszycer and Ester. Scan from archive.

42   New York, Municipal Archives. Death Certificate. Brooklyn, New York. Getzel Holly. Date of birth: 15 December 1876. Date of Death: 27 October 1933. Certificate 21104.

43   Przemysl Archive, Poland. Fond 1731. Kanczuga Births 1851–91. Birth 17 June 1851. Akta 11. Birth: Ester Jacobes. (www.jri-poland).

44   Ancestry.com. Selected U.S. Naturalization Records-Original Documents 1790–1974, Mania Holly. NARA Series: M1879, Roll 704. Petitions 179371-179750. Mania stated that she emigrated to the U.S. from Rotterdam, Holland to New York under the name of Manja Rottmann, on 29 Oct 1907 on the ship *Noordam.*

45   Ancestry.com. New York, Passenger Lists, 1820–1957. Ship: *S.S. Noordam*, sailing from Rotterdam on 19 October 1907 and arriving in New York on 29 October 1907.

46   Ancestry.com. New York Passenger Lists 1820–1957 for Manja Rottman.

47   Ancestry.com. Federal Census 1910. New York, Borough of Manhattan, Ward 13, Enumeration District 775. Address: 52 Lewis Street.

48   Ancestry.com. Federal Census 1920. New York, Borough of Manhattan, Ward 6, Enumeration District 466. Address: 382 Third Street.

49   Ancestry.com. New York State Census 1925. Assembly District 6, Election District 4, Address: 470 East Houston Street.

50   Ancestry.com. Federal Census 1930. New York, Borough of Brooklyn (Coney Island). Address: 2927 W. 29th Street.

51   Ancestry.com. U.S. Naturalization Records Indexes 1794–1995 for Mania Holly. Eastern District Court of New York. Petition 179569. Address: 2927 West 29th St., Brooklyn, N.Y.

52   New York, Municipal Archives. Death Certificate. Manhattan. Certificate 25157. Marion aka Mania Holly. Widow. Address: 10 Monroe Street, New York City. Death: 29 November 1946.

53   Przemysl Archive, Poland. Fond 1731. Kanczuga Births 1851–91, 1904–1910. Birth 1905, akta 6. Symche Tobiasz born to Getzel Holoszycer and Marjem Geiger. (www.jri-poland.org).

54   Alexander Beider. *A Dictionary of Ashkenazic Given Names*. Bergenfield, New Jersey: Avotaynu, 2001. pp. 572–573.

55   Ibid., p. 434.

56   Schmeul Gorr. *Jewish Personal Names*. Bergenfield, New Jersey, Avotaynu, 1992. pp. 75–75. Mina derives from the Hebrew word meaning peaceful or restful.

57   Ancestry.com. Federal Census 1910, Manhattan, Enumeration District 775, Ward 13, 52 Lewis St.

58   Ancestry.com. Selected U.S. Naturalization Records- Original Documents, 1790–1974 for Mina Holly. NARA Series: M1879, Roll 608, Petition 143254. Address: 2927 West 29th Street, Brooklyn, NY.

59   Ancestry.com. U.S. Naturalization Records Indexes, 1794–1995 for Mina Holly. NARA: Index to Naturalization Petitions of the United States District Court for the Eastern District of New York, 1865-1957; Microfilm M1164, Roll 71.

60   Ancestry.com. New York Passenger Lists 1820–1957. Thomas Keenan, store-keeper; ship Santa Paula arriving 2 May 1940 from St.Georges, Bermuda; Thomas Keenan, A.B.; ship Paul Luckenbach arriving 28 Oct 1937 from Los Angeles; Thomas Keenan, A.B.S.; ship Berlanga arriving 4 Nov 1948 from Armuelles, Panama; Thomas M. Keenan, Ch. Officer; ship Thomas Say arriving 6 Feb 1945 from Tunis; Thomas M. Keenan, Sr. Ist Ast. Engineer; ship Brazil arriving 8 Jul 1946 from Le Havre; Thomas M. Keenan, ship Exarch arriving 16 Jan 1936 from Cadiz.

61   FamilySearch.org. Ohio, County Naturalization Records, 1800–1977. Cuyahoga Naturalization Cards 1915-1970. Mina Holly Keenan. .

62   Ancestry.com. U.S. Social Security Death Index, 1935–2014. Thomas Martin Keenan: 21 March 1995, Palm Beach, Florida.

63   Ancestry.com. U.S. Social Security Death Index, 1935–2014. Mina Keenan: March, 1996. New York.

64   Ancestry.com. U.S. Social Security Death Index, 1935–2014. Pearl Holly Bronz. Born 6 May 1909, New York. Died June 1982, Santa Fe, New Mexico.

65   Newspapers.com. Obituary Pearl Holly Bronz, died 2 June 1982. Published 6 June 1982, p.5.

66   Ancestry.com. U.S. School Yearbooks, 1880–2012. Pearl Holly. *The Medical Violet*; Year: 1938. New York University College of Medicine, New York, New York. U.S. School Yearbooks, 1900–1990).

67   Ancestry.com. Virginia Marriage Records 1936-2014. Marriage: Pearl Holly and George Bronz. 15 April 1938, Alexandria, Virginia.

68   George Washington University. Bronz Memorial Fund for Campus Journalism, established 1982 by Pearl b. Holly, MD in memory of her son Stephen Holly Bronz.

69   FamilySearch.org. New York, New York City Municipal Deaths 1795–1949. Death: Max Bronz, 18 June 1911.

70   FamilySearch.org. New York County Naturalization Records, 1791–1980. Petitions for Naturalization. V. 521. No. 123601-123850. Petition for Naturalization: Louis Bronz.

71   Shmuel Spector, editor. *The Encyclopedia of Jewish Life Before and During the Holocaust V. II*. New York: New York University Press, 2001. Pp.604–607.

72   FamilySearch.org. New York, New York City Marriage Records, 1829-1940. Marriage: 30 Dec 1906: Louis Bronz and Sarah Paley.

73   Ancestry.com. Hamburg Passenger Lists 1850–1934 for Sore Paley. Staatsarchiv Hamburg. V.373-71, VIII A I Band 119.

74   Ancestry.com. Record of Aliens Held for Special Inquiry. Arrival of ship Graf Waldersee, 8 June 1901. Freide Paley, dressmaker and 2 daughters.

75   Kasriel Eilender, A Brief History of the Jews in Suwalki. (kehilalinks.jewishgen.org/suwalki/History. htm)

76   Ancestry.com. 1910 US Federal Census: Manhattan Ward 19, New York, New York. Louis Bronz.

77   Ancestry.com. 1920 US Federal Census: Manhattan, New York Assembly District 15, enumeration district 1095. Louis Bronz.

78   FamilySearch.org. 1940 US Federal Census, Essex County, Newark, New Jersey. Ward 9, Address 268 Hawthorne Avenue. Louis Bronz.

79   Ancestry.com. New York, New York Death Index 1949–1965. Death: Louis Bronz 12 June 1949. Cert. 5694.

80   Ancestry.com. New York, New York Death Index 1949–1965. Death: Sarah Bronz, 15 April 1952. Cert. 3492.

81   Ancestry.com. U.S. School Yearbooks, 1880–2012. George Bronz. *The Microcosm*. Year: 1929. U.S., School Yearbooks, 1900–1990).

82   I.J.Carmin Karpman, editor. George Bronx. *Who's Who in World Jewry. A Biographical Dictionary of Outstanding Jews*. New York: Pitman Publishing Corp., 1972. Ancestry.com. Biography and Genealogy Master Index).

83   Ancestry.com. U.S. WWII Draft Cards Young Men 1940-1947. George Bronz.

84   en.wikipedia.org/wiki/Harold_L._Ickes. See *Jewish Refugees in Alaska*. Mr. Ickes proposed in 1938 that Jewish refugees could enter Alaska as Alaska was not yet a state and could bypass immigration quotas.

85   Ancestry.com. 1940 Federal Census.

86   Raphael Medoff. A Thanksgiving Plan to save Europe's Jews. *The Jewish Standard*. 16 Nov 2007.

87   U.S., Register of Civil, Military, and Naval Service, 1863–1959. George Bronz, years 1945, 1947, 1949.

88   Ancestry.com. .

89   George Bronz. The Tariff Commission as a Regulatory Agency. *Columbia Law Review*, v.61, no.3 (March, 1961), pp.463–489.

90   George Bronz. The International Trade Organization Charter. *Harvard Law Review*, v.62, no.7 (May, 1949), pp.1089–1125.

91   *Ciba-Geigy Corporation v. United States*, 79 Cust. Ct. 53 (1977).

92   *Western Dairy Products Inc. v. United States*, C.D. 4506; Court No. 72-12-02554 (1974).

93   Ancestry.com. U.S, Social Security Death Index 1935–2014. George Bronz. Birth: 7 July 1910. Death: April 1976, Washington, D.C.

94   See Affidavit of Support written by George Bronz for Frieda Prisand nee Turnheim.

95   db.yadvashem.org/names/nameDetails.html?itemId=4611389&language=en

96   See Affidavit of Support written by George Bronz for Markus Geiger and his wife Ruchla and their children Clara and Susi.

97   See letter to the German Jewish Aid Committee in London written by George Bronz for Josef and Ester Geiger.

98   See letter written by Charles Geiger 13 July 1939 to Pearl and George Bronz concerning Josef and Ester Geiger.

99   Ancestry.com New York Passenger Lists 1820–1957. Ship: Queen Mary. Departed Southampton, U.K. 31 July 1947, arrived in New York 5 August 1947. U.S. Citizen List: Pearl Bronz born in New York; Stephen born in Washington, D.C. and his sister Elizabeth also born in Washington, D.C. Their address was 2704 36th Place N.W., Washington, D.C.

100   Ancestry.com. U.S. Social Security Death Index, 1935–2014. Stephen Bronz. Born 5 Oct 1941, died Jan 1971.

101   Ancestry.com. U.S. Social Security Death Index, 1935–2014. Born: 18 May, 1912; Died 14 April 2007.

102   Ancestry.com. U.S. Public Records Index, Volume 2. Harry Holly residing 7208 Westwood Drive, Tamarac, Fl.

103   Ancestry.com. U.S., Social Security Death Index, 1935–2014. Rose Holly born 8 Jan 1911 and died July 1974.

104 Ancestry.com. Historical Newspapers, Birth, Marriage and Death Announcements, 1851–2003. The *New York Times,* 26 July 1974. Rose Holly obituary.

105 Ancestry.com. 1930 Federal Census. Castle Shannon, Allegheny County, Pennsylvania. Enumeration district 2-5-3-9. Address: 975 Poplar Avenue. Rose Nassau.

106 FindAGrave.com. Find A Grave Index, 1600s–Current. Harry Holly and Rose Holly. South Florida National Cemetery.

107 National Archives at St. Louis. St. Louis, Missouri. WWII Single Name Final Pay Vouchers. Harry Holly. Request number 2-22521479784.

108 Ancestry. com. U.S. Social Security Death Index, 1935–2014. Esther Holly, born 22 Mar 1915, died Nov 1981.

109 Ancestry.com. Historical Newspapers, Birth, Marriage and Death Announcements, 1851–2003. The New York Times, 12 November 1981. Esther Holly.

110 Ancestry.com. New York, New York, Marriage License Indexes, 1907–2018. Esther Holly and Milton Siegel. Marriage License Date: 1954, Manhattan, New York. License Number 6127.

111 Wikipedia.org. Ethical Movement or the Ethical Culture Movement, founded by Felix Adler. Ethical culture is based on the idea that honoring and living in accordance with ethical principles is central to living meaningful and fulfilling lives.

112 Ancestry.com. New York Passenger Lists 1820–1957. Moses Holoschitzer. S.S. Kronprinz Wilhelm arriving New York 24 May 1905.

113 Ancestry.com. Hamburg Passenger Lists 1850–1934. 29 June 1888. Ship Prague. Hamburg to Amerika via Glasgow. Mechel Holoschitz, Golde, Lazar, Esther, Fischel.

114 Ancestry.com. New York, State and Federal Naturalization Records 1794–1943. Circuit Court of the United States. Southern District of New York. Michael Holschitz. Declaration Date: 12 October 1903.

115 Ancestry.com. New York, New York, Index to Birth Certificates, 1866–1909. Gussie Holoshitzer. Certificate 37232.

116 Ancestry.com. New York, New York, Index to Birth Certificates, 1866–1909. Michal Holoshitzer. Certificate 37232.

117 Ancestry.com. U.S. Social Security Death Index 1935–2014. Pincus Tarnafker. Death: November 1967, last residence Brooklyn, New York.

118 Ancestry.com. Hamburg Passenger Lists 1850–1934 (1 May 1888-30 June 1888). S.S. Prague. Destination New York via Glasgow. Pincus Aron Tarnafker age 18 travelling with Mechel Holoszycer, wife Golde, three children Lazar, Esther, Fischel.

119 Ancestry.com. New York, New York. Extracted Marriage Index 1866–1937. Marriage 19 November 1890 at New York. Pinkas Tarnowker and Pesel Hausman.

120 Ancestry.com. New York, New York, Extracted Death Index 1862–1948. Death 28 April 1923 Pauline Tarnafker. Certificate 3338.

121 Ancestry.com. 1900 United States Federal Census. New York. Enumeration District 0288.

122 www.kanczuga.org. See First Kancziger Aid Society on website.

123 Ancestry.com. 1910 United States Federal Census. New York. Manhattan, Ward 11. Enumeration District 0243.

Chapter Ten

Minnie Geiger and Oscar Weiss

Sections of this chapter include short biographical profiles based on my personal recollections of those individuals who were in my immediate family and who were very dear to me. At the end of this chapter there will be a brief discussion of mtDNA (mitochondrial DNA) research to provide perspective for my deeper ancestral roots based on my maternal lineage.

Beginnings

My maternal grandmother Mindla Geiger was the last of seven children born to Aron Geiger and Hinde Turnheim. Her given name Mindla derives from the He-

Birth record Mindla Turnheim

brew word *menuhah*, meaning peaceful or restful. It is also a feminine form of the masculine name *Menahem* meaning comforter.[1] Mindla was known to us as Minnie. Perhaps she was named for her deceased paternal grandmother Chaje Mindel Geiger née Unger. Grandma Minnie was born 3 April 1887 at Przemyśl, Podkarpackie, Poland at 461 Dobromilska Street; the street name was later changed to Slowackiego Street.[2] I found a website that listed the Przemyśl homeowners for 1899.[3] Meilech Gans, the father-in-law of Grandma's uncle Benjamin Turnheim, was a property owner on Dobromilska and Targowica streets at Przemyśl. My great-grandmother Hinde Geiger, while pregnant with Grandma probably lived with her Turnheim family and gave birth in a house owned by Mr. Gans.

Grandma's family members were among the numerous Hasidic Jews in Galicia. Although there were many Hasidic groups, each group followed a *rebbe* with piety and unswerving allegiance. As a child, Grandma moved with her family from Przemyśl to the smaller town of Błażowa, where the Błażowa (known by

Yiddish speakers as Bluzov) Grand Rabbi Tzvi Elimelech Spira (1841–1924) held court and inspired his devoted followers including my Geiger ancestors.[4] (*See Chapter One: Background*)

Prior to her immigration to the United States in 1904, Grandma was living at Błażowa with her parents Aron Geiger and Hinde Turnheim and her sister Freude Geiger. Grandma's sister Miriem was married 1902 to Getzel Holoszycer from Kańczuga, Podkarpackie, Poland. Minnie's brother Rabbi Abraham Yitzak Geiger was married 1894 to Sprynca Stark also from Kańczuga. Minnie's two older siblings Chaskel Geiger and Israel Geiger immigrated to the United States more than a decade before her immigration.

Top: Minnie Geiger, L: Aron Geiger R: Freude Geiger, Bottom: Salomea Neumark, 1904

Grandma Minnie was an independent woman who was also kind, generous, compassionate, industrious, and loving yet who could also be stern when needed and she did not tolerate nonsense or back talk. I discovered certain facts about her from my genealogical research, information that my mother Sylvia and my aunts Marion and Martha did not know. For example, they never knew where their mother Minnie was born as she always vaguely answered "Austria." They probably never heard that she was born in the city of Przemyśl, Podkarpackie, Poland. The Austria Grandma referred to was known as the Austro-Hungarian Empire that ruled over the Galician territory where she was born and where her family lived. They never saw Grandma's immigration record and so never knew that prior to her immigration to the United States, Grandma was living with her parents at Błażowa, a shtetl in what was called Galicia. Grandma was born 1887 and she was four years older than her birthdate 1891 inscribed on her matsevah.

On her birth record from Przemyśl, Grandma's parents Hinde Turnheim and Aron Geiger were listed as not being legally married as was the case with most Hasidic Jewish birth records at that time since couples were religiously married under the *chupah* and did not register their marriage with civil authorities for several reasons, including avoidance of the steep marriage tax for Jews and the civil requirement that marriages must be registered with the Catholic parish. Hasidic Jews resisted civil registration of marriages as they felt it was a strictly religious and not a state matter. Children born from religious marriages not registered by the state were considered illegitimate by the government and were subject to such restrictions as being unable to inherit property from the father and being assigned to their mother's surname if the father did not appear in person with two witnesses to attest that he was the father of the child. A child considered illegitimate had difficulty obtaining travel documents, business licenses, or owning land.[5] On Grandma's birth record, her mother Hinde Turnheim was listed as the daughter of Hersch and Mariem Turnheim. Grandma was given her mother's surname Turnheim, even though her father was Aron Geiger. By the late 19th and early 20th centuries many couples rectified the question of marriage legitimacy through compliance with civil registration even though they were well past childbearing years. My great-grandparents complied with this regulation so that their children could obtain the necessary travel documents and inherit property.

Immigration

Why did Grandma immigrate to the United States? It is quite possible that she wanted to forge her own destiny, away from the shtetl and the predictable life she would lead if she remained in Galicia. Prior to Grandma's immigration her brother Charles was instrumental in persuading their parents to grant permission for Grandma to immigrate and join him at New York City. He paid for Grandma's ticket and arranged to have her live with his family. Perhaps Charles felt that Minnie would have better marriage prospects in the United States.

Grandma Mindla aka Mina Geiger immigrated to the United States as a second class passenger on a steam ship named *S.S.Moltke* in the Hamburg America Line that departed from Cuxhaven, Germany on 22 October 1904.[6] The Hamburg America line built a large ocean liner terminal at Cuxhaven in 1900 where baggage of first and second class passengers passed through customs at Cuxhaven. Cuxhaven was connected to Hamburg by a special train. This was a major point of departure for German and European emigrants until 1969.[7] The *S.S. Moltke* arrived at New York 1 November 1904.[8] The *S.S. Moltke* was built 1901 at Hamburg by shipbuilders Blohm and Voss. The maiden voyage was made 1902 from Hamburg with stops at Boulogne and Southampton to New York.[9]

The ship manifest contained information that Minnie was going to her brother Charles Geiger at 305–307 Grand Street, Manhattan. Her last residence was Błażowa pov. Rzeszów (Rzesovo on the manifest), that indicated Błażowa was within the administrative district of Rzeszów. Grandma gave her age as 17 years that corresponded with the date on her birth record. Minnie was to be met at Ellis Island by her brother Charles Geiger. In those days, ships would release only unescorted ladies to the care of a relative from the United States especially if they

S.S. Moltke

were young single ladies.

Aunt Martha recalled Grandma's story about her journey as an immigrant to the United States. Grandma Minnie became seasick from the voyage and was unsteady on her feet when she landed at Ellis Island. This was the first time she was away from her family and the first time she was on a ship. When she arrived at Ellis Island, the doctor thought she was crippled because she was so unsteady and so he wrote in chalk a huge "C" on the back of her coat for "crippled", indicating that she would have to be returned to Europe with other sick immigrants. Another female passenger spoke in Yiddish to Grandma and asked her if she was sick. Grandma replied that she was not sick, only unsteady from the sea voyage. The woman asked Grandma if she had someone meeting her and Grandma answered that her brother would meet her. The Yiddish speaking woman then told Grandma to take off her coat and put it back on inside out, so no one would see the "C" and that is how Grandma got through Ellis Island to be greeted by her brother Charles Geiger and begin her new life.

M. Geiger, line 25, ship manifest

Starting A New Life in New York

Grandma initially lived with her brother Charles Geiger and his family.[10] The New York State 1905 census for Manhattan included Charles Geiger, his wife Esther, their three children Marion, Minnie (later known as Minna), Milton, Charles' sister-in-law Minnie Price, Charles' sister Mina (Grandma Minnie) Geiger, and a servant Rose Kessler. The address was 327 E. 68th Street in Manhattan. Tension eventually developed between Grandma and Esther. My cousin Carol Lebeaux z"l, granddaughter of Charles and Esther Geiger, recalled hearing how Esther grew jealous and resentful of Charles's attention to Grandma.

To keep the peace between Charles and Esther, by the time of the 1910 Federal Census Grandma had a new address and lived with her married sister Miriam aka Manya and Getzel Holdschitz (Holoszycer) at 52 Lewis Street in Manhattan, Ward 13, Enumeration District 775.[11] I estimate this move occurred ca. 1908. Grandma and Charles maintained their close sibling relationship until the day Charles died on 24 April 1955. When Charles became ill and bed-ridden, Grandma often went to his apartment to help take care of him until his death. Charles Geiger granted his sister Minnie Weiss née Geiger in January 1948, one half interest and title in the cemetery plot that he purchased from the *landsmanshaften* First Galician Society in 1923.[12] He was buried 1955 in the Weiss-Geiger family plot at Mt. Neboh Cemetery, Glendale, New York. (See the chapter *Chaskel Geiger* and *Esther Mamlock*).

The 1910 Census contained the following information. Grandma's sister Miriam and husband Getzel immigrated to the United States in 1907. Getzel, age 34, was listed as a self-employed egg merchant, and lived with his wife Miriam, age 32, their daughter Minnie age 5, and their 11-month-old baby daughter Pauline. Grandma, age 21, was listed as a sister-in-law; she worked as a dressmaker for a clothing shop. There was also a boarder, Isaac Frankel, age 17, who worked as a cut-

Minnie Geiger ca.1908

ter in a cloak shop. They lived in an apartment at 52 Lewis Street, in a five-story tenement building located at the Lower East Side of Manhattan.[13] (See the chapter *Mariem Geiger and Getzel Holoszycer*)

Marriage

There are two different stories told at different times by Aunt Martha of how Grandma met Grandpa. According to one family story, Grandma worked as a seamstress in a dress shop and a coworker mentioned that she had a good-looking cousin who was interested in getting married. Minnie was interested and arranged to meet him at her brother Charles's apartment. Her future husband Oscar Weiss was impressed by the wealthy surroundings and so thought that Minnie was also well-to-do. Minnie explained that she was a seamstress and worked for a living. They were immediately drawn to one another and fell in love. In another family story, Charles Geiger's wife Esther went to a *shadchen* (matchmaker) to find Grandma a suitable husband.

I found the marriage certificate dated 17 October 1911 for my grandparents Minnie Geiger and Oscar Weiss at the New York City Municipal Archives.[14] Their marriage certificate contained much information such as the names of their parents: Aron Geiger and Hinde Turnheim; Fischel Weiss and Hannie Zuckerberg. Prior to their marriage according to the 1910 Federal Census, Manhattan, New York, Minnie lived with her sister Miriam and brother-in-law Getzel Holoszycer at 52 Lewis Street, Manhattan. Oscar lived with his mother and brother at 18 East 112 Street, Manhattan. Oscar was 30 years of age and was an umbrella manufacturer. Minnie was 22 years of age. If we use her actual birth date of 1887, Grandma would have been 24 years. Oscar's actual age was 35; he was 11 years older than Grandma. A large formal Jewish wedding reception was held at the Lexington Hotel at 109 East 116th Street, Manhattan, probably paid for by Grandma's prosperous brother Charles Geiger.[15] Cousin Arthur provided

Detail of photo p. 265.

me with a photograph of their wedding reception however except for Grandma Minnie and Grandpa Oscar, many guests remain unidentified.

Daily Life in Manhattan and Brooklyn

After their marriage, Grandma began working as a business partner with Grandpa at their umbrella manufacturing business, taking time off only to have her children. Grandma delivered three daughters: Marion born 28 November 1912, my mother Sylvia born 4 June 1914 and Martha born 28 July 1918. Grandma hired a *greener* (newcomer to America) as a nanny to help care for their three children while she went back to work at the factory. The *greener* was a woman who recently arrived from Ellis Island and was often employed as a housekeeper/nanny.

Grandma went to work for the Weiss Umbrella Company first as a seamstress and later as the account and business manager, while Grandpa was the salesman, finding new customers and obtaining orders for the umbrellas. Aunt Martha recalled they were first living at 136 Essex Street in the Lower East Side where they had a store for making and selling the umbrellas and where the family lived in one room behind the store. She told me the family bathed in a large laundry tub and everyone slept near the kitchen for the warmth of the stove. Their evening meal was warmed on a steamer used during the day for pressing umbrella fabric.

Engagement, Oscar and Minnie

1911 Weiss Wedding

1911 Wedding Backrow

The 136 Essex Street location was confirmed on the 1920 Federal census. This census proved difficult to find since Grandpa's name was erroneously transcribed as Aaron Weiss instead of Oscar Weiss.[16] Grandma called herself Yetta instead of Minnie. Grandpa gave his occupation as umbrella manufacturer. The names and ages of their children were: Marion age 7, Sylvia age 5, Martha age 1 year 6 months. They had a live-in servant named Tessie Babenska from Poland. Grandma was working full-time with Grandpa in their umbrella business and Tessie was their housekeeper and children's nanny.

By 1925 Oscar and Minnie with their children Marion, Sylvia, Martha moved to 134 S. 9th Street, Kings County.[17] This address is in Williamsburg, Brooklyn. Grandma did not like to live on the ground floor, so they moved to 142 S. 9th Street, Brooklyn. While they lived in Williamsburg, Aunt Martha recalled truck drivers who delivered blocks of ice for filling ice boxes as this was before refrigerators were in use. Her job was to empty the pail of melting ice under the ice box. She also remembered how delicious fresh milk, cream and rolls tasted, being delivered daily. Laundry was also picked up by a service; cleaned, sorted, and de-

Oscar and Minnie Weiss, Marriage Certificate

livered. Various stores such as the grocery, fish market, kosher poultry and meat markets would also deliver food. She recalled how Grandpa had his shirts laundered at a Chinese laundry because he was the company salesman and needed to be well-groomed and presentable when meeting customers. Chinese laundry owners generously handed out lychee nuts to the children as treats.

By 1930, the family moved to 2000 84th Street, Bensonhurst, Brooklyn.[18] Oscar and Minnie continued to commute daily to Manhattan by public transportation. Grandma Minnie gave her age as 38 and Grandpa gave his age as 49. Their daughters were listed on the census as Marion age 17, Sylvia age 16, Martha age 11 and all were in school. Both Grandma and Grandpa both worked at their umbrella manufacturing business.

Changes in the family were apparent by the 1940 Federal Census. Their new address was 71 Ocean Parkway, Brooklyn and the family consisted of Oscar age 59, Minnie age 49 and their daughter Sylvia age 26, single; everyone worked at the umbrella factory.[19] Their daughters Marion and Martha were married and no longer lived with Grandpa and Grandma. My grandparents occasionally took vacations at Lakewood, New Jersey, and Florida. For entertainment, they also attended the opera and the Yiddish theatre.

Oscar Weiss Umbrella Factory

Oscar Weiss had an older brother Morys Weiss, who was the first in the Weiss family to establish an umbrella manufacturing business at 105 Rivington Street, Manhattan. This information was found on Morys' Naturalization Petition 7 May 1902.[20] Morys probably learned about umbrella manufacturing either in Europe or after he arrived at New York July 1889. Oscar learned the umbrella manufacturing business from his older brother Morys. Oscar eventually opened his own umbrella factory with his younger brother Louis. Oscar Weiss was listed as an umbrella manufacturer with his brother Louis Weiss on a New York City 1912 Directory. The address was 103 Orchard Street located in the Lower East Side of New York. The Trow Directory for New York, 1913 listed

Oscar and Minnie, Brooklyn

both Oscar Weiss Umbrellas and Luis (Louis) Weiss Umbrellas at 84 Ludlow Street, also in the Lower East Side.[21]

Grandma Minnie initially worked as a seamstress at their umbrella factory. She worked a sewing machine and Grandpa Oscar cut the fabric on a cutting table using a pattern to the shape of the umbrella. He used an appliance called a steamer with a funnel that let out steam as the umbrella material was manually pressed. Grandpa fitted umbrella ribs and a center piece to the umbrella fabric then put on the handles. As their business grew additional workers were hired, such as "tippers" who put tips on the ribs of the umbrella and cutters who cut the material for the umbrellas. As told to me by her children, Grandma Minnie soon ran the business side of their umbrella factory since she had mathematical ability and a good mind for numbers. She could calculate material for making umbrellas to the exact inch and so never wasted yardage. Aunt Martha recalled hearing Grandpa exclaim many times "Such a smart Jewish girl I married!" During the Great Depression Grandma Minnie became the manager and her daughter Sylvia (my mother) worked at the factory as their bookkeeper. They occasionally hired other family members who needed employment to work in their factory.

Although Oscar and his brother Louis initially were partners in their umbrella manufacturing business, they later parted ways and became competitors with separate businesses: Oscar Weiss Umbrellas and Louis Weiss Umbrellas. Louis Weiss Umbrellas was listed in a 1942 Manhattan telephone directory at 345 East Houston Street, then in Manhattan Telephone Directories 1946 through 1960 at 258 5th Avenue.[22] A family story was that Louis's wife Jennie Meiselman did not get along with Grandma and there was much quarreling between the two women, so that Oscar and Louis eventually split up their partnership in the umbrella business. There probably were other business matters be-

71 Ocean Parkway, Brooklyn

hind this split. The brothers stopped talking to each other thereafter for the rest of their lives after the break.

The 1933–34 Manhattan Business Directory found in the New York Public Library at 42nd Street listed Oscar and Minnie Weiss umbrella manufacturers located at 37 W. 20th Street, Manhattan. Their home address was 7913 Bay Parkway, Brooklyn. By 1942 Oscar and Minnie moved their umbrella factory to 20 West 22nd Street, Manhattan and the factory remained at that address until my grandmother Minnie's death in 1960. Prior to her death, she continued to work at the umbrella factory, and she managed the business as a widow with few employees, even when post-war Japanese exports of cheap umbrellas flooded the market. Grandma held on to the business until she became too ill at the end of her life. My cousin Mark recalled how Grandma would refuse to leave a customer until she was paid for the delivery of umbrellas. By necessity, she became a tough and uncompromising businesswoman.

My Mom worked at the umbrella factory as a bookkeeper and recalled when the artist Walt Disney appeared at my grandparents' umbrella factory with designs to make Mickey Mouse umbrellas. My grandparents thought that he was a "crazy" man and sent him away telling him to see Louis Weiss who was also an umbrella manufacturer. Instead of turning him away, Louis Weiss recognized that Walt Disney's idea for manufacturing Mickey Mouse umbrellas could become profitable and Louis went on to have enormous financial success with that brand.

My memories about my grandparent's umbrella business were based on my impressions as a child and then as an adolescent visiting the umbrella factory with

(LtoR) Sylvia, Minnie, Martha, Oscar, Marion Weiss ca. 1942

Grandma and Mom. Oscar Weiss Umbrellas was in a loft within an industrial building at 20 West 22nd Street, between Fifth and Sixth Avenues. This building was in an area called the Flatiron District because of proximity to the triangular shaped Flatiron Building at 23rd Street, and Broadway and Fifth Avenue.[23] This area also encompasses the now historic landmark La-dies' Mile Historic District.

The umbrella factory was one of many businesses in an old industrial build-ing, with high ceilings and with windows that were layered with years of grime and dirt from the city. The elevator in their building was manually operated by an elderly man who enjoyed making jokes and who smoked cigars. There was a loud, constant din made by ancient sewing machines usually operated by female Italian immigrants who loudly sang and made coarse jokes as a means of entertaining themselves. There was a man who cut the material and my father also did that job after his discharge from the Army. The "cutter" was respected as a skilled la-borer. The umbrella factory always appeared crowded with rolls of fabrics, huge cones of threads, umbrella ribs and handles. After the umbrellas were made, they were ready to be packaged. Runners would take the packages to whoever ordered them. Payment would be expected upon receipt of the umbrellas.

As a child, I helped screw wooden handles on the umbrellas. A few years later, I helped to test the mechanisms by opening and closing the umbrellas. Umbrella ribs were checked out by Grandma or whoever she delegated. When I had nothing to do and felt restless, I would walk around the building out of curiosity and peered into the open doors to see other factories. Those factories

Oscar and Minnie Weiss, Umbrella Factory

had similar loud industrial noises with people diligently at work.[24] Some of the other businesses in that building were printing presses, leather novelties, tool and die making, engraving, photo services, and advertising.

Memories of Grandma Minnie

Grandma Minnie was a serious no-nonsense type and the opposite personality from Grandpa, who was jovial and outgoing. As an example, after Grandpa Oscar died, Grandma found an enormous quantity of I.O.U.'s in their bank vault from people who owed him money. Grandpa apparently loaned money to help others either in need or to start their businesses. There is a saying that "one hand washes the other" and Grandpa's generosity possibly had a business purpose.

Grandma Minnie was religious, preferring to attend Conservative Jewish services since she did not enjoy Reform services. She especially disliked hearing organ music in shul. On every Yom Kippur, she would fast 24 hours from sundown to sundown the next day and she would spend all day praying at our Conservative synagogue. This preference was based on her Orthodox upbringing in Poland. Years later I learned through my genealogical research that her Geiger family was from a respected, influential, and pious rabbinical lineage, Hasidic and kosher.

I remember Grandma told me after she became a widow and still worked in the factory, a man who owned another business in the same building asked her to marry him, but she refused. She apparently had more than one marriage proposal after her husband's death however she was not interested in marrying anyone else. Aunt Martha told me that Grandpa idolized her and treated her like a "porcelain doll." He insisted that she rest when she came home from work, and he often cooked the evening meal and helped with childcare. When his children asked him what he cooked for his lunches, he would jokingly say "satchel soup" referring to a container of potato soup for his lunch placed in his work satchel.

As their business grew more prosperous, one day Grandpa surprised Grandma by having a diamond merchant come to their apartment to have Grandma choose diamonds for a brooch. Grandma chose three one-carat diamonds and seventy-four sapphires, and this fabulous brooch was passed down from Grandma to Aunt Martha and then to Grandma's granddaughter Olivia. Grandma proudly wore the brooch at weddings and special occasions.

When I visited Grandma at her umbrella factory, we sometimes had lunch together at a local kosher delicatessen where many people spoke Yiddish or read

Yiddish language newspapers. Grandma also took me to the Horn and Hardart automated cafeteria at 57th Street where I was thrilled to put in coins to obtain the foods on display behind the small glass doors. Grandma took her six grandchildren at various times to Radio City Music Hall to see the Rockettes and special movies such as *South Pacific* and *The Ten Commandments*. She took us to lunch at the Russian Tea Room or to Schrafft's followed with rich desserts at the famous

Wood Plaque from Grandma

Rumpelmeyer's. She obviously wanted to spoil her grandchildren and allow herself some pleasure apart from her hard work at the umbrella factory.

I recall how Grandma enjoyed cooking for Jewish holidays; she made an especially delicious gefilte fish. Grandma maintained her close relationship with her brother Charles Geiger until his death. Grandma was very family oriented and must have been sad to never have seen her parents and sister Freude again after she left Europe. When Grandma learned that her mother Hinde died 1931 in Vienna, Austria, she cried in despair and told Mom "Now I am an orphan!" since her father Aron previously died in 1924. I also recall how Grandma would often read from a prayer book called a *siddur*.

Years after Grandpa died, Grandma began to spend winters in Florida. She also paid for us to join her there on certain weeks. She took special delight in showing me off to her friends in Miami. While she was in Florida, and I was home at Brooklyn she would send me gifts from Florida of white chocolate as well as postcards and View Master photo discs of Florida life. The happy ambience of the beaches, ocean, and palm trees were special memories as they were all shared with Grandma. Grandma especially loved sharing Passover holiday celebrations with her daughters and their families. Grandma lived with her daughter Martha and son-in-law Aaron Cantor the last seven years of her life. I enjoyed sitting in Aunt Martha's lovely backyard in Woodmere with Grandma and loved to hear when she sometimes spoke about her life as a happy child in "Austria" hiking in the beautiful mountains near her town.

Mom used to tell me how Grandma could be quite strict and that she was the disciplinarian in the family. Grandma insisted that her children should obey her commands and she would give them a certain look that said she meant business! Grandma was very family minded and she frequently visited with her children and grandchildren as everyone at that time lived in New York City. I also remember Grandma's advice to me: "Do all the good you can, for all the people you can, in every way you can." This sentence signified her moral and spiritual essence that she passed down to me and was symbolized in a wood plaque of the ten commandments that I inherited from Grandma and continue to treasure. Grandma was also the early embodiment of women's liberation, being strongly independent, hard-working, resourceful, persevering, and loving. She continued to be a successful businesswoman during the time when it was mainly a man's world. She was always a strong female role model for our family.

Cousin Memories of Grandma

Cousin Olivia recalled "I remember going with my mother to pick up (Grandma) at the train station and hiding in the back of the car and she pretending I wasn't there and then every day bringing a little present...she was the matriarch we knew..."[25]

Cousin Mark shared "Our wonderful grandmother Minnie—her gifts constant...her strength and caring love to all of us. Minnie taught me how to use her sewing machine at the Woodmere house to taper my pants to be fashionable... threading the bobbin...her taking me to Macy's and to Rockefeller Center during New York's incredible holiday season...I remember her classic dark blue dress with white polka dots...Mom's stories about Minnie not leaving the office of one of her umbrella buyers until she was paid...stubborn and successful. Grandma had a small change purse pinned to the inside of her overcoat that she used to get change out of...I remember her doing that and putting some small amount of money in the hand or pocket of someone sitting on the sidewalk in NYC.[26]

He recalled: "I wish I could have known Oscar as he figured so prominently in my mother Martha's memories as a warm and generous father to her. Keep her memory in our hearts to be influenced with her strength and loving nature."[27]

Cousin Lois wrote "I also have wonderful memories of her especially the show and helping her in the umbrella workshop."[28] She remembered "a snowstorm with Grandma insisting on going to work even when everyone stayed home."[29]

Cousin Arthur recalled Grandma taking him and his sister Lois to the Russian Tea Room for lunch and then to see *South Pacific* with Ezio Pinza. He had another memory of Grandma taking him by train to Nathan's and then to a movie. Arthur sent me a poem that he wrote about Grandma.[30]

> *What A Day*
> *It's over sixty years ago, I*
> *Was six, but it's still fresh*
> *In my mind.*
> *The wonder of it, the*
> *Wonder of her.*
> *My Grandmother, Minnie,*
> *Born in 1887, her shtetl,*
> *Blazowa (Poland), came to the*

United States on her own in 1904
Never to see her parents again.
Independent, always worked along
Side my Grandfather, Oscar,
Hand making and selling umbrellas.
For several years with their three
Daughters, my mother the eldest,
They lived on Essex Street on the
Lower East Side of New York, store
In the front, living in the back.
Even after my Grandfather died in
1946, she continued the business
For another ten years, and I used to
Help in assembling the umbrellas
In her shop, in what is now Chelsea.

(LtoR) Lois, Grandma Minnie, Arthur

Well, on 'that' day Grandma
Picked my sister, Lois, and I up
At our one-bedroom apartment
In Bensonhurst, Brooklyn.
We took the train into Manhattan,
Had lunch at the Russian Tea Room,
Which for us was like being on
Another planet.
Then onto see the musical South Pacific, my
first
Broadway show, and it was
Spectacular, Enzio Pinza the star.
We sat towards the front, on the
Right side.
And, finally, before returning home,
Decadent dessert at the famous
Rumpelmeyer's.
Oh yes, what a day!
I hope she still remembers.

Death

Our beloved Grandma Minnie died 18 May 1960 at 652 Emerson Street, Wood-mere, Nassau, New York. Her death certificate listed immediate cause of death congestive heart failure with arteriosclerotic heart disease.[31] Her date of birth was erroneously given on her death certificate as 28 April 1891. Grandma lived with Aunt Martha and Uncle Aaron at 652 Emerson Street at Woodmere, Nassau County, New York for seven years before her death where she had her own bed-room. She was driven daily by Aunt Martha to the Long Island Railroad to take a commuter train into Manhattan to manage the umbrella factory. She insisted on commuting to her factory despite her health issues or adverse weather condi-tions. Grandma worked up to several weeks prior to her death when she became too ill. She was interred at the Geiger-Weiss family plot, Samaritan Society, at Mt. Neboh Cemetery, Glendale, Queens County, New York. Grandma Minnie was buried next to Grandpa Oscar Weiss. Minnie's brother Charles Geiger was also buried there as well as my parents Sylvia and Frank Gerber and my broth-er David Gerber.[32] Her obituary read "Minnie Weiss, beloved wife of the late Oscar, devoted moth-er of Marion Goshin, Sylvia Ger-ber and Martha Cantor, adored grandmother." Services were held at the Riverside Chapel at Far Rockaway, L.I., New York. Her obituary was published in the *New York Times* 19 May 1960. Grandma Minnie's Hebrew *yahr-zeit* is Iyar-21.

Minnie Weiss Matsevah

The Weiss Family from the Ukraine

My grandfather Oscar Weiss died when I was age 3 so I have little personal mem-ory of him other than family stories and photographs. The date of Grandpa's birth is difficult to confirm as I have not found an actual record of his birth. His son-in-law Aaron Cantor supplied Grandpa's date of birth 11 March 1876 for his death certificate.

Grandpa Oscar (1876–1946) was the fourth of ten children born to Fischel Weiss (1851–1893) from Boryslaw, Ukraine and Hencze Zuckerberg (1852–1936) from Drohobycz, Ukraine. There is a long history of Jews living in Drohobycz from the medieval period to WWII. I refer readers to an excellent website *History of the Jewish Community in Drohobycz, Ukraine* complied by William Fern at kehila-links.jewishgen.org/drohobycz.

I researched the Weiss family for Weiss ancestors from Boryslaw and Drohobycz, for many years. This proved to be a challenge as the name Weiss is extremely common. This brick wall was finally scaled when I submitted my autosomal DNA (atDNA) to the company www.23andme.com. My atDNA matched another individual, Eddy Bikales, who also had Weiss ancestors from the same region. He was estimated to be my third cousin. After comparing family histories, we discovered that we had Yehuda Leib Weiss as our common ancestor. Yehuda Leib Weiss had a daughter Channah who married Moishe Bander. Eddy descended from that Bander branch.[33] Eddy told me that the Bander and Weiss cousins who were descendants of Yehuda Leib Weiss formed the Yehuda Weiss Family Circle in New York during the late 1920s that lasted until the late 1940s. Eddy recalled that his father Norbert came to New York as a penniless Holocaust survivor. Norbert told his son Eddy that a Weiss descendant owned an umbrella factory and bought him a suit so that he could find a job. This descendant was probably my grandfather Oscar Weiss or my great uncle Louis Weiss. (*See Descendants of Yehuda Leib Weiss Tree*).

According to Alexander Beider, the name Yehuda or Judah is associated with "young lion" from Genesis 49:9. The Ashkenazic kinnui, Leyb or Leib is also associated with lion.[34] Yehuda Leib is a double name with the same meaning although men usually used the Hebrew name for religious purposes and kept the secular name for common us-

Oscar Weiss ca.1910

age. I found a death record for Leib Weiss, who died age 68 on 20 December 1882 at Gaje Wyżne and was buried 22 December 1882 at Drohobycz, Ukraine.[35] Gaje Wyżne was a small town in the administrative district of Drohobycz and not far from the large city of Drohobycz.[36] With additional records I confirmed that Leib Weiss was my great-great-grandfather Yehuda Leib Weiss. His occupation was cattle trader.

I located a birth record for one of Oscar Weiss's sisters, Sadye aka Chaje Sara Weiss. She was born 27 December 1882 at Gaje Wyżne to my great-grand-parents Fischel Weiss and Hencze Zuckerberg.[37] I wondered why my pregnant great-grandmother Hencze journeyed to this town and had her baby born there. After finding the death record for Leib Weiss I learned the reason my great-grand-parents were in that town was because Fischel Weiss's father (Yehuda) Leib Weiss died. They gathered there for his funeral and to sit *shiva*. Shiva is a period of mourning for first degree relatives such as parents, children, spouses. It starts immediately after burial and lasts for seven days. Mourners remained at home for the entire time; relatives and friends visited to express their condolences.

Parents for Leib Weiss were listed on his death record of 20 December 1882 at Gaje Wyżne.[38] They were Berko Weiss and Schewa, from Rozdół, Żydaczów, Ukraine, about 34 miles from Drohobycz. As far back as I could research, my Weiss line of ancestors began with my great-great-great-grandparents Berko Weiss (ca. 1796–) and Schewa, then to my great-great-grandparents Yehuda Leib Weiss (1814–1882) and his wife Soske Borgman (1817–1891). My great-grand-parents were Fischel Weiss (1851–1893) and Hencze Zuckerberg (1852–1936); my grandparents were Oscar Weiss (1876–1946) and Minnie Geiger (1887–1960).

Fischel Weiss and Hencze Zuckerberg

My great-grandfather Fischel Weiss (1851–1893) married Hencze Zuckerberg (1852–1936) ca. 1867 at Drohobycz, Ukraine. My great-grandmother Hencze was born in Drohobycz to Mendel Zuckerberg (1823–1888) and Hinde Fraenkel (1828–1895). Hencze's father Mendel Zuckerberg was born at Medenice, Ukraine to Sender Zuckerberg (ca.1789–) and Neche. Medenice was within the admin-istrative district of Drohobycz. It was a shtetl 13 miles from Drohobycz with a small Jewish population of 190, only 7% of the total population. Jews lived in Medenice from the 19th to the beginning of the 20th century. They had their own rabbi, shochet, synagogue and ritual bath. Most Jews of Medenice were employed in commerce.[39]

Leib Weiss, Death Record

Hencze and Fischel were married as teenagers at Drohobycz ca. 1867, and they immediately began raising their large family of ten children, however only seven of the children reached adulthood. The children were all born at Boryslaw: Chulie Weiss (1867–); Morys Weiss (1869–1940); Rosie Weiss (ca. 1875–1943); Oscar Weiss (1876–1946); Annie Weiss (1877–1952); Fannie Weiss (1879–); Ester Weiss (1880–1883); Sadye Weiss (1882 –1963); Louis Weiss (1885–1969); Elio Weiss (1887–1887).

I initially had little information about my great-grandmother Hencze/Hannah/Helen Zuckerberg. Weiss cousins recalled that she was a short, slight woman who lived to 90 years. She was described as feisty and did not mince words. While raising her children as a young widow she was self-employed selling notions as a door-to-door saleswoman. When her children became adults, she would visit them by taxi and order her daughter or son to pay the cab fare. She stayed with each child for a length of time then leave for her visit to her next child. My Weiss cousin Herbert Luckower z"l recalled seeing Hencze when he was a child and he confirmed a photo I have was Hencze. He recalled being at Hencze's death-bed in a nursing home in New York around the time of his bar mitzvah in 1936. I faced a brick wall when after interviewing many Weiss cousins, none knew where Hencze was buried or when she died.

I wanted to know more about Hencze since I was given the Yiddish name Hensha Hinda; I learned through genealogy research that I was named for my great-grandmothers Hencze Weiss née Zuckerberg and Hinde Geiger née Turnheim. My search for finding death information about Hencze continued with trips to the NYC Municipal Archives combing through countless Hannah/Helen/Hennie Weiss death certificates. This was a frustrating experience that did not yield any solid results except to rule out those who were not my great-grandmother.

I decided that I needed another approach to that brick wall. I reasoned that I could try

Hencze Weiss ca.1934

a back door approach to search death certificates of Henze's children for more clues to help me locate her, perhaps she was buried near one of her children. I searched cemetery records for her children Louis Weiss, Sadie Luckower and Rose Brauner and did not find Hencze buried with them. She was not buried in Mt. Neboh Cemetery with her son Oscar Weiss. I then sent away for the death certificate for her son Morys Weiss, who also immigrated to the United States and found he was buried at Mt. Hebron Cemetery, Queens, New York. I researched the Weiss surnames on the Mt. Hebron database and wrote down each row and plot to see if they were buried near Morys.

Hannie Weiss matsevah

To my surprise, I found an Anna Weiss interred at the same plot as Morys. This could be Hencze with Anna as another variation of her given name. I sent for her death certificate from the New York City Municipal Archives and was excited to learn Anna Weiss was indeed my great-grandmother also known as Hannah, Helen, Hennie and now Anna. That is how I discovered my great-grandmother Hencze Weiss née Zuckerberg died 30 April 1936 at age 85. Morys Weiss died 1940 and he was interred at the same burial plot with his mother. Hencze aka Anna Weiss died in a nursing facility, *Home of the Sons and Daughters of Israel*, located in lower Manhattan.[40] Years later the same building became a substance abuse rehabilitation center where I worked although I never knew the history of that building or realized that was where my great-grandmother died.[41]

Boryslaw, Ukraine

Both Boryslaw and Drohobycz were part of Eastern Galicia, now the Ukraine. Boryslaw is 8.7 miles southwest of Drohobycz. Young people from small towns would be drawn to new employment opportunities in larger cities such as Drohobycz and Boryslaw. I discovered an interesting fact about Oscar's paternal grandfather Yehuda Leib Weiss from the death record for his wife Soske Weiss née Borgman. Her death record contained information that she was the widow of Leib, former owner of oil wells at Boryslaw. Her parents Moses Borgman and Estera were innkeepers at Ropczyce, Podkarpackie, Poland. Soske died at age 74, on 19 October 1891 at Boryslaw.[42] Soske's husband Leib Weiss, in addition to being a cattle trader, apparently owned oil wells in Boryslaw.[43] It seemed incredible that my great-great-grandfather Yehuda Leib Weiss could be an oil tycoon! I could not picture a Jew owning an oil well in Galicia and I needed to check out that fact.

Research corroborated this information. Starting from the 1850s Boryslaw became the most important oil center in Europe. The industry of oil production was established and developed by Jews at Boryslaw. Oil even flowed on the surface of the ground. Wax was also found and used in the production of candles. Jews were the first people in that region to refine crude oil and produce oil for illumination. Oil production brought wealth and plenty of work for thousands of Jews who worked hard but also knew how to have a good time! The young men were nicknamed Borislawchik and they were always ready to fight anyone especially Gentiles who tried to take Jewish jobs. However, as devout Hasidim they stopped work on Shabbat and changed their work clothes for their fur hats (*strammel*) and their *Shabatmantle*.[44]

Postcard, Boryslaw Oil fields

Despite the boom of oil supply and demand, the methods for oil extraction were primitive. By the 1890s major Austrian banks started buying up large areas in Boryslaw and introduced modern steam and electrical machinery. The small and medium size oil producers could not compete with larger enterprises and Jews had to sell their wells and mines. This created an economic crisis with thousands of Jews suddenly unemployed. Banks and larger companies practiced anti-Semitic policies by refusing to hire Jewish workers. Gentile workers claimed that all jobs in the oil industry were their exclusive monopoly.[45] The new unemployment among Jews led to increased Jewish immigration from Boryslaw to the United States including my Weiss family.

Weiss Family Immigration

I researched immigration records for my Weiss family on the Hamburg passenger site, and found a record for Oscher Weiss, age 18, traveling with his father Fischel Weiss, age 43, and Oscar's sisters Riwke, age 21, and Hendel, age 9, all from Drohobycz.[46] They departed from Hamburg on 9 March 1892 on the *Warrington* ship to Grimsby, a port in England, where they were going to Liverpool to change to another ship for arrival at New York. With immigrant families the father usually

S.S. Gellert Manifest

travelled first with the oldest children, to be followed later by the mother with their younger children. Fischel Weiss and his children travelled to Liverpool to make a connection with another ship.

I found another ship manifest for the Weiss family that departed from Liverpool, UK 16 March 1892 on the steamship *S.S.Ohio* and arrived at Philadelphia on 27 March 1892.[47] The information on the manifest listed Fischel Weiss, age 43, Oschel age 18 occupation tailor; Rmke age 21 spinster; another name was undecipherable, age 9. All were coming from Galicia and their destination was New York. This record was certainly coincidental with my Weiss ancestors, ages, time frame for the voyage during March 1892 and similar destination for New York, despite preliminary arrival at Philadelphia. The *S.S. Ohio* was built 1872 in Philadelphia by W. Cramp and Sons for the American Line. The steamship made regular Atlantic crossings from Liverpool to Philadelphia.

Another immigration record was discovered for Fischel's wife Hencze, who immigrated from Drohobycz June 1893 with their three children Fanny, Sara (Sadye) and Louis (Leib). Their oldest child Morys was 20 years of age and married. He immigrated separately with his wife Pesel aka Pauline to New York July 1889. Hencze, age 40, travelled with her youngest children Fanny age 9, Sara age 8 and Leib age 7 on the ship the *S.S. Gellert* under the Hamburg America Line that departed Hamburg on 4 June 1893 to New York. They travelled steerage class on the lowest deck, the cheapest and worst accommodations with limited privacy and security, inadequate sanitation, and poor food. The ship arrived at New York on 16 June 1893.[48] Hencze stated that she was married and could read and write. The *S.S. Gellert* was built 1874 in Glasgow by Alexander Stephen and Sons. The ship made regular voyages from Hamburg to New York.[49]

Oscar Weiss Naturalization

My grandfather Osher Weiss (aka Oscar Weiss) began the naturalization process to become an American citizen when he submitted his Declaration of Intention 21 August 1914 to the Supreme Court of New York.[50] He submitted his Petition for Naturalization to the court on 18 October 1919.[51] He took the Oath of Allegiance to the United States of America on 7 February 1921 after renouncing all allegiance to any other state or sovereignty specifically to The Republics of Poland and Austria.[52] His naturalization allowed Grandma Minnie to become a naturalized citizen. Their children Marion, Sylvia and Martha were citizens because they were born in the United States.

U. S. DEPARTMENT OF LABOR
NATURALIZATION SERVICE

No.

73

UNITED STATES OF AMERICA

ORIGINAL

89223 c

PETITION FOR NATURALIZATION

To the Honorable the Supreme Court of the State of New York, First Judicial District:

The petition of .... Osher Weiss ...., hereby filed, respectfully showeth:

First. My place of residence is .... 136 Essex St ...., New York, N. Y.
(Give number and street.)

Second. My occupation is .... Manufacturer

Third. I was born on the ... 64th .. day of ... Jany .... anno Domini 1 .. 879 .. Galicia Austria

Fourth. I emigrated to the United States from ... Hamburg Germany .... on or about the .. 13th .. day of ... March

anno Domini 1 .. 893 .. and arrived in the United States, at the port of ... New York NY ...., on the .. 28th .. day of ... March

anno Domini 1 .. 893 .. on the vessel ... Galle x
(If the alien arrived otherwise than by vessel, the character of conveyance or name of transportation company should be given.)

Fifth. I declared my intention to become a citizen of the United States on the .. 21st .. day of ... August .... anno Domini 1 .. 914

at ... New York New York ..., in the ... Supreme .... Court of ... New York New York

Sixth. I am ... married. My wife's name is ... Minnie ...; she was born on the .. 16th .. of ... May .... anno Domini 1 .. 889

at ... Austria ..., and now resides at ... 136 Essex St ...., New York, N. Y.
(Give number and street.)

I have ... 3 ... children, and the name, date and place of birth, and place of residence of such of said children is as follows:

Miriam 28th November 1912 New York .... נתה דעה

Sylvia 4th June 1914 New York

Martha 28th July 1918 New York

All reside in New York

Seventh. I am not a disbeliever in or opposed to organized government or a member of or affiliated with any organization or body of persons teaching disbelief in or opposed to organized government. I am not a polygamist nor a believer in the practice of polygamy. I am attached to the principles of the Constitution of the United States, and it is my intention to become a citizen of the United States and to renounce absolutely and forever all allegiance and fidelity to any foreign prince, potentate, state, or sovereignty, and particularly to ... The Republic of Poland and Austria ...., of whom at this time I am a subject, and it is my intention to reside permanently in the United States.

Eighth. I am able to speak the English language.

Ninth. I have resided continuously in the United States of America for the term of five years at least, immediately preceding the date of this petition, to wit, since the .. 893 ..

28th .. day of ... March ...., anno Domini 1 ...., and in the State of New York, continuously next preceding the date of this petition,

since the .. 28th .. day of ... march .... anno Domini 1 .. 893 .., being a residence within this State of at least one year next preceding the date of this petition.

Tenth. I have not heretofore made petition for citizenship to any court. (I made petition for citizenship to the .... Court of .... at .... on the .... day of .... anno Domini 1 ...., and the said petition was denied by the said Court for the following reasons and causes, to wit: .... and the cause of such denial has since been cured or removed.)

Attached hereto and made a part of this petition are my declaration of intention to become a citizen of the United States and the certificate from the Department of Labor, together with my affidavit and the affidavits of the two verifying witnesses thereto required by law. Wherefore your petitioner prays that he may be admitted a citizen of the United States of America.

X Osher Weiss
(Complete and true signature of petitioner.)

Declaration of Intention No. 89560 .. and Certificate of Arrival No. .... from Department of Labor filed this .. 18th .. day of ... Oct ...., 191 9

NOTE TO CLERK OF COURT.—If petitioner arrived in the United States on or about June 29, 1906, strike out the words reading "and Certificate of Arrival No. .... from Department of Labor."

AFFIDAVITS OF PETITIONER AND WITNESSES

STATE OF NEW YORK, } ss.:
County of New York,

The aforesaid petitioner being duly sworn, deposes and says that he is the petitioner in the above-entitled proceedings; that he has read the foregoing petition and knows the contents thereof; that the said petition is signed with his full, true name; that the same is true of his own knowledge except as to matters therein stated to be alleged upon information and belief, and that as to those matters he believes it to be true.

X Osher Weiss
(Complete and true signature of petitioner.)

Samuel Weintraub ...., occupation ... Internal Revenue Collector at .. 106 Ludlow St

and Nathan Schultz ...., occupation ... do do do, residing at .. 236 East 5th St

each being severally, duly, and respectively sworn, deposes and says that he is a citizen of the United States of America; that he has personally known

Osher Weiss ...., the petitioner above mentioned, to have resided in the United States continuously immediately preceding the date of filing his petition, since the .. 1st .. day of ... October .... anno Domini 1 .. 914 .., and in the State in which the above-entitled petition is made continuously since the .... 1st .. day of ... oct .... anno Domini 1 .. 914 ..; and that he has personal knowledge that the said petitioner is a person of good moral character, attached to the principles of the Constitution of the United States, and that the petitioner is in every way qualified, in his opinion, to be admitted a citizen of the United States.

Samuel Weintraub
(Signature of witness.)

Nathan Schultz
(Signature of witness.)

[SEAL.]

Subscribed and sworn to before me by the above-named petitioner and witnesses in the office of the Clerk of said Court at New York, N. Y., this

.. 18th .. day of ... October .... anno Domini 191 9

[OVER.]

Abraham Lencher
Special Clerk of the Supreme Court.

Osher Weiss, Naturalization Petition

On his Petition for Naturalization, Grandpa Oscar Weiss indicated that he immigrated on the *S.S. Geller (Gellert)* on 28 March 1893, however it was his mother Hencze with Oscar's three siblings who immigrated on the *S.S. Gellert* during June 1893. On Grandpa Oscar's Declaration of Intention for Naturalization, he listed his birthdate as 6 January 1879 and stated that he was born in Galicia.[53] His naturalization record was in the name of Osher Weiss. In my research I located Weiss birth records from Drohobycz and found Grandpa's sister Feige aka Fanny was born 18 June 1879, therefore ruling out 1879 as his birth year as there was no record or family story of Grandpa having been a twin.[54] He gave his personal information as being 35 years of age, 5 feet 9 inches tall, weighing 174 pounds, color of hair brown and color of eyes blue.

Aunt Martha recalled that Grandpa was born at Boryslaw, in the Drohobycz district, Ukraine, however I did not find his birth record. On his Petition for Naturalization dated 18 October 1919,[55] Grandpa indicated that he immigrated to New York on the ship *Geller* on 28 March 1893, from Hamburg, Germany. Grandpa was living at 136 Essex Street in Manhattan, New York; his wife was Minnie, born 16 May 1889 and they had three children: Miriam (Marion) born 28 November 1912; Sylvia born 4 June 1914 and Martha born 28 July 1918 and that all three children were born at New York.

The Oscar Weiss Family in New York

I found my Weiss family in the 1900 Federal Census for Manhattan, New York, Enumeration District 276.[56] The Weiss family lived at 183 Broome Street in the Lower East Side, Manhattan. My great-grandmother Hencze called herself Annie, listed as a widow, age 48, born March 1852. Grandpa Oscar gave his name as James and his age as 24, his birth September 1875. His brother was listed as Lewis, age 15, born March 1885 and his sisters were listed as Fanny, age 19 born July 1880 and Sadie, age 17 born March 1883. The immigration year for the Weiss family was 1892. For their occupations, Annie and "James" were listed as peddlers. Lewis worked as a clerk, Fanny was a seamstress and Sadie was a saleslady. Mom told me Grandpa's nickname was "Jimmy" and that would fit with this census record. I always thought that Jimmy was an unusual name for an immigrant Jew. Grandpa may have felt he would be more readily accepted by Americans with this nickname.

In the 1905 New York State Census[57] the Weiss family consisted of Hencze then known as Helen, age 52; Oscar age 28; Fannie, age 22; Sadie age 20; and Louis age 18. They all lived at 1653 East 110 Street in Manhattan, New York.

Grandpa Oscar was listed as a hat merchant and his siblings worked as salespersons. Their mother Helen put down "housework" for her occupation. In the 1910 Thirteenth Federal Census for Manhattan, I found Grandpa and his family living at 18 East 112 Street; with his mother Hanna, age 58; Oscar age 31; Sadie age 25; Louis age 23.[58] Grandpa Oscar was listed as selling umbrellas from his own store. Grandpa and his siblings supported their mother. The support of one's aging parents was commonplace before the advent of Social Security.

A Trauma in the Weiss Family

Fischel Weiss matsevah

Changed circumstances in the Weiss household made it necessary for their children to work. This information was based on a family story told to me by my mother and aunts with many details left out. I investigated this story with further research. Soon after his immigration to the United States Fischel Weiss developed serious symptoms that led to a medical diagnosis for a brain tumor. Fischel decided to seek treatment at Vienna, Austria. At that time Vienna had a worldwide reputation for being a famous medical center with outstanding physicians. Fischel left his wife and children in New York to journey to Vienna for treatment at the Vienna General/University Hospital Complex. He unfortunately died at the hospital either during or after brain surgery.

I obtained his death record from Irma Wulz, archivist for the Israelitische Kultus Gemeinde Wien (IKG). His death record contained the

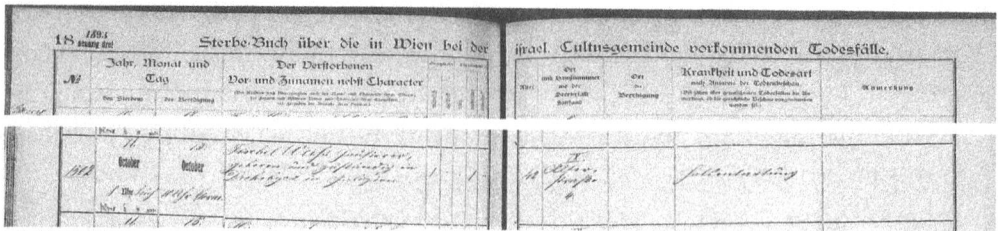

Signatur: Matrikenamt der IKG Wien, A / VIE / IKG / I / BUCH / MA / STERBEBUCH / 135

Death Record, Fischel Weiss IKG

following information: Fischel Weiss, occupation peddler, born at Drohobycz, Galicia, married, died at 42 years, 11 October 1893 at the hospital, cause of death: cancer in the region of the neck/head.[59] He was buried 13 October 1893 in the Jewish section of the Weiner Zentralfriedhof Cemetery, Vienna, Austria: 1 Tor, group 19, row 46, grave 71.[60] The address of the cemetery is District XI, Simmeringer Hauptstrasse 234, Vienna. When Fischel's wife Hencze was notified of his death either she travelled to Vienna herself or she sent money to arrange for Fischel's burial and headstone. Hencze suddenly became a young widow as the sole support of her six children. There was no government help or family assistance. Her children needed to work to help support their family. Aunt Martha recalled that Hencze worked as a door-to-door peddler in New York, selling tablecloths, threads, needles, and pins.

Additional corroborating information was obtained when I obtained a photograph of the matsevah from the IKG for my great-grandfather Fischel Weiss who was buried in the Weiner Zentralfriedhof cemetery at Vienna, Austria. The Hebrew inscription on his dark granite tombstone was difficult to read however I submitted the photo on-line to Viewmate at JewishGen.org. for translation. Fredel Jacobs Fruhman translated the following to English: *Here lies a straightforward and honest man, Efraim Fishel, son of the deceased Yehudah died on the second day of RoshChodesh Cheshvan 5654. May his soul be bound up in the bond of life.*[61] He died 11 October 1893 at Vienna, Austria and was buried 13 October 1893 as confirmed by the official cemetery death record.[62]

WWII

Another document of interest was Oscar Weiss listing himself as age 61 on the 1942 "Old Man's" draft registration card.[63] He gave his birthdate as 11 March 1881 however he was 66 years of age if his actual birth year was 1876; this date was on his death certificate. His address was 71 Ocean Parkway in Brooklyn and his occupation was umbrella manufacturer with his factory being located at 20 West 22nd Street in Manhattan. Older men were required to register for the remote possibility of being drafted during WWII if they were born on or after 28 April 1877 and on or before 16 February 1897. He probably did not know his actual birthdate or felt that he could not prove his actual age.

Death

Grandpa Oscar Weiss died 25 October 1946; his residence was 71 Ocean Parkway, Brooklyn.[64] His age was listed as 70 years, 7 months, and 14 days. His date of birth on his death certificate was given as 11 March 1876; this date was supplied by his son-in-law Aaron Cantor. The death certificate indicated his death was due to natural causes. Mom told me that Grandpa died of prostate cancer. Aunt Martha recalled that he also had uremic poisoning because there was no kidney dialysis at that time. He died at French Hospital, Manhattan after being there 41 days. His father was Efraim aka Fischel and his mother was Hentche Zuckerberg. I found Grandpa's obituary from the *New York Times.*[65]

When I was a toddler Mom wanted me to visit Grandpa at the French hospital before he died however minor children were not permitted to be in the ward. Since it was a Catholic hospital, an obliging nun hid me under her habit so I could visit Grandpa without being turned away. Both Aunt Martha and Mom recalled

Oscar Weiss matsevah

that at Grandpa's funeral there were several hundred people in attendance and one hundred cars in the funeral procession.[66] Besides relatives there were many friends and acquaintances at his funeral as he was highly regarded for his generosity, jovial personality, and kindness. Grandpa Oscar Weiss was buried in the Geiger-Weiss family plot at Mt. Neboh Cemetery, Glendale, Queens, New York. The Hebrew yahrzeit for Oscar Weiss is 30 Tishrei.

Children of Minnie Geiger and Oscar Weiss

Marion Weiss

Miriam aka Marion Goshin née Weiss was the first of three children born to Minnie and Oscar Weiss. She was born on 28 November 1912 at Manhattan, New York.[67] Aunt Marion was a gifted baker and an avid reader of literature. Marion also had a love of teaching children as an elementary school teacher. She learned to play the piano since that was a requirement for a teaching position. I remember the wonderful aroma of her baking and the many delicious cakes and desserts she prepared for the family.

She enjoyed the witty jokes and lively political discussions between her husband Harry, an ardent liberal, and opposing points of views presented by Mom (Sylvia) as the only conservative in the family. Marion was modest about her own accomplishments leaving the limelight to others, especially to her husband. Marion went to P.S. 16 in Williamsburg, Brooklyn. She then went to Eastern District High School in Brooklyn, New York where she met the love of her life, Harry Goshin. They dated while they both went to college in New York City. Marion graduated from Hunter College; Harry graduated from City College of the University of New York.

Mom recalled that her sister Marion was always studious and loved reading and learning. Marion obtained her elementary teacher's license for New York City. She taught elementary grades for many years in New York and in Massachusetts. Whenever she spoke of her teaching, she became animated and enthusiastic. She was a conscientious teacher and enjoyed encouraging her students' curiosity and talents; she especially enjoyed teaching third grade.

Marion and Harry were married 8 September 1935 at Brooklyn, New York during the difficult Great Depression years.[68] Marion lived at 7913 Bay Parkway,

Sylvia and Marion ca. 1919

Marion Weiss, Eastern District HS

Brooklyn with her parents Oscar and Minnie Weiss. Harry lived at 5801 14th Avenue, Brooklyn with his parents Jacob and Lena Goshin. He worked as a salesman. Marion and Harry were married in Brooklyn at Jacob and Lena Goshin's apartment. Marion and Harry struggled financially as many did at that time. They delayed having their first child for six years and then waited another five years before they had their second child. Both Marion and Harry valued higher education with expectations that their children Arthur and Lois would go to college and make something of themselves. They were proud of their children's considerable accomplishments.

Marion was close with her sisters and their families. She even moved with her family to the same apartment complex at Glen Oaks, Queens, New York where we were living. Since we were geographically near Marion and her family we would visit often, sometimes having dinners together and joined one another for the Jewish holidays. This proximity served to reinforce family ties with my cousins and with Marion and Harry. Marion was also persuaded by my parents to

Harry and Marion Goshin, Marriage certificate

Marion and Harry Goshin ca.1936

rent an apartment for the winters in Florida in the same condominium complex where my parents lived at Sunrise, Broward County.

Marion developed chronic emphysema that grew worse over time even though she never smoked. She was, however, exposed to years of second-hand smoke due to her husband Harry's heavy cigarette smoking habit. She eventually died of lung complications and emphysema on 14 January 1996 at Patchogue, Long Island, New York.[69] Both Marion and Harry Goshin are buried together at Beth David Cemetery, Elmont, Queens County, New York in the Rotmistrover Benevolent Society section. Marion and Harry had two children: Lois and Arthur. Both are still living.

Harry Goshin

Tzvi Hersch aka Harry Goshin was the first of two sons born to Jack Goshin and Lena Schuel. He was born 3 January 1912 at his parent's home, Brooklyn, New York. As a child Harry spoke only Yiddish at home until he entered grade school. Harry was an animated and lively person who loved to laugh and make jokes. He also enjoyed arguing over politics. He had a quick wit and a nervous energy. Harry inherited genes enabling him to eat whatever he wanted and remain trim.

According to my cousin Arthur, his father Harry became president of his high school class at Eastern District High School in Brooklyn, New York, and graduated January 1929. Harry went to college and graduated from City College

Harry Goshin, Eastern District High School

of the City University of New York ca. 1933 with a major in accounting. Among his scholastic achievements, he could read and speak Latin and Greek. He became a passionate liberal, was socialistic in philosophy and did not hesitate to speak out on behalf of worker's rights. This viewpoint was typical among students at City College during the 1930s.

Due to the Great Depression, Harry could not find employment in his field, and he worked in the Oscar Weiss Umbrella factory. During WWII Harry worked at Hearn's Department store for several years before opening his own children's clothing store in Bensonhurst, Brooklyn, New York. He later went into partnership and opened a women's and children's clothing store. Harry's father Jacob Goshin was skilled as a professional tailor and taught Harry this skill. Harry made beautiful coats, trousers, and dresses for his family.

Harry met his soulmate Marion while they were both high school students at Eastern District High School. They soon dated steadily and became engaged however, waited to marry until they both graduated from college. They first obtained a marriage license 28 August 1935 at Brooklyn, New York.[70] Harry and Marion married 8 September 1935 at Kings County, New York.[71] When WWII presented a threat, Harry registered for the draft; he received his WWII draft card in October 1940 at Brooklyn, New York. His employer was Hearn's Department Store in Manhattan at 14th Street and 5th Avenue. At that time, Harry and Marion lived at 135 Avenue P, Brooklyn, New York.[72] Cousin Arthur recalled how his father was turned down for active military service due to his medical prescription to wear custom made orthopedic shoes. Harry managed the war bond program at Hearn's Department Store through the war years.

(LtoR) Sylvia, Martha, Marion ca.1930

(LtoR) Harry, Marion, Aaron and Martha

Harry rose to become a store manager for Zayre's discount department stores. This position required Harry and Marion to re-locate to Cleveland, Ohio and Rochester, New York. Harry next re-located to Springfield, Massachusetts where he and Marion lived for ten years. He worked as a district manager and was responsible for eighteen Zayre's stores in the New England area. Aunt Marion enjoyed her work in Springfield as an elementary school teacher. They moved back to New York during their retirement years and lived in an apartment at East Patchogue, Suffolk County, New York. While in retirement Harry volunteered as a mediator. During 1985 they celebrated 50 years of marriage with a large party of relatives and friends. Harry died of lung cancer 23 December 1985 at Patchogue, Suffolk County, New York.[73] He was interred at Beth David Cemetery, Elmont, New York in the Rotmistrover Benevolent Society section.

Goshin Plot, Beth David Cemetery, New York

Arnold Goshin

Harry's younger brother Arnold Goshin (1918–2006) was born 20 May 1918, Brooklyn, New York. He completed his WWII draft card October 1940, and his employer was S.D. Leidesdorf and Company.[74] Arnold enlisted in the Army 28 April 1942. His WWII Army Enlistment Record included information that he had 4 years of college; his occupation was accountant and auditor.[75] He graduated from City College of New York ca. 1939. Arnold became the comptroller for Playtex Corporation. Arnold died 26 September 2006 at Miami, Dade County, Florida.[76] He had no issue.

Jacob Goshin and Lena Schuel

Harry and Arnold were born to Jacob Goschinsky (1890–1978) and Lena Schuel (1890–1951). Jacob (aka Jack) Goschinsky was born 18 February 1890 in Rotmistrovka, Cherkassy, Kiev, Ukraine to Meir Aron Goschinsky and Chava Melnick (Meir Aron's second wife).[77] Much of the Goschinsky family information was obtained from Harry's cousin, Herbert Goshin z"l and from my cousin Arthur Goshin. Meir Aron and Chava had the following children: Jacob, Max, Abraham, Morris, and a daughter. Meir Aron Goschinsky and his first wife (name unknown) had the following children: David and George.

I located the naturalization papers for Jacob Goschinsky. They were found under New York, County Naturalization Records, Kings County, Petitions for Naturalization in www.familysearch.org. His Declaration of Intention for citizenship was submitted 9 September 1915 to the Supreme Court, Bronx County, New York. Jacob Goshin filed his Petition for Naturalization 27 January 1920 in the name of Jacob Goshin however it was noted on his petition that he was also known as Jacob Goschinsky. He took his Oath of Allegiance 14 June 1920.[78] He reported that he immigrated to the USA in 1906 from Liverpool, England on the *Oceanic* 20

Standing: Marion and Harry. Seated: Jack Goshin

Lena Schuel, Immigration

Naturalization Record for Jacob Goschinsky

May 1906 and arrived at New York 12 June 1906. His occupation was Manufacturer of Waists (women's blouses). He resided at 314 South 3rd Street, Brooklyn, New York. His wife Lena Schuel was born 9 December 1890 in Russia. Their children were born in New York; Harry was born 3 January 1912, Manhattan and Arnold was born 20 May 1917(or 1918), Brooklyn.

The 1916 City Directory for New York included Jacob Goschinsky, designer, living at 751 Forest Avenue, New York.[79] The 1920 Federal Census for New York listed Jacob Goshin living at 314 South 3rd Street, Brooklyn. His occupation was operator in a manufacturing business. Lena was home with her children Harry and Arnold. Lena's sister Mollie Schuel lived with the family, and she also worked in a factory as an operator.[80] On the 1930 Federal Census Jacob listed his occupation as foreman for a dress factory; his son Harry was a shipping clerk for a dress factory.[81] Cousin Arthur recalled that his grandfather Jacob was employed as a pattern cutter at Cohen and Goshin, a well-regarded dress manufacturer.

I researched the name George Goshinsky aka Goshin (1885–1963) as a possible Goshin relative. Witnesses for his naturalization petition were Morris Goshin

Jacob Goschinsky and Lena Schuel Marriage Record

and Max Goshin.[82] George Goshin was buried at Mount Zion Cemetery, Queens, New York in the Rotmistroker Plot.[83] Jacob Goshin died 11 January 1978 at Brooklyn, New York.[84] He was interred at Beth David Cemetery, Elmont, New York; section G, block 5, row N, grave 7 in the section Rotmistrover Benevolent Society. This was one of many *landsmanshaften* organizations formed by immigrants who came from similar regions or towns.[85]

Harry's mother Lena Schuel, immigrated at age 16 from Libau, Russia. She was a passenger on the ship *RMS Saxonia* to the United States that departed 15 May 1906 from Liverpool, England and arrived at Boston, Massachusetts 24 May 1906. Her last residence was Libau; her destination was New York City. Her occupation was milliner. Her destination was to her uncle at 670 Gates Avenue, New York City.[86]

The following information was taken from the Marriage Certificate for Jacob Goschinsky and Lena Schuel. After they first applied for a marriage license 14 December 1910, they were married at Manhattan, New York 24 December 1910.[87] Jacob gave his age as 20, his occupation as operator (sewing machine), his birthplace as Kiev, Russia. His father was Meyer Aaron Goschinsky and his mother was Chava Melnick. His address was 199 East 2nd Street, Manhattan. Lena Schuel was living at 103 Essex Street, Manhattan. Her age was 21, her birthplace was Libau, Russia (now in Latvia). Her parents were Hirsch Schuel and Hinde aka Helen Meyeroff (surname was difficult to read).

According to Cousin Arthur, the two brothers Jacob and Max Goschinsky left Rotmistrovka and made their way to Libau, a port city in what is now Latvia. While in Libau, Jacob and Max found a kosher boarding house managed by a woman named Hinde Schuel. Hinde aka Helen and her six children all worked at the boarding house, including Arthur's grandmother Lena and her younger sister Mollie. Lena Schuel died 31 October 1951 at New York.[88] She was buried with her husband Jacob Goshin at Beth David Cemetery, Elmont, New York in the Rotmistrover section. For those who wish to know more about Jewish life in Libau, Latvia I recommend reading a yizkor book written by those who lived and worked there: www.jewishgen.org/yizkor/libau/lib001-html.

Max Goshin and Mollie Schuel

Mollie Schuel, age 16, journeyed from Libau to Liverpool, UK after her older sister Lena. She secured passage on the *S.S. Caronia* that departed from Liverpool 7 November 1908 and arrived at New York 15 November 1908. Her name on the ship manifest was Itte Male Schuel, female, occupation servant. Her nearest relative in Libau was her mother Hinde Schuel. Her birth year was 1892.[89] Mollie was temporarily held as an alien for special inquiry before her admission into the United States. By 1915 Mollie Schuel lived in the Bronx, New York with her sister Lena, brother-in-law Jacob Goshchinsky, Lena and Jacob's son Harry, Jacob's brother Max Goshchinsky and Beckie Schuel.[90]

Max Goshin, Jacob Goshin's younger brother, was born 9 February 1895 at Rotmistrovka, Kiev District, Ukraine. According to both the New York State Census 1925 and the New York Voter List 1924, Max and his family lived in Brooklyn. The 1925 New York State Census included information that Max, Mollie and their daughter Evelyn lived with Mollie's mother Helen aka Hinde Schuel, and her brothers Abraham, Samuel and Isidore Schuel.[91] Max married Lena's younger sister Mollie Schuel 25 December 1922 at Brooklyn, New York.[92] His occupation on his marriage certificate was insurance. Max died 8 November 1958 at Queens County, New York.[93] Sometime after Max died, Mollie moved from New York to Waterbury, Connecticut where she died 23 March 1980 at Torrington, Connecticut.[94] Max and Mollie Goshin had two children: Evelyn Goshin (1923–2013) and Herbert Goshin (1926–2009). Neither Evelyn nor Herbert had issue. On a personal note, Herbert Goshin became a good friend to my family, always friendly, kind, and helpful to my parents.

Sylvia Weiss

Early Years

My mother Sylvia Weiss was born 4 June 1914 at Brooklyn, New York.[95] She was the second of three daughters born to Minnie and Oscar Weiss. Mom's Yiddish name was Soske, for the Hebrew name Sore or Sarah.[96] Her name Sylvia was a kinnui for Soske. I will refer to her as "Mom" in this biography. After years of genealogical research, I discovered that Mom was named after her paternal great-grandmother Soske Weiss née Borgman. (*See Descendants of Yehuda Leib Weiss Family Tree*) Mom's early childhood years were in Williamsburg, Brooklyn. Mom and her sisters Marion and Martha were cared for by a nanny while their parents Minnie and Oscar worked at their umbrella manufacturing business in Manhattan.

Mom delighted in telling me stories about her youth growing up in Williamsburg, Brooklyn and how she was a tomboy, played baseball with boys in her neighborhood and climbed trees. Even as an adult she loved to watch baseball games on television and was an ardent Brooklyn Dodgers fan when the team was based in New York. She loved telling stories of mischievous things she did while growing up, like climbing out her window to meet her friends at night while her parents thought she was fast asleep, teasing her older sister Marion for studying so much while she (Sylvia) had fun with her friends. Mom often told me that she looked forward to summer camp as that was the highlight of her childhood. My grandparents Minnie and Oscar needed to work in their umbrella business all year and so the summers were the time to send the children to a Jewish camp in the country, where they could enjoy themselves, eat Kosher food and where their parents did not have to worry about them staying at home unsupervised in a hot apartment.

Mom had a good ear and love of music. She was given violin lessons and was a violinist for her high school orchestra. She went to New Utrecht High School in Bensonhurst, Brooklyn, New York and graduated in 1932. Her favorite subjects were biology as well as music.[97] She told me about her goal to go to college to study microbiology. Mom did not continue playing her violin as an adult however she always loved listening to show music.

Mom loved to cook, and she did most of the cooking for her working parents. She made sure they had a hot dinner when they came home from work. She would make delicious foods, such as pot roast or brisket with potatoes, followed by a homemade dessert such as noodle pudding. She made mouth-watering dishes using whatever foodstuffs she could find in the kitchen, and she never measured ingredients.

These are some of my personal memories of Mom. She always liked to wear perfume, especially the brand 4711. She loved wearing both costume and fine jewelry. She enjoyed wearing feminine clothing with ruffles, chiffon, soft fabrics, and vibrant colors. Mom had a soprano pitch to her voice; she was often jolly and loved to laugh. She was often vivacious and enjoyed dancing. I recall how she would organize people in a conga line. She would grab pots and pans and bang them together to celebrate New Year's Eve. She was admired for her very pretty face with her beautiful sparkling blue eyes, rosy cheeks, a full "zaftig" figure, and her curvaceous legs. She loved to wear high heels and nylon stockings. As she grew older her hair was a lovely dyed auburn color "Moon Glow" by Clairol. Her skin was smooth with virtually no wrinkles on her face even in her advanced years; she always appeared much younger. She only wore eyeglasses for reading in her senior years. Her hearing remained intact. She was intelligent and her mind was always sharp.

Mom's speech was colorful and peppered with expressions that Leo Rosten categorized in his book as Yinglish; that is, Yiddish words and phrases that were incorporated or used with our English language. Mom could not read or write Yiddish or Hebrew; however, she grew up hearing Yiddish spoken by her parents and so she often spoke this form of Yinglish, causing myself and my brother David to smile and laugh at her peculiar speech that endeared her to us. I can recall her use of certain Yinglish words and phrases and I will add explanation for the meaning of those words from Leo Rosten.[98] Mom used such words as *farpatshket* that Mom pronounced *farpushket* (to be overly ornate); *feh* (disgust, disapproval); *eat a little something* (never a little bit); *fartumelt* (dizzy, confused); *hoch a tchynik* (to talk a great deal, talking nonsense); *bite your tongue* (say no more); *bubbe-mayse* (an old wives tale); *farmisht* (confused); *tchotchke* (a toy or a trinket); *eppes* (something, somewhat, a bit), *live a little* (don't be a puritan or a sad sack or a wet blanket); *gonif* (a thief, a crook or a mischievous bright child); *kineahora* (a magical phrase to ward off the evil eye usually to protect a child or loved one); *knaydlach* (matzo ball dumpling in soup); *pisher* (a young squirt, a bed-wetter, a nobody); *plotz* (to burst, to explode); *schnaps* (brandy or any intoxicating spirit); *shnorrer* (a cheapskate, a beggar); *macher* (a big wheel, someone active in an organization); *balebosteh* (a conscientious and immaculate housewife-cook-laundress-cleaner); *bupkes* (an outrageously inadequate price or proposal, bordering on nothing), *mensh* (a male with admirable character), *a.k.* for *alter kocker* (a crotchety, ineffectual old man); *zaftig* (plump, buxom); *shikker* (drunk).

Mom was age fifteen when the stock market crashed in October 1929 that began a dreadful economic period called the Great Depression (1929–1939) in North America, Europe, and virtually all industrialized areas. The year she graduated New Utrecht High School was 1932 and by then one out of every four U.S. workers was unemployed. The peak of unemployment reached 22% during the mid-1930s. It was an extremely hard time to have gone through, where once there was plenty of money and jobs to sudden massive unemployment and poverty. Mom had to put aside her dreams of college when her parents asked Mom to help them in their umbrella business as their bookkeeper.

Mom continued to work at the umbrella business as a dutiful daughter all through the Great Depression and then into the war years. She was envious of her older sister Marion who went to college. During the Great Depression, people were desperately trying to support themselves by selling apples in the street and her father Oscar Weiss also sold umbrellas wherever he could. Mom's psychology was affected by her life in the Great Depression. All through her adult life she emphasized how one needed to save and not squander money. She saved used envelopes as drawing paper for me. She felt that buying toys was too extravagant. She always shopped at discount stores and tried to get the lowest prices for food and clothing items.

Young Adulthood

By the 1930 Federal Census, Mom with her parents and sisters were living on 84th Street, Bensonhurst, Brooklyn. After Mom's high school graduation, she had a boyfriend, Louis Cowan, who wanted to become a medical doctor. They were dating for a year and then became engaged, however Mr. Cowan's mother felt that Mom was not good enough for her son and she discouraged them from getting married. Louis was drafted in the Army, and he died during WWII. When his mother learned of his death, she knocked at the door of the Weiss household and blamed Mom for "killing" her son because they did not get married. She thought that if they were married, he may not have been in combat. When her

Mom dressed up

father Oscar Weiss heard Mrs. Cowan say those hurtful words, he shouted that she should immediately leave and never come back. Mom was quite distraught about the death of her fiancé; Aunt Martha recalled that Mom never forgot that tragedy.

My grandparents decided to treat Mom and her sister Martha to a cruise in 1939, on the ship *S.S. Volendam* operated by Holland American Line to Cuba and the Bahamas. In those days Cuba was wide open for American tourists and catered to gambling. Mom told me about her experiences, how she was personally escorted by a handsome Cuban chief of police to the nightclub and casino life in Cuba. Mom was impressed by the wealth displayed by the upper-class Cubans and told me how the Cuban women wore furs and diamonds, how they danced to romantic Latin music and how the wealthy Cubans had servants at their beck and call. Mom's trip occurred during the time that Cuba was ruled by the dictator Fulgencio Batista and decades before the revolutionary takeover 1959 by Fidel Castro.

Early War Years

Mom was beautiful, intelligent, and vivacious, frequently dated however no relationship lasted, especially since so many men entered the armed forces as the war went on. By the 1940 Federal Census, Oscar and Minnie Weiss and Mom were living at 71 Ocean Parkway, Brooklyn, New York. This building was new when they moved in as it was built 1936. They probably moved in sometime between 1936 and 1940. The neighborhood is now called the Windsor Terrace section of Brooklyn and the building later became a cooperative.

Following the attack by Japan on Pearl Harbor, Hawaii 7 December 1941, the United States declared war against Japan and the Axis Powers. Thus, the United States officially entered WWII and joined the Allied Forces. Many doctors and nurses were needed and drafted for medical service in the armed forces. The result was an acute shortage of medical staff for stateside hospitals. Mom participated in a special training to become a Nurse's Aide. She was among 607 women who graduated as Nurse's Aides in a ceremony held at Erasmus Hall High School, Brooklyn, New York September 1942.[99] Rather than continue a nursing career, she remained with her elderly parents at their umbrella factory as their bookkeeper.

How Mom met Dad

During the war, Mom decided to volunteer at a USO at Temple Emanuel in New York City. The USO was organized by President Franklin D. Roosevelt in 1941 as an organization to provide soldiers with social support. She met her future husband, my father Frank Gerber, a soldier, during 1942 while he was stationed in the New York City area and on

Mom at Oscar Weiss Umbrella Factory

leave. Mom told me that Dad was an expert ping pong player and he purposely lost games to Mom.

Dad and Mom kept up correspondence, even while he was sent for army training at boot camp. They fell in love; soon Dad proposed marriage to Mom, she accepted, and they began their lifetime love affair. They applied for a marriage license from the New York State Department of Health 22 January 1943. Their marriage certificate recorded they were married 24 January 1943, in the presence of their relatives, at Aits Chaiyim Tree of Life Synagogue on 881 Eastern Parkway, Brooklyn, New York by Rabbi Sigmund J. Rome.[100] Dad wore his Army uniform at their wedding.

Mom met Dad's family in Portland, Maine either before they were married or soon after and her impression of the Gerber family was positive, however Portland was strictly small town and provincial. She thought the party line telephone system in Portland was hilarious because people could listen in to phone con-

Mom and Martha on the Volendam

Standing: Oscar and Minnie, Seated: Sylvia and Martha

versations and thus gossip was rampant. Mom told Dad that she was willing to make their home kosher if he wanted, as she knew he was raised as an orthodox Jew, but Dad did not care either way, so they were never a strictly kosher home but more kosher style. Mom purchased kosher meat and there was absolutely no pork products or shellfish of any kind in our home. She kept two sets of dishes as there was a set used only for Passover. Mom and Dad raised us (myself and my brother David) in Conservative Judaism, and we belonged to a Conservative synagogue at Bellerose, Queens, New York.

Children

Mom became pregnant with me very soon after she and Dad were married to the point that everyone was counting the months to see if I was truly "legitimate". I was born 9 months and six days after their marriage, whew! Dad was sent to Fort Bragg at North Carolina for boot camp soon after their marriage and Mom decided to join him there as an army wife even though she was pregnant. Her memories were not flattering to the south, as she said there was much prej-

udice against northerners and racial discrimination was ubiquitous. There were bathrooms and drinking fountains marked "colored" and "white." Mom being very pregnant, slipped and fell in mud in a town in North Carolina and she said no one would help her get up, as the black people did not want to be seen touching a white woman and the southern whites did not want to help a northerner. Mom returned to Brooklyn, New York where she lived with her parents while Dad was away fighting in Europe.

Life Challenges and Changes

Mom helped care for her beloved father Oscar, who was dying of

Mom holding Judy on a bench

prostate cancer. Mom was close to her father and felt that she was the "apple of his eye." During the time Grandpa Oscar was ill and dying, she helped her father while also tending to my care as a baby. The war years must have been terrible for Mom, as a new mother with a baby, living with her anxious mother and ill father, separated from her beloved husband Frank.

She never knew if she would receive a telegram with bad news. The war was constantly reported on the radio and in the newspapers. Mom did not know where Dad was or if he was still alive or in what condition. They corresponded with each other during the war and Mom used to tell me how Dad's words were so loving and hopeful, however, their letters did not survive except for one post-card from England.

Mom and Dad married

Meanwhile, Dad was away fighting as a soldier in the war until 8 October 1945. He first met me when I was age two years. After the war, when Dad finally came home, Mom told me how he had to have lice picked off him and how exhausted he was. She told me his personality changed after the war, that prior to the war he was gregarious and fun loving. After the war, she noticed that he became introverted and anti-social. Dad may have suffered psychologically during post-war years however there was no understanding or mention of PTSD (post-traumatic stress disorder) or even "battle fatigue." Mom still worked in the umbrella business with her mother after the death of her father and asked Dad to work there as well. Dad did not enjoy the factory work involved in manufacturing umbrellas. He then took a job as a bill collector for magazine subscriptions in a tough Brooklyn neighborhood. Dad seemed unable to anchor himself to any career avenue except to know that he wanted to be self-employed.

Mom and Dad moved to a new housing project at Canarsie, Brooklyn that was a complex of quonset huts built on drained swamps for veterans and their families after the war ended. The quonset huts were aptly named Veteran's Colony and they were erected September 1946. Our address there was 287A 19[101] Lane, Canarsie.[101] The quonset huts were relatively primitive, with coal outside that had to be carried back inside for fuel, with mainly cold water, with huge rats running around and occasionally biting babies. I remember how the veterans shot the rats with guns they brought back from the war. People stayed there because the rent was very affordable for the ex-soldiers. Mom adapted to life there and as she was friendly, made many friends and pushed Dad to socialize with neighbors which he reluctantly did. Mom became pregnant and she delivered a baby boy 16 September 1949. My brother was named David, after Dad's recently deceased father David Gerber.

Mom and Dad wedding, 1943

באחד בשבת בשמנה עשר יום לחדש שבט שנת חמשת אלפים ושבע מאות ושלש
לבריאת עולם למנין שאנו מונין כאן בעיר ברוקלין במדינה אמעריקא הצפונית איך החתן
אפרים בן ר' דוד המכונה נערבער אמר לה להדא בתולתא סאסיא
בת ר' אשר המכונה ווים הוי לי לאנתו כדת משה וישראל ואנא אפלח ואוקיר ואיזון
ואפרנם יתיכי ליכי כהלכות גוברין יהודאין דפלחין ומוקרין וזנין ומפרנסין לנשיהון בקושטא ויהיבנא ליכי מוהר
בתוליכי כסף זוזי מאתן דחזו ליכי מדאוריתא בתולתא דא והוית ליה לאנתו ודין נדוניא דהנעלת ליה מבי
אבוה בין בכסף בין בזהב בין בתכשיטין בנאי דלבושא בשימושי דירה ובשימושי דערסא הכל קבל עליו
אפרים חתן דנן במאה זקוקים כסף צרוף וצבי אפרים חתן דנן והוסיף לה מן דיליה עוד
מאה זקוקים כסף צרוף אחרים כנגדן סך הכל מאתים זקוקים כסף צרוף וכך אמר אפרים חתן דנן
אחריות שטר כתובתא דא ותוספתא דא קבלית עלי ועל ירתי בתראי להתפרע מן כל שפר ארג נכסין
וקנינין דאית לי תחות כל שמיא דקנאי ודעתיד אנא למקנא נכסין דאית אחריות ודלית להון אחריות כלהון יהון
אחראין וערבאין. לפורעי מנהון שטר כתובתא דא ותוספתא דא נדוניא דא ואחריות וחומר שטר כתובתא דא נדוניא דא ותוספתא דין נדוניא דא קבל עליו אפרים
ובמותי מן יומא דנן ולעלם ואחריות שטר כתובתא דא דנן כחומר כל שטרי כתובות ותוספתות דנהגין בבנת ישראל העשויין כתקון חכמינו זכרונם לברכה דלא
כאסמכתא ודלא כטופסי דשטרי וקנינא מן אפרים בן דוד חתן דנן לפרת סאסיא בת ר' אשר בתולתא דא על כל מה דכתוב ומפורש
לעיל במנא דכשר למקנא ביה והכל שריר וקים

This Certificate Witnesseth that

On the **FIRST** day of the week, the **EIGHTEENTH** day of the month **SHEVAT** in the year 57**03**, corresponding to the **TWENTY-FOURTH** of **JANUARY** 19**43**, the holy Covenant of Marriage was entered into at **AITS CHAIYIM - TREE OF LIFE TEMPLE, BROOKLYN, NEW YORK,** between the Bridegroom **FRANK GERBER**, and his Bride **SYLVIA WEISS**

The said Bridegroom made the following declaration to his Bride:

"Be thou my wife according to the law of Moses and Israel. I faithfully promise that I will be a true husband unto thee. I will honor and cherish thee, protect and support thee, and provide all that is necessary for thy sustenance, even as it becometh a Jewish husband to do. I also take upon myself all such further obligations for thy maintenance as are prescribed by our religious statute."

And the said Bride has plighted her troth unto him, in affection and sincerity, and has thus taken upon herself the fulfillment of all the duties incumbent upon a Jewish wife.

This Covenant of Marriage was duly executed and witnessed this day, according to the customs of Israel.

SIGMUND J. ROME, Rabbi

Bride

Witness

Bridegroom

Witness

Sylvia and Frank Gerber, Hebrew marriage certificate

We continued to live at the quonset huts until 1953, when we moved to Glen Oaks Village, Queens, which was a step up for our family.[102] Glen Oaks is middle-class and is a large apartment complex adjoining neighborhoods such as Little Neck, Bellerose, and Floral Park in Queens County, New York. We lived there in a garden apartment, on the second floor at 74–07 255 St., Bellerose, Queens. Dad obtained a job as a circulation manager for the *Long Island Press* newspaper that gave him a measure of self-employment and independence. My brother David and I became latch key children as both parents were working full time and were not home until dinnertime. As the big sister I had the responsibility to take care of David after school, to buy groceries, cook meals, clean our apartment, and help with the laundry.

Mom worked part-time as a school crossing guard while David attended elementary school.[103] She would be friendly but also firm with the children and pedestrians. A local newspaper article described Mom as not only a school crossing guard but also an "encyclopedia," a nurse, and the "mayor" to nearly all the children that crossed Little Neck Parkway. Mom also worked as a cashier for a local department store called *Mays* when we were living in Glen Oaks. I saw her when she was at work. and she told me what to prepare for dinner and supervise David and help him with his homework.

We lived at Glen Oaks when Grandma Minnie died in 1960. We were all devastated by the illness and death of our beloved mother and grandmother Minnie, who died at Martha and Aaron Cantor's home at Woodmere, Nassau County, New York. After my grandmother's death, we moved from Glen Oaks to 150–67 87th Avenue, Jamaica Hills, Queens, New York. Mom was hired full-time as a bill-

Mom and Dad, Carolina honeymoon

er by Harry Goshin's cousin Evelyn Goshin, who was the main accountant for General Switch Company at Greenpoint, Brooklyn. Mom's world consisted of commuting by subway to work in Brooklyn and then purchase groceries on her way home. She cooked dinner, watched television, or talked on the phone. Mom loved to talk on the telephone for hours with her sisters and friends. She was always a light sleeper and preferred to wake up early, often rousing me with a loud "time to wake up"! Mom had a strong appreciation for sculpture and painting; she especially enjoyed Broadway show music.

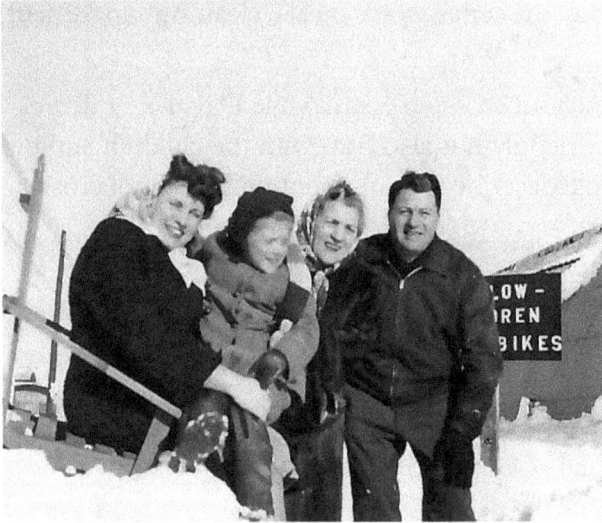

Mom, Judith, Dad and Grandma, 1948

(LtoR) Aaron with Olivia, Marion, Martha, Sylvia, Frank, Judy, and Lois, by a Quonset hut

Family Trauma

A major calamity occurred when my dear brother David tragically died 24 April 1968 in an automobile accident. He was a passenger in the car driven by a class-mate, Stanley Klein, who also died. They were traveling from Florida back to New York for the college spring break. This tragedy turned our lives upside down. My parents were 54 years of age when David died at 18 years of age. We could not stop crying for weeks. We were first in shock, then felt anger and un-relenting grief. Mom was so attached to David; she adored my brother, and he deeply loved his mother.

Months after David's death, my parents discussed how David would have wanted them to be happy, enjoy their lives and not work so hard. My parents made the decision to move from Jamaica Hills to an apartment in midtown Man-hattan. Mom found another job as a biller at Sam Fox Music Publishers in the Broadway area of Manhattan near their apartment where she reconnected with her love of music, especially show music. She enjoyed meeting celebrities at the company who were composers, playwrights, singers, or actors. She was especially impressed by the production of *The Man From La Mancha* and she loved the song *To Dream the Impossible Dream* produced by Sam Fox. Mom either walked or took a bus from their apartment on 310 West 55th Street near Eighth Avenue to Sam Fox Company in the 40s near Broadway. Unfortunately, this move placed a great-er burden for commuting on Dad, as he had to drive from Manhattan to Nassau County, Long Island for his work as a circulation manager for the *Long Island Press*. Dad accepted his longer commute because he wanted Mom to be happy.

Mom and Dad took some cruises in the Caribbean. They went on several tours to Mexico, Portugal, and Morocco. Morocco was by far the most exotic trip; Mom spent endless hours talking about the sights they saw, the rides on top of camels, the snake charmers and the casbah. Despite the travel and entertain-ment, there was always an undercurrent of sorrow for the remainder of her life, as the death of her parents and especially her beloved David rocked her to her foundations. While living in Manhattan, my parents began to earnestly discuss their retirement years. Dad was certain that he wanted to live out his final years in sunny Florida. Mom was less enthused to be there all year but agreed to go to Florida on trips until they finally moved there as permanent residents.

Retirement Years

My parents were still living in Manhattan when at age 63, in 1977, Mom complained of a lump on her neck. She went to see an oncologist at Roosevelt Hospital and was diagnosed with lymphoma, which was Hodgkin's disease. Treatment began early since her lymphoma was still stage 1. Surgery was performed on the lymph nodes in her neck, followed by radiation treatments. After her successful treatments at Roosevelt Hospital, she was motivated to help patients as a hospital volunteer. Mom became a volunteer in the gynecological unit at Roosevelt Hospital and enjoyed her work with the patients.

Mom and Dad decided to move to Florida in 1978 from Manhattan, New York. They were 64 years of age at that time and wanted to live in a warmer climate for their retirement years. They decided to rent a place first to see how they liked living in Florida the year round. They found a lovely large apartment at North Miami Beach, facing the ocean, on a high floor. Mom fell in love with Miami and Florida, and raved about the fantastic weather, sun, beach, warm ocean water, inexpensive lifestyle, and begged us to move there as well. My parents decided to buy a condominium in Florida at Sunrise Lakes Condominiums at Sunrise, Broward County. They purchased a one-bedroom condo, where there was a clubhouse as well as several outdoor pools and a golf course. My parents remained in Florida except for occasional trips north to visit us. They helped me when I delivered our two daughters and when I had a cholecystectomy procedure.

Mom and Dad, 1976

They adored their granddaughters Abby and Jen, counting the days when they could spend time with them either up north or in Florida.

Nearing the End in 1993

Mom had several medical conditions for years including angina pectoris. On 18 February 1993, Mom suddenly suffered a myocardial infarction. She was taken by ambulance to Florida Medical Center Hospital in Lauderdale Lakes, Florida where she underwent a five-vessel coronary artery by-pass graft. The operation took many hours. Her exhausted cardiac surgeon, Dr. Warren Sturman, told Dad and I that at one point he thought he lost her. After she survived that harrowing surgery, I was surprised to hear Mom say that she wished she had died on the operating table as she was in such pain. Her surgeon told me that severe depression often accompanied this surgery. She was in the hospital for six weeks because of complications and needed an intra-aortic balloon pump. She also had congestive heart failure and COPD (chronic obstructive pulmonary disease). After Mom left the hospital, she complained of constant pain in her right leg due to severe peripheral neuropathy. She became permanently non-ambulatory and wheelchair bound. Her doctor recommended Sunrise Rehabilitation Hospital, Sunrise, Florida. Although she had physical therapy, rehabilitation did not make any difference and she remained non-ambulatory and needed to be in a wheelchair.

When she was discharged from the rehabilitation hospital, Dad did his best to take care of her. She was being treated for her various medical problems when Dad fell to the floor in extreme pain. He was suddenly stricken with an enlarged aneurysm on his aorta and was taken by ambulance to Broward Community Hospital. I left my husband Mike in charge of our children in New Hampshire as both parents in Florida simultaneously had serious medical illnesses with no one to help them. I became the primary caregiver for Mom assisting her with everything. I drove her to visit Dad while he underwent cardiac surgery and further care at Florida hospitals. I supervised nursing aides for my mother while at her home but ended up firing them for being careless or irresponsible. I became her only caregiver and I also watched over my father who became extremely ill not only with the ruptured aneurysm but also with sepsis. The autumn of 1993 saw enormous changes happening for my parents as their proverbial roof fell in.

Mom and Dad on boat

I closed out my parent's condo in Sunrise Lakes, packed up only what Mom really wanted to take with her, sold off her furniture, and went with her to close her bank accounts and helped arrange for the sale of their condo. I took her to live with us in New Hampshire. We had Dad flown by a private medical transport airplane with a nurse and respiratory therapist to Whittier Hospital, a special rehabilitation hospital at Methuen, Massachusetts as that was the nearest rehabilitation hospital to our home at Bedford, New Hampshire. It was also the only hospital in the area that would admit Dad in his condition as a chronic ventilator patient. My husband Mike and I drove Mom with her wheelchair and with our children to visit with Dad in the hospital. Mom was evaluated by a rehabilitation doctor in Manchester, New Hampshire who said she was at a nursing home level of care. She remained at a wheelchair level of mobility and needed full assistance with dressing and bathing. Mom needed home care and medical supervision, however she made it clear that she did not want to be placed in a nursing home.

We set up the den in our house on the first floor with a hospital bed, a commode, bathing accessories and a television set. Mike built a wheelchair ramp from our garage to the house. I learned to do most of her care for bathing and dressing, with occasional use of nursing aides. A physical therapist came to the house to give her simple physical exercises. While Dad was in the rehabilitation hospital, I encouraged Mom to attend Easter Seals Senior Day Program three days a week for socialization; a special van came to transport her with her wheelchair to and from the program. Mom tolerated the day program for a few months but made it clear that she preferred to remain at our home. Aunt Martha made a special visit from California to visit Mom while she was so ill. She tried her best to cheer up Mom and gave her exercises to motivate her to walk. After several days of trying without success, Aunt Martha returned to her home in California.

Death

After Dad's death on 5 October 1993 Mom became severely depressed; she stated that she lost her "best friend" and despite living with us, she needed to be hospitalized at the Elliot Hospital psychiatric geriatric unit for severe depression.[104] Mom was admitted on 5 January 1994 and was discharged 2 Feb 1994. Her principal diagnosis was Major Depression, severe, without psychotic features. Her secondary diagnosis was unresolved grief and many diagnoses of a medical nature. Despite our attentions, counseling and medications, Mom no longer wished to live; she refused to eat anything or take her medications. With Dad gone, she felt that she wanted to die and join him and her loved ones who had died before;

she told me she had visions of her loved ones waiting for her. The day before she died, Mom became delirious, and her skin and eyes turned a yellow coloration that was jaundice. I called her psychiatrist who told me to immediately call an ambulance to take her to Catholic Medical Center as that was the closest hospital.

Catholic Medical Center assessed her condition as terminal with all her systems failing. Surgery was ruled out. Mom previously signed a living will and made it clear that she did not want to be kept alive by machines or by heroic means. I was asked by the staff if I wanted her hooked to machines to be kept alive or would I want her to die a natural death. I chose to allow her to go naturally. She never woke from her comatose state. Mom died 28 September 1994 at 80 years of age.[105] The death certificate stated that she died of acute respiratory distress syndrome and acute cholecystitis, however I feel that she also died of a broken heart because her beloved husband of 50 years previously died a year ago and she did not care to continue life without him by her side.

Her funeral was held at Schwartz Brothers, Jeffer Memorial Chapel, Forest Hills, New York. She was buried at Mt. Neboh Cemetery at Glendale, Queens, New York, on 2 October 1994 next to Dad in the Geiger-Weiss burial plot. This burial plot also holds the remains of my brother David, my grandparents Minnie and Oscar Weiss and my great-uncle Charles Geiger. Mom's obituary was published in the *Bulletin News*, Neighborhood Publications, Inc. 13 October 1994 and by the Union Leader, 30 September 1994, Manchester, New Hampshire. Mom was deeply mourned; I will always treasure her memory and her qualities of love, devotion, sincerity, kindness, support and caring. The Hebrew yahrzeit for my mother Sylvia Gerber is 23 Tishrei. Mom and Dad had two children; Judith, still living (the author of this book) and David z"l (1968–1949). Our daughter Jennifer observed following the death of her grandfather Frank: *"My grandmother was devastated. My grandma and grandpa had been the most loving couple I had ever known. They were loyal to each other and loved each other like an old Romeo and Juliet…she grew weaker and weaker… without her husband, she couldn't get the urge to live."* I delivered a eulogy at my mother's funeral recalling how her love and her unselfish devotion to her family fit with Proverbs:31 *"A woman of valor who can find? For her price is far above rubies…. Her children rise up and call her blessed. Her husband also, and he praiseth her…"*

Sylvia Gerber, matsevah

My Grandparents David and Fannie Gerber

My grandfather David Gerber was born 20 May 1872 at Novo-Pavlovka, Kherson guberniya in the southern Ukraine, formerly part of the Russian Empire. Novo-Pavlovka, also known as Novo -Pavlivka, is approximately 81 miles from Odessa. This was a shtetl with a small Jewish population that was devastated during the 1881 and 1905 pogroms. The Jews who remained there during WWII were subsequently murdered and buried in unmarked mass graves.[106] David Gerber was conscripted to serve in the Russian Army for 25 years even though he was the sole support of his wife and children. A family story was David was in the army band and played the tuba. The Russian Army was anti-Semitic, mistreated Jews and refused to provide them with boots or weapons. The Army ordered Jewish soldiers to obtain guns and boots from dead soldiers. David was sent to Siberia under those harsh conditions. He decided to risk his life when he escaped from the Russian Army to journey to the United States. He wanted to join his older brother Abram Gerber who also escaped from the Russian Army but was shot in his leg that left him with a permanent limp. Abram immigrated to the United States and David learned that his brother settled at Portland, Maine.

David's Journey from Russia

Relatives from my Dad's side, aunt Betty Serota z"l and cousin Bessie Gerber, recalled that after David Gerber escaped from the Russian Army, he walked miles without shoes to a German port city where he was able to find passage to Liverpool, England. He secured passage on the ship *S.S.Dominion* that departed from Liverpool, England 9 February 1905 and arrived at the port of Portland, Maine 20 February 1905.[107] The ship was built 1894 in Belfast by Harland and Wolff and owned by the Dominion Line. It was a steamship with regular service from Liverpool to New England and Canada.[108]

I found his name on the passenger list at the UK National Archives at Kew, England when my husband and I visited England in 2006. My search led me to a puzzle when I discovered that David gave a false name as Solomon Gerber on the ship manifest, a false age of 21 and a false marital status as being single. He went incognito as he was probably terrified that the Russian Army would be able to find him to return him to Russia. Russia was still involved in the Russo-Japanese War during the time of David's escape.[109]

When he arrived at Portland, Maine 20 February 1905 he used the same name Solomon Gerber and gave the following information to the immigration officer;

David Gerber manifest, as Solomon

Fanny Gerber, List of Aliens held for special inquiry, 1906

that he was age 29 (he was age 33), married, a tailor, and his passage was paid by his brother Abram. His destination was to his brother Abram Gerber at Portland, Maine.[110] David joined his brother Abram at 57 Middle Street, Portland, Maine where he learned the junk and scrap metal business. David initially worked as a peddler then he later had his own junk and scrap metal business. He first established residence at Portland then sent for his wife Fannie and their two children Morris and Ida.

Fannie's Journey from Russia

Grandma Fannie Gerber was born 1879 to Efroim Gerber and Chava (Eva). Since Efroim Gerber was David Gerber's brother, David and Fannie were uncle and niece. They were married ca.1896 in Russia. According to Gerber relatives and records, their first three children perished during a fire that may have been set during a riot or pogrom. Fannie journeyed from the Ukraine to Liverpool with her two surviving children, Morris, and Ida. Fannie was accompanied by Golda Gerber née Shochet with her child Etta. Golda was married to David's nephew Fishel Gerber who also immigrated to the United States. It is likely the families travelled by train to Germany and from there took a ship to Liverpool. Researchers found that this was a typical immigrant route from the southern Ukraine to England and then to the United States.

Fannie and Golda secured passage to the United States on the *S.S. Celtic* steam ship that departed from Liverpool, England 19 October 1906 and arrived at Ellis Island, New York 28 October 1906.[111] Fannie and her children were detained on Ellis Island until authorities were able to contact David Gerber in Portland, Maine for his affidavits and proof of their marriage, so that she could be released to his custody.

David Gerber's Naturalization

David Gerber first filed his Declaration of Intention for naturalization on 12 September 1924 with the Clerk of the U.S. District Court, Portland, Maine.[112] David stated that he immigrated to the United States from Liverpool on the *S.S.Dominion;* he was a junk dealer, born in Novo Par(v)lovka, Russia on 20 May 1872. He resided at 99 Monument Street, Portland Maine with his wife Fannie Gerber, also born at Novo Par(v)lovka. He arrived at Portland, Maine on 20 February 1905.

David next filed his Petition for Naturalization 2 July 1928 with the following information. Their nine children were: Maurice (1900–1984), Ida (1902–1988),

No. _____

UNITED STATES OF AMERICA

OATH OF ALLEGIANCE

PETITION FOR NATURALIZATION

To the Honorable the ___U.S. District___ Court of ___Maine District___ at ___Portland, Maine___

The petition of ___DAVID GERBER___ hereby filed, respectfully sho

First. My place of residence is ___99 Monument Street, Portland, Maine___ (Give number, street, city or town, and State.)

Second. My occupation is ___Junk Dealer___

Third. I was born on the ___20th___ day of ___May___, anno Domini 1 ___872___ at ___Novo Parlovka, Russia___

Fourth. I emigrated to the United States from ___Liverpool, England___ on or about the ___1st___ day of ___February___ anno Domini 1 ___905___, and arrived in the United States, at the port of ___Portland, Maine___, on the ___20th___ day of ___November___ anno Domini 1 ___905___, on the vessel ___S. S. "Dominion"___ (If the alien arrived otherwise than by vessel, the character of conveyance or name of transportation company should be given.)

Fifth. I declared my intention to become a citizen of the United States on the ___12th___ day of ___September___, anno Domini 19 at ___Portland, Maine___, in the ___U. S. District___ Court of ___Maine District___

Sixth. I am ___married___. My {wife's} name is ___Fannie (Gerber)___ {she} was born on the ___ day of ___, anno Domini 1 at ___Novo Parlovka, Russia___, and now resides at ___99 Monument St., Portland, Maine___ (Give number, street, city or town, and State.)

I have ___9___ children, and the name, date, and place of birth, and place of residence of each of said children is as follows:
Maurice Gerber, born December 8, 1901, at Russia; resides at New York City
Ida Gerber, born October 20, 1903, at Russia; resides at New York City
Rebecca Gerber, born August 3, 1907, at Portland, Maine; resides at Boston, Mass.
Paul Gerber, born March 10, 1909, at Portland, Maine; resides at Portland, Maine (dead)
Salomis Gerber, born March 16, 1911, at Portland, Maine; resides at Portland, Maine
Bessie Gerber, born January 10, 1913, at Portland, Maine; resides at Portland, Maine
Tiank Gerber, born April 12, 1915, at Portland, Maine; resides at Portland, Maine
Isidore Gerber, born Sept. 17, 1917, at Portland, Maine; resides at Portland, Maine
Shirley Gerber, born July 4, 1919, at Portland, Maine; resides at Portland, Maine

Seventh. I am not a disbeliever in or opposed to organized government or a member of or affiliated with any organization or body of persons teaching disbelief in or opp to organized government. I am not a polygamist nor a believer in the practice of polygamy. I am attached to the principles of the Constitution of the United States, and it i intention to become a citizen of the United States and to renounce absolutely and forever all allegiance and fidelity to any foreign prince, potentate, state, or sovereignty, particularly to ___The State of Russia___ of whom at this time I am a subject, and it is my inter to reside permanently in the United States.

Eighth. I am able to speak the English language.

Ninth. I have resided continuously in the United States of America for the term of five years at least immediately preceding the date of this petition, to wit, since ___20th___ day of ___November___, anno Domini 1 ___905___, and in the State of ___Maine___ continuously next preceding the da this petition, since the ___20th___ day of ___November___, anno Domini 1 ___905___, being a residence within this State of at least one year next preceding the of this petition.

Tenth. I have not heretofore made petition for citizenship to any court. (I made petition for citizenship to the ___ Cou ___ at ___, on the ___ day of ___, anno Domini 1 ___, and said petition was denied by the said Court for the following reasons and causes, to wit ___ and the cause of such denial has since been cured or remo

Attached hereto and made a part of this petition are my declaration of intention to become a citizen of the United States and the certificate from the Department of L together with my affidavit and the affidavits of the two verifying witnesses thereto, required by law. Wherefore your petitioner prays that he may be admitted a citizen of the Un States of America.

David Gerber (Complete and true signature of petitioner.)

Declaration of Intention No. ___7327___ and Certificate of Arrival from Department of Labor filed this ___2nd___ day of ___July___, 19 ___25___

NOTE TO CLERK OF COURT.—If petitioner arrived in the United States ON OR BEFORE JUNE 29, 1906, strike out the words reading "and Certificate of Arrival from Department of Labor."

AFFIDAVITS OF PETITIONER AND WITNESSES

United States of America } ss:
District of Maine }

The aforesaid petitioner being duly sworn, deposes and says that he is the petitioner in the above-entitled proceedings; that he has read the foregoing petition and know contents thereof; that the said petition is signed with his full, true name; that the same is true of his own knowledge, except as to matters therein stated to be alleged upon informa and belief, and that as to those matters he believes it to be true.

David Gerber (Complete and true signature of petitioner.)

___Maurice C Gerber___, occupation ___Insurance___, residing at ___9 North St., Portland, Me.___
and ___Morris Epstein___, occupation ___Barrell Dealer___, residing at ___201 Congress St.,___ " "

each being severally, duly, and respectively sworn, deposes and says that he is a citizen of the United States of America; that he has personally known ___
David Gerber

David Gerber, Naturalization Petition

Rebecca aka Rita (1907–1979), Paul (1909–1928), Salomis aka Sally (1911–1991), Bessie aka Betty (1913–2020), Frank (1914–1993), Isidore aka Herbert (1917–1973), Shirley (1919–2012). Two witnesses filed their affidavits for David Gerber's petition: a nephew Maurice Gerber, in the insurance business and Morris Epstein, Barrell Dealer. David gave his Oath of Allegiance to the United States on 2 October 1928 at the US District Court of Maine District, and he became a naturalized citizen.[113]

David insisted that his sons attend Hebrew School and have their bar mitzvahs. Aunt Betty recalled how David and his brother Abram went to *shul* every Saturday morning. At that time, the Jews in Portland, Maine prayed at the orthodox synagogue Shaarey Tphiloh. David also built a sukkah in his backyard so that everyone could eat outside during Succoth. David enjoyed making his own wine, picking Concord grapes in the fall for the Passover holiday in the spring. He had his children wash and mash up the grapes. He also made his own pickles and cider from apples and enjoyed drinking his schnapps. David made sure that his family all had clothing, enough to eat and a roof over their heads. When he was able, he also provided his family with a telephone and a radio. David meted out harsh physical discipline if any of his children dared to disrespect or challenge their parents. He followed the saying "spare the rod, spoil the child." He was a loving husband and a strict but devoted father.

David Gerber died 11 May 1948 at 99 Monument Street, Portland, Maine. The immediate cause of death was cirrhosis of liver accompanied with a condition of arterial sclerotic heart disease.[114] Fannie died 9 August 1955. Her cause of death was Acute Lymphatic Leukemia. Both were buried side by side at Mt. Sinai Cemetery, Portland, Maine.[115] Fannie's obituary was published in the *Portland Evening Press* 10 Aug 1955. Fannie died at her home 18 North Street, Portland, Maine. She was a member of many Jewish women's organizations in Portland. She was known for her Red Cross volunteer work during WWII. She was survived by her three sons: Maurice, Herbert, and Frank and by her five daughters Ida, Rita, Shirley, Sally and Betty.

Gerber matsevah, Mount Sinai

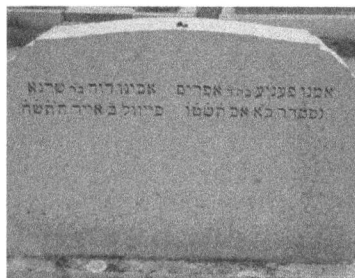

Back of matsevah

Frank Gerber

Early Years

My father Frank Gerber (1914–1993) was the tenth born in a total of twelve children, to parents David and Fannie Gerber. He was born 10 April 1914 at Portland, Maine.[116] Dad was born at home at 455 ½ Fore Street, Portland, Maine. His Hebrew name was Efraim after his maternal grandfather. Dad became a bar mitzvah at age thirteen at the orthodox synagogue Shaarey Tphiloh, as an Orthodox Jew. Dad was raised in a strict manner by his father, who did not tolerate any back talk, cursing or lack of respect. In those days, misbehavior or disrespect was immediately addressed by corporal punishment.

Dad's interests included playing the saxophone well enough to be in the Portland High School band. He told me that during high school he also enjoyed English literature and writing. He had a dream to become a journalist. The description of Dad by his photograph in his high school yearbook *The Totem* read "true as the dial to the sun."

His father, David Gerber, told Dad that after high school graduation, he could continue his studies in college, or continue working in the junk business. When Dad graduated from Portland High School in 1932 it was during the height of the Great Depression. There was massive unemployment in a dreadful economy. Dad needed to help the family, so he decided to put off college and instead he continued working at his father's junk business.

Frank Gerber, birth certificate

War Years

Dad worked for his father's business Gerber and Sons, Portland, Maine after his graduation 1932 from Portland High School until the time he enlisted in the Army on 8 September 1941.[117] He enlisted two months prior to the Japanese attack on Pearl Harbor 7 December 1941 when the United States of America officially declared war and joined the battle against the Axis powers, including Nazi Germany. Dad's civilian occupation on his enlistment papers was as a purchasing agent or buyer, collecting and purchasing resalable waste materials such as metal, rags and paper and operating trucks for 6 years for his father's junk business Gerber and Sons, Portland, Maine. On his Army separation papers dated 8 October 1945, Dad's military specialties were: Basic Training for one month; Light Truck Driver for nine months. As a truck driver he operated a truck to transport military personnel and equipment. He also maintained the vehicles and made minor repairs. When Dad enlisted, he was designated as an Army Bandsman and played the saxophone for one year and three months in the Army Marching Band.[118]

P. H. S. BAND

J. Bennett, A. Briggs, R. Briggs, A. Bowler, V. Bruno, S. Cardilli, T. Cavanaugh, B. Chapman, W. Conley, R. Cousens, E. Cummings, W. Davis, L. Della Valle, J. Doyle, A. Engerowski, C. Farrar, J. Finn, J. Foley, K. Frank, F. Gerber, F. Greenwood, S. Hirshon, W. Holland, H. Ingraham, S. Israelson, R. Lancia, A. Lothrop, H. Marcus, A. Martin, P. Merdek, A. Morris, D. Novick, A. Pacillo, A. Peterson, A. Polito, M. Potter, R. Soule, W. Southard, S. Swartz, H. Thorne, H. Tryon.

Frank Gerber, PHS band 1931

As the war intensified, Dad went from being a musician in the Army Band and was assigned to fight as a soldier in the front lines in England, France, Belgium, Holland, and Germany. Dad was placed in the Third Army under the command of General Patton. He served in Battery C 195th Anti-Aircraft Artillery. He was in the Second Armored Division which was aptly named *Hell on Wheels*.[119] Dad's Honorable Discharge indicated that he participated in the following battles and campaigns: Normandy, the Ardennes, Central Europe, Northern France and in the Rhineland. He was decorated with 7 medals including the European-African-Middle Eastern Service Medal and received another medal for expert rifleman.[120]

Dad fought in the decisive Battle of the Bulge also known as the Ardennes Counter Offensive during the winter of 1944. This battle resulted in 75,000 American casualties and was considered the bloodiest battle for U.S. forces during WWII. Dad served his country honorably and courageously. I honored Dad's wartime service as a soldier by entering his name in the WWII Registry of Remembrances and this was certified on 12 November 2003, as part of the WWII Memorial in Washington, D.C. Also, Dad's name was inscribed on the wall of the WWII History Museum in Wolfeboro, New Hampshire. I

Frank Gerber, June 1932

Dad with soldier WWII

ENLISTED RECORD AND REPORT OF SEPARATION
HONORABLE DISCHARGE

1. LAST NAME - FIRST NAME - MIDDLE INITIAL	2. ARMY SERIAL NO.	3. GRADE	4. ARM OR SERVICE	5. COMPONENT
GERBER FRANK	31 045 155	PVT	CAC (AA)	AUS

6. ORGANIZATION	7. DATE OF SEPARATION	8. PLACE OF SEPARATION
BTRY C 195TH AAA AW BN	8 OCT 45	SEP CTR FT DIX NJ

9. PERMANENT ADDRESS FOR MAILING PURPOSES	10. DATE OF BIRTH	11. PLACE OF BIRTH
71 OCEAN PKWY BKLYN 18 NY	10 APR 14	PORTLAND ME

12. ADDRESS FROM WHICH EMPLOYMENT WILL BE SOUGHT	13. COLOR EYES	14. COLOR HAIR	15. HEIGHT	16. WEIGHT	17. NO. DEPEND.
SEE 9	BROWN	BLACK	5-5½	175 LBS.	2

18. RACE				19. MARITAL STATUS		20. U.S. CITIZEN		21. CIVILIAN OCCUPATION AND NO.
WHITE X	NEGRO	OTHER (specify)	SINGLE	MARRIED X	OTHER (specify)	YES X	NO	BUYER JUNK 1-61.60

MILITARY HISTORY

22. DATE OF INDUCTION	23. DATE OF ENLISTMENT	24. DATE OF ENTRY INTO ACTIVE SERVICE	25. PLACE OF ENTRY INTO SERVICE
8 SEP 41		8 SEP 41	PORTLAND ME

SELECTIVE SERVICE DATA	26. REGISTERED YES X / NO	27. LOCAL S.S. BOARD NO. 1	28. COUNTY AND STATE CUMBERLAND ME	29. HOME ADDRESS AT TIME OF ENTRY INTO SERVICE 99 MONUMENT ST PORTLAND ME

30. MILITARY OCCUPATIONAL SPECIALTY AND NO.	31. MILITARY QUALIFICATION AND DATE (i.e., Infantry, aviation and marksmanship badges, etc.)
TRUCK DRIVER LIGHT 345	M1 MKM 140 10 DEC 43

32. BATTLES AND CAMPAIGNS
ARDENNES, CENTRAL EUROPE, NORMANDY, NORTHERN FRANCE, RHINELAND, GO 33 WD 45 AS AMENDED

33. DECORATIONS AND CITATIONS
EUROPEAN-AFRICAN-MIDDLE EASTERN SERVICE MEDAL

34. WOUNDS RECEIVED IN ACTION
NONE

35.	LATEST IMMUNIZATION DATES				36.	SERVICE OUTSIDE CONTINENTAL U.S. AND RETURN		
SMALLPOX	TYPHOID	TETANUS	OTHER (specify)		DATE OF DEPARTURE	DESTINATION	DATE OF ARRIVAL	
2NOV43	4DEC44	15MAR45	NONE		11 FEB 44	ETO	23 FEB 44	

37.	TOTAL LENGTH OF SERVICE					38. HIGHEST GRADE HELD	23 SEP 45	USA	3 OCT 45
CONTINENTAL SERVICE			FOREIGN SERVICE						
YEARS	MONTHS	DAYS	YEARS	MONTHS	DAYS	PVT			
2	5	8	1	7	23				

39. PRIOR SERVICE	NO FURTHER GRATUITY BENEFIT UNDER TITLE III OF THE SERVICEMEN'S READJUSTMENT ACT OF 1944, AS AMENDED, IS AVAILABLE TO THE PERSON TO WHOM THIS DISCHARGE WAS ISSUED.
NONE	ADMINISTRATOR OF VETERANS AFFAIRS

40. REASON AND AUTHORITY FOR SEPARATION
CONVENIENCE OF THE GOVERNMENT AR 615-365 15 DEC 44 & RR 1-1 DEMOBILIZATION

41. SERVICE SCHOOLS ATTENDED	42. EDUCATION (Years)		
NONE	Grammar 8	High School 4	College 0

PAY DATA

43. LONGEVITY FOR PAY PURPOSES			44. MUSTERING OUT PAY		45. SOLDIER DEPOSIT	46. TRAVEL PAY	47. TOTAL AMOUNT, NAME OF DISBURSING OFFICER
YEARS 4	MONTHS	DAYS	TOTAL $ 300	THIS PAYMENT $ 100	NONE	$ 405	$ 162.95 J HARRIS COL FD

INSURANCE NOTICE

IMPORTANT   IF PREMIUM IS NOT PAID WHEN DUE OR WITHIN THIRTY-ONE DAYS THEREAFTER, INSURANCE WILL LAPSE. MAKE CHECKS OR MONEY ORDERS PAYABLE TO THE TREASURER OF THE U.S. AND FORWARD TO COLLECTIONS SUBDIVISION, VETERANS ADMINISTRATION, WASHINGTON 25, D.C.

48. KIND OF INSURANCE				49. HOW PAID		50. EFFECTIVE DATE OF ALLOTMENT DISCONTINUANCE	51. DATE OF NEXT PREMIUM DUE (One month after 50)	52. PREMIUM DUE EACH MONTH	53. INTENTION OF VETERAN TO		
Nat. Serv. X	U.S. Govt.	None	Allotment	Direct to V.A.			Continue	Continue Only	Discontinue		
X			X	X		30 SEP 45	31 OCT 45	$ 7.10	X		

54. [thumbprint]	55. REMARKS (This space for completion of above items or entry of other items specified in W.D. Directives)
RIGHT THUMB PRINT	LAPEL BUTTON ISSUED 10 DAYS LOST UNDER AW 107 ASR SCORE (2 SEP 45) 104 Recorder's License No. 2227 Issued March 21 1951 Francis J. Sinnott County Clerk

56. SIGNATURE OF PERSON BEING SEPARATED	57. PERSONNEL OFFICER (Type name, grade and organization - signature)
Frank Gerber	J E WHITE JR CAPT AC J E White Jr

WD AGO FORM 53-55
1 November 1944

This form supersedes all previous editions of WD AGO Forms 53 and 55 for enlisted persons entitled to an Honorable Discharge, which will not be used after receipt of this revision.

Frank Gerber, enlisted record

Dad with artillery

Dad in WWII

Dad Fort Hancock, New Jersey 1943

had his name and division inscribed on a paving stone in the veteran's memorial area at the Bedford Village Common, a park in Bedford, New Hampshire. Dad fortunately kept his military papers because a fire in 1973 destroyed most military records held in the National Personnel Records center in St. Louis for the years 1912 to 1959.

Marriage

On one of his leaves, Dad was in New York City, and he went to a USO at Temple Emanuel in Manhattan, where he met Mom. Mom was a volunteer at that USO, to socialize with soldiers and to boost their morale, no doubt also to meet a prospective husband. It must have been love at first sight. Mom was so very pretty and vivacious. She often said how handsome Dad was in uniform. They had a whirlwind courtship because he was scheduled to ship out to the European front. They were married on 24 January 1943, at the Tree of Life Synagogue in Brooklyn, New York, by Rabbi Sigmund Rome in the presence of their family members.[121]

The Newspaper Business

Dad obtained a job as a circulation manager for the *Long Island Press*, a popular local newspaper at that time. He supervised delivery of the newspaper within a certain geographical area in Queens, supervising boys and sometimes girls, to deliver the newspapers. He worked at the newspaper as a district circulation manager for 25 years. He began that job in 1952 when he was 38 years of age until he retired in 1977 at age 63. He won many awards for being a top-notch circulation manager over the years that he worked for the newspaper. He enjoyed his work with other circulation managers and with the children who delivered the newspapers. Perhaps by working as a circulation manager for the newspaper he somehow fulfilled his dream of working for a newspaper, although not as a journalist.

In 1959 Dad was driving with us when he suddenly doubled over in great pain. He drove the car over to the side of the road, got out of the car and fell on the ground writhing in pain. Mom and I flagged down a car and told them we had a medical emergency. An ambulance took my father to the Long Island Jewish Hospital, a very respected and state of the art hospital at that time near our apartment in Glen Oaks. We anxiously waited in the hospital for hours while the surgery proceeded. The surgeon, Dr. Rothenberg, told us that Dad had over 60 gallstones and that many were lodged in his bile duct. The operation became an emergency removal of my father's gallbladder, an operation that took over six hours. Dad thankfully pulled through. He was 45 years of age. Dad spent several weeks in the hospital recuperating and I am certain that Dr. Rothenberg saved his life.

From Glen Oaks, my parents moved to Jamaica Hills in Queens, New York when my brother David began high school at Jamaica High School. I was going to Queens College during the day and would take a bus from our home in Jamaica Hills to Queens College in Flushing, New York. Dad drove to his work as a circulation manager for the *Long Island Press*. He would frequently go to the main building where the *Long Island Press* was printed in Jamaica, to receive the newspapers and then bring them to his office for sorting and inserting advertisements. David and I sometimes went to his office to sort coins and place them in coin bank rolls.

The Unspeakable Tragedy

My brother David was a college student in Florida and accompanied a fellow student as a passenger in his car during the spring break driving from Florida to New York. That evening, 24 April 1968, my parents, and I learned of David's sudden tragic death from an automobile accident where both David and the driver were killed. My parents were totally devastated. Mom was in shock, immobilized and too distraught to do anything. Dad and I needed to go to Florida to identify David's body at the funeral home and arranged to fly his remains back to New York for burial. Dad did not stop crying during the whole trip, on the trip down and on the flight back. I too was devastated and was barely able to focus on what had to be done. Naturally, David's death was so very tragic; my parents and I were in tears for weeks with our grief.

Manhattan

Months after David's death, my parents decided to change their lifestyle and move to Manhattan. They felt that David would have wanted them to enjoy life more fully. They moved to an apartment at 310 West 55th Street in Manhattan, off Eighth Avenue. The neighborhood was near the theatre district, and it contained a mix of people including people in the entertainment industry. Mom often walked to her work as a biller for Sam Fox Music Publishers, which was in the theatre district. Dad had much further to commute, driving from Manhattan to Queens every day and coming home late at night too exhausted to go out. He even fell asleep while tying his shoes. When he came home, he would fall asleep right after dinner. They lived in that apartment building from 1969 to 1978. On the weekends, my parents would take walks in the city including Central Park and Fifth Avenue.

Retirement

When Dad retired in 1977, my parents formed a plan to live out their golden years in Florida. They visited Florida many times and fell in love with that state. Mom was getting treatment for her Hodgkin's disease in Manhattan. After her treatment, they moved permanently to Florida in 1978. They purchased a condominium at Sunrise, Florida. Dad loved living in Florida, especially the warm weather in the winter. He would even tolerate the extreme humidity and heat during the summers. He enjoyed watching television to see how cold it was up north while he was basking in warm weather. Dad appreciated the beautiful tropical vegetation in Florida, the inexpensive lifestyle and having his limited retirement money stretch. Dad also enjoyed living in the predominantly Jewish condominium complex at Sunrise, Florida and he would relate to other Jews especially those from New York. When his sister Betty and brother-in-law Sam Serota moved to Florida close to my parents, they frequently visited with each other.

Memories of Dad

When we were living in the Quonset huts Dad would take delight entertaining us by performing hand stands while riding a bicycle or juggling balls or pulling coins from behind our ears. He told me that as a boy he used to dream of being in a circus. During his adolescence, Dad became adept at playing billiards, snooker, and pool. While in the Army he used his skill to advantage by winning bets. Dad worked as a caddy during high school and enjoyed playing golf as a young man. When he finally retired at age 63 and moved to Florida, I thought that he would pick up golf once again, however he played little golf in Florida. Dad took a part-time job as a park guard to collect entrance fees in a public park and beach. He enjoyed the work as he met many people, and it was relatively stress-free plus gave him something to do with his time. Another pleasure that Dad enjoyed was going to see shows at their condominium complex in Sunrise, Florida. The shows were inexpensive, sometimes featuring well known singers and comedians. He also enjoyed watching television comedy shows such as his favorite *The Honeymooners* with Jackie Gleason. He loved hearing Barbra Streisand and Harry Belafonte sing show music.

When my parents went to the movie theaters, Mom would complain to me that Dad often fell asleep during the movie and that his loud snoring was an embarrassment. She had to constantly nudge him to wake up to stop snoring. Dad did snore loudly and that was due to a broken nose he received from fist fights during his school years in Portland, Maine. He told me about the anti-Semitism of tough Irish youth, who started physical altercations with him because he was a Jew. During one of those fights his nose was broken. This was never treated by surgery.

Dad was humble, philosophical, patient, loyal, stoic, courageous, yet strict with my brother David and I to be respectful and dutiful children. He worshipped Mom, always took her side when she complained about David and I being disrespectful, then Dad punished us. After one of the delicious meals prepared by Mom, he often commented that Mom was a "good looker and a good cooker." He usually remembered Valentine's Day by bringing her a box of chocolate candy. Even though Dad was a man of few words, I could see the deep love he had for her by his adoring facial expression.

A Terminal Illness

During his middle to late seventies, Dad began to develop serious heart conditions. He had several heart attacks, was hospitalized but did not require by-pass surgery. Mom was vigilant about making sure that his diet was fat free and low sodium, however he still loved to eat donuts with coffee. Although Dad smoked cigars for many years, he decided to quit smoking. One day in May 1993 Dad fell to the floor in their condominium in great back pain and was rushed by ambulance to Broward Community Hospital. The medical diagnosis was a large abdominal aortic aneurysm at high risk for rupture. Dad needed a AAA surgical operation to repair the aortic aneurysm before it could burst. If the aneurysm ruptured, then internal bleeding would be life threatening. The larger the aneurysm, the greater the risk of rupture. The operation involved removing the damaged area of the aorta and replacing it with a synthetic tube that would be sewn into place.

Prior to Dad's aneurysm, Mom suffered a myocardial infarction in January 1993. Dad was her caregiver until he became ill. I immediately booked a flight to Florida, as they had no one else to help them and took over both parents' care. The surgeon who operated on my father at Broward Community Hospital told us that the operation was a success, however within days after the operation, Dad developed an internal infection called sepsis or septic shock. This was a bacterial or a fungal infection that infiltrated the site of the operation and relentlessly continued to overwhelm Dad's internal organs. He acquired this infection while in the hospital. The doctors tried every known antibiotic to treat the sepsis without a positive result. Dad's condition grew more serious each day.

Dad waged a courageous battle with death for five months from the time he was operated on in May 1993 to his death 5 October 1993.[122] He remained in the ICU at Broward Community Hospital for weeks and had to have an emergency tracheotomy, then required tubal feeding. He was alert the whole time, except for one instance when he became delirious and hallucinating due to medication. Dad needed to be placed on a ventilator machine as he could not breathe on his own. The hospital staff told me that he could not remain at Broward Community Hospital since he was a chronic rather than an acute care patient so I needed to find another facility that would take him as a chronic care patient on a ventilator.

Ventnor Hospital at Fort Lauderdale agreed to take Dad as a chronic ventilator patient. I had Dad medically transferred to Ventnor. This hospital was depressing, old and clearly a place where chronically ill people on ventilators came before they died. I visited Dad daily and encouraged him to recover. He wanted so much to live, to see his grandchildren Abby and Jenny and meet our dog Billy, he especially wanted to resume his lifestyle with his beloved wife Sylvia. I encouraged his hope for continued life as the alternative was unspeakable. I do not believe that too many men his age in those circumstances would have been so determined to live.

Dad continued to live for five months on ventilators, taking every known antibiotic. Mike and I considered that Dad might possibly survive the infection and so we decided to move both Mom and Dad to where we lived in New Hampshire so that we could see them more often and monitor their treatment from our home. We found out about a medical air flight service, Federal Air Ambulance, complete with a registered nurse and a respiratory therapist, that would be able to provide ambulances and a private airplane to fly Dad from Florida to the Whittier Rehabilitation Hospital at Haverhill, Massachusetts. This hospital agreed to take Dad as a chronic ventilator patient. At that time there was no hospital in New Hampshire that was equipped for this level of care. Whittier was chosen since it was in Haverhill, Massachusetts, only a 45-minute drive from our home.

Whittier Hospital was more cheerful than Ventnor. Dad was placed in a pleasant room with a garden view. Whenever we visited him, he could only talk for a few minutes because he needed to be on the ventilator. We communicated with Dad mainly by his writing on a tablet. After writing questions about the well-being of Mom, myself, Mike and our children Jen and Abby, he then wrote that he always wanted to visit Italy, especially Sicily. He complained of always being hungry as the feeding tube was certainly not even close to eating real food. He said he had a craving for pizza, and it was so sad to know he could not digest real food as his body was still in a struggle with the infection. He required many medical services, including medical doctors specialized in pulmonary and heart disease, also respiratory therapists, nurses, and physical therapists. He wrote "they all say I'm making good progress but I'm still here" and "I hope I can last."

On one of my visits, I saw that he was not in his room. I found out he had a medical crisis and was taken by ambulance to Holy Family Hospital in Haverhill, Massachusetts. I rushed over to that hospital to find out his status. He was in critical condition but was stabilized. I drove home and brought back Mom in her wheelchair, with my family to visit with Dad as I did not know what the ultimate outcome would be. My parents held hands and looked lovingly at each other, assuring one another they would be alright even though they knew that the end was near. Dad was transported back to Whittier and then the awful reality of death came in the form of an urgent telephone call to me on October 5, 1993, to come immediately to Holy Family Hospital as he took a turn for the worse.

I saw his body so still, so tired from his heroic efforts to stay alive. My dear father died 6 October 1993. The immediate cause of death on his death certificate was myocardial infarction. Other conditions contributing to his death were chronic lung disease and respiratory failure. Dad's remains were transported to Goodwin Funeral Home at Manchester, New Hampshire and his funeral was held at the Schwartz Brothers Jeffer Memorial Chapel, Forest Hills, New York. Dad's burial was at Mt. Neboh Cemetery, Glendale, New York where he was laid to rest on 8 October 1993 in the Geiger-Weiss plot next to his beloved son David

Gerber to be joined a year later by his beloved wife Sylvia. His obituary was published 13 October 1993 by Neighborhood Publications, Inc. and by the *Union Leader*, 7 October 1993 Manchester, New Hampshire. The Hebrew yahrzeit for my father, Frank Gerber is 20 Tishrei.

Dad had a kind, loving nature that was sometimes hidden under

Frank Gerber matsevah

a gruff exterior. He fought the battle in WWII with courage and loyalty to his country. He also courageously fought his final battle with death for the last five months of his life during which he was in surgery, in hospitals, on a ventilator, mostly separated from Mom who was also ill and confined to a wheelchair. Dad rarely complained about anything, he was stoic and faced his adversities with courage. He clung to the hope that he would survive until the very end when his body protested and willed him to finally succumb to death. Dad was deeply mourned by all who loved him especially by Mom. We treasured his memory and his deep feelings of love, loyalty, fortitude, and devotion to his family.

David Gerber

Beginnings

My brother David, my only sibling, was the youngest of two children born to Sylvia Weiss and Frank Gerber. He was born 16 September 1949 at Beth-El Hospital, Brooklyn, New York.[123] Beth-El Hospital became Brookdale University Hospital and Medical Center.[124] When David was born, he had "blue baby syndrome." He needed a blood transfusion because he had severe anemia. This transfusion saved his life.[125]

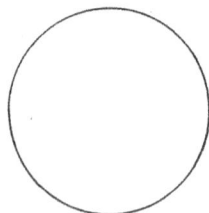

David O. Gerber, birth certificate

David and Judith Quonset Huts

Parents and David

David as Boy Scout

David on tricycle in Quonset Huts

David's Interests

In general, David was healthy; he had flat feet and was left-handed. David was strong, handsome, and tall, with copper color red hair and large blue eyes. He did not have freckles. People commented that he appeared to be Irish in appearance. David had a great sense of humor, was kind, generous, extroverted, popular, fun-loving, and by the time he was in junior high school, he was often sought after by girls. He did not take academics very seriously, often telling me that I was too serious and worked too hard at academic pursuits. He was content with B to C grades. In addition, he was quite athletic. He became an accomplished swimmer and completed the American National Red Cross senior instruction course in lifesaving and water safety course at the YMCA.

David loved playing baseball and he was a star pitcher for a Police Athletic League baseball team. He was fascinated with electronics especially Ham radios. He put together equipment to build his own Ham radio with a goal to become a licensed Ham radio operator. David was especially interested in air travel and told me he had a goal to become a pilot. He learned about all kinds of airplanes and loved to build beautiful model airplanes; I would see them hanging from the ceiling in his bedroom. He became a member of the Civil Air Patrol.

David was also musically inclined. He first learned to play the clarinet then switched to taking music lessons for the trumpet. He had a natural aptitude for music and taught himself to play the organ, piano and guitar. He was so pleased when he could "trill" music on the trumpet. He loved hearing Al Hirt play the trumpet and he admired Louis Armstrong. David was a musician in his Junior High School band and orchestra, also first trumpet for his high school Brooklyn Academy band and orchestra.

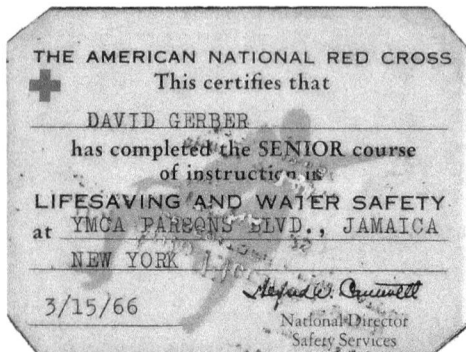

American Red Cross lifesaving course   David Civil Air Patrol

David and Dad, Bar Mitzvah

David cutting challah Bar Mitzvah

Mom and Dad dancing at David's Bar Mitzvah

David HS graduation

David HS graduation portrait

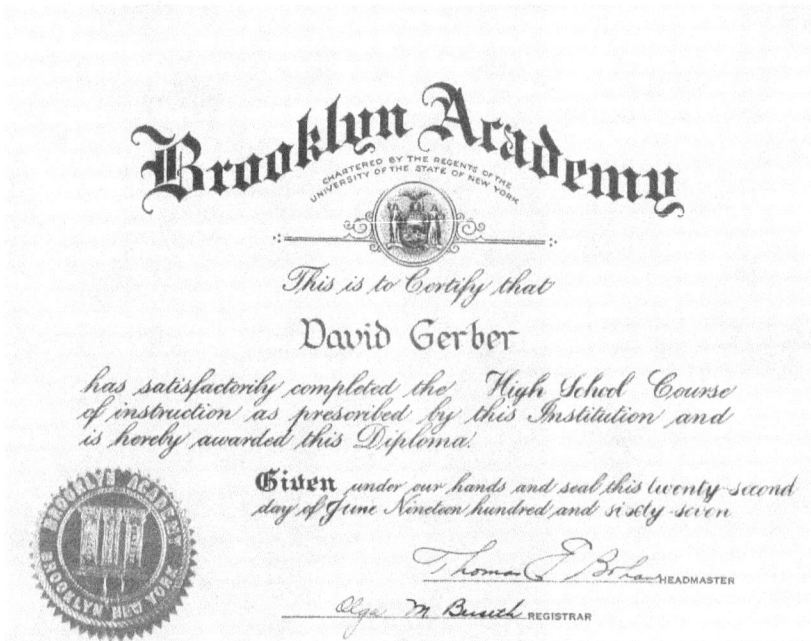

Brooklyn Academy diploma

When I took David with me to hear Vivaldi's *Four Seasons* at Lincoln Center in Manhattan, I could sense his excitement and entrancement with the music. I think that experience opened a new world of classical music for him. He was the organist and trumpeter for his bands such as *Satan and the Forsaken, The Londells, J.Walker and the Pedestrians*. David became the manager of the bands with "gigs" at high school dances and private parties. David inherited his musical talents from his parents as Dad played the saxophone and Mom played the violin.

School Years

David's early childhood years were at 287A 19th Lane, Canarsie, Brooklyn, New York. At that time, we lived at the Quonset Huts, Canarsie, Brooklyn.[126] There was a six-year age difference between us and as the oldest child I was his babysitter with instructions by my parents. When David was four years old, he loved to wear a Davy Crockett hat and play cowboys and Indians, using a cap pistol. He later enjoyed riding a tricycle around our neighborhood at the Quonset Huts.

When David was five years, we moved to Glen Oaks, a middle-class housing complex.[127] The garden apartment buildings were two stories and we lived on the top floor. David started kindergarten, however the very first day of school his teacher called Mom to complain that he blew up a paper bag and popped it during class, causing a loud noise and disrupting the class. David quickly learned to never do that again. David and I would take many long walks, climbing to the top of a hill where we could look out at Glen Oaks and pretend that we were royalty surveying our kingdom. We would play at home, pretending to fly to planets in rocket ships.

David with trumpet

David with guitar

David joined Cub Scouts and Boy Scouts and was an active member, but lost interest as a teenager. While watching television together with our family, David usually positioned himself on the floor by Mom's feet. He idolized Mom and she loved him with all her heart.

It was also in Glen Oaks that my parents joined a conservative synagogue and where David began to attend Hebrew school.[128] David attended faithfully and when he was thirteen years of age, he had his Bar Mitzvah. Dad was very proud of his son David's accomplishment of becoming a Bar Mitzvah perhaps remembering the time he did the same when he lived in Portland, Maine. The religious ceremony at the synagogue was followed by a joyous reception in a restaurant, with music, dancing, a large cake, and of course the candle lighting ceremony. The reception was attended by our relatives, David's friends, and Hebrew school classmates. Everyone was proud of David's accomplishment.

In 1957 Mom wanted David to have a sleep away summer camp experience, but family finances were very tight. There was a department store in Glen Oaks, *Mays*, where Mom worked as a cashier. The Weinstein family owned the department store, and they also owned a Jewish camp, *Camp Crestwood*, at Southington, Connecticut. Mom arranged a deal with the Weinstein family that she and I would manage the snack concession in the camp so that David could attend as a camper without any charge. David was able to have a full summer experience and he especially loved the water sports and canoeing.

In 1963 we moved to Jamaica Hills, Queens, New York into a two-family house that was situated on a hill. Our Chinese landlord, Dr. Tung, a political science professor, and his wife, lived in the apartment on the top floor. The house was near a subway station so that Mom could commute to her work as a biller and Dad, a circulation manager, could drive to Jamaica where he picked up his newspapers at the *Long Island Press* main building. By that time, I was enrolled as an undergraduate at Queens College, Flushing, New York. David went to Jamaica High School however he was coasting along, getting average to below average grades. David had two good friends in that high school, a boy of Italian descent, Johnny, and a boy of Chinese ancestry, Henry. The three young men often socialized with each other and called themselves the Three Musketeers. I can also recall David's austere food preferences, how he would only eat plain spaghetti with no butter or sauce, would only eat salads without any dressing, and liked to eat raw onions. He did not have a sweet tooth and would often forego desserts except for Jell-O. Since he was athletic and active, playing baseball, swimming, riding a bicycle, David certainly did not have a weight issue.

My parents were concerned that David was not achieving his academic potential at Jamaica High School. They decided to send him to a private high school, called the Brooklyn Academy located at downtown Brooklyn, New York. David commuted to the private school by subway. He was enthusiastic about the school and teachers, graduated from Brooklyn Academy with good grades and was bound for college. David preferred to attend a special aeronautics technical school after he graduated from high school; however, my parents wanted David to enter a more "down to earth" field, and so David agreed to matriculate at the Miami Dade Junior College, Miami, Florida to learn hotel business administration. I think that my parents were fearful of David becoming a pilot. After David graduated from Brooklyn Academy, he visited me in Albuquerque, New Mexico when I was in graduate school at the University of New Mexico. He then began college at Miami Dade Junior College in Miami, Florida.

While David was a college student, he sent us letters indicating how homesick he felt. Here is an excerpt from one of the letters that he wrote on 13 February 1968 to Mom and Dad from Florida:

"How about me living with you? I could go to New York City Community College? They have a hotel course there too. I know that I could get in there and it wouldn't be bad living with you and you can keep an eye on me while I go to school. Should I apply?"

Dad, Mom, David, Judith, 1964

David with hotel coworker

Then David added his thoughts about the draft:

"Don't worry about the draft. I am II-S until June '69 and I am sure I will be in a four-year school by then! Meanwhile, a four-year school right now is too expensive. Besides New York Community College is underline free!!"

While at Miami Dade Junior College, David made friends with a classmate Steven Lansky. Steven Lansky had connections with the hotel business and helped David obtain a part-time job at the front desk in the Fontainebleau Hotel at Miami Beach.

David was so impressed as he met many celebrities at the front desk. He wrote:

"I met a lot of stars at Fontainebleau— Frank, Nancy and Tina Sinatra, Will Chamberlain, Jackie Mason, Joi Lansing, George Jessel… last of all (listen to this Dad) Jackie Gleason…I just said hello! I still have time for school. Love, your 'scholar'—David."

SELECTIVE SERVICE SYSTEM

NOTICE OF CLASSIFICATION

This is to certify that

David ___ NMI ___ GERBER

(First name)   (Middle initial)   (Last name)

Selective Service No.

8 | 160 | 49 | 717

is classified in Class ___ II-S

until ___ 9-1968

by Local Board unless otherwise checked below:

☐ by Appeal Board

vote of ___ to ___

☐ by President

NOV 2 4 196

(Date of mailing)

M. H. Gribble

(Member or clerk of local board)

(Registrant's signature)

SSS Form 110 (Rev. 5-25-67)
(Previous printings are obsolete)
(Approval not required)

(Fold along this line)

The law requires you to have this Notice in addition to your Registration Certificate, in your personal possession at all times and to surrender it upon entering active duty in the Armed Forces.

The law requires you to notify your local board in writing within 10 days after it occurs, (1) of every change in your address, physical condition and occupational (including student), marital, family, dependency and military status, and (2) of any other fact which might change your classification.

Any person who alters, forges, knowingly destroys, knowingly mutilates or in any manner changes this certificate or who, for the purpose of false identification or representation, has in his possession a certificate of another or who delivers his certificate to another to be used for such purpose, may be fined not to exceed $10,000 or imprisoned for not more than 5 years, or both.

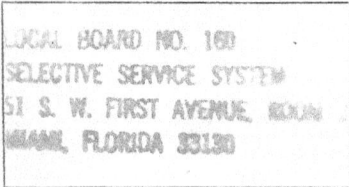

LOCAL BOARD NO. 160
SELECTIVE SERVICE SYSTEM
51 S. W. FIRST AVENUE, ROOM
MIAMI, FLORIDA 33130

(LOCAL BOARD STAMP)
SEE OTHER SIDE

Selective Service classification

David was looking forward to many opportunities and a potentially fulfilling career in hotel management.

A Tragic Sudden Death

On the evening of 24 April 1968, I was relaxing after my work as a teacher in my apartment at Mahopac, New York, watching a television show of Al Jolson singing one of his famous heart-rending songs, *Mamie*. Suddenly a dreadful feeling of doom came over me. Then the phone rang. It was my mother, sobbing hysterically, saying that David was killed that night on his way home for the spring break. He was a passenger in a car driven by a college classmate, Stanley Klein. David was instantly killed when the car ran off the road and crashed into an embankment at Bunnell, Florida off the I-95 highway. Stanley died in the ambulance on the way to the hospital.[129] David was supposed to buy an airplane ticket and fly home during the school spring break. He decided to save the money and instead accompany his classmate Stanley who was driving home to New York.

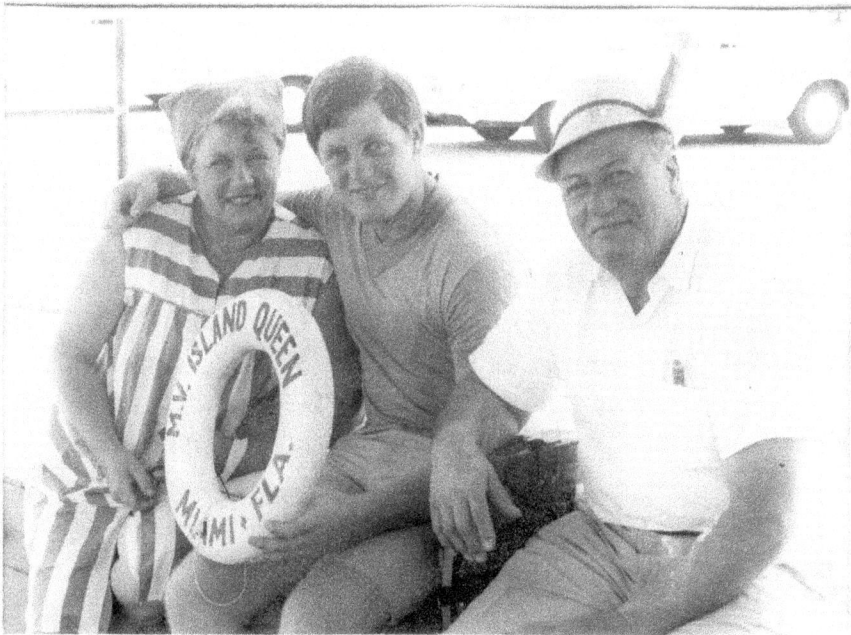

THE ISLAND QUEEN — PIER 5 — MIAMI, FLORIDA

WORLDS FINEST SIGHTSEEING

Mom, David and Dad, Florida 1967

We needed to go to Florida to the funeral home to make an identification of his body and to bring his remains back to New York for burial. Uncle Aaron wrote down the information we needed as to specifics.[130] My mother was in no condition to perform that task. The burden to make identification and transportation plans fell on me and Dad. Our trip to the funeral home was a blur, we made the painful identification, and arranged for David's remains to be transported on the same airplane with us back to New York.[131] Dad and I were in a fog of grief. David's remains were transported to J.S. Garlick Parkside Memorial Chapels Jewish funeral home followed by his burial at Mt. Neboh, in the Geiger-Weiss family plot.[132] David's funeral was attended by many relatives and friends, most of us in shock and grief. His Hebrew yahrzeit is Nisan 26.

Funeral

There were about 85 relatives, friends, and co-workers at my brother David's funeral at Mt. Neboh Cemetery, Queens, New York. People were so shocked and distraught by the news of David's sudden death. We received a tremendous amount of condolence cards and donations to many charities in memory of my brother, as well as sincere and deeply felt personal letters.

David touched all who knew him as a fine, gentle, sincere, sweet young man. Our cousin Mina Keenan wrote:

> *"As I listened to the Rabbi in the funeral parlor, my mind wandered to the last time I saw David. It was just before he graduated high school. He walked with me to the subway station, and we talked about his future and what to expect from life. David was such a good-hearted boy with that winning smile and joy of being alive, I felt as though he considered me a contemporary and not some distant relative to whom he had to pretend a polite regard.*
>
> *When you, Sylvia, told me that he was unmoved by the flattery (which could easily have spoiled another) he received on his part-time job at the luxury hotel (the Fontainebleau), I was not surprised, as I remembered the conversation we had which indicated that he knew the difference between real and phony values.*
>
> *If I were inclined that way, I could easily believe that the heavenly spheres lacked that one bright fair-haired angel with the lovely smile to lead the choir and give it the earthly enthusiasm that only someone in the springtime of life could offer. And that was David."*

Here is the letter written by Mom to the Director of the Brooklyn Academy, Moe Bragin, about David's death:

"With deepest regret I wish to inform you that one of your graduates of 1967 was killed three weeks ago on his way home from college. David Gerber always remembered your school in his conversations to me, his mother. He said that if (it) wasn't for the academy he wouldn't have been the success he was. He took hotel management at the Miami-Dade Junior College. He was very proud that he passed with good grades and was working at the Hotel Fontainebleau and doing very well. They were going to give him an executive job in one year. He had found his goal in life. When he got home he had intentions of visiting your school and telling you all about it.

He was not driving; they had on their seat belts and only went 3 ½ hours out of Miami. They are investigating the accident. The other boy and David were excellent drivers and David's book from the Sportsmanlike Driving was found next to him. You can imagine the shock since he (was) supposed to take the flight Monday night and we were to meet him at Newark Airport. He was a good-natured kid and his friend was driving alone and so changed his mind the last minute. We are all grief stricken of this horrible tragedy. We can hardly believe it ourselves. David was killed in one second, the other boy on the way to the hospital. I know that you will remember him, and he was very happy that your school gave him the chance to make good."

David was so full of life and love, always enthusiastic about his many interests and accomplishments. He completed a senior instructor lifesaving course at the YMCA, joined the Civil Air Patrol, explored his considerable musical abilities, and was interested in Ham radios. He became interested in his emerging career path for hotel management and continued to be modest, courteous, and caring. David especially loved us and we returned our love for him. His young life was so full of promise then was suddenly cut short. The shock and sorrow of losing my beloved brother, my only sibling, who was eighteen years of age at the time of his death, has always been with me and will never disappear.

David Gerber matsevah

Martha Weiss

Beginnings

Martha Cantor née Weiss (1918–2005) was the youngest of three daughters born 28 July 1918 at New York to Minnie Geiger and Oscar Weiss. My mother and her sister Marion doted on Martha as their "kid" sister. Martha would tag along with them wherever they went as children. Aunt Martha recalled that the Weiss family first lived in the back of their store at Manhattan, the family then moved to Brooklyn when Martha was five years of age. They lived at 134 South 9th Street in the Williamsburg section of Brooklyn. The children went to P.S.16 in Williamsburg. Afterwards, they moved to 84th Street in Bensonhurst, then to 7913 Bay Parkway, all in Brooklyn. They acquired a housekeeper who Martha called a "greener kezzina" who was a person just off the boat to work as a housekeeper and a nanny while Oscar and Minnie worked.

I was fortunate to have video-taped Martha during an interview 12 September 2005 while she was visiting her nephew Arthur at New York. She recalled many family details and gave much information. After her visit to New York, Martha flew back to California. She then went on a trip to Sedona, Arizona where she suddenly died 22 September 2005.

Martha recalled hearing from her mother Minnie that her grandfather Aron Geiger owned a tavern and an inn in the "old country" with lawn bowling. Well-to-do travelers would stay at their inn. I have not been able to confirm this information. Martha remembered her father Oscar pulling his three daughters on a sled then taking them to a store for hot cocoa. Oscar enjoyed taking his daughters on a walk across the Williamsburg Bridge and he would buy them hot sweet potatoes wrapped in newspapers to warm their hands. During the summers Oscar and Minnie rented a bungalow at Far

(LtoR) Sylvia, Martha, Marion, ca. 1944

Rockaway beach; Oscar would visit them every night when he was finished with his work. When the children grew older, Oscar and Minnie enrolled their children in Jewish overnight camps. Martha described herself as a tomboy because she loved to play stickball, stoopball, and basketball.

She remembered delicious creamy milk and fresh rolls delivered daily. An ice truck came by to deliver ice for their ice box; when the ice melted the ice box needed to be drained, usually by Martha. A laundry man came to collect their laundry and he brought it back fresh and clean. Groceries including kosher meat and chickens were all delivered to their apartment.

Young Adulthood

Martha graduated from New Utrecht High School in 1935. She took an academic course of study, hoping to enter college, however the Depression years curtailed her plans and so she took salesgirl jobs, at stores such as Bonwit Teller Department Store, working 52 hours a week for $10.

While on the 1939 *Volendam* cruise to Cuba with her sister Sylvia, Martha met a wealthy young man who fell "head over heels" in love with Martha and persisted in courting her. Martha was indeed a beauty with a shapely trim figure. Aunt Martha dated him one evening after the cruise ended and told him that she was already promised to Aaron and that she was not the girl for him.

Martha met Aaron when she worked as a salesgirl at Bonwit Teller Department Store. Martha described how her co-worker Gertrude arranged a blind date of 4 men with 4 women. During this blind date Martha was introduced to Aaron and when she sat down, Aaron laid his head on her lap. The next day, Gertrude came to work saying that Martha mesmerized Aaron, however when Aaron called Martha for a date, she put him off for three weeks saying she was too busy each time. She finally agreed to date Aaron and when he came over, he spoke mainly with her father. They dated for two years and

Martha by a lake

Martha and Aaron wedding

wanted to marry, however their parents told them that they needed to wait until Sylvia was married first as she was older than Martha. Sylvia spoke to her parents and told them that Martha and Aaron should get married before her because they were in love, and she did not have a suitor.

Martha married Aaron on 23 November 1939.[133] They were married by Rabbi Israel Schorr in Kings County, New York and had their honeymoon at the Breakers Hotel at Atlantic City, for only three days because Aaron had to return to work. Martha remembered feeling rice in her coat pockets because they went on their honeymoon right after the wedding. She recalled how cold it was on the boardwalk in Atlantic City and how her knees were feeling frostbite. She had to take a saltwater bath to take down the swelling in her knees. Martha was 21 years old at the time of her marriage.

An Unsubstantiated Family Story

On separate occasions both Aunt Martha and Mom told me a family story that I researched but cannot verify, that there was a cousin connection with a notorious gangster Lepke Buchalter who operated Murder Inc. during the 1930s and 1940s.[134] Martha said that her parents "stayed far away from that family." Neither my mother nor Martha could provide me with specific information, and despite my research, I was unable to find a connection between our family and the Buchalters. Several years before her death, Martha told me she thought the family connection may have been through our Weiss side. Lepke Buchalter's number one hit man was Emanuel (Mendy) Weiss however I could not corroborate if there was a family connection with our Weiss family. The only clues were that both Weiss families were from Drohobycz, Ukraine. Mendy Weiss was buried near my Weiss great uncle Louis Weiss at Mt. Hebron Cemetery, New York. Those were very tenuous leads and probably coincidental. I found a direct descendant from the Mendy Weiss family and asked her if she heard of any other Weiss relatives, however she refused to discuss her family saying it was "all in the past."

Aunt Martha's Memories of Geiger relatives

Martha recalled how her uncle Charles Geiger succeeded in the rescue of his brother Rabbi Abraham Geiger and his family out of Europe during WWII and the Holocaust. She also said that her Uncle Charley looked after Rabbi Abraham Geiger and his family when they arrived in the United States as refugees fleeing from the Holocaust. Martha recalled her uncle Rabbi Abraham Geiger, and his family came to her apartment for dinner and would only eat boiled eggs, herring, and beer with their hands. He was singing and happy to be in the United States, having escaped from certain death in Nazi concentration camps.

Through my research, I now realize that rather than being an unmannered country bumpkin eating with one's hands, Rabbi Abraham Geiger and his family were extremely Orthodox and would not eat non-kosher food or eat from non-kosher dinnerware. Disposable dishes and silverware were not in common use.

Married Life in the Suburbs

Martha reported that sometime after her father Oscar died, her mother Minnie moved in with her family. We often visited Martha and her family when they lived at 652 Emerson Street, Woodmere, Nassau County, New York. Aaron became a successful executive for the Leviton Company. He moved his family from Stuyvesant Town in Manhattan to the upper middle-class suburb of Woodmere. Their colonial style house in Woodmere was quite substantial, with huge hedges surrounding the property, a lush lilac tree and many flowers in their garden.

Martha had a full life at Woodmere; she drove an open convertible during the summer, and I was thrilled to ride in it with her. She belonged to a country club and loved to play golf. She was an expert swimmer and learned to dive as a child but as an adult found that diving affected her sinuses. Martha became an avid yoga practitioner and yoga instructor. She held yoga classes at her apartment when she and Aaron lived at Flushing, Queens. I was so surprised to see her standing on her head! She was physically active up until her last days, practicing various fitness techniques as yoga, chi gong, tai chi. She often told me that keeping fit and active was good for body, mind, and spirit. She religiously practiced what she preached and enjoyed teaching yoga exercises to those interested.

Martha and Aaron loved to travel within the United States. They also enjoying gambling at casinos. Martha told me she loved to shoot "craps" (a dice game) and Aaron preferred the roulette wheel. They took many cruises within the United States and frequented Las Vegas, Reno, Lake Tahoe, and Branson, enjoying shows, gambling, and spending time with their close friends. Martha always maintained her strong connection with her sisters and her nieces and nephews. Martha had a sweet and loving nature with a good sense of humor. She loved to give gifts to her loved ones, and she always had time for her family. She exemplified the power of positive thinking.

Sisters Marion, Sylvia, Martha

Martha Cantor

Martha in a pink jacket

Martha and Aaron Cantor, Laguna Hills

Move to California and Life Changes

Martha and Aaron eventually moved to San Jose, California due to Aaron's transfer from New York as a sales executive for the Leviton Company. Their children Olivia and Mark attended San Jose State University in California. When Martha and Aaron retired, they decided to remain in California since their children Olivia and Mark lived there. When they were ready to retire, they established residence in a large retirement community *Leisure World* at Laguna Hills, California. During retirement Aaron was active in the non-profit organization Service Corps of Retired Executives.[135] Martha continued her swimming, she took college courses for seniors, also yoga and fitness classes. She enjoyed good health; even when she had a stroke in her 60s she was never negative and worked hard at her rehabilitation eventually regaining her full functioning.

One health issue that she could not overcome was macular degeneration that happened during her last two years. She never complained about anything; however, this was a life-changing health issue. She grew depressed about her vision loss and lack of independence. She missed being able to read her books. Instead of driving herself, Martha hired a driver. She obtained the latest visual technology to help with reading to the extent she was able. She supported new research developments in the field of macular degeneration to restore her sight.

Her pride and joy were her children and her many grandchildren. She never grew tired of telling the story of how her daughter Olivia met her future husband Rabbi Shlomo and how they raised their children within the Lubavitch Hasidic Jewish Chabad lifestyle. Martha and Aaron were reform Jews but became kosher when their daughter embraced orthodoxy. Martha also proudly displayed the beautiful glass paperweights made by her artistic son Mark. She delighted in Mark's ability as a professional glass blower. Martha would be amazed to learn that her daughter Olivia's family has grown to 50+ grandchildren and many great-grandchildren. Martha and Aaron Cantor had two children, Olivia, and Mark. Both are still living.

Death

Martha became a caregiver for her husband Aaron when he became ill in the last years of his life. After the death of her husband Aaron, Martha travelled abroad for her first time to France and enjoyed being in a foreign country. She was also spiritually inclined and felt at peace with nature; she often joined local field trips for bird watching. Martha went on a trip to Sedona, Arizona as she felt that was a spiritual place and while there with a friend, she suddenly died on 22 September 2005, due to massive cardio-pulmonary failure.[136] She was deeply mourned by her family who loved her sweet loving nature, kindness, compassion, and wisdom. Martha's funeral was well attended by at least 200 people, including many Hasids, because her son-in-law and her daughter were highly respected Lubavitcher Rebbe Shlomo Schwartz and Rebbetzin Olivia Schwartz in Los Angeles.[137] Martha was buried in section Joshua Garden, row 6, grave 5 at the Home of Peace Cemetery, Los Angeles, California next to her beloved husband Aaron Cantor.

Aaron Cantor

Beginnings

Aaron Cantor was the third of four children, born 29 December 1915 at Newark, New Jersey to Joseph Cantorsky aka Joseph Cantor and Flora Schwartz. He died 2 October 1999 at Laguna Hills, California.[138] Aaron's siblings were as follows: Lawrence Cantor (1908–1985),[139] Gertrude Sachs née Cantor (1913–1992),[140] Maxine Portnoy née Cantor (1921–1975).[141]

Aaron's Parents Joseph Cantor and Flora Schwartz

Aaron's mother Flora Schwartz, was the second of eight children, born 15 April 1886 at New York City to Max and Celia Schwartz. Her parents, Max and Celia,

S.S. Werkendam

immigrated to the United States 1883 from Russia and were married ca. 1883. Max worked as a tailor. Max Schwartz (1861–1920) and Celia Rosenzweig (1858–1944) had the following children: Joseph (1884–); Flora (1886–1949); Isidor (1887–1924); Sarah Sadie (1893–1962); Evelyn (1893–1960); Lillian (1899–1940);

Pennsylvania, Eastern Dis...Naturalization, 1795-1931 > Pennsylvania, Eastern Dis...Naturalization, 1795-1931 > 1927, Petition nos. 084595-085075

Joseph Cantorsky, Declaration of Intention

Hannah (1901–); Zelda (1902–1997). This information was taken from the Simon Family Tree (search.www.ancestry.com) and from the New York 1900 Census for the Borough of Manhattan.[142]

Aaron's father Joseph Cantor's surname was originally Cantorsky, which he changed to Joseph Cantor when he applied for citizenship. I estimate that Flora Schwartz and Joseph Cantorsky were married ca. 1906 at New York. The 1910 Federal Census for Essex County, New Jersey indicated Joseph and Flora Cantor lived at 340 Littleton Avenue, Newark, New Jersey. They had a son, Lawrence, born 1908 at New Jersey. Joseph Cantor worked as a Hat Finisher. [143]

Joseph Cantor's Declaration of Intention was completed 8 November 1920 while he lived at 56 Union Avenue, Brooklyn, New York.[144] He indicated that he was born 1 September 1879 at Kiev, Russia. He immigrated to the United States from Rotterdam, Holland on the *S.S. Werkendam* owned by the Holland America Line. His wife was Flora; his occupation was Hatter. His occupation continued as Hatter consistently throughout his life as seen in subsequent documents.

Joseph Cantorsky aka Cantor completed his Petition for Naturalization 31 May 1927. He resided at 1218 S. 5th Street, Philadelphia, Pennsylvania. Joseph's wife Flora was born 7 July 1886 at New York; their children were: Lawrence born 25 July 1908 at New Jersey; Gertrude born 5 February 1913 at New Jersey; Aaron born 29 October 1915 at New Jersey; Maxine born December 1921 at New York. The two witnesses to his Petition for Naturalization signed the affidavit they personally knew Joseph since 1 May 1922 in Philadelphia. I noted that Joseph stated his wife and their children resided at New York. Joseph Cantorsky signed the Oath of Allegiance 23 September 1927 at Philadelphia, and he became a naturalized citizen.[145]

The family moved from New York City to Newark, New Jersey. The New Jersey State Census for 1915 contained information that Joseph and Flora's children were Lawrence born July 1908 and Gertrude born February 1913 both at New Jersey. The family lived at 340 Littleton Avenue, Newark, New Jersey.[146] Their third child, Aaron Cantor, was born 29 December 1915 at Newark, New Jersey. Their fourth child, Maxine Cantor, was born 12 May 1921 at New York City.

According to Joseph Cantor's 1918 World War I draft registration card his family lived at Newark, New Jersey. He was born at Kiev, Russia; he worked for the Hudson Hat Company at Newark, New Jersey; his wife was Florence Cantor. Their address was 340 Littleton Avenue, Newark, New Jersey.[147] By 1930 the family resided at 4748 Wharton Street, Philadelphia, Pennsylvania. Joseph

Cantor worked for a hat company and his son Larry worked as a salesman for electrical supplies. Their other children were in school.[148] Joseph and Flora Cantor moved from Philadelphia and by 1940 they lived at 956 59th Street, Brooklyn, New York.[149] Their daughter Maxine age 18 lived with them. Joseph worked as a finisher for men's hats, Flora was a dressmaker and Maxine worked as a stenographer.[150] Flora Cantor died 24 November 1949 at Brooklyn, New York.[151] Joseph Cantor died 7 February 1969 at Brooklyn, New York.[152] Both were buried at Mt. Carmel Cemetery, Glendale, Queens, New York in section Kovular Sons of Jacob, 1-A-5-1&2-2.[153]

Aaron and His Upward Journey

Aaron Cantor and Martha Weiss were married 23 November 1939 at Brooklyn, New York.[154] Aaron lived at 956 59th Street, Brooklyn, New York, and he worked as a clerk. Martha lived at 71 Ocean Parkway, Brooklyn, New York; she also worked as a clerk. Information given on the 1940 Federal Census Brooklyn, New York indicated that Martha worked as a clerk in a department store and Aaron worked as a clerk in a dress factory. His highest education grade was the 3rd year of high school and his income given for 1939 was $1500.[155] During WWII, Aaron enlisted on 20 April 1943.[156] Martha told me that she and Aaron lived in Ogden, Utah because Aaron was stationed there. She worked at a clerical job. After the war, they returned to New York and began to raise a family.

Aaron worked for Leviton Company and rose to

Martha and Aaron ca. 1943

(LtoR) Minnie, Martha, Aaron, Sylvia

Aaron Cantor

become a top sales executive. He also worked for Rex Electric Company in sales management. He took special training for salesmanship, and he was ambitious to get ahead to provide for his family. Aaron told me that he read Dale Carnegie's book *How to Win Friends and Influence People* and he participated in a special Dale Carnegie training. Aaron credited the course for giving him the necessary attitude and skills to advance in his work.

While retired Aaron enjoyed mentoring others and was active in SCORE as a volunteer. SCORE is the Service Corps of Retired Executives who volunteer their services to advise small businesses and entrepreneurs. Aaron also took delight in gardening at his home in Leisure World, Laguna, California as that was his hobby for many years. He enjoyed seeing his plants and trees grow and bloom. He also had a wonderful sense of humor.

Aaron and Martha Cantor matsevah

Illness and Death

Aaron's last years of life were difficult as he had several surgeries for cancer, aortic aneurism with bypass surgery and then a pacemaker procedure. Aaron expressed his dissatisfaction with his very restricted diet; his yearning for a kosher frankfurter on a roll was finally fulfilled prior to his death. He deeply loved his beautiful wife Martha, his children Mark and Olivia, and his numerous grandchildren. Aaron died 2 October 1999 at Laguna Hills, California.[157] He was buried next to Martha in section Joshua Garden, row 6, grave 6 at the Home of Peace Cemetery, Los Angeles, California.

MtDNA and My Maternal Ancestral Roots

I submitted my DNA to the company www.familytreedna.org to enhance my genealogical research and was tested for both autosomal (atDNA) and mitochondrial DNA (mtDNA). My goals were to learn more about my origins and to expand knowledge of my family perhaps finding new cousins. Based on my own positive experience I recommend this process for other researchers.

Mitochondria are structures present in the cytoplasm of all human cells. They contain genetic material and enzymes that are important for cell metabolism for converting food to usable energy. They are called the power houses of the cell. The mitochondria are transmitted only from the mother to her children of both sexes however sons do not pass down their mother's mtDNA whereas daughters pass down their mother's mtDNA to their children.[158]

My mtDNA (mitochondrial DNA) was tested to determine my haplogroup or genetic population group for identification of my deep ancestral ethnic and geographic origins. Mitochondrial analysis was focused on specific regions HVR-1 and HVR-2 within the mitochondria because mutations occur more frequently in those regions and can help differentiate specific lineages. Mutations become associated with certain populations in geographic areas for identifying a specific haplogroup.[159]

My mtDNA haplogroup was analyzed to be within Haplogroup K. This haplogroup emerged during the mid-Upper Paleolithic Age approximately 30,000 years–22,000 years before the present in West Asia that includes regions such as the Middle East, the Sinai Peninsula, Mesopotamia, the Levant, Near East and Eastern Mediterranean.[160] In the popular book *The Seven Daughters of Eve* by Bryan Sykes, there was a chapter *Katrine* devoted to the origins of the K haplogroup. She was described as having lived in northern Italy 15,000 years ago on a vast wooded plain from the Po Valley to the Alps.[161] The mitochondrial haplogroup K is found in about 6% of the current populations of Europe and the Near East. Higher percentages > 15 % are seen in the Druze population in Syria and in populations from Lebanon, Israel, Jordan, and Kurdistan.[162]

Further mtDNA analysis revealed that my subclade is K1a1b1a. This is the most frequent K subclade and accounts for 62% of all Ashkenazi Jewish maternal K lineages. The other two subclades within Haplogroup K are K1a9 and K2a2. K1a9 is found in 20% and K2a2 is found in 16% within Ashkenazi maternal K lineages in Jews living today with roots from central and eastern Europe. Those same subclades from Haplogroup K are also seen at lower frequencies in Jewish populations among Sephardic Jews who trace their roots to medieval Spain before the Expulsion of 1492.[163] My maternal ancestry is Ashkenazi as defined by Jews having recent ancestry in central and eastern Europe rather than Jews who have Sephardic ancestry from Iberia or Mizrahim Jews with ancestry from the Near East or from North Africa. This does not exclude the possibility of an unknown ancestor with the same subclade K1a1b1a, who lived in Spain and then migrated to central Europe before or after the Expulsion.

The origins of the Ashkenazi Jewish population originated from the Near East within the last two millennia prior to their migrations to Europe. There were complex changes within the Jewish population due to mutations and population bottlenecks that occurred over centuries. Behar found those changes originated from three different founding ancestral mothers within Haplogroup K: K1a1b1a; K1a9, and K2a2a, and from one founding ancestral mother from Haplogroup N1b.[164] The four founding mothers were likely from a Hebrew/Levantine mtDNA pool, whose descendants migrated to Europe and carried forward their mtDNA variants to 3,500,000 individuals in a time frame of <2 millennia.[165]

Population bottlenecks in the Ashkenazi Jewish population occurred many times during the past 2 millennia. Bottlenecks were groups of a particular population that contracted to a significantly smaller size over a short period of time due to environmental effects or societal changes. The following were bottlenecks of Jews specific to Europe: in the Near East before the initial migration to Europe >1500 years ago; during the migrations of Jews from the Near East to Italy after the 1st century CE; upon the establishment of small Jewish communities in the Rhine Valley during the 8th century CE; and during the 12th century CE when Jews migrated from western to eastern Europe.[166]

Founder effects often occur during bottlenecks. This is when a small group or even one founder can splinter off from the original population. Founders of the new colony can strongly affect future population traits, for example founder effects were estimated to have arisen in the Jewish Pale of Settlement in Lithuania and Belarus during the 16th–19th centuries when endogamy in combination with rapid population growth played a major role in the high frequency of certain genetic diseases observed in the Ashkenazi population today.[167]

My deep mtDNA ancestral roots originated in the Near East. My Jewish ancestors migrated from the Near East to Western Europe probably in the Mediterranean region and then to Poland and Russia. After many generations living in central and eastern Europe they became known as Ashkenazi Jews. I passed down my mitochondrial DNA to our two daughters Abby and Jennifer and it was passed down to our grandchildren Ora and Aaron. My mtDNA was passed down to me by my mother Sylvia Weiss who was born in the United States. Her mtDNA was inherited from our maternal ancestors who were all born in Przemyśl, Podkarpackie, Poland; they were my grandmother Minnie Geiger, great-grandmother Hinde Turnheim, great-great-grandmother Miriam Gems, and great-great-great-grandmother Hinde Marberg.

Descendants of David Gerber

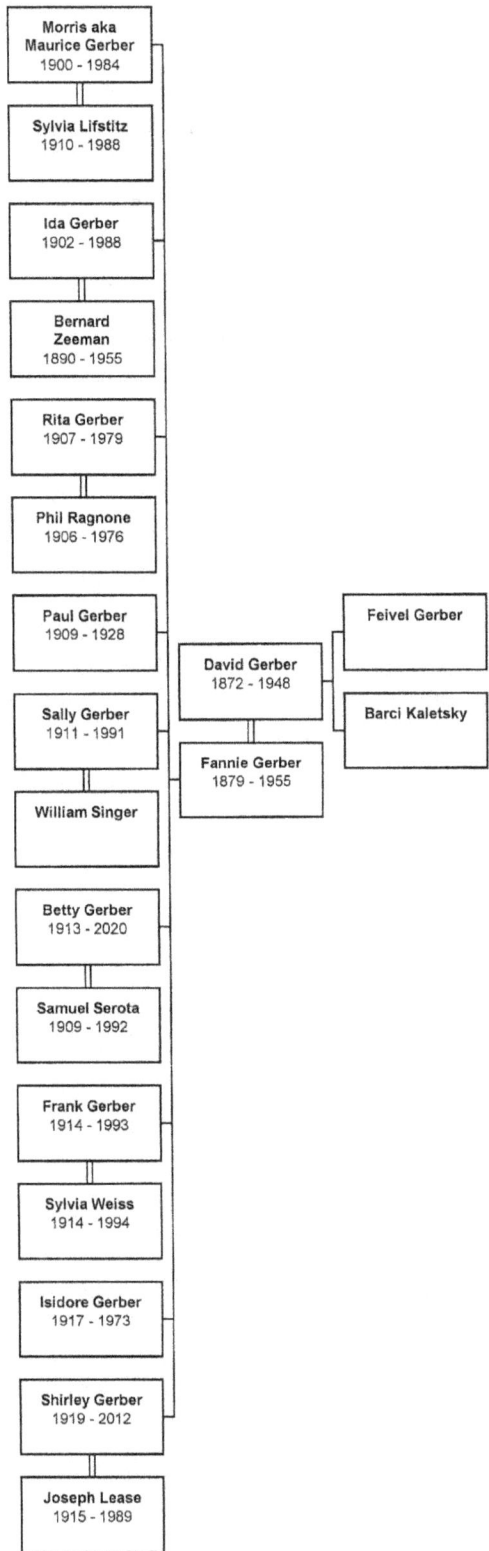

```
┌─────────────────────┐
│   Morris aka        │
│  Maurice Gerber     │
│    1900 - 1984      │
└─────────────────────┘

┌─────────────────────┐
│   Sylvia Lifstitz   │
│    1910 - 1988      │
└─────────────────────┘

┌─────────────────────┐
│    Ida Gerber       │
│    1902 - 1988      │
└─────────────────────┘

┌─────────────────────┐
│     Bernard         │
│     Zeeman          │
│    1890 - 1955      │
└─────────────────────┘

┌─────────────────────┐
│    Rita Gerber      │
│    1907 - 1979      │
└─────────────────────┘

┌─────────────────────┐
│   Phil Ragnone      │
│    1906 - 1976      │
└─────────────────────┘

┌─────────────────────┐                              ┌─────────────────────┐
│    Paul Gerber      │        ┌──────────────────┐  │   Feivel Gerber     │
│    1909 - 1928      │        │   David Gerber   │  └─────────────────────┘
└─────────────────────┘        │    1872 - 1948   │
                               └──────────────────┘
┌─────────────────────┐                              ┌─────────────────────┐
│    Sally Gerber     │        ┌──────────────────┐  │   Barci Kaletsky    │
│    1911 - 1991      │        │   Fannie Gerber  │  └─────────────────────┘
└─────────────────────┘        │    1879 - 1955   │
                               └──────────────────┘
┌─────────────────────┐
│   William Singer    │
└─────────────────────┘

┌─────────────────────┐
│    Betty Gerber     │
│    1913 - 2020      │
└─────────────────────┘

┌─────────────────────┐
│   Samuel Serota     │
│    1909 - 1992      │
└─────────────────────┘

┌─────────────────────┐
│    Frank Gerber     │
│    1914 - 1993      │
└─────────────────────┘

┌─────────────────────┐
│   Sylvia Weiss      │
│    1914 - 1994      │
└─────────────────────┘

┌─────────────────────┐
│   Isidore Gerber    │
│    1917 - 1973      │
└─────────────────────┘

┌─────────────────────┐
│   Shirley Gerber    │
│    1919 - 2012      │
└─────────────────────┘

┌─────────────────────┐
│   Joseph Lease      │
│    1915 - 1989      │
└─────────────────────┘
```

Descendants of Joseph Cantor

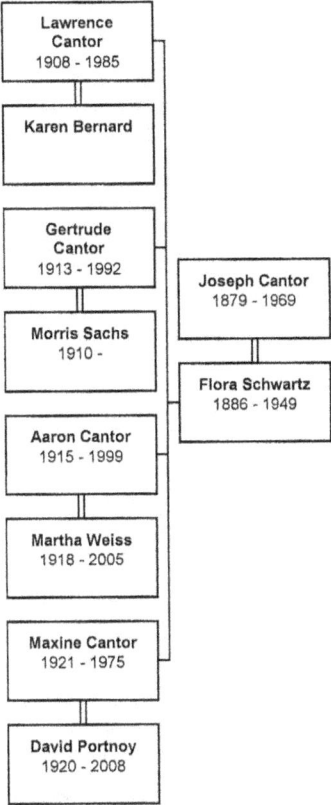

```
Lawrence
Cantor
1908 - 1985
   │
Karen Bernard


Gertrude
Cantor
1913 - 1992                    Joseph Cantor
   │                            1879 - 1969
Morris Sachs                        │
1910 -                         Flora Schwartz
                               1886 - 1949
Aaron Cantor
1915 - 1999


Martha Weiss
1918 - 2005


Maxine Cantor
1921 - 1975
   │
David Portnoy
1920 - 2008
```

Descendants of Meir Aron Goshin

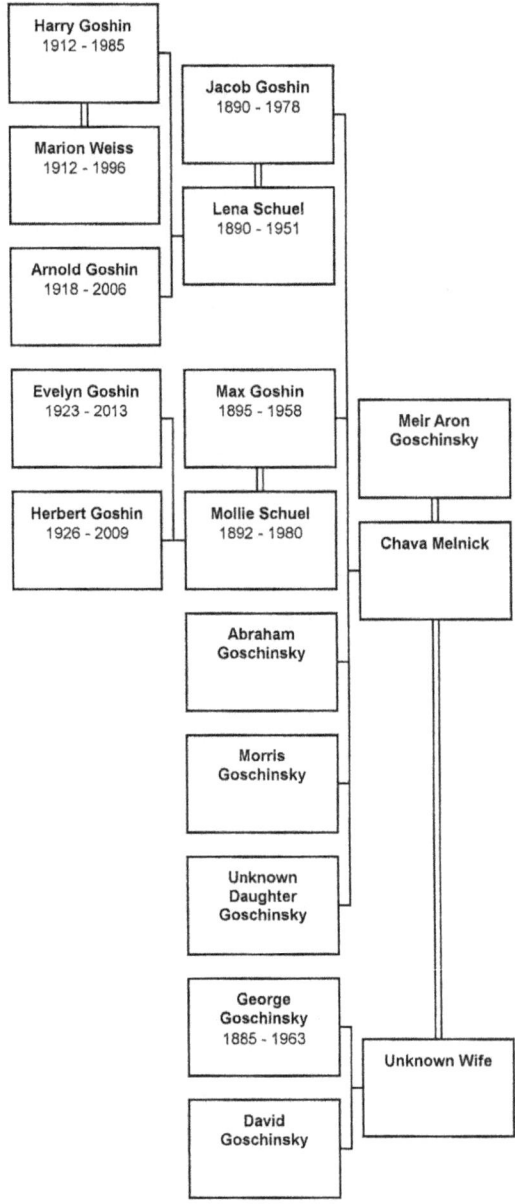

Harry Goshin
1912 - 1985

Marion Weiss
1912 - 1996

Arnold Goshin
1918 - 2006

Jacob Goshin
1890 - 1978

Lena Schuel
1890 - 1951

Evelyn Goshin
1923 - 2013

Herbert Goshin
1926 - 2009

Max Goshin
1895 - 1958

Mollie Schuel
1892 - 1980

Abraham
Goschinsky

Morris
Goschinsky

Unknown
Daughter
Goschinsky

George
Goschinsky
1885 - 1963

David
Goschinsky

Meir Aron
Goschinsky

Chava Melnick

Unknown Wife

Descendants of Minnie Geiger

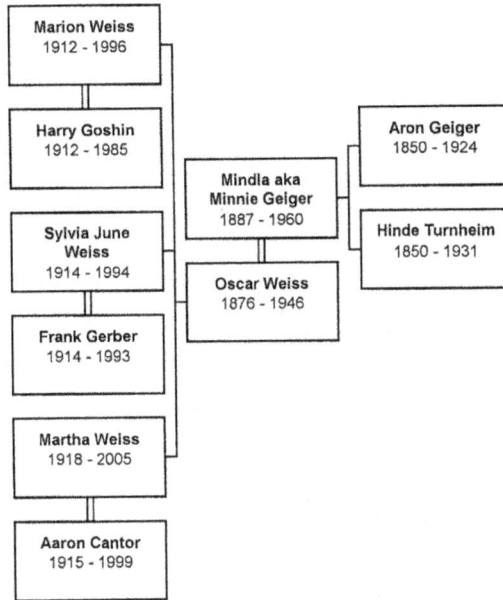

Marion Weiss 1912 - 1996		
Harry Goshin 1912 - 1985		**Aron Geiger** 1850 - 1924
Sylvia June Weiss 1914 - 1994	**Mindla aka Minnie Geiger** 1887 - 1960	**Hinde Turnheim** 1850 - 1931
Frank Gerber 1914 - 1993	**Oscar Weiss** 1876 - 1946	
Martha Weiss 1918 - 2005		
Aaron Cantor 1915 - 1999		

Descendants of Yehuda Leib Weiss

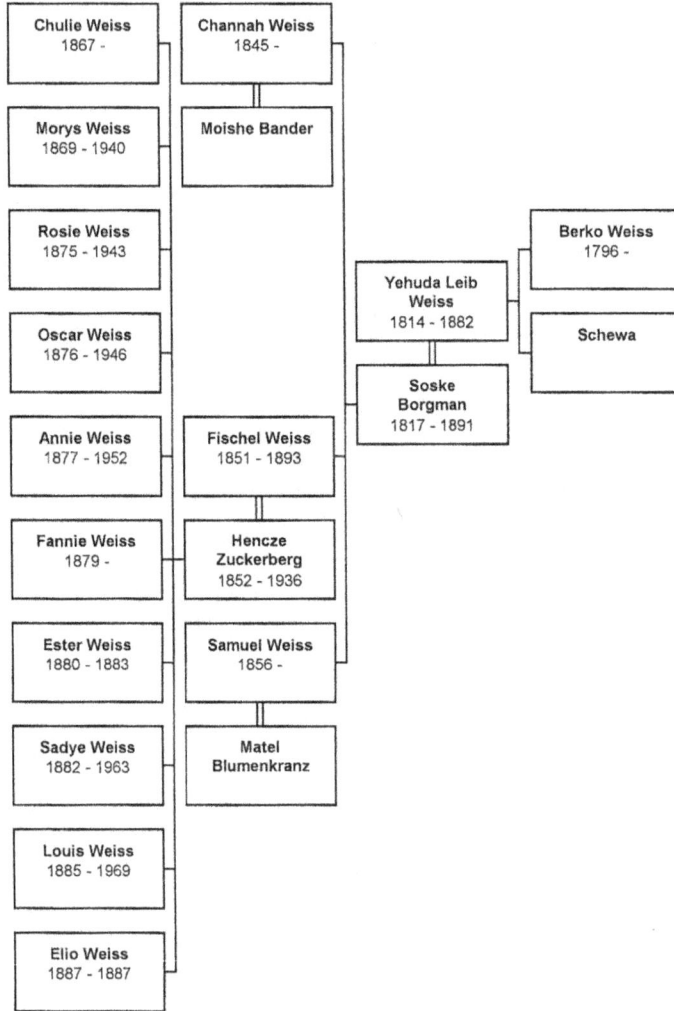

Chulie Weiss 1867 -	**Channah Weiss** 1845 -
Morys Weiss 1869 - 1940	**Moishe Bander**
Rosie Weiss 1875 - 1943	
Oscar Weiss 1876 - 1946	
Annie Weiss 1877 - 1952	**Fischel Weiss** 1851 - 1893
Fannie Weiss 1879 -	**Hencze Zuckerberg** 1852 - 1936
Ester Weiss 1880 - 1883	**Samuel Weiss** 1856 -
Sadye Weiss 1882 - 1963	**Matel Blumenkranz**
Louis Weiss 1885 - 1969	
Elio Weiss 1887 - 1887	

Yehuda Leib Weiss 1814 - 1882

Soske Borgman 1817 - 1891

Berko Weiss 1796 -

Schewa

Endnotes

1   Rabbi Shmuel Gorr. Edited by Chaim Freedman. *Jewish Personal Names-Their Origin, Derivation and Diminutive Forms.* Bergenfield, New Jersey: Avotaynu, Inc. 1992. pp.74–75.

2   Przemysl Archive, Poland. Fond 1924. Przemysl Birth Records 1789–1827, 53-1900. Birth: Mindla Geiger, 1887.

3   /yourjewishgem.blogspot.com/2014/01/1899-przemysl-homeowners-streets-2.html. Jewish Gems' Genealogy- Mining for your Elusive Ancestors. 1899 Przemysl Homeowners Streets.

4   Please see Chapter One; Section: Why My Ancestors Settled in Blazowa.

5   Suzan Wynne. The Galitzianers: the Jews of Galicia, 1772–1918. Suzan Wynne: Kensington, Maryland. 2006. pp.55–63.

6   Ancestry.com. Hamburg Passenger Lists. *S.S.Moltke.* Departing 22 Oct 1904 from Hamburg to New York. Minna Geiger.

7   www.gjenvick.com/passengers/ports.

8   Ancestry.com. New York Passenger Lists. *S.S. Moltke,* arriving 1 Nov 1904. Mina Geiger.

9   Naval History and Heritage Command. (www.history.navy.mil)

10   Ancestry.com. 1905 New York State Census. Election District 4. Assembly District 26. Address: 327 East 68th Street, Manhattan, New York.

11   Ancestry.com. U.S. Federal Census 1910 Manhattan, New York. Ward 13. Enumeration District 775. Lines 13-18.

12   *Landsmanschaften* were immigrant benevolent organizations formed by ex-residents of the same locality or town for mutual aide, hometown aide, and social purposes. Burial sections in cemeteries were often purchased by the organizations including burial plots for sale to members.

13   Ancestry.com. 1910 Federal Census. Manhattan, New York. Ward 13, Enumeration District 775. 52 Lewis Street.

14   Municipal Archives. New York City. Manhattan Marriages. Marriage 17 Oct 1911, Manhattan. Marriage Certificate 23736. Oscar Weiss and Minnie Geiger.

15   Family photograph of the wedding for Minnie Geiger and Oscar Weiss sent to me by cousin Arthur Goshin.

16   Ancestry.com. U.S. Federal Census 1920. Manhattan Assembly District 4, New York. Address 136 Essex Street. Oscar Weiss, Yetta Weiss. (www.ancestry.com).

17   Ancestry.com. New York State Census 1925. Election District 06, Assembly District 04. 134 S. 9th Street.

18   Ancestry.com. U.S. Federal Census 1930. Borough of Brooklyn. Assembly District 16. Enumeration District 24-1415.

19   Ancestry.com. 1940 Federal Census. Kings County. Enumeration District 24-1404. Address: 71 Ocean Parkway.

20   New York, State and Federal Naturalization Records 1794–1943. Morys Weiss. Umbrella Manufacturer. Naturalization Date 7 May 1902. Address 105 Rivington Street, Manhattan.

21   New York Public Library at 42nd. Street, Manhattan Telephone Directory.

22   Ibid.

23   Wikipedia. Flatiron District. Borough of Manhattan. New York City.

24   New York Public Library. Borough of Manhattan Telephone Directories. 1946. Businesses were listed at 20 West 22nd Street including Oscar Weiss Umbrellas.

25   Personal email 9 May 2015.

26   Personal email 5 May 2013

27   Personal email, 10 May 2015.

28   Personal email, 10 May 2015.

29   Personal email, 4 May 2013.

30   Personal email, 10 May 2015

31   Office of Vital Records, New York State Department of Health. Certificate Number 35331. Certificate of Death.

32   Personal papers of Sylvia Gerber. Indenture dated 23 January 1948 made between Charles Geiger and Minnie Weiss. Minnie Weiss paid Charles Geiger one dollar for herself and her heirs for the "one-half right, title share and interest in and to that certain cemetery lot…known and designated in the records of the First Galician Society…contained in the deed dated March 29th, 1923 executed by said First Galician Society to the said Charles Geiger." The document was notarized by Morris Fern, notary public.

33   Personal email correspondence with Eddy Bikales 2015–2016.

34   Alexander Beider. *A Dictionary of Ashkenazic Given Names.* (Bergenfield, New Jersey: Avotaynu) 2001. p. 458.

35   AGAD Archive, Poland. Fond 300. Boryslaw Deaths 1878–1937. Akta 293. Death 1892: Leib Weiss (**www.jri-pl.com**).

36   Brian J. Lenius. *Genealogical Gazetteer of Galicia. 1999.* Canada:Brian J. Lenius.

37   AGAD Archive, Poland. Fond 300. Drohobycz Births 1877–1913. Akta 540. Birth: Chaje Sara. 1882. (www.jri-pl.com).

38   AGAD Archive, Poland. Fond 300. Boryslaw Deaths 1878–1937. Akta 293. Death 1892: Leib Weiss (**www.jri-pl.com**).

39   JewishGen.org. Medenice-Encyclopedia of Jewish Communities in Poland, V.II (Medenychi, Ukraine). Translation of Medenice Chapter from Pinkas Hakehillot Polin. Translator: Jerrold Landau. Project Coordinator Judith C. Goldsmith. Pp. 308–309. Jerusalem: Yad Vashem.

40   New York City. Department of Health. Bureau of Records. Anna Weiss. Death: 30 April 1936. Home of the Sons and Daughters of Israel. 232 East 12th Street, Manhattan, NY. Certificate 10995.

41   Judith Goldsmith. Searching for Hencze. *The Galitzianer.* V. 17, no. 2. February 2010. Pp. 17–19.

42   JewishGen.org. My Viewmate. Translation of death record by Tomasz Jerzy Nowak. 2016.

43   AGAD Archive, Poland. Fond 300. Boryslaw Deaths 1878–1937. Akta 258. Death 1891: Soske Weiss (www.jri-pl.com)

44   Joseph Kitai. Boryslaw, the Oil City. Memorial to the Jews of Drohobycz, Boryslaw, and Surroundings. (Israel, Tel-Aviv, 1959) p. 184. (www.jewishgen.org/yizkor/Drohobycz/dro184.html)

45   Shimon Barak and Barr Dov Youngerman. History of the Jews of Boryslaw. Memorial to the Jews of Drohobycz, Boryslaw and Surroundings.(Israel, Tel-Aviv, 1959) pp. 171–176. (www. jewishgen.org/yizkor/Drohobycz/dro171.html)

46   Ancestry.com. Immigration. Hamburg Passenger Lists. 1850–1934.

47   Ancestry.com. Philadelphia Passenger Lists 1800–1945. Steamship Ohio.

48   Ancestry.com. Immigration. New York Passenger Lists. Also Hamburg Passenger Lists to New York. 1850–1934. S.S. Gellert.

49   **www.norwayheritage.com**

50   Municipal Archives. New York City. Declaration of Intention. Osher Weiss. Certificate # 89560 issued 21 Aug 1914.

51   Municipal Archives. New York City. Petition for Naturalization. Osher Weiss. # 93983 issued 18 October 1919.

52   Municipal Archives. New York City. Oath of Allegiance. Osher Weiss. Certificate of Naturalization #1433443 issued 7 Feb 1921.

53   Municipal Archives. New York City. Naturalization Records. Declaration of Intention Certificate Number 89560.

54   AGAD Archive, Poland. Fond 300. Boryslaw Births 1878–86. Akta 280. Birth: Feige Zukerberg Weiss. 18 June 1879. (**www.jri-pl.com**).

55   Municipal Archives, New York City. Petition for Naturalization. Filed 18 October 1919. Osher Weiss. Oath of Allegiance taken 7 February 1921. Certificate of Naturalization Number 1433443.

56   Ancestry.com. Federal Census 1900. Borough of Manhattan, New York. Ward 4149. Enumeration District 276. Address 183 Broome Street.

57   New York Public Library. New York State Census 1905 .Borough of Manhattan. Address 1653 East 110 Street.

58   Ancestry.com. Federal Census 1910. Borough of Manhattan. Ward 12. Enumeration District 456. Address 18 East 112 St.

59   Irma Wulz, archivist. Archiv der Israelitischen Kultusgemeinde Wien, Vienna, Austria. Matrikenamt der IKG, Wien, A/VIE/IKG/1/Buch/MA/Sterbebuch/135. Death Record for Fischl Weiss: 11 October 1893.

60   Jewishgen.org. JewishGen Online Worldwide Burial Registry (JOWBR). Fischl Weiss.

61   JewishGen.org. My ViewMate. Translation from Hebrew by Fredel Jacobs Fruhman 5 April 2020.

62   Archiv der Israelitischen Kultusgemeinde Wien, Vienna, Austria. Death Date: 11 Oct 1893. Fischel Weiss, born in Drohobycz, Galicia. Married. Age 42. Record sent 5 Jan 2017.

63   Ancestry.com. 1942 draft registration card known as the "Old Man" draft for registering men born on or after 28 April 1877 and on or before 16 February 1897.

64   Municipal Archives, New York City. Oscar Weiss, Death Certificate 22581. Date of death: 25 October 1946. Died in French Hospital, New York of natural causes. Occupation: Umbrella Manufacturer. Burial at Mt. Neboh Cemetery.

65   *New York Times*. Obituaries 26 October 1946, p. 12.

66   *New York Times*, 26 October 1946. P. 12. Obituary for Oscar Weiss stated that he died in his seventieth year, beloved husband of Minnie, devoted father of Marion Goshin, Sylvia Gerber and Martha Cantor, loving brother of Anna Borgman, Fanny Woolf, Sadie Luckower and Louis Weiss and darling grandfather. Interment at Mount Neboh Cemetery.

67   Ancestry.com. New York, New York Birth Index 1910–1965. Birth: Marion Weiss 28 Nov 1912, Manhattan.

68   Municipal Archives. New York City. Marriage Records for Kings County. Harry Goshin and Marion Weiss Marriage Certificate Number 14706. Date of marriage: 8 September 1935.

69   Ancestry.com. U.S., Social Security Death Index, 1935–2014. Death: 24 Jan 1996. Marion Goshin

70   Ancestry.com. New York, New York Marriage License Indexes 1907–2018. Harry Goshin. Marriage License Number 16186.

71   Ancestry.com. New York, New York Extracted Marriage Index 1866–1937. Harry Goshin and Marion Weiss. Marriage 8 September 1935 Certificate 14706.

72   Ancestry.com. U.S. WWII Draft Cards Young Men, 1940–1947 for Harry Goshin.

73   Ancestry.com. U.S. Social Security Death Index, 1935–2014. Death: Dec. 1985. Harry Goshin.

74   Ancestry.com. U.S. WWII Draft Cards Young Men, 1940–1947 for Arnold Goshin.

75   Ancestry.com. U.S. World War II Army Enlistment Records 1938-1946. Arnold Goshin.

76   Ancestry.com. U.S. Social Security Death Index, 1935–2014. Arnold Goshin.

77   Family tree, information and personal papers from Herbert Goshin and Arthur Goshin.

78   FamilySearch.org. New York, County Naturalization Records, 1791–1980, Kings County, Petitions for Naturalization 0 vol 194, no 48101-48350. Petition for Naturalization 27 January 1920. Jacob Goshin.

79   Ancestry.com. U.S. City Directories, 1822–1995. 1916 Directory. Jacob Goschinsky, designer.

80   Ancestry.com. 1920 United States Federal Census, Brooklyn, New York. Brooklyn Assembly District 14. Jacob Goshin.

81   Ancestry.com. 1930 United States Federal Census, Brooklyn, New York, Enumeration District 1183. Jacob Goshin.

82   FamilySearch.org. George Goshinsky. Petition for Naturalization. 12 December 1928. New York Southern District, Naturalization Records, 1824–1946. V. 461. No. 147951-148350.

83   FindAGrave.org. George Goshin. Buried at the Rotmistroker plot, Mt. Zion Cemetery, Maspeth, New York.

84   Ancestry.com. U.S. Social Security Death Index 1935–2014. Death Jan 1978 Brooklyn, NY. Jacob Goshin

85   Rotmistrovka was a shtetl in the Cherkassy uyezd, Kiev gubernia, Ukraine. Rotmistrovka had a Jewish population of 965 Jews in 1863 that grew to 1,785 by 1897, 37% of the total population. Rabbi Yochanan Twersky (1816–1895) became the spiritual leader in Rotmistrovka during the 19th century. He was a grandson of Rebbe Menachem Nachum Twersky of Chernobyl, who was a disciple of the Baal Shem Tov, the founder of Hasidism. Rabbi Yochanan Twersky died at Rotmistrovka and was buried there in an ohel. The ohel is a structure built around a Jewish grave to signify the prominence of the deceased as an important rabbi. Upon his death, his son Rabbi Mordechai Twersky took over spiritual leadership at Rotmistrovka, and it became one of the centers for Hasidism until 1919 when a series of violent pogroms forced many Jews to flee to other cities. Rabbi Mordechai Twersky also fled, and he died 1921 at Palestine. (www.Jewua.org/rotmistrovka)

86   Ancestry.com. Massachusetts, Passenger and Crew Lists, 1820-1963. 1906 Arrival at Boston, Massachusetts. Lina Schuel. S.S. Saxonia.

87   Municipal Archives. New York City. Marriage Records. Manhattan. Marriage: 24 December 1910. Jacob Goschinsky and Lena Schuel. Certificate Number 27.

88   Ancestry.com. New York, New York Death Index 1949-1965. Death: Lena Goshin 31 October 1951, New York.

89   Ancestry.com. New York, U.S., Arriving Passenger and Crew Lists (including Castle Garden and Ellis Island), 1820–1957. Itte Male Schuell. S.S. Caronia. Arrived 15 November 1908, New York.

90   Ancestry.com. New York, State Census, 1915. Assembly District 33.

91   Ancestry.com. New York, State Census, 1925 Max Goshin. Kings County, Assembly District 22.

92   Ancestry.com. N.Y., N.Y., U.S. Extracted Marriage Index, 1866–1937. Marriage Max Goshin and Mollie Schuel.

93   Ancestry.com. New York, New York Death Index, 1949–1965. Death: Max Goshin 8 November 1958.

94   Ancestry.com. Connecticut Death Index, 1949–2012. Mollie Goshin, residence Waterbury, Connecticut; died 23 March 1980 at Torrington, Connecticut.

95   City of New York, Department of Health, Bureau of Records and Statistics. Birth Certificate Number 21766. Sylvia Weiss born 4 June 1914, Brooklyn, New York.

96   Alexander Beider. *A Dictionary of Ashkenazic Given Names.* (Bergenfield, New Jersey: Avotaynu, Inc.) 2001. Pp.574–578.

97   Ancestry.com. Federal Census 1940. Borough of Brooklyn, New York. Ward 12. Enumeration District 24-1404. Address 71 Ocean Parkway.

98   Leo Rosten. *The Joys of Yinglish.* New York: Penguin Books, 1989.

99   Fragment of a newspaper magazine section. 607 Women Complete Nurses' Aide Course. 24 September 1942.

100 New York State Department of Health. Marriage License Number 1406 and Marriage Certificate Number M014634. Frank Gerber and Sylvia Weiss. Marriage 24 January 1943, Tree of Life Temple at 881 Eastern Parkway, Brooklyn, New York. Personal papers from the estate of Frank and Sylvia Gerber.

101 New York City. Brooklyn Telephone Directory, May 1948. Listing for Frank Gerber.

102 New York City, Queens Telephone Directory 1955–1956. Listing for Frank Gerber. Address 74-07 255 St., Bellerose.

103 *Glen Oaks News.* Thursday 28 January 1960. *Sylvia Gerber Makes P.S. 186 Corner Safe for Youngsters.*

104 Elliot Hospital Discharge Summary, Manchester, NH. 17 February 1994. Sylvia Gerber. Attending Physician Walter England.

105 State of New Hampshire. Certified Abstract of a Death Certificate. Sylvia Gerber. Date of Death 28 September 1994. Number 00128412.

106 Novo-Pavlovka. Jewish Cemetery Project, Ukraine. (www.jewishgen.org/cemetery/e-europe/ukra-n.html)

107 National Archives, Kew, U.K. Outgoing Passenger Ships. Solomon Gerber. S.S. Dominion. Leaving Liverpool, U.K. 7 Feb 1905, to Halifax and arrived 20 Feb.1905 at Portland, Maine. (National Archives UK at Kew, England).

108 www.norwayheritage.com

109 worldhistory.us/chinese-history/impact-of-the-russo-japanese-war.php. The war involved the Russian Empire against the Japanese Empire between February 1904 to September 1905. Japan attacked Port Arthur and the Russian fleet. Over the next two years Japan won most naval and land battles. When the war ended in 1905 with the Treaty of Portsmouth, Japan obtained control of Korea. The conflict established Japan as a major power and promoted additional Japanese territorial ambition. The losses suffered by Russia led to the Russian Revolution of 1905.

110 Miscellaneous Atlantic Ports Passenger Lists. 1893–1945. Alien Passengers for the US Immigration Officer at Port of Arrival. Solomon Gerber, S.S. Dominion arrived at Portland, Maine 20 February 1905. (National Archives, Waltham, Massachusetts).

111 National Archives, Kew, UK. Outgoing Passenger Ships. Fannie Gerber and two children. S.S. Celtic. Leaving Liverpool, U.K. 19 Oct 1905, arriving New York, 28 Oct 1906.

112 National Archives, Waltham, Massachusetts. Maine, Federal Naturalization Records, 1787–1952. David Gerber. .Declaration of Intention no. 7327, 12 Sept 1924; Petition for Naturalization 2 July, 1918; Oath of Allegiance 2 October 1928. No. 2844839.

113 Ancestry.com. Maine Federal Naturalization Records 1787–1952. David Gerber.

114 Department of Health, State of Maine. Death Certificate. David Gerber. Date of Death 11 May 1948.

115 Department of Health and Human Services, State of Maine. Death Certificate. Fannie Gerber. Date of Death 7 Aug 1955.

116 Maine Archives, Portland, Maine. Maine, Birth records 1715–1922. Frank Gerber born 10 April 1914 to parents Fannie and David Gerber.

117 National Archives and Records Administration. Military Personnel Records. Record Group 64. U.S. Army II. Army Enlistment Records, 1938–1946. Frank Gerber Enlistment date 8 Sept 1941.

118 Separation Army Qualification Record SWR 55. Frank Gerber. Date of Separation 8 Oct 1945. Separation Center, Fort Dix, New Jersey.

119 Estate of Frank Gerber. Personal papers. Discharge papers, honorable discharge.

120 Enlisted Record and Report of Separation. Honorable Discharge. Length of Service; Continental Service 2 years, 5 months, 8 days; Foreign Service 1 year, 7 months 23 days. United States Army.

121 Certificate of Marriage. Hebrew and English: Frank Gerber and Sylvia Weiss. Date: 24 January 1943. Aits Chayim- Tree of Life Temple, Brooklyn, New York. Rabbi Sigmund Rome.

122 Registry of Vital Records and Statistics. The Commonwealth of Massachusetts. Death Certificate Number 580. Frank Gerber. Date of Death 5 Oct 1993.

123 New York, New York Birth Index 1910–1965. Cert. 40043. David Gerber born 10 Sept 1949, Brooklyn, New York.

124 Brookdale University Hospital and Medical Center, Brooklyn, New York. Beth-El Hospital Center was built 1932 by the Jewish Community in Brownsville, East New York and Canarsie. It was re-named Brookdale Hospital Center in 1963.

125 My mother was Rh Negative and my father was Rh Positive. Although fetal blood circulation and maternal blood circulation are usually separate, Mom's immune system recognized David's blood cells as foreign. In a first pregnancy the immune response by the mother to foreign blood cells is very weak. Because David was her second pregnancy, her antibodies crossed her placenta and attacked and destroyed David's fetal blood, causing a severe problem. The medical terms for this process are isoimmunization, leading to hemolytic disease of the newborn, and the lay term was "blue baby syndrome."

126 New York Public Library. Brooklyn Telephone Directory May 1948. Frank Gerber address: 287A 19th Lane, Canarsie.

127 New York Public Library. Queens Telephone Directory 1955–1956. Frank Gerber address: 74-07 255th Street, Bellerose.

128 www.bellerosejc.org. Bellerose Jewish Center. Address: 254-14 Union Turnpike, Glen Oaks, Queens, New York.

129 Florida Highway Patrol. Driver Exchange Information. Date of Accident: 4/24/68. Location of accident SR9-I95.

130 Information was written on Leviton Manufacturing notepads by Aaron Cantor.

131 Craig Funeral Home, St. Augustine, Florida. Receipt.

132 State of Florida Death Certificate, Flagler County. David Gerber. Cause of Death: head injuries- immediate. Date: 24 April 1968.

133 City Clerk, New York City. Marriage Certificate of Aaron Cantor and Martha Weiss, Number M014632. Dated 23 November 1939.

134 Murder, Inc. was an organized crime group in the 1930's and 40's. They were an enforcement arm of the Italian-American Mafia and Jewish Mob in NYC and elsewhere. The gangsters were mainly from the Brooklyn neighborhoods of Brownsville, East New York, and Ocean Hill. Originally headed by Louis "Lepke" Buchalter and later by Albert Anastasia, Murder, Inc. was responsible for 400-1,000 contract killings. Louis Buchalter, Emanuel Weiss, Louis Capone and others were indicted for the murder of candy store owner Joe Rosen. Lepke, Weiss and Capone were convicted and executed in Sing-Sing prison 4 March 1944. (www.wikipedia.org/wiki/murder_inc)

135 Service Corps of Retired Executives (SCORE) who provide free consultation services and advice to entrepreneurs. (www.wikipedia.org/score)

136 Personal Email to me from Mark Cantor, 26 February 2019.

137 Lubavitcher Rabbi Shlomo Schwartz died 8 February 2017 at Los Angeles. (collive.com)

138 Ancestry.com. U.S., Social Security Death Index, 1935–2014. Aaron Cantor birth 29 December 1915; death 2 October 1999.

139 Ancestry.com. U.S., Social Security Death Index, 1935–2014. Lawrence Kantor birth 22 June 1908; death March 1985.

140 Ancestry.com. U.S., Social Security Death Index, 1935–2014. Gertrude Sachs birth 5 February 1913; death 21 December 1992.

141 Ancestry.com. U.S., Social Security Death Index, 1935–2014. Maxine Portnoy birth 12 May 1921; death July 1975.

142 Ancestry.com. 1900 United States Federal Census. Flora Schwartz.

143 Ancestry.com. 1910 United States Federal Census. Joseph Cantor. Newark, New Jersey. Enumeration District 121, Ward 14.

144 FamilySearch.org. Pennsylvania, Eastern District Petitions for Naturalizations 1795-1931, 1927, Petition Nos. 084595-085075. Joseph Cantorsky.

145 Ibid.

146 FamilySearch.org. New Jersey State Census 1915. Essex, Newark, Ward 14, District 8. Joseph Cantor.

147 FamilySearch.org. United States World War I Draft Registration Cards, 1917–1918. Newark, New Jersey. Joseph Cantor.

148 Ancestry.com. 1930 United States Federal Census. Philadelphia, Pennsylvania. Enumeration District 51-1073. Ward 42. Joseph Cantor.

149 Ancestry.com. Federal Census 1940. Kings County, New York. 9th Ward. Enumeration District 24-990. Address 956 59th Street. Fort Hamilton Parkway.

150 Ancestry.com. 1940 United States Federal Census. Kings County. Ward 9.

151 Ancestry.com. New York, New York, Death Index, 1949–1965. Flora Cantor, died 24 Nov 1949, Brooklyn, New York.

152 Ancestry.com. U.S., Social Security Death Index, 1935–2014. Joseph Cantor.

153 FindAGrave.com. Flora Cantor, burial Mount Carmel Cemetery, Queens, New York.

154 New York State Department of Health. New York City. Marriage Certificate. 19057. Aaron Cantor and Martha Weiss.

155 Ancestry.com. Federal Census 1940. Kings County, New York. Ward 128S. Enumeration District 24-1416. Address 113 Clara Street.

156 Ancestry.com. U.S.World War II Army Enlistment Records, 1938–1946. Aaron Cantor.

157 Ancestry.com. U.S. Social Security Death index, 1935–2014. Aaron Cantor Born 29 Dec 1914, Died 2 Oct 1999.

158 en.wikipedia.org/wiki/mitochondrial_DNA.

159 Understanding Your mtDNAPlus Results. (www.familytreedna.org).

160 Richards, Martin, Vincent Macaulay, Eileen Hickey, Emilce Vega, Bryan Sykes, Valentia Guida, Chiara Rengo, Daniele Sellitto, Fulvio Cruciani, Toomas Kivisild, Richard Villems, MarkThomas, Serge Rychkov, Oksana Rychkov, Yuri Rychkov, Mukaddes Golge, Dimitar Dimitrov, Emmeline Hill, Hans-Jurgen Bandelt. Tracing European Founder Lineages in the Near Eastern mtDNA Pool. *The American Journal of Human Genetics*. Volume 67, Issue 5, November 2000, Pages 1251–1276.

161 Sykes, Bryan. *The Seven Daughters of Eve*. New York: W.W.Norton and Company, 2001. Pp. 252–)259.

162 Simoni, Lucia, Francesc Calafell, Davide Pettener, Jaume Bertranpetit, and Guido Barbujani. Geographic Patterns of mtDNA Diversity in Europe. *American Journal of Human Genetics*, 2000, 66:262-278.

163 Behar, Doron M., Ene Metspalu, Toomas Kivisild, Alessandro Achilli, Yarin Hadid, Shay Tzur, Luisa Pereira, Antonio Amorim, Lluis Quintana-Murci, Kari Majamaa, Corinna Herrnstadt, Neil Howell, Oleg Balanovsky, Ildus Kutuev, Andrey Psenichnov, David Gurwitz, Batsheva Bonne-Tamir, Antonio Torroni, Richard Villems, and Karl Skorecki. The Matrilineal Ancestry of Ashkenazi Jewry: Portrait of a Recent Founder Event. *American Journal of Human Genetics*. V.78, no.3 (2006), pp. 487–97.

164 Ibid., Behar, Doron M. et. al. (2006).

165 Ibid., Behar, Doron M. et. al. (2006).

166 Behar, Doron M., Michael F. Hammer, Daniel Garrigan, Richard Villems, Batsheva Bonne-Tamir, Martin Richards, David Gurwitz, Dror Rosengarten, Matthew Kaplan, Sergio Della Pergola, Lluis Quintana-Murci, and Karl Skorecki. MtDNA evidence for a genetic bottleneck in the early history of the Ashkenazi Jewish Population. *European Journal of Human Genetics* (2004), pp. 1–10.

167 Ibid., Behar, Doron M. et. al. (2006).

Chapter Eleven

Yehezkeil Geiger and Fradal Landesman

This chapter is a discussion of another Geiger family from Błażowa, Podkarpack-ie, Poland. I was first made aware of this family when I met another genealogical researcher Estelle Guzik at the International Jewish Genealogical Convention at Chicago in 2008. Estelle introduced me to her friend, genealogist Suzan Wynne, who was also at the conference and who made a trip with her to Błażowa. Estelle mentioned that she also had a family connection with Błażowa, Podkarpackie, Poland and had a Geiger relative from that town named Oscar Geiger however I had no knowledge of this person in my own Geiger family tree. We compared notes, but nothing "clicked." Yet it was too much of a coincidence that we both had Geiger family connections from Błażowa. Ms. Guzik told me that she was related to Oscar Geiger as his cousin through her great aunt Yehezkeil Geiger's wife, Fradal Landesman. In Ms. Guzik's *Landesman Family Tree-Geiger Branch,* she indicated that Yehezkeil aka Chaskel Geiger from Błażowa was born prior to 1858.[1] I noted that the name Chaskel is a Yiddish Eastern European kinnui for the Hebrew Yehezkeil based on the Biblical prophet Ezekiel.[2] Please refer to the family tree *Descendants of Eliezer Geiger.*

Finding Common Roots

Years later, Suzan Wynne reminded me in an email dated 1 December 2017 of the search she made at Błażowa with Estelle Guzik in 1986 when they hiked up a hill to the Błażowa Jewish cemetery under the watchful eyes of Błażowa residents. Suzan recalled the purpose of their hike was for Estelle Guzik to locate her Geiger family member's grave among the headstones still standing. Their search was curtailed when local "witnesses" followed them believing Jewish treasure was buried in the cemetery.[3]

Estelle Guzik researched and put together the *Landesman Family Tree-Geiger Branch.* She was related to a Geiger family from Błażowa as a descendant from the Landesman family. Fradal Machla Landesman (1867–1924) was married to Yehezkiel/Chaskel Geiger from Błażowa. One of Fradal's sisters, Masha Landes-man, married Elazar Yehuda Guzik who was Estelle's paternal grandfather.

Therefore, Estelle was related to the Geiger family through the marriage of her great aunt Fradal Landesman with Yehezkiel Geiger. She explained that Oscar Geiger born in Błażowa was a first cousin to her father Joseph Guzik and she was a second cousin with Oscar Geiger's daughter Helene Bialik née Geiger.

I spoke with Estelle Guzik by telephone on 6 December 2017. She added that her grandfather Elazar Yehuda Guzik was murdered during the Shoah and her grandmother Masha Landesman preceeded him in death. I searched on www. yadvashem.org website and found corroborating evidence. Her grandfather Lazar Guzik was born in Kombornia, Podkarpackie, Poland in 1866 to Chaim Guzik and Jachet (Yocheved) Finkel. This page of testimony (POT) was submitted to Yad Vashem by Estelle Guzik.[4]

I continued to research Oscar Geiger to find clues about how his Geiger family and my Geiger family may have intersected. When I was on www.myheritage. com website, I found Oscar Geiger included in the *Stern Web Site*. This contact resulted in emails exchanged from 2013 between myself and the Stern family that led me to a greater understanding of our possible connection as cousins. Since there was no definitive paper trail linking our two Geiger families, I asked Doni, one of the Geiger descendants if he would submit his autosomal DNA to FamilyTreeDna to see if there was a genetic match between us. This DNA connection will be discussed at the conclusion of this chapter.

A Geiger Family from Błażowa

According to the *Landesman Family Tree-Geiger Branch* Yehezkiel aka Chaskel Geiger was born before 1858 and lived in Błażowa, Podkarpackie, Poland. His occupation involved wood, probably as a merchant. Yehezkeil aka Chaskel Geiger was born during the same generation as my great-grandfather Aron Geiger (1850–1924). Both were born in Błażowa, both were rabbis and religious teachers. I obtained a photograph of Yehezkiel Geiger's grave and matsevah from the Błażowa Jewish Cemetery, through the research of Israeli students at the Reut School, Jerusalem, Israel.[5] Their project was described on their website www.gidonim.org and involved students travelling to Jewish cemeteries of certain towns in Poland for the purpose of restoration and cataloging graves. I was fortunate that Błażowa was one of the towns they selected.

Yehezkiel Geiger's matsevah inscription from Błażowa indicated he was a rabbi and a religious teacher. The following translation of his matsevah was provided by Rabbi Joshua Segal.[6]

Here (the crown of Torah) lies a man of truth, G-d fearing and avoiding evil. Up-right among men, a perfect man, a faithful friend to those who fear G-d. He remembered his creator through his hospitality. He always observed the mitsvot. Yea, he did the goodness of his maker, Yehezkeil Geiger son of Mr. Eleazer of blessed memory, died the 24th of Elul in the year 5697. May his soul be bound up in the bonds of the living.

Yehezkeil Geiger was born ca. 1857 and he died at Błażowa on 21 August 1937. He was buried in the Błażowa Jewish cemetery. The name of Yehezkeil's

Yehezkeil Geiger matsevah Błażowa

father was Eleazer.[7] Another matsevah photographed from the Błażowa cemetery by the students was for a man with the name Eleazer however the surname
was either eroded away or was omitted. Rabbi Segal translated: *A...man. Died
young. Our teacher the master Eleazer Yekhiel Son of Abraham Moshe.*

I uploaded the photograph to Viewmate at www.jewishgen.org and requested
further translation from the Hebrew. Mr. Kleerekoper responded to my request,
and he translated: *He (Eleazer) was taken to the world above in the prime of his life.* This
phrase was taken to mean half his days and could be applied to anyone who died
before 50 years. In addition, Eleazer Yekhiel was given the title *Morenu Harav*,
our teacher the master. Mr. Kleerekoper noted that Eleazer was conferred with
the religious honorary title at a young age, that indicated he achieved early recognition as a religious scholar. This matsevah with the name Eleazer may be a
coincidence of given names or may be Yehezkeil Geiger's father. If that was the
case, then the given double name Abraham Moshe for Eleazer's father would
take us back another generation, however there were no records or additional ev-

Eliezer matsevah Błażowa

idence to substantiate this theory. Based on a comparison of Geiger family trees, my great-great-grandfather Shlomo David Geiger and Yehezkeil Geiger's father Eleazer were both from Błażowa and were of the same generation. Błażowa had a small population of 893 Jews in 1880 therefore it seemed plausible that both Geiger families were related.[8]

A descendant of Yehezkeil Geiger, Janie, related a family story how Yehezkeil aka Chaskel Geiger participated in a tische for Bluzhover Rebbe Tzvi Elimelech Spira. Chaskel occasionally enjoyed a good drink and then he would get up on a table singing a *niggun* (melody) while dancing on the table. The *tische* was a table prepared for a gathering of Hasidim to celebrate a holiday or Shabbat with speeches on Torah topics and sometimes included mystical passages from the Midrash, Zohar, and Kabbalah. Hasidic melodies were often sung by participants.[9]

Yehezkeil Geiger married Fradal Machla Landesman ca.1884, the daughter of Israel Reuven Landesman and Zelda Rabb. Fradal was born 1866 and she died March 1924 at Błażowa. There was no tombstone found for Fradal among the matsevahs photographed at the Błażowa cemetery. Similiar to the fate of other Jewish cemeteries in Eastern Europe during WWII many matsevahs were destroyed or stolen to be used in construction. Chaskal and Fradal had seven children. They were the following in birth order: Silka; Miriam Ester; Channa Toba; Mojzes Izak (Moshe Yitzchak); Gittel; Oscar (aka Osias Mendel/Yehoshua Menachem); and Mielich. Please refer to the family tree *Descendants of Yehezkeil Geiger*. The following information was obtained from the *Landesman Family Tree-Geiger Branch*.

Children of Yehezkeil Geiger and Fradal Machla Landesman

Silka Geiger

Silka Geiger was born ca.1880 at Błażowa, Podkarpackie, Poland to Yehezkeil Geiger and Fradal Landesman. She married ca. 1899 in Błażowa, Samuel Moses Zins, born 1877 at Sieniawa, Podkarpackie, Poland. He was the son of Selig Zins and Malie Helman.[10] Prior to WWII Silka and her husband Samuel Zins lived in Sieniawa, Poland. Silka and Samuel had nine children including her sister Miriem Esther's two children. Their children were: Lazar born 19 June 1900, Feiga, Barish, David, Yehoshua Mendel, four more children (names unknown).

Before WWII Lazar Zins visited Vienna for medical treatment and stayed with his uncle Oscar Geiger who lived in Vienna. Feiga Zins married her cousin

Yisroel Zins and they lived at Lwów, Poland. Faiga Zins was listed in the Lwów Census of Jewish residents who voted for the Sejm in 1938, the Polish parliament.[11] Barish Zins married Chuna and they had several children. David Zins married Channa, and they had one child. Yehoshua Mendel Zins married Sarah and they had one child.

Silka's aunt Helene Bialik submitted a POT (page of testimony prepared by surviving family or friends) 1999 to Yad Vashem that indicated Silka Zins née Geiger perished during the Holocaust. A POT was submitted by her cousin Estelle Guzik for Samuel Zins 1984.[12] Another POT indicated he was born at Sieniawa and was murdered during the Shoah.[13] Estelle Guzik interviewed Helene Bialik 12 March 1990 in Israel. She learned that both Silka and Samuel Zins were rounded up by the Nazis at Sieniawa, shot in the fields and buried in a mass grave in July 1942. It is presumed that their children died the same time. The Nazis also deported Jews from Sieniawa to the Bełżec death camp at Lubelskie, Poland 20 July 1942.[14]

Miriem Esther Geiger

Miriam Esther Geiger was born ca. 1886 at Błażowa, Podkarpackie, Poland and died ca. 1913 at Błażowa during or after childbirth. She married Moshe Scheiner and they had two children: Chava and Silka. The entire family was murdered during the Holocaust July 1942 at Bełżec, Lubelskie, Poland.[15] A page of testimony (POT) for Yad Vashem was submitted by Estelle Guzik concerning the fate of Moshe Scheiner, who was murdered during the Shoah.[16] Estelle Guzik submitted another POT for Chava, who was single and lived at Błażowa; she was murdered during the Shoah.[17] Silka was born ca. 1913 and perished in the Holocaust. She was married to a man with the surname Nebentzahl.[18]

Channa Tauba Geiger

Channa Tauba Geiger was born 25 February 1887 at Błażowa, Podkarpackie, Poland to Yehezkiel and Fradal Geiger. She married Shaol (Saul) Wolf Ettinger.[19] He was a rabbi and was born 15 May 1874 at Leżajsk, Podkarpackie, Poland and resided in Podgórze, a district within the city of Kraków, Malopolskie, Poland. His occupation was a dayan (rabbinical judge).[20] Their two children were born at Podgórze, Kraków; Yitzchak Ettinger born 29 June 1921 and Fradal Esther Ettinger born 1 August 1924.[21]

Pages of testimony were submitted for Channa Tauba, who was murdered during the Shoah. Her last place of residence was Podgórze and she was a housewife. The Pages of Testimony were submitted by Helene Geiger[22] and Estelle Guzik[23].

Information for Channa Tauba's husband Rabbi Saul Wolf Ettinger was found in the file of persecuted Jews who lived in Kraków with German Identity Cards ("Kennkarte").[24] Their son Yitzchak Ettinger also had a German Identity Card ("Kennkarte").[25] A POT was submitted for Yitzchak Ettinger by Estelle Guzik, who testified that he was murdered during the Shoah.[26] Fradal Esther Ettinger, daughter of Channa Tauba and Saul Wolf Ettinger, was also found among the file of Jews at Kraków with German Identity Cards ("Kennkarte).[27] This entire family likely perished October 1942 at Bełżec, Lubelskie, Poland.[28]

Mojzes Yitzchak (Isak) Geiger

I contacted and exchanged frequent emails since 2013 with Israeli descendants of Mojzes Yitzchak Geiger through www.geni.com and www.myheritage.com. Doni and Janie were most helpful sharing their Geiger family history, photographs, and their *Landesman Family Tree-Geiger Branch* researched by Estelle Guzik. Moses Isak Geiger was born 8 January 1888 at Błażowa, Podkarpackie, Poland to

Kennkartes Wolf Saul and Chana Tauba Ettinger

Yehezkiel Geiger and Fradal Landesman. He served as the *Baal Koreh* and the *Baal Musaf* for the Bluzhova Grand Rabbi Tzvi Elimelech Spira.[29] Mojzes Yitzchak Geiger as the *Baal Musaf* would lead the congregation in prayers after the reading of the Torah on Shabbat and holidays. When he served as the *Baal Koreh*, he chanted specific readings of the Torah. Both *Baal Koreh* and *Baal Musaf* were and still are considered highly prestigious religious positions, especially in the shul of the Bluzhova rabbi.

Mojzes Yitzchak was also a businessman, the proprietor of a confectionary store. His first marriage was to an unknown woman who died either during or before 1910. According to the *Landesman Family Tree* he married a second time to Chaja Itta Stockman, daughter of Berisz Stockman and Judes (Yehudit) Freund, on 5 December 1910 at Pruchnik, Podkarpackie, Poland. A record from JRI-Poland.org listed the birth for Chaja Itta Sztokman born 1881 at Pruchnik to Berisch and Ides Sztokman.[30]

The marriage record for Mojzes Geiger and Chaja Itta Freund was recorded as 1916. Since the birth of their first-born child Mariem Ester was 1912, their religious marriage was probably earlier indicating that December 1910 was the correct date. Their official civil marriage record was 1916, several years after their religious marriage in 1910.[31] Moses Isak and Chaja Itta had the following five children: Miriem Esther born 4 June 1912 at Pruchnik; Ida (Itzel) born 12 April 1914 at Pruchnik; Lazar (Eleazer) born 1916 at Pruchnik and died 1917 at Pruchnik; Riwa Silka born 6 December 1919 at Pruchnik; Beila Malka born 1923 at Pruchnik and died 1924 at Pruchnik.[32]

Pruchnik, Podkarpackie, Poland

Mojzes Yitzchak Geiger and Chaja Itta Stockman raised their family in Pruchnik, Podkarpackie, Poland. Pruchnik is 27 miles east from Błażowa and 11 miles southwest from Jarosław. The earliest references to Jews in Pruchnik was 1563 and 1577. An increase of the Jewish population in Pruchnik began during the First Partition of Poland by Austria during 1772–1810. Jewish families typically had 8–10 children and by 1888 the Jewish population numbered 575 and was 38% of the total population.[33]

By the beginning of the 20th century most businesses in Pruchnik were owned by Jews. They included grocery stores, kosher butcher shops, bakeries, iron works, tannery, and a pharmacy. Jews lived around the market square and surrounding streets. Several Jews owned inns where exhausted wagon drivers and travelers stayed. Jews also held liquor licenses for selling or manufacturing alcoholic beverages.

An anti-Semitic pogrom in Pruchnik occurred November 1918 when peasants robbed and vandalized Jewish owned stores. During WWII the German Nazi army attacked Pruchnik September 1939, and many Jews were shot in forests or at the Catholic cemetery where they were forced to dig their own graves. Most Jews from Pruchnik were deported August 1942 to the Bełżec extermination camp in Poland.[34]

A disturbing reminder of medieval anti-Semitism at Pruchnik was reported by various news agencies during Easter on 21 April 2019 as the entire town of Pruchnik, including children, revived their annual tradition of beating, dragging, hanging, drowning, and burning an effigy of Judas. The effigy was an offensive stereotypical depiction of an Orthodox Jew with *peyos* (side curls), wearing a star of David patch with a long red nose. This action was condemned by the Catholic Church and by many Jewish organizations including the World Jewish Congress.[35]

Moses Isak Geiger and Chaja Itta Stockman

Mojzes Isak, Chaja Itta, Miriem Esther, and Riva Silka all lived in Pruchnik and all perished ca. 1942 at Bełżec, Lubelskie, Poland during the Holocaust. Various pages of testimony (POTs) were submitted by relatives to Yad Vashem. Chaja Itta had a brother Yehoshua Shtokman, who submitted a POT in Hebrew to Yad Vashem for his brother-in-law Moses Geiger and for his sister Chaja Itta.[36] A page of testimony was submitted by Helene Bialik in English for Moses Isak Geiger murdered during the Shoah.[37]

A POT was submitted for Miriem Esther by Helene Bialik as testimony that she was murdered during the Shoah.[38] Another POT was submitted for Riwa Silka by Helene Bialik as testimony of her murder.[39] Much of the following information came from an interview conducted by Estelle Guzik 1990 in Israel with Helene Bialik and was incorporated in Ms. Guzik's *Landesman Family Tree-Geiger Branch*.

Ida Geiger and Mendel Wachsman

Moses Itzak and Chaja Itta Geiger's daughter Ida (Itzel) Geiger was born 12 April 1914 at Pruchnik. She was the sole survivor of her immediate family who escaped death during the Shoah. According to my cousin Janie, her mother Ida left Pruchnik to escape from the Nazi army in 1939 with her uncle, by swimming across the Wislok River. They fled into the forest at the other side of the river and headed towards Soviet-held territory. Ida and her uncle were subsequently arrested, and her uncle was sent to a labor camp during 1940–1941. Ida was released to cousins from her Stockman family who lived at Lviv (Lwów), in the Ukraine.[40] Ida was then deported to Kazan and to Samarkand, Uzbekistan. She recalled seeing the celebrated General Anders mounted on his horse in the refugee camp where she was held.[41]

Ida met her future husband Mendel Wachsman when she was exiled to Uzbekistan. They were married 15 March 1945 at Samarkand, Uzbekistan. Mendel Wachsman was born 28 October 1910 at Łańcut, Podkarpackie, Poland to parents Meyer Wachsman and Yochevet Sprecher. After surviving Siberia and Uzbekistan, Ida and Mendel Wachsman were transferred to a Displaced Persons Camp in Germany.[42]

When WWII ended Ida and Mendel Wachsman departed from Bremerhaven, Germany on the *S.S. General M.B. Stewart* and arrived at New York 2 May 1951. They travelled with their three children: Moses (Moshe Meier) born at Bad-Reichenhall, Germany; Isak (Chaim Yitzchak) born at Eichstaat, Germany and Jacheta aka Jane (Yochevet Miriam) born at Goggingen, Germany. Their youngest child Bernard (Berish Yechezkiel) was born at New York. All are still living.

(LtoR) Unknown Couple, Ida and Mendel Wachsman

Both Mendel and Ida Wachsman submitted their Petitions for Naturalization to the U.S. District Court at New York City. They were both approved for citizenship 11 June 1956.[43] Mendel Wachsman worked for the U.S. Post Office. He made a claim for Social Security benefits 12 April 1976.[44] He died 9 September 1998 and was buried at Har Hamenuchot Cemetery, Jerusalem, Israel. Ida Wachsman née Geiger died 12 September 2013 at New York and was buried at Har Hamenuchot Cemetery, Jerusalem, Israel.

Gittel Geiger

Gittel Geiger was born 1890 at Błażowa, Podkarpackie, Poland to Yehezkiel and Fradal Geiger. She married Joseph Alter Weissblum, born at Leżajsk, Podkarpackie, Poland, son of Elchanan Weissblum and Rachel. Helene Bialik estimated they married before 1922 since their child Esther Malka was born 1922. Gittel and Joseph Weissblum lived at Leżajsk with their family. Joseph Alter Weissblum was a businessman, who managed transportation of merchandise from other towns to Leżajsk. During the Shoah, he was exiled to Siberia and died there of starvation 3 March 1943.[45] He was buried at Bodaybo, Irkutsk, Siberia, Russia.

Ida Wachsman née Geiger, 99th year

Gittel Weissblum was among the Jews rounded up by the Nazis at Sieniawa, Poland during 13 August 1942. She was shot in the fields and buried in a mass grave.[46] This information was reported to Estelle Guzik by Helene Bialik 12 March 1990 and by Frieda Bomrind 3 December 1991.[47] Apparently Josef Weissblum's father Elchanan Weissblum also perished 3 March 1943 at Bodaybo, Irkutsk, Siberia, Russia. Josef Weissblum (Yosef Veisblum) was listed in a Yizkor book to the martyrs of Leżajsk, as having been murdered during the Shoah.[48] A POT for Gittel Weisblum was submitted by Helene Bialik who noted that she was a housewife and lived with her family at Leżajsk prior to her murder.[49]

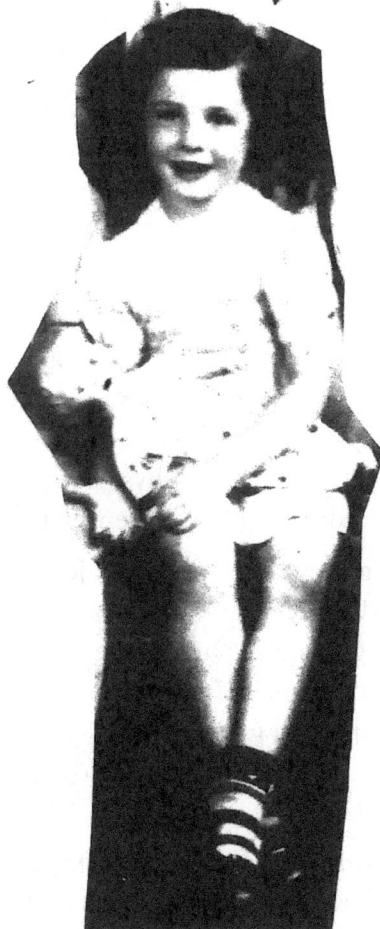

Mendel Wachsman, Ida Wachsman, Janie, 1954 New York

Leżajsk, Podkarpackie, Poland

Leżajsk (Yiddish name Lizhensk) began as a city in 1397 and was located on the banks of the San River. It is approximately 16 miles NNE from Łańcut, 24 miles NE from Rzeszów, 42 miles NE from Błażowa and 37 miles N from Pruchnik. Leżajsk was situated on what was the main water trade route of Lvov-Przemyśl-Jaroslaw-Sandomir-Gdansk. This advantageous location on the banks of the San River was supported by King Zigmont August and he gave the city the rights to build boats for transferring produce and merchandise to Gdansk. The route to Gdansk was circuitous; the San River connected to the Bug River through a tributary and then the Bug River flowed into the Wisla River to Gdansk. Leżajsk grew prosperous with increased trade and annual fairs.

After the Tartars looted and burned the city in 1524, King Sygmund the Elder had the city moved six kilometers further inland at the present location within the San River Valley. Privileges granted to the Jews were reconfirmed by King Jan Sobieski III in 1685. As the city thrived, Jews flocked to Leżajsk to work as merchants, traders, lessees of taverns and inns. Jews dwelt around the market square and side streets; they built a beautiful synagogue and a cheder. By 1880 the Jewish population was 1,868 out of a total population of 4,945 (38%). In 1900 the total population of Leżajsk was 9000 of which 2,760 were Jews (31%). A fire in 1906 destroyed 200 Jewish owned homes, resulting in increased Jewish emigration overseas.[50]

During the interwar period Jews built a library, became members of the city council, owned a bank and several large textile businesses. Many had businesses selling liquor, tobacco, lumber, iron products, as well as restaurants and bakeries. Jews also worked as attorneys, physicians, dentists, and teachers. Leżajsk was extensively destroyed during WWI then looted during November 1918.

The defining event that ended any Jewish presence in Leżajsk was WWII. On 14 September 1939, the synagogue was burned and thus began Nazi persecution and systematic genocide. During the Soviet occupation of Poland many Jews were deported to Siberia. After the Nazis invaded, they confined the few remaining Jews in Leżajsk to a ghetto during 1941. Jews were expelled September 1942 to another ghetto at Tarnogrod and from there were deported to the extermination camp at Bełżec.[51]

Prior to WWII, there was a Jewish golden age in Leżajsk (Yiddish as Lizhensk) that centered around the arrival of Rabbi Elimelech Lipman of Lizhensk (1717–1786) son of Rabbi Eliezer Lipman and Mirel (Miriam). Rabbi Elimelech

Lipman was married twice, his first wife was Shprintze Weissblum and his second wife was Gittel. Hasidic knowledge and culture originated from the founding rabbi of Hasidism; Rabbi Israel ben Eliezer known as the Baal Shem Tov. One of his disciples was Rabbi Dov Ber of Mezeritch who mentored Rabbi Elimelech Lipman of Lizhensk. Rabbi Elimelech's surname is known both as Lipman and Weissblum. He wrote the *Noam Elimelech* and helped to shape a role for mystical leadership in Hasidism.

Many Jews traveled from great distances to visit Leżajsk and hear words from Rabbi Elimelech Lipman Weissblum who was called the Righteous. On the anniversary of his death 21 Adar (Jewish calendar), thousands of Hasids made a pilgrimage to Leżajsk for prayers of healing and redemption at his ohel (a small masonry structure built around a revered grave). This homage continues today by Hasids. Rabbi Elimelech was alleged to declare before his death that any Hasid who prayed at his grave was guaranteed to have his heart's wishes fulfilled.

When the Yahrzeit (anniversary of death) of Rabbi Elimelech occurred, Leżajsk became the center of the Hasidic world. Thousands of Hasidim arrived.

Rabbi Elimelech Lipman Weissblum ohel, Leżajsk

Merchants set up their stalls to sell food, beverages, holy objects and books near the cemetery and the synagogue. Huge crowds gathered around the grave to pour out their requests. This annual excitement would last for several days before and after the Yahrzeit, then when the crowds left, Leżajsk or Lizhensk returned to daily life.[52]

According to Estelle Guzick's interview with Helene Bialik 12 March 1990, Gittel Geiger's husband Joseph Alter Weissblum was a direct descendent of Rabbi Elimelech Weissblum of Leżajsk, one of the founding rabbis of Hasidism in Poland and he was also a nephew of Rabbi Zusha of Anipoli, (1718–1800); indeed, both Rabbi Elimelech Weissblum and Rabbi Zusha were brothers. I researched family histories for Rabbi Elimelech Weissblum in Neil Rosenstein's genealogical volumes *The Unbroken Chain* and on relevant websites without confirmation that Joseph Alter Weissblum was a direct descendant of Rabbi Elimelech Lipman Weissblum.

The only commonalities were the surname Weissblum and the town of Leżajsk. I did find a clue for learning more about a Joseph Weissblum in the Rzeszów 1910 Census. There was a family in the census headed by a widow, Rasche Weissblum, born 1862 at Sanok but belonging to the community of Leżajsk. Her seven children included Joseph Weissblum born 1894 at Leżajsk.[53] The name Rasche was a variation of Rachel. Could this be Josef Weissblum who was later married to Gittel Geiger? Was Rachel Weissblum married to Elchanan Weissblum? Was there a family connection with Rabbi Elimelech Weissblum/Lipman? Without additional evidence, my questions remained unanswered.

Gittel and Joseph Weissblum had one child, Esther Malka Weissblum, born 13 October 1922 at Leżajsk, Poland. Esther Malka survived imprisonment at Siberia during the war.[54] She married Henry (Henech) Schubin, son of Wolf (Zev) Leib Arie Szubin and Fradla Rieder on 26 November 1946. Henry Schubin was born 21 June 1914 at Dukla, Podkarpackie, Poland. Esther Malka and Henry Schubin immigrated to the United States November 1952. Her occupation was doing hand embroidery. The family lived at 1170 42nd Street, Boro Park, Brooklyn, New York.

Their children were: Freida (Fradel Gittel) born 1948 (twin) at Stockholm, Sweden; Joseph Alter born 1948 (twin) at Stockholm, Sweden; William (Zev) born 8 March 1951 at Stockholm, Sweden, died 12 March 1965 in a bicycle accident at Brooklyn, New York. He was buried in Washington Cemetery, Floral Park, Monmouth, New Jersey. Esther Malka Schubin née Weissblum listed her birthdate as 12 June 1922 on her Social Security Application.[55] Her birthdate was listed as 10 June 1922 on the U.S. Social Security Death Index and she died April 1980 in New York.[56] Henry Schubin was listed in the U.S. Social Security Death Index, died 10 March 2010 and his last residence was at Suffern, Rockland County, New York.[57] He died at Lakeland, Camden, New Jersey.[58]

Oscar (Osias Mendel/Yehoshua Menachem) Geiger

After Estelle Guzik mentioned that Oscar Geiger was her Geiger relative from Błażowa, I decided to research his background to learn if there was a connection with my Geiger family from Błażowa. Oscar's name was Osias Mendel Geiger, and he was born 22 June 1891 at Błażowa Podkarpackie, Poland. His Hebrew given name was Yehoshua (Joshua) Menachem Geiger. His parents were Yehezkiel aka Chaskel Geiger and Breitel aka Fradal Landesman.

Oscar Geiger served in the Austrian military medical corps in WWI. He was a medic and worked with a Jewish physician at an Army hospital on the border of Austria and Hungary. After demobilization, he moved to Vienna, Austria. While in Vienna he met and married Matla Mersel 2 July 1922. She was born 10 September 1895 at Radymno, Podkarpackie, Poland to parents Samuel Mersel and Munia aka Miriam Grossman. Oscar and Matla had one child; a daughter named Helene. Matla and Oscar Geiger immigrated to the United States in 1941; Matla died 26 March 1944 in New York City. She was buried at Mt. Hebron cemetery, Queens, New York.[59]

Prior to his immigration to the United States, Oscar Geiger lived in Vienna with his wife and daughter where he became a merchant and proprietor of a

Oscar and Matla Geiger 1929

dry goods store as well as a money lender. The family lived on 68 Klosterneu-burgergasse in Vienna. This location is in the mainly Jewish Leopoldstadt district and was situated near the residence of my Geiger relatives, Rabbis Aron, and Abraham Geiger. My cousin Clara, a granddaughter of Rabbi Abraham Geiger, recalled hearing about the other Geiger family from Błażowa, who also lived at Vienna. She heard they were distant cousins.[60]

The War Changed Everything

Anti-Semitic violence broke out 1938 in Germany and Austria with mobs looting and destroying Jewish property, as well as torturing and murdering Jews. Oscar, Matla and Helene realized that Vienna was no longer safe. They escaped from Vienna 1939 to Italy. Once in Italy they decided to split up, with Helene as the first to leave Europe for the United States. Although their plan was to re-unite safely in the United States, Oscar and Matla were arrested at Milan, Italy during July 1940.[61] Oscar Geiger was subsequently imprisoned at an Italian concentration camp named Lager Isola Gran Sasso, that had very primitive living conditions and scarce food. It was in the mountainous Abruzzo region in Southern Italy east of Rome. While he was held as a prisoner at the camp, Oscar developed angina pectoris.[62] Oscar and Matla were able to obtain American visas that originated from Rome dated 15 May 1941. This action was prior to the Japanese attack on Pearl Harbor 7 December 1941 followed by United States declarations of war against Japan and Germany.

Their visas saved them; Oscar and Matla were listed on the passenger manifest of the ship *S.S. Excalibur* that departed from Lisbon, Portugal 18 July 1941 and arrived at New York on 28 July 1941.[63] Their destination was to their daughter Helene who lived in the Bronx, New York. Helene paid for their passage.[64] I found information about the *S.S. Excalibur*. It was built 1930 at Camden, New Jersey and it was a combination passenger-cargo ship providing regular service from New York City to ports in Europe and the Mediterranean. The ship was renamed the *USS Joseph Hewes* during WWII and became a troop transport for the Navy. It was sunk by German submarines November 1942.[65]

Oscar Geiger filed the SS-5 application for a Social Security Account Number on 20 October 1941.[66] This document indicated after Oscar Geiger arrived at New York, he found employment with Berman Brothers, 49 West 27th Street, in Manhattan, New York. He gave his parents' names as Harry Geiger and Freda Landesman.[67] He also completed a WWII draft registration card for older men born between 1877 and 1897. He was living at 343 East 173 Street, Bronx, New

York. He gave his birth information, 22 June 1891 at Błazowa, Poland and his wife's name as Martha Geiger.[68]

Naturalization

Oscar, Matla aka Martha and their daughter Helene Geiger completed their Declaration of Intention for citizenship on 10 April 1942 at the United States Southern District Court at New York. Oscar stated that he was born at Błażowa, Poland on 22 June 1891. He entered the United States on 28 July 1941, his occupation was a salesman, his physical description was 5 feet 2 inches, 125 pounds, with a fair complexion, hazel eyes, and grey hair. His wife Matla was born at Radymno, Poland on 10 September 1895. They had one child, a daughter, Helene, born 20 September 1923 at Vienna, Austria and she resided at New York.[69] The Affidavit of Witnesses testifying for Oscar Geiger's good moral character and qualifications to become a United States citizen was signed by his daughter Helene Bialik and her husband Rabbi Nathan Bialik living at 947 51st Street, Brooklyn, New York on 21 May 1947. The affidavit also included approval of Oscar Geiger's Certificate of Arrival that indicated he lawfully entered the United States.[70] Oscar Geiger took his Oath of Allegiance 23 June 1947 and became a naturalized citizen.[71]

Oscar Geiger's Quest for Reparations

After the war Austria had a reparation process for Shoah victims. I contacted the Austrian State Archives 2010 with my list of relatives who possibly applied for financial assistance. The Archives promptly sent me records for many of my Geiger relatives. I was amazed at the quantity of records sent and readily found correspondence between Oscar Geiger and the Viennese Assistance Fund for the Politically Persecuted Who Have Their Primary Residence Abroad.[72] This organization was known as Hilfsfonds, their purpose was to provide financial reparation for victims who suffered in the Holocaust. Please understand that most of the correspondence was in German and since I had little knowledge of that language, I used www.googletranslate.com and German dictionaries.

Hilfsfonds as a bureaucratic entity required much documentation from victims including physician's affidavits. Oscar Geiger made an appeal for help and began this process in 1956 with his affidavit and account of why he was seeking financial help.[73] Here is his request translated from the German:

I am 65 years old, a Jew, and had to leave Austria in July 1939 with my wife because of the persecutions. We went first to Milan in July 1940, and I was arrested by the police then taken to the concentration camp Lago Isola Gran Sasso. My wife continued to live in Milan. My nerves and health deteriorated at Lago and I needed medical treatment. Because I was able to present an American visa in June 1941, I was released. We went to the United States where our daughter was living for 1½ years. I am penniless here and we moved in with our daughter who supported us. We were also supported for about two years by HIAS. After that time, I was temporarily working as a salesman and earning about $30 to $35 weekly until a year ago. My wife died 1944 at Bellevue Hospital with a chronic disease whose costs were carried by HIAS. Since the beginning of 1956 I have no income and cannot buy anything. I have no assets or any pension from Austria. I enclose the medical affidavit stating that I am completely unable to work.

This affidavit was signed by Oscar Geiger 26 December 1956, notarized, then sent to Hilfsfonds. His physician Dr. Abraham Lieberson also submitted an affidavit 19 December 1956 testifying that Oscar Geiger was under his care for arteriosclerotic heart disease and angina pectoris that began when he was held prisoner in the Isola del Gran Sasso concentration camp, Italy during 1940–41. Oscar Geiger was considered permanently disabled.

I searched for further information about the Isola del Gran Sasso camp in Italy. I discovered an interesting website istrianet.org. that contained relevant information. When Italy joined the Axis Powers June 1940 the fascist Italian government established 43 concentration camps within Italy. Some were labor camps and others were transit camps where Jews were deported to extermination camps. The concentration camps included Jews, gypsies, homosexuals, and Italian opponents to the Fascist regime of Benito Mussolini. By the end of 1940 there were concentration camps including Isola del Gran Sasso situated in the province of Teramo, in the Abruzzo Region of Italy. This area is now a wildlife refuge and national park.[74]

Another medical report was filed by a Hilfsfonds approved physician Dr. Fritz Einstein, 15 March 1957. This physician evaluated Oscar Geiger's request with the report by Dr. Lieberson. Dr. Einstein decided there was no history of injury, just primitive living quarters and scarce food at the concentration camp. He ruled that any connection of arteriosclerotic heart disease with the Italian concentration camp was improbable, and that Oscar Geiger's medical conditions came with age. He also noted that the angina pectoris was of a moderate degree

UNITED STATES OF AMERICA   518292

DECLARATION OF INTENTION   No.
(Invalid for all purposes seven years after the date hereof)

STATE OF NEW YORK } In the _____ DISTRICT _____ Court
SOUTHERN DISTRICT OF NEW YORK of ____ UNITED STATES ____ NEW YORK ____ at ____

(1) My full, true, and correct name is OSCAR GEIGER formerly Osias Mendel Geiger
(Full, true name, without abbreviation, and any other name which has been used, must appear here)
(2) My present place of residence is 343 East 173 St. NY NY NY
(Number and street)   (City or town)   (State)
(3) My occupation is none   (4) I am 50 years old. (5) I was born on June 22, 1891
                                                                      (Month) (Day)   (Year)
in Blazowa Poland   (6) My personal description is as follows: Sex male
(City or town) (County, district, province, or state) (Country)
color white complexion dark, color of eyes hazel, color of hair hazel, height 5 feet 5 inches, weight 135 pounds,
visible distinctive marks none, race white, present nationality Austria
(7) I am married; the name of my wife or husband is Marta ; we were married 7/2/1922
                                                                                   (Month) (Day) (Year)
at Vienna Austria ; he or she was born at Radymno Poland
(City or town) (State or country)   (City or town) (County, district, province, or state) (Country)
on September 10, 1895 ; and entered the United States at New York NY
   (Month)   (Day)   (Year)   (City or town)   (State)
on July 26, 1941 for permanent residence in the United States, and now resides at 343 East 173 St. NY NY NY
   (Month) (Day) (Year)   (City or town) (County and State)
(8) I have children; and the name, sex, date and place of birth, and present place of residence of each of said children who is living, are as follows:
Helen(f) September 20, 1922 born at Vienna Austria and resides at New York NY

(9) My last place of foreign residence was Rome Italy (10) I emigrated to the United States from
                                            (City or town) (County, district, province, or state) (Country)
Lisbon Portugal (11) My lawful entry for permanent residence in the United States was
            (Country)
at New York NY under the name of Osias Mendel Geiger
   (City or town) (State)
on July 26, 1941 , on the SS Excalibur
   (Month) (Day) (Year)   (Name of vessel or other means of conveyance)
(12) Since my lawful entry for permanent residence I have not been absent from the United States, for a period or periods of 6 months or longer, as follows:

DEPARTED FROM THE UNITED STATES			RETURNED TO THE UNITED STATES		
PORT	DATE (Month, day, year)	VESSEL OR OTHER MEANS OF CONVEYANCE	PORT	DATE (Month, day, year)	VESSEL OR OTHER MEANS OF CONVEYANCE

(13) I have not heretofore made declaration of intention: No. ____, on ____ at ____
(County)   (State)   in the ____ ____
                                       (Month) (Day) (Year)   (City or town)
                                       (Name of court)

(14) It is my intention in good faith to become a citizen of the United States and to reside permanently therein. (15) I will, before being admitted to citizenship, renounce absolutely and forever all allegiance and fidelity to any foreign prince, potentate, state, or sovereignty of whom or which at the time of admission to citizenship I may be a subject or citizen. (16) I am not an anarchist; nor a believer in the unlawful damage, injury, or destruction of property, or sabotage; nor a disbeliever in or opposed to organized government; nor a member of or affiliated with any organization or body of persons teaching disbelief in or opposition to organized government. (17) I certify that the photograph affixed to the duplicate and triplicate hereof is a likeness of me and was signed by me.
I do swear (affirm) that the statements I have made and the intentions I have expressed in this declaration of intention subscribed by me are true to the best of my knowledge and belief: SO HELP ME GOD.

Oscar Geiger
(Original and true signature of declarant without abbreviation, also other name if used)

Subscribed and sworn to (affirmed) before me in the form of oath shown above in the office of the
Clerk of said Court, at New York NY
this 10th day of April , anno Domini 19 42 I hereby certify that
Certification No. 2-241643 from the Commissioner of Immigration and Naturalization, showing the lawful entry for permanent residence of the declarant above named on the date stated in this declaration of intention, has been received by me, and that the photograph affixed to the duplicate and triplicate hereof is a likeness of the declarant.

[SEAL]   GEORGE J. H. FOLLMER
                                          Clerk of the U. S. DISTRICT Court.
                                     By ____ Deputy Clerk.

Oscar Geiger

Form N-315
U. S. DEPARTMENT OF JUSTICE
IMMIGRATION AND NATURALIZATION SERVICE
●16—19119-1   U. S. GOVERNMENT PRINTING OFFICE

Oscar Geiger, Declaration of Intention

as Oscar did not carry nitroglycerin with him. He wrote that Oscar Geiger was not permanently disabled or totally incapable of earning his own living.

After several appeals, Hilfsfonds ruled 3 November 1958 that Oscar Geiger's claim for reparation did not meet their standards for full reparation in certain classification groups A and B. They later placed his request in Groups C and E that allowed him a small amount of money. They mailed him a money order on 1 October 1958. Oscar Geiger received social security from the United States as he obtained a social security number soon after he became a naturalized citizen. Oscar lived with his married daughter Helene Bialik after the death of his wife Matla.

Death

On the Social Security death index, Oscar Geiger was listed as having died 22 October 1986 in Israel.[75] He was buried in the Har Hamenuchot cemetery, Jerusalem, Israel. His daughter Helene and son-in-law Nathan Bialik were buried at the same family plot. The family plot also included the graves of Mendel and Ida Wachsman.[76]

Oscar and Matla's Daughter Helene

Oscar and Matla had one child, Helene (Hinda Zelda), born 20 September 1923 at Vienna, Austria. When the *Anschluss* began her parents made their decision to leave Austria for Italy.[77] Helene departed from Genoa, Italy on the *S.S. Rex* and arrived at New York 9 November 1939.[78] The ship was a luxurious Italian ocean liner owned by the Italian Line. It was a commercial ship that travelled the Mediterranean with voyages to New York during 1931 to June 1940 until Italy entered WWII. The ship was kept out of service then was bombed by RAF aircraft and sank 8 September 1944 in Capodistria Bay, near Trieste.[79]

New York and Citizenship

The 1940 Federal Census indicated Helene Geiger lived with relatives from her mother's side of the family at 27 Marcy Place in the Bronx. The head of the family was her aunt Celia Mersel, age 38, single; who lived with her niece Helene Geiger, age 17, single; brother-in-law Jack Greiner, age 29, married; his wife Hilda née Mersel Greiner, age 30, married and their child Laurie Greiner, age 3 born in Palestine. Everyone else was born in Austria. Celia Mersel worked as a stitcher for wholesale corsets and Jack Greiner worked as a shipping clerk in wholesale auto parts.[80]

Helene was reunited with her parents upon their arrival in the United States 28 July 1941. She resided with her parents at 343 East 173rd. Street, Bronx, New York. She submitted her Declaration of Intention for citizenship on 10 April 1942. She emigrated from Genoa, Italy on the *S.S. Rex* and arrived at New York 9 November 1939.[81] Helene submitted her Declaration of Intention together with her parents on the same day. Her Petition for Naturalization was accepted by the U.S. District Court at New York City on 5 February 1945.[82]

Marriage

Helene married Rabbi Nathan Bialik on 24 February 1946 at Kings County, New York.[83] Helene and Nathan Bialik resided at 956 51st Street, Brooklyn, New York. After Helene married, Oscar moved closer to his daughter at 1153 52nd Street, Brooklyn. Helene's husband Rabbi Nathan Bialik was born 21 January 1918 at Trestine, Poland near Bialystok. His parents were Rabbi Chaim Bialik and Rifka Yalowski. He immigrated to the United States with his parents and sister Lena. He attended Yeshiva Tiferet in Jerusalem. Nathan then studied at Yeshiva Kameniz in Poland 1931–1933 and from 1933–1941 he studied with Rabbi David Leibowitz of the Rabbinic Seminary in Williamsburg, Brooklyn. In 1941, he received *semicha* (rabbinical ordination) from the Union of Orthodox Rabbis of Williamsburg, Brooklyn. Nathan taught Talmud at Yeshiva Eitz Chaim in Boro Park, Brooklyn and in 1965 he took over his father's position as Rabbi for Aron Streit's Matzah bakery. [84] Helene and Rabbi Nathan Bialik had one child, Mordecai aka Martin. Martin and his wife Tova made Aliyah September 1972. They reside in Israel with their children and grandchildren. Martin helpfully sent me family photographs and filled in family history.

Israel

Oscar Geiger together with his daughter Helene and son-in-law Rabbi Nathan Bialik made Aliyah to Israel June 1982. Rabbi Nathan Bialik died 28 September 2000 at Jerusalem, Israel. Helene Bialik née Geiger resided at an assisted living facility at 7 Anna Frank Street, Herzliya, Israel until her death 23 May 2011 at Herzliya, Israel. Both Nathan and Helene Bialik were buried in Har Hamenuchot Cemetery, Jerusalem, Israel. My cousin Elizabeth in Israel spoke with Helene's son Martin. Martin recalled that his grandfather Oscar Geiger told him about Geiger cousins, brothers Abraham and Charles Geiger and how Abraham was a rabbi and gabbai to the Bluzhova rabbi. While in Israel, Helene Bialik filed a POT for her maternal grandfather Schmuel Mersel with the following information.

His wife was Miriam Mersel née Grossman, and his parents were Ascher and Hinda Mersel. Schmuel Mersel was a businessman who lived at Radymno and Dobromil, Poland. He was murdered during the war.[85]

Meilich Geiger

Meilich Geiger was born 1893 at Błażowa, Podkarpackie, Poland to Yehezkeil Geiger and Freda Landesman. He was a businessman and was married 1924 to

Declaration of Intention, Helene Geiger

Tauba Weinstein.[86] Tauba Weinstein was born 1893 at Gorlice to Rechla Fuehrer and Mojzes Weinstein. Meilich and Tauba had two children: Fradl born after 1924 and a son (unknown). Meilich and his family were living at Rzeszów, Podkarpackie, Poland. His niece Helene Bialik and his cousin Estelle Guzik submitted POTs to Yad Vashem Central Database of Shoah Victims' Names for Meilich Geiger.[87] This entire family perished ca. July 1942 at Bełżec, Lubelskie, Poland.[88]

Bełżec, Lubelskie, Poland

So many descendants of this Geiger lineage were murdered by the Nazis during the Holocaust. They were taken from their towns Błażowa, Pruchnik, Leżajsk, Rzeszów, Kraków, Sieniawa and deported to the death camp of Bełżec where they were put to death in gas chambers or shot, beaten, buried alive, and tortured only because they were Jewish.

Establishment of extermination camps was part of the Nazi plan named *Aktion Reinhard*, to expedite the planned genocide of the Jews. The town of Bełżec in Lubelskie, Poland was chosen by the Nazis for logistical reasons since it connected at Rawa Ruska with main railway lines from Lwów, Stanisławów, Rzeszów, Przemyśl, Tarnów and Kraków. The site for the Bełżec death camp was located near the Bełżec railway station. Construction began November 1941 and was completed by the end of February 1942. The Nazis planted large fir and pine trees around the borders of the camp to hide their murderous actions. Bełżec was decommissioned spring 1943.

About 50 Jews escaped from Bełżec and only a handful survived the war. Three survivors provided eyewitness testimony about the extreme cruelty and genocide. Researchers estimated there were at least 434,500 to 600,000 victims murdered at Bełżec, but it is unlikely the precise number will ever be known. A memorial site at Bełżec was opened June 2004 by the Polish government with a museum.[89]

Helene and Nathan Bialik 1990

DNA Study

I found descendants of Moshe Yitzchak Geiger, Janie and Doni, by first accessing www.geni.com and www.myheritage.com. Janie agreed that it was no coincidence that her grandfather Mojzes Yitzchak Geiger and my great-uncle Rabbi Abraham Geiger were both affiliated with the Bluzhova Rabbi in Błażowa. *(See Chapter Abraham Yitzak Geiger and Sprynca Stark).* Given the small population of Jews in Błażowa, it seemed most likely that both Geiger families were related although I was left with the remaining unanswered question how they were related.

My family research revealed that Chaskel/Yehezkeil from Geiger Family (A) was a contemporary of my great-grandfather Aron Geiger from my Geiger Family (B). Yehezkeil's father was Eliezer Geiger born ca.1827 in Poland. Aron Geiger's father was Shlomo David Geiger born ca.1823. Shlomo David Geiger and Eliezer Geiger were contemporaries, both from Błażowa, with the additional circumstantial evidence both families shared the same surname; later generations of both families referred to one another as distant cousins. My great-great-grandfather Shlomo David Geiger and Eliezer Geiger were probably brothers but could also be cousins or uncle and nephew. Through a comparison of the Solomon David Geiger Family Tree (B) with the Eliezer Geiger Family Tree (A) one can observe that both Geiger lineages had comparable dates for each generation.

(LtoR) Standing: Tova, Nathan, Helene. Sitting: Oscar Geiger and grandchildren

I used DNA statistical analysis to see if I could find a genetic relationship between the two families since records and documents were extremely rare or non-existent earlier than 1800. They would have been destroyed during pogroms, wars, fires, floods. Another factor to be considered is the use of surnames by

Jews only began after the Austrian monarch Josef II decree in 1787. Prior to that time, Jews were known by their father's name (patronymic) or less commonly by their mother's name (matronymic), or by occupation, personal characteristic, etc. Searching for relevant Geiger records earlier than 1800 presented as a stumbling block.

I initially asked my first and second cousins descended from my Solomon David Geiger tree, Geiger Family B, to be tested for their autosomal DNA (atD-NA) with the testing company FamilyTreeDna. One purpose was to find matches with unknown cousins to expand knowledge of our family tree. I asked Doni as a descendant from Geiger Family A to have his atDNA tested with FamilyTreeDna and he agreed. In this way, match comparisons could be made between the two Geiger families. I also researched other studies for information on atDNA analysis that would be applicable to our Geiger families Ashkenazi Jewish ethnicity.

Genetic research pertaining to Ashkenazi Jews presented an issue known as endogamy. While this was a factor to be considered, it did not prevent DNA analysis. Ashkenazi Jews taking the FamilyTreeDna Family Finder test for atDNA were found to have more genetic matches than non-Jews.[90] The reason is that Ashkenazi Jews belonged to an endogenous population, where the custom over the centuries was to marry only within their defined religious community. Thus, endogamy of Ashkenazi Jews was based on both religious and cultural traditions to marry other Jews, often close relatives such as cousins or uncles with nieces.

Due to centuries of consanguineous marriages, Ashkenazi Jews are highly inter-related and share more autosomal DNA with each other compared to people from heterogenous populations. Ashkenazi Jews can be traced to a bottleneck of a population of 350 Jews between 25 and 32 generations ago. The bottleneck was followed by rapid exponential expansion of the population. In other words, Ashkenazi Jews will share a larger amount of centimorgans (cMs) with their Ashkenazi matches and will also share more atDNA segments in common. Endogamy then results in predictions for closer cousin relationships than seen in non-endogamous populations.[91]

Another factor to consider was the recombination of atDNA with each generation. The percentage of atDNA inherited from the original ancestor is reduced with each generation. We inherit about 50 percent of our atDNA from each parent; 25 percent of our atDNA from each grandparent; 12.5 percent from each great-grandparent; 6.25 percent from each great-great-grandparent. DNA matches can be found with more distant cousins, but the odds become much smaller to find the common ancestor. [92] All relationships up to and including second cousins can be detected through autosomal DNA. Third and more distant cousin relationships may not always be detected because of the random nature of atDNA inheritance and endogamy. I also had to keep in mind that matches for cousins on such charts as *Cousin Calculator* on FamilySearch.org were normalized for non-endogamous populations.

Keeping those factors in mind, I decided to explore atDNA (autosomal) testing available through FamilyTreeDna for myself and for my 8 other known Geiger descendants from my Geiger family. I compared atDNA from Geiger descendants including myself from Geiger Family B with the known Geiger descendant (DS) from Geiger family (A). The genetic tool Chromosome Browser from FamilyTreeDna was utilized for this study.

The majority of Geiger (B) descendants (7 out of 9) from my family were positive matches with the descendant from Geiger (A) family. I analyzed the Family Finder matches from FamilyTreeDNA for shared atDNA between the Geiger Family A descendant (DS) with the seven descendant matches from Geiger Family B. I decided to focus on only shared atDNA matches for >5 centimorgans. I reasoned that this would help rule out random centimorgan matches or "noise" as I wanted to focus on my specific Geiger lineage.

The ISOGG (International Society of Genetic Genealogy) recommended when using FamilyTreeDna Family Finder data, the percentages of shared cMs can be calculated by dividing the total shared cM by 68. The number 68 is based on estimations that individuals inherit 6800 cM of atDNA or 3400 cM from each parent. If two matches share 425 cM, they share 6.25% DNA and according to the chart from ISOGG *Average Autosomal DNA Shared by Pairs of Relatives* they would be considered first cousins once removed or half first cousins. If two matches share 1700 cM, they would share 25% DNA and would be considered either a grandparent or aunt/uncle or half sibling. [93] Based on my genealogical research, I estimated that matches for atDNA testing for descendants from Geiger Family B with the descendant from Geiger Family A would likely indicate relationships of third or more distant cousins.

Basing total cM>5 matches between DS (Geiger Family A) with each match from Geiger Family B, the shared percentages indicated relationships ranging from third cousin to third cousin once removed or third cousin twice removed. Those figures however were based on the chart from the ISOGG (International

Society of Genetic Genealogy) normalized for non-endogamous populations. When comparing documentation by generations for both Geiger family trees, I estimated that the actual relationships are most likely fourth cousin once removed. The descendant DS from Geiger Family A is a fourth cousin once removed with the descendants from Geiger Family B. *(See Table 1)*

Match	TTL cM >5	TTL cM >10	TTL cm	TTL cm /68	% Shared DNA >5cM		Est. relationship	
JG	35.19	0	35.2	0.51		0.5%	3rdC 1X	
MC	27.7	0	27.7	0.41		0.4%	3rdC 1X	
EL	20.3	0	20.3	0.29		0.3%	3rdC 1X	
DP	27.3	10.14	37.4	0.55		0.6%	3rdC 1X	
GG	17.2	0	17.2	0.25		0.3%	3rdC 1X	
JS	14.5	0	14.5	0.21		0.2%	4thC or 3rd C 2X	
CL	54.3	0	54.3	0.8		0.8%	3rdC or 2nd C 2X	
	Table 1	atDNA matches Geiger Family B with DS Geiger Family A						

Table 1

According to genetic genealogists if two or more matches share a segment on a chromosome in common with each other, they most likely share a common ancestor. Chromosome mapping is a technique used to determine which segments of DNA came from which ancestor. A comparison of Geiger descendants from Geiger Family B with the descendant from Geiger Family A indicated shared segments of DNA on certain shared chromosomes. The shared segments were

Match Name		Chromosome	Start Overlap	End Overlap	Cm>6
CL		2	59001498	67432584	7.78
EL		2	59966246	66868265	6.07
GG		16	64557261	74517469	9.59
EL		16	64557261	74077862	9.16
MC		18	73958207	76116152	6.65
JG		18	73958207	76116152	6.65
CL		18	73958207	76116152	6.65
JS		22	36241136	41732968	8.62
GG		22	36543329	41732968	7.62
JG		22	36543329	41732968	7.62
	Table 2	Triangulations of Geiger Family B with DS Geiger Family A			

Table 2

greater than 6 cM and were on four different chromosomes: 2, 16, 18 and 22. *(See Table 2)*. There were two or more matches on overlapping segments from Geiger Family B on the atDNA chromosome profile of DS. This technique was also used by Jeffrey Mark Paull to prove a genetic relationship between two rabbinical lineages, and he named this phenomenon "chromosome markers".[94] Several descendants who shared segments was additional proof of descent from a common ancestor who lived in the past, even several hundred years ago. This is considered IBD or Identical by Descent.

I also used the analysis technique of triangulation for atDNA to see if I could find additional confirmation of relationship between both Geiger lineages. Triangulation is the comparison of atDNA on a chromosomal segment of atDNA common to three or more people. Matches who have overlapping segments that all match with each other indicate the likelihood they all inherited that segment of DNA from a common ancestor. However due to Ashkenazi Jewish endogamy it is difficult to assign the atDNA to the male or female of the ancestral couple especially in the case of cousin marriages. The atDNA can be from one or both individuals of the ancestral couple in common, such as from Solomon David Geiger and/or Chaje Mindel Unger.

Cousins matching on over-lapping segments who share a common ancestral couple along with well-documented and complete family trees can add credible evidence of descent from an ancestral couple in common.[95] The issue of unidentified common ancestors can also increase the likelihood that shared atDNA may not come from the ancestral couple under study but from other undocumented ancestors. Despite this shortcoming, I feel that triangulation can be a useful tool for determining family relationships among people who had their atDNA tested. There were four different triangulated groups with DS. Three of the groups contained a significant amount of atDNA >10 cM. In addition, two of the triangulated groups had > 3 cousins. These findings are further evidence for a shared ancestor in common with both Geiger Family A and Geiger Family B. *(See Table 3)*

Autosomal DNA can be used as additional information to determine if two or more individuals are genetically related to one another or to compare lineages. Without traditional genealogical information consisting of written documentation or having a paper trail, using DNA alone to identify the common ancestor is still speculative. Despite limitations of having only one descendant from Geiger Family A and working within an endogamous population, there was a high probability that both Geiger families from Błażowa were related based on family trees, available genealogical records, and descendant interviews. In addition, findings from my atDNA research supported my hypothesis there is a genetic relationship between the two Geiger families to establish we are at least fourth cousins.

One should keep in mind that DS was a cousin once removed as he was from a younger generation than the cousins tested from Geiger Family B. The cousin relationship estimation by FamilyTreeDna for cousins with DS was placed as being 5th to remote cousin. This estimation was based on a FamilyTreeDna proprietory algorithm developed by their bioinformatics team that detected and compensated for interrelatedness in Ashkenazi Jewish populations.[96] This population had multiple common ancestral lines and resulted with increased sharing of atDNA. The amount shared would be additive and calculated by adding together the amounts of expected sharing for each known relationship. When there is more than one line of descent in common, there are many smaller identical by descent segments < 5 cM. Another complication is these blocks of smaller segments could be common within the entire population group such as Ashkenazi Jews, referred to as IBS (Identical by State).[97] Although a cousin relationship between the Geiger families A and B may be 4th or 5th to distant cousin, it is my judgment that there is a solid basis for the claim. The common ancestor or ancestors probably existed at least 200 years ago during the early 19th century or the 18th century. It was gratifying to see how atDNA research is a valuable genealogical tool to confirm a cousin relationship between families especially when there are few remaining records.

Match Name	Chromosome	start overlap	end overlap	cM
CL	2	61081798	66868265	5.05
EL	2	61081798	66868265	5.05
GG	16	53636800	83933326	50.16
EL	16	53636800	83933326	50.16
MC	18	69741616	76116152	20.67
JG	18	72112909	76116152	14.37
CL	18	69741616	76116152	20.67
JS	22	33307907	45202574	22.21
GG	22	33307907	45202574	22.21
JG	22	32918748	43343984	17.18

Table 3 Triangulations Shared by Geiger Cousins Matching DS

Table 3

Descendants of Yehezkeil Geiger

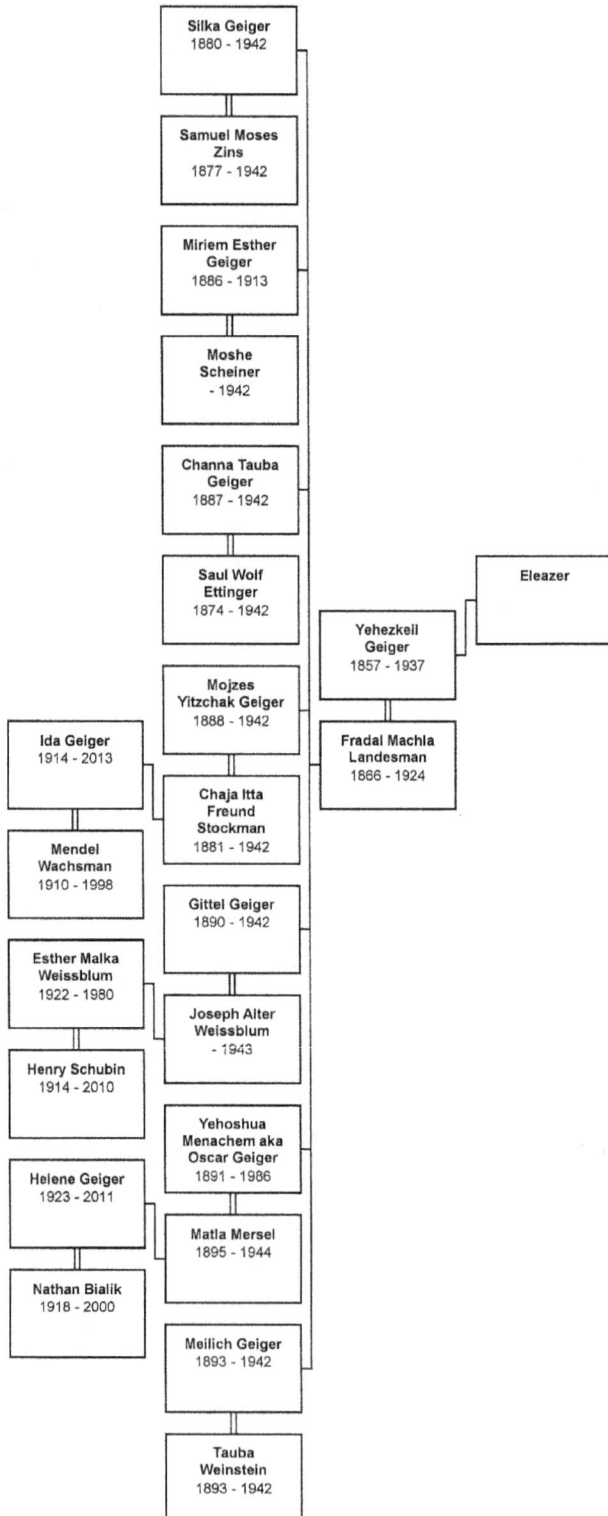

Silka Geiger
1880 - 1942

Samuel Moses Zins
1877 - 1942

Miriem Esther Geiger
1886 - 1913

Moshe Scheiner
- 1942

Channa Tauba Geiger
1887 - 1942

Saul Wolf Ettinger
1874 - 1942

Eleazer

Yehezkeil Geiger
1857 - 1937

Mojzes Yitzchak Geiger
1888 - 1942

Ida Geiger
1914 - 2013

Fradal Machla Landesman
1866 - 1924

Chaja Itta Freund Stockman
1881 - 1942

Mendel Wachsman
1910 - 1998

Gittel Geiger
1890 - 1942

Esther Malka Weissblum
1922 - 1980

Joseph Alter Weissblum
- 1943

Henry Schubin
1914 - 2010

Yehoshua Menachem aka Oscar Geiger
1891 - 1986

Helene Geiger
1923 - 2011

Matla Mersel
1895 - 1944

Nathan Bialik
1918 - 2000

Meilich Geiger
1893 - 1942

Tauba Weinstein
1893 - 1942

Endnotes

1   Ms. Guzik's Landesman Family Tree-Geiger Branch was sent to me by Doni Stern October 2013.

2   Alexander Beider. *A Dictionary of Ashkenazic Given Names*. Avotaynu: Bergenfield, New Jersey, 2001. pp.332–333.

3   Suzan Wynne. Personal email correspondence dated 2 Dec 2017.

4   Yad Vashem. org. Central Database for Shoah Victims' Names. Page of Testimony submitted 1984 by Estelle Guzik, 1984. Lazar Guzik, Item 619998. (yvng.vadvashem.org/nameDetails.html).

5   www.kidum-edu.org.il.

6   Segal, Joshua L., Rabbi. *A Field Guide to Visiting a Jewish Cemetery*. Nashua, New Hampshire: Jewish Cemetery Publishing, 2006. Rabbi Segal generously translated several matsevahs for my research.

7   W. Gunther Plaut, Editor. *The Torah:A Modern Commentary*. New York: Union of American Hebrew Congregations. p. 109. The name Eliezer was based on the biblical proselyte of Abraham, referred to in Genesis 15:2 as the Damascan Eliezer, who was a servant and/or adopted son of Abraham.

8   Shmuel Spector, Editor. Jerrold Landau, Translator. Judith C. Goldsmith, Project Coordinator. Blazowa chapter. Encyclopedia of Jewish Communities in Poland. V.III. (Yad Vashem, Jerusalem). pp. 90–92. www.jewishgen.org/yizkor/pinkas_poland.

9   Wikipedia.org. Tish (Hasidic celebration).

10   JRI-Poland.org. Przemysl Archive, Fond 2001. Sieniawa Births 1869-81. Birth: Samuel Moses Zins, Akta 52. Parents Selig Zins and Malie Helman.

11   Yad Vashem, Central Database of Shoah Victims' Names. List of Jewish residents in Lwow who voted for the Sejm, the Polish parliament in 1938. Faiga Zins, ID 7792739.

12   Yad Vashem, Central Database of Shoah Victims' Names. Page of testimony, submitted by Silka's aunt Helene Bialik for Silka Zins, ID 1062297.

13   Yad Vashem, Central Database of Shoah Victims' Names. Page of testimony, submitted by Estelle Guzik for Samuel Zins, ID 642567.

14   Shmuel Spector, Editor. *The Encyclopedia of Jewish Life Before and During the Holocaust. V.III* (New York: New York University Press, 2001), p. 1180.

15   Shmuel Spector. Editor. *The Encyclopedia of Jewish Life Before and During the Holocaust. V.I* (New York: New York University Press, 2001), p. 156.

16   Yad Vashem, Central Database of Shoah Victims' Names. Page of Testimony, submitted by Estelle Guzik for Moshe Scheiner, ID 723389.

17   Yad Vashem, Central Database of Shoah Victims' Names. Page of testimony, submitted by Estelle Guzik for Chava Silka Scheiner, ID 606777.

18   Landesman Family Tree-Geiger Branch. Prepared by Estelle Guzik.

19   Yad Vashem. Central Database of Shoah Victims' Names. Card File of Jews in Krakow with German identity card ("Kennkarte") nos. 7001-7272 with personal details and photographs. Item ID: 10324360.

20   Yad Vashem. Central Database of Shoah Victims' Names. Card File of Jews in Krakow with German identity card ("Kennkarte") nos. 7001-7272 with personal details and photographs. Item ID: 10324268.

21   Ibid., Ester Ettinger ID: 10324338; Izak Ettinger ID: 10324294.

22   Yad Vashem, Central database of Shoah Victims' Names. Page of Testimony, submitted by Helene Geiger for Toba Ettinger, ID 5650916.

23   Yad Vashem, Central Database of Shoah Victims' Names. Page of Testimony, submitted by Estelle Guzik for Channa Ettinger, ID 1889749.

24   Yad Vashem, Central Database of Shoah Victims' Names. Kennkarte nos. 7001-7272, dated March 1941 for Wolf Ettinger, ID 10324268.

25   Yad Vashem. Central Database of Shoah Victims' Names. Kennkarte nos. 7001-7272, dated March 1941 for Izak Ettinger, ID 10324294.

26   Yad Vashem. Central Database of Shoah Victims' Names. Page of Testimony, submitted by Estelle Guzik for Yitzchak Ettinger, ID 1383189.

27   Yad Vashem. Central Database of Shoah Victims' Names. Kennkarte nos. 7001-7272, dated March 1941 for Ester Ettinger, ID 10324338.

28   Shmuel Spector, Editor. *The Encyclopedia of Jewish Life Before and During the Holocaust*. V.I. (New York: New York University Press, 2001). p. 280.

29   Personal Email dated 16 March 2019 from Janie Stern.

30   JRI-Poland.org. Przemysl Archive. Fond 1761. Pruchnik Births 1871-1905. Birth Chaje Itte Sztokman. 1881. Akta 6.

31   Confidential email.

32   Dates based on unofficial records from Pruchnik not yet in the public domain.

33   szetl.org.pl/en/towns/p.153-pruchnik/gg-and history.

34   Shmuel Spector, Editor. *The Encyclopedia of Jewish Life Before and During the Holocaust*. V. II (New York: New York University Press, 2001). P. 1030.

35   www.project-syndicate.org

36   Vad Vashem, Central Database of Shoah Victims' Names. Page of Testimony, submitted by Yehoshua Shtokman for Moses Geiger, ID 782570.

37   Yad Vashem, Central Database of Shoah Victims' Names. Page of Testimony, submitted by Helene Bialik for Moses Isak Geiger, ID 1082194.

38   Yad Vashem. Central Database of Shoah Victims' Names. Page of Testimony, submitted by Helene Bialik for Miriam Esther Geiger, ID 1038310.

39   Yad Vashem. Central Database of Shoah Victims' Names. Page of Testimony submitted by Helene Geiger for Riva Silka Geiger, ID 1060567.

40   Wikipedia.org. Lviv History. Prior to WWII Lviv had the third largest Jewish population in Poland and numbered almost 100,000 forming 32% of the total population. It was only second to Warsaw as the largest cultural and academic center of Poland. As WWII began, thousands of Jewish war refugees entered Lviv. During the Holocaust when the Nazis held the city, the Lviv Ghetto was established holding 120,000 Jews. Most were deported to the Belzec extermination camp or killed locally.

41   Justice4Poland.com. Evacuation of Polish civilians from the USSR in World War II. The Anders' Army was created in 1941-42 in the Soviet Union under General Władysław Anders. This army consisted of 100,000 Polish POWs released 1941 from Soviet prisons and became known as the Polish II Corps. The army also included thousands of Polish Jews who later separated from Anders' Army when they were in the Middle East to fight for the independence of Israel

42   Bernard Wachsman, interview 10 October 1996 with Estelle Guzik.Landesman Family Tree- Geiger Branch.

43   Ancestry.com. New York, Index for Naturalizations filed in New York City, 1792–1989. Mendel Wachsman. Petition No. 675574; Ida Wachsman Petition no. 675573

44   Ancestry.com. U.S., Social Security Applications and Claims Index, 1936-2007. Mendel Wachsman.

45   Interview Helene Bialik with Estelle Guzik 12 March 1990 and interview Frieda Bomrind 3 December 1991 with Estelle Guzik. Landesman Family Tree-Geiger Branch.

46   Landesman Family Tree-Geiger Branch. Information given by Helene Bialik on 12 March 1990. Tree was passed down to the Stern Family.

47   Landesman Family Tree-Geiger Branch. Information given by Helene Bialik on 12 March 1990 and by Freida Bomrind on 3 December 1991.

48   Yad Vashem. Central Database of Shoah Victims' Names. List of murdered Jews from Yizkor books found in Lezajsk, Yizkor book to the martyrs of Lezajsk, for Yosef Veisblum, 1970. ID 10923776.

49   Yad Vashem. Central Database of Shoah Victims' Names. Page of Testimony, submitted by Helene Bialik for Gittel Weisblum, ID 1057702.

50   *Encyclopedia of Jewish Communities. Pinkas Hakehillot Polin: Lezajsk. V.III.* (Jerusalem, Israel: Yad Vashem). Pp.232–236.

51   Samuel Spector and Geoffrey Wigoder, editors. *The Encyclopedia of Jewish Life Before and During the Holocaust.* (New York: New York University Press, 2001). pp.726–727.

52   Elimelech Honig-Ronen. My Cradle Lizhensk. Translated by Jerrold Landau. The Jews of Lizhensk. (www.jewishgen.org/yizkor/lezajsk).

53   Rzeszow Archive, Fond 1. Rzeszow 1910 Census. Rasche Weissblum widow and seven children, including Joseph Weissblum. (www.jri-poland.org)

54   Landesman Family Tree- Geiger Branch. Information given by Helene Bialik on 12 March 1990.

55   Ancestry.com. U.S., Social Security Applications and Claims Index, 1936–2007. Malka Schubin. Her name was listed as Malka Schubin on June 1954.

56   Ancestry.com. U.S. Social Security Death Index, 1935–2014. Malka Schubin, birthdate 10 June 1922, died April 1980.

57   Ancestry.com. U.S. Social Security Death Index, 1935–2014. Henry Schubin, birthdate 21 Jan 1914, died 10 March 2010.

58   JewishGen.org. Family Tree of the Jewish People: Henoch Henry Schubin. Death: 10 March 2010 at Lakeland, Camden, New Jersey.

59   Mt. Hebron Cemetery, Queens, New York. Mathilda Geiger. Death 26 March 1944. Burial: Ist Radimner Congregation. Grave 25-11-H-3-16. (www.mthebroncemetery.internmentsearch.com).

60   Telephone Interview with Clara Geiger. Date: 25 April 2010.

61   During May 1939 Mussolini signed the Pact of Steel with Hitler, then on 10 June 1940 Italy declared war on France and Great Britain.

62   Osterreichisches Staatarchiv, Vienna, Austria. Hilfsfonds file for Oscar Geiger containing information about his imprisonment during WWII.

63   U.S. Department of Justice. Immigration and Naturalization Service. Certificate of Arrival. Osias Mendel Geiger. S.S. Excalibur arrived in New York 28 July 1941. No. 2 941643.

64   Ancestry.com. New York, Passenger and Crew Lists 1820–1957. Osias Mendel Geiger and Matla Geiger. S.S. Excalibur. Departure from Lisbon 18 July 1941.

65   Wikipedia.org. *USS Joseph Hewes.*

66   Treasury Department. Form SS-5. Application for Social Security Account Number. Oscar Geiger. 20 October 1941.

67   Ancestry.com. New York, Index to Petitions for Naturalization New York City, 1792–1989. Helene Geiger. Petition No. 504629.

68   Ancestry.com. Draft Registration Card. Oscar Geiger. Serial Number 2788.

69   Petition for Naturalization No. 559567. U.S. District Court of Southern District of New York. Oscar Geiger aka Osias Mendel Geiger. Date: 10 April 1942. Declaration of Intention No. 518232. Oscar Geiger. Date: 10 April 1942.

70   U.S. District Court, Southern District of New York. Affidavit of Witnesses and approval of the Certificate of Arrival   Oscar Geiger. Date: 21 May 1947. (www.ancestry.com)

71   U.S. Oath of Allegiance by Oscar Geiger. Petition Granted. Date: 23 June 1947. Certificate: 6708887.

72   Osterreichisches Staatarchiv. Austrian State Archives. Nottendorfergasse 2, A-1030 Wien.

73   Osterreichisches Staatarchiv. Letter by Oscar Geiger in German requesting financial aid from Hilfsfonds for victim war reparations. Dated 26th December 1956. Oscar Geiger's entire file from the Hilfsfonds Records were mailed from the Austrian State Archives, Vienna, Austria upon request by this researcher July 2010.

74   www.istrianet.org/istria/history/1800-present/camps/lager-italy.htm.

75   Social Security Administration. Social Security Death Index. Oscar Geiger. Died October 1986 in Israel.

76   Email from descendant Doni Stern, dated 6 July 2014.

77   Wikipedia.org. Anschluss. The Nazi armed forces crossed the border into Austria and were unopposed by the Austrian military. The Anschluss began with the annexation of Austria into Nazi Germany on 12 March 1938.

78   Ancestry.com. New York, State and Federal Naturalization Records, 1794–1943. Helene Geiger. No. 518281. 10 April 1942.

79   Wikipedia.org. *S.S. Rex.*

80   FamilySearch.org. U.S. Census 1940, New York, Bronx, Assembly District 2. Helene Geiger.

81   New York, State and Federal Naturalization Records 1794–1943. Southern District Court of New York. Declaration of Intention. Helene Geiger. No. 518281.

82   Ancestry.com. New York, Index to Petitions for Naturalization New York City 1792–1989. Helene Geiger. Petition No. 504629.

83   New York, New York, Marriage License Indexes 1907–1995. Helene Geiger and Nathan Bialik Marriage 20 Feb 1946.

84   Landesman Family Tree-Geiger Branch. Prepared by Estelle Guzik.

85   Yad Vashem, Central Database of Shoah Victims' Names. Pages of Testimony, submitted by Helene Bialik for Schmuel Mersel, 1 October 1995, Jerusalem.

86   Rzeszow Archive. Fond 533. Rzeszow Marriages 1896–1914, 17–39. Marriage Meilich Geiger and Tauba Weinstein, 1924. Akta 30. (JRI-Poland.org)

87   Yad Vashem, Central Database of Shoah Victims' Names. Pages of Testimony, submitted by Helen Bialik for Meilach Geiger ID 1038309, Estelle Guzik for Meilach Geiger ID 639905.

88   Shmuel Spector, editor. *The Encyclopedia of Jewish Life Before and During the Holocaust. V.II.* (New York, New York University Press), 2001. p 1112.

89   www.holocaustresearchproject.org.

90   Jeffrey Mark Paull, Gaye Tannenbaum and Jeffrey Briskman. Why Autosomal DNA Test Results are Significantly Different for Ashkenazi Jews. *Avotaynu* V. XXX, no. 1, Spring 2014, p.13.

91   cruwys.blogspot.com. 28 January 2016.

92   Jeffrey Mark Paull and Janet Billstein Akaha. Using Autosomal DNA Analysis to Connect Rabbinical Lineages: A Case Study of the Wertheimer and Wertheim Dynasties. *Avotaynu* V XXV111, no. 4, Winter 2012, p.61.

93   ISOGG Wiki. isogg.org/wiki/autosomal_DNA_Statistics.

94   Jeffrey Mark Paull, Gaye Tannenbaum and Jeffrey Briskman. Why Autosomal DNA Test Results are Significantly Different for Ashkenazi Jews. *Avotaynu* V. XXX, no 1, Spring 2014, pp.16–17.

95   Debbie Parker Wayne, Triangulating Autosomal DNA, National Genealogical Society *NGS Magazine* 42 (October-December 2016): 39–42.

96   learn.familytreedna.com/autosomal-ancestry/universal-dna-matching/ancestors-married-relatives-affect-results/

97   Ibid.

Chapter Twelve

Moses Geiger and Laje

The children born to my 2nd great-grandparents Solomon David Geiger and Chaje Mindel Unger were the following: Aron Geiger; Chaim Yehuda Geiger and Zipora Finder née Geiger. They were discussed in chapters two and three; *Solomon David Geiger and Chaje Mindel Unger* and *Aron Geiger and Hinde Turnheim*. I wondered if my 2nd great-grandparents had additional children. My Geiger ancestors were from Błażowa, Podkarpackie, Poland within the administrative district of Rzeszów, in western Galicia however since there were no surviving vital records from Błażowa, I broadened my search by investigating records from other archives.

My quest led me to additional Geiger birth records found in the Rzeszów Archive, Fond 990, Sokołów Małopolski, Podkarpackie, Poland, Births 1825–1912, from the village of Górno. Górno was a small shtetl with under 100 Jews, 3 miles northeast of the larger town Sokołów Małopolski, where Górno vital records were registered and held. Sokołów Małopolski is 13.7 miles northeast of the administrative city of Rzeszów and 24 miles north from my Geiger ancestral town of Błażowa.[1]

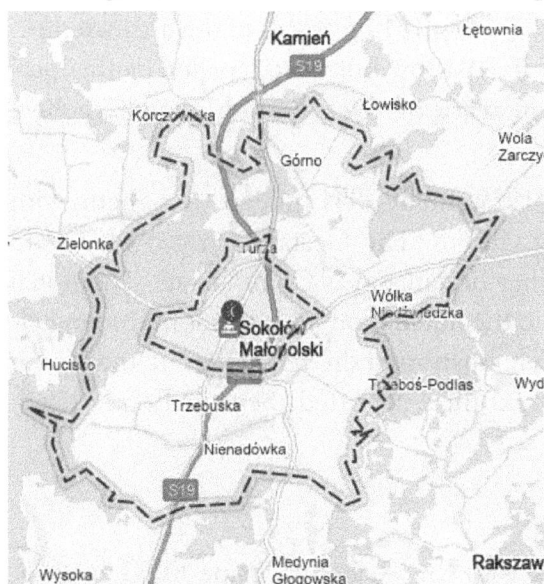

Map of Sokołów and Górno Poland

Sokołów Małopolski

The Jewish population of Sokołów Małopolski, Podkarpackie, Poland in 1890 was 2,155, about 47% out of a total population of 4,609. This town was a regional center of commerce and trade fairs. The first Jews settled in Sokołów Małopolski toward the end of the 17th century and they were innkeepers and lease holders. When the Austrian rule began in 1772 Jews numbered several hundred residents living around the central market square in their own houses. The Jewish population grew and reached its pinnacle during the 1890s.

A catastrophic fire occurred 1904 at Sokołów that destroyed 600 Jewish owned houses, the synagogue, the *mikvah* and the *Beis Midrash*. Jewish communities in the area offered help by sending money, building materials, clothing, and food. The following year an annual fair took place at Górno with Jewish merchants from Sokołów when a fight occurred between a Jewish peddler and a farmer who refused to pay for merchandise. A vicious riot broke out among the farmers who overturned the stalls of the Jews and robbed them of their goods leaving many Jews impoverished and forced to move elsewhere.

Sokołów attracted a growing Hasidic population with influential Hasidic rabbis holding rabbinical seats at Sokołów from the end of the 18th century until the end of WWI. Rabbi Elimelech the son of Rabbi Asher Yeshayahu Horowitz (from the dynasty of Rabbi Naftali-Tzvi Horowitz of Ropszyce) served at Sokołów as head of the rabbinical court and leader of the Hasidic congregation from 1840–1862. Rabbi David the son of Rabbi Moshe Halberstam was rabbi of Sokołów 1900 until WWI.[2]

During WWI the Zionist movement gained growing support in Sokołów. The Bnei Zion organization was organized in 1917 with 150 male and female members. It offered Hebrew studies and collected money for the Land of Israel, also provided funds for the local poor. During 1919 farmers in the area attempted a violent pogrom against the Jews of Sokołów but were repelled by the local police. The inter-war period saw an increase of Jewish youth joining Zionist, Mizrachi and Akiva groups.

Nazis occupied Sokołów October 1939 and by 1941 they set up a ghetto with Jews from Sokołów and surrounding villages. The Gestapo arrived May 1942 and selected certain Jews for murder they designated as Communists. Additional Gestapo arrived June 1942 to complete the liquidation *aktion*, first murdering elderly and handicapped Jews. The Nazis transported the remainder of the Jewish population of Sokołów to Rzeszów and then deported them to Bełżec death camp July 1942.[3]

The Geigers of Górno

I found interesting new birth records with the Geiger surname listed at www.jri-poland.org and subsequently sent a request 2012 using the www.jri-poland.

org form for requesting Jewish Vital Record for copies of the actual Geiger birth documents, to the Rzeszów Archive, database Sokołów Małopolski Births 1825–1912, Fond 990.[4] Those birth documents contained the names of children Chaja Mindel, born 9 June 1897, and Salamon Dawid, born 7 February 1899, to a mother named Chana Geiger from Górno.[5] The names Chaja Mindel Geiger and Salamon Dawid Geiger together on birth records from the same mother with the surname Geiger were uncommon and worth investigating as they were the given names of my 2nd great-grandparents who were deceased prior to those births. There was no mention of Chana Geiger's husband. Birth records from Galicia often indicated that children were born to unwed parents, reflecting the fact that there was a religious marriage that was not registered with the civil authorities. The Austro-Hungarian Empire considered those children to be illegitimate and so were given the maternal surname.

The records that I received from Górno for the Geigers indicated Chana Geiger was the mother and importantly, her parents' names were Moses and Laje Geiger of Górno. I continued my search to find additional records for Chana Geiger's parents. Only their death records were found in the Rzeszów Archive, Fond 990, Sokołów Małopolski, Deaths 1877–1912. There was a Mojzesz Geiger from Górno, who died in 1912 at the age of 71 years, thus born 1841. There was also a Laje Geiger (no surname) from Górno who died in 1912 at the age of 75 years thus born 1837.[6]

The given names chosen by Chana Geiger for her children, Chaje Mindel and Salamon Dawid (Solomon David) led me to further research since parents often named children after deceased relatives such as grandparents. The years fit what I knew about my 2nd great-grandparents Solomon David Geiger and Chaje Mindel Unger from Błażowa; they died several years before the births of Chana Geiger's children. If Chana named her children after her deceased grandparents Solomon David and Chaje Mindel Geiger, then her father Moses Geiger lived at Błażowa and moved to Górno when he married Laje. It seemed quite possible Moses Geiger of Górno was another son of my 2nd great-grandparents Solomon Dawid Geiger and Chaje Mindel Unger, but was there additional evidence to support my hypothesis?

Chana Geiger had additional children; I received birth documents from the Rzeszów Archive for Sara Geiger, born 8 May 1902 at Górno, and Samuel Lemel Geiger, born 27 June 1905 also at Górno.[7] I later discovered Chana had another child, Bluma, born 1908.[8] There were two more birth records from Górno with the names Beinisch (aka Benjamin) Geiger born 1911 and Izaak Geiger born 1911.[9] The latter two birth records represented twin births born at Górno to Chana Geiger. Izaak Geiger died 1912 at three months of age.[10]

I estimated that Chana Geiger was born ca. 1878 if she had her first child at age nineteen. Her father Moses Geiger was born 1841 in the same genera-

Birth record of Chaja Mindel Geiger, p. 1

Birth record of Chaja Mindel Geiger, p. 2

tion as my great-grandfather Aron Geiger. It seemed plausible they were related, perhaps brothers. The Geiger deaths for 1912 in Górno, Sokołów Małopolski included both Moses and Laje Geiger as well as the infant Izaak Geiger. I speculated that a contagious illness or plague may have occurred during 1912 that resulted in deaths at Górno, Sokołów Małopolski.

Birth record of Salamon David Geiger, p. 1

Birth record of Salamon David Geiger, p. 2

　　Birth records from the Rzeszów Archive, Fond 990 for Sokołów Małopolski also indicated Moses and Laje Geiger had two children: Chana Geiger and her sister Ides aka Yehudit Geiger, from Górno. Ides Geiger married Hersz Josef Gruenbaum and their children were: Chaje Roise born 1888; Lana born 1896;

Click to View	Surname	Given Name	Year	Type	Akta	Page / District / Sygnatura	House # / Sex / Age / Born	Date of: Birth / Marriage/Divorce / Death / Registration	Town of: Birth / Marriage / Death / Residence	Cause of Death / Spouse / Spouse Surname	Maiden Name / Patronymic	Other Surnames / Occupation / Father Occupation	Father / Mother	Father Age / Mother Age	Father Town / Mother Town
[GEIGER]	Beinisch	1911	B	65	6	M							Chana GEIGER		Górno

Birth record of Beinisch Geiger 1911

Birth record of Samuel Lemel 1905 p.1

Birth record of Samuel Lemel 1905 p.2

Aron born 1897; Naftali born 1900; Chaskel (Yehezkiel) born 1904; Scheindla born 1907.[11] Note that Chaskel is a kinnui for Yehezkiel, the biblical Ezekiel. Another birth record was found under the surname Gruenbaum for the 1893 birth of a male named Sane.[12] He died 1920 at Sokołów Małopolskie.[13] San(n)e was a kinnui for the biblical Nathaniel.

Yad Vashem Records

My next step was to research Yad Vashem Central Database of Shoah Victims for access to all relevant POT records (Pages of Testimony for victims of the Shoah) for finding descendants of Chana Geiger.[14] New facts became known based on the somber records. Apparently only two of Chana Geiger's children survived the Shoah; Beinisch aka Benjamin Geiger submitted POTs during 1994 and Shmuel Geiger submitted POTs during 1955. Benjamin Geiger's wife Lea Geiger also submitted POTs in 1994 for her parents Vitezlav and Irena Czech. Their photographs were attached with their POT files.[15]

Benjamin Geiger provided a POT for his father Eliezer Valtz. Eliezer was born in 1878 at Nisko, Poland, to parents Tzvi and Yehudit; he was married to Chana née Geiger and lived at Sokołów.

Irena Czech, née Aschkenes

Click to View	Surname	Given Name	Year	Type	Akta	Page # / District / Sygnatura	House # / Sex / Age / Born	Date of: Birth / Marriage/Divorce / Death / Registration	Town of: Birth / Marriage / Death / Residence	Cause of Death / Spouse / Spouse Surname	Maiden Name / Patronymic	Other Surnames / Occupation / Father / Occupation	Father / Mother	Father Age / Mother Age	Father Town / Mother Town	Father Father / Mother Father
	GEIGER	Isak	1912	D	14	17	M / 3m.	M	Górno			Chawa				

Death record of Izaak Geiger 1912

The Central Database of Shoah Victims' Names

Eliezer Valtz

Eliezer Valtz was born in Nisko, Poland in 1878 to Tzvi and Yehudit. He was married to Chana. Prior to WWII he lived in Sokolow, Poland. During the war he was in Sokolow, Poland. Eliezer was murdered/perished in 1942 in Belzec, Poland. This information is based on a Page of Testimony (displayed on left).

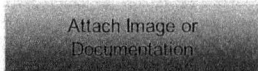

Source:	Pages of Testimony
Last Name:	Valtz
First Name:	Eliezer
Father's First Name:	Tzvi
Mother's First Name:	Yehudit
Gender:	Male
Date of Birth:	1878
Place of Birth:	Nisko,Nisko,Lwow,Poland
Marital Status:	MARRIED
Spouse's First Name:	Chana
Spouse's First Name:	Khana
Permanent Place of Residence:	Sokolow,Poland
Place during the war:	Sokolow,Poland
Place of Death:	Belzec,Rawa Ruska,Lwow,Poland
Date of Death:	1942
Type of material:	Page of Testimony

Eliezer Valtz

Eliezer Valtz was murdered 1942, at the Bełżec Extermination Camp.[16] Benjamin Geiger submitted a POT for his mother Chana Geiger. She was born 1878 to parents Shmuel (aka Moses) and Lea (Laje), married to Eliezer, and prior to WWII she lived and died at Sokołów, Poland.[17]

Benjamin Geiger submitted a POT for his brother David Geiger aka Solomon David Geiger born 1899 at Górno, Sokołów Małopolski, Podkarpackie, Poland to parents Chana and Eliezer. He was murdered by the Nazis at the Bełżec Extermination Camp in 1942. Prior to WWII he lived in Kamień, Poland. A photograph of David Geiger was attached with his file.[18] He was a textile merchant and married to Sara Amsterdam. Shmuel Geiger submitted a POT for David Geiger's wife, Sara Geiger née Amsterdam. She was born at Nisko, Podkarpackie, Poland in 1903 and died 1942 at Treblinka Extermination Camp. Her permanent place of residence was Nisko.[19]

Shmuel Geiger submitted a POT for his sister Sara Geiger. Her parents were Chana and Eliezer. She was married to Yehezkeil Geiger Gruenbaum, her first cousin. There was a discrepancy for her age; on the Yad Vashem record her birth year was 1904, but her birth record from Górno listed 1902. I would take her birth record as reflecting her correct age.[20] Shmuel Geiger submitted a POT for Yehezkeil Geiger Gruenbaum. His parents were Hersz aka Tzvi Gruenbaum and Yehudit aka Ides Geiger. Yehezkeil and Sara resided at Sokołów and he was a merchant. Sara Geiger and Yehezkeil Gruenbaum with their children Tzvi and Yehudit were murdered 1942 at Treblinka.[21]

Shmuel submitted a POT for his sister Bluma Geiger; she was born 1908 at Górno, Sokołów to parents Eliezer aka Volf and Chana. She was married and a merchant.[22] Her permanent place of residence was Sokołów. She was murdered 1942 at Treblinka during the Shoah. Shmuel Geiger also submitted a POT for Bluma's husband Benjamin Weinselbaum. He was born at Łańcut in 1906 and was a merchant; the couple perished with their daughter Khana at Treblinka extermination camp.[23]

Shmuel Geiger submitted a POT for his sister Chaja Mindel Wachtel née Geiger.[24] Shmuel estimated her birth year as 1900; her birth record indicated 1897. Her parents were Eliezer and Chana. She was married. Shmuel Geiger also submitted a POT, for Chaja Mindel's husband Shmuel Yeshiyah Wachtel, born 1898 to parents Yitzhak and Ester, at Leżajsk, Poland. He was a merchant and married to Chaja Mindel Geiger.[25] They were living at Sokołów Małopolski. Chaja Min-

The Central Database of Shoah Victims' Names

David

David Geiger was born in Sokolow, Poland in 1899 to Eliezer and Khana. He was married to Sara. Prior to WWII he lived in Kamien, Poland. During the war he was in Sokolow, Poland. David was murdered/perished in 1942 in Belzec, Poland at the age of 43. This information is based on a Page of Testimony (displayed on left) submitted by his brother.

Attach Image or
Documentation

Source:	Pages of Testimony
Last Name*:	Geiger
First Name:	David
Father's First Name:	Eliezer
Father's First Name:	Volf
Mother's First Name:	Chana
Mother's First Name:	Khana
Mother's Maiden Name*:	Geiger
Gender:	Male
Date of Birth:	1899
Place of Birth:	Sokolow,Poland
Marital Status:	MARRIED
Spouse's First Name:	Sara
Permanent Place of Residence:	Kamien,Nisko,Lwow,Poland
Place during the war:	Sokolow,Poland
Place of Death:	Belzec,Rawa Ruska,Lwow,Poland
Date of Death:	1942

David Geiger

del Geiger and Shmuel Yeshiyah Wachtel with their children Luba, Lea, Anna, Elimelech, and Yona were murdered at Treblinka in 1942.

Shmuel Geiger submitted a POT for his cousin Aron Geiger Gruenbaum born 1896 at Sokołów Małopolski, Poland. Aron's parents were Tzvi (Hersz) Gruenbaum and Yehudit (Ides) Geiger. Aron Geiger Gruenbaum was a merchant and married to Sheindl Hampt.[26] They were murdered 1942 with their four children: Shmuel, Sana, Khaia, and Sima.

Treblinka Extermination Camp

Several Geiger descendants from this Geiger line perished at Treblinka extermination camp during the Holocaust. The Nazis built Treblinka in a remote forest north-east of Warsaw, Poland well hidden from view; it was in operation between July 1942 to October 1943. The Nazis murdered between 700,000 to 900,000 Jews in Treblinka's gas chambers, in fact more Jews died at Treblinka then at any other Nazi extermination camp apart from Auschwitz-Birkenau. Treblinka was one of the three secret extermination camps for Operation Reinhard; the other two were Bełżec and Sobibór. The commandants of Operation Reinhard camps reported directly to Heinrich Himmler, head of the Nazi SS.

An underground Jewish resistance organization at Treblinka succeeded with a prisoner uprising on 2 August 1943. The insurgents unlocked the door to the arsenal with a duplicated key, obtaining 25 rifles, 20 hand grenades and several pistols concealed in a cart to a gravel work detail. The Jews then set fire to all buildings and exploded a tank of gasoline. Armed Jews attacked the main gate and others attempted to climb the fence. Guards used machine gun fire to kill the insurgents however two hundred Jews escaped from the camp. Despite German soldier reinforcements and roadblocks, partisans of the Polish Home Army successfully aided the escapees across the river and Polish villagers helped others to escape. Seventy prisoners survived until the end of the war; some later published their memoirs of Treblinka.[27]

Finding Geiger Descendants

My quest continued to see if there were living Geiger descendants for this family. I sent an inquiry on 12 February 2014 and posted it online at JewishGen. org SIG digests (special interest groups) and the JewishGen.org discussion digest. I quickly received helpful hints and directions to pursue. Events moved quickly since my posting. Brenda Habshush, a genealogist from Israel, located

Lotke, Elisha, and Benjamin Geiger

a living descendant of this Geiger family. She found and interviewed Benjamin Geiger's widow Lea aka Lotke Geiger née Czech, who lived in a home for the elderly at Kibbutz Neve Eitan, Israel.[28] Lotke spoke in Hebrew to Brenda and gave her useful family background. Her entire family from the Czech Republic perished during the Shoah. Lotke was born at Prague, the Czech Republic, and she made Aliyah to Israel then settled at Kibbutz Neve Eitan where she met and married Benjamin Geiger. They had the following children: Elisha, Eliezer, Jacob and Irit. Lotke said that one of her sons, Elisha, left Israel for the United States and lived in Manhattan, New York.

Ben and Lotke Geiger

Brenda Habshush confirmed Benjamin Geiger immigrated to Palestine 1939, lived at Kibbutz Neve Eitan, and died 16 July 1999.[29] He enlisted in the British Army 18 February 1941 as an unmarried man. After the war ended, Benjamin Geiger married Lea 1946 at Kibbutz Neve Eitan. His wife, Lea Czech, was born 1923 at Prague, the Czech Republic. At the time of my inquiry February 2014, Benjamin's wife Lea aka Lotke was still living at Neve Eitan in Israel. Kibbutz Neve Eitan is in the Beit She'an Valley in northern Israel.

I located Elisha in the Manhattan telephone book and then wrote him a letter about my Geiger family research. He confirmed that his parents were Benjamin and Lotke Geiger. He was delighted that he found a cousin; we arranged to meet one another to share family histories at my home in New Hampshire. During that visit 28 September 2014 Elisha brought family photographs, his father's autobiography and discussed his family history. We have been in touch ever since. As it happened, Elisha lived near my cousin Arthur in Manhattan, also a Geiger descendant, and after I introduced them to one another they became good friends.

I was privileged to receive a copy of Benjamin Geiger's autobiography. This document provided additional family information. Benjamin Geiger's father Rabbi Eliezer Valtz was a Belz Hasidic rabbi, a respected town leader and a wholesaler of wheat grain. He descended from Belz Hasidim. Eliezer's father was Rabbi Tzvi Valtz from Tarnograd (1856–1939). When the German Nazi Army occupied Tarnograd they asked the Jews of that town for ten volunteers who were willing to die for their community. Rabbi Tzvi Valtz stepped forward to save his community and the Nazis immediately shot him.[30] Rabbi Tzvi Valtz had a wife named Yehudit who died years before the Shoah.

Information pertaining to Chana Geiger's death was based on birth and death records from the Rzeszów Archive, with family information from her grandson Elisha during a telephone conversation February 2014 and from the autobiography written 1985 by his father Benjamin.[31] Elisha recalled that his grandmother Chana died due to illness after she delivered her twins Benjamin and Izaak born at Sokołów Małopolskie. Based on the death record for her infant son Izaak Geiger in 1912, the death of Chana Geiger probably occurred between 1912–1916.

Elisha provided additional information about the Amsterdam family. His uncle David Geiger was married to Sara Amsterdam. She had a brother Jacob Amsterdam who survived WWII and immigrated to Israel at age 17 years, then immediately joined the Haganah.[32] Jacob fought in every Arab Israeli war. After Israel gained independence as a nation in 1948, he settled at Tel Aviv, where he married and had children. Jacob submitted POTs for his parents Shmayia and Gitze Amsterdam, both murdered 1942 at Bełżec.[33]

Shmuel Geiger Rescued by Oskar Schindler

The other Shoah survivor from this family was Shmuel Geiger. Elisha Geiger recalled that his uncle Shmuel (1905–1977) seldom discussed his Holocaust experience and was usually somber and quiet. There was a number tattooed on Shmuel's arm from a concentration camp. Elisha heard that his uncle Shmuel worked for Oskar Schindler but did not have any details.

I discovered that Shmuel Lemel Geiger was one of the 1,980 essential Jewish workers compiled from lists prepared by Oskar Schindler. Oskar Schindler protected and rescued his Jewish employees from slaughter during the Holocaust. Shmuel was listed as Lemel Geiger, born 1905, and he was a metalworker who survived the Shoah. This information was on www.jewishgen.org and www.ancestry.com websites for Schindler's Lists.[34]

Oskar Schindler (1908–1974) was a Czech industrialist and member of the German Nazi party. He was an opportunist who wanted to build an industrial empire and took control in 1939 of a once Jewish owned enamel factory outside the city of Kraków (in Zabłocie) renaming it The German Enamel Works. This factory produced enamel kitchenware for the Nazi army. He hired Jewish workers who were cheap labor compared to non-Jewish workers. Although Schindler was first motivated by profit, as he learned more about the atrocities committed by the Nazis against the Jews, he began to deeply care about the lives of his Jewish employees.

His goal changed from material considerations to one of protecting his Jewish workforce from their certain deportation and death by the Nazis. As a successful businessman he had an affable personality, resourcefulness, tenacity, courage, and dedication. He saved the lives of his Jewish workers by insisting to the SS that his employees, even those who were elderly, disabled, and children were necessary mechanics and metal workers. Schindler brought them food from the underground economy so they would not starve. Jews wanted to work at his factory because they considered it to be a safer place during the war.[35] By March 1943 the Nazis closed the Jewish ghetto of Kraków and planned to send hundreds of Jews for extermination at the death camp at Plaszów.

Schindler repeatedly bribed Nazi officials to keep his workers from deportation to concentration camps. Schindler bribed Amon Goeth, the notorious SS

commander of the Kraków-Plaszów concentration camp to provide him with Jewish labor
for work in his factory. The Nazis were determined to kill every Jew before the war ended
and that included Schindler's Jewish workers.
Schindler convinced Goeth and other Nazi officials to allow him to move his business enter-
prise and his Jewish workers during October
1944 from the death camp at Plaszów, Poland
to Bruennlitz camp at the Czech Republic,
where they switched from making enamel ware
to anti-tank grenades. This new product produced by his factory served as justification to
the SS for continued employment of his Jewish
workers.

Oskar Schindler

Oskar Schindler often surreptitiously aug-
mented the meager rations allowed by the S.S.
for his workers and by the end of the war, spent his entire fortune on bribes and
on supplies he purchased for his employees. He continued to bribe the SS even
until the Russian Red Army liberated Bruennlitz camp in 1945. Schindler saved at
least 2,000 Jews from certain death through his humanitarian actions.[36] Their descendants survived with many generations living today. The Israeli government
honored Oskar Schindler 1963 by naming him Righteous Among the Nations
in Israel. After his death in West Germany 1974, he was interred at Mount Zion
Catholic cemetery, Jerusalem, Israel. Both a well-known book and film *Schindler's
List* were based on this history.[37]

Shmuel Geiger immigrated to Palestine May 1947. The date suggests that
Shmuel Geiger was on one of the ships allowed by the British bringing refugees
to Palestine.[38] The number tattooed on Shmuel Lemel Geiger's arm was most
probably from the Plaszów death Camp, prior to his transfer arranged by Oskar
Schindler to Bruennlitz. Israeli researchers Jules Feldman, Israel Michaeli and
Saul Sharoni responded to my on-line requests for assistance with Israeli records.
They found that Shmuel Geiger died 26 August 1977 at Israel. Schmuel Lemel
married Gizelle (unknown surname). She was born 15 March 1914, in Romania
and she entered Palestine April 1947. She died 16 April 1993 at Israel. There was
no issue. They lived at Afula located in the Jezreel Valley in northern Israel.

Benjamin Geiger

The following information was based on Benjamin Geiger's fascinating autobiography, included in an Appendix. Elisha Geiger translated the autobiography of his father Benjamin Geiger for me from Hebrew to English. I will summarize the highlights from Benjamin Geiger's autobiography beginning with his birth information.[39] His mother was Chana Geiger. He was born 18 December 1915 as a twin however his twin (Isaac) did not survive. His mother Chana Geiger died June 1916 due to illness when Benjamin was 6 months. There was a difference for birth dates on the archival records from the Rzeszów Archive for Sokołów Małopolski, Górno containing the date of birth for the twins Beinisch and Izaak as 1911.[40] The death of Isaac at 3 months occurred 1912.[41] It is quite possible that Chana Geiger died earlier than 1916 due to illness however no death record was found.

Benjamin explained that his surname Geiger came from his mother because his parents did not register their religious marriage with the civil authorities. Under Austro-Hungarian Empire their children were considered illegitimate and used their Geiger maternal surname. Benjamin recalled relatives telling him about their distinguished Geiger family living long lives who were important and influential rabbis.

Benjamin described how his sister Chaja Mindel at age 13 took care of the house and her younger brothers because her father Eliezer Valtz never re-married after the death of his wife Chana Geiger even though it was not the custom for Jewish widowers with young children to remain unmarried. Benjamin recalled being a target for cruel anti-Semitism in Polish public school from ages 6 through 13. He spent 8 hours daily in public school and then another 4 hours daily in the Jewish cheder. As a young child, Benjamin suffered at the cheder due to an overly strict rabbi until his father intervened. After his bar mitzvah Benjamin went to Tarnów to study in a yeshiva. His father arranged that he was to board with a Jewish family. He was considered as a charity case due to his lack of funds and he was constantly moved to board with other families.

The economic situation grew worse and by 1930 Benjamin left the yeshiva and travelled to Kraków where he joined the Communist youth movement and distributed political flyers. He avoided arrest and returned to Sokołów to confess to his father that he left the yeshiva. To his relief his father was understanding. Benjamin then returned to Kraków and joined the Akiva Zionist movement. This movement prepared Jews for immigration and making Aliyah to Israel. A man from the settlement Neve Eitan in Palestine taught Benjamin agricultural skills on a farm in Kraków. After the Nazis came to power no one could leave Poland to emigrate to Palestine and all Zionist organizations were illegal.

The story of how Benjamin Geiger (b.1911 or b.1915–1999) came to Israel was compelling. Benjamin described how he was a refugee passenger on the last ship bound for Palestine during July 1939. He learned there was a clandestine organization to help Jews escape from Poland. He had only 24 hours to leave and the organization warned him to take nothing with him except the clothes he wore, with no photos or documents. The organization provided him with falsified documents. He decided to take the chance to leave Poland although saying farewell to his family later proved to be traumatic because he never saw his family again. He had to leave behind his three married sisters Sara, Chaja Mindel and Bluma; his brother David; his nine nephews and nieces and his elderly father Eliezer Valtz. The Nazis murdered everyone in his family during the Shoah except for his brother Shmuel who also immigrated to Palestine.

Events Prior to the Formation of the State of Israel

Thousands of Jews fled from the Nazis and entered Palestine still under British rule. The British brokered peace with the Arabs by agreeing to a massive naval and military force to turn back the Jewish refugees from entering Palestine. The British intercepted refugees and sent them to British internment camps located in Cyprus and Mauritius, where they were detained for months and even years.[42] Ships from Europe carrying Jewish refugees had to remain a lengthy distance away from the Palestine coastline. During nightfall refugees jumped from ships to swim to the shore. Jewish organizers were waiting on the shore to help refugees with assistance.

The underground network organized by Jewish organizations was known as *Brichah* ("flight" in Hebrew) and they moved Jews from displaced person camps to ports on the Mediterranean Sea, so they could enter Palestine by boat. This was part of what was known as *Aliyah Bet* or the "second immigration" and were a series of covert operations by Jewish refugees to immigrate illegally to Palestine before and after WWII.

During the 1936–39 Arab revolt in Palestine, the Germans made connections with Arab leaders in Palestine. This led to further cooperation between the Palestinian nationalist movement with Axis Powers during WWII. As fighting broke out in the Middle East in North Africa between the British and the German, the

German Commander Rommel defeated British forces during April 1941 until the British General Montgomery turned the tide of battle at El Alamein, Egypt October 1942. From that point the German Army was on the defensive in North Africa for the rest of the war. The Allied Powers continued to fight the Axis Powers from gaining control of Egypt, the Suez Canal and oil fields.

The Balfour Declaration was written in 1917 as a statement of support by Great Britain for Palestine to be a national home for the Jewish people. This policy became a core component of the British Mandate for Palestine. The League of Nations in 1922 appointed Great Britain temporary administrator for Palestine under the British Mandate for Palestine. The British Mandate granted both Jewish and Arab communities the rights to run their internal affairs. Under increased Arab pressure, the British Mandatory government withdrew from its previous commitment to permit Jewish immigration and land acquisition in Palestine. The British White Papers of 1922, 1930, and 1939 were official reports by the British government following their investigations of Arab riots against British policy in Palestine. The 1939 White Paper limited Jewish immigration to Palestine for five years and added the proviso that Jewish immigration was contingent on Arab consent. The Jewish Agency for Palestine opposed the 1939 White Paper and argued the British "were denying the Jewish people of their rights in the darkest hour of Jewish history."[43]

The United Nations General Assembly adopted Resolution 181 on 29 November 1947 to partition Palestine into an independent Arab state and an independent Jewish state. The Palestinian Arabs and all members of the Arab League rejected that plan. David Ben Gurion who soon became the first Israeli prime minister declared the new independent State of Israel on 14 May 1948.[44] Israel sought membership in the United Nations that was conditional on their acceptance of Resolution 181 (the Partition Plan) and Resolution 194 (a Palestinian right of return and a United Nations claim on Jerusalem). Israel agreed and The United Nations General Assembly then voted in 1949 to approve the recognition of Israel as an independent state and as a member in the General Assembly; the vote was passed with the requisite two-thirds majority.[45] Wars and conflicts between Arabs and Israelis continued: Arab-Israeli War of 1948; Six-Day War of 1967; Yom Kippur War of 1973; Lebanon War of 1982; and Gaza conflicts 2008–2014. Benjamin Geiger including his descendants personally experienced and participated as committed soldier patriots in *Eretz Yisrael* and the establishment of the Jewish state of Israel.

Benjamin Geiger the Soldier and Kibbutznik

Benjamin Geiger entered Palestine in 1939 and went to kibbutz Neve Eitan organized by Polish Jews, where he became oriented to a new life. He lived in a tent and did hard physical labor working hours in the fields in extreme heat. Despite the hardships, Benjamin and other Jewish refugees were enthusiastic and extremely motivated to live as free Jews in Palestine.

British forces asked for Jewish volunteers living in Palestine to join them in their fight against the Nazis. Benjamin Geiger volunteered to be a soldier and enlisted 18 February 1941 as a soldier in the British Army.[46] Fighting continued in the Middle East through the end of WWII in 1945. When the Jewish Infantry Brigade formed in 1944 in Palestine, Benjamin Geiger was one of 5,000 Jewish volunteers.[47] He served in the Engineers Battalion Unit. The Book of Histadrut Army for British Army volunteers 1939–1945 listed Benjamin Geiger as the son of Eliezer.[48]

The mission of the Engineers Battalion Unit was to place mines strategically in the desert to blow up German tanks. Benjamin Geiger became seriously wounded when a land mine exploded under his vehicle. He had a badly fractured

Benyamin Geiger, child of Eliezer	בנימין גייגר [בן/בת] אליעזר

Birth Year:	1915
מקום:	Neve Etan
מקום:	נוה איתן
ארץ מוצא:	פולין
מספר תעודת זהות:	142766
קרבה:	רוק
תאריך עלייה:	1939
קבוצה אתנית:	אשכ׳
Place of Employment (Hebrew):	נוה איתן
Language of Record:	Hebrew
Military ID:	45529
Pluga:	ר.אי.
Enlisted on:	1941-Feb-18

רשומה זו מ ספר המתנדבי ההסתדרות לצבא 1945-1939 (Book of Histadrut Army) Volunteers 1939-1945), חלק מ הצבא הבריטי 1939-1947 1947-1939 (Military British 1939-1947). מאגר מידע, מספר מסמך 447, דף 94, IGRA number 2796. המקור מ ארכיון יד ושם (Yad Vashem Archives). רשומה זו הוסף למנוע החיפוש ב 19 בפברואר 2016.

שתף 💬   הדפס 🖶   סגור ✕

Benjamin Geiger, soldier

Benjamin Geiger, Jewish Brigade

arm, and he underwent multiple surgeries, then needed to recover for months at a Cairo hospital. The Jewish Infantry Brigade was deployed to Italy and Germany in 1945 for further battle against the Axis Powers however Benjamin was not able to continue fighting with his unit due to his injury.

Benjamin returned to kibbutz Neve Eitan, where he met and married Lotke Czech in 1946. They raised their family on the kibbutz. Although Benjamin could not return to active military combat due to his arm injury, he volunteered to serve on guard duty for the Civil Defense Force to prevent Arabs from entering the kibbutz or getting past the border especially during the 1948–49 Arab Israeli War. After the war, Benjamin began a new business venture for the kibbutz by raising carp fish in their fishponds. When he retired at age 68, he returned to Jewish studies taking courses at a Jewish seminary. Benjamin Geiger died 16 July 1999 and was interred at Kibbutz Neve Eitan, Beit She'an Valley, northern Israel.

Lotke Geiger née Czech

Benjamin Geiger's wife Lea aka Lotke Czech was born 1 May 1923 at Prague, Czechoslovakia, the only child born to Vitezlav aka Fritz Czech and Irena

Aschkenes. Fritz Czech was born
30 December 1891 at Prostějov,
Moravia, the Czech Republic. Irena was born 26 September 1901 at
Brno, Moravia, the Czech Republic.
The Nazis captured Fritz and Irena Czech and they perished in the
Lódz ghetto 1944 during the Holocaust. Their daughter Lotke survived
WWII and she began a diary written
in German from the age of ten years
in 1933 until 1947 after her marriage
1946 with Benjamin Geiger. Her diary included her memories about the
German occupation and the changes
for her country and her family.[49] Lotke entered Palestine with a German

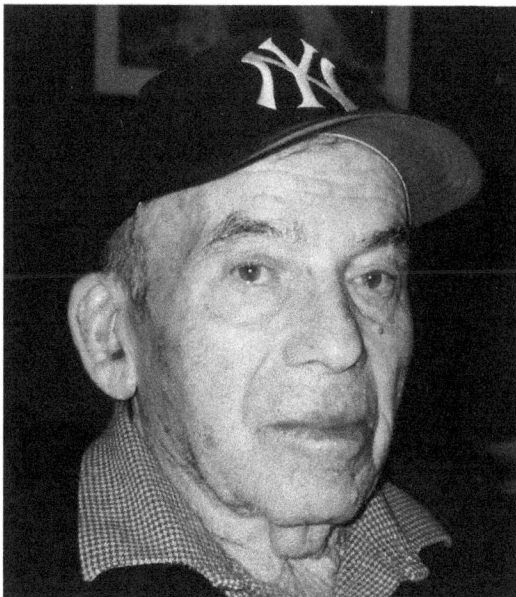

Benjamin Geiger 1999

passport stamped with a Nazi swastika. She was the only person in her family to
escape from the occupied Czech Republic; her entire family was murdered by the
Nazis. Lotke Geiger née Czech died 13 July 2014 and was interred at Kibbutz
Neve Eitan, Beit She'an Valley, northern Israel. Benjamin and Lotke Geiger had
four children: Elisha, Eliezer, Jacob and Irit. They were all born in Israel and are
considered *sabras*.[50] They served in the Israeli army and fought in wars between
the Arabs and Israelis. All are living.

atDNA Study

I wanted to see if a family connection could be confirmed using autosomal DNA
matches from the testing company www.familytreedna.com with myself and my
known Geiger cousins and Elisha. This might clarify if he was a descendant
from my Geiger family. Elisha consented to donate his autosomal (atDNA) to
www.familytreedna.com to determine if there was a genetic relationship with my
Geiger family.

My atDNA research with Ashkenazi Jews led me to consider the issues of
endogamy and recombination of atDNA with every generation. For example,
results of atDNA testing thousands of Ashkenazim by the company www.fam-
ilytreedna.com were found to have more genetic matches than non-Jews.[51] The
history of Ashkenazim was that of a marginalized population often restricted to

live apart from Gentiles for centuries. In addition, Ashkenazim cultural traditions evolved to sanction marriage only within their defined religious community, often to close relatives such as cousins or uncles with nieces.

Due to centuries of consanguineous marriages, Ashkenazim became highly inter-related and therefore shared more autosomal DNA with each other compared to people from heterogenous populations. Genealogists traced Ashkenazim to a bottleneck of a small population of 350 Jews between 25 to 32 generations ago, followed by a rapid exponential expansion of the population. In other words, Ashkenazim will share a larger amount of centimorgans (cMs) with their Ashkenazim matches and will also share more atDNA segments in common.[52]

The recombination of atDNA occurs with each generation and therefore the percentage of atDNA we inherit from the original ancestor is reduced with each generation. We inherit about 50 percent of our atDNA from each parent; 25 percent of our atDNA from each grandparent; 12.5 percent from each great-grandparent; 6.25 percent from each great-great-grandparent. Genealogists can use atDNA matches to find distant cousins, but the odds become much smaller to find the common ancestor.[53] All first and second cousin relationships can be detected through atDNA, however third and more distant cousin relationships may not always be detected because of the random nature of atDNA inheritance and endogamy.

I had a paper trail of clues based on given names coupled with the Geiger surname. Elisha, as another possible descendant, matched 8 out of 9 Geiger descendants from my Geiger lineage including myself. I focused only on shared atDNA matches >5 centimorgans for Elisha with myself and my cousins. I reasoned that this would rule out random centimorgan matches or "noise." The ISOGG (International Society of Genetic Genealogy) recommended when using www.familytreedna.com Family Finder data, the percentages of shared cMs can be calculated by dividing the total shared cM by 68. The number 68 is based on estimations that individuals inherit 6800 cM or 3400 from each parent. If two matches share 425 cM, they share 6.25% DNA and according to the chart from ISOGG *Average Autosomal DNA Shared by Pairs of Relatives* they would be considered first cousins once removed or half first cousins. If two matches share 1700 cM, they would share 25% DNA and would be considered either a grandparent or aunt/uncle or half sibling.[54]

I compared total cMs >5 shared between Elisha with each Geiger descendant match then divided the number by 68 to find percentages of shared DNA.

I referred to the theoretical chart for establishing relationships between matches of autosomal DNA from the ISOGG.[55] The ISOGG matches confirmed that Elisha likely shares a 2nd great-grandparent with myself and my cousins. I also checked those matches with www.familytreedna.com that use their own algorithm to adjust for endogamous populations such as Ashkenazim. Three matches with Elisha were 3rd to 5th cousin.

According to genetic genealogists if two or more matches share a segment on a chromosome in common with each other, they likely share a common ancestor. Therefore, matching atDNA segments between Elisha and my Geiger descendants can be another way to determine descent from a common ancestor. I analyzed the matching segments from chromosomes 9, 11, 12 and 17. Those segments had at least two Geiger descendants matched on the same areas of segments with Elisha *(See Table 1)* This often indicates IBD (Identical by Descent) matching atDNA for cousins sharing a common ancestor.

Match		Chromosome	Start overlap		End overlap		cM>5
DP		9	24288508		33447653		12.68
CL		9	23801127		32384422		11.05
JG		11	60053455		67135592		6.28
MC		11	62288127		67624124		5.08
AG		12	1.20E+08		1.24E+08		5.7
JG		12	1.14E+08		1.20E+08		9.18
MC		12	1.14E+08		1.21E+08		11.35
JS		17	6.98E+07		7.38E+07		10.16
GG		17	6.98E+07		7.36E+07		9.44
		Table 1	Matching Segments with EG				

Table 1

Another genetic analytical tool is triangulation, for comparing atDNA segments common to three or more cousins to see if they all share atDNA on the same or on an overlapping segment on a chromosome. If they do, they form a triangulated group and indicate they all inherited the segment from a common ancestor. I chose to focus on segments of a significant size, >7 to 10 cM, as this would be stronger criteria to suggest that members of the triangulated group probably inherited their shared atDNA from a common ancestor.[56] Due to frequent cousin marriages in the Ashkenazi Jewish population, it is difficult to know if the atDNA segment was from the male or the female or both, such as Solomon David Geiger and/or Chaje Mindel Unger. There were three triangulated groups seen in the atDNA for Elisha with significant segment sizes >10. (*See Table 2*) This finding supported my hypothesis that Elisha shared a common ancestor with my Geiger family.

Match Name	Chromosome		start overlap		end overlap		cM
DP	9		24288508		32095254		10.26
CL	9		24288508		32095254		10.26
JG	11		0				
MC	11		0				
AG	12		0				
JG	12		100454274		128263098		47.6
MC	12		100454274		128263098		47.6
JS	17		65451592		78639702		32.22
GG	17		65451592		78639702		32.22
			Table 2 Triangulations with EG				

Table 2

As previously mentioned, the choice of given names for Chana Geiger's children, Solomon David and Chaje Mindel was compelling circumstantial evidence. This combination of such given double names for two children born from the same mother is uncommon; furthermore, Ashkenazi naming of children is often based on deceased relatives such as grandparents. My theory is that Elisha shared the same 2nd great-grandparents Solomon David Geiger and Chaje Mindel Unger with my Geiger lineage. A comparison of family trees indicated that we are third cousins. In addition, I omitted cM < 5 for my calculations, to weed out randomness, "noise," and inflated amounts of cM due to endogamy. When seen in this perspective, findings for our Geiger cousin relationships were more aligned with the ISOGG chart.

Based on my research, Elisha and his siblings are third cousins with myself and my Geiger cousins. I will conclude that based on the available evidence I collected and atDNA findings, Moses Geiger was a son of my 2nd great-grandparents Solomon David Geiger and Chaje Mindel Unger. Moses Geiger's daughter Chana Valtz née Geiger was contemporary with my grandmother Mindel Weiss née Geiger. Chana's son Benjamin Geiger was contemporary with my mother Sylvia

Gerber née Weiss, and I am contemporary with Benjamin Geiger's son Elisha. It was satisfying to see how a genealogist can utilize atDNA research and matches to substantiate whether previously unknown individuals are genetic descendants from the same family, especially with only incomplete and scant records. This newest branch of Geiger descendants are *sabras* and enrich our family history.

Descendants of Moses Geiger

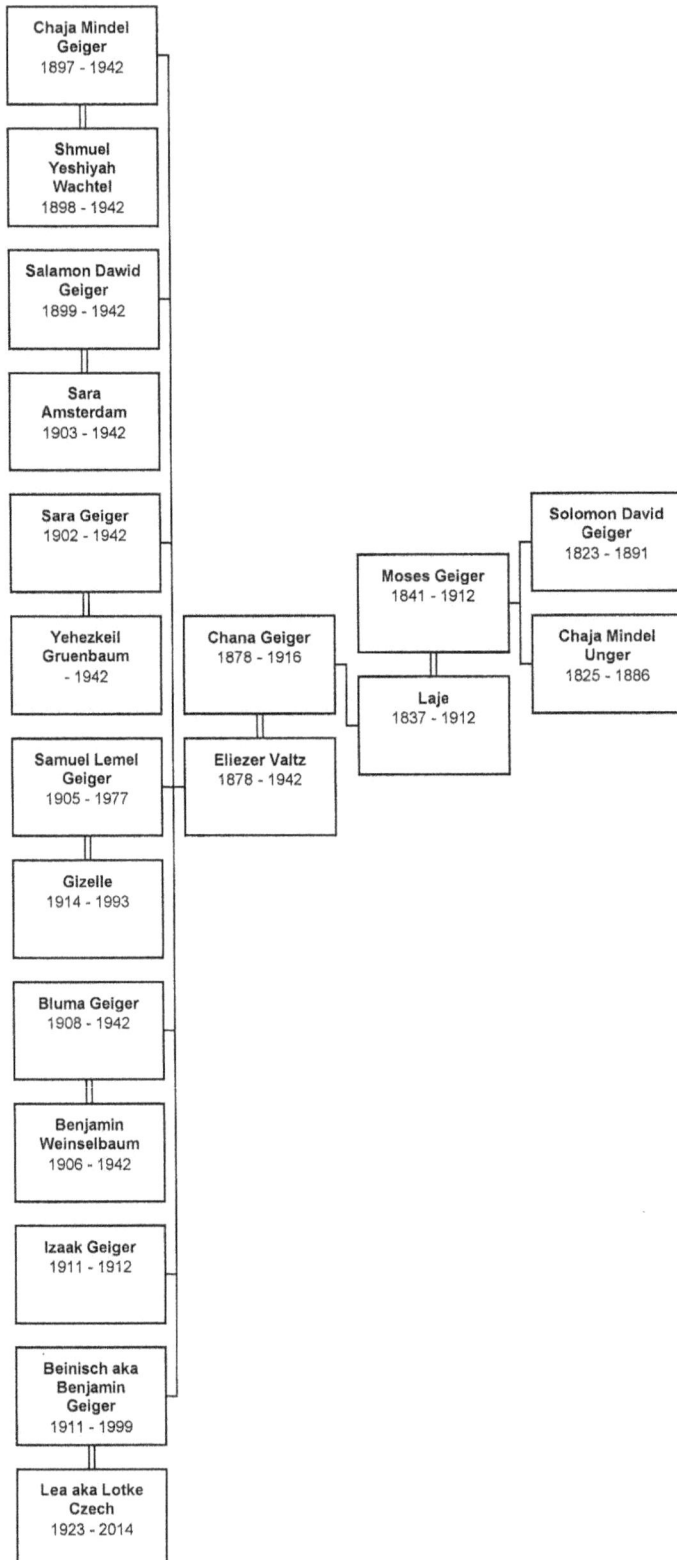

Chaja Mindel Geiger 1897 - 1942		
Shmuel Yeshiyah Wachtel 1898 - 1942		
Salamon Dawid Geiger 1899 - 1942		
Sara Amsterdam 1903 - 1942		
Sara Geiger 1902 - 1942		**Solomon David Geiger** 1823 - 1891
Yehezkeil Gruenbaum - 1942	**Chana Geiger** 1878 - 1916	**Moses Geiger** 1841 - 1912
Samuel Lemel Geiger 1905 - 1977	**Eliezer Valtz** 1878 - 1942	**Laje** 1837 - 1912 — **Chaja Mindel Unger** 1825 - 1886
Gizelle 1914 - 1993		
Bluma Geiger 1908 - 1942		
Benjamin Weinselbaum 1906 - 1942		
Izaak Geiger 1911 - 1912		
Beinisch aka Benjamin Geiger 1911 - 1999		
Lea aka Lotke Czech 1923 - 2014		

Endnotes

1   ¹ KehilaLinks. Prepared by the Kolbuszowa Region Research Group. (www.jewishgen.org).

2   Jerrold Landau, Translator. *Sokolów Malopolski, Poland. Pinkas Hakehillot Polin. Encyclopedia of Jewish Communities, Poland. V.III.* (Jerusalem, Israel: Yad Vashem). p. 277.

3   Ibid., p. 278.

4   Rzeszów Archive, Poland. Sokolow Malopolskie Birth Records 1825-1912. Fond 990. JRI-Poland order form sent 3 May 2012.

5   Rzeszów Archive, Poland. Sokołów Malopolski Births 1825-1912. Fond 990. Birth Chaya Mindel Geiger, Górno, 1897 akta 40, Chana Geiger, mother. Birth of Solomon David Geiger, Górno, 1899 akta 13, Chana Geiger, mother. (www.jri-poland.org).

6   Rzeszów Archive. Sokołów Malopolski Deaths 1877-1912. Fond 990. Death Moses Geiger, Górno, akta 13, 1912; see Death Laja Geiger, Gorno, akta 21, 1912. (www.jri-poland.org).

7   Rzeszów Archive. Sokołów Malopolski Births 1825-1912. Fond 990. Birth of Sara Geiger, Górno, akta 38, 1902; Birth of Samuel Lemel Geiger, Górno, akta 26, 1905. (www.jri-poland.org.)

8   Yad Vashem.org. Central Database of Shoah Victims' Names. Page of Testimony, submitted by Shmuel Geiger, 1955. Death 1942: Bluma Geiger. Item ID 65603.

9   Rzeszów Archive. Sokołów Malopolski Births 1825-1912. Fond 990. Birth of twins Beinisch Geiger, Górno, akta 65, 1911 and Birth of Izaak Geiger, Górno, akta 64, 1911. (www.jri-poland.org).

10 Rzeszów Archive, Sokolów Malopolski Deaths 1877-1912, v. 1894-1913. Fond 990. Death Izaak Geiger, akta 14, 1912. (www.jri-poland.org).

11 Rzeszów Archive. Sokołów Malopolski Births 1825-1912. Fond 990. Mother: Ides Geiger, Births: 1888 Chaje Roise, Akta 122; 1896 Lana, Akta 114; 1897 Aron, Akta 72; 1900 Naftali, Akta 11; 1904 Chaskel, Akta 29; 1907 Scheindla Geiger, Akta 6, 1907. (www.jri-poland.org).

12 Rzeszów Archive. Sokolow Malopolski Births 1825-1912. Fond 990. Parents Hersz Josef Gruenbaum and Judes Geiger. Birth: 1893 Sane, Akta 33.

13 Comments on the birth record indicated Sane died 1920.

14 Yad Vashem.org. The Israeli Knesset enacted the Yad Vashem law in 1953 for collection and publication of testimonies of victims of the Holocaust. Yad Vashem also collects materials documenting and cataloguing Holocaust records. Yad Vashem has a campus on the Mount of Remembrance at Jerusalem. Their online Central Database of Shoah Victims' Names contains close to 3 million victims names in English, Hebrew and Russian. (www.yadvashem.org).

15 Yad Vashem.org. Central Database of Shoah Victims' Names. Pages of testimony submitted by Lea Geiger 1994. Vitezlav Czech, Item 1430876 and Irena Czech item ID 1736025, also see photos. (yvng. vadvashem.org/nameDetails.html).

16 Yad Vashem.org. Central Database of Shoah Victims' Names. Page of testimony submitted by Benjamin Geiger, 1994 for Eliezer Valtz Item 89113.

17 Yad Vashem.org. Central Database of Shoah Victims' Names. Pages of testimony submitted by Benjamin Geiger,1994 for Chana Geiger, Item 1735869.

18 Yad Vashem.org. Central Database of Shoah Victims' Names. Pages of testimony submitted by Benjamin Geiger, 1994 for David Geiger, Item 89111, also see photo. (www.yadvashem.org).

19 Yad Vashem.org. Central Database of Shoah Victims' Names. Page of Testimony submitted by Shmuel Geiger, 1955 for Sara Amsterdam, Item 646749.

20 Yad Vashem.org. Central Database of Shoah Victims' Names. Page of Testimony submitted by Shmuel Geiger, 1955 for Sara Geiger, Item 634065.

21 Yad Vashem.org. Central Database of Shoah Victims' Names. Page of Testimony submitted by Shmuel Geiger, 1955 for Yehezkeil Geiger, Item 65008.

22 Yad Vashem.org. Central Database of Shoah Victims' Names. Page of Testimony submitted by Shmuel Geiger, 1955 for Bluma Geiger, Item 65603.

23   Yad Vashem.org. Central Database of Shoah Victims' Names. Page of Testimony submitted by Shmuel Geiger, 1955 for Benjamin Weinselbaum, Item 65604.

24   Yad Vashem.org. Central Database of Shoah Victims' Names. Page of Testimony submitted by Shmuel Geiger, 1955 for Chaja Wachtel née Geiger, Item 65604.

25   Yad Vashem.org. Central Database of Shoah Victims' Names. Page of Testimony submitted by Shmuel Geiger, 1955 for Shmuel Yeshiyah Wachtel, Item 65607.

26   Yad Vashem.org. Central Database of Shoah Victims' Names. Page of testimony. Submitted by Shmuel Geiger, 1955. Aron Geiger, Item ID 65610.

27   Wikipedia.org. Treblinka Extermination Camp.

28   Wikipedia.org. The Kibbutz Neve Eitan is located at the Beit She'an Valley in Northern Israel. In 2018 the population was 312. It was established November 1938 by Polish Jewish refugees from the Akiva movement.

29   Volunteers 1939-1945. *Book of Histadrut Army 1939–1945; Military British 1939-1947*. Benyamin Geiger, child of Eliezer. IGRA number 2796. (www.yadvashem/archives)

30   International Institute for Holocaust Research. Encyclopedia of the Ghettos. The Surname Valtz was connected to Tarnograd. Prior to 1939 there were 2,500 Jews living there engaged in small businesses. Jewish schools were traditional and orthodox. When the Germans occupied Tarnograd 15 September 1939, many Jews were beaten and one was killed, presumably Tzvi Valtz. A week later the Germans withdrew from Tarnograd but returned to place the Jews within a ghetto. The ghetto was liquidated 2 November 1942. Jews were sent to their destruction at Bełzec Extermination Camp. (www.yadvashem.org).

31   Unpublished Autobiography of Benjamin Geiger written 1985. Translated from the Hebrew to English by his son Elisha Geiger, edited by Judith Goldsmith, October 2014.

32   The Haganah was an underground military organization in Israel 1920-1948. A branch of the Haganah was the Mossad and this group commandeered and sailed 66 ships carrying 70,000 Jewish refugees to Israel during 1945-48. After Israel achieved statehood in 1948, the Haganah was transformed into the Israel Defense Forces. (www.jewishvirtuallibrary.org/the-haganah.)

33   POT Shmayia Amsterdam, b. 1900 Kamien, Poland. POT Gitze Amsterdam, b. 1905 Kamien, Poland. (www.yadvashm.org).

34   JewishGen's Holocaust Database. *Schindler's Lists*. Metalworker. Lemel Geiger, born 1905. (www.jewishgen.org/databases/detail_2.php).

35   Oskar Schindler biography. (en.wikipedia.org/wiki/Oskar_Schindler).

36   Schindler's Lists. (www.jewishgen.org/databases/holocaust)

37   Thomas Keneally. *Schindler's List*. New York: Simon and Schuster. Touchstone book. 1982. A well-known movie by Steven Speilberg *Schindler's List* was based on this book.

38   *New York Times* Archives. Obituary Rudolph Patzert published 21 February 2000. Rudolph Patzert, 88, Transported Jews to Palestine After War. The Arabs waged war against the British 1936-1939, forcing the British to sharply limit European Jews into Palestine. This action by the British to keep Jewish refugees from entering Palestine continued after the war. Zionist organizations smuggled Jews into Palestine and the Paducah was purchased by the Haganah. The captain was an American, Rudolph Patzert, who sided with the Zionists. Fighting broke out between a British destroyer with the Paducah. The British captured the ship and kept the crew and passengers as prisoners in Cyprus for two years after which the refugees finally were able to enter Israel on other ships under British quota ca. 1947.

39   Personal papers of Elisha Geiger. Autobiography of Benjamin Geiger written 1985. Translated from the Hebrew to English by his son Elisha Geiger. Edited by Judith Goldsmith 2014.

40   Rzeszów Archive, Poland. Fond 990. Sokolow Malopolskie, Births 1825-1912. Birth: 1911, Izaak Geiger, Akta 64. Birth: 1911, Beinisch Geiger, Akta 65.

41   JRI-Poland.org. Rzeszów Archive, Poland. Fond 990. Sokolow Malopolskie, Deaths 1877-1912. Death: 1912, Izak Geiger. Akta 14.

42   Jewish Insurgency in Mandatory Palestine (wikipedia.org/wiki/Jewish_insurgency_in_Mandatory_Palestine); also Aliyah Bet (en.wikipedia.org/wiki/Aliyah_Bet).

43   www.jewishvirtuallibrary.org. British Palestine Mandate: British White Papers.

44   Ibid.

45   Wikipedia.org. Israel and the United Nations.

46   Volunteers 1939–1945. *Military British 1939–1947. Book of Histadrut Army 1939–1945*. Benjamin Geiger, child of Eliezer. Enlisted 8 February 1941. Yad Vashem Archives. Record located by Brenda Habshush.

47   Wikipedia.org. The Jewish Brigade. The Jewish brigade was formed 1944 with Jewish volunteers from Palestine and was part of the British Army. Jewish Brigade headquarters was stationed in Egypt with more than 5,000 volunteers organized into three infantry battalions.

48   Volunteers 1939–1945. *Book of Histadrut Army 1939–1945. Military British 1939–1947*. Benjamin Geiger, son of Eliezer. IGRA number 2796. (www.yadvashem/archives).

49   The diary by Lotke was written in German Gothic script and has not been translated at this time.

50   en.wikipedia.org/wiki/sabra_(person). The sabra refers to any Jew born in Israel. The term also alludes to a prickly pear desert plant with a thick skin that conceals a sweet, soft interior. The plant is compared to Israeli Jews who are tough on the outside but sweet on the inside.

51   Jeffrey Mark Paull, Gaye Tannenbaum, and Jeffrey Briskman. Why Autosomal DNA Test Results are Significantly Different for Ashkenazi Jews. Avotaynu V. XXX, no.1, Spring 2014, p.13.

52   cruwys.blogspot.com. 28 January 2016.

53   Jeffrey Mark Paull and Janet Billstein Akaha. Using Autosomal DNA Analysis to Connect Rabbinical Lineages: A Case Study of the Wertheimer and Wertheim Dynasties. Avotaynu V. XXVIII, no. 4, Winter 2012, p.61.

54   ISOGG Wiki. isogg.org/wiki/autosomal_DNA_Statistics.

55   International Society of Genetic Genealogy. Table for Average Autosomal DNA Shared by Pairs of Relatives in Percentages and centiMorgans. (isogg.org/wiki/Autosomal_DNA_Statistics.)

56   Debbie Parker Wayne, Triangulating Autosomal DNA, National Genealogical Society NGS Magazine 42 (October-December 2016): 39–42.

Family Tree

Solomon David Geiger

Generation One

1. **SOLOMON DAVID[1] GEIGER**, born ca. 1823 in Poland; died ca. 1891, Błażowa, Podkarpackie, Poland. Married ca.1840 at Błażowa, Podkarpackie, Poland, CHAJE MINDEL UNGER. She was born ca. 1825 in Poland; died ca. 1886.

Children of Solomon David Geiger and Chaje Mindel Unger:
i. MOSES GEIGER, born 1841, Poland; died 1912, Górno, Sokolów Malopolski, Podkarpackie, Poland. Married ca. 1871 at Górno, Sokolów Malopolski, Podkarpackie, Poland LAJE. She was born ca. 1837; died 1912 Górno.

ii. ARON GEIGER, born 1850, Błażowa, Podkarpackie, Poland; died 1924, Vienna, Austria. Married 1868 at Przemyśl, Podkarpackie, Poland, HINDE TURNHEIM, daughter of Hersch and Mariem Turnheim (née Gems). She was born 1850 in Przemyśl; died 1931 Vienna.

iii. ZIPORA GEIGER, born ca.1860, Błażowa, Podkarpackie, Poland. Married ca. 1885 at Błażowa, Podkarpackie, Poland, LAZAR FINDER, son of Nuchim and Nisli Finder. He was born ca. 1860 Grady, Dabrowa, Malopolskie, Poland.

iv. CHAIM YEHUDA GEIGER, born 1866, Rzeszów, Podkarpackie, Poland; died 8 February 1932, Błażowa, Podkarpackie, Poland. Married 31 August 1902 at Rzeszów, Podkarpackie, Poland, GOLDA LEA GRUENSTEIN. She was born 1870 in Kolbuszowa, Poland; died 1930 at Rzeszów, Poland.

Generation Two

2. **MOSES[2] GEIGER**, (Solomon David[1]), born 1841, Poland; died 1912, Górno, Sokolów Malopolskie, Podkarpackie, Poland. Married ca. 1871 at Górno, Sokolów Malopolskie, Podkarpackie, Poland, LAJE. She was born ca. 1837; died 1912 at Górno, Poland.

Children of Moses Geiger and Laje include:
i. IDES[3] GEIGER (Moses[2], Solomon David[1]), born ca. 1870, Górno, Sokolów

Malopolskie, Podkarpackie, Poland. Married ca. 1887, Górno, Sokolów Malopolskie, Podkarpackie, Poland, HERSZ JOSEF GRUENBAUM, son of Mordko Klinger and Scheindel Grinbaum.

ii. CHANA[3] GEIGER (Moses[2], Solomon David[1]), born 1878, Górno, Sokolów Malopolskie, Podkarpackie, Poland; died ca.1916 in Górno. Married ca. 1896, Górno, Sokolów Malopolskie, Podkarpackie, Poland, ELIEZER VALTZ, son of Tzvi and Yehudit Valtz. He was born 1878 at Nisko, Poland; died 1942 at Belzec, Poland.

3. **ARON[2] GEIGER**, (Solomon David[1]), born 1850, Błażowa, Podkarpackie, Poland; died 17 August 1924, Vienna, Austria. Married 1868 at Przemyśl, Podkarpackie, Poland, HINDE TURNHEIM, daughter of Hersch Turnheim and Mariem Gems. Hinde was born 1 January 1850 at Przemyśl, Poland; died 11 October 1931 at Vienna, Austria.

Children of Aron Geiger and Hinde Turnheim:

i. CHARLES[3] GEIGER (Aron[2], Solomon David[1]), born 1868, Przemyśl, Podkarpackie, Poland; died 24 April 1955, New York, New York. Married 6 March 1894 at New York, New York, ESTHER MAMLOCK daughter of Meyer Mamlock and Caroline Sobel. She was born 14 April 1868 in New York; died 10 January 1944 in New York.

ii. NAFTALE GEIGER (Aron[2], Solomon David[1]), born 29 March 1871, Przemyśl, Podkarpackie, Poland; died 2 April 1877, Przemyśl, Podkarpackie, Poland.

iii. ABRAHAM YITZAK[3] GEIGER (Aron[2], Solomon David[1]), born 19 November 1872, Przemyśl, Podkarpackie, Poland; died 28 September 1946, New York. Married July 1894 at Kańczuga, Podkarpackie, Poland, SPRYNCA STARK daughter of Moses Stark and Sara. She was born 8 June 1870 in Kańczuga; she died 6 February 1945 in New York.

iv. ISRAEL[3] GEIGER (Aron[2], Solomon David[1]), born 16 January 1874, Przemyśl, Podkarpackie, Poland; died 29 April 1933, Chicago, Illinois. Married 27 November 1898 at New York, New York, ESTHER PERLBERG daughter of Elias Perlberg and Sarah Malter. She was born 22 November 1874 in Zabno, Poland; died 12 August 1931 in Chicago, Illinois.

v. MARIEM[3] GEIGER (Aron[2], Solomon David[1]), born 22 February 1880, Przemyśl, Podkarpackie, Poland; died 29 November 1946, New York, New York. Married 31 March 1902 at Błażowa, Podkarpackie, Poland, GETZEL HOLOSZYCER, son of Yakov Holoszycer and Ester Jakubes. He was born 15 December 1876 Kańczuga; died 1 October 1933 in New York.

vi. FREUDE GEIGER (Aron[2], Solomon David[1]), born 23 January 1882, Przemyśl, Podkarpackie, Poland; died ca.1920.

vii. MINNIE³ GEIGER (Aron², Solomon David¹), born 3 April 1887, Przemyśl, Podkarpackie, Poland; died 18 May 1960, New York. Married 17 October 1911 at New York, New York, OSCAR WEISS son of Fischel Weiss and Hannie Zuckerberg. He was born 11 March 1876 in Boryslaw, Ukraine; died 25 October 1946 in New York.

4. **CIPRE AKA ZIPORA² GEIGER** (Solomon David¹), born ca. 1860, Błażowa, Podkarpackie, Poland. Married ca. 1885 at Błażowa, Podkarpackie, Poland, LAZAR FINDER son of Nuchim and Nisli Finder.

Children of Cipre Geiger and Lazar Finder:
i. NECHUMA³ FINDER (Cipre aka Zipora², Solomon David¹), born 27 October 1887, Grądy, Malopolskie, Poland. No further information.

ii. NUCHIM FINDER (Cipre aka Zipora², Solomon David¹), born 28 July 1889, Bagienica, Malopolskie, Poland. No further information.

iii. CHAJA MINDEL FINDER (Cipre aka Zipora², Solomon David¹), born 4 November 1891, Bagienica, Malopolskie, Poland; died 1897, Wola Postolowa, Lisko, Ukraine.

iv. TAUBE FINDER (Cipre aka Zipora², Solomon David¹), born 1897, Wola Postolowa, Lisko, Ukraine; died 1897 at Wola Postolowa, Lisko, Ukraine.

v. ISRAEL BER FINDER (Cipre aka Zipora², Solomon David¹), born 20 June 1895, Bagienica, Malopolskie, Poland; died 1897 at Wola Postolowa, Lisko, Ukraine.

vi. ALTE MARJEM FINDER (Cipre aka Zipora², Solomon David¹), born 25 April 1900, Zurawiczki, Jaroslaw, Podkarpackie, Poland. No further information.

vii. ZECHARJE LEIB FINDER (Cipre aka Zipora², Solomon David¹), born 24 April 1901, Zurawiczki, Jaroslaw, Podkarpackie, Poland. No further information.

5. **CHAIM YEHUDA² GEIGER** (Solomon David¹), born ca.1866, Rzeszów, Podkarpackie, Poland; died 8 February 1932, Błażowa, Podkarpackie, Poland. Married 31 August 1902, at Rzeszów, Podkarpackie, Poland; GOLDA LEA GRUENSTEIN. She was born 1870 in Kolbuszowa, Podkarpackie, Poland; died 1930, Rzeszów, Podkarpackie, Poland.

Children of Chaim Yehuda Geiger and Golda Lea Gruenstein:
i. SOLOMON DAVID³ GEIGER (Chaim Yehuda², Solomon David¹), born 14 February 1892, Rzeszów, Podkarpackie, Poland; died 1898, Rzeszów, Poland.

ii. MARKUS GEIGER (Chaim Yehuda², Solomon David¹), born 1897, Rzeszów,

Podkarpackie, Poland; died 1898, Rzeszów, Podkarpackie, Poland.

iii. BERNARD BERL GEIGER (Chaim Yehuda[2], Solomon David[1]), born 1899, Rzeszów, Podkarpackie, Poland; died 1942, Poland. Married 1923, Rzeszów, Podkarpackie, Poland, FANIA ERNESTYNA GOLDMANN.

iv. CHAIM AKA JOACHIM GEIGER (Chaim Yehuda[2], Solomon David[1]), born 1904, Rzeszów, Podkarpackie, Poland; died 1942, Poland. Married 1928, Rzeszów, Podkarpackie, Poland, RACHELA KREBS.

v. SARAH GEIGER (Chaim Yehuda[2], Solomon David[1]), born 1906, Rzeszów, Podkarpackie, Poland; died 1942, Belzec, Poland. Married, YITZHAK MOSHE GROSS.

vi. CHASKEL GEIGER (Chaim Yehuda[2], Solomon David[1]), born 1908, Rzeszów, Podkarpackie, Poland. No further information.

vii. MENDEL GEIGER (Chaim Yehuda[2], Solomon David[1]), born 1911, Rzeszów, Podkarpackie, Poland. Married 1936, SPRINCA BRUECKNER.

Generation Three

6. **IDES[3] GEIGER** (Moses[2], Solomon David[1]), born ca. 1870, Górno, Sokolów Malopolski, Podkarpackie, Poland; died, Górno, Sokolów Malopolski, Podkarpackie, Poland. She married ca. 1887, Górno, Sokolów Malopolski, Podkarpackie, Poland, HERSZ JOSEF GRUENBAUM, son of Mordko Klinger and Scheindel Grinbaum.

Children of Ides Geiger and Hersz Josef Gruenbaum:
i. CHAJE ROSE[4] GRUENBAUM (Ides[3], Moses[2], Solomon David[1]), born 1888, Górno, Sokolów Malopolski, Podkarpackie, Poland. No further information.

ii. SANE GRUENBAUM (Ides[3], Moses[2], Solomon David[1]), born 1893, Górno, Sokolów Malopolski, Podkarpackie, Poland. He died 1920 at Sokolów, Malopolskie, Poland.

iii. LANA GRUENBAUM (Ides[3], Moses[2], Solomon David[1]), born 1896, Górno, Sokolów Malopolski, Podkarpackie, Poland. No further information.

iv. ARON GRUENBAUM (Ides[3], Moses[2], Solomon David[1]), born 1897, Górno, Sokolów Malopolski, Podkarpackie, Poland; died 1942, Poland. He married at Sokolów Malopolski, Podkarpackie, Poland, SHEINDL HAMPT. She died 1942 in Poland.

v. NAFTALI GRUENBAUM (Ides[3], Moses[2], Solomon David[1]), born 1900,

Górno, Sokolów Malopolski, Podkarpackie, Poland. No further information.

vi. CHASKEL GRUENBAUM (Ides[3], Moses[2], Solomon David[1]), born 1904, Górno, Sokolów Malopolski, Podkarpackie, Poland. Married, Górno, Sokolów Malopolskie, Poland, SARA GEIGER, daughter of Chana Geiger and Eliezer Valtz.

vii. SCHEINDLA GRUENBAUM (Ides[3], Moses[2], Solomon David[1]), born 1907, Górno, Sokolów Malopolski, Podkarpackie, Poland. No further information.

7. **CHANA**[3] **GEIGER** (Moses[2], Solomon David[1]), born 1878, Górno, Sokolów Malopolski, Podkarpackie, Poland; died ca.1916 at Górno, Sokolów Malopolski, Podkarpackie, Poland. She married at Górno, Sokolów Malopolski, Podkarpackie, Poland, ELIEZER VALTZ, son of Tzvi and Yehudit. He was born 1878 in Nisko, Podkarpackie, Poland; died 1942 Belzec, Lubelskie, Poland.

Children of Chana Geiger and Eliezer Valtz:
i. CHAJA MINDEL[4] GEIGER (Chana[3], Moses[2], Solomon David[1]), born 9 June 1897, Górno, Sokolów Malopolski, Podkarpackie, Poland; died 1942 at Treblinka, Poland. Married at Poland, SHMUEL YESHIYAH WACHTEL, son of Yitzhak Wachtel and Ester. He died 1942; Treblinka, Poland.

ii. SHOLOM DAVID GEIGER (Chana[3], Moses[2], Solomon David[1]), born 7 February 1899, Górno, Sokolów Malopolski, Podkarpackie, Poland; died 1942 at Belzec, Poland. Married at Sokolów Malopolski, Podkarpackie, Poland, SARA AMSTERDAM. She was born 1903 at Nisko, Poland; died 1942 at Belzec, Poland.

iii. SARA GEIGER (Chana[3], Moses[2], Solomon David[1]), born 8 May 1902, Górno, Sokolów Malopolski, Podkarpackie, Poland; died 1942 at Treblinka, Poland. Married, Górno, Sokolów Malopolskie, Poland, CHASKEL GRUENBAUM, son of Hersch Josef Gruenbaum and Ides Geiger. Both Sara Geiger and Chaskel Gruenbaum died 1942 at Treblinka, Poland.

iv. SAMUEL LEMEL GEIGER (Chana[3], Moses[2], Solomon David[1]), born 27 June 1905, Górno, Sokolów Malopolski, Podkarpackie, Poland; died 26 August 1977 at Afula, Israel. Married GIZELLE.

v. BLUMA GEIGER (Chana[3], Moses[2], Solomon David[1]), born 8 May 1908, Górno, Sokolów Malopolski, Podkarpackie, Poland; died 1942 at Treblinka, Poland. Married BENJAMIN WEINSELBAUM. He was born 1906 at Lancut, Poland; died 1942 at Treblinka, Poland.

vi. ISAAK GEIGER (Chana[3], Moses[2], Solomon David[1]), born December 1911,

Górno, Sokolów Malopolski, Podkarpackie, Poland; died 1912, Górno, Sokolow Malopolski, Podkarpackie, Poland.

vii. BEINISCH AKA BENJAMIN GEIGER (Chana[3], Moses[2], Solomon David[1]), born December 1911, Górno, Sokolów Malopolski, Podkarpackie, Poland; died 16 July 1999 at Kibbutz Neve Eitan, Israel. Married 1946 at Kibbutz Neve Eitan, Israel, LEAH CZECH, daughter of Vitezlav Fritz Czech and Irena Aschkenes. She was born 1923 in Prague, Czechoslavakia; died 13 July 2014 at Kibbutz Neve Eitan, Israel.

8. **CHASKEL**[3] **GEIGER** (Aron[2], Solomon David[1]), born 18 May 1868, Przemyśl, Podkarpackie, Poland; died 24 April 1955 at New York, New York. Married 6 March 1894 at New York, New York, ESTHER MAMLOCK, daughter of Meyer Mamlock and Caroline Sobel. She was born 14 April 1868 in New York; died 10 January 1944 in New York.

Children of Chaskel Geiger and Esther Mamlock:

i. MARION[4] GEIGER (Chaskel[3], Aron[2], Solomon David[1]), born 10 January 1895, New York, New York; died 3 December 1991 at New York, New York. Married 12 October 1920 at New York, New York, EUGENE MESSNER, son of Emil Messner and Betty Shuster. He was born 27 April 1893 in New York; died 2 October 1965 in New York.

ii. MINNA GEIGER (Chaskel[3], Aron[2], Solomon David[1]), born 3 September 1896, New York, New York; died September 1983 at New York, New York. Married (1) 17 June 1919 at New York, New York, ALBERT M. ROLLAND, son of Jules Rolland and Hattie Metzger. He was born 1891 in Paris, France; died 15 August 1930 in New York. Married (2) 3 July 1932 at Somerville, New Jersey, JESSE DANIEL GIDDING. He was born 5 June 1892 in Millville, New Jersey; died 12 August 1953, Westhampton Beach, Suffolk, New York.

iii. MILTON MARK GEIGER (Chaskel[3], Aron[2], Solomon David[1]), born 27 April 1902, New York, New York; died 29 November 1959 at Minneapolis, Minnesota. Married (1) 5 March 1925 at New York, New York, DOROTHY DUCKER, daughter of Solomon Ducker and Rae Green. Dorothy was born 5 February 1905 at Brooklyn, New York; died 25 June 1991 at Hallandale, Florida. Married (2) 12 January 1937 at Carver, Minnesota, ALMA PETRINE HOLM-REISCHL, daughter of Martin Holm and Julie Arnstad. Alma was born 23 May 1911 in Minnesota; died 2 February 1982, Hennepin, Minnesota.

9. **ABRAHAM YITZAK**[3] **GEIGER** (Aron[2], Solomon David[1]), born 19

November 1872, Przemyśl, Podkarpackie, Poland; died 28 September 1946 at New York, New York. Married July 1894 at Kańczuga, Podkarpackie, Poland, SPRYNCA STARK, daughter of Moses Stark and Sara. She was born 8 June 1870 at Kanczuga, Poland; died 6 February 1945, New York.

Children of Abraham Yitzak Geiger and Sprynca Stark:

i. CHAJIJA AKA MINA[4] GEIGER (Abraham Yitzak[3], Aron[2], Solomon David[1]), born 21 May 1895, Kańczuga, Podkarpackie, Poland; died ca.1958. Married ca. 1938 at Vienna, Austria, KARL NEUMANN.

ii. MORDECHA AKA MAX GEIGER (Abraham Yitzak[3], Aron[2], Solomon David[1]), born 8 March 1898, Błażowa, Podkarpackie, Poland; died 25 February 1981 at New York, New York. Married 31 October 1922 at Vienna, Austria, RUCHLA GINSBERG, daughter Isidore Ginsberg and Schewa. She was born 6 October 1898 in Buczacz, Poland; died 3 September 1973, Brooklyn, New York.

iii. JOSEF GEIGER (Abraham Yitzak[3], Aron[2], Solomon David[1]), born 6 December 1899, Błażowa, Podkarpackie, Poland; died 18 November 1989 at Jerusalem, Israel. Married (1) ca. 1927 at Vienna, Austria, ESTHER SCHONFELD. She was born 26 October 1898 in Bucharest, Romania; died 9 July 1959, London, England. Married (2) ELSA MONDERER October 1960 at Hendon, Middlesex, England.

iv. SZEJWA AKA STELLA GEIGER (Abraham Yitzak[3], Aron[2], Solomon David[1]), born 11 July 1902, Błażowa, Podkarpackie, Poland; died 7 November 1989 at Miami Beach, Florida. Married 29 November 1931, Vienna, Austria, MORRIS STEINBOCH. He was born 20 May 1904 at Tarnow, Poland; died 28 August 1986, Miami Beach, Florida.

10. **ISRAEL**[3] **GEIGER** (Aron[2], Solomon David[1]), born 16 January 1874, Przemyśl, Podkarpackie, Poland; died 29 April 1933 at Chicago, Illinois. Married 27 November 1898 at New York, New York, ESTHER PERLBERG, daughter of Elias Perlberg and Sarah Malter. She was born 22 November 1874, Zabno, Poland; died 12 August 1931, Chicago, Illinois.

Children of Israel Geiger and Esther Perlberg:

i. JENNIE[4] GEIGER (Israel[3], Aron[2], Solomon David[1]), born 7 September 1899, New York, New York; died 10 November 1980 at Oakland, California. Married 19 April 1925 at Chicago, Illinois, ISIDORE AKA FRANCIS RICHARD GLENNER, son of Jacob Glenner and Sarah Mary Joseph. He was born 31

October 1895, Chicago, Illinois; died 4 November 1980, Oakland, California.

ii. ELI GEIGER (Israel[3], Aron[2], Solomon David[1]), born 30 April 1901, New York, New York; died 26 January 1979 at Chicago, Illinois. Married December 1969 at Dade County, Florida, DOROTHY TAMAN, daughter of Benjamin Taman and Elsie Robeek. She was born 18 July 1918, Chicago, Illinois; died 14 May 2008 at Chicago, Illinois.

iii. HARRY GEIGER (Israel[3], Aron[2], Solomon David[1]), born 11 December 1908. Chicago, Illinois; died 10 February 1987 at San Diego, California. Married 6 June 1952 at Chicago, Illinois, BETTY LOUISE NEWMANN. She was born 1922 in Chicago Illinois.;died 26 May 1993, Chicago Illinois.

11. **MARIEM**[3] **GEIGER** (Aron[2], Solomon David[1]), born 22 February 1880, Przemyśl, Podkarpackie, Poland; died 29 November 1946, New York, New York. Married 31 March 1902 at Błażowa, Podkarpackie, Poland, GETZEL HOLOSZYCER, son of Jacob Holoszycer and Ester Jakubes. He was born 15 December 1976 in Kanczuga, Poland; died 1 October 1933 in New York.

Children of Mariem Geiger and Getzel Holoszycer aka Holly:

i. MINA[4] HOLLY (Mariem[3], Aron[2], Solomon David[1]), born 9 February 1905, Kańczuga, Podkarpackie, Poland; died March 1996 at New York, New York. Married 1940 at New York, New York, THOMAS MARTIN KEENAN. He was born 6 March 1916 in Kings County, New York; died 21 March 1995 at West Palm Beach, Florida.

ii. PEARL HOLLY (Mariem[3], Aron[2], Solomon David[1]), born 6 May 1909, New York, New York; died 2 June 1982 at Santa Fe, New Mexico. Married 15 April 1938 at Alexandria, Virginia, GEORGE BRONZ, son of Louis Bronz and Sarah Paley. He was born 7 July 1910 in New York; died April 1976 in Washington, District of Columbia.

iii. HARRY HOLLY (Mariem[3], Aron[2], Solomon David[1]), born 18 May 1912, New York, New York; died 14 April 2007 at Fort Lauderdale, Florida. Married ca. 1942, New York, New York, ROSE NASSAU, daughter of Samuel Nassau and Rebecca. She was born 8 January 1911 in Pennsylvania; died 24 July 1974 at New York.

iv. ESTHER HOLLY (Mariem[3], Aron[2], Solomon David[1]), born 22 March 1915, New York, New York; died 9 November 1981 at New York, New York. Married 1954, New York, New York, MILTON SIEGEL.

12. **MINNIE**[3] **GEIGER** (Aron[2], Solomon David[1]), born 3 April 1887, Przemyśl,

Podkarpackie, Poland; died 18 May 1960 at Woodmere, Nassau County, New York. Married 17 October 1911 at New York, New York, OSCAR WEISS, son of Fischel Weiss and Hannie Zuckerberg. He was born 11 March 1876, Boryslaw, Ukraine; died 25 October 1946, New York.

Children of Minnie Geiger and Oscar Weiss:

i. MARION[4] WEISS (Minnie[3], Aron[2], Solomon David[1]), born 28 November 1912, New York, New York; died 14 January 1996 at Patchogue, Long Island, New York. Married 8 September 1935, Kings County, New York, HARRY GOSHIN, son of Jack Goshin and Lena Schuel. He was born 3 January 1912, Brooklyn, New York; died 23 December 1985, Patchogue, New York.

ii. SYLVIA JUNE WEISS (Minnie[3], Aron[2], Solomon David[1]), born 4 June 1914, Kings County, New York; died 28 September 1994 at Manchester, New Hampshire. Married 24 January 1943, Kings County, New York, FRANK GERBER, son of David Gerber and Fannie Gerber. He was born 10 April 1914, Portland, Maine; died 5 October 1993, Haverhill, Massachusetts.

iii. MARTHA WEISS (Minnie[3], Aron[2], Solomon David[1]), born 28 July 1918, New York, New York; died 22 September 2005 at Sedona, Arizona. Married 23 November 1939, Kings County, New York, AARON CANTOR, son of Joseph Cantor and Flora Schwartz. He was born 29 December 1915, Newark, New Jersey; died 2 October 1999, Laguna Hills, California.

Family Tree

Yehezkeil Geiger

Generation One

1. **YEHEZKEIL¹ GEIGER** was born ca. 1857 in Poland. He died 21 August 1937 in Blazowa, Podkarpackie, Poland. He married FRADAL MACHLA LANDESMAN (daughter of Israel Reuven Landesman and Zelda Rabb) ca. 1884 in Poland. She was born ca. 1866 in Poland. She died March 1924 in Blazowa, Podkarpackie, Poland.

Yehezkeil Geiger and Fradal Machla Landesman had the following children:

i. SILKA² GEIGER (Yehezkeil¹) was born ca. 1885 in Blazowa, Podkarpackie, Poland. She died July 1942 in Sieniawa, Podkarpackie, Poland. She married SAMUEL MOSES ZINS (son of Selig Zins and Malie Helman) ca. 1899 in Blazowa, Podkarpackie, Poland. He was born 1877 in Sieniawa, Podkarpackie, Poland. He died July 1942 in Sieniawa, Podkarpackie, Poland.

ii. MIRIAM ESTHER² GEIGER (Yehezkeil¹) was born ca. 1886 in Blazowa, Podkarpackie, Poland. She died ca. 1913 in Blazowa, Podkarpackie, Poland. She married MOSHE SCHEINER ca. 1910 in Blazowa, Podkarpackie, Poland. He was born in Poland. He died July 1942 in Belzec, Lubelskie, Poland.

iii. CHANNA TAUBA² GEIGER (Yehezkeil¹) was born 25 February 1887 in Blazowa, Podkarpackie, Poland. She died October 1942 in Belzec, Lubelskie, Poland. She married SAUL WOLF ETTINGER about 1919 in Blazowa, Podkarpackie, Poland. He was born 15 May 1874 in Lezajsk, Podkarpackie, Poland. He died October 1942 in Belzec, Lubelskie, Poland.

iv. MOJZES YITZCHAK² GEIGER (Yehezkeil¹) was born 08 January 1888 in Blazowa, Podkarpackie, Poland. He died August 1942 in Belzec, Lubelskie, Poland. He married CHAJA ITTA STOCKMAN (daughter of Berisz Stockman and Yehudit Freund) 05 December 1910 in Pruchnik, Podkarpackie, Poland. She was born 23 June 1890 in Pruchnik, Podkarpackie, Poland. She died August 1942 in Belzec, Lubelskie, Poland.

v. GITTEL GEIGER (Yehezkeil[1]) was born 1890 in Blazowa, Podkarpackie, Poland. She died 13 August 1942 in Sieniawa, Podkarpackie, Poland. She married JOSEPH ALTER WEISSBLUM ca. 1920 in Blazowa, Podkarpackie, Poland. He was born in Lezajsk, Podkarpackie, Poland. He died 03 March 1943 in Bodaybo, Irkutsk, Siberia, Russia.

vi. YEHOSHUA MENACHEM AKA OSCAR GEIGER (Yehezkeil[1]) was born 22 June 1891 in Blazowa, Podkarpackie, Poland. He died 22 October 1986 in Jerusalem, Israel. He married MATLA MERSEL (daughter of Samuel Mersel and Munia Grossman) 02 July 1922 in Vienna, Austria. She was born 10 September 1895 in Radymno, Podkarpackie, Poland. She died 26 March 1944 in New York, New York.

vii. MEILICH GEIGER (Yehezkeil[1]) was born 1893 in Blazowa, Podkarpackie, Poland. He died July 1942 in Belzec, Lubelskie, Poland. He married TAUBA WEINSTEIN (daughter of Mojzesz Weinstein and Rechla Fuehrer) 1924 in Rzeszow, Podkarpackie, Poland. She was born 1893 in Gorlice, Malopolskie, Poland. She died July 1942 in Belzec, Lubelskie, Poland.

Generation Two

2. **SILKA[2] GEIGER** (Yehezkeil[1]) was born about 1885 in Blazowa, Podkarpackie, Poland. She died in July 1942 in Sieniawa, Podkarpackie, Poland. She married SAMUEL MOSES ZINS (son of Selig Zins and Malie Helman) about 1899 in Blazowa, Podkarpackie, Poland. He was born in 1877 in Sieniawa, Podkarpackie, Poland. He died in July 1942 in Sieniawa, Podkarpackie, Poland.

Samuel Moses Zins and Silka Geiger had the following children:
i.   LEIZER[3] ZINS (Silka[2], Yehezkeil[1]) was born 19 June 1900 in Poland. He died July 1942 in Sieniawa, Podkarpackie, Poland.

ii. FEIGA ZINS (Silka[2], Yehezkeil[1]). She died July 1942 in Sieniawa, Podkarpackie, Poland. She married YISROEL ZINS. He died July 1942 in Sieniawa, Podkarpackie, Poland.

iii. BARISH ZINS (Silka[2], Yehezkeil[1]). He died July 1942 in Sieniawa, Podkarpackie, Poland. He married CHUNA.

iv. DAVID ZINS (Silka[2], Yehezkeil[1]). He died July 1942 in Sieniawa, Podkarpackie, Poland. He married CHANNA.

v.   YEHOSHUA MENDEL ZINS (Silka[2], Yehezkeil[1]). He died July 1942 in Sieniawa, Podkarpackie, Poland. He married SARAH.

3. **MIRIAM ESTHER² GEIGER** (Yehezkeil¹) was born about 1886 in Blazowa, Podkarpackie, Poland. She died about 1913 in Blazowa, Podkarpackie, Poland. She married MOSHE SCHEINER about 1910 in Blazowa, Podkarpackie, Poland. He was born in Poland. He died in July 1942 in Belzec, Lubelskie, Poland.

Moshe Scheiner and Miriam Esther Geiger had the following children:
i.   CHAVA³ SCHEINER (Miriam Esther², Yehezkeil¹) was born ca. 1911 in Blazowa, Podkarpackie, Poland. She died July 1942 in Belzec, Lubelskie, Poland.

ii.   SILKA SCHEINER (Miriam Esther², Yehezkeil¹) was born ca. 1913 in Blazowa, Podkarpackie, Poland. She died July 1942 in Belzec, Lubelskie, Poland. She married NEBENTZAHL.

4. **CHANNA TAUBA² GEIGER** (Yehezkeil¹) was born 25 February 1887 in Blazowa, Podkarpackie, Poland. She died October 1942 in Belzec, Lubelskie, Poland. She married SAUL WOLF ETTINGER ca. 1919 in Blazowa, Podkarpackie, Poland. He was born 15 May 1874 in Lezajsk, Podkarpackie, Poland. He died October 1942 in Belzec, Lubelskie, Poland.

Saul Wolf Ettinger and Channa Tauba Geiger had the following children:
i.   YITZCHAK³ ETTINGER (Channa Tauba², Yehezkeil¹) was born 29 June 1921 in Kraków, Malopolskie, Poland. He died October 1942 in Belzec, Lubelskie, Poland.

ii.   FRADL ESTHER ETTINGER (Channa Tauba², Yehezkeil¹) was born 01 August 1924 in Kraków, Malopolskie, Poland. She died October 1942 in Belzec, Lubelskie, Poland.

5. **MOJZES YITZCHAK² GEIGER** (Yehezkeil¹) was born 08 January 1888 in Blazowa, Podkarpackie, Poland. He died August 1942 in Belzec, Lubelskie, Poland. He married CHAJA ITTA STOCKMAN (daughter of Berisz Stockman and Yehudit Freund) 05 December 1910 in Pruchnik, Podkarpackie, Poland. She was born 23 June 1890 in Pruchnik, Podkarpackie, Poland. She died August 1942 in Belzec, Lubelskie, Poland.

Mojzes Yitzchak Geiger and Chaja Itta Stockman had the following children:
i.   MIRIAM ESTHER³ GEIGER (Mojzes Yitzchak², Yehezkeil¹) was born 04 June 1912 in Pruchnik, Podkarpackie, Poland. She died August 1942 in Belzec, Lubelskie, Poland.

ii. ITZEL AKA IDA GEIGER (Mojzes Yitzchak[2], Yehezkeil[1]) was born 12 April 1914 in Pruchnik, Podkarpackie, Poland. She died 12 September 2013 in New York. She married MENDEL WACHSMAN (son of Meyer Wachsman and Yochevet Sprecher) 15 March 1945 in Samarkand, Uzbekistan. He was born 28 October 1910 in Lancut, Podkarpackie, Poland. He died 09 September 1998 in New York.

iii. ELIEZER GEIGER (Mojzes Yitzchak[2], Yehezkeil[1]) was born ca. 1917 in Pruchnik, Podkarpackie, Poland. He died ca. 1918 in Pruchnik, Podkarpackie, Poland.

iv. RIVA SILKA GEIGER (Mojzes Yitzchak[2], Yehezkeil[1]) was born 06 December 1919 in Pruchnik, Podkarpackie, Poland. She died August 1942 in Belzec, Lubelskie, Poland.

v.   MALKA BAYLA GEIGER (Mojzes Yitzchak[2], Yehezkeil[1]) was born ca. 1922 in Pruchnik, Podkarpackie, Poland. She died ca. 1923 in Pruchnik, Podkarpackie, Poland.

6. **GITTEL[2] GEIGER** (Yehezkeil[1]) was born 1890 in Blazowa, Podkarpackie, Poland. She died 13 August 1942 in Sieniawa, Podkarpackie, Poland. She married JOSEPH ALTER WEISSBLUM ca. 1920 in Blazowa, Podkarpackie, Poland. He was born in Lezajsk, Podkarpackie, Poland. He died 03 March 1943 in Bodaybo, Irkutsk, Siberia, Russia.

Joseph Alter Weissblum and Gittel Geiger had the following child:
i. ESTHER MALKA[3] WEISSBLUM (Gittel[2], Yehezkeil[1]) was born 13 October 1922 in Lezajsk, Podkarpackie, Poland. She died 13 April 1980 in New York, New York. She married HENOCH SCHUBIN (son of Wolf Leib Arie Schubin and Fradel Malie Meisner-Rieder) 26 November 1946. He was born 21 June 1914 in Dukla, Podkarpackie, Poland. He died 10 March 2010 in Lakeland, Camden, New Jersey.

7. **YEHOSHUA MENACHEM AKA OSCAR[2] GEIGER** (Yehezkeil[1]) was born 22 June 1891 in Blazowa, Podkarpackie, Poland. He died 22 October 1986 in Jerusalem, Israel. He married MATLA MERSEL (daughter of Samuel Mersel and Munia Grossman) 02 July 1922 in Vienna, Austria. She was born 10 September 1895 in Radymno, Podkarpackie, Poland. She died 26 March 1944 in New York, New York.

Yehoshua Menachem Geiger and Matla Mersel had the following child:

i. HINDA ZELDA AKA HELENE³ GEIGER (Yehoshua Menachem², Yehezkeil¹) was born 20 September 1923 in Vienna, Austria. She died 23 May 2011 in Herzliya, Israel. She married NATHAN BIALIK (son of Chaim Bialik and Rifka Yalowski) 24 February 1946 in Kings County, New York. He was born 21 January 1918 in Trestine, Poland. He died 28 September 2000 in Jerusalem, Israel.

8. **MEILICH² GEIGER** (Yehezkeil¹) was born 1893 in Blazowa, Podkarpackie, Poland. He died July 1942 in Belzec, Lubelskie, Poland. He married TAUBA WEINSTEIN (daughter of Mojzesz Weinstein and Rechla Fuehrer) 1924 in Rzeszow, Podkarpackie, Poland. She was born 1893 in Gorlice, Malopolskie, Poland. She died July 1942 in Belzec, Lubelskie, Poland.

Meilich Geiger and Tauba Weinstein had the following children:

i. FRADAL³ GEIGER (Meilich², Yehezkeil¹) was born ca. 1925 in Poland. She died July 1942 in Belzec, Lubelskie, Poland.

ii. MALE GEIGER (Meilich², Yehezkeil¹) was born ca. 1926 in Poland. He died July 1942 in Belzec, Lubelskie, Poland.

Generation Three

9. **ITZEL AKA IDA³ GEIGER** (Mojzes Yitzchak², Yehezkeil¹) was born 12 April 1914 in Pruchnik, Podkarpackie, Poland. She died 12 September 2013 in New York. She married MENDEL WACHSMAN (son of Meyer Wachsman and Yochevet Sprecher) 15 March 1945 in Samarkand, Uzbekistan. He was born 28 October 1910 in Lancut, Podkarpackie, Poland. He died 09 September 1998 in New York.

Mendel Wachsman and Itzel Geiger had the following children:

i. MOSHE MEIR⁴ WACHSMAN (Itzel³, Mojzes Yitzchak², Yehezkeil¹) was born in Bad-Reichenhall, Berchtesgadener Land, Bayern, Germany.

ii. CHAIM YITZCHAK WACHSMAN (Itzel³, Mojzes Yitzchak², Yehezkeil¹) was born in Eichstaat, Bavaria, Germany.

iii. YOCHEVET MIRIAM WACHSMAN (Itzel³, Mojzes Yitzchak², Yehezkeil¹) was born in Goggingen, Stuttgart, Germany.

iv. BERISH YECHEZKIEL WACHSMAN (Itzel³, Mojzes Yitzchak², Yehezkeil¹) was born in New York, New York.

10. **ESTHER MALKA³ WEISSBLUM** (Gittel², Yehezkeil¹) was born 13 October 1922 in Lezajsk, Podkarpackie, Poland. She died 13 April 1980 in New York, New York. She married HENOCH SCHUBIN (son of Wolf Leib Arie Schubin and Fradel Malie Meisner-Rieder) 26 November 1946. He was born 21 June 1914 in Dukla, Podkarpackie, Poland. He died 10 March 2010 in Lakeland, Camden, New Jersey.

Henoch Schubin and Esther Malka Weissblum had the following children:
i.   ZEV ARYE ELCHONON⁴ SCHUBIN (Esther Malka³, Gittel², Yehezkeil¹) was born 08 March 1951 in Stockholm, Sweden. He died 12 March 1965 in Kings County, New York.

ii.   FRADAL GITTEL SCHUBIN (Esther Malka³, Gittel², Yehezkeil¹).

iii. JOSEPH ALTER SCHUBIN (Esther Malka³, Gittel², Yehezkeil¹).

11. **HINDA ZELDA AKA HELENE³ GEIGER** (Yehoshua Menachem,² Yehezkeil¹) was born 20 September 1923 in Vienna, Austria. She died 23 May 2011 in Herzliya, Israel. She married NATHAN BIALIK (son of Chaim Bialik and Rifka Yalowski) 24 February 1946 in Kings County, New York. He was born 21 January 1918 in Trestine, Poland. He died 28 September 2000 in Jerusalem, Israel.

Nathan Bialik and Hinda Zelda Geiger had the following child:
i.   MORDECHAI DANIEL⁴ BIALIK (Hinda Zelda³, Yehoshua Menachem², Yehezkeil¹) was born in Kings County, New York.

Family Tree

Isak Holoszycer

Generation One

1. **ISAK[1] HOLOSZYCER** was born ca. 1819 in Kanczuga, Podkarpackie, Poland. He died 2 December 1890 in Kanczuga, Podkarpackie, Poland. He married PESSEL FROMMER 11 September 1870 in Kanczuga, Podkarpackie, Poland. She was born ca. 1818 in Kanczuga, Podkarpackie, Poland. She died ca. 1888 in Kanczuga, Podkarpackie, Poland.

Isak Holoszycer and Pessel Frommer had the following children:

i. AMALIE[2] HOLOSZYCER (Izak[1]) was born 1843 in Kanczuga, Podkarpackie, Poland. She died ca. 1905 in Kanczuga, Podkarpackie, Poland. She married JOEL JUDA TARNAFKER ca. 1863 in Kanczuga, Podkarpackie, Poland. He was born ca. 1845 in Kanczuga, Podkarpackie, Poland.

ii. JAKOB[2] HOLOSZYCER (Izak[1]) was born 1850 in Kanczuga, Podkarpackie, Poland. He married ESTER JACOBES (daughter of Laser Jacobes and Sime) ca. 1870 in Kanczuga, Podkarpackie, Poland. She was born 17 June 1851 in Kanczuga, Podkarpackie, Poland.

iii. MECHEL[2] HOLOSZYCER (Izak[1]) was born 2 April 1858 in Kanczuga, Podkarpackie, Poland. He married GOLDA C. KROPF (daughter of Schyja Kropf and Perly). She was born 1861 in Jaroslaw, Podkarpackie, Poland.

iv. CHANE HOLOSZYCER (Izak[1]) was born 16 August 1861 in Kanczuga, Podkarpackie, Poland. She died 1905 in Kanczuga, Podkarpackie, Poland.

Generation Two

2. **AMALIE[2] HOLOSZYCER** (Izak[1]) was born 1843 in Kanczuga, Podkarpackie, Poland. She died ca. 1905 in Kanczuga, Podkarpackie, Poland. She married JOEL JUDA TARNAFKER ca. 1863 in Kanczuga, Podkarpackie, Poland. He was born ca. 1845 in Kanczuga, Podkarpackie, Poland.

Joel Juda Tarnafker and Amalie Holoszycer had the following children:

i. MALKE[3] TARNAFKER (Amalie[2], Izak[1]) was born 1863 in Kanczuga, Podkarpackie, Poland. She died 1864 in Kanczuga, Podkarpackie, Poland.

ii. CHAJE RUCHEL TARNAFKER (Amalie[2], Izak[1]) was born 02 April 1865 in Kanczuga, Podkarpackie, Poland. She married MARCUS HOLOSZYCER (son of Jakob Holoszycer and Ester Jacobes) 27 May 1905 in Kanczuga, Podkarpackie, Poland. He was born 1871 in Kanczuga, Podkarpackie, Poland.

iii. PINCUS ARON TARNAFKER (Amalie[2], Izak[1]) was born 10 August 1869 in Kanczuga, Podkarpackie, Poland. He died November 1967 in New York, New York. He married PESEL DEBORAH HAUSMAN 19 November 1890 in New York. She was born 1870. She died 28 April 1923 in Bronx, New York.

iv. CIWIE TARNAFKER (Amalie[2], Izak[1]) was born 18 March 1873 in Kanczuga, Podkarpackie, Poland.

v. GETZEL TARNAFKER (Amalie[2], Izak[1]) was born 21 January 1875 in Kanczuga, Podkarpackie, Poland.

vi. CHANA TARNAFKER (Amalie[2], Izak[1]) was born 1878 in Kanczuga, Podkarpackie, Poland. She married RUBEN WESTREICH ca. 1904 in Kanczuga, Podkarpackie, Poland. He was born 1904 in Kanczuga, Podkarpackie, Poland.

vii. HERSCH CHAJEM TARNAFKER (Amalie[2], Izak[1]) was born 20 March 1885 in Kanczuga, Podkarpackie, Poland.

3. **JAKOB[2] HOLOSZYCER** (Isak[1]) was born 1850 in Kanczuga, Podkarpackie, Poland. He married ESTER JACOBES (daughter of Laser Jacobes and Sime) ca. 1870 in Kanczuga, Podkarpackie, Poland. She was born 17 June 1851 in Kanczuga, Podkarpackie, Poland.

Jakob Holoszycer and Ester Jacobes had the following children:

i. MARCUS[3] HOLOSZYCER (Jacob[2], Izak[1]) was born 1871 in Kanczuga, Podkarpackie, Poland. He married (1) CHAJE RUCHEL TARNAFKER (daughter of Joel Juda Tarnafker and Amalie Holoszycer) 27 May 1905 in Kanczuga, Podkarpackie, Poland. She was born 02 April 1865 in Kanczuga, Podkarpackie, Poland.

ii. FREIDA HOLOSZYCER (Jacob[2], Izak[1]) was born 23 December 1872 in Kanczuga, Podkarpackie, Poland. She died 1933 in Krakow, Malopolskie, Poland. She married CHAIM WALD (son of Josef Wald and Teme Sara Klinger) 26 December 1896 in Rzeszow, Podkarpackie, Poland. He was born 1873 in Rzeszow, Podkarpackie, Poland. He died 1923 in Rzeszow, Podkarpackie, Poland.

iii. GETZEL HOLOSZYCER HOLLY (Jacob[2], Izak[1]) was born 21 December 1876 in Kanczuga, Podkarpackie, Poland. He died 27 October 1933 in Kings County, New York. He married MARIEM GEIGER (daughter of Aron Geiger and Hinde Turnheim) 1902 probably at Blazowa, Podkarpackie, Poland. She was born 22 February 1880 in Przemysl, Podkarpackie, Poland. She died 29 November 1946 in Manhattan, New York, New York.

iv. MOSES HOLOSZYCER (Jacob[2], Izak[1]) was born 04 August 1879 in Kanczuga, Podkarpackie, Poland.

v. RYKA MARJEM HOLOSZYCER (Jacob[2], Izak[1]) was born 27 July 1882 in Kanczuga, Podkarpackie, Poland. She died 16 February 1883 in Kanczuga, Podkarpackie, Poland.

vi. EFROIM HOLOSZYCER (Jacob[2], Izak[1]) was born 01 December 1884 in Kanczuga, Podkarpackie, Poland. He died 24 December 1887 in Kanczuga, Podkarpackie, Poland.

vii. SIME HOLOSZYCER (Jacob[2], Izak[1]) was born 1887 in Kanczuga, Podkarpackie, Poland.

viii. ISAAC HOLOSZYCER (Jacob[2], Izak[1]) was born October 1890 in Kanczuga, Podkarpackie, Poland. He died 02 December 1890 in Kanczuga, Podkarpackie, Poland.

4. **MECHEL[2] HOLOSZYCER** (Izak[1]) was born 2 April 1858 in Kanczuga, Podkarpackie, Poland. He married GOLDA C. KROPF (daughter of Schyja Kropf and Perly). She was born 1861 in Jaroslaw, Podkarpackie, Poland.

Mechel Holoszycer and Golda C. Kropf had the following children:
i. ESTER[3] HOLOSZYCER (Mechel[2], Izak[1]) was born 13 September 1882 in Kanczuga, Podkarpackie, Poland.

ii. LAZAR HOLOSZYCER (Jacob[2], Izak[1]) was born 14 September 1884 in Kanczuga, Podkarpackie, Poland.

iii. DAVID HERSCH HOLOSZYCER (Jacob[2], Izak[1]) was born 22 January 1887 in Kanczuga, Podkarpackie, Poland.

iv. GETZEL HOLOSZYCER (Jacob[2], Izak[1]) was born ca. 1905 in New York.

Generation Three

5. **CHAJE RUCHEL³ TARNAFKER** (Amalie², Isak¹) was born 02 April 1865 in Kanczuga, Podkarpackie, Poland. She married MARCUS HOLOSZYCER (son of Jakob Holoszycer and Ester Jacobes) 27 May 1905 in Kanczuga, Podkarpackie, Poland. He was born 1871 in Kanczuga, Podkarpackie, Poland.

Marcus Holoszycer and Chaje Ruchel Tarnafker had the following children:
i.   JOSEF MAJER⁴ HOLOSZYCER (Chaje Ruchel³, Amalie², Izak¹) was born 08 May 1885 in Kanczuga, Podkarpackie, Poland.

ii. ISAAC HOLOSZYCER (Chaje Ruchel³, Amalie², Izak¹) was born 20 September 1890 in Kanczuga, Podkarpackie, Poland.

iii. DAVID HOLOSZYCER (Chaje Ruchel³, Amalie², Izak¹) was born 27 September 1894 in Kanczuga, Podkarpackie, Poland. He died 24 August 1897 in Kanczuga, Podkarpackie, Poland.

iv. EFRAIM HOLOSZYCER (Chaje Ruchel³, Amalie², Izak¹) was born 1900 in Kanczuga, Podkarpackie, Poland.

v.   AMALIE HOLOSZYCER (Chaje Ruchel³, Amalie², Izak¹) was born 1905 in Kanczuga, Podkarpackie, Poland.

6. **PINCUS ARON³ TARNAFKER** (Amalie², Isak¹) was born 10 August 1869 in Kanczuga, Podkarpackie, Poland. He died November 1967 in New York, New York. He married PESEL DEBORAH HAUSMAN 19 November 1890 in New York. She was born 1870. She died 28 April 1923 in Bronx, New York.

Pincus Aron Tarnafker and Pesel Deborah Hausman had the following children:
i.   ROSE⁴ TARNAFKER (Pincus Aron³, Amalie², Izak¹) was born 15 November 1891 in New York. She married SAM MESSENGER 26 February 1913 in New York.

ii. YETTA TARNAFKER (Pincus Aron³, Amalie², Izak¹) was born 06 December 1893 in New York. She married SAM LABOR ca. 1915 in New York. He was born 1892.

iii. IRVING TARNAFKER TANNER (Pincus Aron³, Amalie², Izak¹) was born 13 May 1895 in New York. He died 26 December 1973 in Valley Stream, Nassau, New York. He married SADIE LINDNER 06 June 1920 in Bronx, New York. She was born 04 October 1892 in New York. She died 09 May 1970.

iv. FRANCES TARNAFKER (Pincus Aron[3], Amalie[2], Izak[1]) was born 09 July 1900 in New York. She died 28 December 1903 in New York.

v. MOLLIE TARNAFKER (Pincus Aron[3], Amalie[2], Izak[1]) was born 09 November 1902 in New York. She married CHARLIE SOLOMON 22 October 1922 in Bronx, New York.

vi. SAMUEL TARNAFKER (Pincus Aron[3], Amalie[2], Izak[1]) was born 25 September 1905 in New York. He died 17 January 1965 in Memphis, Shelby, Tennessee. He married SARAH VOLMAN 16 December 1928 in Memphis, Shelby, Tennessee. She was born 20 May 1908. She died 14 October 1993 in Cordoba.

vii. BENNIE TARNAFKER (Pincus Aron[3], Amalie[2], Izak[1]) was born 16 January 1908 in New York. He married YETTA EISENBERG 03 May 1924 in New York. She was born 1872 in New York.

7. **CHANA[3] TARNAFKER** (Amalie[2], Isak[1]) was born 1878 in Kanczuga, Podkarpackie, Poland. She married RUBIN WESTREICH ca. 1904 in Kanczuga, Podkarpackie, Poland.

Rubin Westreich and Chana Tarnafker had the following child:
i. CHAJA[4] WESTREICH (Chana[3], Amalie[2], Izak[1]) was born in 1905 in Kanczuga, Podkarpackie, Poland.

8. **MARCUS[3] HOLOSZYCER** (Jakob[2], Isak[1]) was born 1871 in Kanczuga, Podkarpackie, Poland. He married (1) CHAJE RUCHEL TARNAFKER (daughter of Joel Juda Tarnafker and Amalie Holoszycer) 27 May 1905 in Kanczuga, Podkarpackie, Poland. She was born 02 April 1865 in Kanczuga, Podkarpackie, Poland.

Marcus Holoszycer and Chaje Ruchel Tarnafker had the following children:
i. JOSEF MAJER[4] HOLOSZYCER (Marcus[3], Jakob[2], Isak[1]) was born 08 May 1885 in Kanczuga, Podkarpackie, Poland.

ii. ISAAC HOLOSZYCER (Marcus[3], Jakob[2], Isak[1]) was born 20 September 1890 in Kanczuga, Podkarpackie, Poland.

iii. DAVID HOLOSZYCER (Marcus[3], Jakob[2], Isak[1]) was on 27 September 1894 in Kanczuga, Podkarpackie, Poland. He died 24 August 1897 in Kanczuga, Podkarpackie, Poland.

iv. EFRAIM HOLOSZYCER (Marcus[3], Jakob[2], Isak[1]) was born 1900 in Kanczuga, Podkarpackie, Poland.

v. AMALIE HOLOSZYCER (Marcus[3], Jakob[2], Isak[1]) was born 1905 in Kanczuga, Podkarpackie, Poland.

9. **FREIDA[3] HOLOSZYCER** (Jakob[2], Isak[1]) was born 23 December 1872 in Kanczuga, Podkarpackie, Poland. She died 1933 in Krakow, Malopolskie, Poland. She married CHAIM WALD (son of Josef Wald and Teme Sara Klinger) 26 December 1896 in Rzeszow, Podkarpackie, Poland. He was born 1873 in Rzeszow, Podkarpackie, Poland. He died 1923 in Rzeszow, Podkarpackie, Poland.

Chaim Wald and Freda Holoszycer had the following children:
i. MOSHE WALD[4] YAARI (Freida[3], Jakob[2], Isak[1]) was born 23 February 1895 in Kanczuga, Podkarpackie, Poland. He died 1983 in Israel. He married CHAYA RIVKA HOROWITZ (daughter of Alter Josef Horowitz and Feiga Leia). She was born 1898 in Rzeszów, Podkarpackie, Poland. She died 29 December 1966 in Israel.

ii. MEIR WALD YAARI (Freida[3], Jakob[2], Isak[1]) was born 24 April 1897 in Kanczuga, Podkarpackie, Poland. He died 21 February 1987 in Merhavia, Israel. He married ANDA KARP. She was born 04 January 1902 in Brody, Ukraine. She died 14 June 1993 in Merhavia, Israel.

iii. TOBIAS LAZAR WALD (Freida[3], Jakob[2], Isak[1]) was born 1907 in Rzeszow, Poland. He married FAIGA MINDEL AMSTER (daughter of Yaakov Amster and Chaya Sara). She was born 1911 in Sanok, Podkarpackie, Poland.

iv. ESTHER WALD (Freida[3], Jakob[2], Isak[1]) was born 1911 in Rzeszow, Poland.

10. **GETZEL HOLOSZYCER[3] HOLLY** (Jakob[2], Isak[1]) was born 21 December 1876 in Kanczuga, Podkarpackie, Poland. He died 27 October 1933 in Kings County, New York. He married MARIEM GEIGER (daughter of Aron Geiger and Hinde Turnheim) 1902 in Poland. She was born 22 February 1880 in Przemysl, Podkarpackie, Poland. She died 29 November 1946 in Manhattan, New York, New York.

Getzel Holoszycer Holly and Mariem Geiger had the following children:
i. MINA HOLOSZYCER[4] HOLLY (Getzel[3], Jakob[2], Isak[1]) was born 09 February 1905 in Poland. She died March 1996 in New York. She married THOMAS M. KEENAN in 1940 in New York.

ii. PAULINE AKA PEARL HOLOSZYCER HOLLY (Getzel[3], Jakob[2], Isak[1]) was born 06 May 1909 in New York, New York. She died June 1982 in Santa Fe, New Mexico. She married GEORGE BRONZ 15 April 1938 in Virginia. He was born 07 July 1910 in New York, New York. He died April 1976 in Washington, District of Columbia.

iii. HARRY HOLOSZYCER HOLLY (Getzel[3], Jakob[2], Isak[1]) was born 18 May 1912 in New York, New York. He died 14 April 2007 in Fort Lauderdale, Broward County, Florida. He married ROSE NASSAU about 1942 in New York. She was born 08 January 1911 in Pennsylvania. She died 24 July 1974 in New York.

iv. ESTHER HOLOSZYCER HOLLY (Getzel[3], Jakob[2], Isak[1]) was born 22 March 1915 in New York, New York. She died 09 November 1981 in New York, New York. She married MILTON SIEGEL in 1954 in New York.

Family Tree

Solomon Turnheim

Generation One

1. **SOLOMON**[1] **TURNHEIM**, born ca. 1797 in Jaroslaw, Podkarpackie, Poland; died ca. 1857 in Poland. Married ca. 1814 at Jaroslaw, Podkarpackie, Poland, SARA FEIGE.

Children of Solomon Turnheim and Sara Feige:
i. MALIE[2] TURNHEIM, born 1815 in Poland; died 1892, Jaroslaw, Podkarpackie, Poland. Married ca. 1833 at Jaroslaw, Podkarpackie, Poland, DAVID ATLAS, son of Sender Atlas and Feige.

ii. HERSCH TURNHEIM, born 1818 in Jaroslaw, Podkarpackie, Poland; died ca. 1882 in Poland. Married 1836 at Przemysl, Podkarpackie, Poland, MARIEM GEMS, daughter of Gronem Gems and Hinde Marberg.

iii. DAVID TURNHEIM, born 1820 in Jaroslaw, Podkarpackie, Poland; died 1883, Jaroslaw, Poland. Married ca. 1842, CHANE RUCHEL LEBENBRAUN, daughter of Moses Herz Lebenbraun and Basche Reisel.

Generation Two

2. **MALIE**[2] **TURNHEIM** (Solomon[1]), born 1815, Poland; died 1892, Jaroslaw, Podkarpackie, Poland. Married ca. 1833 at Jaroslaw, Podkarpackie, Poland, DAVID ATLAS, son of Sender Atlas and Feige.

Children of Malie[2] Turnheim and David Atlas:
i. JACOB[3] ATLAS, born ca. 1834, Jaroslaw, Podkarpackie, Poland; died 1889, Poland. Married 23 February 1882 at Przemysl, Podkarpackie, Poland, ZLATE TURNHEIM, daughter of Hersch Turnheim and Mariem Gems.

ii. WOLF ATLAS, born 1838, Poland; died 1894, Jaroslaw, Podkarpackie, Poland.

iii. JOSEPH ATLAS, born 1840, Poland; died 1894, Jaroslaw, Podkarpackie, Poland.

iv. SENDER ATLAS, born 1851, Poland; died 1889, Jaroslaw, Podkarpackie, Poland.

3. **HERSCH**[2] **TURNHEIM** (Solomon[1]), born 1818, Jaroslaw, Podkarpackie, Poland; died ca. 1882 in Poland. Married 1836 at Przemysl, Podkarpackie, Poland, MARIEM GEMS, daughter of Gronem Gems and Hinde Marberg.

Children of Hersch[2] Turnheim and Mariem Gems:
i. ZLATE[3] TURNHEIM, born November 1839, Przemysl, Podkarpackie, Poland; died Przemysl, Poland. Married 23 February 1882 at Przemysl, Polkarpackie, Poland, JACOB ATLAS, son of Malie Turnheim and David Atlas.

ii. BARUCH TURNHEIM, born 1844 Przemysl, Podkarpackie, Poland; died 1914, Drohobycz, Ukraine. Married 5 December 1887 at Drohobycz, Ukraine, CHANE KREPPEL, daughter of Chaim Kreppel and Chaje Wegner.

iii. HINDE TURNHEIM, born 1 January 1850, Przemysl, Podkarpackie, Poland; died 11 October 1931, Vienna, Austria. Married 1868, Przemysl, Podkarpackie, Poland, ARON GEIGER, son of Solomon David Geiger and Chaje Mindel Unger.

iv. MOSES TURNHEIM, born 1852, Przemysl, Podkarpackie, Poland; died 6 January 1890, Przemysl, Podkarpackie, Poland. Married 1874 at Bolechow, Poland, SARA HEJNDEL, daughter of Josef Hejndel and Rachel.

v. BENJAMIN TURNHEIM, born 8 August 1854, Przemysl, Podkarpackie, Poland; died 18 April 1930, Przemysl, Podkarpackie, Poland. Married 3 December 1882, Przemysl, Podkarpackie, Poland, CHAJE REISEL GANS, daughter of Meilech Gans and Sara Rifka Feldstein.

vi. SIMON TURNHEIM, born 7 December 1857, Przemysl, Podkarpackie, Poland; died 1858, Przemysl, Podkarpackie, Poland.

vii. SCHULEM TURNHEIM, born 7 December 1857, Przemysl, Podkarpackie, Poland; died 29 August 1925, Vienna, Austria. Married (1) 29 June 1879 SABINA PILPEL, daughter of Herza Pilpel and Chaji Gideli Hand. She died ca. 1887. Married (2) 6 December 1887 LEA TURNHEIM, daughter of Baruch Turnheim and Chane Kreppel.

4. **DAVID**[2] **TURNHEIM** (Solomon[1]), born 1820 in Jaroslaw, Podkarpackie, Poland; died 1883, Jaroslaw, Poland. Married ca. 1842, Jaroslaw, Podkarpackie, Poland, CHANE RUCHEL LEBENBRAUN, daughter of Moses Herz Lebenbraun and Basche Reisel.

Children of David[2] Turnheim and Chane Ruchel Lebenbraun:
i. JOSEPH[3] TURNHEIM, born 1843, Jaroslaw, Podkarpackie, Poland; died 1890, Poland. Married 1866, Przemysl, Podkarpackie, Poland, RACHEL GLANZ, daughter of Israel Glanz.

ii. JACOB TURNHEIM, born 1850, Jaroslaw, Podkarpackie, Poland; Married ca. 1889, Przemysl, Podkarpackie, Poland, TILLIE TURNHEIM, daughter of Joseph Turnheim and Rachel Glanz.

iii. DEBORA TURNHEIM, born 1852, Jaroslaw, Podkarpackie, Poland; died 1892, Przemysl, Podkarpackie, Poland. Married 1884, Jaroslaw, Podkarpackie, Poland, LEIBA TIRK, son of Hersch Tirk and Diene.

iv. LEIB TURNHEIM, born 1858, Jaroslaw, Podkarpackie, Poland. Married 25 November 1885, Tarnow, Poland, ESTER HANDGRIFF, daughter of Chiel Dawid Handgriff and Feige Eisenberg.

Generation Three

5. **ZLATE**[3] **TURNHEIM** (Malie[2], Solomon[1]), born ca. 1834, Jaroslaw, Podkarpackie, Poland; died 1889, Poland. Married 23 February 1882 at Przemysl, Podkarpackie, Poland, JACOB ATLAS, son of Malie Turnheim and David Atlas.

Children of Zlate Turnheim and Jacob Atlas:
i. SCHIE[4] ATLAS, born 9 June 1856, Przemysl, Podkarpackie, Poland.

ii. FEIGE ATLAS, born 1859, Przemysl, Podkarpackie, Poland. Married 7 March 1882, Przemysl, ISRAEL ANGERMAN, son of Hirsch Angerman and Ester.

iii. JOSEF[4] ATLAS, born 8 December 1865, Przemysl, Podkarpackie, Poland. Married 1896, Rzeszow, Podkarpackie, Poland, MALCIA GLEICHER, daughter of Hersch Gleicher and Mindel Meister.

iv. MARIM ATLAS, born 16 October 1875, Przemysl Podkarpackie, Poland. Married 19 June 1899, Przemysl, Podkarpackie, Poland, SIMON MANDEL, son of Josef Mandel and Surka Katzner.

6. **BARUCH**[3] **TURNHEIM** (Hersch[2], Solomon[1]), born 1844 Przemysl, Podkarpackie, Poland; died 1914, Drohobycz, Ukraine. Married 5 December 1887, Drohobycz, Ukraine, CHANE KREPPEL, daughter of Chaim Kreppel and Chaje Wegner.

Children of Baruch Turnheim and Chane Kreppel:
i. LEA[4] TURNHEIM, born 1866, Przemysl, Podkarpackie, Poland. Married 6 December 1887, Drohobycz, Ukraine, SCHULEM TURNHEIM, son of Hersch Turnheim and Mariem Gems.

ii. ETEL[4] TURNHEIM, born 1870, Drohobycz, Ukraine. Married 8 July 1900, Drohobycz, Ukraine, MOSES DAVID SCHINDLER, son of Abraham Schindler and Ryfki Gottlieb.

iii. RYSCHE TURNHEIM, born 1874, Drohobycz, Ukraine; died 14 February 1896, Drohobycz, Ukraine.

iv. MARYEM TURNHEIM, born 19 June 1879, Drohobycz, Ukraine.

7. **HINDE³ TURNHEIM** (Hersch², Solomon¹), born 1 January 1850, Przemysl, Podkarpackie, Poland; died 11 October 1931, Vienna, Austria. Married 1868, Przemysl, Podkarpackie, Poland, ARON GEIGER, son of Solomon David Geiger and Chaje Mindel Unger.

Children of Hinde Turnheim and Aron Geiger:
i. CHASKEL⁴ GEIGER, born 18 May 1868, Przemysl, Podkarpackie, Poland; died 24 April 1955, New York, New York. Married 6 March 1894, New York, New York, ESTHER MAMLOCK, daughter of Meyer Mamlock and Caroline Sobel.

ii. NAFTALE GEIGER, born 29 March 1871, Przemysl, Podkarpackie, Poland; died 1879. Przemysl, Podkarpackie, Poland.

iii. ABRAHAM YITZAK GEIGER, born 26 November 1872, Przemysl, Podkarpckie, Poland; died 28 September 1946, New York, New York. Married July 1894, Kanczuga, Podkarpackie, Poland, SPRYNCA STARK, daughter of Moses Stark and Sara.

iv. ISRAEL GEIGER, born 16 January 1874, Przemysl, Podkarpackie, Poland; died 29 April 1933, Chicago, Illinois. Married 27 November 1898, New York, New York, ESTHER PERLBERG, daughter of Elias Perlberg and Sarah Malter.

v. MARIEM GEIGER, born 22 February 1880, Przemysl, Podkarpackie, Poland; died 29 November 1946, New York, New York. Married 31 March 1902, Blazowa, Podkarpackie, Poland, GETZEL HOLOSZYCER, son of Jacob Holoszycer and Esther Jakubes.

vi. FREUDE GEIGER, born 23 January 1882, Przemysl, Podkarpackie, Poland; died ca. 1920.

vii. MINDLA GEIGER, born 3 April 1887, Przemysl, Podkarpackie, Poland; died 18 May 1960, Woodmere, New York. Married 17 October 1911, New York, New York, OSCAR WEISS, son of Fischel Weiss and Hannie Zuckerberg.

8. **MOSES³ TURNHEIM** (Hersch², Solomon¹), born 1852, Przemysl, Poland; died 6 January 1890, Przemysl, Poland. Married 17 January 1874, Bolechow, Ukraine, SARA HENDEL, daughter of Jozef Hendel and Rechel.

Children of Moses Turnheim and Sara Hendel:
i. CHANA⁴ TURNHEIM, born 1880, Przemysl, Podkarpackie, Poland died 1887.

ii. JOSEF TURNHEIM, born 1882, Przemysl, Podkarpackie, Poland; died 15 July 1942, Przemysl, Podkarpackie, Poland. He married 1910, Sieniawa, Poland, EDKA SCHMIDT.

iii. Ester Turnheim, born 1885, Przemysl, Podkarpackie, Poland; died 1895.

9. **BENJAMIN³ TURNHEIM** (Hersch², Solomon¹), born 8 August 1854, Przemysl, Podkarpackie, Poland; died 18 April 1930, Przemysl, Podkarpackie, Poland. Married 3 December 1882, Przemysl, Podkarpackie, Poland, CHAJE REISEL GANS, daughter of Meilech Gans and Sara Rifka Feldstein.

Children of Benjamin Turnheim and Chaje Reisel Gans:
i. FREUDE AKA FRANCESCA⁴ TURNHEIM, born 22 July 1875, Przemysl, Podkarpackie, Poland; Married 3 June 1895, Przemysl, Podkarpackie, Poland, HERZIL SCHONBACH, son of Samuel Moses Schonbach and Blima.

ii. MARJEM TURNHEIM, born 9 February 1877, Przemysl, Podkarpackie, Poland; died 12 October 1880, Przemysl, Podkarpackie, Poland.

iii. DEBORA TURNHEIM, born 22 April 1878, Przemysl, Podkarpackie, Poland; died 14 July 1959, New York, New York. Married 7 June 1898, Przemysl, Podkarpackie, Poland, DAVID NEUMARK, son of Solomon Neumark and Shifra Schutz.

iv. SAMUEL TURNHEIM, born 4 October 1879, Przemysl, Podkarpackie, Poland; died 20 August 1957, Przemysl, Podkarpackie, Poland. Married 1908, Ivano-Frankivsk, Ukraine, SALCIA ELIZA HALPERN, daughter of Nuchim Halpern and Ruchel.

v. SALOMON TURNHEIM, born 21 November 1881, Przemysl, Podkarpackie, Poland; died 28 January 1960, Louisville, Kentucky. Married ca. 1915, Louisville, Kentucky, FANNIE GOODMAN.

vi. MATHIAS TURNHEIM, born 20 February 1886, Przemysl, Podkarpackie, Poland; died 8 March 1920, Przemysl, Podkarpackie, Poland. Married ca. 1906, Przemysl, Podkarpackie, Poland, LOTI SILVERBUSH.

10. **SCHULEM³ TURNHEIM** (Hersch², Solomon¹), born 7 December 1857, Przemysl, Podkarpackie, Poland; died 29 August 1925, Vienna, Austria. Married (1) 29 June 1879, Lwow, Ukraine, SABINA PILPEL, daughter of Hersz Jona Pilpel and Chaje Gittel Hand. She died between 1885 to 1887. Married (2) 6 December 1887, Drohobycz, Ukraine, LEA TURNHEIM, daughter of Baruch Turnheim and Chane Kreppel.

Children of Schulem Turnheim and Sabina Pilpel:
i. MARYA⁴ TURNHEIM, born 18 May 1880, Lwow, Ukraine; died 1941.

ii. KELMAN JOZEF TURNHEIM, born 8 November 1881, Lwow, Ukraine; died 1964. He married EMILIA HEINE. They had two sons, Hans, and Leopold Turnheim.

iii. SIGMUND SOLOMON TURNHEIM, born 1883, Przemysl, Podkarpackie, Poland; died 7 November 1909, Vienna, Austria.

iv. LEA LORKA TURNHEIM, born 10 October 1884, Lwow, Ukraine; died 19 February 1975 in Vienna, Austria.

Children of Schulem Turnheim and Lea Turnheim:
i. FREIDA⁴ TURNHEIM, born 11 August 1889, Przemysl, Podkarpackie, Poland; died October 1942, Poland. Married 1925, Vienna, Austria, BETZALEL PRISAND, son of Abraham Prisand and Esther.

ii. MALKA ELIZBIETA TURNHEIM, born 6 October 1894 at Przemyśl, Podkarpackie, Poland; died 1896 at 2 years.

iii. HUGO TURNHEIM, born 2 May 1890, Vienna, Austria; died 1966, Israel. Married Anda.

iv. VALERIE TURNHEIM, born 9 June 1891, Vienna, Austria.

v. MAX TURNHEIM, born 24 June 1892, Vienna, Austria.

vi. ERNEST TURNHEIM, born 14 April 1896, Przemysl, Podkarpackie, Poland; died 1973 in Israel. He married TOVA ALEXANDROVITZ.

vii. HEDWIG TURNHEIM, born 30 March 1898, Vienna, Austria; died 4 January 1963 in England.

viii. WALTER TURNHEIM, born 22 June 1899, Vienna, Austria; died 1985 in Tel Aviv, Israel. He married HANNA NEUBAUER. They had two sons, Amiel and Joel Turnheim.

ix. FRIEDRICH TURNHEIM, born 7 April 1902, Vienna, Austria; died 5 December 1980, Vienna, Austria. He married IRENE WEISS. She was born 15 October 1907 and died 3 January 2007. They had two sons, Georg and Fred Turnheim. Both are still living.

11. **JOSEPH³ TURNHEIM** (David², Solomon¹), born 1843, Jaroslaw, Podkarpackie, Poland; died 1890, Poland. Married 1866, Przemysl, Podkarpackie, Poland, RACHEL GLANZ, daughter of Israel Glanz.

Children of Joseph Turnheim and Rachel Glanz:
i. FREUDE⁴ TURNHEIM, born 1864, Przemysl, Podkarpackie, Poland.

ii. LIEB AKA LEON TURNHEIM, born 19 January 1866, Przemysl, Podkarpackie, Poland. Married 26 July 1899, Lwow, Ukraine, ANTONINA TAUBA KALMUS, daughter of Nusyn Kalmus and Risie Thorn.

iii. TILLIE TURNHEIM, born 1867, Przemysl, Podkarpackie, Poland; died 1909, Przemysl, Podkarpackie, Poland. Married ca. 1890, Przemysl, Podkarpackie, Poland, JACOB TURNHEIM, son of David Turnheim and Chane Lebenbraun.

12. **JACOB[3] TURNHEIM** (David[2], Solomon[1]), born 1850; married Tillie Turnheim, daughter of Joseph Turnheim and Rachel Glanz.

Children of Jacob Turnheim and Tillie Turnheim:
i. JOSEF[4] TURNHEIM, born 1890, Jaroslaw, Poland; died 1890.

ii. DAVID TURNHEIM, born 28 August 1891, Jaroslaw, Poland.

iii. MORITZ TURNHEIM, born 1900.

iv. ISIDOR TURNHEIM, born 1893; died 1894.

v. ANNA TURNHEIM, born 1895, Bircza.

13. **DEBORA[3] TURNHEIM** (David[2], Solomon[1]), born 1851, Zolynia, Poland; died 3 December 1892, Przemysl, Podkarpackie, Poland. Married 1884, Jaroslaw, Podkarpackie, Poland, LEIBA TIRK, son of Hersch Tirk and Diene.

Children of Debora Turnheim and Leiba Tirk:
i. BETTY[4] TIRK, born 1878, Jaroslaw, Podkarpackie, Poland.

ii. SIGMUND TIRK, born 1879, Jaroslaw, Podkarpackie, Poland.

iii. ALEXANDER TIRK, born 1880, Jaroslaw, Podkarpackie, Poland; died 1880, Jaroslaw, Podkarpackie, Poland.

12. **LEIB[3] TURNHEIM** (David[2], Solomon[1]), born 1858, Jaroslaw, Podkarpackie, Poland. Married 25 November 1885, Tarnow, Poland, ESTER HANDGRIFF, daughter of Chiel Dawid Handgriff and Feige Eisenberg.

Children of Leib Turnheim and Ester Handgriff:
i. SALI[4] FRANCZISKA TURNHEIM, born 27 December 1886, Tarnow, Poland, married Chaim Klein 21 October 1906, Tarnow, Poland. CHAIM KLEIN AKA SCHLACHET was born at Nowy Sacz, Krakow, Poland, son of Maier Nathan Schlachet and Ester Klein.

ii. MARYA TURNHEIM, born 11 February 1888, Tarnow, Poland, married CHAIM HOCHHAUSER 4 December 1910, Tarnow, Poland. She died 21 April 1984, Cochabamba, Bolivia. Chaim was born 25 February 1884, Poland, the son of Abraham Dawid Hochhauser and Czarna Luftglas. He died 13 August 1943, Cochabamba, Bolivia.

iii. ABRAHAM CHUNE TURNHEIM, born 27 July 1889, Tarnow., Poland He was murdered during the Shoah.

iv. ANNA TURNHEIM, born 1892, Tarnow, Poland; died 1893 Tarnow, Poland.

v. EDWARD TURNHEIM, born 1894, Tarnow, Poland. He was a merchant in Tarnow and murdered during the Shoah.

vi. GIZELA TURNHEIM, born 1897, Tarnow; died 1900, Tarnow, Poland.

vii. JOZEF TURNHEIM, born 8 January 1899, Tarnow, Poland; died 8 April 1915.

viii. MAURYCY TURNHEIM, born 1901, Tarnow, Poland.

ix. MENASHE JUDA AKA MAKS JULIUSZ TURNHEIM, born 1903, Tarnow, Poland.

x. SALOMON TURNHEIM, born 1907, Tarnow, Poland. He was murdered during the Shoah.

Generation Four

13. **KELMAN JOZEF**[4] **TURNHEIM** (Schulem[3], Hersch[2], Solomon[1]), born 8 November 1881, Lwow, Ukraine; died 1964. He married EMILIA HEINE. They had two sons Hans and Leopold Turnheim.

    Children of Kelman Jozef Turnheim and Emilia Heine:
    i. HANS[5] TURNHEIM, born 11 April 1913, Vienna, Austria, married MELI. He died at Salzburg, Austria. They had two sons, Heinz and Klaus Turnheim.
    ii. LEOPOLD TURNHEIM, born 28 August 1911, Vienna, Austria, married HENRIETTE DRUCKER. He died 23 July 2012, Vienna, Austria. They had two children, Maria and Michael Turnheim.

14. **WALTER**[4] **TURNHEIM** (Schulem[3], Hersch[2], Solomon[1]), born 22 June 1899, Vienna, Austria; died 1985 in Tel Aviv, Israel. He married HANSI NEUBAUER and they immigrated to Israel in 1932–34. They had two sons, Amiel and Joel Turnheim.

15. **FRIEDRICH**[4] **TURNHEIM** (Schulem[3], Hersch[2], Solomon[1]), born 7 April 1902, Vienna, Austria; died 5 December 1980, Vienna, Austria, married IRENE WEISS. She was born 15 October 1907 and died 3 January 2007. They had two sons, Georg and Fred Turnheim. During the rise of the Nazis, Friedrich joined

the Communist party and was arrested in 1933. He escaped from prison in 1934 and fled to Kharkiv, Soviet Union where he lived until 1945 after WWII ended then returned to Vienna.

16. **CHASKEL**[4] **GEIGER** (Hinde[3] Turnheim, Hersch[2], Solomon[1]), born 18 May 1868, Przemyśl, Poland; died 24 April 1955 at New York, New York. Married 6 March 1894 at New York, New York, ESTHER MAMLOCK, daughter of Meyer Mamlock and Caroline Sobel.

Children of Chaskel Geiger and Esther Mamlock:
i. MARION[5] GEIGER, born 10 January 1895, New York, New York; died 3 December 1991 at New York, New York. Married 12 October 1920 at New York, New York, EUGENE MESSNER, son of Emil Messner and Betty Shuster.

ii. MINNA GEIGER, born 3 September 1896, New York, New York; died September 1983 at New York, New York. Married (1) 17 June 1919 at New York, New York, ALBERT M. ROLLAND, son of Jules Rolland and Hattie Metzger. Married (2) 3 July 1932 at Somerville, New Jersey, JESSE DANIEL GIDDING.

iii. MILTON MARK GEIGER, born 27 April 1902, New York, New York; died 29 November 1959 at Minneapolis, Minnesota. Married (1) 5 March 1925 at New York, New York, DOROTHY DUCKER, daughter of Solomon Ducker and Rae Green. Married (2) 12 January 1937 at Carver, Minnesota, ALMA PETRINE HOLM-REISCHL, daughter of Martin Holm and Julie Arnstad.

17. **ABRAHAM YITZAK**[4] **GEIGER** (Hinde[3] Turnheim, Hersch[2], Solomon[1]), born 19 November 1872, Przemyśl, Poland; died 28 September 1946 at New York, New York. Married July 1894 at Kańczuga, Podkarpackie, Poland, SPRYNCA STARK, daughter of Moses Stark and Sara.

Children of Abraham Yitzak Geiger and Sprynca Stark:
i. CHAJIJA AKA MINA[5] GEIGER, born 21 May 1895, Kańczuga, Podkarpackie, Poland; died ca.1958. Married ca. 1938 at Vienna, Austria, KARL NEUMANN.

ii. MORDECHA AKA MAX GEIGER, born 8 March 1898, Błażowa, Podkarpackie, Poland; died 25 February 1981 at New York, New York. Married 31 October 1922 at Vienna, Austria, RUCHLA GINSBERG, daughter Isidore Ginsberg and Schewa.

iii. JOSEF GEIGER, born 6 December 1899, Błażowa, Podkarpackie, Poland; died 18 November 1989 at Jerusalem, Israel. Married (1) ca. 1927 at Vienna, Austria, ESTHER SCHONFELD; Married (2) October 1960 at London, England, ELSIE MONDERER.

iv. SZEJWA AKA STELLA GEIGER, born 11 July 1902, Błażowa, Podkarpackie, Poland; died 7 November 1989 at Miami Beach, Florida. Married ca. 1934 at Vienna, Austria, MORRIS STEINBOCH.

18. **ISRAEL[4] GEIGER** (Hinde[3] Turnheim, Hersch[2], Solomon[1]), born 16 January 1874, Przemyśl, Podkarpackie, Poland; died 29 April 1933 at Chicago, Illinois. Married 27 November 1898 at New York, New York, ESTHER PERLBERG, daughter of Elias Perlberg and Sarah Malter.

Children of Israel Geiger and Esther Perlberg:
i. JENNIE[5] GEIGER, born 7 September 1899, New York, New York; died 10 November 1980 at Oakland, California. Married 19 April 1925 at Chicago, Illinois, ISIDORE AKA FRANCIS RICHARD GLENNER, son of Jacob Glenner and Sarah Mary Joseph.

ii. ELI GEIGER, born 30 April 1901, New York, New York; died 26 January 1979 at Chicago, Illinois. Married December 1969 at Dade County, Florida, DOROTHY TAMAN.

iii. HARRY GEIGER, born 11 December 1908. Chicago, Illinois; died 10 February 1987 at San Diego, California. Married 6 June 1952 at Chicago, Illinois, BETTY LOUISE NEWMANN.

19. **MARIEM[4] GEIGER** (Hinde[1] Turnheim, Hersch[2], Solomon[1]), born 22 February 1880, Przemyśl, Podkarpackie, Poland; died 29 November 1946, New York, New York. Married 31 March 1902 at Błażowa, Podkarpackie, Poland, GETZEL HOLOSZYCER, son of Jacob Holoszycer and Ester Jakubes.

Children of Mariem Geiger and Getzel Holoszycer aka Holly:
i. MINA[5] HOLLY, born 9 February 1905, Kańczuga, Podkarpackie, Poland; died March 1996 at New York, New York. Married 1940 at New York, New York, THOMAS MARTIN KEENAN.

ii. PEARL HOLLY, born 6 May 1909, New York, New York; died 2 June 1982 at Santa Fe, New Mexico. Married 15 April 1938 at Alexandria, Virginia, GEORGE BRONZ, son of Louis Bronz and Sarah Paley.

iii. HARRY HOLLY, born 18 May 1912, New York, New York; died 14 April 2007 at Fort Lauderdale, Florida. Married ca. 1942, New York, New York, ROSE NASSAU, daughter of Samuel Nassau and Rebecca.

iv. ESTHER HOLLY, born 22 March 1915, New York, New York; died 9 November 1981 at New York, New York. Married 1954, New York, New York, MILTON SIEGEL.

20. **MINDLA AKA MINNIE**[4] **GEIGER** (Hinde[3] Turnheim, Hersch[2], Solomon[1]), born 3 April 1887, Przemyśl, Podkarpackie, Poland; died 18 May 1960 at Woodmere, Nassau County, New York. Married 17 October 1911 at New York, New York, OSCAR WEISS, son of Fischel Weiss and Hannie Zuckerberg.

Children of Minnie Geiger and Oscar Weiss:
i. MARION[5] WEISS, born 28 November 1912, New York, New York; died 14 January 1996 at Patchogue, Long Island, New York. Married 8 September 1935, Kings County, New York, HARRY GOSHIN, son of Jack Goshin and Lena Schuel.

ii. SYLVIA JUNE WEISS, born 4 June 1914, Kings County, New York; died 28 September 1994 at Manchester, New Hampshire. Married 24 January 1943, Kings County, New York, FRANK GERBER, son of David Gerber and Fannie Gerber.

iii. MARTHA WEISS, born 28 July 1918, New York, New York; died 22 September 2005 at Sedona, Arizona. Married 23 November 1939, Kings County, New York, AARON CANTOR, son of Joseph Cantor and Flora Schwartz.

21. **DEBORA**[4] **TURNHEIM** (Benjamin[3], Hersch[2], Solomon[1]), born 22 April 1878, Przemysl, Podkarpackie, Poland; died 14 July 1959, New York, New York. Married 7 June 1898, Przemysl, Podkarpackie, Poland, DAVID NEUMARK, son of Solomon Neumark and Shifra Schutz.

Children of Debora Turnheim and David Neumark:
i. SALOMEA[5] NEUMARK, born 11 September 1899, Rakonice, Warsaw, Poland; died 11 March 1985, Israel. Married 3 October 1921, New York, New York, JOSEPH BRAININ, son of Reuben Brainin and Masha Amsterdam.

ii. MARTHA NEUMARK, born 5 May 1904, Berlin, Germany; died 21 September 1981, New York, New York. Married 16 September 1924, Marion, Indiana, HARRISON GOLDBERG AKA HENRY MONTOR.

iii. IMMANUEL KANT NEUMARK, born 23 April 1914, Cincinnati, Ohio; died 2 November 1993, Miami, Florida. Married ca. 1938, New York, New York, RUTH SCHMERLER, daughter of Elias Schmerler and Bertha.

22. **SALOMON**[4] **TURNHEIM** (Benjamin[3], Hersch[2], Solomon[1]), born 21 November 1881, Przemysl, Podkarpackie, Poland; died 28 January 1960, Louisville, Kentucky. Married ca. 1915, Louisville, Kentucky, FANNIE GOODMAN.

Children of Salomon Turnheim and Fannie Goodman:

i. JOSEPH HENRY[5] TURNHEIM, born 13 February 1916, Louisville, Kentucky; died 25 June 1974, Louisville, Kentucky. Married ca. 1942, Louisville, Kentucky, BETTY ZELLNER, daughter of Carl Zellner and Freda Rutman.

23. **MATHIAS[4] TURNHEIM** (Benjamin[3], Hersch[2], Solomon[1]), born 20 February 1886, Przemysl, Podkarpackie, Poland; died 8 March 1920, Przemysl, Podkarpackie, Poland. Married, Przemysl, Podkarpackie, Poland, LOTI SILVERBUSH.

Children of Mathias Turnheim and Loti Silverbush:

i. MIRIAM[5] TURNHEIM, born 30 July 1920, Przemysl, Podkarpackie, Poland; died 23 March 2003, Haifa, Israel. Married in Israel, MENDEL ROSENBAUM AKA ROTEM.

24. **TILLIE[4] TURNHEIM** (Joseph[3], David[2], Solomon[1]), born 1867, Przemysl, Podkarpackie, Poland; died 1909, Przemysl, Podkarpackie, Poland. Married ca. 1889, Przemysl, Podkarpackie, Poland, JACOB TURNHEIM, son of David Turnheim and Chane Ruchel Lebenbraun.

Children of Tillie Turnheim and Jacob Turnheim:

i. JOSEF[5] TURNHEIM, born 1890, Jaroslaw, Podkarpackie, Poland; died 1890, Jaroslaw, Podkarpackie, Poland.

ii. DAVID TURNHEIM, born 28 August 1891, Jaroslaw, Podkarpackie, Poland; died 25 May 1942, Poland.

iii. ISIDOR TURNHEIM, born 1893, Jaroslaw, Podkarpackie, Poland; died 1894, Jaroslaw, Podkarpackie, Poland.

iv. ANNA TURNHEIM, born 1895, Jaroslaw, Podkarpackie, Poland.

v. MORITZ TURNHEIM, born 1900, Jaroslaw, Podkarpackie, Poland.

Family Tree

Yehuda Leib Weiss

Generation One

1. **YEHUDA LEIB[1] WEISS** was born ca. 1814 in Rozdil, Zydaczow, Ukraine. He died 20 December 1882 in Gaje Wyzne, Ukraine. He married SOSKE BORGMAN (daughter of Moses Borgman and Estasy Kahane) ca. 1843 in Boryslaw, Ukraine. She was born 1817 in Ukraine. She died 19 October 1891 in Boryslaw, Ukraine.

Yehuda Leib Weiss and Soske Borgman had the following children:
i. FISCHEL[2] WEISS (Yehuda Leib[1]) was born 1851 in Boryslaw, Ukraine. He died 11 October 1893 in Vienna, Austria. He married HENCZE ZUCKERBERG (daughter of Mendel Zuckerberg and Hinde Fraenkel) ca. 1869 in Drohobycz, Ukraine. She was born 1852 in Drohobycz, Ukraine. She died 30 April 1936 in Manhattan, New York, New York.

ii. CHANNA WEISS[2] (Yehuda Leib[1]) was born ca. 1845 in Boryslaw, Ukraine. She died ca. 1918. She married MOSES BANDER (son of Iser Bander and Beily). He was born 1840 in Boryslaw, Ukraine. He died 1902 in Boryslaw, Ukraine.

iii. SAMUEL WEISS[2] (Yehuda Leib[1]) was born 06 July 1856 in Boryslaw, Ukraine. He married MATEL BLUMENKRANZ.

Generation Two

2. **FISCHEL[2] WEISS** (Yehuda Leib[1]) was born 1851 in Boryslaw, Ukraine. He died 11 October 1893 in Vienna, Austria. He married HENCZE ZUCKERBERG (daughter of Mendel Zuckerberg and Hinde Fraenkel) ca. 1869 in Drohobycz, Ukraine. She was born 1852 in Drohobycz, Ukraine. She died 30 April 1936 in Manhattan, New York, New York.

Fischel Weiss and Hencze Zuckerberg had the following children:

i. OSCAR[3] WEISS (Fischel[2], Yehuda Leib[1]) was born 11 March 1876 in Boryslaw, Ukraine. He died 25 October 1946 in Manhattan, New York, New York. He married MINNIE GEIGER (daughter of Aron Geiger and Hinde Turnheim) on 17 October 1911 in Manhattan, New York, New York. She was born on 04 April 1887 in Przemysl, Podkarpackie, Poland. She died on 18 May 1960 in Woodmere, Nassau, New York.

ii. ESTER WEISS (Fischel[2], Yehuda Leib[1]) was born 28 June 1880. She died 25 April 1883 in Drohobycz, Ukraine.

iii. LOUIS WEISS (Fischel[2], Yehuda Leib[1]) was born 14 January 1885 in Boryslaw, Ukraine. He died 09 March 1969 in Brooklyn, New York. He married JENNIE MEISELMAN. She was born 06 April 1892. She died 05 April 1974.

iv. MORYS WEISS (Fischel[2], Yehuda Leib[1]) was born 08 November 1869 in Drohobych, Ukraine. He died 03 November 1940 in New York, New York. He married PAULINE MESSER (daughter of Henry Messer and Sophia Zwillich) ca. 1892. She was born 06 March 1873. She died 25 December 1946 in New York.

v. FANNIE WEISS (Fischel[2], Yehuda Leib[1]) was born 18 June 1879 in Boryslaw, Ukraine. She married PHILLIP HARRY WOLF (son of Isaac Wolf and Perla Tepper) 27 December 1905 in New York, New York. He was born ca. 1874.

vi. SADYE WEISS (Fischel[2], Yehuda Leib[1]) was born 29 December 1882 in Gaje Wyzne, Ukraine. She died 01 November 1963 in New York, New York. She married MORRIS LUCKOWER 23 March 1913 in New York. He was born 03 September 1881. He died 30 May 1969 in New York City.

vii. CHANNA AKA ANNIE WEISS (Fischel[2], Yehuda Leib[1]) was born 1877 in Drohobycz, Ukraine. She died November 1952 in Bronx, Bronx, New York. She married JACOB BORGMAN (son of Abraham Hersh Borgman and Sara Friedman) 04 July 1898. He was born 26 January 1875. He died 20 November 1931 in New York.

viii. ROSIE WEISS (Fischel[2], Yehuda Leib[1]) was born ca. 1875. She died 1 Apr 1943 in Bronx, New York. She married KALMAN HERMAN BRAUNER (son of Munisch Brauner and Yudes Berger). He was born 1866 in Rychcice, Ukraine. He died 26 September 1947 in New York.

ix. ELIO WEISS (Fischel[2], Yehuda Leib[1]) was born 1887. He died 1887.

3. CHANNA²WEISS (Yehuda Leib¹) was born ca. 1845 in Boryslaw, Ukraine. She died ca. 1918. She married MOSES BANDER (son of Iser Bander and Beily). He was born 1840 in Boryslaw, Ukraine. He died 1902 in Boryslaw, Ukraine.

Moses Bander and Channa Weiss had the following children:
i. MEIR³ BANDER (Channa², Yehuda Leib¹) was born 1866 in Boryslaw, Ukraine. He died 1941 in Ukraine. He married CHAJA RACHEL KASSER (daughter of Isak Kasser and Ester). She was born ca. 1861. She died 1929 in Boryslaw, Ukraine.

ii. SCHAJE BANDER (Channa², Yehuda Leib¹) was born ca. 1870 in Boryslaw, Ukraine. He married JENTE KIMELHEIM (daughter of Chaim Shmuel Kimelheim and Udli Beily Fink) 05 February 1917 in Boryslaw, Ukraine. She was born ca. 1875 in Ukraine.

iii. ESTER BANDER (Channa², Yehuda Leib¹) was born 1878. She died 1880.

iv. JUDA HERSH BANDER (Channa², Yehuda Leib¹) was born 21 December 1881 in Boryslaw, Ukraine.

v. BERTA RACHEL BANDER (Channa², Yehuda Leib¹) was born 1896. She died 1942. She married SALOMON BIKALES. He was born 1887. He died 1942.

vi. FEIGE BANDER (Channa², Yehuda Leib¹) was born 1900 in Boryslaw, Ukraine. She died 1943. She married PAUL KRAUT. He died in 1943.

4. SAMUEL³ WEISS (Yehuda Leib¹) was born 06 July 1856 in Boryslaw, Ukraine. He married MATEL BLUMENKRANZ.

Samuel Weiss and Matel Blumenkranz had the following children:
i. MOSES MARCUS⁴ WEISS (Samuel², Yehuda Leib¹) was born 1880 in Boryslaw, Ukraine. He died 1880.

ii. ITTE MALIA WEISS (Samuel², Yehuda Leib¹) was born 1882 in Boryslaw, Ukraine.

iii. ESTHER WEISS (Samuel², Yehuda Leib¹) was born 1885 in Boryslaw, Ukraine.

Generation Three

5. **OSCAR³ WEISS** (Fischel², Yehuda Leib¹) was born 11 March 1876 in Boryslaw, Ukraine. He died 25 October 1946 in Manhattan, New York, New York. He married MINNIE GEIGER (daughter of Aron Geiger and Hinde Turnheim) 17 October 1911 in Manhattan, New York, New York. She was born 04 April 1887 in Przemysl, Podkarpackie, Poland. She died 18 May 1960 in Woodmere, Nassau, New York.

Oscar Weiss and Minnie Geiger had the following children:

i. MARION⁴ WEISS (Oscar³, Fischel², Yehuda Leib¹) was born 28 November 1912 in New York, New York. She died 14 January 1996 in Patchogue, Long Island, New York. She married TZVI HERSH AKA HARRY GOSHIN (son of Jacob Goshin and Lena Schuel) 08 September 1935 in Brooklyn, New York. He was born 03 January 1912 in Brooklyn, New York. He died 23 December 1985 in Patchogue, New York.

ii. SYLVIA WEISS (Oscar³, Fischel², Yehuda Leib¹) was born 04 June 1914 in Brooklyn, New York. She died 28 September 1994 in Manchester, New Hampshire. She married FRANK GERBER (son of David Gerber and Fannie Gerber) 24 January 1943 in Brooklyn, New York. He was born 10 April 1914 in Portland, Maine. He died 05 October 1993 in Haverhill, Essex, Massachusetts.

iii. MARTHA WEISS (Oscar³, Fischel², Yehuda Leib¹) was born 28 July 1918 in New York. She died 22 September 2005 in Sedona, Coconino, Arizona. She married AARON CANTOR (son of Joseph Cantor and Flora Schwartz) 23 November 1939 in New York, New York. He was born 29 December 1915 in Newark, New Jersey. He died 02 October 1999 in Laguna Hills, Orange, California.

6. **LOUIS³ WEISS** (Fischel², Yehuda Leib¹) was born 14 January 1885 in Boryslaw, Ukraine. He died 09 March 1969 in Brooklyn, New York. He married JENNIE MEISELMAN. She was born 06 April 1892. She died 05 April 1974.

Louis Weiss and Jennie Meiselman had the following child:

i. SYDONIA⁴ WEISS (Louis³, Fischel², Yehuda Leib¹) was born on 11 December 1914 in Kings County, New York. She died on 29 June 2003 in Pompano Beach, Florida. She married SAMUEL VINIG. He was born on 24 August 1911. He died on 13 June 1980 in Kings County, New York.

7. **MORYS³ WEISS** (Fischel², Yehuda Leib¹) was born 08 November 1869 in Drohobych, Ukraine. He died 03 November 1940 in New York, New York. He married PAULINE MESSER (daughter of Henry Messer and Sophia Zwillich) ca. 1892. She was born 06 March 1873. She died 25 December 1946 in New York.

Morys Weiss and Pauline Messer had the following children:

i. MAX⁴ WEISS (Morys³, Fischel², Yehuda Leib¹) was born 12 May 1893 in Jersey City, New Jersey. He died 15 September 1955 in Manhattan, New York, New York. He married JOHANNA FIEBERT (daughter of Louis R. Fiebert and Clara Von Gelden) 1916. She was born 02 August 1896. She died 01 June 1983 in New York, New York.

ii. SIDNEY SIGMUND WEISS (Morys³, Fischel², Yehuda Leib¹) was born 13 September 1902 in New York. He died 1963 in Haverstraw, Rockland, New York. He married BLANCHE MARGULIES (daughter of Pincus Margulies and Fanny K. Stern) 29 May 1930 in Kings County, New York. She was born 1904. She died 08 December 1992 in Middleton, Orange, New York.

iii. HELEN W. WEISS (Morys³, Fischel², Yehuda Leib¹) was born 06 March 1898. She died 11 November 1984. She married EZRA EPSTEIN. He was born 29 April 1893. He died 04 March 1980 in Florida.

iv. NORCIA WEISS (Morys³, Fischel², Yehuda Leib¹) was born 24 March 1903 in New York City. She married HARRY KATZ 04 August 1925 in New York City. He died October 1969.

8. **FANNIE³ WEISS** (Fischel², Yehuda Leib¹) was born 18 June 1879 in Boryslaw, Ukraine. She married PHILLIP HARRY WOLF (son of Isaac Wolf and Perla Tepper) 27 December 1905 in New York, New York. He was born ca. 1874.

Phillip Harry Wolf and Fannie Weiss had the following child:

i. ELEANOR HELEN⁴ WOLF (Fannie³, Fischel², Yehuda Leib¹) was born 26 November 1911 in Jersey City, New Jersey. She died 19 March 1994 in New Jersey. She married (1) EDMOND B. MARKHEIM (son of Samuel Markheim and Amelia Benjamin) 24 June 1934 in Bronx County, New York. He was born 1909. He died 29 August 1942 in New York, New York. She married (2) HAROLD SCHWARTZ. He was born 24 March 1903. He died September 1974 in Rutherford, Bergen, New Jersey.

9. **SADYE³ WEISS** (Fischel², Yehuda Leib¹) was born 29 December 1882 in Gaje Wyzne, Ukraine. She died 01 November 1963 in New York, New York. She married MORRIS LUCKOWER 23 March 1913 in New York. He was born 03 September 1881. He died 30 May 1969 in New York City.

Morris Luckower and Sadye Weiss had the following children:
i. FRANCIS⁴ LUCKOWER (Sadye³, Fischel², Yehuda Leib¹) was born 01 February 1914 in New York. He died 24 February 1995 in North Miami Beach, Dade, Florida. He married NORMA WORKMAN 14 January 1940 in New York, New York. She was born 05 March 1918 in New York. She died 18 September 1983 in North Miami Beach, Dade, Florida.

ii. HERBERT LUCKOWER (Sadye³, Fischel², Yehuda Leib¹) was born 29 April 1923 in New York. He died 24 February 2011 in Harrison, New York. He married IDA M. BURGER. She was born 04 March 1936 in New York.

iii. SEYMOUR EMANUEL LUCKOWER (Sadye³, Fischel², Yehuda Leib¹) was born 10 August 1915 in Bronx, New York. He died 19 November 1940 in Melbourne, Victoria, Australia.

iv. VIRGINIA LUCKOWER (Sadye³, Fischel², Yehuda Leib¹) was born 08 May 1926 in New York. She died 20 July 2010 in Cape Coral, Florida. She married JOSEPH BERKE (son of Barney Berke and Rebecca Finkel). He was born 08 May 1923. He died August 1973 in New Jersey.

10. **CHANNA AKA ANNIE³ WEISS** (Fischel², Yehuda Leib¹) was born 1877 in Drohobycz, Ukraine. She died November 1952 in Bronx, Bronx, New York. She married JACOB BORGMAN (son of Abraham Hersh Borgman and Sara Friedman) 04 July 1898. He was born 26 January 1875. He died 20 November 1931 in New York.

Jacob Borgman and Channa aka Annie Weiss had the following children:
i. SANFORD⁴ BORGMAN (Channa aka Annie³, Fischel², Yehuda Leib¹) was born 20 December 1906 in New York. He died August 1976 in Florida. He married SYLVIA GOLDIN (daughter of Gedalia Goldin and Channe Greenberg) 29 December 1927 in Bronx County, New York. She was born 08 March 1911 in Kings County, New York. She died 1996 in Miami Beach, Dade, Florida.

ii. MILTON BORGMAN (Channa aka Annie³, Fischel², Yehuda Leib¹) was born 03 February 1905 in New York. He died 13 January 1989 in Nassau County, New York. He married EDITH A. BLUMENTHAL (daughter of Ruben Blumenthal and Jennie Danziger) in Bronx, Bronx, New York. She was born 18 May 1906 in New York. She died 1995 in New York.

iii. NETTIE BORGMAN (Channa aka Annie[3], Fischel[2], Yehuda Leib[1]) was born ca. 1910 in New York. She died 03 March 1989. She married ABE LEVINE ca. 1939 in New York. He was born ca. 1907 in New York. He died 26 February 1985 in New York.

iv. LILLIAN BORGMAN (Channa aka Annie[3], Fischel[2], Yehuda Leib[1]) was born 1902.

11. **ROSIE[3] WEISS** (Fischel[2], Yehuda Leib[1]) was born ca. 1875. She died 01 April 1943 in Bronx, New York. She married KALMAN HERMAN BRAUNER (son of Munisch Brauner and Yudes Berger). He was born 1866 in Rychcice, Ukraine. He died 26 September 1947 in New York.

Kalman Herman Brauner and Rosie Weiss had the following children:
i.   FISCHEL[4] BRAUNER (Rosie[3], Fischel[2], Yehuda Leib[1]) was born 22 April 1898 in Drohobycz, Ukraine. He died 09 September 1898 in Drohobycz, Ukraine.

ii. MAX BRAUNER (Rosie[3], Fischel[2], Yehuda Leib[1]) was born 22 June 1899 in New York. He died October 1976 in New York. He married RHODA MERFOGEL. She was born 26 October 1904. She died 09 March 1997 in Roanoke, Virginia.

iii. CHAJE SARA BRAUNER (Rosie[3], Fischel[2], Yehuda Leib[1]) was born 1902 in Rychcice, Ukraine.

iv. MARCUS BRAUNER (Rosie[3], Fischel[2], Yehuda Leib[1]) was born 22 May 1904 in Ukraine. He died 10 September 1905 in Drohobycz, Ukraine.

v.   SADIE BRAUNER (Rosie[3], Fischel[2], Yehuda Leib[1]) was born 28 February 1905 in Ukraine. She married LOUIS SMITH. He was born ca. 1904 in Russia.

vi. SYLVIA BRAUNER (Rosie[3], Fischel[2], Yehuda Leib[1]) was born 08 September 1906 in Poland. She died 1997. She married JULIUS LOWENSTEIN. He was born ca. 1905 in Germany.

vii. IDA BRAUNER (Rosie[3], Fischel[2], Yehuda Leib[1]) was born ca. 1912. She died 2004.

viii. NETTIE BRAUNER (Rosie[3], Fischel[2], Yehuda Leib[1]) was born 16 June 1918 in New York. She died 04 January 2009 in New York. She married HARRY HOROWITZ.

12. MEIR³ BANDER (Channa², Yehuda Leib¹) was born 1866 in Boryslaw, Ukraine. He died 1941 in Ukraine. He married CHAJA RACHEL KASSER (daughter of Isak Kasser and Ester). She was born ca. 1861. She died 1929 in Boryslaw, Ukraine.

Meir Bander and Chaja Rachel Kasser had the following children:
i.   SAMUEL⁴ BANDER (Meir³, Channa², Yehuda Leib¹)was born ca. 1891 in Boryslaw, Ukraine. He died 25 May 1892 in Boryslaw, Ukraine.

ii.   SOSCHE BANDER (Meir³, Channa², Yehuda Leib¹) was born 1894 in Boryslaw, Ukraine. She died 1895 in Boryslaw, Ukraine.

iii.   RUCHEL BANDER (Meir³, Channa², Yehuda Leib¹) was born 10 February 1896 in Boryslaw, Ukraine.

iv.   FEIGE ROSA BANDER (Meir³, Channa², Yehuda Leib¹) was born 1898 in Boryslaw, Ukraine.

v. MOISHE BANDER (Meir³, Channa², Yehuda Leib¹) was born 14 February 1903 in Boryslaw, Ukraine. He died 1943 in Drohobycz, Ukraine. He married JULIA.

vi. HERSCH BANDER (Meir³, Channa², Yehuda Leib¹) was born 02 September 1904 in Boryslaw, Ukraine. He died 13 February 1991 in New York. He married IDA BRESLER. She was born 1902. She died 1971.

13. SCHAJE³ BANDER (Channa², Yehuda Leib¹) was born ca. 1870 in Boryslaw, Ukraine. He married JENTE KIMELHEIM (daughter of Chaim Shmuel Kimelheim and Udli Beily Fink) 05 February 1917 in Boryslaw, Ukraine. She was born ca. 1875 in Ukraine.

Schaje Bander and Jente Kimelheim had the following children:
i.   LEIB⁴ BANDER (Schaje³, Channa², Yehuda Leib¹) was born 13 October 1901 in Boryslaw, Ukraine. He married RIFKA MEHR (daughter of Israel Mehr and Sara Neche Auslander) 05 June 1928 in Boryslaw, Ukraine. She was born 1906.

ii.   MOSES BANDER (Schaje³, Channa², Yehuda Leib¹) was born 19 January 1904 in Boryslaw, Ukraine.

iii.   CHAJE SURE BANDER (Schaje³, Channa², Yehuda Leib¹) was born 30 May 1906 in Boryslaw, Ukraine. She died 24 June 1906 in Boryslaw, Ukraine.

iv.   BLIME BANDER (Schaje³, Channa², Yehuda Leib¹) was born 18 July 1907 in Boryslaw, Ukraine. She married MENDEL ISAK HALLER (son of Abraham Fuchs and Liebe Haller) 15 December 1932 in Boryslaw, Ukraine.

v.   IZAK BANDER (Schaje³, Channa², Yehuda Leib¹) was born 19 March 1910 in Boryslaw, Ukraine.

vi.   ZOFIA BANDER (Schaje³, Channa², Yehuda Leib¹) was born 18 December 1915 in Boryslaw, Ukraine.

14. **BERTA RACHEL³ BANDER** (Channa², Yehuda Leib¹ Weiss) was born in 1896. She died 1942. She married SALOMON BIKALES. He was born 1887. He died 1942.

Salomon Bikales and Berta Rachel Bander had the following children:
i.   RICHARD⁴ BIKALES (Berta Rachel³, Channa², Yehuda Leib¹) was born 1921. He died 2003. He married CHARLOTTE NESTEL. She was born 1920. She died 2001.

ii.   NORBERT BIKALES (Berta Rachel³, Channa², Yehuda Leib¹). He married GERDA BIERZONSKI.

5.   **FEIGE³ BANDER** (Channa², Yehuda Leib¹) was born 1900 in Boryslaw, Ukraine. She died 1943. She married PAUL KRAUT. He died 1943.

Paul Kraut and Feige Bander had the following children:
i.   ISAAC⁵ KRAUT (Feige³, Channa², Yehuda Leib¹) was born 1928 in Lwow, Ukraine. He died 1943.

ii.   MALE KRAUT (Feige³, Channa², Yehuda Leib¹) was born 1931. He died 1943.

Bibliography and References

A.A. Aliev. "Origin of Jewish Clusters of E1b1b1 (M35) Haplogroup." *The Russian Journal of Genetic Genealogy*, 2010.

Alexander Beider. *A Dictionary of Ashkenazic Given Names*. Bergenfield, NJ: Avotaynu, 2001.

---. *A Dictionary of Jewish Surnames from Galicia*. Bergenfield, NJ: Avotaynu, 2004.

---. *A Dictionary of Jewish Surnames from the Kingdom of Poland*. Teaneck, NJ: Avotaynu, 1996.

Harold T. Betteridge, Editor. *The New Cassell's German Dictionary*. New York: Funk and Wagnalls Company, 1965.

Ellen Levy-Coffman. "A Mosaic of People: the Jewish Story and a Reassessment of the DNA Evidence." *Journal of Genetic Genealogy*, 2005.

Max I. Dimont. *Jews, God and History*. New York: New American Library, 1962.

Simon M. Dubnow. *History of the Jews in Russia and Poland, from the Earliest Times Until the Present Day, Volume I*. Philadelphia, PA: Jewish Publication Society of America, 1918.

Simon M. Dubnow. *History of the Jews in Russia and Poland, from the Earliest Times Until the Present Day, Volume II*. Philadelphia, PA: Jewish Publication Society of America, 1946.

Yaffa Eliach. *Hasidic Tales of the Holocaust*. First Vintage Books Edition, 1988.

Jon Entine. *Abraham's Children*. New York: Grand Central Publishing, 2007.

Josef Fraenkel, Editor. *The Jews of Austria*. London: Valentine, Mitchell and Co., 1967.

Judith R. Franzin. *A Translation Guide to 19th-Century Polish-Language Civil Registration Documents*. 3rd edition. Northbrook, IL: Jewish Genealogical Society of Illinois, 2009.

Saul Friedlander. *Nazi Germany and the Jews. Volume I. The Years of Persecution, 1933-1939*. New York: Harper Perennial, 1997.

Sir Martin Gilbert. *The Atlas of Jewish History*. New York: William Morrow and Co., Inc., 1969.

Shmuel Gorr. Chaim Freedman, Editor. *Jewish Personal Names. Their Origin, Derivation and Diminutive Forms*. Bergenfield, NJ: Avotaynu, 1992.

Ruth Ellen Gruber. *Jewish Life in East-Central Europe, Yesterday and Today*. New York: John Wiley and Sons, Inc., 1994.

Estelle M. Guzik, Editor. *Genealogical Resources in New York*. New York: Jewish Genealogical Society, Inc., 2003.

Pinkas Hakehillot Polin: *Encyclopedia of Jewish Communities, Poland*. Jerusalem, Israel: Yad Vashem.

John J. Hartman and Jacek Krochmal, Editors. *I Remember Every Day…the Fates of the Jews of Przemyśl During World War II. Przemyśl*, Poland: Ganset, 2002.

Irving Howe. *How We Lived: A Documentary of Immigrant Jews in America*. New York: Ricard Marek Publishers, 1979.

Irving Howe. *World of Our Fathers*. New York: New York University Press, 2005.

Paul J. Jacobi. Emanuel Elyasaf, Editor. *The Jacobi Papers: Genealogical Studies of Leading Ashkenazi Families. Vol. 1*. New Haven, CT: Avotaynu, 2019.

Janina Jaślan and Jan Stanisławski, Editors. *Compact Polish and English Dictionary*. New York: McGraw-Hill, 1981.

Alter Kacyzne. *Poyln-Jewish Life in the Old Country*. New York: Henry Holt and Company, 1999.

Thomas Keneally. *Schindler's List*. New York: Simon and Schuster, 1982.

John D. Klier and Shlomo Lambroza, Editors. *Pogroms. Anti-Jewish Violence in Modern Russian History*. Cambridge, UK: Cambridge University Press, 1992.

Arthur Kurzweil. *From Generation to Generation. How to Trace Your Jewish Genealogy and Family History*. San Francisco, CA: Jossey-Bass, 2004.

Brian J. Lenius. *Genealogical Gazetteer of Galicia*. Selkirk, Manitoba, Canada: Brian J. Lenius, 1999.

Nolan Menachemson. *A Practical Guide to Jewish Cemeteries*. Bergenfield, NJ: Avotaynu, 2007.

Pamela S. Nadell. *Women Who Would be Rabbis: A History of Women's Ordination, 1889-1985*. Boston, MA: Beacon Press, 1998.

Jeffrey Mark Paull, Gaye Tannenbaum and Jeffrey Briskman. "Why Autosomal DNA Rest Results Are Significantly Different for Ashkenazi Jews." New Haven, CT: *Avotaynu*, XXX, No.1, Spring 2014.

W. Gunther Plaut, Editor. *The Torah: A Modern Commentary*. New York: Jewish Publication Society, 1981.

Neil Rosenstein. *The Unbroken Chain*. Lakewood, NJ: C.I.S. Publishers, 1990.

Leo Rosten. *The Joys of Yinglish*. New York: Penguin Books, 1989.

Sallyann Amdur Sack and Gary Mokotoff, Editors. *Avotaynu Guide to Jewish Genealogy*. Bergenfield, NJ: Avotaynu, 2004.

Jonathan D. Shea and William F. Hoffman. *Following the Paper Trail: A Multilingual Translation Guide*. Teaneck, NJ: Avotaynu, 1994.

Jonathan D. Shea and William F. Hoffman. *In Their Words: A Genealogist's Translation Guide to Polish, German, Latin, and Russian Documents. Volume I: Polish*. New Britain, CT: Language and Lineage Press, 2007.

Joshua L. Segal. *A Field Guide to Visiting a Jewish Cemetery*. Nashua, NH: Jewish Cemetery Publishing LLC, 2007.

David R. Semmel. *11ᵗʰ of Av*. Lexington, KY: David R. Semmel, 2010.

Ilana Shamir and Shlomo Shavit, Editors. *Encyclopedia of Jewish History*. Israel: Masada Publishers, 1986.

Megan Smolenyak Smolenyak and Ann Turner. *Trace Your Roots With DNA: Using Genetic Tests to Explore Your Family Tree*. Rodale Inc., 2004.

Shmuel Spector, Editor in Chief and Geoffrey Wigoder, Consulting Editor. *The Encyclopedia of Jewish Life Before and During the Holocaust. Volumes 1, 2, 3*. New York: New York University Press, 2001.

Jits Van Straten. *The Origin of Ashkenazi Jewry*. Berlin, Germany: Walter de Gruyter GmbH & Co., 2011.

Henrietta Szold, Editor. *American Jewish Yearbook 5668 9 September 1907–25 September 1908*. Philadelphia, PA: Jewish Publication Society of America.

Debbie Parker Wayne. "Triangulating Autosomal DNA." *National Genealogical Society Magazine*, 2016.

Miriam Weiner. *Jewish Roots in Poland*. New York: YIVO Institute for Jewish Research, 1997.

Nisson Wolpin, Editor. *Torah Luminaries: A Treasury of Biographical Sketches*. Brooklyn, New York: Mesorah Publications, 1994.

Piotr Wrobel. *The Jews of Galicia Under Austrian-Polish Rule, 1867–1918*. Boston, MA: Cambridge University Press, 1994.

David S. Wyman. *The Abandonment of the Jews-:America and the Holocaust 1941–1945*. New York: Pantheon Books, 1984.

Suzan Wynne. *The Galitzianers-the Jews of Galicia 1772–1918*. Kensington, MD: Suzan Wynne, 2006.

Photo Sources and Credits

Chapter 6

Chapter 7

p. 263   Top image: www.gjenvick.com, Bottom image: www.ancestry.com New York Passenger Lists 1820-1957.

p. 265   Left image: courtesy of Arthur Goshin; Right images: details from photo on p. 37.

p. 266   Courtesy of Elizabeth Lifschitz

p. 267   www.ancestry.com. U.S. Naturalization Records 1794-1995.

p. 268   Top image: www.ancestry.com. U.S. Naturalization Records Indexes; Bottom left image: courtesy of Judith Goldsmith; Bottom right image: courtesy of Mt. Zion Cemetery, Maspeth, Queens, New York

p. 270   www.ancestry.com. Selected U.S. Naturalization Records 1790-1974.

p. 271   Left image: courtesy of Judith Goldsmith; Right image: www.metmuseumofart.org.

p. 272   www.ancestry.com. U.S. School Yearbooks 1900-1990. New York University College of Medicine.

p. 273   www.ancestry.com. Virginia Marriage Records 1936-2014.

p. 274   www.ancestry.com. U.S. School Yearbooks 1880-2012. City College of New York.

p. 277   Courtesy of Elizabeth Lifschitz.

p. 279   Courtesy of Elizabeth Lifschitz

p. 280   Courtesy of Elizabeth Lifschitz

p. 281   Top image: courtesy of Elizabeth Lifschitz; Bottom left image: courtesy of Judith Goldsmith; Bottom right image: courtesy of Dan Holly

p. 283   Courtesy of Elizabeth Lifschitz

p. 284   Courtesy of Judith Goldsmith

Chapter 10

p. 294   www.jri-pl.org. Przemysl Archive, Poland. Przemysl Birth Records 1853-1900.

p. 295   Detail from image on p. 37.

p. 297   www.gjenvick.com

p. 298   www.ancestry.com. New York Passenger Lists. *S.S. Moltke*, 1904.

p. 299   Estate of Sylvia Gerber

p. 300   Detail from image on p. 265.

p. 301   Estate of Sylvia Gerber

p. 302   Both images courtesy of Arthur Goshin.

p. 303   New York Municipal Archives. Manhattan Marriages.

p. 304   Estate of Sylvia Gerber

p. 305   www.streeteasy.com

p. 306   Estate of Sylvia Gerber

p. 307   Estate of Sylvia Gerber

p. 309   Courtesy of Judith Goldsmith

p. 312   Estate of Marion Goshin

p. 313   Courtesy of Judith Goldsmith

p. 314   Estate of Sylvia Gerber

p. 316   www.jri-pl.com. Boryslaw Deaths.

p. 317   Estate of Sylvia Gerber

p. 318   Courtesy of Judith Goldsmith

p. 319   www.forgottengalicia.com/the-galician-petroleum-industry.

p. 320   www.ancestry.com. Immigration, Hamburg Passenger Lists to New York 1850-1934.

p. 322   New York Municipal Archive. Petitions for Naturalization. Osher Weiss.

p. 324   Both images courtesy of Israelitische Kultus Gemeinde, Vienna (IKG).

p. 326   Courtesy of Judith Goldsmith

p. 327   Left image: estate of Sylvia Gerber; Right image: courtesy of Lois Chertoff.

p. 328   New York Municipal Archive. Brooklyn, Marriage Records.

p. 329   Courtesy of Lois Chertoff

p. 330   Courtesy of Arthur Goshin

p. 331   Left image: estate of Sylvia Gerber, Right image: estate of Marion Goshin

p. 332   Courtesy of Judith Goldsmith

p. 333   Courtesy of Judith Goldsmith

p. 334   Top image: www.ancestry.com. Massachusetts, Passenger and Crew Lists. *S.S. Saxonia;* Bottom image: www.familysearch.org. New York, Petitions for Naturalization.

p. 335   New York Municipal Archive. Manhattan, Marriage Records.

p. 340   Estate of Sylvia Gerber

p. 341   Detail from image on p. 307.

p. 342   Both images: estate of Sylvia Gerber

p. 343   Estate of Sylvia Gerber

p. 344   Estate of Sylvia Gerber

p. 345   Estate of Sylvia Gerber

p. 346   Estate of Sylvia Gerber

p. 347   Estate of Sylvia Gerber

p. 348   Both images: estate of Sylvia Gerber

p. 350   Courtesy of Judith Goldsmith

p. 351   Courtesy of Judith Goldsmith

p. 353   Courtesy of Judith Goldsmith

p. 355   Top image: National Archives, Kew, UK. Bottom image: www.ancestry.com, Immigration Records

p. 357   National Archives, Waltham, Massachusetts. Maine Federal Naturalization Records 1787-1952.

p. 358   Courtesy of Judith Goldsmith

p. 359   Maine Archives, Portland, Maine. Birth Records 1715-1922.

p. 360   Estate of Frank Gerber. Portland HS yearbook *The Totem.*

p. 361   Both images: estate of Frank Gerber

p. 362   Estate of Frank Gerber

p. 363   Estate of Frank Gerber

p. 369   Courtesy of Judith Goldsmith

p. 370   Estate of Sylvia Gerber

p. 371   All images: estate of Sylvia Gerber

p. 372   Both images: estate of David Gerber

p. 373   All images: estate of Sylvia Gerber

p. 374   All images: estate of David Gerber

p. 375   Both images: estate of David Gerber

p. 377   Estate of Sylvia Gerber

p. 378   All images: estate of David Gerber

p. 379   Estate of Sylvia Gerber

p. 381   Courtesy of Judith Goldsmith

p. 382   Estate of Martha Cantor

p. 383   Estate of Martha Cantor

p. 384   Estate of Martha Cantor

p. 387   Top image: estate of Martha Cantor; Middle images: courtesy of Judith Goldsmith; Bottom image: courtesy of Mark Cantor

p. 389   www.kustvaartforum.com

p. 390   www.familysearch.org. Eastern District Petitions for Naturalizations 1795-1931.

p. 392   Courtesy of Mark Cantor

p. 393   Estate of Martha Cantor

p. 394   Top image: courtesy of Mark Cantor, Bottom image: courtesy of Judith Goldsmith

Chapter 11

p. 412   www.gidonim.org

p. 413   www.gidonim.org

p. 416   National Archives, Krakow, Poland. Applications for the Issuance of Identity Cards, Kennkarten, for Jews, 1941.

p. 419   Courtesy of Jane Stern

p. 420   Courtesy of Jane Stern

p. 421   Courtesy of Jane Stern

p. 423   Jewish Cemetery, Lezajsk, Poland. www.wikimediacommons.org. Photographer Emmanuel Dyan.

p. 425   Courtesy of Martin Bialik

p. 429   www.familysearch.org. Naturalizations, U.S. District Court of Southern District, New York

p. 432   www.familysearch.org. Naturalizations, U.S. District Court of Southern District, New York

p. 433   Courtesy of Martin Bialik

p. 434   Courtesy of Martin Bialik

Chapter 12

p. 445   www.bing.com. Map of Sokolow, Poland.

p. 448   www.jri-pl.org. Rzeszow Archive, Poland. Sokolow Malopolskie Birth Records 1825-1912.

p. 449   www.jri-pl.org. Rzeszow Archive, Poland. Sokolow Malopolskie Birth Records 1825-1912.

p. 450   www.jri-pl.org. Rzeszow Archive, Poland. Sokolow Malopolskie Birth Records 1825-1912.

p. 451   Top image: www.yadvashem.org. Bottom image: www.jri-pl.org.

p. 452   www.yadvashem.org.

p. 454   www.yadvashem.org

p. 456   All images: courtesy of Elisha Geiger

p. 459   www.wikimediacommons. Unknown photographer.

p. 463   Courtesy of Brenda Habshush

p. 464   Courtesy of Elisha Geiger

p. 465   Courtesy of Elisha Geiger

Appendix A

Geiger and Bronz Letters

UNITED STATES OF AMERICA)
:
DISTRICT OF COLUMBIA)
:
CITY OF WASHINGTON)

AFFIDAVIT OF SUPPORT

I, GEORGE BRONZ, BEING DULY SWORN, DEPOSE AND SAY:

1. I reside at 116 - 19th Street S.E., Washington, D. C.

2. I am a native born citizen of the United States. I was born in the City of New York, State of New York, *on July 7, 1910.* I have resided continuously in the United States since my birth.

3. It is my intention and desire to have Frieda Prisand, nee Turnheim, residing at Wien II, Taborstrasse 21a/19, Germany, come to the United States for permanent residence here. Frieda Prisand is my wife's cousin.

4. I am employed as Principal Attorney in the Department of Agriculture, Government of the United States, at a salary of $5600 per year. There are attached hereto copies of my latest appointment notices, duly certified by the official custodian of the personnel records of the Department of Agriculture. Although I do not have civil service status, I have been continuously employed in the Federal service since August, 1933, and expect to continue in that employment indefinitely. My business address is Department of Agriculture, Washington, D. C.

5. My wife is now partially dependent upon me for support. However, she holds the degree of Doctor of Medicine and expects to be entirely self-supporting as soon as she has completed her hospital training. My mother is partially dependent upon me for support since my father's earnings are not sufficient to maintain her in comfortable fashion. I have no children and

-2-

there are no persons dependent upon me for support, except those mentioned herein.

6. I am willing and able to receive, maintain and support Frieda Prisand after her immigration into the United States and hereby assume such obligation and guarantee that she will not, at any time, become a burden upon any community in the United States.

7. I make this affidavit voluntarily and freely, for the purpose of inducing the American Consul to issue a visa to Frieda Prisand so that she may enter the United States for permanent residence.

_____

Subscribed and sworn to before me this _____ day of _____ 1938.

_____
                                                        Notary Public

My commission expires: _____

July 19th, 1939

Dear Uncle Charles:

I am sorry we did not reply sooner to your letter but it took me a few days to collect some information here.

I spoke to a Jewish Agency here which handles matters of this sort and they told me that the English Committee is not accepting any affidavits, letters or assurances. What they require is a substantial amount of cash. Under English law, she tells me, immigrants coming into England to await their turn under American quotas are not permitted to work in England. Therefore, there must be cash available for their support. The Committee asks that you deposit with them about $2200 or $2400 for two people which will support them for two years. The English Committee then makes weekly or monthly payments to the immigrants for their support and refunds any balance to the person who put up the money. This Washington Agency supplied me with a form of application. I have filled the form in partly, but I don't have full information about the Geigers, so I am leaving the top and bottom of the form for you to fill out. The Washington Agency suggests that you see a Miss Levine at the National Refugee Service, 165 West 46th Street, New York.

On the assumption that this information is incorrect, I am sending you the sort of letter which you suggested so that it will be available, if it will be helpful. If there is anything more I can do, please do not hesitate to call upon me.

Lots of love to Aunt Ester and your children, from Pearl and me.

July 19, 1939

German Jewish Aid Committee,
   52, Bedford Way,
      London, W. C. 1.
         England.

                Reference No. 1 M/24582.
                Immigration Department.

Gentlemen:

    Josef Geiger and his wife Ester Geiger are seeking to enter England for residence there until they will be permitted to enter the United States under quota restrictions. They have asked for your assistance in securing admission for them to England and giving the necessary guarantees that these immigrants will not become a public charge in England.

    I have executed affidavits required under the Immigration Regulations of the United States, which have been filed with the proper Consuls, giving assurance, under oath, that I am willing, able and ready to receive, maintain and support Josef Geiger, and his wife Ester, after their immigration into the United States and I have guaranteed that they will not, at any time, become a burden upon any community in the United States. I hereby give the same assurance and assume the same obligations with respect to their immigration into England, pending their admission to the United States, and I hereby guarantee that they will not, at any time, become a burden upon any community in England.

    I am attaching hereto copies of the Affidavits which I executed for the American Consul for these two immigrants. These affidavits give full information about the immigrants and about my financial responsibility.

                  Very truly yours,

Enclosures   George Bronz

GB:ew

AFFIDAVIT OF SUPPORT

UNITED STATES OF AMERICA)
)
DISTRICT OF COLUMBIA   )   ss:
)
CITY OF WASHINGTON   )

I, George Bronz, being duly sworn, depose and say:

1. I reside at 3925 Davis Place, N. W., Washington, D. C.

2. I am a native-born citizen of the United States. I was born in the City of New York, State of New York, on July 7, 1910. I have resided continuously in the United States since my birth.

3. It is my intention and desire to have Marcus (or Markus) Geiger, his wife Ruchla Geiger, and their children Clara and Susi, formerly residing in Vienna, Germany, and now temporarily residing in Marseilles, France, come to the United States for permanent residence here. Marcus Geiger is my wife's first cousin. Marcus Geiger was born in Balsowa (or Blozowa or Blazowa), County of Rzeszow, Poland, about 1898. Ruchla, Clara and Susi Geiger were born in Austria in 1898, 1926 and 1931 respectively.

4. I am employed as Chief Legal Adviser, Consumers' Counsel Division in the Department of the Interior, Government of the United States, at a salary of $6500 per year. There is attached hereto a copy of my latest appointment notice, duly certified by the official custodian of the personnel records of the Consumers' Counsel Division. Although I do not have civil service status, I have been continuously

employed in the Federal service since August 1933, and expect to
continue in that employment indefinitely. My business address
is Department of the Interior, Washington, D. C.

5. My wife is a licensed physician and is now employed
on the faculty of the George Washington University School of
Medicine at a salary of $1200 per year. My parents are largely
dependent upon me for support, since neither of them is gainfully
employed, but they have a small income from other sources. I have
no children and there are no persons dependent upon me for support,
except those mentioned herein. I have had no difficulty in meeting
the obligations mentioned herein and, in addition, am accumulating
savings so that I believe I shall be able readily to carry out this
additional obligation.

6. I am willing and able to receive, maintain and support
Marcus Geiger, his wife, and their children after their immigration
into the United States and hereby assume such obligations and
guarantee that none of them will at any time become a burden upon
any community in the United States.

7. While I do not know Marcus Geiger, his wife or children
personally, I am familiar with their reputations in the communities
in which they have lived and among their friends and relatives, of
which I have been advised by persons who knew them intimately abroad
and by Americans who visited them from time to time.

8. To the best of my information and belief, from the
sources indicated above, Marcus Geiger and his wife, Ruchla, and
their children are all of excellent and unimpeachable character; none
of them has ever been arrested or otherwise charged with any crime;
none of them has ever been engaged in political activities; none of

them is an agent for any foreign government.

9. I shall consider myself fully responsible for these four applicants if they are admitted to the United States, and to the best of my ability I shall see that they do not become involved in any political activities or become members of any political organizations which are in any way under foreign control.

10. I make this affidavit voluntarily and freely for the purpose of inducing the American Consul at ~~Marseilles, France,~~ *Vienna, Germany,* or any other American Consul to whom this affidavit may be presented, to issue *a* visa to ~~Marcus, Ruchla, Clara and Susi Geiger~~ *Frieda Prisand* so that ~~they~~ *she* may enter the United States for permanent residence.

_____

Subscribed and sworn to before me this ____ day of March, 1941.

_____
Notary Public

My commission expires _____

UNITED STATES
DEPARTMENT OF THE INTERIOR
OFFICE OF THE SOLICITOR
WASHINGTON

CONSUMERS' COUNSEL
DIVISION

April 9, 1941

MEMORANDUM for Mr. Guy W. Numbers,

Assistant Director of Personnel.

Confirming our telephone conversation may I ask if you
would be so good as to have prepared for me a copy of my
latest appointment notice (dated about February, 1940) certified under the seal of the Department? This is for trans-
mittal to the American Consul at Marseilles, France. I would
be grateful to you if this could be prepared before the end
of business tomorrow, since the State Department will send it
by diplomatic pouch if I get it to them the first thing Friday
morning. If you will have me called at Branch 4406 when the
document is ready I will send for it.

George Brons,

Chief Legal Adviser.

UNITED STATES
DEPARTMENT OF THE INTERIOR
OFFICE OF THE SOLICITOR
WASHINGTON

CONSUMERS' COUNSEL
DIVISION

April 10, 1941

Consul of the United States of America,

Marseilles,

France.

Dear Sir;

Several weeks ago I executed an Affidavit of Support on behalf of Marcus Geiger and his family and sent it to him. Now he advises me that your office does not consider it satisfactory because it is a "copy" rather than the "original".

Since the affidavit proper which I sent to him was an original, I assume that the objection is to the appended carbon copy of my Notice of Employment to my present position in the Interior Department. I am therefore enclosing another copy of my Notice of Employment certified under the seal of the Interior Department in regular form according to statute. I hope this will be satisfactory and I should be deeply grateful to you for any assistance you could render in expediting the granting of visas to this family.

Very truly yours,

George Bronz,
Chief Legal Adviser

Enclosure

Monday 12/5/38

Dear Pearl & George

Glad to know that you intend to visit us shortly as we all are lonesome for you.

Our cousin Dora Neumark told me that you may be able to help in getting some affidavits for our relatives abroad.

I have 13 of them to take care of. so far I succeeded in sending 5 affid. but it seems that I am at the ropes end.

Here are 3 very important people in need of affid namely

RUCHLA GEIGER born 10/6 1898 in BUCZACZ POLAND, Vienna citizen wife of Marcus Geiger

Their children KLARA GEIGER born 7/8. 1926 and SUSI " " 4/9 1931

2.

Markus has an affid, but it is very urgent that the rest of his family get affid also so that they at least get out of Vienna. Their present address is

MARKUS GEIGER
DARWINGASSE 35/18. II WIEN
~~Germany~~

even those of them who have affid. can not get here for a long time, but at least it helps them a lot.

Please do all you possible can to help me in the matter as it almost drive me crazi.

Hope and pray you will succeed

Love from all

Uncle chas.

Margot is having her Tonsels removed to-day.

New York July 13ᵗ 1939

Dear Pearl and George

Sorry could not see you when you
were last in N.Y.

I received a letter from my
brother in London stating that his
son Josef and wife must
leave Milano Italy shortly
or be deported back to
germany. If I am not mistaken
you have send them afidavits
for this country, as it may
take years before they reach
the quota. he my brother is
trying hard to take them to
London meantime and has
also procured a good job for
Josef but the jewish committee
wants asurance of some kind
that they will not become a
public charge. I visited the
authrities here in reference
to this and they advise me that
the party that send them the
offidavit can do so by
making a statement that it

7/13

will look out off for their support
while in England, untill they
reach their qmota for the u.s.
Will therefore ask you that
you send me the above
mentioned instrument, you
can easely find out from
the refugee committee at
Washington or other office
how same is to be worded
and address same to
German Jewish Committee
London Re: Josef Geiger & Wife
Ref. N° 117/24582, Immigration dept.
and I will forward same
to London.
This is only a matter of form
as I will keep you free from
any obligation as to their
support e.t.c.   you practicaly
risk nothing outside of helping
a near relative from going
back to hell.
Hope you are well and will
be here soon again
               Love from us all,
                    uncle chas.

Thursd 7/17/41 New York

Dear Pearl & George.

I saw mr. Sams to-day,.
The 6 piece bedroom suit
Bed. chest. dresser & mirror, chair
and 2 night stand will cost
you $185.50 delivered to your
door by the R.R. Co. shipped
direct from the factory at
no charge for freight.
If you have to pay freight
charges same will be deducted
from above price.
I asked him to make sure
if the factory has the pieces
in stock he will know
within a few days, and
if satisfactory to you
I will then give shipping
instruction as pr your order.

- 2 -   7/17/41

I am sending you under
seperate cover a sample of
carpet which I believe is of
a better quality than the one
you sellected.

size 12ʃ X 21ʃ including
binding & the cushion lining
will cost you about
$125.00

If you have a sample
from Berber compare the
two. I may be wrong.

I am getting all the date
to gether for the affidavit of
support for Josef & Erna Geiger.
please let me know if on
the original affidavit her
name is given Erna, Esther
or both names. and if posible,
send me 1 form b. July 1941
from Dept of State for my record.

With love from all
Uncle Chas

NY. Wedn July 30ᵗ 1941

Dear George and Pearl

at last I am home again after a
poor vacation, as I did not
feel well the week up at Sp. Val.
I am getting too sweet to suit me.
plenty of sugar. I was to a
good doctor yesterday for a general
check up but will know the
results in a few days.

I was glad to receive your letter
and all paragraphs noted.

I agree with your decision.
let me Know the number of
the H&W bedroom suit as I will
g have the bedding house get
the right size for the main
bed. as measures differ.
as to the box spring on legs would
like to Know the collor of the legs.
I believe you will want maple.
the spring & Mattress about 36" or
39" let me Know the size wanted

I believe the enclosed bunch
of papers will cover all you want

- 2 -   7/30/40

for Josef & Erna or Esther.
Please George look them over.
Brother abraham askes me to plead
with you to do all you can to expedite
matters, advise him as soon as
cable to europe is one the way
so that he can cable to Josef.
and to send him the bill or amount
of your cash outlay.

Pearl, I showed your letter to
Marion & Minne, they will be
glad ∧to Washington for your
house warming!

to motor

With best wishes and love
from all
                    Uncle Chas.

New York Feb. 10ᵗ 42

Dear George

    The enclosed were forwarded to me by my brother Abraham asking me to send them to you with request that you be good enough and apply to the immigration authorities for a hearing re: Joseph & his wife, And when same is granted in due time, that you show them the photos of the parents, pleading that they are sick and old. And wish to have Joseph and his wife here soon as possible.

    I am sure that you will do all you can to comply with their request.

    I assure you dear George That I am very reluctent of troubling you, but what else can I do.

1.

Mr. Richard B. Barton is handling the matter for them, he is one day a week in his New York office.

With love to you. Pearl and baby from Aunte Esther and self.

Sincerely yours
Uncle Chas.

New York Dec. 18ᵗ 1942

Dear George.

On receipt of your recent letter I got in tuch with my brother abraham. he imidiatly wrote to Josef to try and get an affidavit from the Polish representative at London,

Abraham wants to Know if it would do that he, his daughter, son and son in law could make sworn affidavits to their positive Knowledge that Josef is a polish subject, if that would be accepted. If that meets with your aproval would you please send copy for such instrument and they would notarise same.

I realy hate to trouble you but I see no other way out if it and would therefore ask you for your kind indolgence.

Perhaps in the spring of 1943 we would visit you as we would like to see your home, especially Steve before he looses his baby charm.

With love to you all and best wishes for a happy new year from us all.

Sincerely

Uncle Chas.

New York 16ᵗʰ March 1943

Dear George,

We returned last week from Lakewood
where we got rid of colds. & feel O.K.
I got your letter of 6ᵗʰ inst before me;
You ask for reference letters for Uncle
Abraham, They are enclosed herewith
also one letter of same character
for myself. and statement from
the Mutual Benefit Life omited
in my last mail to you
I arrived at the New York port
but do not remember the name
of the ship
I derive my income from
dividends on my investments
and from interest on bonds &
mortgages.
As to definite shipping arrangements, they can't be made

3/16/43

here. but soon as Josef
gets the visais in London
he will make all shipping
arrangements out there with
the moneys we will cable him.
In any event the american
consul at London will not
hand him the visais untill
he shows S.S. tickets for
their passage to America.
    Aunte Esther and I are
talking about our visit
to you which we hope will
be in the very near future.
    with love to you all
                Uncle Chas.
P.S.
    Please acknowledge imidiatly
    receipt of this letter & enclosures.
4 enclosures

New York Feb. 4th 1943

Dear George,

At last I am mailing you the papers re: Josef Geiger and his wife.

I suggest, on my brothers affidavit paragraph 7 you substitute instead of businessman in paper: manufacturer of paper bags, handling Machinery, etc.

About shipping space that could be arrangment, I will see my brother on Sunday and will take the matter up with him and will advise you.

My brother has written Joseph to get affidavit from polish authorities in London re: his polish citizenship, he will no doubt obtain same. it is only a question of a little time on account mail irregularity.

I will obtain some character affi-davits if necessary and will forward them to you. with love to you all

P1 Uncle Chas

I am enclosing some copies which I used in bringing the Steinbocks over here, these where I prepared by my friend and accountant Mr. Metz. you may want them I thought. also, statements from my bank. my broker, N.Y. Life. Equitable Life, Metropolitan Life and M. L. I Bens S. & T. S.

excuse myself it is easier for me to write Machinery and having earlier copy of this letter.

for myself

CHARLES GEIGER 585 West ~~~~ ~~~   February 1st 1943

Collateral loan			
6350			
1750			
4600			

Collateral loan
6350
1750
4600

Cash in Bank 1,433.11   Chase National Bank

Collateral equity .   4,600.-   "   "   "

Insurance policy   12,936   New York Life Insurance Co.
       51 Madison Ave N.Y.

"   "   3,088.02   Metropolitan Life Ins. Co
       1 Madison Ave N.Y.

"   "   2,314.85   Mutual Benefit Life Ins Co
       New ark N J

"   "   1,502.50   Equitable Life Assurance Soc,
       393 Seventh Ave N.Y.

Real property   50% interest in
       Chasol Co. N.C. -
       a New York Corporation
       property assessed for 80,000.-
       net equity 19,000

9,500.   my interest

1,433.	11		
4,600			Hirsch Lilienthal & Co
12,936		12,700 -	members of Stock Exchange
3,088.	02		25 Broad St N.Y.C.
2,314	85	.500.	US Victory Bonds
1,502	50		
9,500.			
12,700			
500			

October 30, 1940
1059- -53rd S t.
Brooklyn, N. Y .

Dear George:

I am enclosing the forms for affidavits for my son
Joseph. You made this affidavit two years ago and the American
Counsul in London demand a renewal of same.

D ta:

Joseph Geiger Born in Balzowa, Polland age
    Dec. 6, 1899.
Esther Schonfeld, Born in Bucarest-1898
Their present address:

16 Courtleigh
    Bridge Lane
        London N. W. 11
            Golders Green, London, Eng.

I would appreciate it very much if you would be so
kind as to take care of same immediately because of the terrible
conditions there and I would like to take them out as soon as
p ossible.

When you are in New York, I shall be very happy to
thank you personally. Please fill out the forms and return to
me.

With kindest regards to Pearl,

Love from all,
Abraham Geiger

P.S.
Enclosed sample
of letter of friendship

March 2 - 1943

Dear Pearl & George!

I am very much surprised that I did'nt hear from you about the papers from my son Josef. –

Yesterday I received from Josef a letter as following:

" I was at the Polish Consulate
" in London and asked him
" to certify my citizenship. The
" Consulate was very much surprised
" because it is the first time that
" somebody asks a certification
" for this purpose. – He told me
" to make a Photostate copy of
" my passport, which I send you
" enclosed. – I hope that will
" do and I will soon get the visa."

I send you enclosed this Photocopy and please, dear George try the best and I hope you will succeede now. –

Best regards from all and love your Uncle

Bobbi Abraham Geiger

Phone Windsor 6-3796

Rabbi Isak Halberstam
of
Congregation Chevra Bnai Moshe Halberstam
5120 Fort Hamilton Parkway
Brooklyn, N. Y.

הרב יצחק האלבערשטאם
בן הרב הצדיק מבּארדיוב ז"ל
נכד ה"ק מסאנז ונכד ה"ק מסיגעט ומאיחעל זצ"ל
חתן הצדיק מריבּאטשנצש וצ"ל
רב דחברה בני משה האלבערשטאם

January 26, 1943

To Whom It May Concern:

I, an American citizen, hereby certify that
Mr. Joseph Geiger, who is at present residing at
16 Courtleigh Bridge Lane, London N.W. 11, England,
is very well known to me from my native town of
Blazowa, Poland. To the best of my knowledge, he
is now a Polish citizen. He was born in Blazowa,
Poland, and has never changed his Polish citizenship.

Any courtesy shown in the above case will be
greatly appreciated.

Respectfully yours,

Rabbi Isak Halberstam

RABBI ISAK HALBERSTAM

Sept. 27 - 1941

Dear Pearl & George!

Many thanks for your Bestwishes
to the New Year. - We hope now, that you are
all right. - May the New Year bring you health
and happiness. -

Dear George, I received a letter from
my brother from Marseille, he wrote me
that he is in a very big danger. He asked
me to do everything what is possible to help
him to come out of this hell. He has got
some money here and he told me to
spend it for this purpose. - His Affidavits
are allready since a few weeks in the State
Departement of Washington. - He got 2 very good
sponsors. The Name of the one sponsor is
Morris Ullmann, Diamonddealer, Brooklyn. -
He is a brother of my brothers wife, a wealthy
man. - The other sponsor is also very rich. -
The Name of my brother is:

wife: Josef STEINBOCK, MARSEILLE, 5 RUE NOUVELLE,
       MELANIE — " — née Ullmann, same address;
       Only what he needs is a push in
the Visa-Departement. -

/.

Please Dear George, maybe you can advise me somebody to make his intervention in the Visa-Departement. – My brother wrote me, that a 10-20 people received the visa in Marseille, only in account of the intervention in Washington

Don't be angry with me, that I trouble you again, but as you know I am very desperate and I have'nt got no body in Washington. –

Thank you very very much in advance, I hope you will help me in this case. –

Many regards from all.

Your
Harris Steinbock

Appendix B

Autobiography of Benjamin Geiger

The Autobiography of Benjamin Geiger was written in 1985

Translated from the Hebrew to English by his son Elisha Geiger

Edited by Judith Goldsmith

October 2014

I, Benjamin Geiger, was born on 18 December 1915 in the town of Sokolow in Poland.[1] I was born as a twin but my twin did not survive. My mother, Chana Geiger, died in June 1916 due to illness when I was about six months of age. She would have been about 38 years of age. My father, Rabbi Eliezer Valtz, did not want to re-marry after her death. My family was very religious and my father was the town leader. My father would tell the people what was going on in the world and how it would affect Jews. He would also discuss with the people what they could do to protect themselves.

My siblings were: Bluma born 1908, Chaja Mindel born 9 June 1897, Sara born 8 May 1902, Solomon David born 7 Feb 1899, Shmuel Lemel born 26 Sept 1905. My brother, Solomon David aka David Geiger, married Sara Amsterdam. David Geiger had a large textile business and house in Kamien, Poland. It was a stone house on the main road and the family lived in the back. The house was originally owned by the Amsterdam family. Sara was an aunt to Jacob Amsterdam. I went to Poland in 1992 to see the house, however it no longer exists because a gas station was erected on the site.

When my town and region was under the Austrian rule, Jews were treated relatively well. Then when Poland became an independent nation in 1918 after WWI, Jews were subject to anti-Semitism and much mistreatment. I remember sitting by my father when I was four years of age and listening to his stories. Then I was told that I must attend a cheder to study Hebrew and the Torah. This was a traumatic experience for me as a young child because the teacher was extremely stern and strict. Young children were taught as if they were adults. I became quite upset in the cheder and my father must have known of my suffering because he made a visit to the cheder to speak with the teacher. After that, the teacher went easier on me. My father, although strict, never hit me.

My father remained a widower without re-marrying, however this was against common practice. We children appreciated this as we did not have to contend with a step-mother. I was sent to a Polish school at six years of age and it was there that I witnessed deep seated Polish anti-Semitism. Polish children were taught to hate Jews and I was often assaulted by Polish children during the time I attended the Polish public school from ages six to thirteen. I spent eight hours a day in the public school and then in the evenings another four hours a day in the cheder, thus making twelve hours a day of study and education. After my bar mitzvah at age thirteen I was supposed to attend a yeshiva in Tarnow. My father could not afford the tuition so he arranged that I would board with a well-to-do Jewish families. This turned out to be a very difficult situation as I would be moved around every night to another house. I was poorly treated since I was a poor Jew and considered as a charity case.

By 1930 there rose a very bad economic situation and I became interested in the Zionist and Communist youth movements. I joined some friends and I left the yeshiva to travel to Krakow to join the Communist movement. We gave out flyers about the movement in the streets of Krakow, but we were unable to find work there. I returned to tell my father that I had left the yeshiva. My father was understanding. I returned to Krakow and found work in a store. By 1935 I was 20 years of age and my three sisters, Sara, Chaja Mindel and Bluma were married and my brother David was also married.

While I was in Krakow, I joined the Akiva movement, to immigrate to Israel. This was a religious but not an orthodox movement. In order to prepare people for immigration, the movement stressed that people needed to learn agriculture skills by working on a farm for one year. The agricultural work was taught by a man from Palestine, from a settlement called Neve Eitan. When the Nazis came to power, no one could leave Poland to go to Palestine. Any Zionist organization was illegal and any immigration was impossible because the Nazis prevented anyone from obtaining visas. In addition, the British closed the doors for anyone trying to enter Palestine.

I was very fortunate to be able to enter Palestine in July 1933, on the last ship leaving. This is how it happened. I learned of an underground system but only had 24 hours to leave. I decided to take the chance to escape and I had to say good-bye to my family members, a very traumatic experience. My three sisters had nine children between them. My father was frail at this time and he remained with his family. I was instructed to take nothing with me except the clothes I was wearing; no photos, no documents. I was given a false name on a document in order to leave Poland. I never saw my family again.

My brother Shmuel also survived the Shoah but he was a broken man.[2] He and his wife Giselle lived in Afula. They did not have children. He immigrated to Israel in May, 1947.

In Palestine, I worked at the settlement kibbutz Neve Eitan. We lived in tents and endured hard physical labor in the fields in the extreme heat. We were enthusiastic and were very motivated to succeed. Palestine was governed by the British and since this was during WWII, they asked for Jewish volunteers to help them fight against the German army. The British army bases were in Egypt. I volunteered and joined the Jewish Infantry Brigade. We were active during 1944–1945 and I served in the Engineers Battalion Unit. Our job was to place mines in strategic places to blow up and stop the German tanks.

I became wounded during one of the battles and my arm was broken in several places. I was taken to a hospital in Cairo in 1944 and was there for a year. My battalion went on to fight in Italy and then to Germany. Even though I wanted to continue in the fighting, I was kept back. After the war was over, I returned to the kibbutz Neve Eitan where I met my wife Lotke. We were married in 1946 and a year later our son Elisha was born in 1947. There was continued fighting as a war broke out with the Arabs in 1948.[3] Lotke and I had three more children: Eliezer born 1950, Jacob born 1952, Irit born 1956.

I concentrated on finding a new business venture for the kibbutz and so organized raising carp fish in fish ponds on the kibbutz. I preferred to work outdoors until I retired at age 68. Our sons bravely fought in the 1967 war and the Yom Kippur war of 1973. Our children all married and we have many grandchildren.

When I was retired I once again returned to Jewish studies by taking free courses in a Jewish seminary. I looked into continuing to work in a plastic factory on Neve Eitan that opened in 1985 but I did not like to sit all day in the air-conditioned factory. I preferred to work outdoors and to raise the fish in the fish ponds.

My surname Geiger comes from my mother's side since my parents did not register their marriage with the civil authorities. My parents were married religiously as orthodox Jews; we all took the name Geiger. My grandparents used to tell me about the distinguished Geiger family living long lives and who were also influential rabbis. My paternal grandfather, Tzvi Valtz, told me that he would pray for me every day and will see me once again in Jerusalem. He was born in 1856 and in 1939, when he was age 83, the Germans asked the Jews for 10 volunteers who were willing to die for the town of Tarnogrod. My grandfather immediately stepped forward and he was shot on the spot.[4] It is very possible that he was the first Jew who was murdered by the Germans in Tarnogrod.

My father came from a long line of Belz Hasidim. Tarnogrod had many Belz Hasidim living there. The Belz Hasidim were against the idea of Israel and against Zionism. My father's mother Yedudit died earlier at a young age. My paternal grandparents sometimes visited us however I did not get to know them very well.

When my sister Chaja was about the age of 13, she took care of our house and myself and my brother Shmuel. Our father was strict and very religious. We had very little money but we were never hungry. Our father, besides being a rabbi, was also a wholesaler of wheat grain that he would purchase from farmers. I remember how Jews were so badly treated by the Cossacks during pogroms. Sara later married and she had two small children, ages four and two. Sara and her family all died in Treblinka during the Shoah. My brother Shmuel Geiger came to Israel and he and I both gave Pages of Testimony to Yad Vashem concerning the fates of our family members.

My sisters Sara, Bluma and their families were all murdered during the Shoah at Treblinka. My sister-in-law Sara was also murdered in Treblinka in 1942. My sister Chaja and her husband Yeshayahu Veinshtok as well as my brother David also died in the Shoah, in 1942 at Bełżec. My father, Eliezer Volf Valtz, was murdered in 1942 also at Belzec. My brother Shmuel and I managed to survive the Shoah and to live in Israel. Shmuel died 26 August 1977.[5]

Endnotes

1   A researcher, James Dale, informed me that Sokolow Malopolski is 24 miles north of Blazowa.

2   www.jewishgen.org/databases/holocaust/0126 Schindlers-lists.html. Research indicated that Shmuel Lemel Geiger worked for Oskar Schindler in his factory called the German Enamel Works in Krakow as a metal worker. Against tremendous odds, Schindler moved most of his Jewish workers in October 1944 to Czechoslovakia to the Bruennlitz camp, that was liberated by the Russian Red army in 1945.

3   Lotke's maiden name was Czech and she was born 1923 in Prague.

4   www.yadvashem.org. International Institute for Holocaust Research. Encyclopedia of the Ghettos. In researching the Shoah Database of names, the surname Valtz was connected with the shtetl of Tarnograd. There were 2,500 Jews living there engaged in small businesses. Jewish schools were traditional and ortho-dox. When the Germans occupied Tarnograd on 15 September 1939, many Jews were beaten and one of them was killed. A week later, the Germans withdrew from Tarnograd, but then returned to force the Jews into a ghetto. This ghetto was liquidated on 2 November 1942. Remaining Jews were sent to Belzec for annihilation.

5   Benjamin Geiger died 16 July 1999. His wife Lotke died 13 July 2014. Both are buried at kibbutz Neve Eitan, Israel. Please note that records for the murdered family members were found in Yad Vashem in the Central Database of Shoah Victims' Names.

Appendix C

Relatives Murdered During the Holocaust
May They Never be Forgotten

compiled by Judith C. Goldsmith

Vitezlav aka Fritz Czech

Irena Czech née Aschkenes

Jacob Bander

Moishe Bander

Berta Rachel Bikales née Bander

Salomon Bikales

Chana Tauba Ettinger née Geiger

Shaul Wolf Ettinger

Fradl Esther Ettinger

Yitzchak Ettinger

Abraham Wolf Finder

Beila Finder née Gemeiner

Bernard Berl Geiger

Chaya Ita Geiger née Stockman

Chaim Yehuda Geiger

David Geiger

Fradal Geiger née Landesman

Joachim Geiger

Marcus Geiger

Meilich Geiger

Moshe Yitzak Geiger

Riva Silka Geiger

Sara Geiger

Sara Geiger née Amsterdam

Tauba Geiger née Weinstein

Schewa Ginsberg

Isidore Ginsberg

Aron Geiger Gruenbaum

Sheindel Gruenbaum née Hampt

Schmuel Gruenbaum

Sana Gruenbaum

Chaya Yehudit Gruenbaum

Tzvi Gruenbaum

Sima Gruenbaum

Yehezkeil Geiger Gruenbaum

Elazar Yehuda Guzik

Marya Hochhauser née Turnheim	Tzvi Valtz
Chaim Klein	Chaya Veinshtok née Geiger
Sali Klein née Turnheim	Yeshayahu Veinshtok
Feige Kraut née Bander	Chaja Mindel Wachtel née Geiger
Isaac Kraut	Shmuel Yeshiyah Wachtel
Paul Kraut	Luba Wachtel
Rachela Geiger née Krebs	Lea Wachtel
Salomon Samuel Mersel	Anna Wachtel
Silka Nebentzahl née Scheiner	Elimelech Wachtel
Nebentzahl	Yona Wachtel
Betzalel Prisand	Bluma Weinselbaum née Geiger
Freida Prisand née Turnheim	Benjamin Weinselbaum
Chava Scheiner	Chana Weinselbaum
Moshe Scheiner	Gittel Weissblum née Geiger
Etel Schindler	Elchanan Weissblum
Moses David Schindler	Josef Alter Weissblum
Salomon Schlachet	Beirisch Zins
Mrs. Schlachet née Spira	Channah Zins
Josef Steinboch	Chuna Zins
Lotta Turnheim née Trattner	David Zins
David Turnheim	Feige Zins
Edka Turnheim	Lazar Zins
Edward Turnheim	Yisrael Zins
Ernest Chuna Turnheim	Sara Zins
Josef Turnheim	Samuel Moses Zins
Leon Turnheim	Silka Zins née Geiger
Eliezer Volf Valtz	Yehoshua Mendel Zins

Index

About the Researcher:

Dr. Judith C. Goldsmith

Judith Goldsmith née Gerber was born in Brooklyn, New York in 1943, the granddaughter of Jewish immigrants to the United States from the Austro-Hungarian and Russian Empires. She was always curious about her family history even during her multifaceted professional life as an artist, art educator, art therapist and social worker. Her academic background includes an undergraduate degree from Queens College, CUNY, New York and graduate degrees in both art education and social work, with an Ed.D. from Teachers College, Columbia University, New York and an M.S.W. from Salem State University, Salem, Massachusetts. Judith Goldsmith worked in such diverse places as public schools, substance abuse rehabilitation centers, mental hospitals, a prison, and community mental health facilities.

After raising her family and during her retirement years she was able to increase the amount of time she could devote to her genealogical research and writing. Her journey into genealogy opened new avenues for understanding and appreciating her ancestors. Her genealogical research focused on her maternal lineages that were organized, meticulously and comprehensively presented in her book *My Galitzianer Ancestors: Geiger and Turnheim Families from Subcarpathia Province, Poland* including family trees, family charts, images and maps.

www.ingramcontent.com/pod-product-compliance
Lightning Source LLC
Chambersburg PA
CBHW080127270326
41926CB00021B/4385